Business Data Communications and Networking

Twelfth Edition

Jerry FitzGerald
Jerry FitzGerald & Associates

Alan Dennis
Indiana University

Alexandra Durcikova
University of Oklahoma

WILEY

To my beautiful wife Kelly

AD

VICE PRESIDENT AND EXECUTIVE PUBLISHER   *Don Fowley*
EXECUTIVE EDITOR   *Beth Lang Golub*
EDITORIAL ASSISTANT   *Jayne Ziemba*
SPONSORING EDITOR   *Mary O'Sullivan*
PROJECT EDITOR   *Ellen Keohane*
MARKETING MANAGER   *Margaret Barrett*
MARKETING ASSISTANT   *Elisa Wong*
SENIOR PRODUCT DESIGNER   *Lydia Cheng*
ASSOCIATE EDITOR   *Christina Volpe*
PHOTO EDITOR   *James Russiello*
SENIOR DESIGNER   *Maureen Eide*
ASSOCIATE PRODUCTION MANAGER   *Joyce Poh*
SENIOR PRODUCTION EDITOR   *Yee Lyn Song*
PRODUCTION SERVICES   *Sangeetha Parthasarathy/Laserwords*
COVER DESIGNER   *Wendy Lai*
COVER CREDIT   *© Rawpixel / iStockphoto*

This book was set in Times Roman by Laserwords Private Limited, Chennai, India and manufactured by RR Donnelley Harrisonburg. The cover was printed by RR Donnelley Harrisonburg.

This book is printed on acid-free paper. ∞

Founded in 1807, John Wiley & Sons, Inc., has been a valued source of knowledge and understanding for more than 200 years, helping people around the world meet their needs and fulfill their aspirations. Our company is built on a foundation of principles that include responsibility to the communities we serve and where we live and work. In 2008, we launched a Corporate Citizenship Initiative, a global effort to address the environmental, social, economic, and ethical challenges we face in our business. Among the issues we are addressing are carbon impact, paper specifications and procurement, ethical conduct within our business and among our vendors, and community and charitable support. For more information, please visit our website: www.wiley.com/go/citizenship.

Library of Congress Cataloging-in-Publication Data

FitzGerald, Jerry, 1936-
  Business data communications and networking / Jerry FitzGerald, Jerry FitzGerald & Associates, Alan Dennis, Indiana University, Alexandra Durcikova, University of Arizona. – Twelfth edition.
    pages cm
  Includes bibliographical references and index.
  ISBN 978-1-118-89168-1 (paperback)
 1. Data transmission systems. 2. Computer networks. 3. Office practice–Automation. I. Dennis, Alan.
II. Durcikova, Alexandra. III. Title.
  TK5105.F577 2015
  004.6–dc23

                              2014023087

Printed in the United States of America
10 9 8 7

ABOUT THE AUTHORS

Alan Dennis is professor of information systems in the Kelley School of Business at Indiana University and holds the John T. Chambers Chair in Internet Systems. The Chambers Chair was established to honor John Chambers, president and chief executive officer of Cisco Systems, the worldwide leader of networking technologies for the Internet.

Prior to joining Indiana University, Alan spent nine years as a professor at the University of Georgia, where he won the Richard B. Russell Award for Excellence in Undergraduate Teaching. He has a bachelor's degree in computer science from Acadia University in Nova Scotia, Canada, and an MBA from Queen's University in Ontario, Canada. His PhD in management of information systems is from the University of Arizona. Prior to entering the Arizona doctoral program, he spent three years on the faculty of the Queen's School of Business.

Alan has extensive experience in the development and application of groupware and Internet technologies and co-founded Courseload, an electronic textbook company whose goal is to improve learning and reduce the cost of textbooks. He has won many awards for theoretical and applied research and has published more than 150 business and research articles, including those in *Management Science, MIS Quarterly, Information Systems Research, Academy of Management Journal, Organization Behavior and Human Decision Making, Journal of Applied Psychology, Communications of the ACM,* and *IEEE Transactions of Systems, Man, and Cybernetics.* His first book was *Getting Started with Microcomputers,* published in 1986. Alan is also an author of two systems analysis and design books published by Wiley. He is the cochair of the Internet Technologies Track of the Hawaii International Conference on System Sciences. He has served as a consultant to BellSouth, Boeing, IBM, Hughes Missile Systems, the U.S. Department of Defense, and the Australian Army.

Alexandra Durcikova is an Assistant Professor at the Price College of Business, University of Oklahoma. Alexandra has a PhD in management information systems from the University of Pittsburgh. She has earned a MSc degree in solid state physics from Comenius University, Bratislava, worked as an experimental physics researcher in the area of superconductivity and as an instructor of executive MBA students prior to pursuing her PhD. Alexandra's research interests include knowledge management and knowledge management systems, the role of organizational climate in the use of knowledge management systems, knowledge management system characteristics, governance mechanisms in the use of knowledge management systems, and human compliance with security policy and characteristics of successful phishing attempts within the area of network security. Her research appears in *Information Systems Research, Journal of Management Information Systems, Information Systems Journal, Journal of Organizational and End User Computing, International Journal of Human-Computer Studies, International Journal of Human-Computer Studies,* and *Communications of the ACM.*

Alexandra has been teaching business data communications to both undergraduate and graduate students for several years. In addition, she has been teaching classes on information technology strategy and most recently won the Dean's Award for Undergraduate Teaching Excellence while teaching at the University of Arizona.

Dr. Jerry FitzGerald wrote the early editions of this book in the 1980s. At the time, he was the principal in Jerry FitzGerald & Associates, a firm he started in 1977.

PREFACE

The field of data communications has grown faster and become more important than computer processing itself. Though they go hand in hand, the ability to communicate and connect with other computers and mobile devices is what makes or breaks a business today. There are three trends that support this notion. First, the wireless LAN and Bring-Your-Own-Device (BYOD) allow us to stay connected not only with the workplace but also with family and friends. Second, computers and networks are becoming an essential part of not only computers but also devices we use for other purpose, such as kitchen appliances. This web of things allows you to set the thermostat in your home from your mobile phone, can help you cook a dinner, or eventually can allow you to drive to work without ever touching the steering wheel. Lastly, we see that a lot of life is moving online. At first this started with games, but education, politics, and activism followed swiftly. Therefore, understanding how networks work; how they should be set up to support scalability, mobility, and security; and how to manage them is of utmost importance to any business. This need will call not only for engineers who deeply understand the technical aspects of networks but also for highly social individuals who embrace technology in creative ways to allow business to achieve a competitive edge through utilizing this technology. So the call is for you who are reading this book—you are at the right place at the right time!

PURPOSE OF THIS BOOK

Our goal is to combine the fundamental concepts of data communications and networking with practical applications. Although technologies and applications change rapidly, the fundamental concepts evolve much more slowly; they provide the foundation from which new technologies and applications can be understood, evaluated, and compared.

This book has two intended audiences. First and foremost, it is a university textbook. Each chapter introduces, describes, and then summarizes fundamental concepts and applications. Management Focus boxes highlight key issues and describe how networks are actually being used today. Technical Focus boxes highlight key technical issues and provide additional detail. Mini case studies at the end of each chapter provide the opportunity to apply these technical and management concepts. Hands-on exercises help to reinforce the concepts introduced in the chapter. Moreover, the text is accompanied by a detailed Instructor's Manual that provides additional background information, teaching tips, and sources of material for student exercises, assignments, and exams. Finally, our Web page contains supplements to our book.

Second, this book is intended for the professional who works in data communications and networking. The book has many detailed descriptions of the technical aspects of communications, along with illustrations where appropriate. Moreover, managerial, technical, and sales personnel can use this book to gain a better understanding of fundamental concepts and trade-offs not presented in technical books or product summaries.

WHAT'S NEW IN THIS EDITION

The twelfth edition maintains the three main themes of the eleventh edition, namely, (1) how networks work (Chapters 1–5); (2) network technologies (Chapters 6–10); and network security and management (Chapters 11 and 12). In the new edition, we removed older technologies and replaced them with new ones. Accordingly, new hands-on activities and questions have been added at the end of each chapter that guide students in understanding how to select technologies to build a network that would support an organization's business needs. In addition to this overarching change, the twelfth edition has five major changes from the eleventh edition:

First, we revised Chapter 1 to explain the three main themes of the book and to help students better understand why they should care about them.

The second major change is that this edition focuses on the design of networks. We introduce a comprehensive framework for network design in Chapter 6 that is supported by an ongoing case study at the ends of Chapters 6–10 that walks the students through network design step by step.

This modification leads to the third change: Chapters 6–12 are designed in a way that can be used for a "flipped classroom" style of teaching as well as the traditional lecture approach. Students are motivated to learn about LANs and WLANs (Chapter 7), BNs (Chapter 8), WANs (Chapter 9), and the Internet (Chapter 10) because they are designing a network for an organization.

Fourth, Chapter 5 has a detailed discussion with three new hands-on activities that describe subnetting for IPv4 and one activity that focuses on IPv6.

Finally, Chapter 11, which discusses network security, introduces a new framework for risk assessment that builds on currently accepted industry standards. It walks students through risk assessment in an easily comprehensible way.

LAB EXERCISES
www.wiley.com/college/fitzgerald

This edition includes an online lab manual with many hands-on exercises that can be used in a networking lab. These exercises include configuring servers and other additional practical topics.

ONLINE SUPPLEMENTS FOR INSTRUCTORS
www.wiley.com/college/fitzgerald

Instructor's supplements comprise an Instructor's Manual that includes teaching tips, war stories and answers to end-of-chapter questions, a Test Bank that includes true-false, multiple choice, short answer, and essay test questions for each chapter, and Lecture Slides in PowerPoint for classroom presentations. All are available on the instructor's book companion site.

E-BOOK

Wiley E-Text: Powered by VitalSource offers students continuing access to materials for their course. Your students can access content on a mobile device, online from any Internet-connected computer, or by a computer via download. With dynamic features built into this e-text, students can search across content, highlight, and take notes that they can share with teachers and classmates. Readers will also have access to interactive images and embedded podcasts. Visit www.wiley.com/college/fitzgerald for more information.

ACKNOWLEDGMENTS

Our thanks to the many people who helped in preparing this edition. Specifically, we want to thank the staff at John Wiley & Sons for their support, including Ellen Keohane, Mary O'Sullivan, Elizabeth Pearson, and Yee Lyn Song.

We also want to thank the reviewers whose comments helped us improve this book:

Hans-Joachim Adler, University of Texas at Dallas
Zenaida Bodwin, Northern Virginia Community College
Thomas Case, Georgia Southern University
Jimmie Cauley II, University of Houston
Rangadhar Dash, University of Texas at Arlington
Bob Gehling, Auburn University, Montgomery
Joseph Hasley, Metropolitan State University of Denver
William G. Heninger, Brigham Young University
Robert Hogan, University of Alabama
Margaret Leary, Northern Virginia Community College
Eleanor T. Loiacono, Worcester Polytechnic Institute
Mohamed Mahgoub, New Jersey Institute of Technology
Brad Mattocks, California Lutheran University
Carlos Oliveira, University of California Irvine
Don Riley, University of Maryland
Joseph H. Schuessler, Tarleton State University
Myron Sheu, California State University, Dominguez Hills
Jean G. Smith, Technical College of the Lowcountry
James Stephenson, Western International University
Manjit Taneja, Northern Virginia Community College
Mehmet Ulema, Manhattan College
Jingguo Wang, University of Texas, Arlington
Cartmell Warrington, SUNY Orange
Qing Yan, Grantham University
Shahid Zaheer, Fairleigh Dickinson University

Alan Dennis
Bloomington, Indiana
www.kelley.indiana.edu/ardennis
Alexandra Durcikova
Norman, Oklahoma

CONTENTS

CHAPTER 1

INTRODUCTION TO DATA COMMUNICATIONS

This chapter introduces the basic concepts of data communications. It describes why it is important to study data communications and introduces you to the three fundamental questions that this book answers. Next, it discusses the basic types and components of a data communications network. Also, it examines the importance of a network model based on layers. Finally, it describes the three key trends in the future of networking.

OBJECTIVES

- Be aware of the three fundamental questions this book answers
- Be aware of the applications of data communications networks
- Be familiar with the major components of and types of networks
- Understand the role of network layers
- Be familiar with the role of network standards
- Be aware of three key trends in communications and networking

OUTLINE

1.1 INTRODUCTION

What Internet connection should you use? Cable modem or DSL (formally called Digital Subscriber Line)? Cable modems are supposedly faster than DSL, providing data speeds of 50 Mbps to DSL's 1.5–25 Mbps (million bits per second). One cable company used a tortoise to represent DSL in advertisements. So which is faster? We'll give you a hint. Which won the race in the fable, the tortoise or the hare? By the time you finish this book, you'll understand which is faster and why, as well as why choosing the right company as your **Internet service provider (ISP)** is probably more important than choosing the right technology.

Over the past decade or so, it has become clear that the world has changed forever. We continue to forge our way through the Information Age—the second Industrial Revolution, according to John Chambers, CEO (chief executive officer) of Cisco Systems, Inc., one of the world's leading networking technology companies. The first Industrial Revolution revolutionized the way people worked by introducing machines and new organizational forms. New companies and industries emerged, and old ones died off.

The second Industrial Revolution is revolutionizing the way people work through networking and data communications. The value of a high-speed data communications network is that it brings people together in a way never before possible. In the 1800s, it took several weeks for a message to reach North America by ship from England. By the 1900s, it could be transmitted within the hour. Today, it can be transmitted in seconds. Collapsing the *information lag* to Internet speeds means that people can communicate and access information anywhere in the world regardless of their physical location. In fact, today's problem is that we cannot handle the quantities of information we receive.

Data communications and networking is a truly global area of study, both because the technology enables global communication and because new technologies and applications often emerge from a variety of countries and spread rapidly around the world. The World Wide Web, for example, was born in a Swiss research lab, was nurtured through its first years primarily by European universities, and exploded into mainstream popular culture because of a development at an American research lab.

One of the problems in studying a global phenomenon lies in explaining the different political and regulatory issues that have evolved and currently exist in different parts of the world. Rather than attempt to explain the different paths taken by different countries, we have chosen simplicity instead. Historically, the majority of readers of previous editions of this book have come from North America. Therefore, although we retain a global focus on technology and its business implications, we focus mostly on North America.

This book answers three fundamental questions.

First, how does the Internet work? When you access a Web site using your computer, laptop, iPad, or smart phone, what happens so that the page opens in your Web browser? This is the focus in Chapters 1–5. The short answer is that the software on your computer (or any device) creates a message composed in different software languages (HTTP, TCP/IP, and Ethernet are common) that requests the page you clicked. This message is then broken up into a series of smaller parts that we call packets. Each packet is transmitted to the nearest router, which is a special-purpose computer whose primary job is to find the best route for these packets to their final destination. The packets move from router to router over the Internet until they reach the Web server, which puts the packets back together into the same message that your computer created. The Web server reads your request and then sends the page back to you in the same way—by composing a message using HTTP, TCP/IP, and Ethernet and then sending it as a series of smaller packets back through the Internet that the software on your computer puts together into the page you requested. You might have heard a news story that the U.S. or Chinese government can read your email or see what Web sites you're visiting. A more shocking truth is that the person sitting next you at a coffee shop might be doing exactly the same thing—reading all the packets that come from or go to your laptop. How is this possible, you ask? After finishing Chapter 5, you will know exactly how this is possible.

Second, how do I design a network? This is the focus of Chapters 6–10. We often think about networks in four layers. The first layer is the Local Area Network, or the LAN (either wired or wireless), which enables users like you and me to access the network. The second is the backbone network that connects the different LANs within a building. The third is the core network that connects different buildings on a company's campus. The final layer is connections we have to the other campuses within the organization and to the Internet. Each of these layers has slightly different concerns, so the way we design networks for them and the technologies we use are slightly different. Although this describes the standard for building corporate networks, you will have a much better understanding of how your wireless router at home works. Perhaps more importantly, you'll learn why buying the newest and fastest wireless router for your house or apartment is probably not a good way to spend your money.

Finally, how do I manage my network to make sure it is secure, provides good performance, and doesn't cost too much? This is the focus of Chapters 11 and 12. Would it surprise you to learn that most companies spend between $1,500 and $3,500 per computer per year on network management and security? Yup, we spend way more on network management and security each year than we spend to buy the computer in the first place. And that's for well-run networks; poorly run networks cost a lot more. Many people think network security is a technical problem, and to some extent, it is. However, the things people do and don't do cause more security risks than not having the latest technology. According to Symantec, one of the leading companies that sells antivirus software, about half of all security threats are not prevented by their software. These threats are called targeted attacks, such as phishing attacks (which are emails that look real but instead take you to fake Web sites) or ransomware (software apps that appear to be useful but actually lock your computer and demand a payment to unlock it). Therefore, network management is as much a people management issue as it is a technology management issue.

By the time you finish this book, you'll understand how networks work, how to design networks, and how to manage networks. You won't be an expert, but you'll be ready to enter an organization or move on to more advanced courses.

MANAGEMENT
FOCUS

1-1 Career Opportunities

It's a great time to be in information technology (IT)! The technology-fueled new economy has dramatically increased the demand for skilled IT professions. According to the U.S. Bureau of Labor Statistics, the second fastest growing occupation is data communications and networking analyst, which is expected to grow by 53% by 2018 and create 150,000 new jobs with an annual median salary of $71,100—not counting bonuses. There are two reasons for this growth. First, companies have to continuously upgrade their networks and thus need skilled employees to support their expanding IT infrastructure. Second, people are spending more time on their mobile devices, and because employers are allowing them to use these personal devices at work (i.e., BYOD, or bring your own device), the network infrastructure has to support the data that flow from these devices as well as making sure that they don't pose a security risk.

With a few years of experience, there is the possibility to work as an information systems manager, for which the median annual pay is as high as $117,780. An information systems manager plans, coordinates, and directs IT-related activities in such a way that they can fully support the goals of any business. Thus, this job requires a good understanding not only of the business but also of the technology so that appropriate and reliable technology can be implemented at a reasonable cost to keep everything operating smoothly and to guard against cybercriminals.

Because of the expanding job market for IT and networking-related jobs, certifications become important. Most large vendors of network technologies, such as the Microsoft Corporation and Cisco Systems Inc., provide certification processes (usually a series of courses and formal exams) so that individuals can document their knowledge. Certified network professional often earn $10,000 to $15,000 more than similarly skilled uncertified professionals—provided that they continue to learn and maintain their certification as new technologies emerge.

Adapted from: http://jobs.aol.com, "In Demand Careers That Pay $100,00 a Year or More"; www.careerpath.com, "Today's 20 Fastest-Growing Occupations"; www.cnn.com, "30 Jobs Needing Most Workers in Next Decade."

1.2 DATA COMMUNICATIONS NETWORKS

Data communications is the movement of computer information from one point to another by means of electrical or optical transmission systems. Such systems are often called *data communications networks*. This is in contrast to the broader term *telecommunications*, which includes the transmission of voice and video (images and graphics) as well as data and usually implies longer distances. In general, data communications networks collect data from personal computers and other devices and transmit those data to a central server that is a more powerful personal computer, minicomputer, or mainframe, or they perform the reverse process, or some combination of the two. Data communications networks facilitate more efficient use of computers and improve the day-to-day control of a business by providing faster information flow. They also provide message transfer services to allow computer users to talk to one another via email, chat, and video streaming.

TECHNICAL FOCUS   1-1 Internet Domain Names

*I*nternet address names are strictly controlled; otherwise, someone could add a computer to the Internet that had the same address as another computer. Each address name has two parts, the computer name and its domain. The general format of an Internet address is therefore computer.domain. Some computer names have several parts separated by periods, so some addresses have the format computer.computer.computer.domain. For example, the main university Web server at Indiana University (IU) is called www.indiana.edu, whereas the Web server for the Kelley School of Business at IU is www.kelley.indiana.edu.

Since the Internet began in the United States, the American address board was the first to assign domain names to indicate types of organizations. Some common U.S. domain names are

EDU   for an educational institution, usually a university
COM   for a commercial business
GOV   for a government department or agency
MIL   for a military unit
ORG   for a nonprofit organization

As networks in other countries were connected to the Internet, they were assigned their own domain names. Some international domain names are

CA   for Canada
AU   for Australia
UK   for the United Kingdom
DE   for Germany

New top-level domains that focus on specific types of businesses continue to be introduced, such as

AERO   for aerospace companies
MUSEUM   for museums
NAME   for individuals
PRO   for professionals, such as accountants and lawyers
BIZ   for businesses

Many international domains structure their addresses in much the same way as the United States does. For example, Australia uses *EDU* to indicate academic institutions, so an address such as xyz.edu.au would indicate an Australian university.

For a full list of domain names, see www.iana.org/root/db.

1.2.1 Components of a Network

There are three basic hardware components for a data communications network: a server (e.g., personal computer, mainframe), a client (e.g., personal computer, terminal), and a circuit (e.g., cable, modem) over which messages flow. Both the server and client also need special-purpose network software that enables them to communicate.

The **server** stores data or software that can be accessed by the clients. In client-server computing, several servers may work together over the network with a client computer to support the business application.

The **client** is the input-output hardware device at the user's end of a communication circuit. It typically provides users with access to the network and the data and software on the server.

The **circuit** is the pathway through which the messages travel. It is typically a copper wire, although fiber-optic cable and wireless transmission are becoming common. There are many devices in the circuit that perform special functions such as switches and routers.

Strictly speaking, a network does not need a server. Some networks are designed to connect a set of similar computers that share their data and software with each other. Such networks are called **peer-to-peer networks** because the computers function as equals, rather than relying on a central server to store the needed data and software.

Figure 1-1 shows a small network that has four personal computers (clients) connected by a **switch** and **cables** (circuit). In this network, messages move through the switch to and from the computers. All computers share the same circuit and must take turns sending messages. The **router** is a special device that connects two or more networks. The router enables computers on this network to communicate with computers on other networks (e.g., the Internet).

The network in Figure 1-1 has three servers. Although one server can perform many functions, networks are often designed so that a separate computer is used to provide different services. The **file server** stores data and software that can be used by computers on the network. The **print server**, which is connected to a printer, manages all printing requests from the clients on the network. The **Web server** stores documents and graphics that can be accessed from any Web browser, such as Internet Explorer. The Web server can respond to requests from computers on this network or any computer on the Internet. Servers are

FIGURE 1-1

Example of a local area network (LAN)

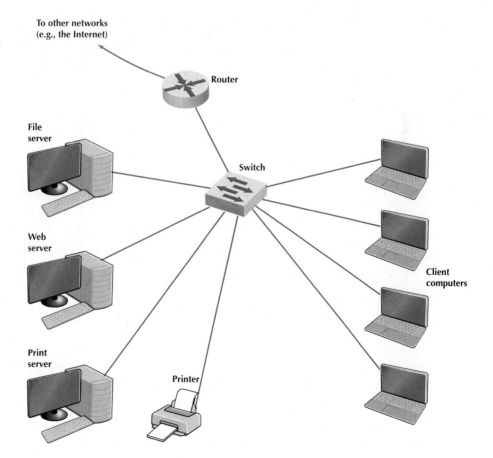

usually personal computers (often more powerful than the other personal computers on the network) but may be minicomputers or mainframes.

1.2.2 Types of Networks

There are many different ways to categorize networks. One of the most common ways is to look at the geographic scope of the network. Figure 1-2 illustrates four types of networks: local area networks (LANs), backbone networks (BNs), and wide area networks (WANs). The distinctions among these are becoming blurry because some network technologies now used in LANs were originally developed for WANs, and vice versa. Any rigid classification of technologies is certain to have exceptions.

A **local area network (LAN)** is a group of computers located in the same general area. A LAN covers a clearly defined small area, such as one floor or work area, a single building, or a group of buildings. The upper left diagram in Figure 1-2 shows a small LAN located in the records building at the former McClellan Air Force Base in Sacramento. LANs support high-speed data transmission compared with standard telephone circuits, commonly

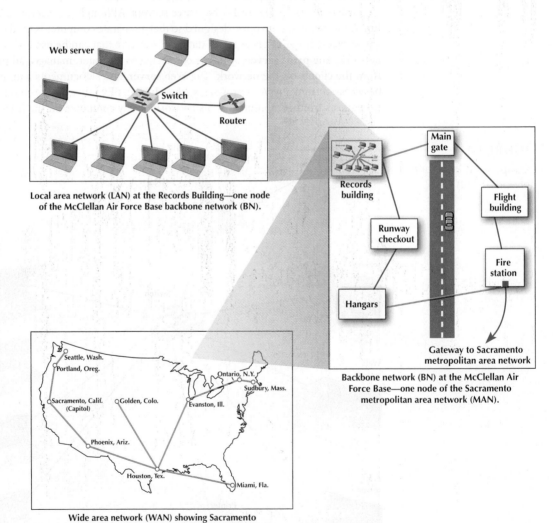

Local area network (LAN) at the Records Building—one node of the McClellan Air Force Base backbone network (BN).

Backbone network (BN) at the McClellan Air Force Base—one node of the Sacramento metropolitan area network (MAN).

Wide area network (WAN) showing Sacramento connected to nine other cities throughout the United States.

FIGURE 1-2 The hierarchical relationship of a local area network (LAN) to a backbone network (BN) to a wide area network (WAN)

operating 100 million bits per second (100 Mbps). LANs and wireless LANs are discussed in detail in Chapter 6.

Most LANs are connected to a **backbone network (BN)**, a larger, central network connecting several LANs, other BNs, MANs, and WANs. BNs typically span from hundreds of feet to several miles and provide very high-speed data transmission, commonly 100 to 1,000 Mbps. The second diagram in Figure 1-2 shows a BN that connects the LANs located in several buildings at McClellan Air Force Base. BNs are discussed in detail in Chapter 7.

Wide area networks (WANs) connect BNs and MANs (see Figure 1-2). Most organizations do not build their own WANs by laying cable, building microwave towers, or sending up satellites (unless they have unusually heavy data transmission needs or highly specialized requirements, such as those of the Department of Defense). Instead, most organizations lease circuits from IXCs (e.g., AT&T, Sprint) and use those to transmit their data. WAN circuits provided by IXCs come in all types and sizes but typically span hundreds or thousands of miles and provide data transmission rates from 64 Kbps to 10 Gbps. WANs are discussed in detail in Chapter 8.

Two other common terms are **intranets** and **extranets**. An intranet is a LAN that uses the same technologies as the Internet (e.g., Web servers, Java, HTML [Hypertext Markup Language]) but is open to only those inside the organization. For example, although some pages on a Web server may be open to the public and accessible by anyone on the Internet, some pages may be on an intranet and therefore hidden from those who connect to the Web server from the Internet at large. Sometimes an intranet is provided by a completely separate Web server hidden from the Internet. The intranet for the Information Systems Department at Indiana University, for example, provides information on faculty expense budgets, class scheduling for future semesters (e.g., room, instructor), and discussion forums.

An extranet is similar to an intranet in that it, too, uses the same technologies as the Internet but instead is provided to invited users outside the organization who access it over the Internet. It can provide access to information services, inventories, and other internal organizational databases that are provided only to customers, suppliers, or those who have paid for access. Typically, users are given passwords to gain access, but more sophisticated technologies such as smart cards or special software may also be required. Many universities provide extranets for Web-based courses so that only those students enrolled in the course can access course materials and discussions.

1.3 NETWORK MODELS

There are many ways to describe and analyze data communications networks. All networks provide the same basic functions to transfer a message from sender to receiver, but each network can use different network hardware and software to provide these functions. All of these hardware and software products have to work together to successfully transfer a message.

One way to accomplish this is to break the entire set of communications functions into a series of **layers**, each of which can be defined separately. In this way, vendors can develop software and hardware to provide the functions of each layer separately. The software or hardware can work in any manner and can be easily updated and improved, as long as the interface between that layer and the ones around it remains unchanged. Each piece of hardware and software can then work together in the overall network.

There are many different ways in which the network layers can be designed. The two most important network models are the Open Systems Interconnection Reference (OSI) model and the Internet model. The Internet model is the most commonly used of the two; few people use the OSI model, although understand it is commonly required for network certification exams.

1.3.1 Open Systems Interconnection Reference Model

The **Open Systems Interconnection Reference model** (usually called the **OSI model** for short) helped change the face of network computing. Before the OSI model, most commercial networks used by businesses were built using nonstandardized technologies developed by one vendor (remember that the Internet was in use at the time but was not widespread and certainly was not commercial). During the late 1970s, the International Organization for Standardization (ISO) created the Open System Interconnection Subcommittee, whose task was to develop a framework of standards for computer-to-computer communications. In 1984, this effort produced the OSI model.

The OSI model is the most talked about and most referred to network model. If you choose a career in networking, questions about the OSI model will be on the network certification exams offered by Microsoft, Cisco, and other vendors of network hardware and software. However, you will probably never use a network based on the OSI model. Simply put, the OSI model never caught on commercially in North America, although some European networks use it, and some network components developed for use in the United States arguably use parts of it. Most networks today use the Internet model, which is discussed in the next section. However, because there are many similarities between the OSI model and the Internet model, and because most people in networking are expected to know the OSI model, we discuss it here. The OSI model has seven layers (see Figure 1-3).

Layer 1: Physical Layer The *physical layer* is concerned primarily with transmitting data bits (zeros or ones) over a communication circuit. This layer defines the rules by which ones and zeros are transmitted, such as voltages of electricity, number of bits sent per second, and the physical format of the cables and connectors used.

Layer 2: Data Link Layer The *data link layer* manages the physical transmission circuit in layer 1 and transforms it into a circuit that is free of transmission errors as far as layers above are concerned. Because layer 1 accepts and transmits only a raw stream of bits without understanding their meaning or structure, the data link layer must create and recognize message boundaries; that is, it must mark where a message starts and where it ends. Another major task of layer 2 is to solve the problems caused by damaged, lost, or duplicate messages so the succeeding layers are shielded from transmission errors. Thus, layer 2 performs error detection and correction. It also decides when a device can transmit so that two computers do not try to transmit at the same time.

FIGURE 1-3

Network models.
OSI = Open Systems
Interconnection
Reference

OSI Model	Internet Model	Groups of Layers	Examples
7. Application Layer		*Application Layer*	Internet Explorer and Web pages
6. Presentation Layer	5. Application Layer		
5. Session Layer			
4. Transport Layer	4. Transport Layer	*Internetwork Layer*	TCP/IP software
3. Network Layer	3. Network Layer		
2. Data Link Layer	2. Data Link Layer	*Hardware Layer*	Ethernet port, Ethernet cables, and Ethernet software drivers
1. Physical Layer	1. Physical Layer		

Layer 3: Network Layer The *network layer* performs routing. It determines the next computer to which the message should be sent so it can follow the best route through the network and finds the full address for that computer if needed.

Layer 4: Transport Layer The *transport layer* deals with end-to-end issues, such as procedures for entering and departing from the network. It establishes, maintains, and terminates logical connections for the transfer of data between the original sender and the final destination of the message. It is responsible for breaking a large data transmission into smaller packets (if needed), ensuring that all the packets have been received, eliminating duplicate packets, and performing flow control to ensure that no computer is overwhelmed by the number of messages it receives. Although error control is performed by the data link layer, the transport layer can also perform error checking.

Layer 5: Session Layer The *session layer* is responsible for managing and structuring all sessions. Session initiation must arrange for all the desired and required services between session participants, such as logging on to circuit equipment, transferring files, and performing security checks. Session termination provides an orderly way to end the session, as well as a means to abort a session prematurely. It may have some redundancy built in to recover from a broken transport (layer 4) connection in case of failure. The session layer also handles session accounting so the correct party receives the bill.

Layer 6: Presentation Layer The *presentation layer* formats the data for presentation to the user. Its job is to accommodate different interfaces on different computers so the application program need not worry about them. It is concerned with displaying, formatting, and editing user inputs and outputs. For example, layer 6 might perform data compression, translation between different data formats, and screen formatting. Any function (except those in layers 1 through 5) that is requested sufficiently often to warrant finding a general solution is placed in the presentation layer, although some of these functions can be performed by separate hardware and software (e.g., encryption).

Layer 7: Application Layer The *application layer* is the end user's access to the network. The primary purpose is to provide a set of utilities for application programs. Each user program determines the set of messages and any action it might take on receipt of a message. Other network-specific applications at this layer include network monitoring and network management.

1.3.2 Internet Model

The network model that dominates current hardware and software is a more simple five-layer **Internet model**. Unlike the OSI model that was developed by formal committees, the Internet model evolved from the work of thousands of people who developed pieces of the Internet. The OSI model is a formal standard that is documented in one standard, but the Internet model has never been formally defined; it has to be interpreted from a number of standards.[1] The two models have very much in common (see Figure 1-3); simply put, the Internet model collapses the top three OSI layers into one layer. Because it is clear that the Internet has won the "war," we use the five-layer Internet model for the rest of this book.

Layer 1: The Physical Layer The **physical layer** in the Internet model, as in the OSI model, is the physical connection between the sender and receiver. Its role is to transfer a series

[1] Over the years, our view of the Internet layers has evolved, as has the Internet itself. It's now clear that most of the Internet community thinks about networks using a five-layer view, so we'll use it as well. As of this writing, however, Microsoft uses a four-layer view of the Internet for its certification exams.

of electrical, radio, or light signals through the circuit. The physical layer includes all the *hardware* devices (e.g., computers, modems, and switches) and physical *media* (e.g., cables and satellites). The physical layer specifies the type of connection and the electrical signals, radio waves, or light pulses that pass through it. Chapter 3 discusses the physical layer in detail.

Layer 2: The Data Link Layer The **data link layer** is responsible for moving a message from one computer to the next computer in the network path from the sender to the receiver. The data link layer in the Internet model performs the same three functions as the data link layer in the OSI model. First, it controls the physical layer by deciding when to transmit messages over the media. Second, it formats the messages by indicating where they start and end. Third, it detects and may correct any errors that have occurred during transmission. Chapter 4 discusses the data link layer in detail.

Layer 3: The Network Layer The **network layer** in the Internet model performs the same functions as the network layer in the OSI model. First, it performs routing, in that it selects the next computer to which the message should be sent. Second, it can find the address of that computer if it doesn't already know it. Chapter 5 discusses the network layer in detail.

Layer 4: The Transport Layer The **transport layer** in the Internet model is very similar to the transport layer in the OSI model. It performs two functions. First, it is responsible for linking the application layer software to the network and establishing end-to-end connections between the sender and receiver when such connections are needed. Second, it is responsible for breaking long messages into several smaller messages to make them easier to transmit and then recombining the smaller messages back into the original larger message at the receiving end. The transport layer can also detect lost messages and request that they be resent. Chapter 5 discusses the transport layer in detail.

Layer 5: Application Layer The **application layer** is the application software used by the network user and includes much of what the OSI model contains in the application, presentation, and session layers. It is the user's access to the network. By using the application software, the user defines what messages are sent over the network. Because it is the layer that most people understand best and because starting at the top sometimes helps people understand better, Chapter 2 begins with the application layer. It discusses the architecture of network applications and several types of network application software and the types of messages they generate.

Groups of Layers The layers in the Internet are often so closely coupled that decisions in one layer impose certain requirements on other layers. The data link layer and the physical layer are closely tied together because the data link layer controls the physical layer in terms of when the physical layer can transmit. Because these two layers are so closely tied together, decisions about the data link layer often drive the decisions about the physical layer. For this reason, some people group the physical and data link layers together and call them the **hardware layers**. Likewise, the transport and network layers are so closely coupled that sometimes these layers are called the **internetwork layer**. See Figure 1-3. When you design a network, you often think about the network design in terms of three groups of layers: the hardware layers (physical and data link), the internetwork layers (network and transport), and the application layer.

1.3.3 Message Transmission Using Layers

Each computer in the network has software that operates at each of the layers and performs the functions required by those layers (the physical layer is hardware, not software). Each layer in the network uses a formal language, or **protocol**, that is simply a set of rules that

FIGURE 1-4 Message transmission using layers. IP = Internet Protocol;
HTTP = Hypertext Transfer Protocol; TCP = Transmission Control Protocol

define what the layer will do and that provides a clearly defined set of messages that software at the layer needs to understand. For example, the protocol used for Web applications is HTTP (Hypertext Transfer Protocol, which is described in more detail in Chapter 2). In general, all messages sent in a network pass through all layers. All layers except the physical layer create a new **Protocol Data Unit (PDU)** as the message passes through them. The PDU contains information that is needed to transmit the message through the network. Some experts use the word *packet* to mean a PDU. Figure 1-4 shows how a message requesting a Web page would be sent on the Internet.

Application Layer First, the user creates a message at the application layer using a Web browser by clicking on a link (e.g., get the home page at www.somebody.com). The browser translates the user's message (the click on the Web link) into HTTP. The rules of HTTP define a specific PDU—called an HTTP packet—that all Web browsers must use when they request a Web page. For now, you can think of the HTTP packet as an envelope into which the user's message (*get the Web page*) is placed. In the same way that an envelope placed in the mail needs certain information written in certain places (e.g., return address, destination address), so too does the HTTP packet. The Web browser fills in the necessary information in the HTTP packet, drops the user's request inside the packet, then passes the HTTP packet (containing the Web page request) to the transport layer.

Transport Layer The transport layer on the Internet uses a protocol called TCP (Transmission Control Protocol), and it, too, has its own rules and its own PDUs. TCP is responsible for breaking large files into smaller packets and for opening a connection to the server for the transfer of a large set of packets. The transport layer places the HTTP packet inside a TCP PDU (which is called a TCP segment), fills in the information needed by the TCP segment, and passes the TCP segment (which contains the HTTP packet, which, in turn, contains the message) to the network layer.

Network Layer The network layer on the Internet uses a protocol called IP (Internet Protocol), which has its rules and PDUs. IP selects the next stop on the message's route through the network. It places the TCP segment inside an IP PDU, which is called an IP packet, and passes the IP packet, which contains the TCP segment, which, in turn, contains the HTTP packet, which, in turn, contains the message, to the data link layer.

Data Link Layer If you are connecting to the Internet using a LAN, your data link layer may use a protocol called Ethernet, which also has its own rules and PDUs. The data link layer formats the message with start and stop markers, adds error checking information, places the IP packet inside an Ethernet PDU, which is called an Ethernet frame, and instructs the physical hardware to transmit the Ethernet frame, which contains the IP packet, which contains the TCP segment, which contains the HTTP packet, which contains the message.

Physical Layer The physical layer in this case is network cable connecting your computer to the rest of the network. The computer will take the Ethernet frame (complete with the IP packet, the TCP segment, the HTTP packet, and the message) and send it as a series of electrical pulses through your cable to the server.

When the server gets the message, this process is performed in reverse. The physical hardware translates the electrical pulses into computer data and passes the message to the data link layer. The data link layer uses the start and stop markers in the Ethernet frame to identify the message. The data link layer checks for errors and, if it discovers one, requests that the message be resent. If a message is received without error, the data link layer will strip off the Ethernet frame and pass the IP packet (which contains the TCP segment, the HTTP packet, and the message) to the network layer. The network layer checks the IP address and, if it is destined for this computer, strips off the IP packet and passes the TCP segment, which contains the HTTP packet and the message, to the transport layer. The transport layer processes the message, strips off the TCP segment, and passes the HTTP packet to the application layer for processing. The application layer (i.e., the Web server) reads the HTTP packet and the message it contains (the request for the Web page) and processes it by generating an HTTP packet containing the Web page you requested. Then the process starts again as the page is sent back to you.

The Pros and Cons of Using Layers There are three important points in this example. First, there are many different software packages and many different PDUs that operate at different layers to successfully transfer a message. Networking is in some ways similar to the Russian *matryoshka*, nested dolls that fit neatly inside each other. This is called *encapsulation*, because the PDU at a higher level is placed inside the PDU at a lower level so that the lower-level PDU encapsulates the higher-level one. The major advantage of using different software and protocols is that it is easy to develop new software, because all one has to do is write software for one level at a time. The developers of Web applications, for example, do not need to write software to perform error checking or routing, because those are performed by the data link and network layers. Developers can simply assume those functions are performed and just focus on the application layer. Likewise, it is simple to change the software at any level (or add new application protocols), as long as the interface between that layer and the ones around it remains unchanged.

Second, it is important to note that for communication to be successful, each layer in one computer must be able to communicate with its matching layer in the other computer. For example, the physical layer connecting the client and server must use the same type of electrical signals to enable each to understand the other (or there must be a device to translate between them). Ensuring that the software used at the different layers is the same is accomplished by using *standards*. A standard defines a set of rules, called *protocols*, that explain exactly how hardware and software that conform to the standard are required to operate. Any hardware and software that conform to a standard can communicate with any other hardware and software that conform to the same standard. Without standards, it would be virtually impossible for computers to communicate.

Third, the major disadvantage of using a layered network model is that it is somewhat inefficient. Because there are several layers, each with its own software and PDUs, sending a message involves many software programs (one for each protocol) and many PDUs. The PDUs add to the total amount of data that must be sent (thus increasing the time it takes to transmit), and the different software packages increase the processing power needed in computers. Because the protocols are used at different layers and are stacked on top of one another (take another look at Figure 1-4), the set of software used to understand the different protocols is often called a **protocol stack**.

1.4 NETWORK STANDARDS

1.4.1 The Importance of Standards

Standards are necessary in almost every business and public service entity. For example, before 1904, fire hose couplings in the United States were not standard, which meant a fire department in one community could not help in another community. The transmission of electric current was not standardized until the end of the nineteenth century, so customers had to choose between Thomas Edison's direct current (DC) and George Westinghouse's alternating current (AC).

The primary reason for standards is to ensure that hardware and software produced by different vendors can work together. Without networking standards, it would be difficult—if not impossible—to develop networks that easily share information. Standards also mean that customers are not locked into one vendor. They can buy hardware and software from any vendor whose equipment meets the standard. In this way, standards help to promote more competition and hold down prices.

The use of standards makes it much easier to develop software and hardware that link different networks because software and hardware can be developed one layer at a time.

1.4.2 The Standards-Making Process

There are two types of standards: *de jure* and *de facto*. A *de jure* standard is developed by an official industry or a government body and is often called a formal standard. For example, there are *de jure* standards for applications such as Web browsers (e.g., HTTP, HTML), for network layer software (e.g., IP), for data link layer software (e.g., Ethernet IEEE 802.3), and for physical hardware (e.g., V.90 modems). *De jure* standards typically take several years to develop, during which time technology changes, making them less useful.

De facto standards are those that emerge in the marketplace and are supported by several vendors but have no official standing. For example, Microsoft Windows is a product of one company and has not been formally recognized by any standards organization, yet it is a *de facto* standard. In the communications industry, *de facto* standards often become *de jure* standards once they have been widely accepted.

The *de jure standardization process* has three stages: specification, identification of choices, and acceptance. The *specification* stage consists of developing a nomenclature and identifying the problems to be addressed. In the *identification of choices* stage, those working on the standard identify the various solutions and choose the optimum solution from among the alternatives. *Acceptance*, which is the most difficult stage, consists of defining the solution and getting recognized industry leaders to agree on a single, uniform solution. As with many other organizational processes that have the potential to influence the sales of hardware and software, standards-making processes are not immune to corporate politics and the influence of national governments.

International Organization for Standardization One of the most important standards-making bodies is the *International Organization for Standardization (ISO)*,[2] which makes technical recommendations about data communication interfaces (see www.iso.org). ISO is based in Geneva, Switzerland. The membership is composed of the national standards organizations of each ISO member country.

International Telecommunications Union—Telecommunications Group The **Telecommunications Group (ITU-T)** is the technical standards-setting organization of the United Nations International Telecommunications Union, which is also based in Geneva (see www.itu.int). ITU is composed of representatives from about 200 member countries. Membership was originally focused on just the public telephone companies in each country, but a major reorganization in 1993 changed this, and ITU now seeks members among public- and private-sector organizations who operate computer or communications networks (e.g., RBOCs) or build software and equipment for them (e.g., AT&T).

American National Standards Institute The **American National Standards Institute (ANSI)** is the coordinating organization for the U.S. national system of standards for both technology and nontechnology (see www.ansi.org). ANSI has about 1,000 members from both public and private organizations in the United States. ANSI is a standardization organization, not a standards-making body, in that it accepts standards developed by other organizations and publishes them as American standards. Its role is to coordinate the development of voluntary national standards and to interact with ISO to develop national standards that comply with ISO's international recommendations. ANSI is a voting participant in the ISO.

Institute of Electrical and Electronics Engineers The **Institute of Electrical and Electronics Engineers (IEEE)** is a professional society in the United States whose Standards Association (IEEE-SA) develops standards (see www.standards.ieee.org). The IEEE-SA is probably most known for its standards for LANs. Other countries have similar groups; for example, the British counterpart of IEEE is the Institution of Electrical Engineers (IEE).

Internet Engineering Task Force The IETF sets the standards that govern how much of the Internet will operate (see www.ietf.org). The IETF is unique in that it doesn't really have official memberships. Quite literally anyone is welcome to join its mailing lists, attend its meetings, and comment on developing standards. The role of the IETF and other Internet organizations is discussed in more detail in Chapter 8; also, see the box entitled "How Network Protocols Become Standards."

[2]You're probably wondering why the abbreviation is *ISO*, not *IOS*. Well, *ISO* is a word (not an acronym) derived from the Greek *isos*, meaning "equal." The idea is that with standards, all are equal.

MANAGEMENT FOCUS

1-2 How Network Protocols Become Standards

*T*here are many standards organizations around the world, but perhaps the best known is the **Internet Engineering Task Force (IETF)**. IETF sets the standards that govern how much of the Internet operates.

The IETF, like all standards organizations, tries to seek consensus among those involved before issuing a standard. Usually, a standard begins as a protocol (i.e., a language or set of rules for operating) developed by a vendor (e.g., HTML [Hypertext Markup Language]). When a protocol is proposed for standardization, the IETF forms a working group of technical experts to study it. The working group examines the protocol to identify potential problems and possible extensions and improvements, then issues a report to the IETF.

If the report is favorable, the IETF issues a **Request for Comment (RFC)** that describes the proposed standard and solicits comments from the entire world. Most large software companies likely to be affected by the proposed standard prepare detailed responses. Many "regular" Internet users also send their comments to the IETF.

The IETF reviews the comments and possibly issues a new and improved RFC, which again is posted for more comments. Once no additional changes have been identified, it becomes a proposed standard.

Usually, several vendors adopt the proposed standard and develop products based on it. Once at least two vendors have developed hardware or software based on it and it has proven successful in operation, the proposed standard is changed to a draft standard. This is usually the final specification, although some protocols have been elevated to Internet standards, which usually signifies mature standards not likely to change.

The process does not focus solely on technical issues; almost 90% of the IETF's participants work for manufacturers and vendors, so market forces and politics often complicate matters. One former IETF chairperson who worked for a hardware manufacturer has been accused of trying to delay the standards process until his company had a product ready, although he and other IETF members deny this. Likewise, former IETF directors have complained that members try to standardize every product their firms produce, leading to a proliferation of standards, only a few of which are truly useful.

Sources: "How Networking Protocols Become Standards," *PC Week,* March 17, 1997; "Growing Pains," *Network World,* April 14, 1997.

MANAGEMENT FOCUS

1-3 Keeping Up with Technology

*T*he data communications and networking arena changes rapidly. Significant new technologies are introduced and new concepts are developed almost every year. It is therefore important for network managers to keep up with these changes.

There are at least three useful ways to keep up with change. First and foremost for users of this book is the Web site for this book, which contains updates to the book, additional sections, teaching materials, and links to useful Web sites.

Second, there are literally hundreds of thousands of Web sites with data communications and networking information. Search engines can help you find them. A good initial starting point is the telecom glossary at www.atis.org. Two other useful sites are networkcomputing.com and zdnet.com.

Third, there are many useful magazines that discuss computer technology in general and networking technology in particular, including *Network Computing, Data Communications, Info World, Info Week,* and *CIO Magazine.*

FIGURE 1-5

Some common data communications standards. HTML = Hypertext Markup Language; HTTP = Hypertext Transfer Protocol; IMAP = Internet Message Access Protocol; IP = Internet Protocol; LAN = local area network; MPEG = Motion Picture Experts Group; POP = Post Office Protocol; TCP = Transmission Control Protocol

Layer	Common Standards
5. Application layer	HTTP, HTML (Web) MPEG, H.323 (audio/video) SMTP, IMAP, POP (e-mail)
4. Transport layer	TCP (Internet and LANs)
3. Network layer	IP (Internet and LANs)
2. Data link layer	Ethernet (LAN) Frame relay (WAN) T1 (MAN and WAN)
1. Physical layer	RS-232C cable (LAN) Category 5 cable (LAN) V.92 (56 Kbps modem)

1.4.3 Common Standards

There are many different standards used in networking today. Each standard usually covers one layer in a network. Some of the most commonly used standards are shown in Figure 1-5. At this point, these models are probably just a maze of strange names and acronyms to you, but by the end of the book, you will have a good understanding of each of these. Figure 1-5 provides a brief road map for some of the important communication technologies we discuss in this book.

For now, there is one important message you should understand from Figure 1-5: For a network to operate, many different standards must be used simultaneously. The sender of a message must use one standard at the application layer, another one at the transport layer, another one at the network layer, another one at the data link layer, and another one at the physical layer. Each layer and each standard is different, but all must work together to send and receive messages.

Either the sender and receiver of a message must use the same standards or, more likely, there are devices between the two that translate from one standard into another. Because different networks often use software and hardware designed for different standards, there is often a lot of translation between different standards.

1.5 FUTURE TRENDS

The field of data communications has grown faster and become more important than computer processing itself. Both go hand in hand, but we have moved from the computer era to the communication era. Three major trends are driving the future of communications and networking.

1.5.1 Wireless LAN and BYOD

The rapid development of mobile devices, such as smart phones and tablets, has encouraged employers to allow their employees to bring these devices to work and use them to access data, such as their work email. This movement, called bring your own device, or BYOD, is a great way to get work quickly, saves money, and makes employees happy. But BYOD also brings its own problems. Employers need to add or expand their Wireless Local Area Networks (WLANS) to support all these new devices.

Another important problem is security. Employees bring these devices to work so that they can access not only their email but also other critical company assets, such as information about their clients, suppliers, or sales. Employers face myriad decisions about how to manage access to company applications for BYOD. Companies can adopt two main approaches: (1) native apps or (2) browser-based technologies. **Native apps** require an app to be developed for each application that an employee might be using for every potential device that the employee might use (e.g., iPhone, Android, Windows). The **browser-based** approach (often referred to as responsive design using HTML5) doesn't create an app but rather requires employees to access the application through a Web browser. Both these approaches have their pros and cons, and only the future will show which one is the winner.

What if an employee loses his or her mobile phone or tablet so that the application that accesses critical company data now can be used by anybody who finds the device? Will the company's data be compromised? Device and data loss practices now have to be added to the general security practices of the company. Employees need to have apps to allow their employer to wipe their phones clean in case of loss so that no company data are compromised (e.g., SOTI's MobiControl). In some cases, companies require the employee to allow monitoring of the device at all times, to ensure that security risks are minimized. However, some argue that this is not a good practice because the device belongs to the employee, and monitoring it 24/7 invades the employee's privacy.

1.5.2 The Web of Things

Telephones and computers used to be separate. Today voice and data have converged into unified communications, with phones plugged into computers or directly into the LAN using Voice over Internet Protocol (VOIP). Vonage and Skype have taken this one step further and offer telephone service over the Internet at dramatically lower prices than traditional separate landline phones, whether from traditional phones or via computer microphones and speakers.

Computers and networks can also be built into everyday things, such as kitchen appliances, doors, and shoes. In the future, the Web will move from being a Web of computers to also being a Web of Things with which we interact using a computer. All this interaction will happen seamlessly, without human intervention. And we will get used to seeing our shoes tell us how far we walked, our refrigerator telling us what food we need to buy, and our locks opening and closing without physical keys and telling us who entered and left at what times.

The Web of Things is already under way. For example, Microsoft has an Envisioning Center that focuses on creating the future of work and play (it is open to the public). At the Envisioning Center, a person can communicate with his or her colleagues through digital walls that enable the person to visualize projects through simulation and then rapidly move to execution of ideas. In the home of the future, anyone can, for example, be a chef and adapt recipes based on dietary needs or ingredients in the pantry (see Figure 1-6) through the use of Kinect technology.

Google is another leading innovator in the Web of Things. Google has been developing a self-driving car for several years. This self-driving car not only passes a standard driving test but also spends less time in near-collision states on public roads in California and Nevada. Of course, for such a car to appear in other states, technology has to be installed that allows the car to "see" the road. Other car developers started installing computer technology that not only parallel parks the car but also applies brakes to avoid collisions.

1.5.3 Massively Online

You have probably heard of massively multiplayer online games, such as World of Warcraft, where you can play with thousands of players in real time. Well, today not only games

FIGURE 1-6

Microsoft's Envisioning Center—Smart Stovetop that helps you cook without getting in your way

Source: Smart Stovetop, Microsofts Envisioning Center, Used with permission by Microsoft.

are massively online. Education is massively online. Khan Academy, Lynda.com, or Code Academy have Web sites that offer thousands of education modules for children and adults in myriad fields to help them learn. Your class very likely also has an online component. You may even use this textbook online and decide whether your comments are for you only, for your instructor, or for the entire class to read. In addition, you may have heard about massive open online courses, or MOOC. MOOC enable students who otherwise wouldn't have access to elite universities to get access to top knowledge without having to pay the tuition. These classes are offered by universities, such as Stanford, UC Berkeley, MIT, UCLA, and Carnegie Mellon, free of charge and for no credit (although at some universities, you can pay and get credit toward your degree).

Politics has also moved massively online. President Obama reached out to the crowds and ordinary voters not only through his Facebook page but also through Reddit and Google Hangouts. Many other politicians use social computing to reach potential voters. Finally, massively online allows activists to reach masses of people in a very short period of time to initiate change. Examples of use of YouTube videos or Facebook for activism include the Arab Spring, Kony 2012, or the use of sarin gas in Syria.

So what started as a game with thousands of people being online at the same time is being reinvented for good use in education, politics, and activism. Only the future will show what humanity can do with what massively online has to offer.

What these three trends have in common is that there will be an increasing demand for professionals who understand development of data communications and networking infrastructure to support this growth. There will be more and more need to build faster and more secure networks that will allow individuals and organizations to connect to resources, probably stored on cloud infrastructure (either private or public). This need will call not only for engineers who deeply understand the technical aspects of networks but also for highly social individuals who embrace technology in creative ways to allow business to achieve a competitive edge through utilizing this technology. So the call is for you who are reading this book—you are in the right place at the right time!

1.6 IMPLICATIONS FOR MANAGEMENT

At the end of each chapter, we provide key implications for management that arise from the topics discussed in the chapter. We draw implications that focus on improving the management of networks and information systems as well as implications for the management of the organization as a whole.

FIGURE 1-7

One server farm with more than 1,000 servers

Source: © zentilia/iStockphoto

There are three key implications for management from this chapter. First, networks and the Internet change almost everything. The ability to quickly and easily move information from distant locations and to enable individuals inside and outside the firm to access information and products from around the world changes the way organizations operate, the way businesses buy and sell products, and the way we as individuals work, live, play, and learn. Companies and individuals who embrace change and actively seek to apply networks and the Internet to better improve what they do will thrive; companies and individuals who do not will gradually find themselves falling behind.

Second, today's networking environment is driven by standards. The use of standard technology means an organization can easily mix and match equipment from different vendors. The use of standard technology also means that it is easier to migrate from older technology to a newer technology, because most vendors designed their products to work with many different standards. The use of a few standard technologies rather than a wide range of vendor-specific proprietary technologies also lowers the cost of networking because network managers have fewer technologies they need to learn about and support. If your company is not using a narrow set of industry-standard networking technologies (whether those are *de facto* standards such as Windows, open standards such as Linux, or *de jure* standards such as 802.11n wireless LANs), then it is probably spending too much money on its networks.

Third, as the demand for network services and network capacity increases, so too will the need for storage and server space. Finding efficient ways to store all the information we generate will open new market opportunities. Today, Google has almost a million Web servers (see Figure 1-7). If we assume that each server costs an average of $1000, the money large companies spend on storage is close to $1Billion. Capital expenditure of this scale is then increased by money spent on power and staffing. One way companies can reduce this amount of money is to store their data using cloud computing.

SUMMARY

Introduction The information society, where information and intelligence are the key drivers of personal, business, and national success, has arrived. Data communications is the principal enabler of the rapid information exchange and will become more important than the use of computers themselves in the future. Successful users of data communications, such as Wal-Mart, can gain significant competitive advantage in the marketplace.

Network Definitions A local area network (LAN) is a group of computers located in the same general area. A backbone network (BN) is a large central network that connects almost everything on a single company site. A metropolitan area network (MAN) encompasses a city or county area. A wide area network (WAN) spans city, state, or national boundaries.

Network Model Communication networks are often broken into a series of layers, each of which can be defined separately, to enable vendors to develop software and hardware that can work together in the overall network. In this book, we use a five-layer model. The application layer is the application software used by the network user. The transport layer takes the message generated by the application layer and, if necessary, breaks it into several smaller messages. The network layer addresses the message and determines its route through the network. The data link layer formats the message to indicate where it starts and ends, decides when to transmit it over the physical media, and detects and corrects any errors that occur in transmission. The physical layer is the physical connection between the sender and receiver, including the hardware devices (e.g., computers, terminals, and modems) and physical media (e.g., cables and satellites). Each layer, except the physical layer, adds a Protocol Data Unit (PDU) to the message.

Standards Standards ensure that hardware and software produced by different vendors can work together. A *de jure* standard is developed by an official industry or a government body. *De facto* standards are those that emerge in the marketplace and are supported by several vendors but have no official standing. Many different standards and standards-making organizations exist.

Future Trends At the same time as the use of BYOD offers efficiency at the workplace, it opens up the doors for security problems that companies need to consider. Our interactions with colleagues and family will very likely change in the next 5–10 years because of the Web of Things, where devices will interact with each other without human intervention. Finally, massively online not only changed the way we play computer games but also showed that humanity can change its history.

KEY TERMS

QUESTIONS

1. How can data communications networks affect businesses?
2. Discuss three important applications of data communications networks in business and personal use.
3. How do local area networks (LANs) differ from wide area networks (WANs) and backbone networks (BNs)?
4. What is a circuit?
5. What is a client?
6. What is a server?
7. Why are network layers important?
8. Describe the seven layers in the OSI network model and what they do.
9. Describe the five layers in the Internet network model and what they do.
10. Explain how a message is transmitted from one computer to another using layers.
11. Describe the three stages of standardization.
12. How are Internet standards developed?
13. Describe two important data communications standards-making bodies. How do they differ?
14. What is the purpose of a data communications standard?
15. What are three of the largest interexchange carriers (IXCs) in North America?
16. Discuss three trends in communications and networking.
17. Why has the Internet model replaced the Open Systems Interconnection Reference (OSI) model?
18. In the 1980s, when we wrote the first edition of this book, there were many, many more protocols in common use at the data link, network, and transport layers than there are today. Why do you think the number of commonly used protocols at these layers has declined? Do you think this trend will continue? What are the implications for those who design and operate networks?
19. The number of standardized protocols in use at the application layer has significantly increased since the 1980s. Why? Do you think this trend will continue? What are the implications for those who design and operate networks?
20. How many bits (not bytes) are there in a 10-page text document? Hint: There are approximately 350 words on a double-spaced page.

EXERCISES

A. Investigate the long-distance carriers (interexchange carriers [IXCs]) and local exchange carriers (LECs) in your area. What services do they provide, and what pricing plans do they have for residential users?
B. Discuss the issue of communications monopolies and open competition with an economics instructor and relate his or her comments to your data communication class.
C. Find a college or university offering a specialized degree in telecommunications or data communications and describe the program.
D. Describe a recent data communication development you have read about in a newspaper or magazine and how it may affect businesses.
E. Investigate the networks in your school or organization. Describe the important local area networks (LANs) and backbone networks (BNs) in use (but do not describe the specific clients, servers, or devices on them).
F. Use the Web to search the Internet Engineering Task (IETF) Web site (www.ietf.org). Describe one standard that is in the request for comment (RFC) stage.
G. Discuss how the revolution/evolution of communications and networking is likely to affect how you will work and live in the future.
H. Investigate the pros and cons of developing native apps versus taking a browser-based approach.

MINICASES

I. **Global Consultants** John Adams is the chief information officer (CIO) of Global Consultants (GC), a very large consulting firm with offices in more than 100 countries around the the world. GC is about to purchase a set of several Internet-based financial software packages that will be installed in all of their offices. There are no standards at the application layer for financial software but several software companies that sell financial software (call them group A) use one *de facto* standard to enable their software to work with one another's software. However, another group of financial software companies (call them group B) use a different *de facto* standard. Although both groups have software packages that GC could use, GC would really prefer to buy one package from group A for one type of financial analysis and one package from group B for a different type of financial analysis. The problem, of course, is that then the two packages cannot communicate and GC's staff would end up having to type the same data into both packages. The alternative is to buy two packages from the same group—so that data could be easily shared—but that would mean having to settle for second best for one of the packages. Although there have been some reports in the press about the two groups of companies working together to develop one common standard that will enable software to work together, there is no firm agreement yet. What advice would you give Adams?

II. **Atlas Advertising** Atlas Advertising is a regional advertising agency with offices in Boston, New York, Providence, Washington, D.C., and Philadelphia. 1. Describe the types of networks you think they would have (e.g., LANs, BNs, WANs) and where they are likely to be located. 2. What types of standard protocols and technologies do you think they are using at each layer (e.g., see Figure 1-5)?

III. **Consolidated Supplies** Consolidated Supplies is a medium-sized distributor of restaurant supplies that operates in Canada and several northern U.S. states. They have 12 large warehouses spread across both countries to service their many customers. Products

arrive from the manufacturers and are stored in the warehouses until they are picked and put on a truck for delivery to their customers. The networking equipment in their warehouses is old and is starting to give them problems; these problems are expected to increase as the equipment gets older. The vice president of operations, Pat McDonald, would like to replace the existing LANs and add some new wireless LAN technology into all the warehouses, but he is concerned that now may not be the right time to replace the equipment. He has read several technology forecasts that suggest there will be dramatic improvements in networking speeds over the next few years, especially in wireless technologies. He has asked you for advice about upgrading the equipment. Should Consolidated Supplies replace all the networking equipment in all the warehouses now, should it wait until newer networking technologies are available, or should it upgrade some of the warehouses this year, some next year, and some the year after, so that some warehouses will benefit from the expected future improvements in networking technologies?

IV. **Asia Importers** Caisy Wong is the owner of a small catalog company that imports a variety of clothes and houseware from several Asian countries and sells them to its customers over the Web and by telephone through a traditional catalog. She has read about the convergence of voice and data and is wondering about changing her current traditional, separate, and rather expensive telephone and data services into one service offered by a new company that will supply both telephone and data over her Internet connection. What are the potential benefits and challenges that Asia Importers should consider in making the decision about whether to move to one integrated service?

CASE STUDY

NEXT-DAY AIR SERVICE

See the book companion site at www.wiley.com/college/fitzgerald.

HANDS-ON ACTIVITY 1A

Convergence at Home

We talked about the convergence of voice, video, and data into unified communications. The objective of this Activity is for you to experience this convergence.

1. Yahoo! Instant Messenger is one of the many tools that permit the convergence of voice, video, and text data over the Internet. Use your browser to

FIGURE 1-8 Voice, video, and data in Yahoo! Instant Messenger

connect to messenger.yahoo.com and sign up for Yahoo! Instant Messenger, then download and install it—or use the tool of your choice (Skype is another good tool). Buy an inexpensive Webcam with a built-in microphone.

2. Get your parents to do the same.

3. Every weekend, talk to your parents using IM text, voice, and video (see Figure 1-8). It's free, so there's no phone bill to worry about, and the video will make everyone feel closer. If you want to feel even closer, connect to them and just leave the voice and video on while you do your homework; no need to talk, just spend time together online.

Deliverable

A log of your conversations showing the date and time of the conversation, the person(s) you spoke with, and how long the conversation lasted.

HANDS-ON ACTIVITY 1B

Seeing the PDUs in Your Messages

We talked about how messages are transferred using layers and the different Protocol Data Units (PDUs) used at each layer. The objective of this Activity is for you to see the different PDUs in the messages that you send. To do this, we'll use Wireshark, which is one of the world's foremost network protocol analyzers, and is the *de facto* standard that most professional and education institutions use today. It is used for network troubleshooting, network analysis, software and communications protocol development, and general education about how networks work.

Wireshark enables you to see all messages sent by your computer, as well as some or all of the messages sent by other computers on your LAN, depending on how your LAN is designed. Most modern LANs are designed to prevent you from eavesdropping on other computer's messages, but some older ones still permit this. Normally, your computer will ignore the messages that are not addressed for your computer, but Wireshark enables you to eavesdrop and read messages sent to and from other computers.

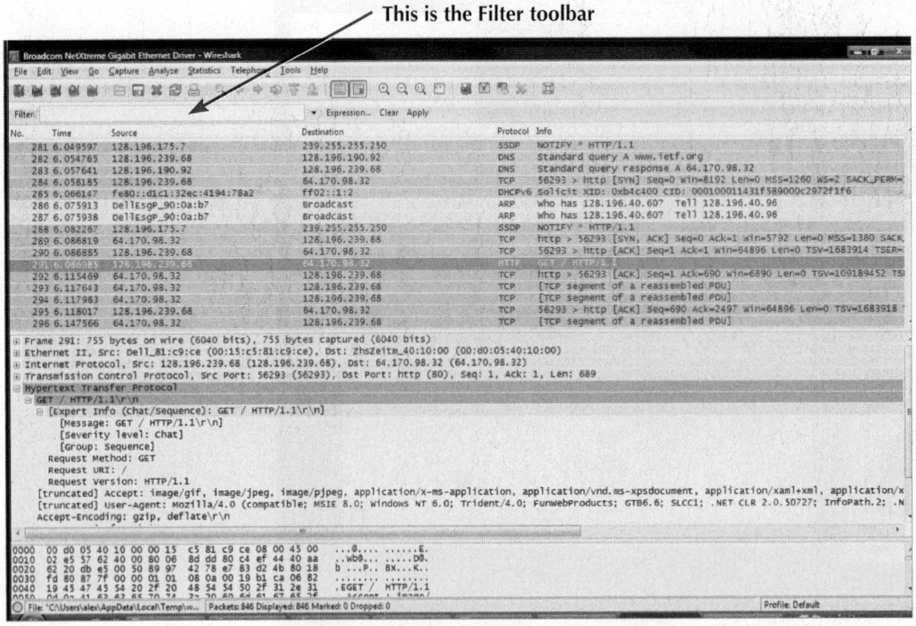

This is the Filter toolbar

FIGURE 1-9 Wireshark capture

Wireshark is free. Before you start this activity, download and install it from www.wireshark.org.

1. Start Wireshark.

2. Click on Capture and then Interfaces. Click the Start button next to the active interface (the one that is receiving and sending packets). Your network data will be captured from this moment on.

3. Open your browser and go to a Web page that you have not visited recently (a good one is www.iana.org).

4. Once the Web page has loaded, go back to Wireshark and stop the packet capture by clicking on Capture and then Stop (the hot key for this is Ctrl + E).

5. You will see results similar to those in Figure 1-9. There are three windows below the tool bar:

   a. The top window is the Packet List. Each line represents a single message or packet that was captured by Wireshark. Different types of packets will have different colors. For example, HTTP packets are colored green. Depending on how busy your network is, you may see a small number of packets in this window or a very large number of packets.

   b. The middle window is the Packet Detail. This will show the details for any packet you click on in the top window.

   c. The bottom window shows the actual contents of the packet in hexadecimal format, so it is usually hard to read. This window is typically used by network programmers to debug errors.

6. Let's take a look at the packets that were used to request the Web page and send it to your computer. The application layer protocol used on the Web is HTTP, so we'll want to find the HTTP packets. In the Filter toolbar, type http and hit enter.

7. This will highlight all the packets that contain HTTP packets and will display the first one in Packet Detail window. Look at the Packet Detail window in Figure 1-9 to see the PDUs in the message we've highlighted. You'll see that it contains an Ethernet II Frame, an IP packet, a TCP segment, and an HTTP packet. You can see inside any or all of these PDUs by clicking on the +box in front of them. In Figure 1-9, you'll see that we've clicked the +box in front of the HTTP packet to show you what's inside it.

Deliverables

1. List the PDU at layers 2, 3, and 4 that were used to transmit your HTTP GET packet.

   a. Locate your HTTP Get packet in the Packet List and click on it.

   b. Look in the Packet Detail window to get the PDU information.

2. How many different HTTP GET packets were sent by your browser? Not all the HTTP packets are GET packets, so you'll have to look through them to answer this question.

3. List at least five other protocols that Wireshark displayed in the Packet List window. You will need to clear the filter by clicking on the "Clear" icon that is on the right of the Filter toolbar.

CHAPTER 2

APPLICATION LAYER

The application layer (also called layer 5) is the software that enables the user to perform useful work. The software at the application layer is the reason for having the network because it is this software that provides the business value. This chapter examines the five fundamental types of application architectures used at the application layer (host-based, client-based, client-server, cloud-based, and peer-to-peer). It then looks at the Internet and the primary software application packages it enables: the Web, email, Telnet, and instant messaging.

OBJECTIVES

- Understand host-based, client-based, client-server, and cloud-based application architectures
- Understand how the Web works
- Understand how email works
- Be aware of how Telnet and instant messaging work

OUTLINE

2.1 INTRODUCTION

Network applications are the software packages that run in the application layer. You should be quite familiar with many types of network software, because it is these application packages that you use when you use the network. In many respects, the only reason for having a network is to enable these applications.

In this chapter, we first discuss five basic architectures for network applications and how each of those architectures affects the design of networks. Because you probably have a good understanding of applications such as the Web and word processing, we will use those as examples of different application architectures. We then examine several common applications used on the **Internet** (e.g., Web, email) and use those to explain how application software interacts with the networks. By the end of this chapter, you should have a much better understanding of the application layer in the network model and what exactly we meant when we used the term *protocol data unit* in Chapter 1.

2.2 APPLICATION ARCHITECTURES

In Chapter 1, we discussed how the three basic components of a network (client computer, server computer, and circuit) worked together. In this section, we will get a bit more specific about how the client computer and the server computer can work together to provide application software to the users. An **application architecture** is the way in which the functions of the application layer software are spread among the clients and servers in the network.

The work done by any application program can be divided into four general functions. The first is **data storage**. Most application programs require data to be stored and retrieved, whether it is a small file such as a memo produced by a word processor or a large database such as an organization's accounting records. The second function is **data access logic**, the processing required to access data, which often means database queries in SQL (structured query language). The third function is the **application logic** (sometimes called business logic), which also can be simple or complex, depending on the application. The fourth function is the **presentation logic**, the presentation of information to the user and the acceptance of the user's commands. These four functions—data storage, data access logic, application logic, and presentation logic—are the basic building blocks of any application.

There are many ways in which these four functions can be allocated between the client computers and the servers in a network. There are five fundamental application architectures in use today. In **host-based architectures**, the server (or host computer) performs virtually all of the work. In **client-based architectures**, the client computers perform most of the work. In **client-server architectures**, the work is shared between the servers and clients. In **cloud-based architectures**, the cloud provides services (software, platform, and/or infrastructure) to the client. In **peer-to-peer architectures**, computers are both clients and servers and thus share the work. Although the client-server architecture is the dominant application architecture, cloud-based architecture is becoming the runner-up because it offers rapid scalability and deployability of computer resources.

TECHNICAL FOCUS

2-1 Cloud Computing Deployment Models

When an organization decides to use cloud-based architecture, it needs to decide on which deployment model will it use. There are three deployment models from which to choose:

- **Private cloud** As the name suggests, private clouds are created for the exclusive use of a single private organization. The cloud (hardware and software) would be hosted by the organization in a private data center. This deployment model provides the highest levels of control, privacy, and security. This model is often used by organizations needing to satisfy regulations posed by regulators, such as in the financial and health care industries.
- **Public cloud** This deployment model is used by multiple organizations that share the same cloud resources. The level of control is lower than in private clouds, and many companies are concerned with the security of their data. However, this deployment model doesn't require any upfront capital investment, and the selected service can be up and running in a few days. Public clouds are a good choice when a lot of people in the organization are using the same application. Because of this, the most frequently used software as a service (SaaS) is email. For example, many universities have moved to this model for their students.

- **Community cloud** This deployment model is used by organizations that have a common purpose. Rather than each organization creating its own private cloud, organizations decide to collaborate and pool their resources. Although this cloud is not private, only a limited number of companies have access to it. Community clouds are considered to be a subset of public clouds. Therefore, community clouds realize the benefits from cloud infrastructure (such as speed of deployment) with the added level of privacy and security that private clouds offer. This deployment model is often used in the government, health care, and finance industries, members of which have similar application needs and require a very high level of security.

  Sometimes an organization will choose to use only one of these deployment models for all its cloud-based applications. This strategy is called a **pure strategy**, such as a pure private cloud strategy or a pure public cloud strategy. In other cases, the organization is best supported by a mix of public, private, and community clouds for different applications. This strategy is called a **hybrid cloud strategy**. A hybrid cloud strategy allows the organization to take advantage of the benefits that these different cloud deployment models offer. For example, a hospital can use Gmail for its email application (public cloud) but a private cloud for patient data, which require high security. The downside of a hybrid cloud strategy is that an organization has to deal with different platforms and **cloud providers**. However, the truth is that this strategy offers the greatest flexibility, so most organizations eventually end up with this strategy.

2.2.1 Host-Based Architectures

The very first data communications networks developed in the 1960s were host-based, with the server (usually a large mainframe computer) performing all four functions. The clients (usually terminals) enabled users to send and receive messages to and from the host computer. The clients merely captured keystrokes, sent them to the server for processing, and accepted instructions from the server on what to display (see Figure 2-1).

This very simple architecture often works very well. Application software is developed and stored on the one server along with all data. If you've ever used a terminal, you've used a host-based application. There is one point of control, because all messages flow through the one central server. In theory, there are economies of scale, because all computer resources are centralized (but more on cost later).

There are two fundamental problems with host-based networks. First, the server must process all messages. As the demands for more and more network applications grow, many servers become overloaded and unable to quickly process all the users' demands. Prioritizing users' access becomes difficult. Response time becomes slower, and network managers are required to spend increasingly more money to upgrade the server. Unfortunately, upgrades to the mainframes that usually are the servers in this architecture are "lumpy." That is, upgrades come in large increments and are expensive (e.g., $500,000); it is difficult to upgrade "a little."

2.2.2 Client-Based Architectures

In the late 1980s, there was an explosion in the use of personal computers. Today, more than 90% of most organizations' total computer processing power now resides on personal computers, not in centralized mainframe computers. Part of this expansion was fueled by a number of low-cost, highly popular applications such as word processors, spreadsheets, and presentation graphics programs. It was also fueled in part by managers' frustrations with application software on host mainframe computers. Most mainframe software is not as easy to use as personal computer software, is far more expensive, and can take years to develop. In the late 1980s, many large organizations had application development backlogs of

FIGURE 2-1

Host-based architecture

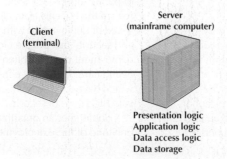

Client
(terminal)

Server
(mainframe computer)

Presentation logic
Application logic
Data access logic
Data storage

FIGURE 2-2

Client-based architecture

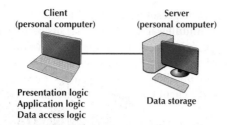

Client
(personal computer)

Server
(personal computer)

Presentation logic
Application logic
Data access logic

Data storage

2 to 3 years; that is, getting any new mainframe application program written would take years. New York City, for example, had a 6-year backlog. In contrast, managers could buy personal computer packages or develop personal computer-based applications in a few months.

With client-based architectures, the clients are personal computers on a LAN, and the server is usually another personal computer on the same network. The application software on the client computers is responsible for the presentation logic, the application logic, and the data access logic; the server simply stores the data (Figure 2-2).

This simple architecture often works very well. If you've ever used a word processor and stored your document file on a server (or written a program in Visual Basic or C that runs on your computer but stores data on a server), you've used a client-based architecture.

The fundamental problem in client-based networks is that all data on the server must travel to the client for processing. For example, suppose the user wishes to display a list of all employees with company life insurance. All the data in the database (or all the indices) must travel from the server where the database is stored over the network circuit to the client, which then examines each record to see if it matches the data requested by the user. This can overload the network circuits because far more data are transmitted from the server to the client than the client actually needs.

2.2.3 Client-Server Architectures

Most applications written today use client-server architectures. Client-server architectures attempt to balance the processing between the client and the server by having both do some of the logic. In these networks, the client is responsible for the presentation logic, whereas the server is responsible for the data access logic and data storage. The application logic may either reside on the client, reside on the server, or be split between both.

Figure 2-3 shows the simplest case, with the presentation logic and application logic on the client and the data access logic and data storage on the server. In this case, the client software accepts user requests and performs the application logic that produces database requests that are transmitted to the server. The server software accepts the database requests, performs the data access logic, and transmits the results to the client. The client software accepts the results and presents them to the user. When you used a Web browser to get pages from a Web server, you used a client-server architecture. Likewise, if you've ever written a program that uses SQL to talk to a database on a server, you've used a client-server architecture.

For example, if the user requests a list of all employees with company life insurance, the client would accept the request, format it so that it could be understood by the server, and transmit it to the server. On receiving the request, the server searches the database for all requested records and then transmits only the matching records to the client, which would then present them to the user. The same would be true for database updates; the client accepts the request and sends it to the server. The server processes the update and responds (either accepting the update or explaining why not) to the client, which displays it to the user.

One of the strengths of client-server networks is that they enable software and hardware from different vendors to be used together. But this is also one of their disadvantages, because it can be difficult to get software from different vendors to work together. One solution to this problem is **middleware**, software that sits between the application software on the client and the application software on the server. Middleware does two things. First, it provides a standard way of communicating that can translate between software from different vendors. Many middleware tools began as translation utilities that enabled messages sent from a specific client tool to be translated into a form understood by a specific server tool.

The second function of middleware is to manage the message transfer from clients to servers (and vice versa) so that clients need not know the specific server that contains the application's data. The application software on the client sends all messages to the middleware, which forwards them to the correct server. The application software on the client is therefore protected from any changes in the physical network. If the network layout changes (e.g., a new server is added), only the middleware must be updated.

There are literally dozens of standards for middleware, each of which is supported by different vendors and each of which provides different functions. Two of the most important standards are Distributed Computing Environment (DCE) and Common Object Request Broker Architecture (CORBA). Both of these standards cover virtually all aspects of the client-server architecture but are quite different. Any client or server software that conforms to one of these standards can communicate with any other software that conforms to the same standard. Another important standard is Open Database Connectivity (ODBC), which provides a standard for data access logic.

Two-Tier, Three-Tier, and *n*-Tier Architectures There are many ways in which the application logic can be partitioned between the client and the server. The example in Figure 2-3 is one of the most common. In this case, the server is responsible for the data and the client, the application and presentation. This is called a **two-tier architecture**, because it uses only two sets of computers, one set of clients and one set of servers.

A **three-tier architecture** uses three sets of computers, as shown in Figure 2-4. In this case, the software on the client computer is responsible for presentation logic, an application server is responsible for the application logic, and a separate database server is responsible for the data access logic and data storage.

N-tier architecture uses more than three sets of computers. In this case, the client is responsible for presentation logic, a database server is responsible for the data access logic and data storage, and the application logic is spread across two or more different sets of servers. Figure 2-5 shows an example of an *n*-tier architecture of a groupware product called TCB Works developed at the University of Georgia. TCB Works has four major components. The first is the Web browser on the client computer that a user uses to access the system and enter commands (presentation logic). The second component is a Web server that responds to the user's requests, either by providing HTML pages and graphics (application logic) or by sending the request to the third component, a set of 28 C programs that perform various functions such as adding comments or voting (application logic). The fourth component is a database server that stores all the data (data access logic and data storage). Each of these four components is separate, making it easy to spread the different components on different servers and to partition the application logic on two different servers.

FIGURE 2-3

Two-tier client-server architecture

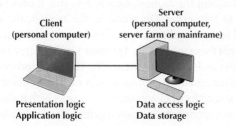

Client
(personal computer)

Server
(personal computer,
server farm or mainframe)

Presentation logic
Application logic

Data access logic
Data storage

FIGURE 2-4

Three-tier client-server
architecture

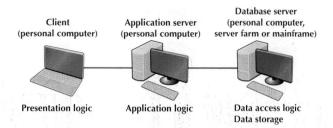

The primary advantage of an *n*-tier client-server architecture compared with a two-tier architecture (or a three-tier compared with a two-tier) is that it separates the processing that occurs to better balance the load on the different servers; it is more scalable. In Figure 2-5, we have three separate servers, which provides more power than if we had used a two-tier architecture with only one server. If we discover that the application server is too heavily loaded, we can simply replace it with a more powerful server, or even put in two application servers. Conversely, if we discover the database server is underused, we could put data from another application on it.

There are two primary disadvantages to an *n*-tier architecture compared with a two-tier architecture (or a three-tier with a two-tier). First, it puts a greater load on the network. If you compare Figures 2-3, 2-4, and 2-5, you will see that the *n*-tier model requires more communication among the servers; it generates more network traffic so you need a higher capacity network. Second, it is much more difficult to program and test software in *n*-tier architectures than in two-tier architectures because more devices have to communicate to complete a user's transaction.

Thin Clients versus Thick Clients Another way of classifying client-server architectures is by examining how much of the application logic is placed on the client computer. A **thin-client** approach places little or no application logic on the client (e.g., Figure 2-5), whereas a **thick-client** (also called *fat-client*) approach places all or almost all of the application logic on the client (e.g., Figure 2-3). There is no direct relationship between thin and fat client and two-, three- and *n*-tier architectures. For example, Figure 2-6 shows a typical Web architecture: a two-tier architecture with a thin client. One of the biggest forces favoring thin clients is the Web.

Thin clients are much easier to manage. If an application changes, only the server with the application logic needs to be updated. With a thick client, the software on all of the

FIGURE 2-5

The *n*-tier client-server
architecture

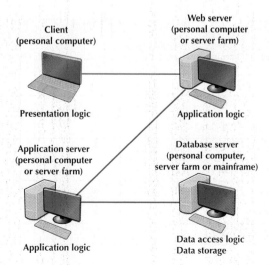

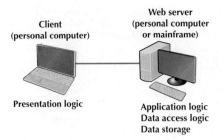

clients would need to be updated. Conceptually, this is a simple task; one simply copies the new files to the hundreds of affected client computers. In practice, it can be a very difficult task.

Thin-client architectures are the future. More and more application systems are being written to use a Web browser as the client software, with Java Javascriptor AJAX (containing some of the application logic) downloaded as needed. This application architecture is sometimes called the **distributed computing model**. The thin-client architecture also enables **cloud-based architecture**, which is discussed next.

2.2.4 Cloud Computing Architectures

The traditional client-server architecture can be complicated and expensive to deploy. Every application has to be hosted on a server so that it can fulfill requests from potentially thousands of clients. An organization has hundreds of applications, so running a successful client-server architecture requires a variety of software and hardware and the skilled personnel who can build and maintain this architecture.

Cloud computing architectures are different because they outsource part or all of the infrastructure to other firms that specialize in managing that infrastructure. There are three common cloud-based architecture models. Figure 2-7 summarizes these three models and compares them to the client-server architecture.

The first column of this figure shows the thin-client client-server architecture, in which the organization manages the entire application software and hardware. In addition to the software components we've discussed previously (the application logic, data access logic, and the data themselves), the servers need an operating system (e.g., Windows, Linux). Most companies also use virtualization software to install many virtual or logical servers on the

Who manages which parts	Thin-Client Client-Server		Infrastructure as a Service		Platform as a Service		Software as a Service	
	Internal	Outsourced	Internal	Outsourced	Internal	Outsourced	Internal	Outsourced
Application Logic	X		X		X			X
Data Storage	X		X		X			X
Data Access Logic	X		X			X		X
Operating System	X		X			X		X
Virtualization Software	X		X			X		X
Server Hardware	X			X		X		X
Storage Hardware	X			X		X		X
Network Hardware	X			X		X		X

FIGURE 2-8

One row of a server farm at Indiana University
Source: Courtesy of the author, Alan Dennis

same physical computer. This software (VMware is one of the leaders) creates a separate partition on the physical server for each of the logical servers. Each partition has its own operations system and its own server software and works independently from the other partitions.

This software must run on some hardware, which includes a server, a storage device, and the network itself. The server may be a large computer or a **server farm**. A server farm is a cluster of computers linked together so that they act as one computer. Requests arrive at the server farm (e.g., Web requests) and are distributed among the computers so that no one computer is overloaded. Each computer is separate so that if one fails, the sever farm simply bypasses it. Server farms are more complex than single servers because work must be quickly coordinated and shared among the individual computers. Server farms are very scalable because one can always add another computer. Figure 2-8 shows one row of a server farm at Indiana University. There are seven more rows like this one in this room, and another room contains about the same number.

Many companies use separate storage devices instead of the hard disks in the servers themselves. These storage devices are special-purpose hard disks designed to be very large and very fast. The six devices on the left of Figure 2-8 comprise a special storage device called a **storage area network** (SAN).

Software as a Service (SaaS) SaaS is one of the three cloud computing models. With SaaS, an organization outsources the entire application to the cloud provider (see the last column of Figure 2-7) and uses it as any other application that is available via a browser (thin client). SaaS is based on **multitenancy**. This means that rather than having many copies of the same application, there is only one application that everybody shares, yet everybody can customize it for his or her specific needs. Imagine a giant office building in which all people share the infrastructure (water, A/C, electricity) but can customize the offices they are renting. The customers can customize the app and don't have to worry about upgrades, security, or underlying infrastructure because the cloud provider does it all. The most frequently used SaaS application is email. At Indiana University, all student email is outsourced to Google's Gmail. Customer relationship management (CRM) from Salesforce.com is another very commonly used SaaS.

Platform as a Service (PaaS) PaaS is another of the three cloud computing models. What if there is an application you need but no cloud provider offers one you like? You can build your own application and manage your own data on the cloud infrastructure provided by your cloud supplier. This model is called Platform as a Service (PaaS). The developers in your organization decide what programming language to use to develop the application of choice. The needed hardware and software infrastructure, called the platform, is rented from the cloud provider (see Figure 2-7). In this case, the organization manages the application and its own data but uses the database software (data access logic) and operating system provided by the cloud provider. PaaS offers a much faster development and deployment of custom applications at a fraction of the cost required for the traditional client-server architecture. PaaS providers include Amazon Elastic Cloud Compute (EC2), Microsoft Windows Azure, and Google App Engine.

Infrastructure as a Service (IaaS) As you can see in Figure 2-7, with IaaS, the cloud provider manages the hardware, including servers, storage, and networking components. The organization is responsible for all the software, including operating system (and virtualization software), database software, and its applications and data. IaaS is sometimes referred to also as **HaaS**, or **Hardware as a Service**, because in this cloud model, only the hardware is provided; everything else is up to the organization. This model allows a decrease in capital expenditures for hardware and maintaining the proper environment (e.g., cooling) and redundancy, and backups for data and applications. Providers of IaaS are Amazon Web Services, Microsoft Windows Azure, and Akamai.

In conclusion, cloud computing is a technology that fundamentally changed the way we think about applications in that they are rented and paid for as a service. The idea is the same as for utilities—water, gas, cable, and phone. The provider of the utility builds and is running the infrastructure; you plug in and sign up for a type of service. Sometimes you pay as you go (water, gas), or you sign up for a level of service (phone, cable).

2.2.5 Peer-to-Peer Architectures

Peer-to-peer (P2P) architectures are very old, but their modern design became popular in the early 2000s with the rise of P2P file sharing applications (e.g., Napster). With a P2P architecture, all computers act as both a client and a server. Therefore, all computers perform all four functions: presentation logic, application logic, data access logic, and data storage (see Figure 2-9). With a P2P file sharing application, a user uses the presentation, application, and data access logic installed on his or her computer to access the data stored on another computer in the network. With a P2P application sharing network (e.g., grid computing such as seti.org), other users in the network can use others' computers to access application logic as well.

The advantage of P2P networks is that the data can be installed anywhere on the network. They spread the storage throughout the network, even globally, so they can be very resilient to the failure of any one computer. The challenge is finding the data. There must be some central server that enables you to find the data you need, so P2P architectures

FIGURE 2-9

Peer-to-peer architecture

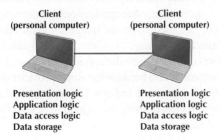

| Client
(personal computer) | Client
(personal computer) |

Presentation logic
Application logic
Data access logic
Data storage

Presentation logic
Application logic
Data access logic
Data storage

often are combined with a client-server architecture. Security is a major concern in most P2P networks, so P2P architectures are not commonly used in organizations, except for specialized computing needs (e.g., grid computing).

2.2.6 Choosing Architectures

Each of the preceding architectures has certain costs and benefits, so how do you choose the "right" architecture? In many cases, the architecture is simply a given; the organization has a certain architecture, and one simply has to use it. In other cases, the organization is acquiring new equipment and writing new software and has the opportunity to develop a new architecture, at least in some part of the organization.

Almost all new applications today are client-server applications. Client-server architectures provide the best **scalability**, the ability to increase (or decrease) the capacity of the servers to meet changing needs. For example, we can easily add or remove application servers or database servers depending on whether we need more or less capacity for application software or database software and storage.

Client-server architectures are also the most reliable. We can use multiple servers to perform the same tasks, so that if one server fails, the remaining servers continue to operate and users don't notice problems.

Finally, client-server architectures are usually the cheapest because many tools exist to develop them. And lots of client-server software exists for specific parts of applications so we can more quickly buy parts of the application we need. For example, no one writes Shopping Carts anymore; it's cheaper to buy a Shopping Carts software application and put it on an application server than it is to write your own.

Client-server architectures also enable **cloud computing**. As we mentioned in Section 2.2.4, companies may choose to run a software as a service (SaaS) because of low price and high scalability as compared to traditional client-server architecture hosted at home. One major issue that companies face when choosing SaaS is the security of the data. Each company has to evaluate the risk of its data being compromised and select its cloud provider carefully. However, SaaS is gaining popularity and companies are becoming more and more accustomed to this solution.

MANAGEMENT

FOCUS

2-1 Cloud Computing with Salesforce.com

Salesforce.com, the world's number one cloud platform, is the poster child for cloud computing. Companies used to buy and install software for customer relationship management (CRM), the process of identifying potential customers, marketing to them, converting them into customers, and managing the relationship to retain them. The software and needed servers were expensive and took a long time to acquire and install. Typically, only large firms could afford it.

Salesforce.com changed this by offering a cloud computing solution. The CRM software offered by salesforce.com resides on the salesforce.com servers. There is no need to buy and install new hardware or software. Companies just pay a monthly fee to access the software over the Internet. Companies can be up and running in weeks, not months, and it is easy to scale from a small implementation to a very large one. Because salesforce.com can spread its costs over so many users, they can offer deals to small companies that normally wouldn't be able to afford to buy and install their own software. Salesforce is a very competitive organization that is keeping up with the mobile world too. In fall 2013, it announced the "Salesforce $1 Million Hackathon," where hundreds of teams competed to build the next killer mobile app on the Salesforce platform. Yup, the winning team will walk away with $1 million! Although we don't know the winner of this largest single hackathon, the reader can discover this easily by googling it.

2.3 WORLD WIDE WEB

The Web was first conceived in 1989 by Sir Tim Berners-Lee at the European Particle Physics Laboratory (CERN) in Geneva. His original idea was to develop a database of information on physics research, but he found it difficult to fit the information into a traditional database. Instead, he decided to use a *hypertext* network of information. With hypertext, any document can contain a link to any other document.

CERN's first Web browser was created in 1990, but it was 1991 before it was available on the Internet for other organizations to use. By the end of 1992, several browsers had been created for UNIX computers by CERN and several other European and American universities, and there were about 30 Web servers in the entire world. In 1993, Marc Andreessen, a student at the University of Illinois, led a team of students that wrote Mosaic, the first graphical Web browser, as part of a project for the university's National Center for Supercomputing Applications (NCSA). By the end of 1993, the Mosaic browser was available for UNIX, Windows, and Macintosh computers, and there were about 200 Web servers in the world. Today, no one knows for sure how many Web servers there are. There are more than 250 million separate Web sites, but many of these are hosted on the same servers by large hosting companies such as godaddy.com or Google sites.

2.3.1 How the Web Works

The Web is a good example of a two-tier client-server architecture (Figure 2-10). Each client computer needs an application layer software package called a **Web browser**. There are many different browsers, such as Microsoft's Internet Explorer. Each server on the network that will act as a Web server needs an application layer software package called a **Web server**. There are many different Web servers, such as those produced by Microsoft and Apache.

To get a page from the Web, the user must type the Internet **uniform resource locator (URL)** for the page he or she wants (e.g., www.yahoo.com) or click on a link that provides the URL. The URL specifies the Internet address of the Web server and the directory and name of the specific page wanted. If no directory and page are specified, the Web server will provide whatever page has been defined as the site's home page.

For the requests from the Web browser to be understood by the Web server, they must use the same standard **protocol** or language. If there were no standard and each Web browser used a different protocol to request pages, then it would be impossible for a Microsoft Web browser to communicate with an Apache Web server, for example.

The standard protocol for communication between a Web browser and a Web server is **Hypertext Transfer Protocol (HTTP)**. To get a page from a Web server, the Web browser issues a special packet called an **HTTP request** that contains the URL and other information about the Web page requested (see Figure 2-10). Once the server receives the HTTP request,

FIGURE 2-10

How the Web works

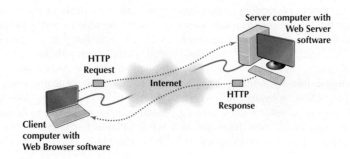

it processes it and sends back an **HTTP response**, which will be the requested page or an error message (see Figure 2-10).

This request-response dialogue occurs for every file transferred between the client and the server. For example, suppose the client requests a Web page that has two graphic images. Graphics are stored in separate files from the Web page itself using a different file format than the HTML used for the Web page (in JPEG [Joint Photographic Experts Group] format, for example). In this case, there would be three request-response pairs. First, the browser would issue a request for the Web page, and the server would send the response. Then, the browser would begin displaying the Web page and notice the two graphic files. The browser would then send a request for the first graphic and a request for the second graphic, and the server would reply with two separate HTTP responses, one for each request.

2.3.2 Inside an HTTP Request

The HTTP request and HTTP response are examples of the packets we introduced in Chapter 1 that are produced by the application layer and sent down to the transport, network, data link, and physical layers for transmission through the network. The HTTP response and HTTP request are simple text files that take the information provided by the application (e.g., the URL to get) and format it in a structured way so that the receiver of the message can clearly understand it.

An HTTP request from a Web browser to a Web server has three parts. The first two parts are required; the last is optional. The parts are

- The **request line**, which starts with a command (e.g., get), provides the Web page, and ends with the HTTP version number that the browser understands; the version number ensures that the Web server does not attempt to use a more advanced or newer version of the HTTP standard that the browser does not understand.
- The **request header**, which contains a variety of optional information such as the Web browser being used (e.g., Internet Explorer) and the date.
- The **request body**, which contains information sent to the server, such as information that the user has typed into a form.

Figure 2-11 shows an example of an HTTP request for a page on our Web server, formatted using version 1.1 of the HTTP standard. This request has only the request line and

FIGURE 2-11

An example of a request from a Web browser to a Web server using the HTTP (Hypertext Transfer Protocol) standard

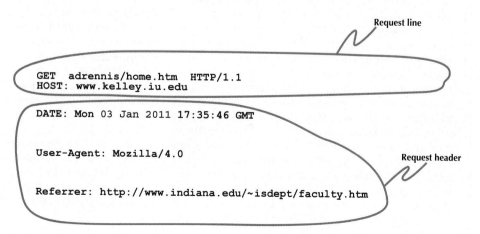

Request line

```
GET  adrennis/home.htm  HTTP/1.1
HOST: www.kelley.iu.edu

DATE: Mon 03 Jan 2011 17:35:46 GMT


User-Agent: Mozilla/4.0


Referrer: http://www.indiana.edu/~isdept/faculty.htm
```

Request header

the request header, because no request body is needed for this request. This request includes the date and time of the request (expressed in Greenwich Mean Time [GMT], the time zone that runs through London) and name of the browser used (Mozilla is the code name for the browser). The "Referrer" field means that the user obtained the URL for this Web page by clicking on a link on another page, which in this case is a list of faculty at Indiana University (i.e., www.indiana.edu/~isdept/faculty.htm). If the referrer field is blank, then it means the user typed the URL himself or herself. You can see inside HTTP headers yourself at www.rexswain.com/httpview.html.

2.3.3 Inside an HTTP Response

The format of an HTTP response from the server to the browser is very similar to the HTTP request. It, too, has three parts, with the first required and the last two optional:

- The **response status**, which contains the HTTP version number the server has used, a status code (e.g., *200* means "OK"; *404* means "not found"), and a reason phrase (a text description of the status code).
- The **response header**, which contains a variety of optional information, such as the Web server being used (e.g., Apache), the date, and the exact URL of the page in the response.
- The **response body**, which is the Web page itself.

Figure 2-12 shows an example of a response from our Web server to the request in Figure 2-11. This example has all three parts. The response status reports "OK," which means the requested URL was found and is included in the response body. The response header provides the date, the type of Web server software used, the actual URL included in the response body, and the type of file. In most cases, the actual URL and the requested URL are the same, but not always. For example, if you request an URL but do not specify a file name (e.g., www.indiana.edu), you will receive whatever file is defined as the home page for that server, so the actual URL will be different from the requested URL.

MANAGEMENT FOCUS

2-2 Top Players in Cloud Email

Among the wide variety of applications that organizations are using, email is most frequently deployed as SaaS. Four major industry players provide email as SaaS: Google, Microsoft, USA.NET, and Intermedia. Although cloud-based email seems to appeal more to smaller companies, it provides a cost-effective solution for organizations with up to 15,000 users (as a rule of thumb). Google was the first company to enter this market and offered Google Apps, Calendar, and 30 Gb of storage in addition to email. Microsoft entered this market in 2008 and offered Microsoft Office 365. Microsoft offers not only email but the whole MS Office suite. And of course, all the office applications are accessible from multiple devices. USA.NET is a SaaS company that offers Microsoft Exchange and robust security features that meet the federal and industry regulations, such as FINRA and HIPAA. It services approximately 6,000 organizations worldwide that provide financial, health care, energy, and critical infrastructure services. In addition, USA.NET offers Security-as-a-Service platform from the cloud. Finally, Intermedia, which was founded in 1995, is the largest Microsoft-hosted Exchange provider. This was the first company to offer Hosted Microsoft Exchange, and today, it has 90,000 customers and more than 700,000 users. Just like Microsoft, Intermedia delivers the Office Suite in the cloud.

The prices for the services these companies offer differ quite a bit. The cheapest of these four companies is Google, starting at $4.17 per user per month. However, these are basic prices that increase with the number of features and services added.

FIGURE 2-12

An example of a response from a Web server to a Web browser using the HTTP standard

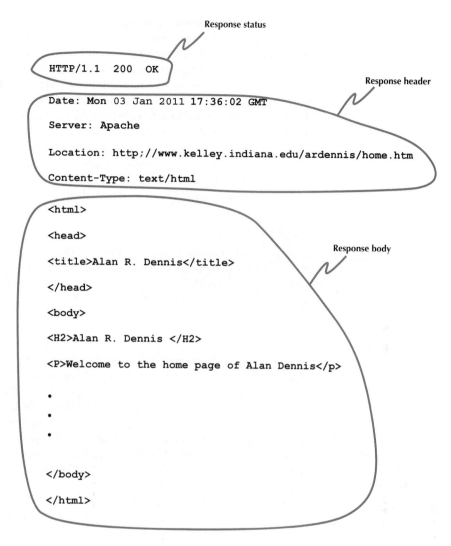

Response status

```
HTTP/1.1   200   OK
```

Response header

```
Date: Mon 03 Jan 2011 17:36:02 GMT

Server: Apache

Location: http;//www.kelley.indiana.edu/ardennis/home.htm

Content-Type: text/html
```

Response body

```
<html>

<head>

<title>Alan R. Dennis</title>

</head>

<body>

<H2>Alan R. Dennis </H2>

<P>Welcome to the home page of Alan Dennis</p>

•

•

•

</body>

</html>
```

The response body in this example shows a Web page in **Hypertext Markup Language (HTML)**. The response body can be in any format, such as text, Microsoft Word, Adobe PDF, or a host of other formats, but the most commonly used format is HTML. HTML was developed by CERN at the same time as the first Web browser and has evolved rapidly ever since. HTML is covered by standards produced by the IETF, but Microsoft keeps making new additions to HTML with every release of its browser, so the HTML standard keeps changing.

2.4 ELECTRONIC MAIL

Electronic mail (or **email**) was one of the earliest applications on the Internet and is still among the most heavily used today. With email, users create and send messages to one user, several users, or all users on a **distribution list**. Most email software enables users to send text messages and attach files from word processors, spreadsheets, graphics programs, and so on. Many email packages also permit you to filter or organize messages by priority.

Several standards have been developed to ensure compatibility between different email software packages. Any software package that conforms to a certain standard can send messages that are formatted using its rules. Any other package that understands that particular standard can then relay the message to its correct destination; however, if an email package receives a mail message in a different format, it may be unable to process it correctly. Many email packages send using one standard but can understand messages sent in several different standards. The most commonly used standard is SMTP (Simple Mail Transfer Protocol). Other common standards are X.400 and CMC (Common Messaging Calls). In this book, we will discuss only SMTP, but CMC and X.400 both work essentially the same way. SMTP, X.400, and CMC are different from one another (in the same way that English differs from French or Spanish), but several software packages are available that translate between them, so that companies that use one standard (e.g., CMC) can translate messages they receive that use a different standard (e.g., SMTP) into their usual standard as they first enter the company and then treat them as "normal" email messages after that.

2.4.1 How Email Works

The **Simple Mail Transfer Protocol (SMTP)** is the most commonly used email standard simply because it is the email standard used on the Internet. Email works similarly to how the Web works, but it is a bit more complex. SMTP email is usually implemented as a two-tier thick client-server application, but not always. We first explain how the normal two-tier thick client architecture works and then quickly contrast that with two alternate architectures.

Two-Tier Email Architecture With a two-tier thick client-server architecture, each client computer runs an application layer software package called a **mail user agent**, which is usually more commonly called an email client (Figure 2-12). There are many common email client software packages such as Eudora and Outlook. The user creates the email message using one of these email clients, which formats the message into an SMTP packet that includes information such as the sender's address and the destination address.

The user agent then sends the SMTP packet to a mail server that runs a special application layer software package called a **mail transfer agent**, which is more commonly called mail server software (see Figure 2-13).

This email server reads the SMTP packet to find the destination address and then sends the packet on its way through the network—often over the Internet—from mail server to mail server, until it reaches the mail server specified in the destination address (see Figure 2-13). The mail transfer agent on the destination server then stores the message in the receiver's mailbox on that server. The message sits in the mailbox assigned to the user who is to receive the message until he or she checks for new mail.

The SMTP standard covers message transmission between mail servers (i.e., mail server to mail server) and between the originating email client and its mail server. A different standard is used to communicate between the receiver's email client and his or her mail server. Two commonly used standards for communication between email client and mail server are **Post Office Protocol (POP)** and **Internet Message Access Protocol (IMAP)**. Although there are several important technical differences between POP and IMAP, the most noticeable difference is that before a user can read a mail message with a POP (version 3) email client, the email message must be copied to the client computer's hard disk and deleted from the mail server. With IMAP, email messages can remain stored on the mail server after they are read. IMAP therefore offers considerable benefits to users who read their email from many different computers (e.g., home, office, computer labs) because they no longer need to worry about having old email messages scattered across several client computers; all email is stored on the server until it is deleted.

In our example in Figure 2-13, when the receiver next accesses his or her email, the email client on his or her computer contacts the mail server by sending an IMAP or a POP packet that asks for the contents of the user's mailbox. In Figure 2-13, we show this as an

FIGURE 2-13

How SMTP (Simple Mail Transfer Protocol) email works. IMAP = Internet Message Access Protocol; LAN = local area network

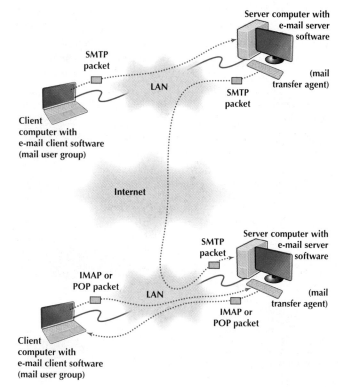

IMAP packet, but it could just as easily be a POP packet. When the mail server receives the IMAP or POP request, it converts the original SMTP packet created by the message sender into a POP or an IMAP packet that is sent to the client computer, which the user reads with the email client. Therefore, any email client using POP or IMAP must also understand SMTP to create messages. POP and IMAP provide a host of functions that enable the user to manage his or her email, such as creating mail folders, deleting mail, creating address books, and so on. If the user sends a POP or an IMAP request for one of these functions, the mail server will perform the function and send back a POP or an IMAP response packet that is much like an HTTP response packet.

Three-Tier Thin Client-Server Architecture The three-tier thin client-server email architecture uses a Web server and Web browser to provide access to your email. With this architecture, you do not need an email client on your client computer. Instead, you use your Web browser. This type of email is sometimes called *Web-based email* and is provided by a variety of companies such as Hotmail and Yahoo!.

You use your browser to connect to a page on a Web server that lets you write the email message by filling in a form. When you click the send button, your Web browser sends the form information to the Web server inside an HTTP request (Figure 2-14). The Web server runs a program (written in C or Perl, for example) that takes the information from the HTTP request and builds an SMTP packet that contains the email message. Although not important to our example, it also sends an HTTP response back to the client. The Web server then sends the SMTP packet to the mail server, which processes the SMTP packet as though it came from a client computer. The SMTP packet flows through the network in the same manner as before. When it arrives at the destination mail server, it is placed in the receiver's mailbox.

When the receiver wants to check his or her mail, he or she uses a Web browser to send an HTTP request to a Web server (see Figure 2-14). A program on the Web server (in C or

FIGURE 2-14

Inside the Web. HTTP =
Hypertext Transfer
Protocol; IMAP =
Internet Message Access
Protocol; LAN = local
area network; SMTP =
Simple Mail Transfer
Protocol

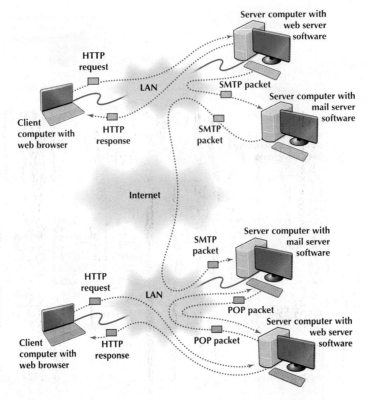

Perl, for example) processes the request and sends the appropriate POP request to the mail server. The mail server responds with a POP packet, which a program on the Web server converts into an HTTP response and sends to the client. The client then displays the email message in the Web browser *Web-based email.*

TECHNICAL

FOCUS | **2-2 SMTP Transmission**

SMTP (Simple Mail Transfer Protocol) is an older protocol, and transmission using it is rather complicated. If we were going to design it again, we would likely find a simpler transmission method. Conceptually, we think of an SMTP packet as one packet. However, SMTP mail transfer agents transmit each element within the SMTP packet as a separate packet and wait for the receiver to respond with an "OK" before sending the next element.

For example, in Figure 2-15, the sending mail transfer agent would send the *from* address and wait for an OK from the receiver. Then it would send the *to* address and wait for an OK. Then it would send the date, and so on, with the last item being the entire message sent as one element.

A simple comparison of Figures 2-13 and 2-14 will quickly show that the three-tier approach using a Web browser is much more complicated than the normal two-tier approach. So why do it? Well, it is simpler to have just a Web browser on the client computer rather than to require the user to install a special email client on his or her computer and then set up the special email client to connect to the correct mail server using either POP or IMAP. It is simpler for the user to just type the URL of the Web server

FIGURE 2-15

An example of an email message using the SMTP (Simple Mail Transfer Protocol) standard

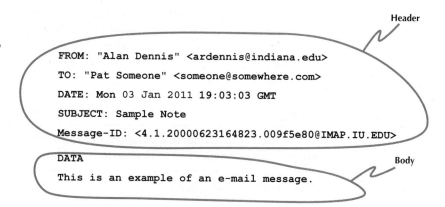

providing the mail services into his or her browser and begin using mail. This also means that users can check their email from a public computer anywhere on the Internet.

It is also important to note that the sender and receiver do not have to use the same architecture for their email. The sender could use a two-tier client-server architecture, and the receiver, a host-based or three-tier client-server architecture. Because all communication is standardized using SMTP between the different mail servers, how the users interact with their mail servers is unimportant. Each organization can use a different approach.

In fact, there is nothing to prevent one organization from using all three architectures simultaneously. At Indiana University, email is usually accessed through an email client (e.g., Microsoft Outlook) but is also accessed over the Web because many users travel internationally and find it easier to borrow a Web browser with Internet access than to borrow an email client and set it up to use the Indiana University mail server.

2.4.2 Inside an SMTP Packet

SMTP defines how message transfer agents operate and how they format messages sent to other message transfer agents. An SMTP packet has two parts:

- The **header**, which lists source and destination email addresses (possibly in text form [e.g., "Pat Smith"]) as well as the address itself (e.g., psmith@somewhere.com), date, subject, and so on.
- The **body**, which is the word *DATA*, followed by the message itself.

Figure 2-15 shows a simple email message formatted using SMTP. The header of an SMTP message has a series of fields that provide specific information, such as the sender's email address, the receiver's address, date, and so on. The information in quotes on the *from* and *to* lines is ignored by SMTP; only the information in the angle brackets is used in email addresses. The *message ID* field is used to provide a unique identification code so that the message can be tracked. The message body contains the actual text of the message itself.

2.4.3 Attachments in Multipurpose Internet Mail Extension

As the name suggests, SMTP is a simple standard that permits only the transfer of text messages. It was developed in the early days of computing, when no one had even thought about using email to transfer nontext files such as graphics or word processing documents. Several standards for nontext files have been developed that can operate together with SMTP, such as **Multipurpose Internet Mail Extension (MIME)**, uuencode, and binhex.

Each of the standards is different, but all work in the same general way. The MIME software, which exists as part of the email client, takes the nontext file such as a PowerPoint graphic file, and translates each byte in the file into a special code that looks like regular text. This encoded section of "text" is then labeled with a series of special fields understood by SMTP as identifying a MIME-encoded attachment and specifying information about the attachment (e.g., name of file, type of file). When the receiver's email client receives the SMTP message with the MIME attachment, it recognizes the MIME "text" and uses its MIME software (that is part of the email client) to translate the file from MIME "text" back into its original format.

2.5 OTHER APPLICATIONS

There are literally thousands of applications that run on the Internet and on other networks. Most application software that we develop today, whether for sale or for private internal use, runs on a network. We could spend years talking about different network applications and still cover only a small number.

A Day in the Life: Network Manager

It was a typical day for a network manager. It began with the setup and troubleshooting for a videoconference. Videoconferencing is fairly routine activity but this one was a little different; we were trying to videoconference with a different company who used different standards than we did. We attempted to use our usual Web-based videoconferencing but could not connect. We fell back to videoconferencing over telephone lines, which required bringing in our videoconferencing services group. It took two hours but we finally had the technology working.

The next activity was building a Windows database server. This involved installing software, adding a server into our ADS domain, and setting up the user accounts. Once the server was on the network, it was critical to install all the security patches for both the operating system and database server. We receive so many security attacks that it is our policy to install all security patches on the same day that new software or servers are placed on the network or the patches are released.

After lunch, the next two hours was spent in a boring policy meeting. These meetings are a necessary evil to ensure that the network is well-managed. It is critical that users understand what the network can and can't be used for, and our ability to respond to users' demands. Managing users' expectations about support and use rules helps ensure high user satisfaction.

The rest of the day was spent refining the tool we use to track network utilization. We have a simple intrusion detection system to detect hackers, but we wanted to provide more detailed information on network errors and network utilization to better assist us in network planning.

Source: With thanks to Jared Beard

Fortunately, most network application software works in much the same way as the Web or email. In this section, we will briefly discuss only three commonly used applications: Telnet, instant messaging (IM), and video conferencing.

2.5.1 Telnet

Telnet enables users to log in to servers (or other clients). It requires an application layer program on the client computer and an application layer program on the server or host computer. Once Telnet makes the connection from the client to the server, you must use the account name and password of an authorized user to log in.

Although Telnet was developed in the very early days of the Internet (actually, the very first application that tested the connectivity on ARPANET was Telnet), it is still widely used today. Because it was developed so long ago, Telnet assumes a host-based architecture. Any key strokes that you type using Telnet are sent to the server for processing, and then the server instructs the client what to display on the screen.

One of the most frequently used Telnet software packages is PuTTY. PuTTY is open source and can be downloaded for free (and in case you're wondering, the name does not stand for anything, although TTY is a commonly used abbreviation for "terminal" in UNIX-based systems).

The very first Telnet applications posed a great security threat because every key stroke was sent over the network as plain text. PuTTY uses secure shell (SSH) encryption when communicating with the server so that no one can read what is typed. An additional advantage of PuTTY is that it can run on multiple platforms, such as Windows, Mac, or Linux. Today, PuTTY is routinely used by network administrators to log in to servers and routers to make configuration changes.

MANAGEMENT

2-3 Tagging People

FOCUS

*J*oseph Krull has a chip on his shoulder—well, in his shoulder to be specific. Krull is one of a small but growing number of people who have a Radio Frequency Identification (RFID) chip implanted in their bodies.

RFID technology has been used to identify pets, so that lost pets can be easily reunited with their owners. Now, the technology is being used for humans.

Krull has a blown left pupil from a skiing accident. If he were injured in an accident and unable to communicate, an emergency room doctor might misinterpret his blown pupil as a sign of a major head injury and begin drilling holes to relieve pressure. Now doctors can use the RFID chip to identify Krull and quickly locate his complete medical records on the Internet.

Critics say such RFID chips pose huge privacy risks because they enable any firms using RFID to track users such as Krull. Retailers, for example, can track when he enters and leaves their stores.

Krull doesn't care. He believes the advantages of having his complete medical records available to any doctor greatly outweigh the privacy concerns.

Tagging people is no longer the novelty it once was; in fact, today it is a U.S. Food and Drug Administration approved procedure. More that 10% of all RFID research projects worldwide involve tagging people. There are even do-it-yourself RFID tagging kits available—not that we would recommend them (www.youtube.com/watch?v=vsk6dJr4wps).

Besides the application to health records, RFID is also being used for security applications, even something as simple as door locks. Imagine having an RFID-based door lock that opens automatically when you walk up to it because it recognizes the RFID tag in your body.

Adapted from: *NetworkWorld*, ZDNet, and GizMag.com

2.5.2 Instant Messaging

One of the fastest growing Internet applications has been **instant messaging (IM)**. With IM, you can exchange real-time typed messages or chat with your friends. Some IM software also enables you to verbally talk with your friends in the same way as you might use the telephone or to use cameras to exchange real-time video in the same way you might use a videoconferencing system. Several types of IM currently exist, including Google Talk and AOL Instant Messenger.

Instant messaging works in much the same way as the Web. The client computer needs an IM client software package, which communicates with an IM server software package that runs on a server. When the user connects to the Internet, the IM client software package sends an IM request packet to the IM server informing it that the user is now online. The IM client software package continues to communicate with the IM server to monitor what

FIGURE 2-16

How instant messaging (IM) works. LAN = local area network

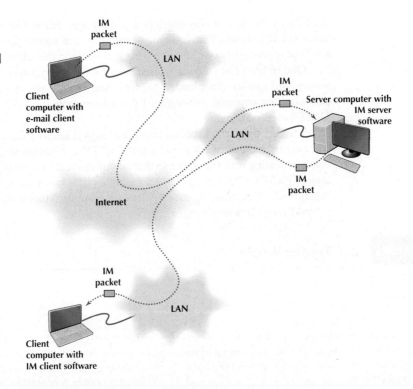

other users have connected to the IM server. When one of your friends connects to the IM server, the IM server sends an IM packet to your client computer so that you now know that your friend is connected to the Internet. The server also sends a packet to your friend's client computer so that he or she knows that you are on the Internet.

With the click of a button, you can both begin chatting. When you type text, your IM client creates an IM packet that is sent to the IM server (Figure 2-16). The server then retransmits the packet to your friend. Several people may be part of the same chat session, in which case the server sends a copy of the packet to all of the client computers. IM also provides a way for different servers to communicate with one another, and for the client computers to communicate directly with each other. Additionaly, IM will do voice and video.

2.5.3 Videoconferencing

Videoconferencing provides real-time transmission of video and audio signals to enable people in two or more locations to have a meeting. In some cases, videoconferences are held in special-purpose meeting rooms with one or more cameras and several video display monitors to capture and display the video signals (Figure 2-17). Special audio microphones and speakers are used to capture and play audio signals. The audio and video signals are combined into one signal that is transmitted though a MAN or WAN to people at the other location. Most of this type of videoconferencing involves two teams in two separate meeting rooms, but some systems can support conferences of up to eight separate meeting rooms. Some advanced systems provide telepresence, which is of such high quality that you feel you are face-to-face with the other participants.

The fastest growing form of videoconferencing is **desktop videoconferencing**. Small cameras installed on top of each computer permit meetings to take place from individual offices (Figure 2-18). Special application software (e.g., Yahoo! IM, Skype, Net Meeting) is installed on the client computer and transmits the images across a network to application

FIGURE 2-17

A Cisco telepresence system

Source: Courtesy Cisco Systems, Inc. Unauthorized use not permitted

FIGURE 2-18

Desktop videoconferencing

Source: Courtesy Cisco Systems, Inc. Unauthorized use not permitted

software on a videoconferencing server. The server then sends the signals to the other client computers that want to participate in the videoconference. In some cases, the clients can communicate with one another without using the server. The cost of desktop videoconferencing ranges from less than $20 per computer for inexpensive systems to more than $1,000 for high-quality systems. Some systems have integrated conferencing software with desktop videoconferencing, enabling participants to communicate verbally and, by using applications such as white boards, to attend the same meeting while they are sitting at the computers in their offices.

The transmission of video requires a lot of network capacity. Most videoconferencing uses data compression to reduce the amount of data transmitted. Surprisingly, the most common complaint is not the quality of the video image but the quality of the voice transmissions. Special care needs to be taken in the design and placement of microphones and speakers to ensure quality sound and minimal feedback.

Most videoconferencing systems were originally developed by vendors using different formats, so many products were incompatible. The best solution was to ensure that all hardware and software used within an organization was supplied by the same vendor and to hope that any other organizations with whom you wanted to communicate used the same equipment. Today, three standards are in common use: **H.320**, **H.323**, and **MPEG-2** (also called ISO 13818-2). Each of these standards was developed by different organizations and is supported by different products. They are not compatible, although some application software packages understand more than one standard. H.320 is designed for room-to-room videoconferencing over high-speed telephone lines. H.323 is a family of standards designed for desktop videoconferencing and just simple audio conferencing over the Internet. MPEG-2 is designed for faster connections, such as a LAN or specially designed, privately operated WAN.

Webcasting is a special type of one-directional videoconferencing in which content is sent from the server to the user. The developer creates content that is downloaded as needed by the users and played by a plug-in to a Web browser. At present, there are no standards for Webcast technologies, but the products by RealNetworks.com are the *de facto* standards.

2.6 IMPLICATIONS FOR MANAGEMENT

The first implication for management from this chapter is that the primary purpose of a network is to provide a worry-free environment in which applications can run. The network itself does not change the way an organization operates; it is the applications that the network enables that have the potential to change organizations. If the network does not easily enable a wide variety of applications, this can severely limit the ability of the organization to compete in its environment.

The second implication is that over the past few years there has been a dramatic increase in the number and type of applications that run across networks. In the early 1990s, networks primarily delivered email and organization-specific application traffic (e.g. accounting transactions, database inquiries, inventory data). Today's traffic contains large amounts of email, Web packets, videoconferencing, telephone calls, instant messaging, music, and organization-specific application traffic. Traffic has been growing much more rapidly than expected, and each type of traffic has different implications for the best network design, making the job of the network manager much more complicated. Most organizations have seen their network operating costs grow significantly even though the cost per packet (i.e., the cost divided by the amount of traffic) has dropped significantly over the last 10 years. Experts predict that by 2015, video will be the most common type of traffic on the Web, passing email and Web, which are the leading traffic types today.

MANAGEMENT FOCUS

2-4 Cloud-Hosted Virtual Desktops

While cloud computing started on the server side, it quickly is moving to the client side—the desktop. Imagine that you work for a multinational organization and fly several times a year to different parts of the world to do your job. Your organization doesn't want you to travel with a laptop because they fear that you can lose the laptop with the data on it but they want you to be able to log in to any desktop in any office around the world and have your desktop appear on the screen. Well, with the cloud technology, this is possible, and many companies are taking advantage of this new service. Could you guess its name? Yes, Desktop-as-a-Service (DaaS). Several companies offer DaaS without the infrastructure cost and with reduced complexity of deploying desktops. This service works as a monthly subscription service and includes data center hardware and facilities and also security. Dell DaaS on Demand and Amazon WorkSpaces are among the service providers of Daas.

SUMMARY

Application Architectures There are four fundamental application architectures. In host-based networks, the server performs virtually all of the work. In client-based networks, the client computer does most of the work; the server is used only for data storage. In client-server networks, the work is shared between the servers and clients. The client performs all presentation logic, the server handles all data storage and data access logic, and one or both perform the application logic. With peer-to-peer networks, client computers also play the role of a server. Client-server networks can be cheaper to install and often better balance the network loads but are more complex to develop and manage. Cloud computing is a form of client-server architecture.

World Wide Web One of the fastest growing Internet applications is the Web, which was first developed in 1990. The Web enables the display of rich graphical images, pictures, full-motion video, and sound. The Web is the most common way for businesses to establish a presence on the Internet. The Web has two application software packages: a Web browser on the client and a Web server on the server. Web browsers and servers communicate with one another using a standard called HTTP. Most Web pages are written in HTML, but many also use other formats. The Web contains information on just about every topic under the sun, but finding it and making sure the information is reliable are major problems.

Electronic Mail With email, users create and send messages using an application-layer software package on client computers called user agents. The user agent sends the mail to a server running an application-layer software package called a mail transfer agent, which then forwards the message through a series of mail transfer agents to the mail transfer agent on the receiver's server. Email is faster and cheaper than regular mail and can substitute for telephone conversations in some cases. Several standards have been developed to ensure compatibility between different user agents and mail transfer agents such as SMTP, POP, and IMAP.

KEY TERMS

application architecture, 27
application logic, 27
client-based architecture, 27
client-server architecture, 27
cloud computing, 35
cloud provider, 28
cloud-based architectures, 27
data access logic, 27
data storage, 27
desktop videoconferencing, 46
distributed computing model, 32
email, 39
H.320, 48
H.323, 48

host-based architecture, 27
HTTP request, 36
HTTP response, 37
Hypertext Markup Language (HTML), 39
Hypertext Transfer Protocol (HTTP), 36
Infrastructure as a Service (IaaS), 34
instant messaging (IM), 45
Internet, 26
Internet Message Access Protocol (IMAP), 40
mail transfer agent, 40
mail user agent, 40
middleware, 30
MPEG-2, 48
Multipurpose Internet Mail Extension (MIME), 43

multitenancy, 33
n-tier architecture, 30
peer-to-peer architecture, 27
Platform as a Service (Paas), 34
Post Office Protocol (POP), 40
presentation logic, 27
protocol, 36
request body, 37
request header, 37
request line, 37
response body, 38
response header, 38
response status, 38
scalability, 35
server farm, 33

Simple Mail Transfer Protocol (SMTP), 40
SMTP body, 43
SMTP header, 43
Software as a Service (SaaS), 33
storage area network (SAN), 33
Telnet, 44
thick client, 31
thin client, 31
three-tier architecture, 30
two-tier architecture, 30
uniform resource locator (URL), 36
Videoconferencing, 46
Web browser, 36
Webcasting, 48
Web server, 36

QUESTIONS

1. What are the different types of application architectures?
2. Describe the four basic functions of an application software package.
3. What are the advantages and disadvantages of host-based networks versus client-server networks?
4. What is middleware, and what does it do?
5. Suppose your organization was contemplating switching from a host-based architecture to client-server. What problems would you foresee?
6. Which is less expensive: host-based networks or client-server networks? Explain.
7. Compare and contrast two-tier, three-tier, and *n*-tier client-server architectures. What are the technical differences, and what advantages and disadvantages does each offer?
8. How does a thin client differ from a thick client?
9. What are the benefits of cloud computing?
10. Compare and contrast the three cloud computing models.
11. What is a network computer?
12. For what is HTTP used? What are its major parts?
13. For what is HTML used?
14. Describe how a Web browser and Web server work together to send a Web page to a user.
15. Can a mail sender use a two-tier architecture to send mail to a receiver using a three-tier architecture? Explain.
16. Describe how mail user agents and mail transfer agents work together to transfer mail messages.
17. What roles do SMTP, POP, and IMAP play in sending and receiving email on the Internet?
18. What are the major parts of an email message?
19. What is a virtual server?
20. What is Telnet, and why is it useful?
21. What is cloud computing?
22. Explain how instant messaging works.
23. Compare and contrast the application architecture for videoconferencing and the architecture for email.
24. Which of the common application architectures for email (two-tier client server, Web-based) is "best"? Explain.
25. Some experts argue that thin-client client-server architectures are really host-based architectures in disguise and suffer from the same old problems. Do you agree? Explain.

EXERCISES

A. Investigate the use of the major architectures by a local organization (e.g., your university). Which architecture(s) does it use most often and what does it see itself doing in the future? Why?
B. What are the costs of thin client versus thick client architectures? Search the Web for at least two different studies and be sure to report your sources. What are the likely reasons for the differences between the two?
C. Investigate which companies are the most reliable cloud computing providers for small business.
D. What application architecture does your university use for email? Explain.
E. Investigate the options for having your private cloud as an individual. Hint: Try the Apple Web site.

MINICASES

I. **Deals-R-Us Brokers (Part 1)** Fred Jones, a distant relative of yours and president of Deals-R-Us Brokers (DRUB), has come to you for advice. DRUB is a small brokerage house that enables its clients to buy and sell stocks over the Internet, as well as place traditional orders by phone or fax. DRUB has just decided to offer a set of stock analysis tools that will help its clients more easily pick winning stocks, or so Fred tells you. Fred's information systems department has presented him with two alternatives for developing the new tools. The first alternative will have a special tool developed in C++ that clients will download onto their computers to run. The tool will communicate with the DRUB server to select data to analyze.

The second alternative will have the C++ program running on the server, the client will use his or her browser to interact with the server.

    a. Classify the two alternatives in terms of what type of application architecture they use.

    b. Outline the pros and cons of the two alternatives and make a recommendation to Fred about which is better.

II. **Deals-R-Us Brokers (Part 2)** Fred Jones, a distant relative of yours and president of Deals-R-Us Brokers (DRUB), has come to you for advice. DRUB is a small brokerage house that enables its clients to buy and sell stocks over the Internet, as well as place traditional orders by phone or fax. DRUB has just decided to install a new email package. The IT department offered Fred two solutions. First, it could host the email in-house using Microsoft Exchange Server. The second solution would be to use one of the cloud-based providers and completely outsource the company email. The IT department also explained to Fred that both solutions would allow users to access email on their desktops and laptops and also on their smart devices.

    a. *Briefly* explain to Fred, in layperson's terms, the differences between the two.

    b. Outline the pros and cons of the two alternatives and make a recommendation to Fred about which is better.

III. **Accurate Accounting** Diego Lopez is the managing partner of Accurate Accounting, a small accounting firm that operates a dozen offices in California. Accurate Accounting provides audit and consulting services to a growing number of small- and medium-sized firms, many of which are high technology firms. Accurate Accounting staff typically spend many days on-site with clients during their consulting and audit projects, but has increasingly been using email and instant messenger (IM) to work with clients. Now, many firms are pushing Accurate Accounting to adopt videoconferencing. Diego is concerned about what videoconferencing software and hardware to install. While Accurate Accounting's email system enables it to exchange email with any client, using IM has proved difficult because Accurate Accounting has had to use one IM software package with some companies and different IM software with others. Diego is concerned that videoconferencing may prove to be as difficult to manage as IM. "Why can't IM work as simply as email?" he asks. "Will my new videoconferencing software and hardware work as simply as email, or will it be IM all over again?" Prepare a response to his questions.

IV. **Ling Galleries** Howard Ling is a famous artist with two galleries in Hawaii. Many of his paintings and prints are sold to tourists who visit Hawaii from Hong Kong and Japan. He paints 6–10 new paintings a year, which sell for $50,000 each. The real money comes from the sales of prints; a popular painting will sell 1,000 prints at a retail price of $1,500 each. Some prints sell very quickly, while others do not. As an artist, Howard paints what he wants to paint. As a businessman, Howard also wants to create art that sells well. Howard visits each gallery once a month to talk with clients, but enjoys talking with the gallery staff on a weekly basis to learn what visitors say about his work and to get ideas for future work. Howard has decided to open two new galleries, one in Hong Kong and one in Tokyo. How can the Internet help Howard with the two new galleries?

CASE STUDY

NEXT-DAY AIR SERVICE

See the book companion site at www.wiley.com/college/fitzgerald.

HANDS-ON ACTIVITY 2A

Looking Inside Your HTTP Packets

Figures 2-11 and 2-12 show you inside one HTTP request and one HTTP response that we captured. The objective of this Activity is for you to see inside HTTP packets that you create.

1. Use your browser to connect to www.rexswain.com/httpview.html. You will see the screen in Figure 2-19.

2. In box labeled URL, type any URL you like and click Submit. You will then see something like the screen in Figure 2-20. In the middle of the screen, under the label "Sending Request:" you will see the exact HTTP packet that your browser generated.

3. If you scroll this screen down, you'll see the exact HTTP response packet that the server sent back to you. In Figure 2-21, you'll see the response from the Indiana University Web server. You'll notice that at the time we did this, Indiana University was using the Apache Web server.

4. Try this on several sites around the Web to see what Web server they use. For example, Microsoft uses the Microsoft IIS Web server, while Cisco uses Apache. Some companies set their Web servers not to release this information.

Deliverables

Do a print screen from two separate Web sites that shows your HTTP requests and the servers' HTTP responses.

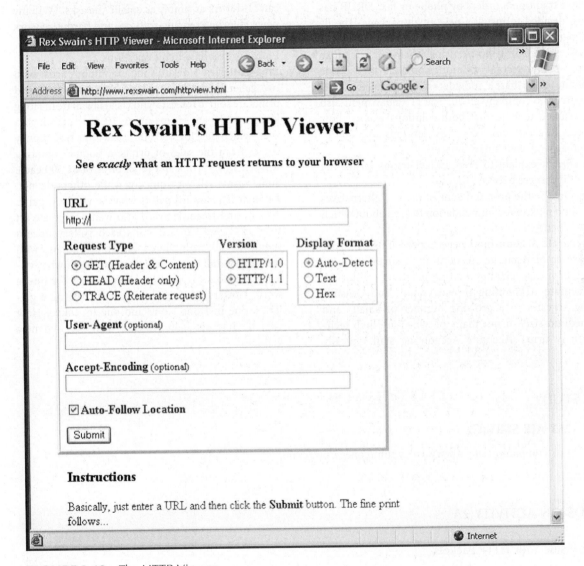

FIGURE 2-19 The HTTP Viewer

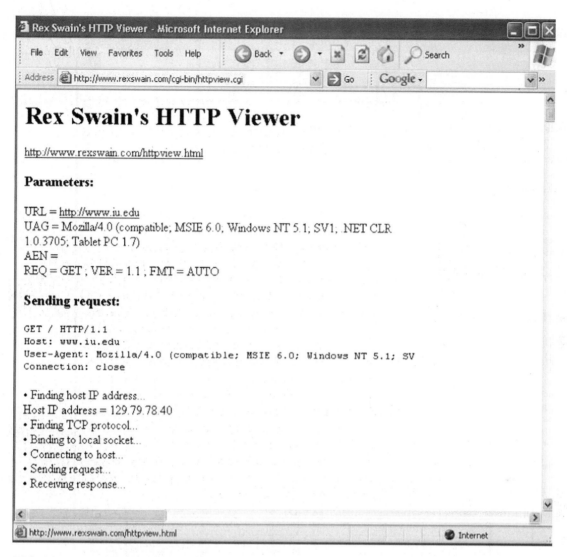

FIGURE 2-20   Looking inside an HTTP request

HANDS-ON ACTIVITY 2B

Tracing Your Email

Most email today is spam, unwanted commercial email, or phishing, fake email designed to separate you from your money. Criminals routinely send fake emails that try to get you to tell them your log-in information for your bank or your PayPal account, so they can steal the information, log-in as you, and steal your money.

It is very easy to fake a return address on an email, so simply looking to make sure that an email has a valid sender is not sufficient to ensure that the email was actually sent by the person or company that claims to have sent it. However, every SMTP email packet contains information in its header about who actually sent the email.

FIGURE 2-21 Looking inside an HTTP response

You can read this information yourself, or you can use a tool designed to simplify the process for you. The objective of this Activity is for you to trace an email you have received to see if the sending address on the email is actually the organization that sent it.

There are many tools you can use to trace your email. We like a tool called eMail Tracker Pro, which has a free version that lasts 15 days.

1. Go to www.emailtrackerpro.com and download and install eMail Tracker Pro.

2. Login to your email and find an email message you want to trace. I recently received an email supposedly from Wachovia Bank; the sender's email address was aw-login@wachovia.com.

3. After you open the email, find the option that enables you to view the Internet header or source of the message (in Microsoft Outlook, click the Options tab and look at the bottom of the box that pops up). Figure 2-22 shows the email I received and how to find the SMTP header (which Outlook

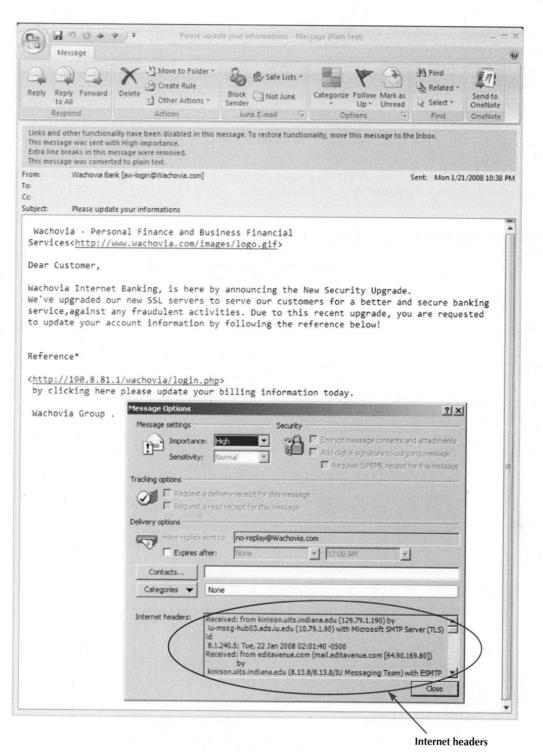

Internet headers

FIGURE 2-22 Viewing the SMTP packet header

calls the Internet header). Copy the entire SMTP header to the clipboard.

4. Start eMail Tracker Pro. Select Trace an email, and paste the SMTP header into the box provided. Click Trace to start the trace.

5. It may take up to 30 seconds to trace the email, so be patient. Figure 2-23 shows the results from the email I received. The email supposedly from Wachovia Bank was actually from a company named Musser and Kouri Law whose primary contact is Musser Ratliff, CPA, which uses SBC in Plano, Texas, as its Internet service provider. We suspect that someone broke into this company's network and used their email server without permission, or fraudulently used this company's name and contact information on its domain registration.

Deliverables

Trace one email. Print the original email message and the trace results.

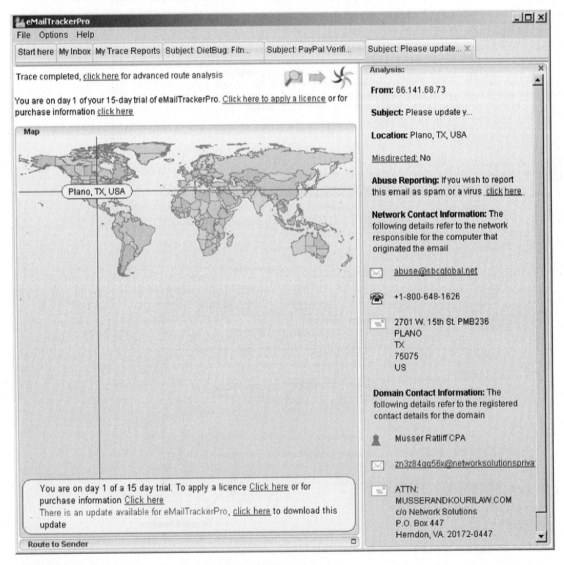

FIGURE 2-23 Viewing the source of the SMTP packet

Source: http://www.visualware.com/contact.html

HANDS-ON ACTIVITY 2C

Seeing SMTP and POP PDUs

We've discussed about how messages are transferred using layers and the different protocol data units (PDUs) used at each layer. The objective of this Activity is for you to see the different PDUs in the messages that you send. To do this, we'll use Wireshark, which is one of the world's foremost network protocol analyzers, and is the

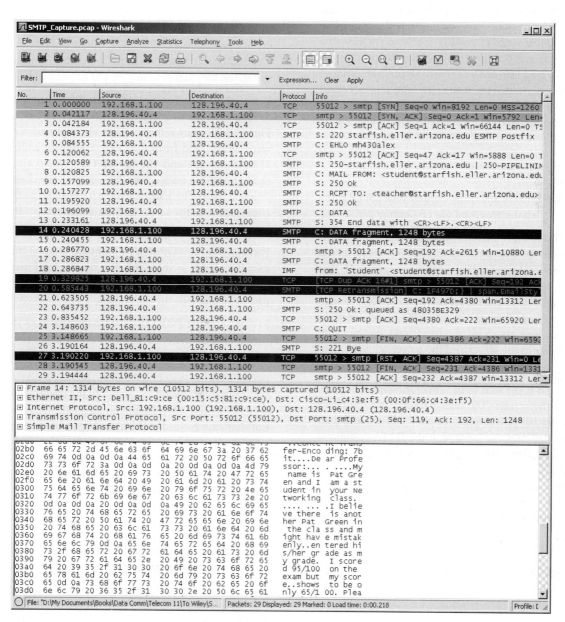

FIGURE 2-24 SMTP packets in Wireshark

de facto standard that most professional and education institutions use today. It is used for network troubleshooting, network analysis, software and communications protocol development, and general education about how networks work. Wireshark enables you to see all messages sent by your computer and may also let you see the messages sent by other users on your LAN (depending on how your LAN is configured).

For this activity you can capture your own SMTP and POP packets using Wireshark, or use two files that we've created by capturing SMTP and POP packets. We'll assume you're going to use our files. If you'd like to capture your own packets, read Hands-On Activity 1B in Chapter 1 and use your two-tier email client to create and send an email message instead of your Web browser. If you'd like to use our files, go to the Web site for this book and download the two files: *SMTP Capture.pkt* and *POP3 Capture.pkt*.

Part 1: SMTP

1. Start Wireshark and either capture your SMTP packets or open the file called *SMTP Capture.pkt*.

2. We used the email software on our client computer to send an email message to our email server. Figure 2-24 shows the packets we captured that were sent to and from the client computer (called 192.168.1.100) and the server (128.196.40.4) to send this message from the client to the server. The first few packets are called the handshake, as the client connects to the server and the server acknowledges it is ready to receive a new email message.

3. Packet 8 is the start of the email message that identifies the sender. The next packet from the client (packet 10) provides the recipient address and then the email message starts with the DATA command (packet 12) and is spread over several packets (14, 15, and 17) because it is too large to fit in one Ethernet frame. (Remember that the sender's transport layer breaks up large messages into several smaller TCP segments for transmission and the receiver's transport layer reassembles the segments back into the one SMTP message.)

4. Packet 14 contains the first part of the message that the user wrote. It's not that easy to read, but by looking in the bottom window, you can see what the sender wrote.

Deliverables

1. List the information in the SMTP header (to, from, date, subject, message ID#).

2. Look through the packets to read the user's message. List the user's actual name (not her email address), her birth date, and her SSN.

3. Some experts believe that sending an email message is like sending a postcard. Why? How secure is SMTP email? How could security be improved?

Part 2: POP

1. Start Wireshark and either capture your SMTP packets or open the file called *POP3 Capture.pkt*. (Note: Depending on the version of Wireshark you are using, the file extension may by pkt or pcap.)

2. We used the email software on our client computer to read an email message that was our email server. Figure 2-25 shows the packets we captured that were sent to and from the client computer (called 128.196.239.91) and the server (128.192.40.4) to send an email message from the server to the client. The first few packets are called the handshake, as the client logs in to the server and the server accepts the log in.

3. Packet 12 is the POP STAT command (status) that asks the server to show the number of email messages in the user's mailbox. The server responds in packet 13 and tells the client there is one message.

4. Packet 16 is the POP LIST command that asks the server to send the client a summary of email messages, which it does in packet 17.

5. Packet 18 is the POP RETR command (retrieve) that asks the server to send message 1 to the client. Packets 20, 22, and 23 contain the email message. It's not that easy to read, but by looking in the bottom window for packet 20, you can see what the sender wrote. You can also expand the POP packet in the middle packet detail window (by clicking on the + box in front of it), which is easier to read.

Deliverables

1. Packets 5 through 11 are the log-in process. Can you read the user id and passwords? Why or why not?

2. Look through the packets to read the user's message. List the user's actual name (not her email address), her birth date, and her SSN.

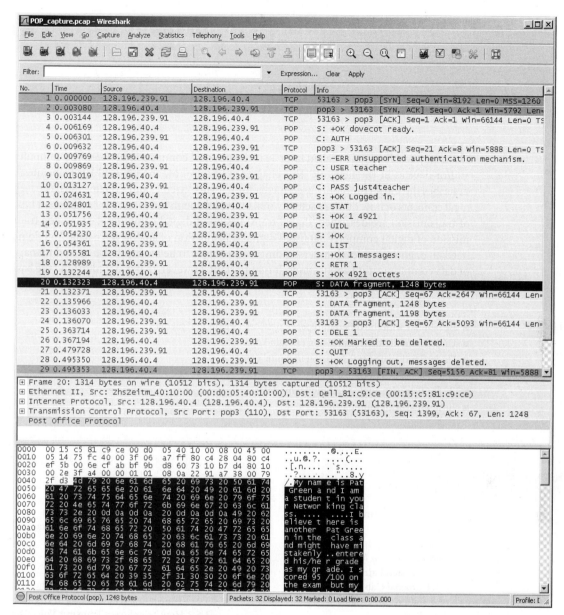

FIGURE 2-25 POP packets in Wireshark

CHAPTER 3

PHYSICAL LAYER

The physical layer (also called layer 1) is the physical connection between the computers and/or devices in the network. This chapter examines how the physical layer operates. It describes the most commonly used media for network circuits and explains the basic technical concepts of how data are actually transmitted through the media. Three different types of transmission are described: digital transmission of digital computer data, analog transmission of digital computer data, and digital transmission of analog voice data. You do not need an engineering-level understanding of the topics to be an effective user and manager of data communication applications. It is important, however, that you understand the basic concepts, so this chapter is somewhat technical.

OBJECTIVES

- Be familiar with the different types of network circuits and media
- Understand digital transmission of digital data
- Understand analog transmission of digital data
- Understand digital transmission of analog data
- Be familiar with analog and digital modems
- Be familiar with multiplexing

OUTLINE

3.1 INTRODUCTION

This chapter examines how the physical layer operates. The physical layer is the network hardware including servers, clients, and circuits, but in this chapter we focus on the circuits and on how clients and servers transmit data through them. The circuits are usually a combination of both physical media (e.g., cables, wireless transmissions) and special-purpose devices that enable the transmissions to travel through the media. Special-purpose devices such as switches and routers are discussed in Chapters 6 and 8.

The word **circuit** has two very different meanings in networking, and sometimes it is hard to understand which meaning is intended. Sometimes, we use the word *circuit* to refer to the **physical circuit**—the actual wire—used to connect two devices. In this case, we are referring to the physical media that carry the message we transmit, such as the twisted pair wire used to connect a computer to the LAN in an office. In other cases, we are referring to a **logical circuit** used to connect two devices, which refers to the transmission characteristics of the connection, such as when we say a company has a T1 connection into the Internet. In this case, T1 refers not to the physical media (i.e., what type of wire is used) but rather to how fast data can be sent through the connection.[1] Often, each physical circuit is also a logical circuit, but sometimes it is possible to have one physical circuit—one wire—carry several separate logical circuits, or to have one logical circuit travel over several physical circuits.

There are two fundamentally different types of data that can flow through the circuit: *digital* and *analog*. Computers produce digital data that are binary, either on or off, 0 or 1. In contrast, telephones produce analog data whose electrical signals are shaped like the sound waves they transfer; they can take on any value in a wide range of possibilities, not just 0 or 1.

Data can be transmitted through a circuit in the same form they are produced. Most computers, for example, transmit their digital data through digital circuits to printers and other attached devices. Likewise, analog voice data can be transmitted through telephone networks in analog form. In general, networks designed primarily to transmit digital computer data tend to use digital transmission, and networks designed primarily to transmit analog voice data tend to use analog transmission (at least for some parts of the transmission).

Data can be converted from one form into the other for transmission over network circuits. For example, digital computer data can be transmitted over an analog telephone circuit by using a modem. A **modem** at the sender's computer translates the computer's digital data into analog data that can be transmitted through the voice communication circuits, and a second modem at the receiver's end translates the analog transmission back into digital data for use by the receiver's computer.

Likewise, it is possible to translate analog voice data into digital form for transmission over digital computer circuits using a device called a **codec**. Once again, there are two codecs, one at the sender's end and one at the receiver's end. Why bother to translate voice into digital? The answer is that digital transmission is "better" than analog transmission. Specifically, digital transmission offers five key benefits over analog transmission:

- Digital transmission produces fewer errors than analog transmission. Because the transmitted data are binary (only two distinct values), it is easier to detect and correct errors.
- Digital transmission permits higher maximum transmission rates. Fiber-optic cable, for example, is designed for digital transmission.
- Digital transmission is more efficient. It is possible to send more data through a given circuit using digital rather than analog transmission.
- Digital transmission is more secure because it is easier to encrypt.
- Finally, and most importantly, integrating voice, video, and data on the same circuit is far simpler with digital transmission.

For these reasons, most long-distance telephone circuits built by the telephone companies and other common carriers over the past decades use digital transmission. In the future, most transmissions (voice, data, and video) will be sent digitally.

---

[1] Don't worry about what a T1 circuit is at this point. All you need to understand is that a T1 circuit is a specific type of circuit with certain characteristics, the same way we might describe gasoline as being unleaded or premium. We discuss T1 circuits in Chapter 9.

Regardless of whether digital or analog transmission is used, transmission requires the sender and receiver to agree on two key parameters. First, they have to agree on the *symbols* that will be used: What pattern of electricity, light, or radio wave will be used to represent a 0 and a 1. Once these symbols are set, the sender and receiver have to agree on the **symbol rate**: How many symbols will be sent over the circuit per second? Analog and digital transmissions are different, but both require a commonly agreed on set of symbols and a symbol rate.

In this chapter, we first describe the basic types of circuits and examine the different media used to build circuits. Then we explain how data are actually sent through these media using digital and analog transmission.

3.2 CIRCUITS

3.2.1 Circuit Configuration

Circuit configuration is the basic physical layout of the circuit. There are two fundamental circuit configurations: point-to-point and multipoint. In practice, most complex computer networks have many circuits, some of which are point-to-point and some of which are multipoint.

Figure 3-1 illustrates a **point-to-point circuit**, which is so named because it goes from one point to another (e.g., one computer to another computer). These circuits sometimes are called *dedicated circuits* because they are dedicated to the use of these two computers. This type of configuration is used when the computers generate enough data to fill the capacity of the communication circuit. When an organization builds a network using point-to-point circuits, each computer has its own circuit running from itself to the other computers. This can get very expensive, particularly if there is some distance between the computers. Despite the cost, point-to-point circuits are used regularly in modern wired networks to connect clients to switches, switches to switches and routers, and routers to routers. We will discuss in detail these circuits in Chapter 7.

Figure 3-2 shows a **multipoint circuit** (also called a *shared circuit*). In this configuration, many computers are connected on the same circuit. This means that each must share the circuit with the others. The disadvantage is that only one computer can use the circuit at

FIGURE 3-1
Point-to-point circuit

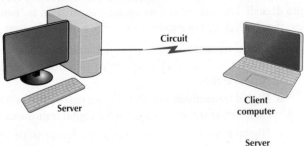

FIGURE 3-2
Multipoint circuit

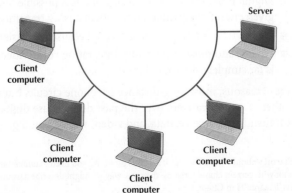

a time. When one computer is sending or receiving data, all others must wait. The advantage of multipoint circuits is that they reduce the amount of cable required and typically use the available communication circuit more efficiently. Imagine the number of circuits that would be required if the network in Figure 3-2 were designed with separate point-to-point circuits. For this reason, multipoint configurations are cheaper than point-to-point circuits. Thus, multipoint circuits typically are used when each computer does not need to continuously use the entire capacity of the circuit or when building point-to-point circuits is too expensive. Wireless circuits are almost always multipoint circuits because multiple computers use the same radio frequencies and must take turns transmitting.

3.2.2 Data Flow

Circuits can be designed to permit data to flow in one direction or in both directions. Actually, there are three ways to transmit: simplex, half-duplex, and full-duplex (Figure 3-3).

Simplex transmission is one-way transmission, such as that with radios and TVs.

Half-duplex transmission is two-way transmission, but you can transmit in only one direction at a time. A half-duplex communication link is similar to a walkie-talkie link; only one computer can transmit at a time. Computers use *control signals* to negotiate which will send and which will receive data. The amount of time half-duplex communication takes to switch between sending and receiving is called **turnaround time** (also called **retrain time** or reclocking time). The turnaround time for a specific circuit can be obtained from its technical specifications (often between 20 and 50 milliseconds). Europeans sometimes use the term *simplex circuit* to mean a half-duplex circuit.

With **full-duplex transmission**, you can transmit in both directions simultaneously, with no turnaround time.

How do you choose which data flow method to use? Obviously, one factor is the application. If data always need to flow only in one direction (e.g., from a remote sensor to a host computer), then simplex is probably the best choice. In most cases, however, data must flow in both directions.

The initial temptation is to presume that a full-duplex channel is best; however, each circuit has only so much capacity to carry data. Creating a full-duplex circuit means that the circuit offers full capacity both ways simultaneously. In some cases, it makes more sense to build a set of simplex circuits in the same way a set of one-way streets can increase the speed of traffic. In other cases, a half-duplex circuit may work best. For example, terminals

FIGURE 3-3

Simplex, half-duplex, and full-duplex transmissions

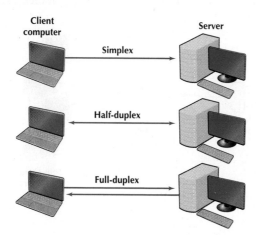

connected to mainframes often transmit data to the host, wait for a reply, transmit more data, and so on, in a turn-taking process; usually, traffic does not need to flow in both directions simultaneously. Such a traffic pattern is ideally suited to half-duplex circuits.

3.2.3 Multiplexing

Multiplexing means to break one high-speed physical communication circuit into several lower-speed logical circuits so that many different devices can simultaneously use it but still "think" that they have their own separate circuits (the multiplexer is "*transparent*"). It is multiplexing without multiplexing, the Internet would have collapsed in the 1990s.

Multiplexing often is done in multiples of 4 (e.g., 8, 16). Figure 3-4 shows a four-level multiplexed circuit. Note that two multiplexers are needed for each circuit: one to combine the four original circuits into the one multiplexed circuit and one to separate them back into the four separate circuits.

The primary benefit of multiplexing is to save money by reducing the amount of cable or the number of network circuits that must be installed. For example, if we did not use multiplexers in Figure 3-4, we would need to run four separate circuits from the clients to the server. If the clients were located close to the server, this would be inexpensive. However, if they were located several miles away, the extra costs could be substantial.

There are four types of multiplexing: frequency division multiplexing (FDM), time division multiplexing (TDM), statistical time division multiplexing (STDM), and wavelength division multiplexing (WDM).

Frequency Division Multiplexing **FDM** can be described as dividing the circuit "horizontally" so that many signals can travel a single communication circuit simultaneously. The circuit is divided into a series of separate channels, each transmitting on a different frequency, much like a series of different radio or TV stations. All signals exist in the media at the same time, but because they are on different frequencies, they do not interfere with each other.

Time Division Multiplexing **TDM** shares a communication circuit among two or more computers by having them take turns, dividing the circuit vertically, so to speak.

Statistical Time Division Multiplexing STDM is the exception to the rule that the capacity of the multiplexed circuit must equal the sum of the circuits it combines. STDM allows more terminals or computers to be connected to a circuit than does FDM or TDM. If you have four computers connected to a multiplexer and each can transmit at 64 Kbps, then you should have a circuit capable of transmitting 256 Kbps (4 × 64 Kbps). However, not all computers will be transmitting continuously at their maximum transmission speed.

FIGURE 3-4
Multiplexed circuit

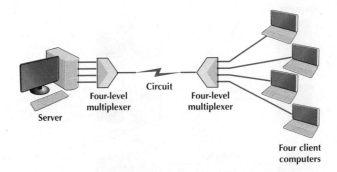

Users typically pause to read their screens or spend time typing at lower speeds. Therefore, you do not need to provide a speed of 256 Kbps on this multiplexed circuit. If you assume that only two computers will ever transmit at the same time, 128 Kbps will be enough. STDM is called *statistical* because selection of transmission speed for the multiplexed circuit is based on a statistical analysis of the usage requirements of the circuits to be multiplexed.

Wavelength Division Multiplexing WDM is a version of FDM used in fiber-optic cables. When fiber-optic cables were first developed, the devices attached to them were designed to use only one color of light generated by a laser or LED.

Light has different frequencies (i.e., colors), so rather than building devices to transmit using only one color, why not send multiple signals, each in a different frequency, through the same fiber-optic cable? By simply attaching different devices that could transmit in the full spectrum of light rather than just one frequency, the capacity of the existing fiber-optic cables could be dramatically increased, with no change to the physical cables themselves.

One technology that you may have come across that uses multiplexing is DSL. **DSL** stands for **digital subscriber line**, and it allows for simultaneous transmission of voice (phone calls), data going to the Internet (called upstream data), and data coming to your house from the Internet (called downstream data). With DSL, a DSL modem is installed at the customer's home or office, and another DSL modem is installed at the telephone company switch closet. The modem is first an FDM device that splits the physical circuit into three logical circuits (phone, upstream data, and downstream data). TDM is then used within the two data channels to provide a set of one or more individual channels that can be used to carry different data. A combination of amplitude and phase modulation is used in the data circuits to provide the desired data rate. You will learn more about DSL in Chapter 10.

MANAGEMENT	**3-1 Structured Cabling EIA/TIA 568-B**
FOCUS	

In 1995, the Telecommunications Industry Association (TIA) and Electronic Industries Alliance (EIA) came up with the first standard to create structured cabling, called TIA/EIA 568-A. This standard defined the minimum requirements for internal telecommunications wiring within buildings and between buildings on one campus. This standard was updated and changed many times, and today the accepted standard is TIA/EIA 568-B, which came out in 2002. This standard has six subsystems:

1. **Building entrance:** the point where external cabling and wireless connects to the internal building wiring and equipment room
2. **Equipment room (ER):** the room where network servers and telephone equipment would be stored
3. **Telecommunications closet:** the room that contains the cable termination points and the distribution frames
4. **Backbone cabling:** the cabling that interconnects telecommunication closets, equipment rooms, and building entrances within a building; also, this refers to cabling between buildings
5. **Horizontal cabling:** the cabling that runs from the telecommunications closet to each LAN
6. **Work area:** the cabling where the computers, printers, patch cables, jacks, and so on, are located

This standard describes what the master cabling document should look like (which would describe each of the six areas discussed previously) and applies for both twisted pair and fiber-optic cabling.

MANAGEMENT **3-2 Undersea Fiber-Optic Cables**

FOCUS

Perhaps you were wondering what happens when you send an email from the United States to Europe. How is your email transmitted from one continent to another? It most likely travels through one of the submarine cables that connect America and Europe. A neat interactive submarine cable map can be found at http://www.submarinecablemap.com.

This map shows you each cable's name, ready-for-service (RFS) date, length, owners, Web site (if any), and landing points. Each cable on this map has a capacity of at least 5 Gbps.

Actually, the first submarine telecommunication cable was laid in the 1850s and carried telegraphy traffic. Today, we use fiber-optic cable that carries phone, Internet, and private data as digital data.

So now you may ask yourself, how do these cables get laid on the seabed? Submarine cables are laid using special cable-layer ships—these are factories that produce the cable on board and then have equipment to lay and bury the cable. The cable-layer ships get as close as possible to the shore where the cable will be connected. A messenger line is sent out from the ship using a work boat that takes it to the shore.

Once the cable is secured on shore, the installation process under the sea can begin. A 30 ton sea plow with the cable in it (think about a needle and thread) is then tossed overboard and lands on the seabed. The plow then buries the cable under the sea bed at a required burial depth (up to 3 meters). The simultaneous lay-and-bury of the cable continues until an agreed position, after which the cable is surface laid until reaching its destination.

3.3 COMMUNICATION MEDIA

The *medium* (or *media*, if there is more than one) is the physical matter or substance that carries the voice or data transmission. Many different types of transmission media are currently in use, such as copper (wire), glass or plastic (fiber-optic cable), or air (radio, microwave, or satellite). There are two basic types of media. **Guided media** are those in which the message flows through a physical medium such as a twisted pair wire, coaxial cable, or fiber-optic cable; the medium "guides" the signal. **Wireless media** are those in which the message is broadcast through the air, such as microwave or satellite.

In many cases, the circuits used in WANs are provided by the various common carriers who sell usage of them to the public. We call the circuits sold by the common carriers *communication services*. Chapter 9 describes specific services available in North America. The following sections describe the medium and the basic characteristics of each circuit type, in the event you were establishing your own physical network, whereas Chapter 9 describes how the circuits are packaged and marketed for purchase or lease from a common carrier. If your organization has leased a circuit from a common carrier, you are probably less interested in the media used and more interested in whether the speed, cost, and reliability of the circuit meet your needs.

3.3.1 Twisted Pair Cable

One of the most commonly used types of guided media is **twisted pair cable**, insulated pairs of wires that can be packed quite close together (Figure 3-5). The wires usually are twisted to minimize the electromagnetic interference between one pair and any other pair in the bundle. Your house or apartment probably has a set of two twisted pair wires (i.e., four wires) from it to the telephone company network. One pair is used to connect your telephone; the other pair is a spare that can be used for a second telephone line. The twisted

FIGURE 3-5

Category 5e twisted pair
wire
Source: Courtesy of Belkin
International, Inc.

pair cable used in LANs are usually packaged as four sets of pairs, as shown in Figure 3-5, whereas bundles of several thousand wire pairs are placed under city streets and in large buildings. The specific types of twisted pair cable used in LANs, such as Cat 5e and Cat 6, are discussed in Chapter 7.

3.3.2 Coaxial Cable

Coaxial cable is a type of guided medium that is quickly disappearing (Figure 3-6). Coaxial cable has a copper core (the inner conductor) with an outer cylindrical shell for insulation. The outer shield, just under the shell, is the second conductor. Because they have additional shielding provided by their multiple layers of material, coaxial cables are less prone to interference and errors than basic low-cost twisted pair wires. Coaxial cables cost about three times as much as twisted pair wires but offer few additional benefits other than better shielding. One can also buy specially shielded twisted pair wire that provides the same level of quality as coaxial cable but at half its cost. For this reason, few companies are installing coaxial cable today, although some still continue to use existing coaxial cable that was installed years ago.

3.3.3 Fiber-Optic Cable

Although twisted pair is the most common type of guided medium, **fiber-optic cable** also is becoming widely used. Instead of carrying telecommunication signals in the traditional

FIGURE 3-6

Coaxial cables. Thinnet
and Thicknet Ethernet
cables (right) - 1. center
core, 2. dielectric insu-
lator, 3. metallic shield,
4. plastic jacket and
cross-sectional view (left)
Source: Courtesy of Tim Kloske

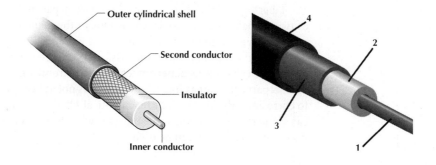

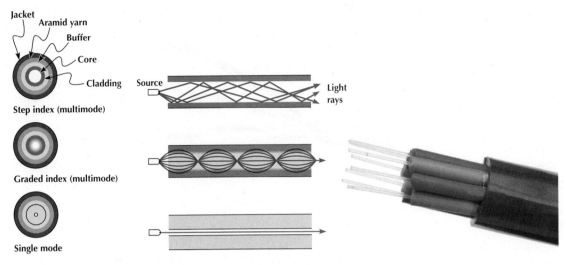

FIGURE 3-7 Fiber-optic cable
Source: © Hugh Threlfall/Alamy

electrical form, this technology uses high-speed streams of light pulses from lasers or LEDs (light-emitting diodes) that carry information inside hair-thin strands of glass called optical fibers. Figure 3-7 shows a fiber-optic cable and depicts the optical core, the cladding (metal coating), and how light rays travel in optical fibers.

The earliest fiber-optic systems were *multimode*, meaning that the light could reflect inside the cable at many different angles. Multimode cables are plagued by excessive signal weakening (attenuation) and dispersion (spreading of the signal so that different parts of the signal arrive at different times at the destination). For these reasons, early multimode fiber was usually limited to about 500 meters. Graded-index multimode fiber attempts to reduce this problem by changing the refractive properties of the glass fiber so that as the light approaches the outer edge of the fiber, it speeds up, which compensates for the slightly longer distance it must travel compared with light in the center of the fiber. Therefore, the light in the center is more likely to arrive at the same time as the light that has traveled at the edges of the fiber. This increases the effective distance to just under 1,000 meters.

Single-mode fiber-optic cables transmit a single direct beam of light through a cable that ensures the light reflects in only one pattern, in part because the core diameter has been reduced from 50 microns to about 5 to 10 microns. This smaller-diameter core allows the fiber to send a more concentrated light beam, resulting in faster data transmission speeds and longer distances, often up to 100 kilometers. However, because the light source must be perfectly aligned with the cable, single-mode products usually use lasers (rather than the LEDs used in multimode systems) and therefore are more expensive.

Fiber-optic technology is a revolutionary departure from the traditional copper wires of twisted pair cable or coaxial cable. One of the main advantages of fiber optics is that it can carry huge amounts of information at extremely fast data rates. This capacity makes it ideal for the simultaneous transmission of voice, data, and image signals. In most cases, fiber-optic cable works better under harsh environmental conditions than do its metallic counterparts. It is not as fragile or brittle, it is not as heavy or bulky, and it is more resistant to corrosion. Also, in case of fire, an optical fiber can withstand higher temperatures than can copper wire. Even when the outside jacket surrounding the optical fiber has melted, a fiber-optic system still can be used.

3.3.4 Radio

One of the most commonly used forms of wireless media is *radio;* when people used the term *wireless*, they usually mean **radio transmission**. When you connect your laptop into the network wirelessly, you are using radio transmission. Radio data transmission uses the same basic principles as standard radio transmission. Each device or computer on the network has a radio receiver/transmitter that uses a specific frequency range that does not interfere with commercial radio stations. The transmitters are very low power, designed to transmit a signal only a short distance, and are often built into portable computers or handheld devices such as phones and personal digital assistants. Wireless technologies for LAN environments, such as IEEE 802.1x, are discussed in more detail in Chapter 7.

MANAGEMENT	3-3 Boingo Hot Spots Around the World
FOCUS	

*P*erhaps you have come across Boingo while trying to find a wireless connection in an airport between flights. Boingo is a wireless Internet service provider (WISP) that is different than many free wifi connections that you can get at airports or coffee shops because it offers a secure connection (specifically, a VPN or WPA service that can be configured on your device, but more about this in Chapter 11). This secure connection is now offered in 7,000 U.S. locations and 13,000 international locations and as in-flight wifi on some international carriers.

Their monthly rates start at $9.94 for laptops and $7.95 for other mobile devices. Boingo also offers 1-, 2-, and 3-hour plans in case you don't travel frequently and don't need a monthly subscription. To find Boingo hot spots, you need to download an app on your phone or laptop, and the app will alert you if there is an available wifi connection in your area. The app will even chart a graph that will show you signal strength in real time.

Adapted from: Boingo.com, cnet.com

3.3.5 Microwave

Microwave transmission is an extremely high-frequency radio communication beam that is transmitted over a direct line-of-sight path between any two points. As its name implies, a microwave signal is an extremely short wavelength, thus the word *micro*-wave. Microwave radio transmissions perform the same functions as cables. For example, point A communicates with point B via a through-the-air microwave transmission path, instead of a copper wire cable. Because microwave signals approach the frequency of visible light waves, they exhibit many of the same characteristics as light waves, such as reflection, focusing, or refraction. As with visible light waves, microwave signals can be focused into narrow, powerful beams that can be projected over long distances. Just as a parabolic reflector focuses a searchlight into a beam, a parabolic reflector also focuses a high-frequency microwave into a narrow beam. Towers are used to elevate the radio antennas to account for the earth's curvature and maintain a clear line-of-sight path between the two parabolic reflectors; see Figure 3-8.

This transmission medium is typically used for long-distance data or voice transmission. It does not require the laying of any cable, because long-distance antennas with microwave repeater stations can be placed approximately 25–50 miles apart. A typical long-distance antenna might be 10 feet wide, although over shorter distances in the inner cities, the dish antennas can be less than 2 feet in diameter. The airwaves in larger cities are becoming congested because so many microwave dish antennas have been installed that they interfere with one another.

FIGURE 3-8

A microwave tower. The round antennas are microwave antennas and the straight antennas are cell phone antennas
Source: © Matej Pribelsky / iStockphoto

3.3.6 Satellite

Satellite transmission is similar to microwave transmission, except instead of transmission involving another nearby microwave dish antenna, it involves a satellite many miles up in space. Figure 3-9 depicts a geosynchronous satellite. *Geosynchronous* means that the

FIGURE 3-9

Satellites in operation

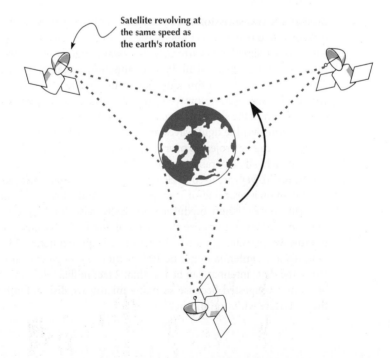

Satellite revolving at the same speed as the earth's rotation

satellite remains stationary over one point on the earth. One disadvantage of satellite transmission is the *propagation delay* that occurs because the signal has to travel out into space and back to earth, a distance of many miles that even at the speed of light can be noticeable. Low earth orbit (LEO) satellites are placed in lower orbits to minimize propogation delay. Satellite transmission is sometimes also affected by *raindrop attenuation* when satellite transmissions are absorbed by heavy rain. It is not a major problem, but engineers need to work around it.

MANAGEMENT
FOCUS

3-4 Satellite Communications Improve Performance

*B*oyle Transportation hauls hazardous materials nationwide for both commercial customers and the government, particularly the U.S. Department of Defense. The Department of Defense recently mandated that hazardous materials contractors use mobile communications systems with up-to-the-minute monitoring when hauling the department's hazardous cargoes.

After looking at the alternatives, Boyle realized that it would have to build its own system. Boyle needed a relational database at its operations center that contained information about customers, pickups, deliveries, truck location, and truck operating status. Data are distributed from this database via satellite to an antenna on each truck. Now, at any time, Boyle can notify the designated truck to make a new pickup via the bidirectional satellite link and record the truck's acknowledgment.

Each truck contains a mobile data terminal connected to the satellite network. Each driver uses a keyboard to enter information, which transmits the location of the truck. These satellite data are received by the main offices via a leased line from the satellite earth station.

This system increased productivity by an astounding 80% over 2 years; administration costs increased by only 20%.

3.3.7 Media Selection

Which media are best? It is hard to say, particularly when manufacturers continue to improve various media products. Several factors are important in selecting media.

- The *type of network* is one major consideration. Some media are used only for WANs (microwaves and satellite), whereas others typically are not (twisted pair, coaxial cable, and radio), although we should note that some old WAN networks still use twisted pair cable. Fiber-optic cable is unique in that it can be used for virtually any type of network.

- *Cost* is always a factor in any business decision. Costs are always changing as new technologies are developed and as competition among vendors drives prices down. Among the guided media, twisted pair wire is generally the cheapest, coaxial cable is somewhat more expensive, and fiber-optic cable is the most expensive. The cost of the wireless media is generally driven more by distance than any other factor. For very short distances (several hundred meters), radio is the cheapest; for moderate distances (several hundred miles), microwave is cheapest; and for long distances, satellite is cheapest.

- *Transmission distance* is a related factor. Twisted pair wire coaxial cable and radio can transmit data only a short distance before the signal must be regenerated. Twisted pair wire and radio typically can transmit up to 100–300 meters, and coaxial cable typically between 200 and 500 meters. Fiber optics can transmit up to 75 miles, and new types of fiber-optic cable can reach more than 600 miles.

■ *Security* is primarily determined by whether the media are guided or wireless. Wireless media (radio, microwave, and satellite) are the least secure because their signals are easily intercepted. Guided media (twisted pair, coaxial, and fiber optics) are more secure, with fiber optics being the most secure.

■ *Error rates* are also important. Wireless media are most susceptible to interference and thus have the highest error rates. Among the guided media, fiber optics provides the lowest error rates, coaxial cable the next best, and twisted pair cable the worst, although twisted pair cable is generally better than the wireless media.

■ *Transmission speeds* vary greatly among the different media. It is difficult to quote specific speeds for different media because transmission speeds are constantly improving and because they vary within the same type of media, depending on the specific type of cable and the vendor. In general, twisted pair cable and coaxial cable can provide data rates of between 1 Mbps (1 million bits per second) and 1 Gbps (1 billion bits per second), whereas fiber-optic cable ranges between 1 Gbps and 40 Gbps. Radio, microwave, and satellite generally provide 10–100 Mbps.

3.4 DIGITAL TRANSMISSION OF DIGITAL DATA

All computer systems produce binary data. For these data to be understood by both the sender and receiver, both must agree on a standard system for representing the letters, numbers, and symbols that compose messages. The **coding scheme** is the language that computers use to represent data.

3.4.1 Coding

A *character* is a symbol that has a common, constant meaning. A character might be the letter *A* or *B*, or it might be a number such as *1* or *2*. Characters also may be special symbols such as *?* or &. Characters in data communications, as in computer systems, are represented by groups of *bits* that are binary zeros (0) and ones (1). The groups of bits representing the set of characters that are the "alphabet" of any given system are called a *coding scheme*, or simply a *code*.

A *byte* is a group of consecutive bits that is treated as a unit or character. One byte normally is composed of 8 bits and usually represents one character; however, in data communications, some codes use 5, 6, 7, 8, or 9 bits to represent a character. For example, representation of the character *A* by a group of 8 bits (say, 01 000 001) is an example of coding.

There are three predominant coding schemes in use today. **United States of America Standard Code for Information Interchange (USASCII,** or, more commonly, **ASCII)** is the most popular code for data communications and is the standard code on most microcomputers. There are two types of ASCII; one is a 7-bit code that has 128 valid character combinations, and the other is an 8-bit code that has 256 combinations. The number of combinations can be determined by taking the number 2 and raising it to the power equal to the number of bits in the code because each bit has two possible values, a 0 or a 1. In this case $2^7 = 128$ characters or $2^8 = 256$ characters.

A second commonly used coding scheme is **ISO 8859**, which is standardized by the International Standards Organization. ISO 8859 is an 8-bit code that includes the ASCII codes plus non-English letters used by many European languages (e.g., letters with accents). If you look closely at Figure 2.21, you will see that HTML often uses ISO 8859.

Unicode is the other commonly used coding scheme. There are many different versions of Unicode. UTF-8 is an 8-bit version which is very similar to ASCII. UTF-16, which uses 16 bits per character (i.e., 2 bytes, called a "word"), is used by Windows. By using more bits, UTF-16 can represent many more characters beyond the usual English or Latin characters, such as Cyrillic or Chinese.

FIGURE 3-10

Binary numbers used to represent different characters using ASCII

Character	ASCII
A	01000001
B	01000010
C	01000011
D	01000100
E	01000101
a	01100001
b	01100010
c	01100011
d	01100100
e	01100101
1	00110001
2	00110010
3	00110011
4	00110100
!	00100001
$	00100100

We can choose any pattern of bits we like to represent any character we like, as long as all computers understand what each bit pattern represents. Figure 3-10 shows the 8-bit binary bit patterns used to represent a few of the characters we use in ASCII.

3.4.2 Transmission Modes

Parallel **Parallel transmission** is the way the internal transfer of binary data takes place inside a computer. If the internal structure of the computer is 8 bit, then all 8 bits of the data element are transferred between main memory and the central processing unit simultaneously on 8 separate connections. The same is true of computers that use a 32-bit structure; all 32 bits are transferred simultaneously on 32 connections.

TECHNICAL FOCUS   **3-1 Basic Electricity**

*T*here are two general categories of electrical current: direct current and alternating current. *Current* is the movement or flow of electrons, normally from positive (+) to negative (−). The plus (+) or minus (−) measurements are known as **polarity**. *Direct current* (DC) travels in only one direction, whereas *alternating current* (AC) travels first in one direction and then in the other direction.

A copper wire transmitting electricity acts like a hose transferring water. We use three common terms when discussing electricity. *Voltage* is defined as electrical pressure—the amount of electrical force pushing electrons through a circuit. In principle, it is the same as pounds per square inch in a water pipe. *Amperes* (amps) are units of electrical flow, or volume. This measure is analogous to gallons per minute for water. The *watt* is the fundamental unit of electrical power. It is a rate unit, not a quantity. You obtain the wattage by multiplying the volts by the amperes.

Figure 3-11 shows how all 8 bits of one character could travel down a parallel communication circuit. The circuit is physically made up of eight separate wires, wrapped in one outer coating. Each physical wire is used to send 1 bit of the 8-bit character. However, as far as the user is concerned (and the network for that matter), there is only one circuit; each of

FIGURE 3-11

Parallel transmission of an 8-bit code

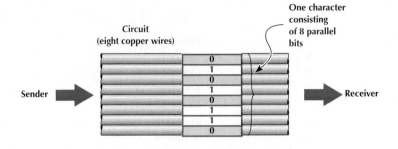

FIGURE 3-12

Serial transmission of an 8-bit code

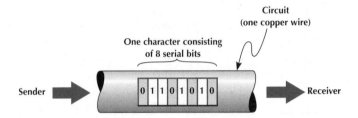

the wires inside the cable bundle simply connects to a different part of the plug that connects the computer to the bundle of wire.

Serial **Serial transmission** means that a stream of data is sent over a communication circuit sequentially in a bit-by-bit fashion, as shown in Figure 3-12. In this case, there is only one physical wire inside the bundle, and all data must be transmitted over that one physical wire. The transmitting device sends one bit, then a second bit, and so on, until all the bits are transmitted. It takes n iterations or cycles to transmit n bits. Thus, serial transmission is considerably slower than parallel transmission—eight times slower in the case of 8-bit ASCII (because there are 8 bits). Compare Figure 3-12 with Figure 3-11.

3.4.3 Digital Transmission

Digital transmission is the transmission of binary electrical or light pulses in that it only has two possible states, a 1 or a 0. The most commonly encountered voltage levels range from a low of +3/−3 to a high of +24/−24 volts. Digital signals are usually sent over wire of no more than a few thousand feet in length.

All digital transmission techniques require a set of symbols (to define how to send a 1 and a 0) and the symbol rate (how many symbols will be sent per second).

Figure 3-13 shows five types of digital transmission techniques. With **unipolar** signaling, the voltage is always positive or negative (like a DC current). Figure 3-13 illustrates a unipolar technique in which a signal of 0 volts (no current) is used to transmit a zero and a signal of +5 volts is used to transmit a 1.

An obvious question at this point is this: If 0 volts means a zero, how do you send no data? This is discussed in detail in Chapter 4. For the moment, we will just say that there are ways to indicate when a message starts and stops, and when there are no messages to send, the sender and receiver agree to ignore any electrical signal on the line.

To successfully send and receive a message, both the sender and receiver have to agree on how often the sender can transmit data—that is, on the *symbol rate*. For example, if the symbol rate on a circuit is 64 **Kilo Hertz (KHz)** (64,000 symbols per second), then the sender changes the voltage on the circuit once every $1/64{,}000$ of a second and the receiver must examine the circuit every $1/64{,}000$ of a second to read the incoming data.

FIGURE 3-13

Unipolar, bipolar, and Manchester signals (digital)

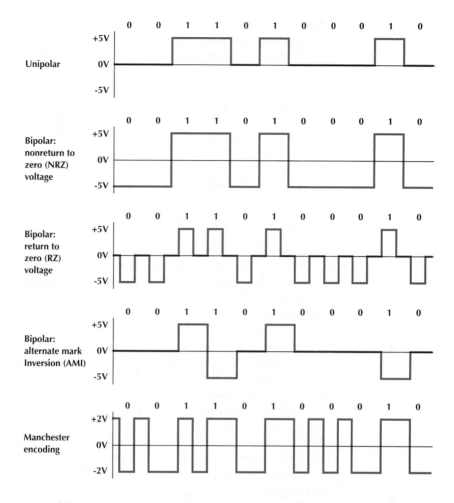

In **bipolar** signaling, the ones and zeros vary from a plus voltage to a minus voltage (like an AC current). The first bipolar technique illustrated in Figure 3-13 is called nonreturn to zero (NRZ) because the voltage alternates from +5 volts (a symbol indicating a 1) to −5 volts (a symbol indicating a 0) without ever returning to 0 volts. The second bipolar technique in this figure is called return to zero (RZ) because it always returns to 0 volts after each bit before going to +5 volts (the symbol for a 1) or −5 volts (the symbol for a 0). The third bipolar technique is called alternate mark inversion (AMI) because a 0 is always sent using 0 volts, but 1s alternate between +5 volts and −5 volts. AMI is used on T1 and T3 circuits. In Europe, bipolar signaling sometimes is called *double current* signaling because you are moving between a positive and negative voltage potential.

In general, bipolar signaling experiences fewer errors than unipolar signaling because the symbols are more distinct. Noise or interference on the transmission circuit is less likely to cause the bipolar's +5 volts to be misread as a −5 volts than it is to cause the unipolar's 0 volts to be misread as a +5 volts. This is because changing the polarity of a current (from positive to negative, or vice versa) is more difficult than changing its magnitude.

3.4.4 How Ethernet Transmits Data

The most common technology used in LANs is Ethernet;[2] if you are working in a computer lab on campus, you are most likely using Ethernet. Ethernet uses digital transmission over

---

[2]If you don't know what Ethernet is, don't worry. We will discuss Ethernet in Chapter 6.

either serial or parallel circuits, depending on which version of Ethernet you use. One version of Ethernet that uses serial transmission requires 1/10,000,000 of a second to send one symbol; that is, it transmits 10 million symbols (each of 1 bit) per second. This gives a data rate of 10 Mbps, and if we assume that there are 8 bits in each character, this means that about 1.25 million characters can be transmitted per second in the circuit.

Ethernet uses **Manchester encoding**, which is a special type of bipolar signaling in which the signal is changed from high to low or from low to high in the middle of the signal. A change from high to low is used to represent a 0, whereas the opposite (a change from low to high) is used to represent a 1. See Figure 3-13. Manchester encoding is less susceptible to having errors go undetected, because if there is no transition in midsignal, the receiver knows that an error must have occurred.

3.5 ANALOG TRANSMISSION OF DIGITAL DATA

Telephone networks were originally built for human speech rather than for data. They were designed to transmit the electrical representation of sound waves, rather than the binary data used by computers. There are many occasions when data need to be transmitted over a voice communications network. Many people working at home still use a modem over their telephone line to connect to the Internet.

The telephone system (commonly called **POTS** for **plain old telephone service**) enables voice communication between any two telephones within its network. The telephone converts the sound waves produced by the human voice at the sending end into electrical signals for the telephone network. These electrical signals travel through the network until they reach the other telephone and are converted back into sound waves.

Analog transmission occurs when the signal sent over the transmission media continuously varies from one state to another in a wave-like pattern much like the human voice. Modems translate the digital binary data produced by computers into the analog signals required by voice transmission circuits. One modem is used by the transmitter to produce the analog signals and a second by the receiver to translate the analog signals back into digital signals.

The sound waves transmitted through the voice circuit have three important characteristics (see Figure 3-14). The first is the height of the wave, called **amplitude**. Amplitude is measured in decibels (dB). Our ears detect amplitude as the loudness or volume of sound. Every sound wave has two parts, half above the zero amplitude point (i.e., positive) and half below (i.e., negative), and both halves are always the same height.

The second characteristic is the length of the wave, usually expressed as the number of waves per second, or **frequency**. Frequency is expressed in hertz (Hz).[3] Our ears detect frequency as the pitch of the sound. Frequency is the inverse of the length of the sound

FIGURE 3-14

Sound wave

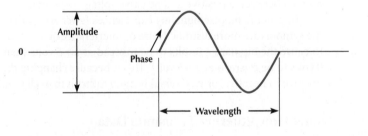

---

[3]Hertz is the same as "**cycles per second**"; therefore, 20,000 Hertz is equal to 20,000 cycles per second. One hertz (HZ) is the same as 1 cycle per second. One kilohertz (KHZ) is 1,000 cycles per second (kilocycles), 1 megahertz (MHZ) is 1 million cycles per second (megacycles), and 1 gigahertz (GHZ) is 1 billion cycles per second.

wave, so that a high frequency means that there are many short waves in a 1-second interval, whereas a low frequency means that there are fewer (but longer) waves in 1 second.

The third characteristic is the **phase**, which refers to the direction in which the wave begins. Phase is measured in the number of degrees (°). The wave in Figure 3-14 starts up and to the right, which is defined as a 0° phase wave. Waves can also start down and to the right (a 180° phase wave), and in virtually any other part of the sound wave.

3.5.1 Modulation

When we transmit data through the telephone lines, we use the shape of the sound waves we transmit (in terms of amplitude, frequency, and phase) to represent different data values. We do this by transmitting a simple sound wave through the circuit (called the **carrier wave**) and then changing its shape in different ways to represent a 1 or a 0. *Modulation* is the technical term used to refer to these "shape changes." There are three fundamental modulation techniques: amplitude modulation, frequency modulation, and phase modulation. Once again, the sender and receiver have to agree on what symbols will be used (what amplitude, frequency, and phase will represent a 1 and a 0) and on the symbol rate (how many symbols will be sent per second).

Basic Modulation With **amplitude modulation (AM)** (also called **amplitude shift keying [ASK]**), the amplitude or height of the wave is changed. One amplitude is the symbol defined to be 0, and another amplitude is the symbol defined to be a 1. In the AM shown in Figure 3-15, the highest amplitude symbol (tallest wave) represents a binary 1 and the lowest amplitude symbol represents a binary 0. In this case, when the sending device wants to transmit a 1, it would send a high-amplitude wave (i.e., a loud signal). AM is more susceptible to noise (more errors) during transmission than is frequency modulation or phase modulation.

Frequency modulation (FM) (also called **frequency shift keying [FSK]**) is a modulation technique whereby each 0 or 1 is represented by a number of waves per second (i.e., a different frequency). In this case, the amplitude does not vary. One frequency (i.e., a certain number of waves per second) is the symbol defined to be a 1, and a different frequency (a different number of waves per second) is the symbol defined to be a 0. In Figure 3-16, the higher frequency wave symbol (more waves per time period) equals a binary 1, and the lower frequency wave symbol equals a binary 0.

Phase modulation (PM) (also called **phase shift keying [PSK]**) is the most difficult to understand. *Phase* refers to the direction in which the wave begins. Until now, the waves we have shown start by moving up and to the right (this is called a 0° phase wave). Waves can also start down and to the right. This is called a phase of 180°. With phase modulation, one phase symbol is defined to be a 0 and the other phase symbol is defined to be a 1. Figure 3-17

FIGURE 3-15
Amplitude modulation

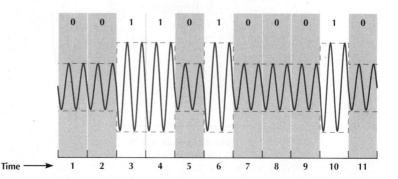

FIGURE 3-16

Frequency modulation

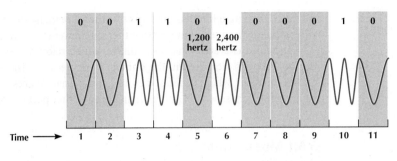

FIGURE 3-17

Phase modulation

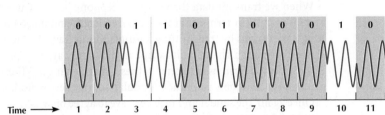

shows the case where a phase of 0° symbol is defined to be a binary 0 and a phase of 180° symbol is defined to be a binary 1.

Sending Multiple Bits Simultaneously Each of the three basic modulation techniques (AM, FM, and PM) can be refined to send more than 1 bit at one time. For example, basic AM sends 1 bit per wave (or *symbol*) by defining two different amplitudes, one for a 1 and one for a 0. It is possible to send 2 bits on one wave or symbol by defining four different amplitudes. Figure 3-18 shows the case where the highest-amplitude wave is defined to be a symbol representing 2 bits, both 1s. The next highest amplitude is the symbol defined to mean first a 1 and then a 0, and so on.

This technique could be further refined to send 3 bits at the same time by defining eight different symbols, each with different amplitude levels or 4 bits by defining 16 symbols, each with different amplitude levels, and so on. At some point, however, it becomes very difficult to differentiate between the different amplitudes. The differences are so small that even a small amount of noise could destroy the signal.

This same approach can be used for FM and PM. Two bits could be sent on the same symbol by defining four different frequencies, one for 11, one for 10, and so on, or by defining four phases (0°, 90°, 180°, and 270°). Three bits could be sent by defining symbols

FIGURE 3-18

Two-bit amplitude modulation

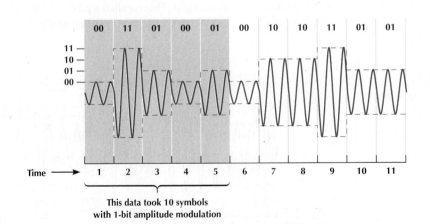

with eight frequencies or eight phases (0°, 45°, 90°, 135°, 180°, 225°, 270°, and 315°). These techniques are also subject to the same limitations as AM; as the number of different frequencies or phases becomes larger, it becomes difficult to differentiate among them.

It is also possible to combine modulation techniques—that is, to use AM, FM, and PM techniques on the same circuit. For example, we could combine AM with four defined amplitudes (capable of sending 2 bits) with FM with four defined frequencies (capable of sending 2 bits) to enable us to send 4 bits on the same symbol.

One popular technique is **quadrature amplitude modulation (QAM)**. QAM involves splitting the symbol into eight different phases (3 bits) and two different amplitudes (1 bit), for a total of 16 different possible values. Thus, one symbol in QAM can represent 4 bits, while 256-QAM sends 8 bits per symbol. 64-QAM and 256-QAM are commonly used in digital TV services and cable modem Internet services.

Bit Rate versus Baud Rate versus Symbol Rate The terms **bit rate** (i.e., the number bits per second transmitted) and **baud rate** are used incorrectly much of the time. They often are used interchangeably, but they are not the same. In reality, the network designer or network user is interested in bits per second because it is the bits that are assembled into characters, characters into words and, thus, business information.

A *bit* is a unit of information. A *baud* is a unit of signaling speed used to indicate the number of times per second the signal on the communication circuit changes. Because of the confusion over the term *baud rate* among the general public, ITU-T now recommends the term *baud rate* be replaced by the term *symbol rate*. The bit rate and the symbol rate (or baud rate) are the same only when 1 bit is sent on each symbol. For example, if we use AM with two amplitudes, we send 1 bit on one symbol. Here, the bit rate equals the symbol rate. However, if we use QAM, we can send 4 bits on every symbol; the bit rate would be four times the symbol rate. If we used 64-QAM, the bit rate would be six times the symbol rate. Virtually all of today's modems send multiple bits per symbol.

3.5.2 Capacity of a Circuit

The data capacity of a circuit is the fastest rate at which you can send your data over the circuit in terms of the number of bits per second. The **data rate** (or bit rate) is calculated by multiplying the number of bits sent on each symbol by the maximum symbol rate. As we discussed in the previous section, the number of bits per symbol depends on the modulation technique (e.g., QAM sends 4 bits per symbol).

The maximum symbol rate in any circuit depends on the bandwidth available and the signal-to-noise ratio (the strength of the signal compared with the amount of noise in the circuit). The **bandwidth** is the difference between the highest and the lowest frequencies in a band or set of frequencies. The range of human hearing is between 20 Hz and 14,000 Hz, so its bandwidth is 13,880 Hz. The maximum symbol rate for analog transmission is usually the same as the bandwidth as measured in hertz. If the circuit is very noisy, the maximum symbol rate may fall as low as 50% of the bandwidth. If the circuit has very little noise, it is possible to transmit at rates up to the bandwidth.

Digital transmission symbol rates can reach as high as two times the bandwidth for techniques that have only one voltage change per symbol (e.g., NRZ). For digital techniques that have two voltage changes per symbol (e.g., RZ, Manchester), the maximum symbol rate is the same as the bandwidth.

Standard telephone lines provide a bandwidth of 4,000 Hz. Under perfect circumstances, the maximum symbol rate is therefore about 4,000 symbols per second. If we were to use basic AM (1 bit per symbol), the maximum data rate would be 4,000 **bits per second (bps)**. If we were to use QAM (4 bits per symbol), the maximum data rate would be 4 bits per symbol × 4,000 symbols per second = 16,000 bps. A circuit with a 10 MHz bandwidth using 64-QAM could provide up to 60 Mbps.

3.5.3 How Modems Transmit Data

The **modem** (an acronym for _mo_dulator/_dem_odulator) takes the digital data from a computer in the form of electrical pulses and converts them into the analog signal that is needed for transmission over an analog voice-grade circuit. There are many different types of modems available today from dial-up modems to cable modems. For data to be transmitted between two computers using modems, both need to use the same type of modem. Fortunately, several standards exist for modems, and any modem that conforms to a standard can communicate with any other modem that conforms to the same standard.

A modem's data transmission rate is the primary factor that determines the throughput rate of data, but it is not the only factor. **Data compression** can increase throughput of data over a communication link by literally compressing the data. **V.44**, the ISO standard for data compression, uses **Lempel–Ziv encoding**. As a message is being transmitted, Lempel–Ziv encoding builds a dictionary of two-, three-, and four-character combinations that occur in the message. Anytime the same character pattern reoccurs in the message, the index to the dictionary entry is transmitted rather than sending the actual data. The reduction provided by V.44 compression depends on the actual data sent but usually averages about 6:1 (i.e., almost six times as much data can be sent per second using V.44 as without it).

3.6 DIGITAL TRANSMISSION OF ANALOG DATA

In the same way that digital computer data can be sent over analog telephone networks using analog transmission, analog voice data can be sent over digital networks using digital transmission. This process is somewhat similar to the analog transmission of digital data. A pair of special devices called _codecs_ (_co_de/_dec_ode) is used in the same way that a pair of modems is used to translate the data to send across the circuit. One codec is attached to the source of the signal (e.g., a telephone or the local loop at the end office) and translates the incoming analog voice signal into a digital signal for transmission across the digital circuit. A second codec at the receiver's end translates the digital data back into analog data.

3.6.1 Translating from Analog to Digital

Analog voice data must first be translated into a series of binary digits before they can be transmitted over a digital circuit. This is done by sampling the amplitude of the sound wave at regular intervals and translating it into a binary number. Figure 3-19 shows an example where eight different amplitude levels are used (i.e., each amplitude level is represented by 3 bits). The top diagram shows the original signal, and the bottom diagram shows the digitized signal.

A quick glance will show that the digitized signal is only a rough approximation of the original signal. The original signal had a smooth flow, but the digitized signal has jagged "steps." The difference between the two signals is called **quantizing error**. Voice transmissions using digitized signals that have a great deal of quantizing error sound metallic or machinelike to the ear.

There are two ways to reduce quantizing error and improve the quality of the digitized signal, but neither is without cost. The first method is to increase the number of amplitude levels. This minimizes the difference between the levels (the "height" of the "steps") and results in a smoother signal. In Figure 3-19, we could define 16 amplitude levels instead of eight levels. This would require 4 bits (rather than the current 3 bits) to represent the amplitude, thus increasing the amount of data needed to transmit the digitized signal.

No amount of levels or bits will ever result in perfect-quality sound reproduction, but in general, 7 bits ($2^7 = 128$ levels) reproduces human speech adequately. Music, on the other hand, typically uses 16 bits ($2^{16} = 65,536$ levels).

FIGURE 3-19

Pulse amplitude
modulation (PAM)

The signal (original wave) is quantized
into 128 pulse amplitudes (PAM). In this
example we have used only eight pulse amplitudes
for simplicity. These eight amplitudes can be
depicted by using only a 3-bit code instead
of the 8-bit code normally used to encode
each pulse amplitude.

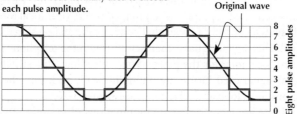

After quantizing, samples are taken at
specific points to produce amplitude
modulated pulses. These pulses are then
coded. Because we used eight pulse
levels, we only need three binary
positions to code each pulse.[1] If we
had used 128 pulse amplitudes, then a
7-bit code plus one parity bit would
be required.

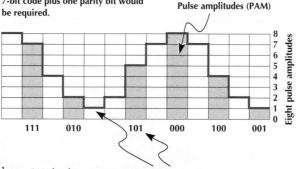

[1]001 = PAM level 1
010 = PAM level 2
011 = PAM level 3
100 = PAM level 4
101 = PAM level 5
110 = PAM level 6
111 = PAM level 7
000 = PAM level 8

For digitizing a voice signal, 8,000 samples
per second are taken. These 8,000 samples
are then transmitted as a serial stream of
0s and 1s. In our case 8,000 samples times
3 bits per sample would require a 24,000
bps transmission rate. In reality, 8 bits per
sample times 8,000 samples requires a
64,000 bps transmission rate.

The second method is to sample more frequently. This will reduce the "length" of each "step," also resulting in a smoother signal. To obtain a reasonable-quality voice signal, one must sample at least twice the highest possible frequency in the analog signal. You will recall that the highest frequency transmitted in telephone circuits is 4,000 Hz. Thus, the methods used to digitize telephone voice transmissions must sample the input voice signal at a minimum of 8,000 times per second. Sampling more frequently than this (called *oversampling*) will improve signal quality. RealNetworks.com, which produces Real Audio and other Web-based tools, sets its products to sample at 48,000 times per second to provide higher quality. The iPod and most CDs sample at 44,100 times per second and use 16 bits per sample to produce almost error-free music. Some other MP3 players sample less frequently and use fewer bits per sample to produce smaller transmissions, but the sound quality may suffer.

3.6.2 How Telephones Transmit Voice Data

When you make a telephone call, the telephone converts your analog voice data into a simple analog signal and sends it down the circuit from your home to the telephone company's network. This process is almost unchanged from the one used by Bell when he invented the telephone in 1876. With the invention of digital transmission, the common carriers (i.e., the telephone companies) began converting their voice networks to use digital transmission. Today, all of the common carrier networks use digital transmission, except in the **local loop** (sometimes called the *last mile*), the wires that run from your home or business to the telephone switch that connects your local loop into the telephone network. This **switch** contains a codec that converts the analog signal from your phone into a digital signal. This digital signal is then sent through the telephone network until it hits the switch for the local loop for the person you are calling. This switch uses its codec to convert the digital signal used inside the phone network back into the analog signal needed by that person's local loop and telephone. See Figure 3-20.

There are many different combinations of sampling frequencies and numbers of bits per sample that could be used. For example, one could sample 4,000 times per second using 128 amplitude levels (i.e., 7 bits) or sample at 16,000 times per second using 256 levels (i.e., 8 bits).

The North American telephone network uses **pulse code modulation (PCM)**. With PCM, the input voice signal is sampled 8,000 times per second. Each time the input voice signal is sampled, 8 bits are generated.[4] Therefore, the transmission speed on the digital circuit must be 64,000 bps (8 bits per sample × 8,000 samples per second) to transmit a voice signal when it is in digital form. Thus, the North American telephone network is built using

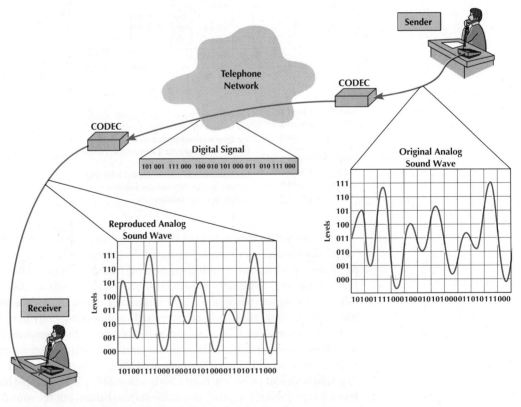

FIGURE 3-20   Pulse amplitude modulation (PAM)

---

[4]Seven of those bits are used to represent the voice signal, and 1 bit is used for control purposes.

millions of 64 Kbps digital circuits that connect via codecs to the millions of miles of analog local loop circuits into the users' residences and businesses.

3.6.3 How Instant Messenger Transmits Voice Data

A 64 Kbps digital circuit works very well for transmitting voice data because it provides very good quality. The problem is that it requires a lot of capacity.

Adaptive differential pulse code modulation (ADPCM) is the alternative used by IM and many other applications that provide voice services over lower-speed digital circuits. ADPCM works in much the same way as PCM. It samples incoming voice signals 8,000 times per second and calculates the same 8-bit amplitude value as PCM. However, instead of transmitting the 8-bit value, it transmits the *difference* between the 8-bit value in the last time interval and the current 8-bit value (i.e., how the amplitude has *changed* from one time period to another). Because analog voice signals change slowly, these changes can be adequately represented by using only 4 bits. This means that ADPCM can be used on digital circuits that provide only 32 Kbps (4 bits per sample × 8,000 samples per second = 32,000 bps).

Several versions of ADPCM have been developed and standardized by the ITU-T. There are versions designed for 8 Kbps circuits (which send 1 bit 8,000 times per second) and 16 Kbps circuits (which send 2 bits 8,000 times per second), as well as the original 32 Kbps version. However, there is a trade-off here. Although the 32 Kbps version usually provides as good a sound quality as that of a traditional voice telephone circuit, the 8 Kbps and 16 Kbps versions provide poorer sound quality.

3.6.4 Voice over Internet Protocol (VoIP)

Voice over Internet Protocol (**VoIP**, pronounced "voyp") is commonly used to transmit phone conversations over digital networks. VoIP is a relatively new standard that uses digital telephones with built-in codecs to convert analog voice data into digital data (see Figure 3-21). Because the codec is built into the telephone, the telephone transmits digital data and therefore can be connected directly into a local area network, in much the same manner as a typical computer. Because VoIP phones operate on the same networks as computers, we can reduce the amount of wiring needed; with VoIP, we need to operate and maintain only one network throughout our offices, rather than two separate networks—one for voice and one for data. However, this also means that data networks with VoIP phones

FIGURE 3-21

VoIP phone

Source: Courtesy Cisco Systems, Inc. Unauthorized use not permitted

must be designed to operate in emergencies (to enable 911 calls) even when the power fails; they must have uninterruptable power supplies (UPS) for all network circuits.

One commonly used VoIP standard is G.722 wideband audio, which is a version of ADPCM that operates at 64 Kbps. It samples 8,000 times per second and produces 8 bits per sample.

Because VoIP phones are digital, they can also contain additional capabilities. For example, high-end VoIP phones often contain computer chips to enable them to download and install small software applications so that they can function in many ways like computers.

3.7 IMPLICATIONS FOR MANAGEMENT

In the past, networks used to be designed so that the physical cables transported data in the same form in which the data were created: Analog voice data generated by telephones used to be carried by analog transmission cables and digital computer data used to be carried by digital transmission cables. Today, it is simple to separate the different types of data (analog voice or digital computer) from the actual physical cables used to carry the data. In most cases, the cheapest and highest-quality media are digital, which means that most data today are transmitted in digital form. Thus, the convergence of voice and video and data at the physical layers is being driven primarily by business reasons: Digital is better.

The change in physical layers also has implications for organizational structure. Voice data used to be managed separately from computer data because they use different types of networks. As the physical networks converge, so too do the organizational units responsible for managing the data. Today, more organizations are placing the management of voice telecommunications into their information systems organizations.

This also has implications for the telecommunications industry. Over the past few years, the historical separation between manufacturers of networking equipment used in organizations and manufacturers of networking equipment used by the telephone companies has crumbled. There have been some big winners and losers in the stock market from the consolidation of these markets.

SUMMARY

Circuits Networks can be configured so that there is a separate circuit from each client to the host (called a point-to-point configuration) or so that several clients share the same circuit (a multipoint configuration). Data can flow through the circuit in one direction only (simplex), in both directions simultaneously (full duplex), or by taking turns so that data sometimes flow in one direction and then in the other (half duplex). A multiplexer is a device that combines several simultaneous low-speed circuits on one higher-speed circuit so that each low-speed circuit believes it has a separate circuit. In general, the transmission capacity of the high-speed circuit must equal or exceed the sum of the low-speed circuits.

Communication Media Media are either guided, in that they travel through a physical cable (e.g., twisted pair wires, coaxial cable, or fiber-optic cable), or wireless, in that they are broadcast through the air (e.g., radio, microwave, or satellite). Among the guided media, fiber-optic cable can transmit data the fastest with the fewest errors and offers greater security but costs the most; twisted pair wire is the cheapest and most commonly used. The choice of wireless media depends more on distance than on any other factor; radio is cheapest for short distances, microwave is cheapest for moderate distances, and satellite is cheapest for long distances.

Digital Transmission of Digital Data Digital transmission (also called baseband transmission) is done by sending a series of electrical (or light) pulses through the media. Digital transmission is preferred to analog transmission because it produces fewer errors; is more efficient; permits higher maximum transmission rates; is more secure; and simplifies the integration of voice, video, and data on the same circuit. With unipolar digital transmission, the voltage changes between 0 volts to represent a binary 0 and some positive value (e.g., +15 volts) to represent a binary 1. With bipolar digital transmission, the voltage changes polarity (i.e., positive or negative) to represent a 1 or a 0. Bipolar is less susceptible to errors. Ethernet uses Manchester encoding, which is a version of unipolar transmission.

Analog Transmission of Digital Data Modems are used to translate the digital data produced by computers into the analog signals for transmission in today's voice communication circuits. Both the sender and receiver need to have a modem. Data are transmitted by changing (or modulating) a carrier sound wave's amplitude (height), frequency (length), or phase (shape) to indicate a binary 1 or 0. For example, in amplitude modulation, one amplitude is defined to be a 1 and another amplitude is defined to be a 0. It is possible to send more than 1 bit on every symbol (or wave). For example, with amplitude modulation, you could send 2 bits on each wave by defining four amplitude levels. The capacity or maximum data rate that a circuit can transmit is determined by multiplying the symbol rate (symbols per second) by the number of bits per symbol. Generally (but not always), the symbol rate is the same as the bandwidth, so bandwidth is often used as a measure of capacity. V.44 is a data compression standard that can be combined with any of the foregoing types of modems to reduce the amount of data in the transmitted signal by a factor of up to six. Thus, a V.92 modem using V.44 could provide an effective data rate of $56,000 \times 6 = 336,000$ bps.

Digital Transmission of Analog Data Because digital transmission is better, analog voice data are sometimes converted to digital transmission. Pulse code modulation (PCM) is the most commonly used technique. PCM samples the amplitude of the incoming voice signal 8,000 times per second and uses 8 bits to represent the signal. PCM produces a reasonable approximation of the human voice, but more sophisticated techniques are needed to adequately reproduce more complex sounds such as music.

KEY TERMS

adaptive differential pulse code modulation (ADPCM), 83
American Standard Code for Information Interchange (ASCII), 72
amplitude modulation (AM), 77
amplitude shift keying (ASK), 77
amplitude, 76
analog transmission, 76
bandwidth, 79

baud rate, 79
bipolar, 75
bit rate, 79
bits per second (bps), 79
carrier wave, 77
circuit, 61
circuit configuration, 62
coaxial cable, 67
codec, 61
coding scheme, 72
cycles per second, 76
data compression, 80
data rate, 79

digital subscriber line (DSL), 65
digital transmission, 74
fiber-optic cable, 67
frequency division multiplexing (FDM), 64
frequency modulation (FM), 77
frequency shift keying (FSK), 77
frequency, 76
full-duplex transmission, 63

guided media, 66
half-duplex transmission, 63
ISO 8859, 72
Kilo Hertz (KHz), 74
Lempel-Ziv encoding, 80
local loop, 82
logical circuit, 61
Manchester encoding, 76
microwave transmission, 69
modem, 80
multipoint circuit, 62

QUESTIONS

1. How does a multipoint circuit differ from a point-to-point circuit?
2. Describe the three types of data flows.
3. Describe three types of guided media.
4. Describe four types of wireless media.
5. How do analog data differ from digital data?
6. Clearly explain the differences among analog data, analog transmission, digital data, and digital transmission.
7. Explain why most telephone company circuits are now digital.
8. What is coding?
9. Briefly describe three important coding schemes.
10. How are data transmitted in parallel?
11. What feature distinguishes serial mode from parallel mode?
12. How does bipolar signaling differ from unipolar signaling? Why is Manchester encoding more popular than either?
13. What are three important characteristics of a sound wave?
14. What is bandwidth? What is the bandwidth in a traditional North American telephone circuit?
15. Describe how data could be transmitted using amplitude modulation.
16. Describe how data could be transmitted using frequency modulation.
17. Describe how data could be transmitted using phase modulation.
18. Describe how data could be transmitted using a combination of modulation techniques.
19. Is the bit rate the same as the symbol rate? Explain.
20. What is a modem?
21. What is quadrature amplitude modulation (QAM).
22. What is 64-QAM?
23. What factors affect transmission speed?
24. What is oversampling?
25. Why is data compression so useful?
26. What data compression standard uses Lempel–Ziv encoding? Describe how it works.
27. Explain how pulse code modulation (PCM) works.
28. What is quantizing error?
29. What is the term used to describe the placing of two or more signals on a single circuit?
30. What is the purpose of multiplexing?
31. How does DSL (digital subscriber line) work?
32. Of the different types of multiplexing, what distinguishes
    a. frequency division multiplexing (FDM)?
    b. time division multiplexing (TDM)?
    c. statistical time division multiplexing (STDM)?
    d. wavelength division multiplexing (WDM)?
33. What is the function of inverse multiplexing (IMUX)?
34. If you were buying a multiplexer, would you choose TDM or FDM? Why?
35. Some experts argue that modems may soon become obsolete. Do you agree? Why or why not?
36. What is the maximum capacity of an analog circuit with a bandwidth of 4,000 Hz using QAM?
37. What is the maximum data rate of an analog circuit with a 10 MHz bandwidth using 64-QAM and V.44?
38. What is the capacity of a digital circuit with a symbol rate of 10 MHz using Manchester encoding?
39. What is the symbol rate of a digital circuit providing 100 Mbps if it uses bipolar NRz signaling?
40. What is VoIP?

EXERCISES

A. Investigate the costs of dumb terminals, network computers, minimally equipped personal computers, and top-of-the-line personal computers. Many equipment manufacturers and resellers are on the Web, so it's a good place to start looking.

B. Investigate the different types of cabling used in your organization and where they are used (e.g., LAN, backbone network).

C. Three terminals (T_1, T_2, T_3) are to be connected to three computers (C_1, C_2, C_3) so that T_1 is connected to C_1, T_2 to C_2, and T_3 to C_3. All are in different cities. T_1 and C_1 are 1,500 miles apart, as are T_2 and C_2, and T_3 and C_3. The points T_1, T_2, and T_3 are 25 miles apart, and the points C_1, C_2, and C_3 also are 25 miles apart. If telephone lines cost $1 per mile, what is the line cost for three?

D. Investigate different types of satellite communication services that are provided today.

E. Draw how the bit pattern 01101100 would be sent using
    a. Single-bit AM
    b. Single-bit FM
    c. Single-bit PM
    d. Two-bit AM (i.e., four amplitude levels)
    e. Two-bit FM (i.e., four frequencies)
    f. Two-bit PM (i.e., four different phases)
    g. Single-bit AM combined with single-bit FM
    h. Single-bit AM combined with single-bit PM
    i. Two-bit AM combined with two-bit PM

F. If you had to download a 20-page paper of 400 K (bytes) from your professor, approximately how long would it take to transfer it over the following circuits? Assume that control characters add an extra 10% to the message.
    a. Dial-up modem at 33.6 Kbps
    b. Cable modem at 384 Kbps
    c. Cable modem at 1.5 Mbps
    d. If the modem includes V.44 data compression with a 6:1 data compression ratio, what is the data rate in bits per second you would actually see in choice c?

MINICASES

I. Eureka! (Part 1) Eureka! is a telephone- and Internet-based concierge service that specializes in obtaining things that are hard to find (e.g., Super Bowl tickets, first-edition books from the 1500s, Fabergé eggs). It currently employs 60 staff members who collectively provide 24-hour coverage (over three shifts). They answer the phones and respond to requests entered on the Eureka! Web site. Much of their work is spent on the phone and on computers searching on the Internet. The company has just leased a new office building and is about to wire it. What media would you suggest the company install in its office and why?

II. Eureka! (Part 2) Eureka! is a telephone- and Internet-based concierge service that specializes in obtaining things that are hard to find (e.g., Super Bowl tickets, first-edition books from the 1500s, Fabergé eggs). It currently employs 60 staff members who work 24 hours per day (over three shifts). Staff answer the phone and respond to requests entered on the Eureka! Web site. Much of their work is spent on the phone and on computers searching on the Internet. What type of connections should Eureka! consider from its offices to the outside world, in terms of phone and Internet? Outline the pros and cons of each alternative below and make a recommendation. The company has three alternatives:

1. Should the company use standard voice lines but use DSL for its data ($40 per month per line for both services)?
2. Should the company separate its voice and data needs, using standard analog services for voice but finding some advanced digital transmission services for data ($40 per month for each voice line and $300 per month for a circuit with 1.5 Mbps of data)?
3. Should the company search for all digital services for both voice and data ($60 per month for an all-digital circuit that provides two phone lines that can be used for two voice calls, one voice call and one data call at 64 Kbps, or one data call at 128 Kbps)?

III. Eureka! (Part 3) Eureka! is a telephone- and Internet-based concierge service that specializes in obtaining things that are hard to find (e.g., Super Bowl tickets, first-edition books from the 1500s,

Fabergé eggs). It currently employees 60 staff members who work 24 hours per day (over three shifts). Staff members answer phone calls and respond to requests entered on the Eureka! Web site. Currently, each staff member has a desktop PC with two monitors and a twisted pair connection (Cat5e) that offers speeds up to 100 Mbps. Some employees made a suggestion to the CEO of Eureka! to upgrade their connection to a fiber-optic cable that can provide speeds up to 1 Gbps. What do you think about this idea? How easy (difficult) is it to change wiring from twisted pair to fiber optic? Can we use the same network cards in the PCs, or do we need to change them? How much would this change cost?

IV. **Speedy Package** Speedy Package is a same-day package delivery service that operates in Chicago. Each package has a shipping label that is attached to the package and is also electronically scanned and entered into Speedy's data network when the package is picked up and when it is delivered. The electronic labels are transmitted via a device that operates on a cell phone network. 1. Assuming that each label is 1,000 bytes long, how long does it take to transmit one label over the cell network, assuming that the cell phone network operates at 144 kbps (144,000 *bits* per second) and that there are 8 bits in a byte? 2. If Speedy were to upgrade to the new, faster digital phone network that transmits data at 200 Kbps (200,000 *bits* per second), how long would it take to transmit a label?

V. **Boingo** Reread Management Focus 3.2. What other alternatives can travelers consider? How is Boingo different from other companies offering hot spots, such as T-Mobile or AT&T?

CASE STUDY

NEXT-DAY AIR SERVICE

See the Web site at www.wiley.com/college/fitzgerald.

HANDS-ON ACTIVITY 3A

Looking Inside Your Cable

One of the most commonly used types of local network cable is Category 5 unshielded twisted pair cable, commonly called "Cat 5." Cat 5 (and an enhanced version called Cat 5e) are used in Ethernet LANs. If you have installed a LAN in your house or apartment, you probably used Cat 5 or Cat 5e.

Figure 3-22 shows a picture of a typical Cat 5 cable. Each end of the cable has a connector called an RJ-45 connector that enables the cable to be plugged into a computer or network device. If you look closely at the connector, you will see there are eight separate "pins." You might think that this would mean the Cat 5 can transmit data in parallel, but it doesn't do this. Cat 5 is used for serial transmission.

If you have an old Cat 5 cable (or are willing to spend a few dollars to buy cheap cable), it is simple to take the connector off. Simply take a pair of scissors and cut through the cable a few inches from the connector. Figure 3-23 shows the same Cat 5 cable with the connector cut off. You can see why twisted pair is called twisted pair: A single Cat 5 cable contains four separate sets of twisted pair wires for a total of eight wires.

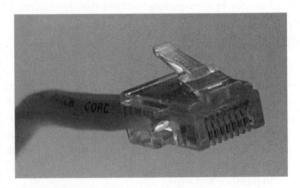

FIGURE 3-22 Cat 5 cable

Unfortunately, this picture is in black and white so it is hard to see the different colors of the eight wires inside the cable. Figure 3-24 lists the different colors of the wires and what they are used for under the EIA/TIA 568B standard (the less common 568A standard uses the pins in different ways). One pair of wires (connected to pins 1 and 2) is used

FIGURE 3-23   Inside a Cat 5 cable
Source: Courtesy of Belkin International, Inc.

to transmit data from your computer into the network. When your computer transmits, it sends the same data on both wires; pin 1 (transmit+) transmits the data normally and pin 2 (transmit−) transmits the same data with reversed polarity. This way, if an error occurs, the hardware will likely detect a different signal on the two cables. For example, if there is a sudden burst of electricity with a positive polarity (or a negative polarity), it will change only one of the transmissions from negative to positive (or vice versa) and leave the other transmission unchanged. Electrical pulses generate a magnetic field that has very bad side effects on the other wires. To minimize this, the two transmit wires are twisted together so that the other wires in the cable receive both a positive and a negative polarity magnetic field from the wires twisted around each other, which cancel each other out.

Figure 3-24 also shows a separate pair of wires for receiving transmissions from the network (pin 3 [receive+] and pin 6 [receive−]). These wires work exactly the same way as transmit+ and transmit− but are used by the network to send data to your computer. You'll notice that they are also twisted together in one pair of wires, even though they are not side by side on the connector.

Figure 3-24 shows the pin functions from the viewpoint of your computer. If you think about it, you'll quickly realize that the pin functions at the network end of the cable are reversed; that is, pin 1 is receive+ because it is the wire that the network uses to receive the transmit+ signal from your computer. Likewise, pin 6 at the network end is the transmit− wire because it is the wire on which your computer receives the reversed data signal.

The separate set of wires for transmitting and receiving means that Cat 5 is designed for full-duplex transmission. It can send and receive at the same time because one set of wires is used for sending data and one set is used for receiving data. However, Cat 5 is not often used this way. Most hardware that uses Cat 5 is designed to operate in a half-duplex mode, even though the cable itself is capable of full duplex.

You'll also notice that the other four wires in the cable are not used. Yes, that's right; they are simply wasted.

Deliverable

Find a Cat 5 or Cat 5e cable and record what color wires are used for each pin.

Pin number	Color (EIA/TIA 568B standard)	Name
1	White with orange stripe	Transmit +
2	Orange with white stripe or solid orange	Transmit −
3	White with green stripe	Receive +
4	Blue with white stripe or solid blue	Not used
5	White with blue stripe	Not used
6	Green with white stripe or solid green	Receive −
7	White with brown stripe or solid brown	Not used
8	Brown with white stripe or solid brown	Not used

FIGURE 3-24   Pin connection for Cat 5 at the computer end

HANDS-ON ACTIVITY 3B

Making MP3 Files

MP3 files are good examples of analog-to-digital conversion. It is simple to take an analog signal—such as your voice—and convert it into a digital file for transmission or playback. In this activity, we will show you how to record your voice and see how different levels of digital quality affect the sound.

First, you need to download a sound editor and MP3 converter. One very good sound editor is Audacity—and it's free. Go to audacity.sourceforge.net and download and install the audacity software. You will also need the plug-in called LAME (an MP3 encoder), which is also free and available at lame.sourceforge.net.

Use Audacity to record music or your voice (you can use a cheap microphone). Audacity records in very high quality, but will produce MP3 files in whatever quality level you choose.

Once you have the file recorded, you can edit the Preferences to change the File Format to use in saving the MP3 file. Audacity/LAME offers a wide range of qualities. Try recording at least three different quality levels. For example, for high quality, you could use 320 Kbps, which means the recording uses 320 Kbps of data per second. In other words, the number of samples per second times the number of bits per sample equals 320 Kbps. For regular quality, you could use 128 Kbps. For low quality, you could use 16 Kbps.

Create each of these files and listen to them to hear the differences in quality produced by the quantizing error. The differences should be most noticeable for music. A recording at 24 Kbps is often adequate for voice, but music will require a better quality encoding.

Deliverable

1. Produce three MP3 files of the same music or voice recording at three different quality levels.

2. List the size of each file.

3. Listen to each file and describe the quality differences you hear (if any).

HANDS-ON ACTIVITY 3C

Making a Cat 5e Patch Cable

A patch cable is a cable that runs a short distance (usually less than 10 feet) that connects a device into a wall jack, a patch panel jack, or a device. If you have a desktop computer, you're using a patch cable to connect it into your Ethernet LAN. Patch cables are relatively inexpensive (usually $10 or less), but compared to the cost of their materials, they are expensive (the materials usually cost less than $1). Because it is relatively easy to make a patch cable, many companies make their own in order to save money.

To make your own patch cable, you will need a crimper, some Cat 5e cable, two RJ45 connectors, and a cable tester (optional). See Figure 3-25.

1. Using the cutter on the crimping tool, cut a desired length of Cat 5e cable.

2. Insert the end of the cable into the stripper and gently press on the cable while rotating it to remove the outer insulation of the cable. Be careful not to cut the twisted pairs inside. After removing the outer insulation, visually inspect the twisted pairs for damage. Do this on both ends of your cable. If any of the cables are damaged, you need to cut them and start over.

3. Untwist the twisted pairs and straighten them. Once they are straightened, put them into this order: orange-white, orange, green-white, blue, blue-white, green, brown-white, brown.

4. Hold the cable in your right hand; the orange-white wire should be closest to you. Hold the RJ45 connector in your left hand with the little "handle" on the bottom.

5. Insert the wires inside the connector all the way to the end—you should be able to see the colors of the wires when you look at the front of the connector. Make sure that the wires don't change order. The white insulation should be about 1/3 of the way inside the connector. (If you used the stripper on the tool properly, the length of the wires will be exactly as needed to fit to the RJ45 connector.)

6. Now you are ready to crimp the connector. Insert the RJ45 connector to the crimper and press really hard. This will push the gold contacts on the connector onto the twisted pairs.

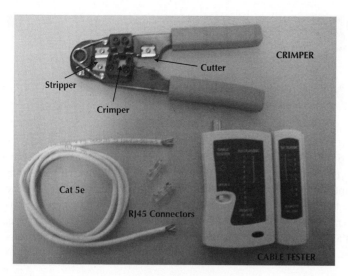

FIGURE 3-25 Tools and materials for making a patch cable

7. Crimp the other end of the cable by repeating steps 4 through 7.

8. The final step is to test your cable. Turn on the cable tester and insert both ends of the patch cable into the tester. If you see the flashing light going down the indicators 1 through 8, not skipping any number or changing the order, you made a fully functional patch cable. If you don't have a cable tester, you can use the cable to connect your computer into an Ethernet LAN. If you're able to use the LAN, the cable is working.

Deliverable

A working patch cable.

CHAPTER 4

DATA LINK LAYER

The data link layer (also called layer 2) is responsible for moving a message from one computer or network device to the next computer or network device in the overall path from sender or receiver. It controls the way messages are sent on the physical media. Both the sender and receiver have to agree on the rules, or *protocols*, that govern how they will communicate with each other. A *data link protocol* determines who can transmit at what time, where a message begins and ends, and how a receiver recognizes and corrects a transmission error. In this chapter, we discuss these processes as well as several important sources of errors.

OBJECTIVES

- Understand the role of the data link layer
- Become familiar with two basic approaches to controlling access to the media
- Become familiar with common sources of error and their prevention
- Understand three common error detection and correction methods
- Become familiar with several commonly used data link protocols

OUTLINE

4.1 INTRODUCTION

In Chapter 1, we introduced the concept of layers in data communications. The data link layer sits between the physical layer (hardware such as the circuits, computers, and multiplexers described in Chapter 3) and the network layer (which performs addressing and routing, as described in Chapter 5).

The data link layer is responsible for sending and receiving messages to and from other computers. Its job is to reliably move a message from one computer over one circuit to the next computer where the message needs to go.

The data link layer performs two main functions and therefore is often divided into two sublayers. The first sublayer (called the **logical link control [LLC] sublayer**) is the data link layer's connection to the network layer above it. At the sending computer, the LLC sublayer software is responsible for communicating with the network layer software (e.g., IP) and for taking the network layer Protocol Data Unit (PDU)—usually an IP packet—and surrounding it with a data link layer PDU—often an Ethernet frame. At the receiving computer, the LLC sublayer software removes the data link layer PDU and passes the message it contains (usually an IP packet) to the network layer software.

The second sublayer (called the **media access control [MAC] sublayer**) controls the physical hardware. The MAC sublayer software at the sending computer controls how and when the physical layer converts bits into the physical symbols that are sent down the circuit. At the receiving computer, the MAC sublayer software takes the data link layer PDU from the LLC sublayer, converts it into a stream of bits, and controls when the physical layer actually transmits the bits over the circuit. At the receiving computer, the MAC sublayer receives a stream of bits from the physical layer and translates it into a coherent PDU, ensures that no errors have occurred in transmission, and passes the data link layer PDU to the LLC sublayer.

Both the sender and receiver have to agree on the rules or *protocols* that govern how their data link layers will communicate with each other. A *data link protocol* performs three functions:

- Controls when computers transmit (*media access control*)
- Detects and corrects transmission errors (*error control*)
- Identifies the start and end of a message by using a PDU (*message delineation*)

4.2 MEDIA ACCESS CONTROL

Media access control refers to the need to control when computers transmit. With point-to-point full-duplex configurations, media access control is unnecessary because there are only two computers on the circuit, and full duplex permits either computer to transmit at any time.

Media access control becomes important when several computers share the same communication circuit, such as a point-to-point configuration with a half-duplex configuration that requires computers to take turns or a multipoint configuration in which several computers share the same circuit. Here, it is critical to ensure that no two computers attempt to transmit data at the same time—but if they do, there must be a way to recover from the problem. There are two fundamental approaches to media access control: contention and controlled access.

4.2.1 Contention

With **contention**, computers wait until the circuit is free (i.e., no other computers are transmitting) and then transmit whenever they have data to send. Contention is commonly used in Ethernet LANs.

As an analogy, suppose that you are talking with some friends. People listen, and if no one is talking, they can talk. If you want to say something, you wait until the speaker is done and then you try to talk. Usually, people yield to the first person who jumps in at the precise moment the previous speaker stops. Sometimes two people attempt to talk at the same time, so there must be some technique to continue the conversation after such a verbal collision occurs.

4.2.2 Controlled Access

With **controlled access** controls the circuit and determines which clients can transmit at what time. There are two commonly used controlled access techniques: access requests and polling.

With the **access request** technique, client computers that want to transmit send a request to transmit to the device that is controlling the circuit (e.g., the wireless access point). The controlling device grants permission for one computer at a time to transmit. When one computer has permission to transmit, all other computers wait until that computer has finished, and then, if they have something to transmit, they use a contention technique to send an access request.

The access request technique is like a classroom situation in which the instructor calls on the students who raise their hands. The instructor acts like the controlling access point. When they want to talk, students raise their hands and the instructor recognizes them so they can contribute. When they have finished, the instructor again takes charge and allows someone else to talk. And of course, just like in a classroom, the wireless access point can choose to transmit whenever it likes.

Polling is the process of sending a signal to a client computer that gives it permission to transmit. With polling, the clients store all messages that need to be transmitted. Periodically, the controlling device (e.g., a wireless access point) *polls* the client to see if it has data to send. If the client has data to send, it does so. If the client has no data to send, it responds negatively, and the controller asks another client if it has data to send.

There are several types of polling. With **roll-call polling**, the controller works consecutively through a list of clients, first polling client 1, then client 2, and so on, until all are polled. Roll-call polling can be modified to select clients in priority so that some get polled more often than others. For example, one could increase the priority of client 1 by using a polling sequence such as 1, 2, 3, 1, 4, 5, 1, 6, 7, 1, 8, 9.

Typically, roll-call polling involves some waiting because the controller has to poll a client and then wait for a response. The response might be an incoming message that was waiting to be sent, a negative response indicating nothing is to be sent, or the full "time-out period" may expire because the client is temporarily out of service (e.g., it is malfunctioning or the user has turned it off). Usually, a timer "times out" the client after waiting several seconds without getting a response. If some sort of fail-safe time-out is not used, the circuit poll might lock up indefinitely on an out-of-service client.

With **hub polling** (often called **token passing**), one device starts the poll and passes it to the next computer on the multipoint circuit, which sends its message and passes the poll to the next. That computer then passes the poll to the next, and so on, until it reaches the first computer, which restarts the process again.

4.2.3 Relative Performance

Which media access control approach is best: controlled access or contention? There is no simple answer. The key consideration is throughput—which approach will permit the most amount of user data to be transmitted through the network.

In general, contention approaches work better than controlled approaches for small networks that have low usage. In this case, each computer can transmit when necessary, without waiting for permission. Because usage is low, there is little chance of a collision. In contrast, computers in a controlled access environment must wait for permission, so even if no other computer needs to transmit, they must wait for the poll.

The reverse is true for large networks with high usage: Controlled access works better. In high-volume networks, many computers want to transmit, and the probability of a collision using contention is high. Collisions are very costly in terms of throughput because they waste circuit capacity during the collision and require both computers to retransmit later. Controlled access prevents collisions and makes more efficient use of the circuit, and although response time does increase, it does so more gradually (Figure 4-1).

The key to selecting the best access control technique is to find the crossover point between controlled and contention. Although there is no one correct answer, because it depends on how many messages the computers in the network transmit, most experts believe that the crossover point is often around 20 computers (lower for busy computers,

FIGURE 4-1

Relative response times

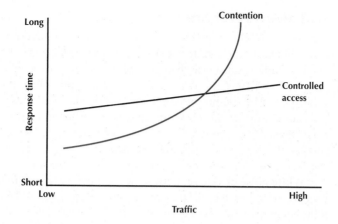

higher for less-busy computers). For this reason, when we build shared multipoint circuits like those often used in LANs or wireless LANs, we try to put no more than 20 computers on any one shared circuit.

4.3 ERROR CONTROL

Before learning the control mechanisms that can be implemented to protect a network from errors, you should realize that there are *human errors* and *network errors*. Human errors, such as a mistake in typing a number, usually are controlled through the application program. Network errors, such as those that occur during transmission, are controlled by the network hardware and software.

There are two categories of network errors: *corrupted data* (data that have been changed) and *lost data*. Networks should be designed to (1) prevent, (2) detect, and (3) correct both corrupted data and lost data. We begin by examining the sources of errors and how to prevent them and then turn to error detection and correction.

Network errors are a fact of life in data communications networks. Depending on the type of circuit, they may occur every few hours, minutes, or seconds because of noise on the lines. No network can eliminate all errors, but most errors can be prevented, detected, and corrected by proper design. Inter-Exchange Carriers (IXCs) that provide data transmission circuits provide statistical measures specifying typical **error rates** and the pattern of errors that can be expected on the circuits they lease. For example, the error rate might be stated as 1 in 500,000, meaning there is 1 bit in error for every 500,000 bits transmitted.

Normally, errors appear in bursts. In a **burst error**, more than 1 data bit is changed by the error-causing condition. In other words, errors are not uniformly distributed in time. Although an error rate might be stated as 1 in 500,000, errors are more likely to occur as 100 bits every 50,000,000 bits. The fact that errors tend to be clustered in bursts rather than evenly dispersed is both good and bad. If the errors were not clustered, an error rate of 1 bit in 500,000 would make it rare for 2 erroneous bits to occur in the same character. Consequently, simple character-checking schemes would be effective at detecting errors. When errors are #ore or less evenly distrib#ted, it is not di#ficult to gras# the me#ning even when the error #ate is high, as it is in this #entence (1 charac#er in 20). But burst errors are the rule rather than the exception, often obliterating 100 or more bits at a time. This makes it more difficult to recover the meaning, so more reliance must be placed on error detection and correction methods. The positive side is that there are long periods of error-free transmission, meaning that very few messages encounter errors.

4.3.1 Sources of Errors

Line noise and *distortion* can cause data communication errors. The focus in this section is on electrical media such as twisted pair wire and coaxial cable, because they are more likely to suffer from noise than are optical media such as fiber-optic cable. In this case, noise is undesirable electrical signals (for fiber-optic cable, it is undesirable light). Noise is introduced by equipment or natural disturbances, and it degrades the performance of a communication circuit. Noise manifests itself as extra bits, missing bits, or bits that have been "flipped" (i.e., changed from 1 to 0 or vice versa). Figure 4-2 summarizes the major sources of error and ways to prevent them. The first six sources listed there are the most important; the last three are more common in analog rather than digital circuits.

White noise or **Gaussian noise** (the familiar background hiss or static on radios and telephones) is caused by the thermal agitation of electrons and therefore is inescapable. Even if the equipment were perfect and the wires were perfectly insulated from any and all external interference, there still would be some white noise. White noise usually is not a problem unless it becomes so strong that it obliterates the transmission. In this case, the strength of the electrical signal is increased so it overpowers the white noise; in technical terms, we increase the signal-to-noise ratio.

Impulse noise (sometimes called *spikes*) is the primary source of errors in data communications. It is heard as a click or a crackling noise and can last as long as $1/100$ of a second. Such a click does not really affect voice communications, but it can obliterate a group of data, causing a burst error. At 1.5 Mbps, 15,000 bits would be changed by a spike of $1/100$ of a second. Some of the sources of impulse noise are voltage changes in adjacent lines, lightning flashes during thunderstorms, fluorescent lights, and poor connections in circuits.

Cross-talk occurs when one circuit picks up signals in another. A person experiences cross-talk during telephone calls when she or he hears other conversations in the background. It occurs between pairs of wires that are carrying separate signals, in multiplexed links carrying many discrete signals, or in microwave links in which one antenna picks up a minute reflection from another antenna. Cross-talk between lines increases with increased communication distance, increased proximity of the two wires, increased signal strength, and higher-frequency signals. Wet or damp weather can also increase cross-talk. Like white noise, cross-talk has such a low signal strength that it normally is not bothersome.

Echoes are the result of poor connections that cause the signal to reflect back to the transmitting equipment. If the strength of the echo is strong enough to be detected, it causes errors. Echoes, like cross-talk and white noise, have such a low signal strength that they normally are not bothersome. Echoes can also occur in fiber-optic cables when connections between cables are not properly aligned.

Attenuation is the loss of power a signal suffers as it travels from the transmitting computer to the receiving computer. Some power is absorbed by the medium or is lost before

FIGURE 4-2

Sources of errors and ways to minimize them

Source of Error	What Causes It	How to Prevent It
White noise	Movement of electrons	Increase signal strength
Impulse noise	Sudden increases in electricity (e.g., lightning)	Shield or move the wires
Cross-talk	Multiplexer guardbands too small or wires too close together	Increase the guardbands or move or shield the wires
Echo	Poor connections	Fix the connections or tune equipment
Attenuation	Gradual decrease in signal over distance	Use repeaters or amplifiers
Intermodulation noise	Signals from several circuits combine	Move or shield the wires

it reaches the receiver. As the medium absorbs power, the signal becomes weaker, and the receiving equipment has less and less chance of correctly interpreting the data. This power loss is a function of the transmission method and circuit medium. High frequencies lose power more rapidly than do low frequencies during transmission, so the received signal can thus be distorted by unequal loss of its component frequencies. Attenuation increases as frequency increases or as the diameter of the wire decreases.

Intermodulation noise is a special type of cross-talk. The signals from two circuits combine to form a new signal that falls into a frequency band reserved for another signal. This type of noise is similar to harmonics in music. On a multiplexed line, many different signals are amplified together, and slight variations in the adjustment of the equipment can cause intermodulation noise. A maladjusted modem may transmit a strong frequency tone when not transmitting data, thus producing this type of noise.

In general, errors are more likely to occur in wireless, microwove, or satellite transmission than transmission through cables. Therefore, error detection is more important when using radiated media than guided media. Impulse noise is the most frequent cause of errors in today's networks. Unfortunately, as the next section describes, it could be very difficult to determine what caused this type of error.

4.3.2 Error Prevention

Obviously, **error prevention** is very important. There are many techniques to prevent errors (or at least reduce them), depending on the situation. *Shielding* (protecting wires by covering them with an insulating coating) is one of the best ways to prevent impulse noise, cross-talk, and intermodulation noise. Many different types of wires and cables are available with different amounts of shielding. In general, the greater the shielding, the more expensive the cable and the more difficult it is to install.

Moving cables away from sources of noise (especially power sources) can also reduce impulse noise, cross-talk, and intermodulation noise. For impulse noise, this means avoiding lights and heavy machinery. Locating communication cables away from power cables is always a good idea. For cross-talk, this means physically separating the cables from other communication cables.

Cross-talk and intermodulation noise are often caused by improper multiplexing. Changing multiplexing techniques (e.g., from FDM [Frequency Division Multiplexing] to TDM [Time Division Multiplexing]) or changing the frequencies or size of the guardbands in FDM can help.

Many types of noise (e.g., echoes, white noise) can be caused by poorly maintained equipment or poor connections and splices among cables. This is particularly true for echo in fiber-optic cables, which is almost always caused by poor connections. The solution here is obvious: Tune the transmission equipment and redo the connections.

To avoid attenuation, telephone circuits have **repeaters** or **amplifiers** spaced throughout their length. The distance between them depends on the amount of power lost per unit length of the transmission line. An amplifier takes the incoming signal, increases its strength, and retransmits it on the next section of the circuit. They are typically used on analog circuits such as the telephone company's voice circuits. The distance between the amplifiers depends on the amount of attenuation, although 1- to 10-mile intervals are common. On analog circuits, it is important to recognize that the noise and distortion are *also* amplified, along with the signal. This means some noise from a previous circuit is regenerated and amplified each time the signal is amplified.

Repeaters are commonly used on digital circuits. A repeater receives the incoming signal, translates it into a digital message, and retransmits the message. Because the message is recreated at each repeater, noise and distortion from the previous circuit are not amplified. This provides a much cleaner signal and results in a lower error rate for digital circuits.

MANAGEMENT **4-1 Finding the Source of Impulse Noise**

FOCUS

*S*everal years ago, the University of Georgia radio station received FCC (Federal Communications Commission) approval to broadcast using a stronger signal. Immediately after the station started broadcasting with the new signal, the campus backbone network (BN) became unusable because of impulse noise. It took 2 days to link the impulse noise to the radio station, and when the radio station returned to its usual broadcast signal, the problem disappeared.

However, this was only the first step in the problem. The radio station wanted to broadcast at full strength, and there was no good reason for why the stronger broadcast should affect the BN in this way. After 2 weeks of effort, the problem was discovered. A short section of the BN ran above ground between two buildings. It turned out that the specific brand of outdoor cable we used was particularly tasty to squirrels. They had eaten the outer insulating coating off of the cable, making it act like an antennae to receive the radio signals. The cable was replaced with a steel-coated armored cable so the squirrels could not eat the insulation. Things worked fine when the radio station returned to its stronger signal.

4.3.3 Error Detection

It is possible to develop data transmission methodologies that give very high **error-detection** performance. The only way to do error detection is to send extra data with each message. These error-detection data are added to each message by the data link layer of the sender on the basis of some mathematical calculations performed on the message (in some cases, error-detection methods are built into the hardware itself). The receiver performs the same mathematical calculations on the message it receives and matches its results against the error-detection data that were transmitted with the message. If the two match, the message is assumed to be correct. If they don't match, an error has occurred.

In general, the larger the amount of error-detection data sent, the greater the ability to detect an error. However, as the amount of error-detection data is increased, the throughput of useful data is reduced, because more of the available capacity is used to transmit these error-detection data and less is used to transmit the actual message itself. Therefore, the **efficiency** of data throughput varies inversely as the desired amount of error detection is increased.

Three well-known *error-detection methods* are parity checking, checksum, and cyclic redundancy checking.

Parity Checking   One of the oldest and simplest error-detection methods is *parity*. With this technique, one additional bit is added to each byte in the message. The value of this additional **parity bit** is based on the number of 1s in each byte transmitted. This parity bit is set to make the total number of 1s in the byte (including the parity bit) either an even number or an odd number. Figure 4-3 gives an example.

A little thought will convince you that any single error (a switch of a 1 to a 0, or vice versa) will be detected by parity, but it cannot determine which bit was in error. You will know an error occurred, but not what the error was. But if *two* bits are switched, the **parity check** will not detect any error. It is easy to see that parity can detect errors only when an odd number of bits have been switched; any even number of errors cancel one another out. Therefore, the probability of detecting an error, given that one has occurred, is only about 50%. Many networks today do not use parity because of its low error-detection rate. When parity is used, protocols are described as having **odd parity** or **even parity**.

FIGURE 4-3

Using parity for error detection

> Assume we are using even parity with 8-bit ASCII.
> The letter *V* in 8-bit ASCII is encoded as 01101010.
> Because there are four 1's (an even number), parity is set to 0.
> This would be transmitted as 011010100.
>
> Assume we are using even parity with 8-bit ASCII.
> The letter *W* in 8-bit ASCII is encoded as 00011010.
> Because there are three 1's (an odd number), parity is set to 1.
> This would be transmitted as 000110101.

Checksum With the **checksum** technique, a checksum (typically 1 byte) is added to the end of the message. The checksum is calculated by adding the decimal value of each character in the message, dividing the sum by 255, and using the remainder as the checksum. The receiver calculates its own checksum in the same way and compares it with the transmitted checksum. If the two values are equal, the message is presumed to contain no errors. Use of checksum detects close to 95% of the errors for multiple-bit burst errors.

Cyclic Redundancy Check One of the most popular error-checking schemes is **cyclic redundancy check (CRC)**. It adds 8, 16, 24, or 32 bits to the message. With CRC, a message is treated as one long binary number, P. Before transmission, the data link layer (or hardware device) divides P by a fixed binary number, G, resulting in a whole number, Q, and a remainder, R/G. So, $P/G = Q + R/G$. For example, if $P = 58$ and $G = 8$, then $Q = 7$ and $R = 2$. G is chosen so that the remainder, R, will be either 8 bits, 16 bits, 24 bits, or 32 bits.[1]

The remainder, R, is appended to the message as the error-checking characters before transmission. The receiving hardware divides the received message by the same G, which generates an R. The receiving hardware checks to ascertain whether the received R agrees with the locally generated R. If it does not, the message is assumed to be in error.

Cyclic redundancy check performs quite well. The most commonly used CRC codes are CRC-16 (a 16-bit version), CRC-CCITT (another 16-bit version), and CRC-32 (a 32-bit version). The probability of detecting an error is 100% for all errors of the same length as the CRC or less. For example, CRC-16 is guaranteed to detect errors if 16 or fewer bits are affected. If the burst error is longer than the CRC, then CRC is not perfect but is close to it. CRC-16 will detect about 99.998% of all burst errors longer than 16 bits, whereas CRC-32 will detect about 99.99999998% of all burst errors longer than 32 bits.

4.3.4 Error Correction via Retransmission

Once error has been detected, it must be corrected. The simplest, most effective, least expensive, and most commonly used method for error correction is retransmission. With retransmission, a receiver that detects an error simply asks the sender to retransmit the message until it is received without error. This is often called **Automatic Repeat reQuest (ARQ)**. There are two types of ARQ: stop-and-wait and continuous.

Stop-and-Wait ARQ With **stop-and-wait ARQ**, the sender stops and waits for a response from the receiver after each data packet. After receiving a packet, the receiver sends either an

---

[1]CRC is actually more complicated than this because it uses polynominal division, not "normal" division as illustrated here. Ross Williams provides an excellent tutorial on CRC at www.ross.net/crc/crcpaper.html.

FIGURE 4-4

Stop-and-wait ARQ
(Automatic Repeat
reQuest).
ACK = acknowledgment;
NAK = negative
acknowledgment

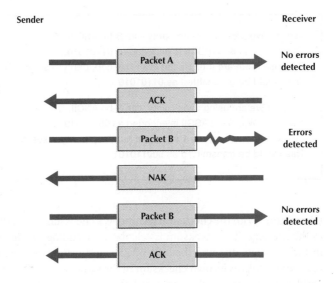

acknowledgment (ACK), if the packet was received without error, or a **negative acknowl-edgment (NAK)**, if the message contained an error. If it is an NAK, the sender resends the previous message. If it is an ACK, the sender continues with the next message. Stop-and-wait ARQ is by definition a half-duplex transmission technique (Figure 4-4).

Continuous ARQ With **continuous ARQ**, the sender does not wait for an acknowledgment after sending a message; it immediately sends the next one. Although the messages are being transmitted, the sender examines the stream of returning acknowledgments. If it receives an NAK, the sender retransmits the needed messages. The packets that are retransmitted may be only those containing an error (called **Link Access Protocol for Modems [LAP-M]**) or may be the first packet with an error and all those that followed it (called **Go-Back-N ARQ**). LAP-M is better because it is more efficient.

Continuous ARQ is by definition a full-duplex transmission technique, because both the sender and the receiver are transmitting simultaneously. (The sender is sending messages, and the receiver is sending ACKs and NAKs.) Figure 4-5 illustrates the flow of messages on a communication circuit using continuous ARQ. Continuous ARQ is sometimes called **sliding window** because of the visual imagery the early network designers used to think about continuous ARQ. Visualize the sender having a set of messages to send in memory stacked in order from first to last. Now imagine a window that moves through the stack from first to last. As a message is sent, the window expands to cover it, meaning that the sender is waiting for an ACK for the message. As an ACK is received for a message, the window moves forward, dropping the message out of the bottom of the window, indicating that it has been sent and received successfully.

Continuous ARQ is also important in providing **flow control**, which means ensuring that the computer sending the message is not transmitting too quickly for the receiver. For example, if a client computer was sending information too quickly for a server computer to store a file being uploaded, the server might run out of memory to store the file. By using ACKs and NAKs, the receiver can control the rate at which it receives information. With stop-and-wait ARQ, the receiver does not send an ACK until it is ready to receive more packets. In continuous ARQ, the sender and receiver usually agree on the size of the sliding window. Once the sender has transmitted the maximum number of packets permitted in the sliding window, it cannot send any more packets until the receiver sends an ACK.

FIGURE 4-5

Continuous ARQ
(Automatic Repeat
reQuest).
ACK = acknowledgment;
NAK = negative
acknowledgment

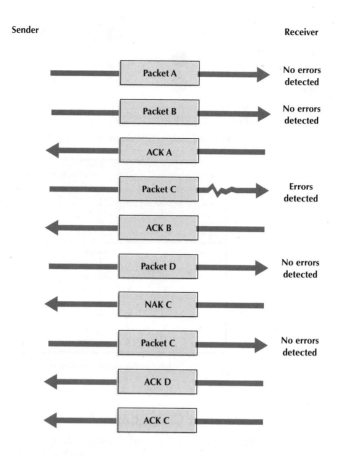

TECHNICAL	4-1 How Forward Error Correction Works
FOCUS	

*T*o see how error-correcting codes work, consider the example of a forward error checking code in Figure 4-6, called a **Hamming code**, after its inventor, R. W. Hamming. This code is a very simple approach, capable of correcting 1-bit errors. More sophisticated techniques (e.g., Reed–Solomon) are commonly used today, but this will give you a sense of how they work.

The Hamming code associates even parity bits with unique combinations of data bits. With a 4-data-bit code as an example, a character might be represented by the data-bit configuration 1010. Three parity bits, P_1, P_2, and P_4, are added, resulting in a 7-bit code, shown in the upper half of Figure 4-6. Notice that the data bits (D_3, D_5, D_6, D_7) are 1010 and the parity bits (P_1, P_2, P_4) are 101.

As depicted in the upper half of Figure 4-6, parity bit P_1 applies to data bits D_3, D_5, and D_7. Parity bit P_2 applies to data bits D_3, D_6, and D_7. Parity bit P_4 applies to data bits D_5, D_6, and D_7. For the example, in which D_3, D_5, D_6, D_7 = 1010, P_1 must equal 1 because there is only a single 1 among D_3, D_5, and D_7 and parity must

be even. Similarly, P_2 must be 0 because D_3 and D_6 are 1s. P_4 is 1 because D_6 is the only 1 among D_5, D_6, and D_7.

Now, assume that during the transmission, data bit D_7 is changed from a 0 to a 1 by line noise. Because this data bit is being checked by P_1, P_2, and P_4, all three parity bits now show odd parity instead of the correct even parity. D_7 is the only data bit that is monitored by all three parity bits; therefore, when D_7 is in error, all three parity bits show an incorrect parity. In this way, the receiving equipment can determine which bit was in error and reverse its state, thus correcting the error without retransmission.

The lower half of the figure is a table that determines the location of the bit in error. A 1 in the table means that the corresponding parity bit indicates a parity error. Conversely, a 0 means the parity check is correct. These 0s and 1s form a binary number that indicates the numeric location of the erroneous bit. In the previous example, P_1, P_2, and P_4 checks all failed, yielding 111, or a decimal 7, the subscript of the erroneous bit.

FIGURE 4-6

Hamming code for
forward error correction

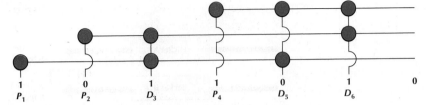

1	0	1	1	0	1	0
P_1	P_2	D_3	P_4	D_5	D_6	

Checking relations between parity bits (*P*) and data bits (*D*)

√ = Corresponding parity check is correct X = Corresponding parity check fails			Determines in which bit the error occured
P_4	P_2	P_1	
√	√	√	→ no error
√	√	X	→ P_1
√	X	√	→ P_2
√	X	X	→ D_3
X	√	√	→ P_4
X	√	X	→ D_5
X	X	√	→ D_6
X	X	X	→ D_7

Interpreting parity bit patterns

4.3.5 Forward Error Correction

Forward error correction uses codes containing sufficient redundancy to prevent errors by detecting and correcting them at the receiving end *without* retransmission of the original message. The redundancy, or extra bits required, varies with different schemes. It ranges from a small percentage of extra bits to 100% redundancy, with the number of error-detecting bits roughly equaling the number of data bits. One of the characteristics of many error-correcting codes is that there must be a minimum number of error-free bits between bursts of errors.

Forward error correction is commonly used in satellite transmission. A round trip from the earth station to the satellite and back includes a significant delay. Error rates can fluctuate depending on the condition of equipment, sunspots, or the weather. Indeed, some weather conditions make it impossible to transmit without some errors, making forward error correction essential. Compared with satellite equipment costs, the additional cost of forward error correction is insignificant.

4.3.6 Error Control in Practice

In the OSI model (see Chapter 1), error control is defined to be a layer-2 function—it is the responsibility of the data link layer. However, in practice, we have moved away from this. Most network cables—especially LAN cables—are very reliable, and errors are far less common than they were in the 1980s.

Therefore, most data link layer software used in LANs (i.e., Ethernet) is configured to detect errors, but *not* correct them. Any time a packet with an error is discovered, it is simply discarded. Wireless LANs and some WANs, where errors are more likely, still perform both error detection and error correction.

The implication from this is that error correction must be performed by software at higher layers. This software must be able to detect lost packets (i.e., those that have been discarded) and request the sender to retransmit them. This is commonly done by the transport layer using continuous ARQ, as we shall see in the next chapter.

4.4 DATA LINK PROTOCOLS

In this section, we outline several commonly used data link layer protocols, which are summarized in Figure 4-7. Here we focus on message delineation, which indicates where a message starts and stops, and the various parts or *fields* within the message. For example, you must clearly indicate which part of a message or packet of data is the error-control portion; otherwise, the receiver cannot use it properly to determine if an error has occurred. The data link layer performs this function by adding a PDU to the packet it receives from the network layer. This PDU is called a *frame*.

4.4.1 Asynchronous Transmission

Asynchronous transmission is often referred to as *start–stop transmission* because the transmitting computer can transmit a character whenever it is convenient, and the receiving computer will accept that character. It is typically used on point-to-point full-duplex circuits (i.e., circuits that have only two computers on them), so media access control is not a concern. If you use VT100 protocol, or connect to a UNIX or Linux computer using Telnet, chances are you are using asynchronous transmission.

With asynchronous transmission, each character is transmitted independently of all other characters. To separate the characters and synchronize transmission, a **start bit** and a **stop bit** are put on the front and back of *each* individual character. For example, if we are using 7-bit ASCII with even parity, the total transmission is 10 bits for each character (1 start bit, 7 bits for the letter, 1 parity bit, 1 stop bit).

The start bit and stop bit are the opposite of each other. Typically, the start bit is a 0 and the stop bit is a 1. There is no fixed distance between characters because the terminal transmits the character as soon as it is typed, which varies with the speed of the typist. The recognition of the start and stop of each message (called **synchronization**) takes place for each individual character because the start bit is a signal that tells the receiver to start sampling the incoming bits of a character so the data bits can be interpreted into their proper character structure. A stop bit informs the receiver that the character has been received and resets it for recognition of the next start bit.

When the sender is waiting for the user to type the next character, no data are sent; the communication circuit is idle. This idle time really is artificial—some signal always must

Protocol	Size	Error Detection	Retransmission	Media Access
Asynchronous transmission	1	Parity	Continuous ARQ	Full Duplex
Synchronous protocols				
SDLC	*	16-bit CRC	Continuous ARQ	Controlled Access
HDLC	*	16-bit CRC	Continuous ARQ	Controlled Access
Ethernet	*	32-bit CRC	Stop-and-wait ARQ	Contention
PPP	*	16-bit CRC	Continuous ARQ	Full Duplex

*Varies depending on the message length.

ARQ = Automatic Repeat reQuest; CRC = cyclical redundancy check; HDLC = high-level data link control; PPP = Point-to-Point Protocol; SDLC = synchronous data link control.

FIGURE 4-7   Protocol summary

FIGURE 4-8

Asynchronous
transmission.
ASCII = United States of
America Standard Code
for Information
Interchange

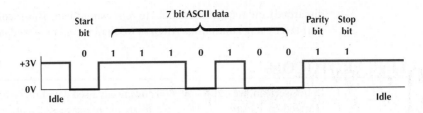

be sent down the circuit. For example, suppose we are using a unipolar digital signaling technique where +5 volts indicates a 1 and 0 volts indicates a 0 (see Chapter 3). Even if we send 0 volts, we are still sending a signal, a 0 in this case. Asynchronous transmission defines the *idle signal* (the signal that is sent down the circuit when no data are being transmitted) as the same as the stop bit. When the sender finishes transmitting a letter and is waiting for more data to send, it sends a continuous series of stop bits. Figure 4-8 shows an example of asynchronous transmission.

Some older protocols have two stop bits instead of the traditional single stop bit. The use of both a start bit and a stop bit is changing; some protocols have eliminated the stop bit altogether.

4.4.2 Synchronous Transmission

With **synchronous transmission**, all the letters or data in one group of data are transmitted at one time as a block of data. This block of data is called a **frame**. For example, a terminal or personal computer will save all the keystrokes typed by the user and transmit them only when the user presses a special "transmit" key. In this case, the start and end of the entire frame must be marked, not the start and end of each letter. Synchronous transmission is often used on both point-to-point and multipoint circuits. For multipoint circuits, each packet must include a destination address and a source address, and media access control is important.

The start and end of each frame (synchronization) sometimes is established by adding synchronization characters (SYN) to the start of the frame. Depending on the protocol, there may be anywhere from one to eight SYN characters. After the SYN characters, the transmitting computer sends a long stream of data that may contain thousands of bits. Knowing what code is being used, the receiving computer counts off the appropriate number of bits for the first character, assumes this is the first character, and passes it to the computer. It then counts off the bits for the second character, and so on.

In summary, asynchronous data transmission means each character is transmitted as a totally independent entity with its own start and stop bits to inform the receiving computer that the character is beginning and ending. Synchronous transmission means whole blocks of data are transmitted as frames after the sender and the receiver have been synchronized.

There are many protocols for synchronous transmission. We discuss four commonly used synchronous data link protocols.

Synchronous Data Link Control *Synchronous data link control (SDLC)* is a mainframe protocol developed by IBM in 1972 that is still in use today. It uses a controlled-access media access protocol. If you use a 3270 protocol, you're using SDLC.

Figure 4-9 shows a typical SDLC *frame*. Each SDLC frame begins and ends with a special bit pattern (01111110), known as the *flag*. The *address field* identifies the destination. The length of the address field is usually 8 bits but can be set at 16 bits; all computers on the same network must use the same length. The *control field* identifies the kind of frame that is being transmitted, either information or supervisory. An *information frame* is used for the transfer and reception of messages, frame numbering of contiguous frames, and the like.

FIGURE 4-9

SDLC (synchronous data
link control) frame layout

Flag	Address	Control	Message	Frame check sequence	Flag
8 bits	8 bits	8 bits	Variable length	32 bits	8 bits

A *supervisory frame* is used to transmit acknowledgments (ACKs and NAKs). The *message field* is of variable length and is the user's message. The *frame check sequence field* is a 32-bit CRC code (some older versions use a 16-bit CRC).

High-Level Data Link Control **High-level data link control (HDLC)** is a formal standard developed by the ISO often used in WANs. HDLC is essentially the same as SDLC, except that the address and control fields can be longer. HDLC also has several additional benefits that are beyond the scope of this book, such as a larger sliding window for continuous ARQ. It uses a controlled-access media access protocol. One variant, **Link Access Protocol–Balanced (LAP-B)**, uses the same structure as HDLC but is a scaled-down version of HDLC (i.e., provides fewer of those benefits mentioned that are "beyond the scope of this book"). A version of HDLC called Cisco HDLC (cHDLC) includes a network protocol field. cHDLC and HDLC have gradually replaced SDLC.

Ethernet **Ethernet** is a very popular LAN protocol, conceived by Bob Metcalfe in 1973 and developed jointly by Digital, Intel, and Xerox in the 1970s. Since then, Ethernet has been further refined and developed into a formal standard called **IEEE 802.3ac**. There are several versions of Ethernet in use today. Ethernet uses a contention media access protocol.

There are several standard versions of Ethernet. Figure 4.10a shows an Ethernet 803.3ac frame. The frame starts with a 7-byte *preamble*, which is a repeating pattern of ones and zeros (10101010). This is followed by a *start of frame delimiter*, which marks the start of the frame. The *destination address* specifies the receiver, whereas the *source address* specifies the sender. The *length* indicates the length in 8-bit bytes of the message portion of the frame. The *VLAN tag* field is an optional 4-byte address field used by virtual LANs (VLANs), which are discussed in Chapter 7. The Ethernet frame uses this field only when VLANs are in use; otherwise the field is omitted, and the length field immediately follows the source address field. When the VLAN tag field is in use, the first 2 bytes are set to the number 24,832 (hexadecimal 81-00), which is obviously an impossible packet length. When Ethernet sees this length, it knows that the VLAN tag field is in use. When the length is some other value, it assumes that VLAN tags are not in use and that the length field immediately follows the source address field. The *DSAP* and *SSAP* are used to pass control information between the sender and receiver. These are often used to indicate the type of network layer protocol the packet contains (e.g., TCP/IP or IPX/SPX, as described in Chapter 5). The *control field* is used to hold the frame sequence numbers and ACKs and NAKs used for error control, as well as to enable the data link layers of communicating computers to exchange other

Preamble	Start of Frame	Destination Address	Source Address	VLAN Tag	Length	DSAP	SSAP	Control	Data	Frame Check Sequence
7 bytes	1 byte	6 bytes	6 bytes	4 bytes	2 bytes	1 byte	1 byte	1-2 bytes	46-1,500 bytes	4 bytes

FIGURE 4.10a   Ethernet 802.3ac frame layout

FIGURE 4.10b

Ethernet II frame layout

Preamble	Start of Frame	Destination Address	Source Address	Type	Data	Frame Check Sequence
7 bytes	1 byte	6 bytes	6 bytes	2 bytes	46-1,500 bytes	4 bytes

FIGURE 4-11

PPP frame layout

Flag	Address	Control	Protocol	Data	Frame Check Sequence	Flag
1 byte	1 byte	1 byte	2 bytes	Variable Length	2 or 4 bytes	1 byte

control information. The last 2 bits in the first byte are used to indicate the type of control information being passed and whether the control field is 1 or 2 bytes (e.g., if the last 2 bits of the control field are 11, then the control field is 1 byte in length). In most cases, the control field is 1-byte long. The maximum length of the message is about 1,500 bytes. The frame ends with a CRC-32 *frame check sequence* used for error detection.

Ethernet II is another commonly used version of Ethernet. Like SDLC, it uses a preamble to mark the start of the frame. It has the same source and destination address format as Ethernet 802.3ac. The type field is used to specify an ACK frame or the type of network layer packet the frame contains (e.g., IP). The data and frame check sequence fields are the same as Ethernet 802.3ac. Ethernet II has an unusual way of marking the end of a frame. It uses bipolar signaling to send 1s (positive voltage) and 0s (negative voltage); see Chapter 3. When the frame ends, the sending computer transmits no signal for 96 bits (i.e., neither a 0 or a 1). After these 96 bits have been on no signal, the sending computer then transmits the next frame, which starts with a preamble, and so on. It is possible that in the time that the computer is sending no signal, some other computer could jump in and begin transmitting. In fact, this 96-bit pause is designed to prevent any one computer from monopolizing the circuit.

Newer versions of these two types of Ethernet permit jumbo frames with up to 9,000 bytes of user data in the message field. Some vendors are experimenting with super jumbo frames that can hold up to 64,000 bytes. Jumbo frames are common for some types of Ethernet such as gigabit Ethernet (see Chapter 6).

Point-to-Point Protocol **Point-to-Point Protocol (PPP)** was developed in the early 1990s and is often used in WANs. It is designed to transfer data over a point-to-point circuit but provides an address so that it can be used on multipoint circuits. Figure 4-11 shows the basic layout of a PPP frame, which is very similar to an SDLC or HDLC frame. The frame starts with a flag and has a 1-byte address (which is not used on point-to-point circuits). The control field is typically not used. The protocol field indicates what type of data packet the frame contains (e.g., an IP packet). The data field is variable in length and may be up to 1,500 bytes. The frame check sequence is usually a CRC-16 but can be a CRC-32. The frame ends with a flag.

A Day in the Life: Network Support Technician

When a help call arrives at the help desk, the help desk staff (first-level support) spends up to 10 minutes attempting to solve the problem. If they can't, then the problem is passed to the second-level support, the network support technician.

A typical day in the life of a network support technician starts by working on computers from the day before. Troubleshooting usually begins with a series of diagnostic tests to eliminate hardware problems. The next step, for a laptop, is to remove the hard disk and replace it with a hard disk containing a correct standard image. If the computer passes those tests, then the problem is usually software. Then the fun begins.

Once a computer has been fixed, it is important to document all the hardware and/or software changes to help track problem computers or problem software. Sometimes a problem is new but relatively straightforward to correct once it has been diagnosed. In this case, the technician will change the standard support process followed by the technicians working at the help desk to catch the problem before it is escalated to the network support technicians. In other cases, a new entry is made into the organization's technical support knowledge base so that if another technician (or user) encounters the problem, it is easier for him or her to diagnose and correct the problem. About 10% of the network technician's time is spent documenting solutions to problems.

Network support technicians also are the ones who manage new inventory and set up and configure new computers as they arrive from the manufacturer. In addition, they are responsible for deploying new software and standard desktop images across the network. Many companies also set aside standard times for routine training; in our case, every Friday, several hours are devoted to regular training.

Source: With thanks to Doug Strough

4.5 TRANSMISSION EFFICIENCY

One objective of a data communication network is to move the highest possible volume of accurate information through the network. The higher the volume, the greater the resulting network's efficiency and the lower the cost. Network efficiency is affected by characteristics of the circuits such as error rates and maximum transmission speed, as well as by the speed of transmitting and receiving equipment, the error-detection and control methodology, and the protocol used by the data link layer.

Each protocol we discussed uses some bits or bytes to delineate the start and end of each message and to control error. These bits and bytes are necessary for the transmission to occur, but they are not part of the message. They add no value to the user, but they count against the total number of bits that can be transmitted.

Each communication protocol has both information bits and overhead bits. **Information bits** are those used to convey the user's meaning. **Overhead bits** are used for purposes such as error checking and marking the start and end of characters and packets. A parity bit used for error checking is an overhead bit because it is not used to send the user's data; if you did not care about errors, the overhead error checking bit could be omitted and the users could still understand the message.

Transmission efficiency is defined as the total number of information bits (i.e., bits in the message sent by the user) divided by the total bits in transmission (i.e., information bits plus overhead bits). For example, let's calculate the transmission efficiency of asynchronous transmission. Assume we are using 7-bit ASCII. We have 1 bit for parity, plus 1 start bit and 1 stop bit. Therefore, there are 7 bits of information in each letter, but the total bits per letter is 10 (7 + 3). The efficiency of the asynchronous transmission system is 7 bits of information divided by 10 total bits, or 70%.

In other words, with asynchronous transmission, only 70% of the data rate is available for the user; 30% is used by the transmission protocol. If we have a communication circuit using a dial-up modem receiving 56 Kbps, the user sees an effective data rate (or throughput) of 39.2 Kbps. This is very inefficient.

We can improve efficiency by reducing the number of overhead bits in each message or by increasing the number of information bits. For example, if we remove the stop bits from asynchronous transmission, efficiency increases to $\frac{7}{9}$, or 77.8%. The throughput of a dial-up modem at 56 Kbps would increase 43.6 Kbps, which is not great but is at least a little better.

The same basic formula can be used to calculate the efficiency of synchronous transmission. For example, suppose we are using SDLC. The number of information bits is calculated by determining how many information characters are in the message. If the message portion of the frame contains 100 information characters and we are using an 8-bit code, then there are $100 \times 8 = 800$ bits of information. The total number of bits is the 800 information bits plus the overhead bits that are inserted for delineation and error control. Figure 4-9 shows that SDLC has a beginning flag (8 bits), an address (8 bits), a control field (8 bits), a frame check sequence (assume we use a CRC-32 with 32 bits), and an ending flag (8 bits). This is a total of 64 overhead bits; thus, efficiency is $800/(800 + 64) = 92.6\%$. If the circuit provides a data rate of 56 Kbps, then the effective data rate available to the user is about 51.9 Kbps.

This example shows that synchronous networks usually are more efficient than asynchronous networks and that some protocols are more efficient than others. The longer the message (1,000 characters as opposed to 100), the more efficient the protocol. For example, suppose the message in the SDLC example were 1,000 bytes. The efficiency here would be 99.2%, or $8,000/(8000 + 64)$, giving an effective data rate of about 55.6 Kbps.

The general rule is that the larger the message field, the more efficient the protocol. So why not have 10,000-byte or even 100,000-byte packets to really increase efficiency? The answer is that anytime a frame is received containing an error, the entire frame must be retransmitted. Thus, if an entire file is sent as one large packet (e.g., 100 K) and 1 bit is received in error, all 100,000 bytes must be sent again. Clearly this is a waste of capacity. Furthermore, the probability that a frame contains an error increases with the size of the frame; larger frames are more likely to contain errors than are smaller ones, simply because of the laws of probability.

Thus, in designing a protocol, there is a trade-off between large and small frames. Small frames are less efficient but are less likely to contain errors and cost less (in terms of circuit capacity) to retransmit if there is an error (Figure 4-12).

Throughput is the total number of information bits received per second, after taking into account the overhead bits and the need to retransmit frames containing errors. Generally speaking, small frames provide better throughput for circuits with more errors, whereas larger frames provide better throughput in less-error-prone networks. Fortunately, in most real networks, the curve shown in Figure 4-12 is very flat on top, meaning that there is a range of frame sizes that provide almost optimum performance. Frame sizes vary greatly among different networks, but the ideal frame size tends to be between 2,000 and 10,000 bytes.

So why are the standard sizes of Ethernet frames about 1,500 bytes? Because Ethernet was standardized many years ago, when errors were more common. Jumbo and super jumbo frame sizes emerged from higher speed, highly error free fiber-optic networks.

FIGURE 4-12

Frame size effects on throughput

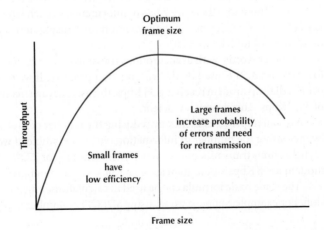

4-2 Sleuthing for the Right Frame Size

Optimizing performance in a network, particularly a client–server network, can be difficult because few network managers realize the importance of the frame size. Selecting the right—or the wrong—frame size can have greater effects on performance than anything you might do to the server.

Standard Commercial, a multinational tobacco and agricultural company, noticed a decrease in network performance when they upgraded to a new server. They tested the effects of using frame sizes between 500 bytes and 32,000 bytes. In their tests, a frame size of 512 bytes required a total of 455,000 bytes transmitted over their network to transfer the test messages. In contrast, the 32,000-byte frames were far more efficient, cutting the total data by 44% to 257,000 bytes.

However, the problem with 32,000-byte frames was a noticeable response time delay because messages were saved until the 32,000-byte frames were full before transmitting.

The ideal frame size depends on the specific application and the pattern of messages it generates. For Standard Commercial, the ideal frame size appeared to be between 4,000 and 8,000. Unfortunately, not all network software packages enable network managers to fine-tune frame sizes in this way.

Adapted from: "Sleuthing for the Right Packet Size," *InfoWorld*, January 16, 1995.

Calculating the actual *throughput* of a data communications network is complex because it depends not only on the efficiency of the data link protocol but also on the error rate and number of retransmissions that occur. *Transmission rate of information bits (TRIB)* is a measure of the effective number of information bits that is transmitted over a communication circuit per unit of time. The basic TRIB equation from ANSI is shown in Figure 4-13, along with an example.

4.6 IMPLICATIONS FOR MANAGEMENT

You can think of the data link layer protocol as the fundamental "language" spoken by networks. This protocol must be compatible with the physical cables that are used, but in many cases the physical cables can support a variety of different protocols. Each device on the network speaks a particular data link layer protocol. In the past, literally dozens of protocols were used; each protocol was custom-tailored to specific needs of the devices and application software in use. Where different devices or cables from different parts of the organization were connected, we used a translator to convert from the data link protocol spoken by one device into the protocol spoken by another device.

As the Internet has become more prominent and as it has become more important to move data from one part of an organization to the other, the need to translate among different data link layer protocols has become more and more costly. It is now more important to provide a few widely used protocols for all networks than to custom-tailor protocols to the needs of specific devices or applications. Today, businesses are moving rapidly to reduce the number of different protocols spoken by their networking equipment and converge on a few standard protocols that are used widely throughout the network.

We still do use different protocols in different parts of the network where there are important reasons for doing so. For example, local area networks often have different needs than wide area networks, so their data link layer protocols typically are still different, but even here we are seeing a few organizations move to standardize protocols.

This move to standardize data link layer protocols means that networking equipment and networking staff need to understand fewer protocols—their job is becoming simpler,

---

FORMULA FOR CALCULATING TRIB

$$TRIB = \frac{\text{Number of information bits accepted}}{\text{Total time required to get the bits accepted}}$$

$$TRIB = \frac{K(M - C)\,(1 - P)}{(M/R) + T}$$

where K = information bits per character

M = frame length in characters

R = data transmission rate in characters per second

C = average number of noninformation characters per frame (control characters)

P = probability that a frame will require retransmission because of error

T = time between frames in seconds, such as modem delay/turnaround time on half duplex and propagation delay on satellite transmission. This is the time required to reverse the direction of transmission from send to receive or receive to send on a half-duplex circuit. It can be obtained from the modem specification book and may be referred to as *reclocking time*

The following TRIB example shows the calculation of throughput assuming a 4,800-bps half-duplex circuit:

$$TRIB = \frac{7(400 - 10)\,(1 - 0.01)}{(400/600) + 0.025} = 3,908 \text{ bits per second}$$

where K = 7 bits per character (information)

M = 400 characters per frame

R = 600 characters per second (derived from 4,800 bps divided by 8 bits/character)

C = 10 control characters per frame

P = 0.01 (10^{-2}) or 1 retransmission per 100 blocks transmitted—1%

T = 25 milliseconds (0.025) turnaround time

If all factors in the calculation remain constant except for the circuit, which is changed to full duplex (no turnaround time delays, T = 0), then the TRIB increases to 4,504 bps.

Look at the equation where the turnaround value (T) is 0.025. If there is a further propagation delay time of 475 milliseconds (0.475), this figure changes to 0.500. For demonstrating how a satellite channel affects TRIB, the total delay time is now 500 milliseconds. Still using the figures above (except for the new 0.500 delay time), we reduce the TRIB for our half-duplex satellite link to 2,317 bps, which is almost half of the full-duplex (no turnaround time) 4,054 bps.

FIGURE 4-13 Calculating TRIB (transmission rate of information bits)

which in turn means that the cost to buy and maintain network equipment and to train networking staff is gradually decreasing (and the side benefit to students is that there are fewer protocols to learn!). The downside, of course, is that some applications may take longer to run over protocols are not perfectly suited to them. As network capacities in the physical layer continue to increase, this has proven to be far less important than the significant cost savings that can be realized from standardization.

SUMMARY

Media Access Control Media access control refers to controlling when computers transmit. There are three basic approaches. With roll-call polling, the server polls client computers to see if they have data to send; computers can transmit only when they have been polled. With hub polling or token passing, the computers themselves manage when they can transmit by passing a token to one other; no computer can transmit unless it has the token. With contention, computers listen and transmit only when no others are transmitting. In general, contention approaches work better for small networks that have low levels of usage, whereas polling approaches work better for networks with high usage.

Sources and Prevention of Error Errors occur in all networks. Errors tend to occur in groups (or bursts) rather than 1 bit at a time. The primary sources of errors are impulse noises (e.g., lightning), cross-talk, echo, and attenuation. Errors can be prevented (or at least reduced) by shielding the cables; moving cables away from sources of noise and power sources; using repeaters (and, to a lesser extent, amplifiers); and improving the quality of the equipment, media, and their connections.

Error Detection and Correction All error-detection schemes attach additional error-detection data, based on a mathematical calculation, to the user's message. The receiver performs the same calculation on incoming messages, and if the results of this calculation do not match the error-detection data on the incoming message, an error has occurred. Parity, checksum, and CRC are the most common error-detection schemes. The most common error-correction technique is simply to ask the sender to retransmit the message until it is received without error. A different approach, forward error correction, includes sufficient information to allow the receiver to correct the error in most cases without asking for a retransmission.

Message Delineation Message delineation means to indicate the start and end of a message. Asynchronous transmission uses start and stop bits on each letter to mark where they begin and end. Synchronous techniques (e.g., SDLC, HDLC, Ethernet, PPP) group blocks of data together into frames that use special characters or bit patterns to mark the start and end of entire messages.

Transmission Efficiency and Throughput Every protocol adds additional bits to the user's message before sending it (e.g., for error detection). These bits are called overhead bits because they add no value to the user; they simply ensure correct data transfer. The efficiency of a transmission protocol is the number of information bits sent by the user divided by the total number of bits transferred (information bits plus overhead bits). Synchronous transmission provides greater efficiency than does asynchronous transmission. In general, protocols with larger frame sizes provide greater efficiency than do those with small frame sizes. The drawback to large frame sizes is that they are more likely to be affected by errors and thus require more retransmission. Small frame sizes are therefore better suited to error-prone circuits, and large frames to error-free circuits.

KEY TERMS

QUESTIONS

1. What does the data link layer do?
2. What is media access control, and why is it important?
3. Under what conditions is media access control unimportant?
4. Compare and contrast roll-call polling, hub polling (or token passing), and contention.
5. Which is better, controlled access or contention? Explain.
6. Define two fundamental types of errors.
7. Errors normally appear in _____, which is when more than 1 data bit is changed by the error-causing condition.
8. Is there any difference in the error rates of lower-speed lines and higher-speed lines?
9. Briefly define *noise*.
10. Describe four types of noise. Which is likely to pose the greatest problem to network managers?
11. How do amplifiers differ from repeaters?
12. What are three ways of reducing errors and the types of noise they affect?
13. Describe three approaches to *detecting* errors, including how they work, the probability of detecting an error, and any other benefits or limitations.
14. Briefly describe how even parity and odd parity work.
15. Briefly describe how checksum works.
16. How does CRC work?
17. How does forward error correction work? How is it different from other error-correction methods?
18. Under what circumstances is forward error correction desirable?
19. Compare and contrast stop-and-wait ARQ and continuous ARQ.
20. Which is the simplest (least sophisticated) protocol described in this chapter?
21. Describe the frame layouts for SDLC, Ethernet, and PPP.
22. What is transmission efficiency?
23. How do information bits differ from overhead bits?
24. Are stop bits necessary in asynchronous transmission? Explain by using a diagram.
25. During the 1990s, there was intense competition between two technologies (10-Mbps Ethernet and 16-Mbps token ring) for the LAN market. Ethernet was promoted by a consortium of vendors, whereas token ring was primarily an IBM product, even though it was standardized. Ethernet won, and no one talks about token ring anymore. Token ring used a hub-polling-based approach. Outline a number of reasons why Ethernet might have won. Hint: The reasons were both technical and business.
26. Under what conditions does a data link layer protocol need an address?
27. Are large frame sizes better than small frame sizes? Explain.
28. What media access control technique does your class use?
29. Show how the word "HI" would be sent using asynchronous transmission using even parity (make assumptions about the bit patterns needed). Show how it would be sent using Ethernet.

EXERCISES

A. Draw how a series of four separate messages would be *successfully* sent from one computer to another if the first message were transferred without error, the second were initially transmitted with an error, the third were initially lost, and the ACK for the fourth were initially lost.

B. How efficient would a 6-bit code be in asynchronous transmission if it had 1 parity bit, 1 start bit, and 2 stop bits? (Some old equipment uses 2 stop bits.)

C. What is the transmission rate of information bits if you use ASCII (8 bits plus 1 parity bit), a 1,000-character frame, 56 Kbps modem transmission speed, 20 control characters per frame, an error rate of 1%, and a 30-millisecond turnaround time? What is the TRIB if you add a half-second delay to the turnaround time because of satellite delay?

D. Search the Web to find a software vendor that sells a package that supports each of the following protocols: SDLC, HDLC, Ethernet, and PPP (i.e., one package that supports SDLC, another [or the same] for HDLC, and so on).

E. Investigate the network at your organization (or a service offered by an IXC) to find out the average error rates.

F. What is the efficiency if a 100-byte file is transmitted using Ethernet? A 10,000-byte file?

G. What is the propagation delay on a circuit using a LEO satellite orbiting 500 miles above the earth if the speed of the signal is 186,000 miles per second? If the satellite is 22,000 miles above the earth?

H. Suppose you are going to connect the computers in your house or apartment. What media would you use? Why? Would this change if you were building a new house?

MINICASES

I. Smith, Smith, Smith, and Smith Smith, Smith, Smith, and Smith is a regional accounting firm that is putting up a new headquarters building. The building will have a backbone network that connects eight LANs (two on each floor). The company is very concerned with network errors. What advice would you give regarding the design of the building and network cable planning that would help reduce network errors?

II. Worldwide Charity Worldwide Charity is a charitable organization whose mission is to improve education levels in developing countries. In each country where it is involved, the organization has a small headquarters and usually 5 to 10 offices in outlying towns. Staff members communicate with one another via email on older computers donated to the organization. Because Internet service is not reliable in many of the towns in these countries, the staff members usually phone headquarters and use a very simple Linux email system that uses a server-based network architecture. They also upload and download files. What range of frame sizes is likely to be used?

III. Industrial Products Industrial Products is a small light-manufacturing firm that produces a variety of control systems for heavy industry. It has a network

that connects its office building and warehouse that has functioned well for the last year, but over the past week, users have begun to complain that the network is slow. Clarence Hung, the network manager, did a quick check of the number of orders over the past week and saw no real change, suggesting that there has been no major increase in network traffic. What would you suggest that Clarence do next?

IV. Alpha Corp. Alpha Corp. is trying to decide the size of the connection it needs to the Internet. The company estimates that it will send and receive a total of about 1,000 emails per hour and that each email message is about 1,500 bytes in size. The company also estimates that it will send and receive a total of about 3,000 Web pages per hour and that each page is about 40,000 bytes in size. 1. Without considering transmission efficiency, how large an Internet connection would you recommend in terms of bits per second (assuming that each byte is 8 bits in length)? 2. Assuming they use a synchronous data link layer protocol with an efficiency of about 90%, how large an Internet connection would you recommend? 3. Suppose Alpha wants to be sure that its Internet connection will provide sufficient capacity the next two years. How large an Internet connection would you recommend?

CASE STUDY

NEXT-DAY AIR SERVICE

See the Web site at www.wiley.com/college/fitzgerald.

HANDS-ON ACTIVITY 4A

Capturing Packets on Your Network

In this chapter, we discussed several data link layer protocols, such as SDLC and Ethernet. The objective of this Activity is for you to see the data link layer frames in action on your network.

Wireshark is one of the many tools that permit users to examine the frames in their network. It is called a packet sniffer because it enables you to see inside the frames and packets that your computer sends, as well as the frames and packets sent by other users on your LAN. In other words, you can eavesdrop on the other users on your LAN to see what Web sites they visit and even the email they send. We don't recommend using it for this reason, but it is important that you understand that someone else could be using Ethereal to sniff your packets to see and record what you are doing on the Internet.

1. Use your browser to connect to www.wireshark.org and download and install the Wireshark software.

2. When you start Wireshark you will see a screen like that in Figure 4-14, minus the two smaller windows on top.

    a. Click Capture
    b. Click Interfaces
    c. Click the Capture button beside your Wireshark connection (wireless LAN or traditional LAN).

3. Wireshark will capture all packets moving through your LAN. To make sure you have something to see, open your Web browser and visit one or two Web sites. After you have captured packets for 30–60 seconds, return to Wireshark and click Stop.

4. Figure 4-15 shows the packets captured on my home network. The top window in Wireshark displays the complete list of packets in chronological order. Each packet is numbered; I've scrolled the window, so the first packet shown is packet 11. Wireshark lists the time, the source IP address, the destination IP address, the protocol, and some additional information about each packet. The IP addresses will be explained in more detail in the next chapter.

    For the moment, look at packet number 16, the second HTTP packet from the top. I've clicked on

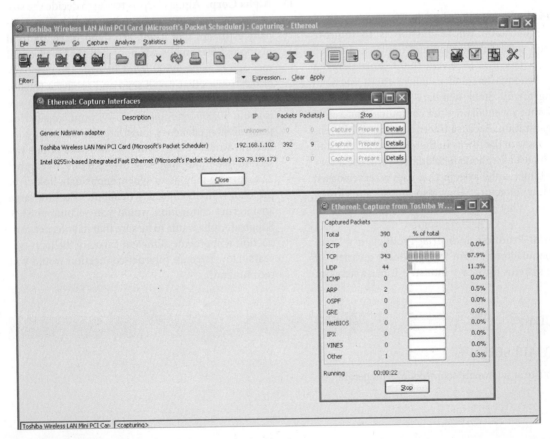

FIGURE 4-14 Capturing packets with Wireshark

this packet, so the middle window shows the inside of the packet. The first line in this second window says the frame (or packet if you prefer) is 1091 bytes long. It contains an Ethernet II packet, an Internet Protocol (IP) packet, a Transmission Control Protocol (TCP) packet, and a Hypertext Transfer Protocol (HTTP) packet. Remember in Chapter 1 that Figure 1.4 described how each packet was placed inside another packet as the message moved through the layers and was transmitted.

Click on the plus sign (+) in front of the HTTP packet to expand it. Wireshark shows the contents of the HTTP packet. By reading the data inside the HTTP packet, you can see that this packet was an HTTP request to my.yahoo.com that contained a cookie. If you look closely, you'll see that the sending computer was a Tablet PC—that's some of the optional information my Web browser (Internet Explorer) included in the HTTP header.

The bottom window in Figure 4-15 shows the exact bytes that were captured. The section highlighted in gray shows the HTTP packet. The numbers on the left show the data in hexadecimal format, whereas the data on the right show the text

version. The data before the highlighted section are the TCP packet.

From Chapter 2, you know that the client sends an HTTP request packet to request a Web page, and the Web server sends back an HTTP response packet. Packet number 25 in the top window in Figure 4-15 is the HTTP response sent back to my computer by the Yahoo! server. You can see that the destination IP address in my HTTP request is the source IP address of this HTTP packet.

5. Figure 4-15 also shows what happens when you click the plus sign (+) in front of the Ethernet II packet to expand it. You can see that this Ethernet packet has a destination address and source address (e.g., 00:02:2d:85:cb:e0).

Deliverables

1. List the layer 2, 3, 4, and 5 PDUs that are used in your network to send a request to get a Web page.

2. List the source and destination Ethernet addresses on the message.

3. What value is in the Ethernet type field in this message? Why?

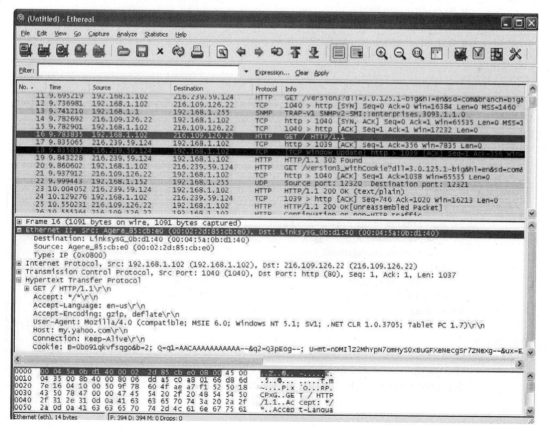

FIGURE 4-15 Analyzing packets with Wireshark

CHAPTER 5

NETWORK AND TRANSPORT LAYERS

The network layer and transport layer are responsible for moving messages from end to end in a network. They are so closely tied together that they are usually discussed together. The transport layer (layer 4) performs three functions: linking the application layer to the network, segmenting (breaking long messages into smaller packets for transmission), and session management (establishing an end-to-end connection between the sender and receiver). The network layer (layer 3) performs two functions: routing (determining the next computer to which the message should be sent to reach the final destination) and addressing (finding the address of that next computer). There are several standard transport and network layer protocols that specify how packets are to be organized, in the same way that there are standards for data link layer packets. However, only one protocol is in widespread use today: Transmission Control Protocol/Internet Protocol (TCP/IP), the protocol used on the Internet. This chapter takes a detailed look at how TCP/IP works.

OBJECTIVES

- Be aware of the TCP/IP protocols
- Be familiar with linking to the application layer, segmenting, and session management
- Be familiar with addressing
- Be familiar with routing
- Understand how TCP/IP works

OUTLINE

5.1 INTRODUCTION

The transport and network layers are so closely tied together that they are almost always discussed together. For this reason, we discuss them in the same chapter. TCP/IP is the most commonly used set of transport and network layer protocols, so this chapter focuses exclusively on TCP/IP.

The transport layer links the application software in the application layer with the network and is responsible for the end-to-end delivery of the message. The transport layer accepts outgoing messages from the application layer (e.g., Web, email, and so on, as described in Chapter 2) and segments them for transmission. Figure 5-1 shows the application layer software producing an SMTP packet that is split into two smaller TCP segments by the transport layer. The Protocol Data Unit (PDU) at the transport layer is called a **segment**. The network layer takes the messages from the transport layer and routes them through the network by selecting the best path from computer to computer through the network (and adds an IP packet). The data link layer adds an Ethernet frame and instructs the physical layer hardware when to transmit. As we saw in Chapter 1, each layer in the network has its own set of protocols that are used to hold the data generated by higher layers, much like a set of *matryoshka* (nested Russian dolls).

The network and transport layers also accept incoming messages from the data link layer and organize them into coherent messages that are passed to the application layer. For example, as in Figure 5-1, a large email message might require several data link layer frames to transmit. The transport layer at the sender would break the message into several smaller segments and give them to the network layer to route, which in turn gives them to the data link layer to transmit. The network layer at the receiver would receive the individual packets from the data link layer, process them, and pass them to the transport layer, which would reassemble them into the one email message before giving it to the application layer.

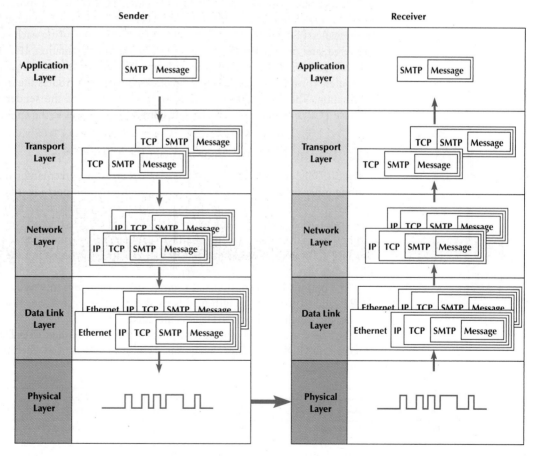

FIGURE 5-1 Message transmission using layers. HTTP = Hypertext Transfer Protocol; IP = Internet Protocol; TCP = Transmission Control Protocol

In this chapter, we provide a brief look at the transport and network layer protocols, before turning our attention to how TCP/IP works. We first examine the transport layer functions. Addressing and routing are performed by the transport layer and network layers working together, so we will discuss them together rather than separate them according to which part is performed by the transport layer and which by the network layer.

5.2 TRANSPORT AND NETWORK LAYER PROTOCOLS

There are different transport/network layer protocols, but one family of protocols, TCP/IP, dominates. Each transport and network layer protocol performs essentially the same functions, but each is incompatible with the others unless there is a special device to translate between them. In this chapter, we focus only on TCP/IP. A good overview of protocols, at all layers, is available at www.protocols.com.

The **Transmission Control Protocol/Internet Protocol (TCP/IP)** was developed for the U.S. Department of Defense's Advanced Research Project Agency network (ARPANET) by Vinton Cerf and Bob Kahn in 1974. TCP/IP is the transport/network layer protocol used on the Internet. It is the world's most popular protocol set, used by almost all BNs and WANs. TCP/IP allows reasonably efficient and error-free transmission. Because it performs error checking, it can send large files across sometimes unreliable networks with great assurance that the data will arrive uncorrupted. TCP/IP is compatible with a variety of data link protocols, which is one reason for its popularity.

As the name implies, TCP/IP has two parts. TCP is the transport layer protocol that links the application layer to the network layer. It performs segmenting: breaking the data into smaller PDUs called segments, numbering them, ensuring each segment is reliably delivered, and putting them in the proper order at the destination. IP is the network layer protocol and performs addressing and routing. IP software is used at each of the intervening computers through which the message passes; it is IP that routes the message to the final destination. The TCP software needs to be active only at the sender and the receiver, because TCP is involved only when data comes from or goes to the application layer.

5.2.1 Transmission Control Protocol (TCP)

A typical TCP segment has a 192-bit header (24 bytes) of control information (Figure 5-2). Among other fields, it contains the source and destination port identifier. The destination port tells the TCP software at the destination to which application layer program the application layer packet should be sent, whereas the source port tells the receiver which application layer program the packet is from. The TCP segment also provides a sequence number so that the TCP software at the destination can assemble the segments into the correct order and make sure that no segments have been lost.

The options field is optional and rarely used. Therefore this results in a 20-byte-long TCP header. The header length field is used to tell the receiver how long the TCP packet is—that is, whether the options field is included.

TCP/IP has a second type of transport layer protocol called **User Datagram Protocol (UDP)**. UDP PDUs are called datagrams. Typically, UDP is used when the sender needs to

Source port	Destination port	Sequence number	ACK number	Header length	Unused	Flags	Flow control	CRC–16	Urgent pointer	Options	User data
16 bits	16 bits	32 bits	32 bits	4 bits	3 bits	9 bits	16 bits	16 bits	16 bits	32 bits	Varies

FIGURE 5-2 Transmission Control Protocol (TCP) segment. ACK = acknowledgment; CRC = cyclical redundancy check

send a single small packet to the receiver (e.g., for a DNS request, which we discuss later in this chapter). When there is only one small packet to be sent, the transport layer doesn't need to worry about segmenting the outgoing messages or reassembling them upon receipt, so transmission can be faster. A UDP datagram has only four fields (8 bytes of overhead) plus the application layer packet: source port, destination port, length, and a CRC-16. Unlike TCP, UDP does not check for lost messages, so occasionally a UDP datagram is lost and the message must be resent. Interestingly, it is not the transport layer that decides whether TCP or UDP is going to be used. This decision is left to the engineer who is writing the application.

5.2.2 Internet Protocol (IP)

The Internet Protocol (IP) is the network layer protocol. Network layer PDUs are called packets. Two forms of IP are currently in use. The older form is IP version 4 (IPv4), which also has a 192-bit header (24 bytes) (Figure 5-3). This header contains source and destination addresses, packet length, and packet number. Similar to the TCP header, the options field is rarely used, and therefore the header is usually 20 bytes long.

IP version 4 is being replaced by IPv6, which has a 320-bit header (40 bytes) (Figure 5-4). The primary reason for the increase in the packet size is an increase in the address size from 32 bits to 128 bits. IPv6's simpler packet structure makes it easier to perform routing and supports a variety of new approaches to addressing and routing.

Development of the IPv6 came about because IP addresses were being depleted on the Internet. IPv4 has a 4-byte address field, which means there is a theoretical maximum of about 4.2 billion addresses. However, about 500 million of these addresses are reserved and cannot be used, and the way addresses were assigned in the early days of the Internet means that a small number of companies received several million addresses, even when they didn't need all of them. With the increased growth in Internet users, and the explosion in mobile Internet devices, current estimates project that we will run out of IPv4 addresses sometime in 2011.

Internet Protocol version 6 uses a 16-byte-long address which provides a theoretical maximum of 3.4×10^{38} addresses—more than enough for the foreseeable future. IPv4 uses decimals to express addresses (e.g., 128.192.55.72), but IPv6 uses hexadecimal (base 16) like Ethernet to express addresses, which makes it slightly more confusing to use. Addresses are eight sets of 2-byte numbers (e.g., 2001:0890:0600:00d1:0000:0000:abcd:f010), but because this can be long to write, there is a IPv6 "compressed notation" that eliminates the leading zeros within each block and blocks that are all zeros. So the preceding IPv6 address could also be written as 2001:890:600:d1: :abcd:f010.

Version number	Header length	Type of service	Total length	Identifiers	Flags	Packet offset	Hop limit	Protocol	CRC 16	Source address	Destination address	Options	User data
4 bits	4 bits	8 bits	16 bits	16 bits	3 bits	13 bits	8 bits	8 bits	16 bits	32 bits	32 bits	32 bits	Varies

FIGURE 5-3 Internet Protocol (IP) packet (version 4). CRC = cyclical redundancy check

Version number	Priority	Flow name	Total length	Next header	Hop limit	Source address	Destination address	User data
4 bits	4 bits	24 bits	16 bits	8 bits	8 bits	128 bits	128 bits	Varies

FIGURE 5-4 Internet Protocol (IP) packet (version 6)

Adoption of IPv6 has been slow. Most organizations have not felt the need to change because IPv6 provides few benefits other than the larger address space and requires their staff to learn a whole new protocol. In most cases, the shortage of addresses on the Internet doesn't affect organizations that already have Internet addresses, so there is little incentive to convert to IPv6. Most organizations that implement IPv6 also run IPv4, and IPv6 is not backward-compatible with IPv4, which means that all network devices must be changed to understand both IPv4 and IPv6. The cost of this conversion, along with the few benefits it provides to organizations that do convert, has led a number of commentators to refer to this as the IPv6 "mess." To encourage the move to IPv6, the U.S. government required all of its agencies to convert to IPv6 on their WANs and backbone networks by June 2008, but the change was not completed on time.

The size of the message field depends on the data link layer protocol used. TCP/IP is commonly combined with Ethernet. Ethernet has a maximum packet size of 1,492 bytes, so the maximum size of a TCP message field if IPv4 is used is 1,492 − 24 (the size of the TCP header) − 24 (the size of the IPv4 header) = 1,444.

5.3 TRANSPORT LAYER FUNCTIONS

The transport layer links the application software in the application layer with the network and is responsible for segmenting large messages into smaller ones for transmission and for managing the session (the end-to-end delivery of the message). One of the first issues facing the application layer is to find the numeric network address of the destination computer. Different protocols use different methods to find this address. Depending on the protocol—and which expert you ask—finding the destination address can be classified as a transport layer function, a network layer function, a data link layer function, or an application layer function with help from the operating system. In all honesty, understanding how the process works is more important than memorizing how it is classified. The next section discusses addressing at the network layer and transport layer. In this section, we focus on three unique functions performed by the transport layer: linking the application layer to the network layer, segmenting, and session management.

5.3.1 Linking to the Application Layer

Most computers have many application layer software packages running at the same time. Users often have Web browsers, email programs, and word processors in use at the same time on their client computers. Likewise, many servers act as Web servers, mail servers, FTP servers, and so on. When the transport layer receives an incoming message, the transport layer must decide to which application program it should be delivered. It makes no sense to send a Web page request to email server software.

With TCP/IP, each application layer software package has a unique **port address**. Any message sent to a computer must tell TCP (the transport layer software) the application layer port address that is to receive the message. Therefore, when an application layer program generates an outgoing message, it tells the TCP software its own port address (i.e., the **source port address**) and the port address at the destination computer (i.e., the **destination port address**). These two port addresses are placed in the first two fields in the TCP segment (see Figure 5-2).

Port addresses can be any 16-bit (2-byte) number. So how does a client computer sending a Web request to a Web server know what port address to use for the Web server? Simple. On the Internet, all port addresses for popular services such as the Web, email, and FTP have been standardized. Anyone using a Web server should set up the Web server with a port address of 80, which is called the well-known port. Web browsers, therefore, automatically generate a port address of 80 for any Web page you click on. FTP servers use

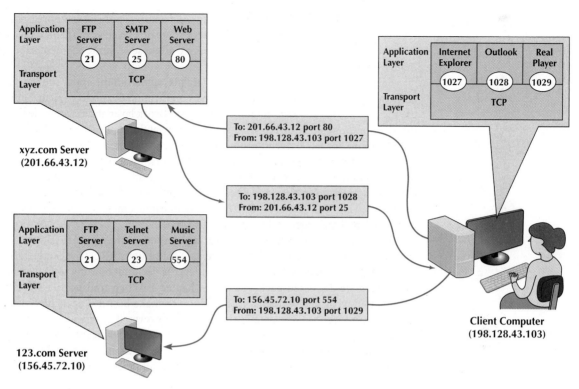

FIGURE 5-5 Linking to application layer services

port 21, Telnet 23, SMTP 25, and so on. Network managers are free to use whatever port addresses they want, but if they use a nonstandard port number, then the application layer software on the client must specify the correct port number.[1]

Figure 5-5 shows a user running three applications on the client (Internet Explorer, Outlook, and RealPlayer), each of which has been assigned a different port number, called a temporary port number (1027, 1028, and 7070, respectively). Each of these can simultaneously send and receive data to and from different servers and different applications on the same server. In this case, we see a message sent by Internet Explorer on the client (port 1027) to the Web server software on the xyz.com server (port 80). We also see a message sent by the mail server software on port 25 to the email client on port 1028. At the same time, the RealPlayer software on the client is sending a request to the music server software (port 554) at 123.com.

5.3.2 Segmenting

Some messages or blocks of application data are small enough that they can be transmitted in one frame at the data link layer. However, in other cases, the application data in one "message" are too large and must be broken into several frames (e.g., Web pages, graphic images). As far as the application layer is concerned, the message should be transmitted and received as one large block of data. However, the data link layer can transmit only messages

---

[1]One way to make a Web server private would be to use a different port number (e.g., 8080). Any Web browser wanting to access this Web server would then have to explicitly include the port number in the URL (e.g., http://www.abc.com:8080).

of certain lengths. It is therefore up to the sender's transport layer to break the data into several smaller segments that can be sent by the data link layer across the circuit. At the other end, the receiver's transport layer must receive all these separate segments and recombine them into one large message.

Segmenting means to take one outgoing message from the application layer and break it into a set of smaller segments for transmission through the network. It also means to take the incoming set of smaller segments from the network layer and reassemble them into one message for the application layer. Depending on what the application layer software chooses, the incoming packets can either be delivered one at a time or held until all packets have arrived and the message is complete. Web browsers, for example, usually request delivery of packets as they arrive, which is why your screen gradually builds a piece at a time. Most email software, conversely, usually requests that messages be delivered only after all packets have arrived and TCP has organized them into one intact message, which is why you usually don't see email messages building screen by screen.

The TCP is also responsible for ensuring that the receiver has actually received all segments that have been sent. TCP therefore uses continuous ARQ (see Chapter 4).

One of the challenges at the transport layer is deciding how big to make the segments. Remember, we discussed packet sizes in Chapter 4. When transport layer software is set up, it is told what size segments it should use to make best use of its own data link layer protocols (or it chooses the default size of 536). However, it has no idea what size is best for the destination. Therefore, the transport layer at the sender negotiates with the transport layer at the receiver to settle on the best segment sizes to use. This negotiation is done by establishing a TCP connection between the sender and receiver.

5.3.3 Session Management

A **session** can be thought of as a conversation between two computers. When the sending computer wants to send a message to the receiver, it usually starts by establishing a session with that computer. The sender transmits the segments in sequence until the conversation is done, and then the sender ends the session. This approach to session management is called *connection-oriented* messaging.

Sometimes, the sender only wants to send one short information message or a request. In this case, the sender may choose not to start a session but just send the one quick message and move on. This approach is called *connectionless messaging*.

Connection-Oriented Messaging **Connection-oriented messaging** sets up a *TCP connection* (also called a session) between the sender and receiver. To establish a connection, the transport layer on both the sender and the receiver must send a SYN (synchronize) and receive a ACK (acknowledgement) segment. This process starts with the sender (usually a client) sending a SYN to the receiver (usually a server). The server responds with an ACK for the sender's/client's SYN and then sends its own SYN. SYN is usually a randomly generated number that identifies a packet. The last step is when the client sends an ACK for the server's SYN. This is called the *three-way handshake*, and this process also contains the segment size negotiation.

Once the connection is established, the segments flow between the sender and receiver. TCP uses the continuous ARQ (sliding window) technique described in Chapter 4 to make sure that all segments arrive and to provide flow control.

When the transmission is complete, the session is terminated using a *four-way handshake*. Because TCP/IP connection is a full-duplex connection, each side of the session has to terminate the connection independently. The sender (i.e., the client) will start by sending with a FIN to inform the receiver (i.e., the server) that is finished sending data. The server acknowledges the FIN sending an ACK. Then the server sends a FIN to the client. The connection is successfully terminated when the server receives the ACK for its FIN.

Connectionless Messaging Connectionless messaging means each packet is treated separately and makes its own way through the network. Unlike connection-oriented routing, no connection is established. The sender simply sends the packets as separate, unrelated entities, and it is possible that different packets will take different routes through the network, depending on the type of routing used and the amount of traffic. Because packets following different routes may travel at different speeds, they may arrive out of sequence at their destination. The sender's network layer, therefore, puts a sequence number on each packet, in addition to information about the message stream to which the packet belongs. The network layer must reassemble them in the correct order before passing the message to the application layer.

Transmission Control Protocol/Internet Protocol can operate either as connection-oriented or connectionless. When connection-oriented messaging is desired, TCP is used. When connectionless messaging is desired, the TCP segment is replaced with a User Datagram Protocol (UDP) packet. The UDP header is much smaller than the TCP header (only 8 bytes).

Connectionless is most commonly used when the application data or message can fit into one single message. One might expect, for example, that because HTTP requests are often very short, they might use UDP connectionless rather than TCP connection-oriented messaging. However, HTTP always uses TCP. All of the application layer software we have discussed so far uses TCP (HTTP, SMTP, FTP, Telnet). UDP is most commonly used for control messages such as addressing (DHCP [Dynamic Host Configuration Protocol], discussed later in this chapter), routing control messages (RIP [Routing Information Protocol], discussed later in this chapter), and network management (SNMP [Simple Network Management Protocol], discussed in Chapter 12).

Quality of Service Quality of Service (QoS) routing is a special type of connection-oriented messaging in which different connections are assigned different priorities. For example, videoconferencing requires fast delivery of packets to ensure that the images and voices appear smooth and continuous; they are very time dependent because delays in routing seriously affect the quality of the service provided. Email packets, conversely, have no such requirements. Although everyone would like to receive email as fast as possible, a 10-second delay in transmitting an email message does not have the same consequences as a 10-second delay in a videoconferencing packet.

With QoS routing, different *classes of service* are defined, each with different priorities. For example, a packet of videoconferencing images would likely get higher priority than would an SMTP packet with an email message and thus be routed first. When the transport layer software attempts to establish a connection (i.e., a session), it specifies the class of service that connection requires. Each path through the network is designed to support a different number and mix of service classes. When a connection is established, the network ensures that no connections are established that exceed the maximum number of that class on a given circuit.

QoS routing is common in certain types of networks (e.g., ATM, as discussed in Chapter 8). The Internet provides several QoS protocols that can work in a TCP/IP environment. **Resource Reservation Protocol (RSVP)** and **Real-Time Streaming Protocol (RTSP)** both permit application layer software to request connections that have certain minimum data transfer capabilities. As one might expect, RTSP is geared toward audio/video streaming applications, whereas RSVP is more general purpose.

Both QoS protocols, RSVP and RTSP, are used to create a connection (or session) and request a certain minimum guaranteed data rate. Once the connection has been established, they use **Real-Time Transport Protocol (RTP)** to send packets across the connection. RTP contains information about the sending application, a packet sequence number, and a time stamp so that the data in the RTP packet can be synchronized with other RTP packets by the application layer software, if needed.

With a name like Real-Time *Transport* Protocol, one would expect RTP to replace TCP and UDP at the transport layer. It does not. Instead, RTP is combined with UDP. (If you read the previous paragraph carefully, you noticed that RTP does not provide source and destination port addresses.) This means that each real-time packet is first created using RTP and then surrounded by a UDP datagram, before being handed to the IP software at the network layer.

5.4 ADDRESSING

Before you can send a message, you must know the destination address. It is extremely important to understand that each computer has several addresses, each used by a different layer. One address is used by the data link layer, another by the network layer, and still another by the application layer.

When users work with application software, they typically use the application layer address. For example, in Chapter 2, we discussed application software that used Internet addresses (e.g., www.indiana.edu). This is an **application layer address** (or a *server name*). When a user types an Internet address into a Web browser, the request is passed to the network layer as part of an application layer packet formatted using the HTTP protocol (Figure 5-6) (see Chapter 2).

The network layer software, in turn, uses a **network layer address**. The network layer protocol used on the Internet is IP, so this Web address (www.indiana.edu) is translated into an IP address that is 4 bytes long when using IPv4 (e.g., 129.79.127.4) (Figure 5-6). This process is similar to using a phone book to go from someone's name to his or her phone number.[2]

The network layer then determines the best route through the network to the final destination. On the basis of this routing, the network layer identifies the **data link layer address** of the next computer to which the message should be sent. If the data link layer is running Ethernet, then the network layer IP address would be translated into an Ethernet address. Chapter 3 shows that Ethernet addresses are 6 bytes in length, so a possible address might be 00-0F-00-81-14-00 (Ethernet addresses are usually expressed in hexadecimal) (Figure 5-6). Data link layer addresses are needed only on multipoint circuits that have more than one computer on them. For example, many WANs are built with point-to-point circuits that use PPP as the data link layer protocol. These networks do not have data link layer addresses.

5.4.1 Assigning Addresses

In general, the data link layer address is permanently encoded in each network card, which is why the data link layer address is also commonly called the *physical address* or the

FIGURE 5-6

Types of addresses

Address	Example Software	Example Address
Application layer	Web browser	www.kelley.indiana.edu
Network layer	Internet Protocol	129.79.127.4
Data link layer	Ethernet	00-0C-00-F5-03-5A

[2]If you ever want to find out the IP address of any computer, simply enter the command *ping*, followed by the application layer name of the computer at the command prompt (e.g., ping www.indiana.edu).

MAC address. This address is part of the hardware (e.g., Ethernet card) and can never be changed. Hardware manufacturers have an agreement that assigns each manufacturer a unique set of permitted addresses, so even if you buy hardware from different companies, it will never have the same address. Whenever you install a network card into a computer, it immediately has its own data link layer address that uniquely identifies it from every other computer in the world.

Network layer addresses are generally assigned by software. Every network layer software package usually has a configuration file that specifies the network layer address for that computer. Network managers can assign any network layer addresses they want. It is important to ensure that every computer on the same network has a unique network layer address so that every network has a standards group that defines what network layer addresses can be used by each organization.

Application layer addresses (or server names) are also assigned by a software configuration file. Virtually all servers have an application layer address, but most client computers do not. This is because it is important for users to easily access servers and the information they contain, but there is usually little need for someone to access someone else's client computer. As with network layer addresses, network managers can assign any application layer address they want, but a network standards group must approve application layer addresses to ensure that no two computers have the same application layer address. Network layer addresses and application layer addresses go hand in hand, so the same standards group usually assigns both (e.g., www.indiana.edu at the application layer means 129.79.78.4 at the network layer). It is possible to have several application layer addresses for the same computer. For example, one of the Web servers in the Kelley School of Business at Indiana University is called both www.kelley.indiana.edu and www.kelley.iu.edu.

| MANAGEMENT FOCUS | 5-1 Final Countdown for IPv4 |

*T*he address space for IPv4 is running out very quickly. Although early predictions suggested that we would run out of IPv4 address space in early 2011, these didn't materialize. The American Registry for Internet Numbers (ARIN), which is in charge of the IPv4 address space, created a four-phased countdown plan. Phase 1 started in February 2011, when ARIN started assigning addresses in the last/eight address block. Phase 2 began in September 2012, when only three/eight address blocks remained. At the time of writing, we are in Phase 3, which started in August 2013 with the last two remaining/eight blocks. Phase 4 will start when ARIN reaches the last/eight address block. You can monitor the decreasing number of IPv4 addresses on twitter (@IPv4Countdown).

However, even after all the IPv4 addresses are depleted, ARIN is ready to help organizations that need IPv4 addresses. ARIN created a service that allows organizations to transfer IPv4 addresses they don't need to another organization. If a transfer is not available, organizations will be put on a waiting list. The reality, however, is that we are counting down to the inevitable end of IPv4, also called the "IPcalypse" by the supporters of IPv6, who can't wait for the world to convert to IPv6.

Adapted from: www.arin.net

Internet Addresses No one is permitted to operate a computer on the Internet unless he or she uses approved addresses. **ICANN (Internet Corporation for Assigned Names and Numbers)** is responsible for managing the assignment of network layer addresses (i.e., IP addresses) and application layer addresses (e.g., www.indiana.edu). ICANN sets the rules by which new *domain names* (e.g., .com, .org, .ca, .uk) are created and IP address numbers are assigned to users. ICANN also directly manages a set of Internet domains (e.g., .com, .org, .net) and authorizes private companies to become domain name registrars for those domains. Once authorized, a registrar can approve requests for application layer addresses and assign IP numbers for those requests. This means that individuals and organizations wishing to register an Internet name can use any authorized registrar for the domain they choose, and different registrars are permitted to charge different fees for their registration services. Many registrars are authorized to issue names and addresses in the ICANN managed domains, as well as domains in other countries (e.g., .ca, .uk, .au).

Several application layer addresses and network layer addresses can be assigned at the same time. IP addresses are often assigned in groups, so that one organization receives a set of numerically similar addresses for use on its computers. For example, Indiana University has been assigned the set of application layer addresses that end in indiana.edu and iu.edu and the set of IP addresses in the 129.79.x.x range (i.e., all IP addresses that start with the numbers 129.79).

The IP protocol defines the address space that can be used on the Internet. The address space is the total number of addresses available. In general, if a protocol uses N bits to define an address, the available space is 2^N (because each bit can be either 1 or 0). Specifically, IPv4 uses 32 bits (4 bytes) to define an address, and therefore the number of available addresses is $2^{32} = 4,294,967,296$, or approximately 4.3 billion.

These 4.3 billion addresses in the IPv4 address space are divided into **Internet address classes**. Although this terminology is considered to be old, you can still run into people who use it. Figure 5-7 shows the address ranges for each class of addresses. There are three classes of addresses that can be assigned to organizations: Class A, Class B, and Class C. Addresses are assigned into a particular class by the value of the first byte (the original standard used the term "octet" to mean a "byte," so you may see documents using the term "octet"). For example, Class A addresses can have any number between 1 and 126 in the first byte.

The first byte can be any number from 0 to 255 (for an explanation, refer to Hands-On Activity 5C). Figure 5-7 shows that there are some numbers in the first byte range that are not assigned to any address range. An address starting with 0 is not allowed. The 127 address range is reserved for a computer to communicate with itself and is called the **loopback**. Loopback is used mostly by developers and system administrators when testing software. Addresses starting from 224 are **reserved addresses** that should not be used on IP networks. Addresses from 224 to 239 belong to Class D and are reserved for **multicasting,** which is sending messages to a group of computers rather than to one computer (which is normal) or every computer on a network (called broadcast). Addresses from 240 to 254 belong to Class E and are reserved for experimental use. Some companies use the Class E addresses for multicasting internal content in addition to the Class D addresses. Addresses starting with 255 are reserved for **broadcast messages** (which are explained in more detail in the last section of this chapter).

Class	First byte	Byte allocation	Start Address	End Address	Number of Networks	Number of Hosts
A	1-126	Network.Host.Host.Host	1.0.0.0	126.255.255.255	128 (2^7)	16,777,216 (2^{24})
B	128-191	Network.Network.Host.Host	128.0.0.0	191.255.255.255	16,384 (2^{14})	65,536 (2^{16})
C	192-223	Network.Network.Network.Host	192.0.0.0	223.255.255.255	2,097,152 (2^8)	256 (2^8)

FIGURE 5-7 IPv4 public address space

FIGURE 5-8

IPv4 private address space

Class	IP Address Range	Classful Description	Slash Notation	Number of Hosts
A	10.0.0.0 – 10.255.255.255	One Class A address	10.0.0.0/8	16,777,216
B	172.16.0.0. – 172.31.255.255	16 Class B addresses	172.16.0.0/16	1,048,576
C	192.168.0.0 – 192.168.255.255	256 Class C addresses	192.168.0.0/24	65,536

Within each class, there is a set of addresses that are labeled as **private IPv4 address space** (see Figure 5-8). This address space can be used internally by organizations, but routers on the Internet do not route packets that use private addresses (they simply discard them). For this reason, private addresses are often used to increase security. An organization will assign private addresses to its computers so that hackers can't send messages to them. However, these computers need to be able to send messages to other computers on the Internet. The organization has special devices (called NAT firewalls) that translate the private addresses on messages that these computers send into valid public addresses for use on the Internet. We talk more about NAT firewalls and the use of private addresses in Chapter 11. The computer you're using right now probably has a private IP address (see Hands-On Activity 5A).

Figure 5-8 also shows how the newer terminology **classless addressing** is used. Classless addressing uses a slash to indicate the address range (it's also called *slash notation*). For example, 128.192.1.0 is a Class B address, so the first 2 bytes (16 bits) are to be used for the network address and the next 2 bytes (third and fourth bytes) are allocated for host addresses. Using the slash notation, one would identify this network as 128.192.1.0/16. However, a network administrator may decide that rather than allocating 16 bits for the network, it would be more beneficial to allocate 24 bits, and the remaining 8 bits would be used for clients. Therefore, the network would be identified as 128.192.1.0/24. We discuss more about bit allocation for a network and hosts when we discuss subnetting.

One of the problems with the current address system is that the Internet is quickly running out of addresses. Although the 4-byte address of IPv4 provides more than 4 billion possible addresses, the fact that they are assigned in sets significantly limits the number of usable addresses. For example, the address range owned by Indiana University includes about 65,000 addresses, but the university will probably not use all of them.

The IP address shortage was one of the reasons behind the development of IPv6, discussed previously. Once IPv6 is in wide use, the current Internet address system will be replaced by a totally new system based on 16-byte addresses. Most experts expect that all the current 4-byte addresses will simply be assigned an arbitrary 12-byte prefix (e.g., all zeros) so that the holders of the current addresses can continue to use them.

Subnets Each organization must assign the IP addresses it has received to specific computers on its networks. To make the IP address assignment more functional, we use an addressing hierarchy. The first part of the address defines the network, and the second part of the address defines a particular computer or host on the network. However, it is not efficient to assign every computer to the same network. Rather, subnetworks or subnets are designed on the network that subdivide the network into logical pieces. For example, suppose a university has just received a set of addresses starting with 128.192.x.x. It is customary to assign all the computers in the same LAN numbers that start with the same first three digits, so the business school LAN might be assigned 128.192.56.x, which means all the computers in that LAN would have IP numbers starting with those numbers (e.g., 128.192.56.4, 128.192.56.5, and so on) (Figure 5-9). The subnet ID for this LAN then is

FIGURE 5-9

Address subnets

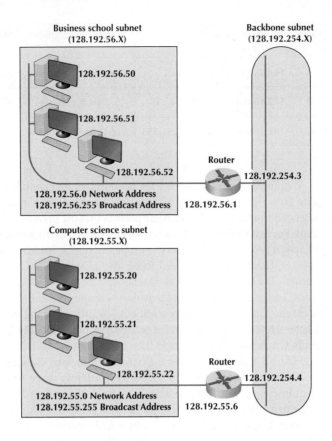

128.192.56. Two addresses on this subnet cannot be assigned as IP address to any computer. The first address is 128.192.56.0, and this is the network address. The second address is 128.192.56.255, which is the broadcast address. The computer science LAN might be assigned 128.192.55.x, and likewise, all the other LANs at the university and the BN that connects them would have a different set of numbers. Similar to the business school LAN, the computer science LAN would have a subnet ID 128.192.55. Thus, 128.192.55.0 and 128.192.55.255 cannot be assigned to any computer on this network because they are reserved for the network address and broadcast address.

Routers connect two or more subnets so they have a separate address on each subnet. Without routers, the two subnets would not be able to communicate. The routers in Figure 5-9, for example, have two addresses each because they connect two subnets and must have one address in each subnet.

Although it is customary to use the first 3 bytes of the IP address to indicate different subnets, it is not required. Any portion of the IP address can be designated as a subnet by using a **subnet mask**. Every computer in a TCP/IP network is given a subnet mask to enable it to determine which computers are on the same subnet (i.e., LAN) that it is on and which computers are outside of its subnet. Knowing whether a computer is on your subnet is very important for message routing, as we shall see later in this chapter.

For example, a network could be configured so that the first 2 bytes indicated a subnet (e.g., 128.184.x.x), so all computers would be given a subnet mask giving the first 2 bytes as the subnet indicator. This would mean that a computer with an IP address of 128.184.22.33 would be on the same subnet as 128.184.78.90.

IP addresses are binary numbers, so partial bytes can also be used as subnets. For example, we could create a subnet that has IP addresses between 128.184.55.1

and 128.184.55.127, and another subnet with addresses between 128.184.55.128 and 128.184.55.254.

Dynamic Addressing To this point, we have said that every computer knows its network layer address from a configuration file that is installed when the computer is first attached to the network. However, this leads to a major network management problem. Any time a computer is moved or its network is assigned a new address, the software on each individual computer must be updated. This is not difficult, but it is very time consuming because someone must go from office to office, editing files on each individual computer.

The easiest way around this is **dynamic addressing**. With this approach, a server is designated to supply a network layer address to a computer each time the computer connects to the network. This is commonly done for client computers but usually not for servers.

TECHNICAL

FOCUS

5-1 Subnet Masks

Subnet masks tell computers what part of an Internet Protocol (IP) address is to be used to determine whether a destination is on the same subnet or on a different subnet. A subnet mask is a 4-byte binary number that has the same format as an IP address and is not routable on the network. A 1 in the subnet mask indicates that that position is used to indicate the subnet. A zero indicates that it is not. Therefore, a mask can only contain a continuous stream of ones.

A subnet mask of 255.255.255.0 means that the first 3 bytes indicate the subnet; all computers with the same first 3 bytes in their IP addresses are on the same subnet. This is because 255 expressed in binary is 11111111.

In contrast, a subnet mask of 255.255.0.0 indicates that the first 2 bytes refer to the same subnet.

Things get more complicated when we use partial-byte subnet masks. For example, suppose the subnet mask was 255.255.255.128. In binary numbers, this is expressed as

11111111.11111111.11111111.10000000

This means that the first 3 bytes plus the first bit in the fourth byte indicate the subnet address.

Likewise, a subnet mask of 255.255.254.0 would indicate the first 2 bytes plus the first 7 bits of third byte indicate the subnet address, because in binary numbers, this is

11111111.11111111.11111110.00000000

The bits that are ones are called *network bits* because they indicate which part of an address is the network or subnet part, whereas the bits that are zeros are called *host bits* because they indicate which part is unique to a specific computer or host.

The most common standard for dynamic addressing is **Dynamic Host Configuration Protocol (DHCP)**. DHCP does not provide a network layer address in a configuration file. Instead, there is a special software package installed on the client that instructs it to contact a DHCP server to obtain an address. In this case, when the computer is turned on and connects to the network, it first issues a broadcast DHCP message that is directed to any DHCP server that can "hear" the message. This message asks the server to assign the requesting computer a unique network layer address. The server runs a corresponding DHCP software package that responds to these requests and sends a message back to the client, giving it its network layer address (and its subnet mask).

The DHCP server can be configured to assign the same network layer address to the computer (on the basis of its data link layer address) each time it requests an address, or it can *lease* the address to the computer by picking the "next available" network layer address from a list of authorized addresses. Addresses can be leased for as long as the computer is connected to the network or for a specified time limit (e.g., 2 hours). When the lease expires, the client computer must contact the DHCP server to get a new address. Address leasing is commonly used by ISPs for dial-up users. ISPs have many more authorized users than they have authorized network layer addresses because not all users can log in at the same time. When a user logs in, his or her computer is assigned a temporary TCP/IP address that is reassigned to the next user when the first user hangs up.

Dynamic addressing greatly simplifies network management in non-dial-up networks, too. With dynamic addressing, address changes need to be made only to the DHCP server, not to each individual computer. The next time each computer connects to the network or whenever the address lease expires, the computer automatically gets the new address.

5.4.2 Address Resolution

To send a message, the sender must be able to translate the application layer address (or server name) of the destination into a network layer address and in turn translate that into a data link layer address. This process is called **address resolution**. There are many different approaches to address resolution that range from completely decentralized (each computer is responsible for knowing all addresses) to completely centralized (there is one computer that knows all addresses). TCP/IP uses two different approaches, one for resolving application layer addresses into IP addresses and a different one for resolving IP addresses into data link layer addresses.

Server Name Resolution Server name resolution is the translation of application layer addresses into network layer addresses (e.g., translating an Internet address such as www.yahoo.com into an IP address such as 204.71.200.74). This is done using the **Domain Name Service (DNS)**. Throughout the Internet a series of computers called **name servers** provides DNS services. These name servers have address databases that store thousands of Internet addresses and their corresponding IP addresses. These name servers are, in effect, the "directory assistance" computers for the Internet. Anytime a computer does not know the IP number for a computer, it sends a message to the name server requesting the IP number.

Whenever you register an Internet application layer address, you must inform the registrar of the IP address of the name server that will provide DNS information for all addresses in that name range. For example, because Indiana University owns the indiana.edu name, it can create any name it wants that ends in that suffix (e.g., www.indiana.edu, www.kelley.indiana.edu, abc.indiana.edu). When it registers its name, it must also provide the IP address of the DNS server that it will use to provide the IP addresses for all the computers within this domain name range (i.e., everything ending in indiana.edu). Every organization that has many servers also has its own DNS server, but smaller organizations that have only one or two servers often use a DNS server provided by their ISP. DNS servers are maintained by network managers, who update their address information as the network changes. DNS servers can also exchange information about new and changed addresses among themselves, a process called *replication*.

When a computer needs to translate an application layer address into an IP address, it sends a special DNS request packet to its DNS server.[3] This packet asks the DNS server to send to the requesting computer the IP address that matches the Internet application layer address provided. If the DNS server has a matching name in its database, it sends back a special DNS response packet with the correct IP address. If that DNS server does not have

---

[3]DNS requests and responses are usually short, so they use UDP as their transport layer protocol. That is, the DNS requests are passed to the transport layer, which surrounds them in a UDP datagram before handing them to the network layer.

that Internet address in its database, it will issue the same request to another DNS server elsewhere on the Internet.[4]

For example, if someone at the University of Toronto were to ask for a Web page on the server (www.kelley.indiana.edu) at Indiana University, the software on the Toronto client computer would issue a DNS request to the University of Toronto DNS server, called the **resolving name server** (Figure 5-10). This DNS server probably would not know the IP address of our server, so it would send a DNS request to one of the DNS **root servers** that it knows. The root server would respond to the resolving name server with a DNS response that said "I don't know the IP address you need, but ask this DNS server," and it would include the IP address of the **top level domain** (TLD) server for the requested Web site (in this case, the .edu TLD server, because the destination Web site is in the .edu domain). The resolving name server would then send a DNS request to the .edu TLD server. The .edu TLD domain server would respond with a DNS response that tells the resolving name server to ask the **authoritative name server** for indiana.edu and provides its IP address. The resolving name server would send a DNS request to the authoritative name server for indiana.edu. The authoritative name server would then respond to the resolving name server with the needed IP address, and the resolving name server would send a DNS response to the client computer with the IP address.

This is why it sometimes takes longer to access certain sites. Most DNS servers know only the names and IP addresses for the computers in their part of the network. Some store

FIGURE 5-10
How the DNS system works

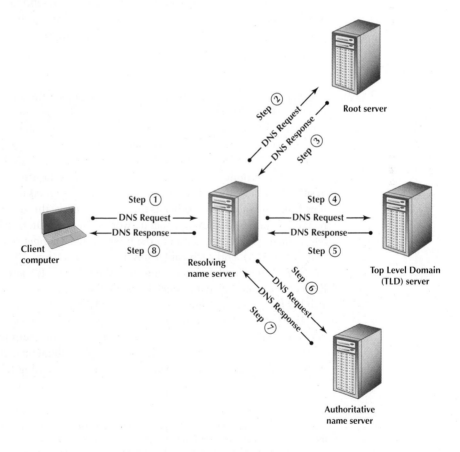

[4]This is called recursive DNS resolution. DNS servers can also use iterative DNS resolution, whereby the client is told that the DNS server does not know the desired address but is given the IP address of another DNS server that can be used to find the address. The client then issues a new DNS request to that DNS server.

frequently used addresses (e.g., www.yahoo.com). If you try to access a computer that is far away, it may take a while before your computer receives a response from the resolving name server.

Once your application layer software receives an IP address, it is stored on your computer in a DNS cache. This way, if you ever need to access the same computer again, your computer does not need to contact its resolving name server. The DNS cache is routinely deleted whenever you turn off your computer.

Data Link Layer Address Resolution To actually send a message on a multipoint circuit, the network layer software must know the data link layer address of the receiving computer. The final destination may be far away (e.g., sending from Toronto to Indiana). In this case, the network layer would *route* the message by selecting a path through the network that would ultimately lead to the destination. (Routing is discussed in the next section.) The first step on this route would be to send the message to its router.

To send a message to another computer in its subnet, a computer must know the correct data link layer address. In this case, the TCP/IP software sends a **broadcast message** to all computers in its subnet. A broadcast message, as the name suggests, is received and processed by all computers in the same LAN (which is usually designed to match the IP subnet). The message is a specially formatted request using **Address Resolution Protocol (ARP)** that says, "Whoever is IP address xxx.xxx.xxx.xxx, please send me your data link layer address." The software in the computer with that IP address then sends an ARP response with its data link layer address. The sender transmits its message using that data link layer address. The sending computer also stores the data link layer address in its address table for future use.[5]

5.5 ROUTING

Routing is the process of determining the route or path through the network that a message will travel from the sending computer to the receiving computer. In some networks (e.g., the Internet), there are many possible routes from one computer to another. In other networks (e.g., internal company networks), there may only be one logical route from one computer to another.[6] In either case, some device has to route messages through the network.

Routing is done by special devices called routers. **Routers** are usually found at the edge of subnets because they are the devices that connect subnets together and enable messages to flow from one subnet to another as the messages move through the network from sender to receiver. Figure 5-11 shows a small network with two routers, R1 and R2. This network has five subnets, plus a connection to the Internet. Each subnet has its own range of addresses (e.g., 10.10.51.x), and each router has its IP address (e.g., 10.10.1.1). The first router (R1) has four connections, one to the Internet, one to router R2, and one to each of two subnets. Each connection, called an **interface**, is numbered from 0 to 3. The second router (R2) has also has four interfaces, one that connects to R1 and three that connect to other subnets.

Every router has a routing table that specifies how messages will travel through the network. In its simplest form, the routing table is a two-column table. The first column lists every network or computer that the router knows about, and the second column lists the interface that connects to it. Figure 5-12 shows the routing tables that might be used by

---

[5]It would be reasonable at this point to guess that because ARP requests and responses are small, they use UDP in the same way that DNS requests and responses do. But they don't. Instead, ARP packets replace both TCP/UDP and IP and are placed directly into the data link layer frame with no transport or network layer PDUs.

[6]If you ever want to find out the route through the Internet from your computer to any other computer on the Internet, simply enter the command *tracert* followed by the application layer name of the computer at the command line (e.g., tracert www.indiana.edu).

FIGURE 5-11

A small corporate
network

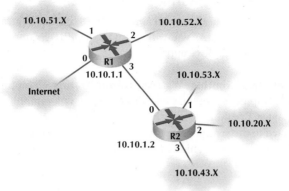

FIGURE 5-12

Sample routing tables

Router R1's Routing Table

Network Address	Interface
10.10.51.0 to 10.10.51.255	1
10.10.52.0 to 10.10.52.255	2
10.10.53.0 to 10.10.53.255	3
10.10.20.0 to 10.10.20.255	3
10.10.43.0 to 10.10.43.255	3
10.10.1.2	3
All other addresses	0

Router R2's Routing Table

Network Address	Interface
10.10.1.1	0
10.10.53.0 to 10.10.53.255	1
10.10.20.0 to 10.10.20.255	2
10.10.43.0 to 10.10.43.255	3
All other addresses	0

routers in Figure 5-11. The first entry in R1's routing table says that any message with an IP address in the range from 10.10.51.0 to 10.10.51.255 should be sent out on interface 1.

A router uses its routing table to decide where to send the messages it receives. Suppose a computer in the 10.10.43.x subnet sends an HTTP request for a Web page that is located on the company's Web server, which is in the 10.10.20.x subnet (let's say the Web server has an IP address of 10.10.20.10). The computer would send the message to its router, R2. R2 would look at the IP address on the IP packet and search its routing table for a matching address. It would search through the table, from top to bottom, until it reached the third entry, which is a range of addresses that contains the Web server's address (10.10.20.10). The matching interface is number 2, so R2 would transmit the message on this interface.

The process would be similar if the same computer were to request a page somewhere on the Internet (e.g., www.yahoo.com). The computer would send the message to its router, R2. R2 would look at the IP address on the IP packet (www.yahoo.com has an IP address of 69.147.125.65) and search its routing table for a matching entry. It would look at the first four entries and not find a match. It would reach the final entry that says to send a message with any other address on interface 0, so R2 would transmit this message on interface 0 to router R1.

The same process would be performed by R1. It would search through its routing table for an address that matched 69.147.125.65 and not find it. When it reaches the final entry, R1 knows to send this message on interface 0 into the Internet.

5.5.1 Types of Routing

There are three fundamental approaches to routing: centralized routing, static routing, and dynamic routing. As you will see in the TCP/IP Example section later in this chapter, the Internet uses all three approaches.

Centralized Routing With **centralized routing**, all routing decisions are made by one central computer or router. Centralized routing is commonly used in host-based networks (see Chapter 2), and in this case, routing decisions are rather simple. All computers are connected to the central computer, so any message that needs to be routed is simply sent to the central computer, which in turn retransmits the message on the appropriate circuit to the destination.

Static Routing **Static routing** is decentralized, which means that all computers or routers in the network make their own routing decisions following a formal routing protocol. In MANs and WANs, the routing table for each computer is developed by its individual network manager (although network managers often share information). In LANs or backbones, the routing tables used by all computers on the network are usually developed by one individual or a committee. Most decentralized routing protocols are self-adjusting, meaning that they can automatically adapt to changes in the network configuration (e.g., adding and deleting computers and circuits).

With static routing, routing decisions are made in a fixed manner by individual computers or routers. The routing table is developed by the network manager, and it changes only when computers are added to or removed from the network. For example, if the computer recognizes that a circuit is broken or unusable (e.g., after the data link layer retry limit has been exceeded without receiving an acknowledgment), the computer will update the routing table to indicate the failed circuit. If an alternate route is available, it will be used for all subsequent messages. Otherwise, messages will be stored until the circuit is repaired. Static routing is commonly used in networks that have few routing options that seldom change.

Dynamic Routing With **dynamic routing** (or *adaptive routing*), routing decisions are made in a decentralized manner by individual computers. This approach is used when there are multiple routes through a network, and it is important to select the best route. Dynamic routing attempts to improve network performance by routing messages over the fastest possible route, away from busy circuits and busy computers. An initial routing table is developed by the network manager but is continuously updated by the computers themselves to reflect changing network conditions.

With **distance vector dynamic routing**, routers count the number of **hops** along a route. A hop is one circuit, so that router R1 in Figure 5-11 would know it could reach a computer in the 10.10.52.X subnet in one hop, and a computer in the 10.10.43.X subnet in 2 hops, by going through R2. With this approach, computers periodically (usually every 1 to 2 minutes) exchange information on the hop count and sometimes on the relative speed of the circuits in route and how busy they are with their neighbors.

With **link state dynamic routing**, computers or routers track the number of hops in the route, the speed of the circuits in each route, and how busy each route is. In other words, rather than knowing just a route's distance, link state routing tries to determine how fast each possible route is. Each computer or router periodically (usually every 30 seconds or when a major change occurs) exchanges this information with other computers or routers in the network (not just their neighbors) so that each computer or router has the most accurate information possible. Link state protocols are preferred to distance vector protocols in large networks because they spread more reliable routing information throughout the entire network when major changes occur in the network. They are said to *converge* more quickly.

There are two drawbacks to dynamic routing. First, it requires more processing by each computer or router in the network than does centralized routing or static routing. Computing resources are devoted to adjusting routing tables rather than to sending messages, which can slow down the network. Second, the transmission of routing information "wastes" network capacity. Some dynamic routing protocols transmit status information very frequently, which can significantly reduce performance.

5.5.2 Routing Protocols

A routing protocol is a protocol that is used to exchange information among computers to enable them to build and maintain their routing tables. You can think of a routing protocol as the language that is used to build the routing tables in Figure 5-12. When new paths are added or paths are broken and cannot be used, messages are sent among computers using the routing protocol.

It can be useful to know all possible routes to a given destination. However, as a network gets quite large, knowing all possible routes becomes impractical; there are simply too many possible routes. Even at some modest number of computers, dynamic routing protocols become impractical because of the amount of network traffic they generate. For this reason, networks are often subdivided into autonomous systems of networks.

An **autonomous system** is simply a network operated by one organization, such as IBM or Indiana University, or an organization that runs one part of the Internet. Remember that we said the Internet was simply a network of networks. Each part of the Internet is run by a separate organization such as AT&T, MCI, and so on. Each part of the Internet or each large organizational network connected to the Internet can be a separate autonomous system.

The computers within each autonomous system know about the other computers in that system and usually exchange routing information because the number of computers is kept manageable. If an autonomous system grows too large, it can be split into smaller parts. The routing protocols used inside an autonomous system are called **interior routing protocols**.

Protocols used between autonomous systems are called **exterior routing protocols**. Although interior routing protocols are usually designed to provide detailed routing information about all or most computers inside the autonomous systems, exterior protocols are designed to be more careful in the information they provide. Usually, exterior protocols provide information about only the preferred or the best routes rather than all possible routes.

There are many different protocols that are used to exchange routing information. Five are commonly used on the Internet: Border Gateway Protocol (BGP), Internet Control Message Protocol (ICMP), Routing Information Protocol (RIP), Intermediate System to Intermediate System (IS-IS) Open Shortest Path First (OSPF), and Enhanced Interior Gateway Routing Protocol (EIGRP).

Border Gateway Protocol (BGP) is a dynamic distance vector exterior routing protocol used on the Internet to exchange routing information between autonomous systems—that is, large sections of the Internet. Although BGP is the preferred routing protocol between Internet sections, it is seldom used inside companies because it is large, complex, and often hard to administer.

Internet Control Message Protocol (ICMP) is the simplest interior routing protocol on the Internet. ICMP is simply an error-reporting protocol that enables computers to report routing errors to message senders. ICMP also has a very limited ability to update routing tables.[7]

---

[7]ICMP is the protocol used by the ping command.

TECHNICAL FOCUS

5-2 Routing on the Internet

The Internet is a network of autonomous system networks. Each autonomous system operates its own interior routing protocol while using Border Gateway Protocol (BGP) as the exterior routing protocol to exchange information with the other autonomous systems on the Internet. Although there are a number of interior routing protocols, Open Shortest Path First (OSPF) is the preferred protocol, and most organizations that run the autonomous systems forming large parts of the Internet use OSPF.

Figure 5-13 shows how a small part of the Internet might operate. In this example, there are six autonomous systems (e.g., Sprint, AT&T), three of which we have shown in more detail. Each autonomous system has a **border router** that connects it to the adjacent autonomous systems and exchanges route information via BGP. In this example, autonomous system A is connected to autonomous system B, which in turn is connected to autonomous system C. A is also connected to C via a route through systems D and E. If someone in A wants to send a message to someone in C, the message should be routed through B because it is the fastest route. The autonomous systems must share route information via BGP so that the border routers in each system know what routes are preferred. In this case, B would inform A that there is a route through it to C (and a route to E), and D

would inform A that it has a route to E, but D would not inform A that there is a route through it to C. The border router in A would then have to decide which route to use to reach E.

Each autonomous system can use a different interior routing protocol. In this example, B is a rather simple network with only a few devices and routes, and it uses RIP, a simpler protocol in which all routers broadcast route information to their neighbors every minute or so. A and C are more complex networks and use OSPF. Most organizations that use OSPF create a special router called a **designated router** to manage the routing information. Every 15 minutes or so, each router sends its routing information to the designated router, which then broadcasts the revised routing table information to all other routers. If no designated router is used, then every router would have to broadcast its routing information to all other routers, which would result in a very large number of messages. In the case of autonomous system C, which has seven routers, this would require 42 separate messages (seven routers each sending to six others). By using a designated router, we now have only 12 separate messages (the six other routers sending to the designated router, and the designated router sending the complete set of revised information back to the other six).

Routing Information Protocol (RIP) is a dynamic distance vector interior routing protocol that is commonly used in smaller networks, such as those operated by one organization. The network manager uses RIP to develop the routing table. When new computers are added, RIP simply counts the number of computers in the possible routes to the destination and selects the route with the least number. Computers using RIP send broadcast messages every minute or so (the timing is set by the network manager) announcing their routing status to all other computers. RIP is used by both TCP/IP and IPX/SPX.

Intermediate System to Intermediate System (IS-IS) is a link state interior routing protocol that is commonly used in large networks. IS-IS is an ISO protocol that has been added to many TCP/IP networks.

Open Shortest Path First (OSPF) is a dynamic hybrid interior routing protocol that is commonly used on the Internet. It uses the number of computers in a route as well as network traffic and error rates to select the best route. OSPF is more efficient than RIP because it normally doesn't use broadcast messages. Instead, it selectively sends status update messages directly to selected computers or routers. OSPF is the preferred interior routing protocol used by TCP/IP.

Enhanced Interior Gateway Routing Protocol (EIGRP) is a dynamic hybrid interior routing protocol developed by Cisco and is commonly used inside organizations. Hybrid means that it has some features that act like distance vector protocols and some other features that act like link-state protocols. As you might expect, EIGRP is an improved version of **Interior Gateway Routing Protocol (IGRP)**. EIGRP records information about a route's transmission capacity, delay, reliability, and load. EIGRP is unique in that computers or

FIGURE 5-13

Routing on the Internet with Border Gateway Protocol (BGP), Open Shortest Path First (OSPF), and Routing Information Protocol (RIP)

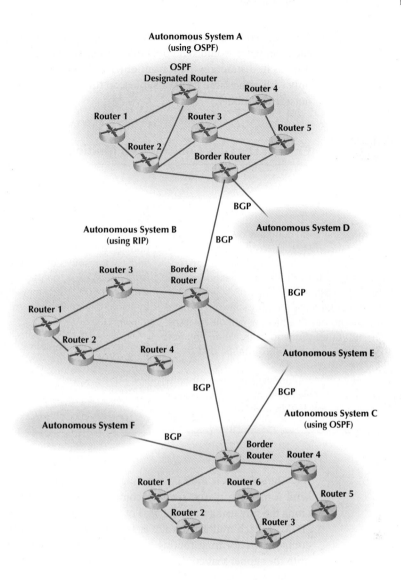

routers store their own routing tables as well as the routing tables for all of their neighbors so they have a more accurate understanding of the network.

5.5.3 Multicasting

The most common type of message in a network is the transmission between two computers. One computer sends a message to another computer (e.g., a client requesting a Web page). This is called a **unicast message**. Earlier in the chapter, we introduced the concept of a *broadcast message* that is sent to all computers on a specific LAN or subnet. A third type of message called a **multicast message** is used to send the same message to a group of computers.

Consider a videoconferencing situation in which four people want to participate in the same conference. Each computer could send the same voice and video data from its camera to the computers of each of the other three participants using unicasts. In this case, each computer would send three identical messages, each addressed to the three different computers. This would work but would require a lot of network capacity. Alternately, each computer could send one broadcast message. This would reduce network traffic (because each computer would send only one message), but every computer on the network would process it, distracting them from other tasks. Broadcast messages usually are transmitted only within the same LAN or subnet, so this would not work if one of the computers were outside the subnet.

MANAGEMENT	5-2 Captain D's Gets Cooking with Multicast
FOCUS	

Captain D's has more than 500 company owned and franchised fast-food restaurants across North America. Each restaurant has a small low-speed satellite link that can send and receive data at speeds similar to broadband Internet access (384 Kbps to 1.2 Mbps).

Captain D's used to send its monthly software updates to each of its restaurants one at a time, which meant transferring each file 500 times, once to each restaurant. You don't have to be a network wizard to realize that this is slow and redundant.

Captain D's now uses multicasting to send monthly software updates to all its restaurants at once. What once took hours is now accomplished in minutes.

Multicasting also enables Captain D's to send large human resource file updates each week to all restaurants and to transmit computer-based training videos to all restaurants each quarter. The training videos range in size from 500–1000 megabytes, so without multicasting it would be impossible to use the satellite network to transmit the videos.

Adapted from: "Captain D's Gets Cooking with Multicast from XcelleNet," www.xcellenet.com, 2004.

The solution is multicast messaging. Computers wishing to participate in a multicast send a message to the sending computer or some other computer performing routing along the way using a special type of packet called **Internet Group Management Protocol (IGMP)**. Each multicast group is assigned a special IP address to identify the group. Any computer performing routing knows to route all multicast messages with this IP address onto the subnet that contains the requesting computer. The routing computer sets the data link layer address on multicast messages to a matching multicast data link layer address. Each requesting computer must inform its data link layer software to process incoming messages with this multicast data link layer address. When the multicast session ends (e.g., the videoconference is over), the client computer sends another IGMP message to the organizing computer or the computer performing routing to remove it from the multicast group.

5.5.4 The Anatomy of a Router

There is a huge array of software and hardware that makes the Internet work, but the one device that is indispensable is the router. The router has three main functions: (1) it determines a path for a packet to travel over, (2) it transmits the packet across the path, and (3) it supports communication between a wide variety of devices and protocols. Now we will look inside a router to see how these three functions are supported by hardware and software.

Routers are essentially special-purpose computers that consist of a CPU (central processing unit), memory (both volatile and nonvolatile), and ports or interfaces that connect to them to the network and/or other devices so that a network administrator can communicate with them. What differentiates routers from computers that we use in our everyday lives is that they are diskless and they don't come with a monitor, keyboard, and mouse. They don't have these because they were designed to move data rather than display it.

There are three ways that a network manager can connect to a router and configure and maintain it: (1) console port, (2) **network interface port**, and (3) auxiliary port (see Figure 5-14). When the router is turned on for the very first time, it does not have an IP address assigned, so it cannot communicate on the network. Because of this, the **console port**, also called the *management port*, is used to configure it. A network manager would use a blue rollover cable (not the Ethernet cable) to connect the router's console port to a computer that has terminal emulation software on it. The network manager would use this software to communicate with the router and perform the basic setup (e.g., IP address assignment, routing protocol selection). Once the basic setup is done, the network manager can log in to the router from any computer using the network interface using TCP/IP and Telnet with Secure Shell (SSH). Although routers come with an **auxiliary port** that allows an administrator to log via a direct, nonnetwork connection (e.g., using modems), this connection is rarely used today.

A router, just like a computer, must have an operating system so that it can be configured. The operating system that is used in about 90% of routers is the **Cisco Internetwork Operating Systems (IOS)**, although other operating systems exist too. IOS uses a command line interface rather than a graphical user **interface**. The network manager uses IOS commands to create a configuration file (also a config file) that defines how the router will operate. The config file can contain the type of routing protocol to be used, the interfaces that are active/enabled and those that are down, and what type of encryption is used. The

FIGURE 5-14

Anatomy of a router

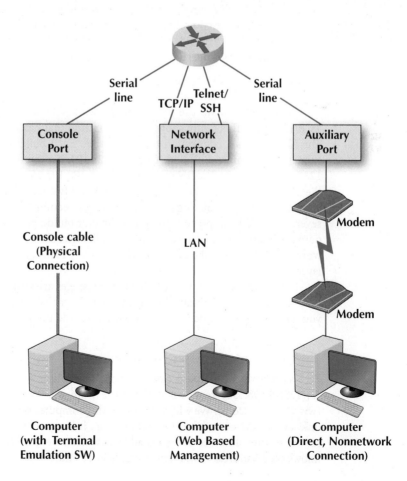

config file is central to a router's operation, and the IOS refers to it hundreds of times per second to tell the router how to do its job.

The other important file is the **Access Control List (ACL)**, which plays an important role in network security. The ACL defines what types of packets should be routed and what types of packets should be discarded. The ACL is discussed in more detail in Chapter 10 on security.

5.6 TCP/IP EXAMPLE

This chapter has discussed the functions of the transport and network layers: linking to the application layer, segmenting, session management, addressing, and routing. In this section, we tie all of these concepts together to take a closer look at how these functions actually work using TCP/IP.

When a computer is installed on a TCP/IP network (or dials into a TCP/IP network), it must be given four pieces of network layer addressing and routing information before it can operate. This information can be provided by a configuration file, or via a DHCP server. The information is

1. Its IP address
2. A subnet mask, so it can determine what addresses are part of its subnet
3. The IP address of a DNS server, so it can translate application layer addresses into IP addresses
4. The IP address of an IP **gateway** (commonly called a router) leading outside of its subnet, so it can route messages addressed to computers outside of its subnet (this presumes the computer is using static routing and there is only one connection from it to the outside world through which all messages must flow; if it used dynamic routing, some routing software would be needed instead)

These four pieces of information are the minimum required. A server would also need to know its application layer address.

In this section, we use the simple network shown in Figure 5-15 to illustrate how TCP/IP works. This figure shows an organization that has four LANs connected by a BN. The BN also has a connection to the Internet. Each building is configured as a separate subnet. For example, Building A has the 128.192.98.x subnet, whereas Building B has the 128.192.95.x subnet. The BN is its own subnet: 128.192.254.x. Each building is connected to the BN via a router that has two IP addresses and two data link layer addresses, one for the connection into the building and one for the connection onto the BN. The organization has several Web servers spread throughout the four buildings. The DNS server and the router onto the Internet are located directly on the BN itself. For simplicity, we assume that all networks use Ethernet as the data link layer and only focus on Web requests at the application layer.

In the next sections, we describe how messages are sent through the network. For the sake of simplicity, we initially ignore the need to establish and close TCP connections. Once you understand the basic concepts, we will then add these in to complete the example.

5.6.1 Known Addresses, Same Subnet

Let's start with the simplest case. Suppose that a user on a client computer in Building A (128.192.98.130) requests a Web page from the Web server in the same building (www1.anyorg.com). We will assume that this computer knows the network layer and data link layer addresses of the Web server (e.g., it has previously requested pages from this server, so the addresses are in its address tables). Because the application layer software knows the IP address of the server, it uses its IP address, not its application layer address.

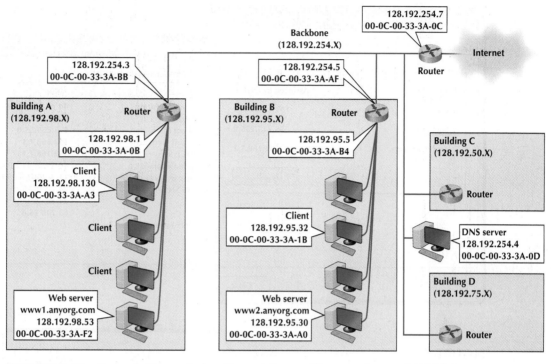

FIGURE 5-15   Example Transmission Control Protocol/Internet Protocol (TCP/IP) network

---

TECHNICAL   **5-3 Finding Your Computer's TCP/IP Settings**
FOCUS

*I*f your computer can access the Internet, it must use TCP/IP. In Windows, you can find out your TCP/IP settings by looking at their *properties*. Click on the **Start** button and then select **Control Panel** and then select **Network Connections.** Double click on your **Local Area Connection** and then click the **Support** tab.

This will show you your computer's IP address, subnet mask, and gateway, and whether the IP address is assigned by a DHCP server. Figure 5-16 shows this information for one of our computers.

If you would like more information, you can click on the **Details** button. This second window shows the same information, plus the computer's Ethernet address (called

the physical address), as well as information about the DHCP lease and the DNS servers available.

Try this on your computer. If you have your own home network with your own router, there is a chance that your computer has an IP address very similar to ours or someone else's in your class—or the same address, in fact. How can two computers have the same IP address? Well, they can't. This is a security technique called *network address translation* in which one set of "private" IP addresses is used inside a network and a different set of "public" IP addresses is used by the router when it sends the messages onto the Internet. Network address translation is described in detail in Chapter 11.

In this case, the application layer software (i.e., Web browser) passes an HTTP packet containing the user request to the transport layer software requesting a page from 128.192.98.53. The transport layer software (TCP) would take the HTTP packet, add a TCP segment, and then hand it to the network layer software (IP). The network layer software will compare the destination address (128.192.98.53) to the subnet mask (255.255.255.0) and discover that this computer is on its own subnet. The network layer software will then search its data link layer address table and find the matching data link layer address

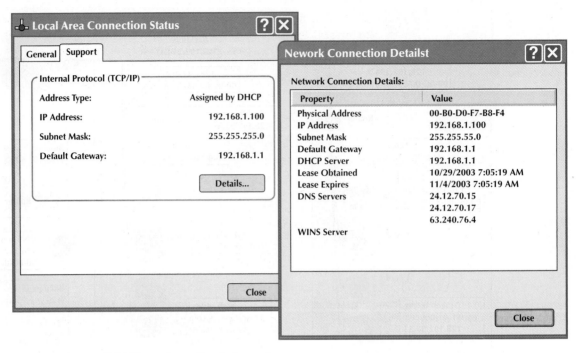

FIGURE 5-16 TCP/IP configuration information

(00-0C-00-33-3A-F2). The network layer would then attach an IP packet and pass it to the data link layer, along with the destination Ethernet address. The data link layer would surround the frame with an Ethernet frame and transmit it over the physical layer to the Web server (Figure 5-17).

The data link layer on the Web server would perform error checking before passing the HTTP packet with the TCP segment and IP packet attached to its network layer software. The network layer software (IP) would then process the IP packet, see that it was destined to this computer, and pass it to the transport layer software (TCP). This software would process the TCP segment, see that there was only one packet, and pass the HTTP packet to the Web server software.

The Web server software would find the page requested, attach an HTTP packet, and pass it to its transport layer software. The transport layer software (TCP) would break the Web page into several smaller segments, each less than 1,500 bytes in length, and attach a TCP segment (with a number to indicate the order) to each. Each smaller segment would then go to the network layer software, get an IP packet attached that specified the IP address of the requesting client (128.192.98.130), and be given to the data link layer with the client's Ethernet address (00-0C-00-33-3A-A3) for transmission. The data link layer on the server would transmit the frames in the order in which the network layer passed them to it.

FIGURE 5-17

Packet nesting. HTTP = Hypertext Transfer Protocol; IP = Internet Protocol; TCP = Transmission Control Protocol

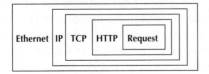

The client's data link layer software would receive the frames, perform error checking, and pass the IP packets inside them to the network layer. The network layer software (IP) would check to see that the packets were destined for this computer and pass the TCP segments they contained to the transport layer software. The transport layer software (TCP) would assemble the separate segments, in order, back into one Web page and pass the HTTP packet in turn to the Web browser to display on the screen.

5.6.2 Known Addresses, Different Subnet

Suppose this time that the same client computer wanted to get a Web page from a Web server located somewhere in Building B (www2.anyorg.com). Again, assume that all addresses are known and are in the address tables of all computers. In this case, the application layer software would pass an HTTP packet to the transport layer software (TCP) with the Internet address of the destination www2.anyorg.com: 128.192.95.30. The transport layer software (TCP) would make sure that the request fit in one segment and hand it to the network layer. The network layer software (IP) would then check the subnet mask and would recognize that the Web server is located outside of its subnet. Any messages going outside the subnet must be sent to the router (128.192.98.1), whose job it is to process the message and send the message on its way into the outside network. The network layer software would check its address table and find the Ethernet address for the router. It would therefore set the data link layer address to the router's Ethernet address on this subnet (00-0C-00-33-3A-0B) and pass the IP packet to the data link layer for transmission. The data link layer would add the Ethernet frame and pass it to the physical layer for transmission.

The router would receive the message and its data link layer would perform error checking and send an acknowledgment before passing the packet to the network layer software (IP). The network layer software would read the IP address to determine the final destination. The router would recognize that this address (128.192.95.30) needed to be sent to the 128.192.95.x subnet. It knows the router for this subnet is 128.192.254.5. It would pass the packet back to its data link layer, giving the Ethernet address of the router (00-0C-00-33-3A-AF).

This router would receive the message (do error checking, etc.) and read the IP address to determine the final destination. The router would recognize that this address (128.192.95.30) was inside its 128.192.95.x subnet and would search its data link layer address table for this computer. It would then pass the packet to the data link layer along with the Ethernet address (00-0C-00-33-3A-A0) for transmission.

The www2.anyorg.com Web server would receive the message and process it. This would result in a series of TCP/IP packets addressed to the requesting client (128.192.98.130). These would make their way through the network in reverse order. The Web server would recognize that this IP address is outside its subnet and would send the message to the 128.192.95.5 router using its Ethernet address (00-0C-00-33-3A-B4). This router would then send the message to the router for the 128.192.98.x subnet (128.192.254.3) using its Ethernet address (00-0C-00-33-3A-BB). This router would in turn send the message back to the client (128.192.98.130) using its Ethernet address (00-0C-00-33-3A-A3).

This process would work in the same way for Web servers located outside the organization on the Internet. In this case, the message would go from the client to the 128.192.98.x router, which would send it to the Internet router (128.192.254.7), which would send it to its Internet connection. The message would be routed through the Internet, from router to router, until it reached its destination. Then the process would work in reverse to return the requested page.

5.6.3 Unknown Addresses

Let's return to the simplest case (requesting a Web page from a Web server on the same subnet), only this time we will assume that the client computer does not know the network layer or data link layer address of the Web server. For simplicity, we will assume that the client knows the data link layer address of its subnet router, but after you read through this example, you will realize that obtaining the data link layer address of the subnet router is straightforward. (It is done the same way as the client obtains the data link layer address of the Web server.)

Suppose the client computer in Building A (128.192.98.130) wants to retrieve a Web page from the www1.anyorg.com Web server but does not know its addresses. The Web browser realizes that it does not know the IP address after searching its IP address table and not finding a matching entry. Therefore, it issues a DNS request to the name server (128.192.254.4). The DNS request is passed to the transport layer (TCP), which attaches a UDP datagram and hands the message to the network layer.

Using its subnet mask, the network layer (IP) will recognize that the DNS server is outside of its subnet. It will attach an IP packet and set the data link layer address to its router's address.

The router will process the message and recognize that the 128.192.254.4 IP address is on the BN. It will transmit the packet using the DNS server's Ethernet address.

The name server will process the DNS request and send the matching IP address back to the client via the 128.198.98.x subnet router.

The IP address for the desired computer makes its way back to the application layer software, which stores it in its IP table. It then issues the HTTP request using the IP address for the Web server (128.192.98.53) and passes it to the transport layer, which in turn passes it to the network layer. The network layer uses its subnet mask and recognizes that this computer is on its subnet. However, it does not know the Web server's Ethernet address. Therefore, it broadcasts an ARP request to all computers on its subnet, requesting that the computer whose IP address is 128.192.98.53 respond with its Ethernet address.

This request is processed by all computers on the subnet, but only the Web server responds with an ARP packet giving its Ethernet address. The network layer software on the client stores this address in its data link layer address table and sends the original Web request to the Web server using its Ethernet address.

This process works the same for a Web server outside the subnet, whether in the same organization or anywhere on the Internet. If the Web server is far away (e.g., Australia), the process will likely involve searching more than one name server, but it is still the same process.

5.6.4 TCP Connections

Whenever a computer transmits data to another computer, it must choose whether to use a connection-oriented service via TCP or a connectionless service via UDP. Most application layer software such as Web browsers (HTTP), email (SMTP), FTP, and Telnet use connection-oriented services. This means that before the first packet is sent, the transport layer first sends a SYN segment to establish a session. Once the session is established, then the data packets begin to flow. Once the data are finished, the session is closed with a FIN segment.

In the preceding examples, this means that the first packet sent is really a SYN segment, followed by a response from the receiver accepting the connection, and then the packets as described earlier. There is nothing magical about the SYN and FIN segments; they are addressed and routed in the same manner as any other packets. But they do add to the complexity and length of the example.

A special word is needed about HTTP packets. When HTTP was first developed, Web browsers opened a separate TCP session for each HTTP request. That is, when they requested a page, they would open a session, send the single packet requesting the Web page, and close the session at their end. The Web server would open a session, send as many packets as needed to transmit the requested page, and then close the session. If the page included graphic images, the Web browser would open and close a separate session for each request. This requirement to open and close sessions for each request was time consuming and not really necessary. With the newest version of HTTP, Web browsers open one session when they first issue an HTTP request and leave that session open for all subsequent HTTP requests to the same server.

5.6.5 TCP/IP and Network Layers

In closing this chapter, we want to return to the layers in the network model and take another look at how messages flow through the layers. Figure 5-18 shows how a Web request message from a client computer in Building A would flow through the network layers in the different computers and devices on its way to the server in Building B.

The message starts at the application layer of the sending computer (the client in Building A), shown in the upper left corner of the figure, which generates an HTTP packet. This packet is passed to the transport layer, which surrounds the HTTP packet with a TCP segment. This is then passed to the network layer, which surrounds it with an IP frame that includes the IP address of the final destination (128.192.95.30). This in turn is passed to the

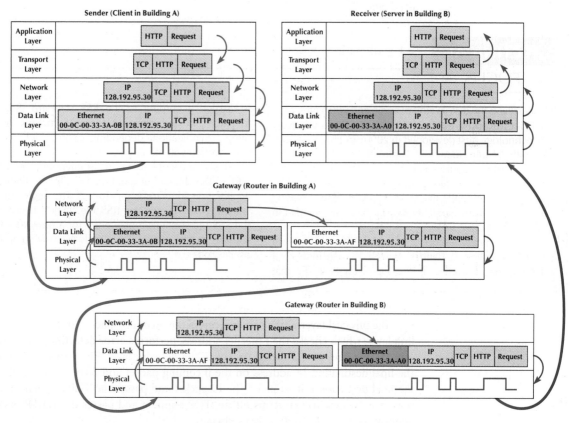

FIGURE 5-18 How messages move through the network layers.
Note: The addresses in this example are destination addresses

data link layer, which surrounds it within an Ethernet frame that also includes the Ethernet address of the next computer to which the message will be sent (00-0C-00-33-3A-0B). Finally, this is passed to the physical layer, which converts it into electrical impulses for transmission through the cable to its next stop—the router that serves as the gateway in Building A.

When the message arrives at the router in Building A, its physical layer translates it from electrical impulses into digital data and passes the Ethernet frame to the data link layer. The data link layer checks to make sure that the Ethernet frame is addressed to the router, performs error detection, strips off the Ethernet frame, and passes its contents (the IP packet) to the network layer. The routing software running at the network layer looks at the destination IP address, determines the next computer to which the packet should be sent, and passes the outgoing packet down to the data link layer for transmission. The data link layer surrounds the IP packet with a completely new Ethernet frame that contains the destination address of the next computer to which the packet will be sent (00-0C-00-33-3A-AF). In Figure 5-18, this new frame is shown in a different color. This is then passed to the physical layer, which transmits it through the network cable to its next stop—the router that serves as the gateway in Building B.

When the message arrives at the router in Building B, it goes through the same process. The physical layer passes the incoming packet to the data link layer, which checks the destination Ethernet address, performs error detection, strips off the Ethernet frame, and passes the IP packet to the network layer software. The software determines the next destination and passes the IP packet back to the data link layer, which adds a completely new Ethernet frame with the destination address of its next stop (00-0C-00-33-3A-A0)—its final destination.

TECHNICAL FOCUS

5-4 Podcasting

*P*odcasting is the distribution of audio and video files (e.g., MP3 files) over the Internet. Podcasting uses a relatively old technology (first developed in 2000), but became popular with the introduction of Apple's iPod.

Podcasting requires two things: the content and a channel description file that describes the content. The content is usually MP3 files, audio and/or video. Creating MP3 files is fairly straightforward—see the Hands-On Activity in Chapter 3.

The channel description file describes the overall set of files, called a channel, as well as each individual MP3 file that is available. This file is an XML file that is created according to the **RSS** standard (RSS stands for Rich Site Summary, RDF Site Summary, or Really Simple Syndication, depending upon which version of the standard you read).

Users subscribe to a podcast channel by entering the URL of the channel description RSS file into their favorite aggregation software (e.g., iTunes). The aggregation software regularly reads the RSS file. When it notices that the RSS file contains a new entry for a new MP3 file, the software automatically downloads the new content to the user's iPod.

The physical layer at the server receives the incoming packet and passes it to the data link layer, which checks the Ethernet address, performs error detection, removes the Ethernet frame, and passes the IP packet to the network layer. The network layer examines the final destination IP address on the incoming packet and recognizes that the server is the final destination. It strips off the IP packet and passes the TCP segment to the transport layer, which in turn strips off the TCP segment and passes the HTTP packet to the application layer (the Web server software).

There are two important things to remember from this example. First, at all gateways (i.e., routers) along the way, the packet moves through the physical layer and data link layer up to the network layer, but no higher. The routing software operates at the network layer, where it selects the next computer to which the packet should be sent, and passes the packet back down through the data link and physical layers. These three layers are involved at all computers and devices along the way, but the transport and application layers are only involved at the sending computer (to create the application layer packet and the TCP segment) and at the receiving computer (to understand the TCP segment and process the application layer packet). Inside the TCP/IP network itself, messages only reach layer 3—no higher.

Second, at each stop along the way, the Ethernet frame is removed and a new one is created. The Ethernet frame lives only long enough to move the message from one computer to the next and then is destroyed. In contrast, the IP packet and the packets above it (TCP and application layer) never change while the message is in transit. They are created and removed only by the original message sender and the final destination.

5.7 IMPLICATIONS FOR MANAGEMENT

The implications from this chapter are similar in many ways to the implications from Chapter 4. There used to be several distinct protocols used at the network and transport layers, but as the Internet has become an important network, most organizations are moving to the adoption of TCP/IP as the single standard protocol at the transport and network layers. This is having many of the same effects described in Chapter 4: The cost of buying and maintaining networking equipment and the cost of training networking staff are steadily decreasing. However, as we move closer to running out of IPv4 addresses, more organizations will move to IPv6. This will cost a lot, but most organizations will see little business value from the change.

As TCP/IP becomes the dominant transport and network layer protocol for digital data, telephone companies who operate large non-TCP/IP-based networks to carry voice traffic are beginning to wonder whether they too should make the switch to TCP/IP. This has significant financial implications for companies that manufacture large networking equipment used in these networks.

SUMMARY

Transport and Network Layer Protocols TCP/IP are the standard transport and network protocols used today. They perform addressing (finding destination addresses), routing (finding the "best" route through the network), and segmenting (breaking large messages into smaller packets for transmission and reassembling them at the destination).

Transport Layer The transport layer (TCP) uses the source and destination port addresses to link the application layer software to the network. TCP is also responsible for segmenting—breaking large messages into smaller segments for transmission and reassembling them at the receiver's end. When connection-oriented routing is needed, TCP establishes a connection or session from the sender to the receiver. When connectionless routing is needed, TCP is replaced with UDP. Quality of service provides the ability to prioritize packets so that real-time voice packets are transmitted more quickly than simple email messages.

Addressing Computers can have three different addresses: application layer address, network layer address, and data link layer address. Data link layer addresses are usually part of the hardware, whereas network layer and application layer addresses are set by software. Network layer and application layer addresses for the Internet are assigned by Internet registrars. Addresses within one organization are usually assigned so that computers in the same LAN or subnet have similar addresses, usually with the same first 3 bytes. Subnet masks are used to indicate whether the first 2 or 3 bytes (or partial bytes) indicate the same subnet. Some networks assign network layer addresses in a configuration file on the client computer, whereas others use dynamic addressing, in which a DHCP server assigns addresses when a computer first joins the network.

Address Resolution Address resolution is the process of translating an application layer address into a network layer address or translating a network layer address into a data link layer address. On the Internet, network layer resolution is done by sending a special message to a DNS server (also called a *name server*) that asks for the IP address (e.g., 128.192.98.5) for a given Internet address (e.g., www.kelley.indiana.edu). If a DNS server does not have an entry for the requested Internet address, it will forward the request to another DNS server that it thinks is likely to have the address. That server will either respond or forward the request to another DNS server, and so on, until the address is found or it becomes clear that the address is unknown. Resolving data link layer addresses is done by sending an ARP request in a broadcast message to all computers on the same subnet that asks the computer with the requested IP address to respond with its data link layer address.

Routing Routing is the process of selecting the route or path through the network that a message will travel from the sending computer to the receiving computer. With centralized routing, one computer performs all the routing decisions. With static routing, the routing table is developed by the network manager and remains unchanged until the network manager updates it. With dynamic routing, the goal is to improve network performance by routing messages over the fastest possible route; an initial routing table is developed by the network manager but is continuously updated to reflect changing network conditions, such as message traffic. BGP, RIP, ICMP, EIGRP, and OSPF are examples of dynamic routing protocols.

TCP/IP Example In TCP/IP, it is important to remember that the TCP segments and IP packets are created by the sending computer and never change until the message reaches its final destination. The IP packet contains the original source and ultimate destination address for the packet. The sending computer also creates a data link layer frame (e.g., Ethernet) for each message. This frame contains the data link layer address of the current computer sending the packet and the data link layer address of the next computer in the route through the network. The data link layer frame is removed and replaced with a new frame at each computer at which the message stops as it works its way through the network. Thus, the source and destination data link layer addresses change at each step along the route, whereas the IP source and destination addresses never change.

KEY TERMS

Access Control List (ACL), 140
address resolution, 130
Address Resolution Protocol (ARP), 132
addressing, 147
application layer address, 124
authoritative name server, 131

autonomous systems, 135
auxiliary port, 139
Border Gateway Protocol (BGP), 135
border router, 136
broadcast message, 132
centralized routing, 134
Cisco IOS, 139
classless addressing, 127

Connectionless messaging, 123
connection-oriented messaging, 122
console port, 139
data link layer address, 124
designated router, 136
destination port address, 120

distance vector dynamic routing, 134
Domain Name Service (DNS), 130
dynamic addressing, 129
Dynamic Host Configuration Protocol (DHCP), 129
dynamic routing, 134

QUESTIONS

1. What does the transport layer do?
2. What does the network layer do?
3. What are the parts of TCP/IP and what do they do? Who is the primary user of TCP/IP?
4. Compare and contrast the three types of addresses used in a network.
5. How is TCP different from UDP?
6. How does TCP establish a session?
7. What is a subnet and why do networks need them?
8. What is a subnet mask?
9. How does dynamic addressing work?
10. What benefits and problems does dynamic addressing provide?
11. What is address resolution?
12. How does TCP/IP perform address resolution from URLs into network layer addresses?
13. How does TCP/IP perform address resolution from IP addresses into data link layer addresses?
14. What is routing?
15. How does decentralized routing differ from centralized routing?
16. What are the differences between connectionless and connection-oriented messaging?
17. What is a session?
18. What is QoS routing and why is it useful?
19. Compare and contrast unicast, broadcast, and multicast messages.
20. Explain how multicasting works.

21. Explain how the client computer in Figure 5-16 (128.192.98.xx) would obtain the data link layer address of its subnet router.
22. Why does HTTP use TCP and DNS use UDP?
23. How does static routing differ from dynamic routing? When would you use static routing? When would you use dynamic routing?
24. What type of routing does a TCP/IP client use? What type of routing does a TCP/IP gateway use? Explain.
25. What is the transmission efficiency of a 10-byte Web request sent using HTTP, TCP/IP, and Ethernet? Assume the HTTP packet has 100 bytes in addition to the 10-byte URL. Hint: Remember from Chapter 4 that *efficiency = user data/total transmission size*.
26. What is the transmission efficiency of a 1,000-byte file sent in response to a Web request HTTP, TCP/IP, and Ethernet? Assume the HTTP packet has 100 bytes in addition to the 1,000-byte file. Hint: Remember from Chapter 4 that *efficiency = user data/total transmission size*.
27. What is the transmission efficiency of a 5,000-byte file sent in response to a Web request HTTP, TCP/IP, and Ethernet? Assume the HTTP packet has 100 bytes in addition to the 5,000-byte file. Assume that the maximum packet size is 1,200 bytes. Hint: Remember from Chapter 4 that *efficiency = user data/total transmission size*.
28. Describe the anatomy of a router. How does a router differ from a computer?

EXERCISES

A. Would you recommend dynamic addressing for your organization? Why?

B. Look at your network layer software (either on a LAN or dial-in) and see what options are set—but don't change them! You can do this by using the RUN command to run winipcfg. How do these match the fundamental addressing and routing concepts discussed in this chapter?

C. Suppose a client computer (128.192.95.32) in Building B in Figure 5-15 requests a large Web page from the server in Building A (www1.anyorg.com). Assume that the client computer has just been turned on and does not know any addresses other than those in its configuration tables. Assume that all gateways and Web servers know all network layer and data link layer addresses.

    a. Explain what messages would be sent and how they would flow through the network to deliver the Web page request to the server.

    b. Explain what messages would be sent and how they would flow through the network as the Web server sent the requested page to the client.

    c. Describe, but do not explain in detail, what would happen if the Web page contained several graphic images (e.g., GIF [Graphics Interchange Format] or JPEG files).

D. Network Solutions provides a service to find who owns domain names and IP addresses. Go to www.networksolutions.com/whois. Find the owner of

    a. books.com

    b. TV.com

    c. 74.128.18.22

    d. 129.79.78.188

E. What is the subnet portion of the IP address and what is the subnet mask for the following:

    a. 12.1.0.0/16

    b. 12.1.0.0/24

    c. 12.1.0.0/20

    d. 12.1.0.0/28

F. You might be wondering how the first bytes for each address range were picked. Why do you think Class A's first byte is 1–126, Class B's byte is 128–191, and Class C's byte is 192–223?

MINICASES

I. Central University Suppose you are the network manager for Central University, a medium-sized university with 13,000 students. The university has 10 separate colleges (e.g., business, arts, journalism), 3 of which are relatively large (300 faculty and staff members, 2,000 students, and 3 buildings) and 7 of which are relatively small (200 faculty and staff, 1,000 students, and 1 building). In addition, there are another 2,000 staff members who work in various administration departments (e.g., library, maintenance, finance) spread over another 10 buildings. There are 4 residence halls that house a total of 2,000 students. Suppose the university has the 128.100.xxx.xxx address range on the Internet. How would you assign the IP addresses to the various subnets? How would you control the process by which IP addresses are assigned to individual computers? You will have to make some assumptions to answer both questions, so be sure to state your assumptions.

II. Connectus Connectus is a medium-sized Internet Service Provider (ISP) that provides Internet access and data communication services to several dozen companies across the United States and Canada. Connectus provides fixed data connections for clients'

offices in about 50 cities and an internal network that connects them. For reliability purposes, all centers are connected with at least two other centers so that if one connection goes down, the center can still communicate with the network. Predicting access volume is difficult because it depends on how many sales representatives are in which city. Connectus currently uses RIP as its routing protocol but is considering moving to OSPF. Should it stay with RIP or move to OSPF? Why?

III. Old Army Old Army is a large retail store chain operating about 1,000 stores across the United States and Canada. Each store is connected into the Old Army data network, which is used primarily for batch data transmissions. At the end of each day, each store transmits sales, inventory, and payroll information to the corporate head office in Atlanta. The network also supports email traffic, but its use is restricted to department managers and above. Because most traffic is sent to and from the Atlanta headquarters, the network is organized in a hub and spoke design. The Atlanta office is connected to 20 regional data centers, and each regional center is in turn connected to the 30–70 stores in its region. Network volumes have been growing, but at a fairly predictable rate, as the number of stores and overall sales volume increase. Old Army currently uses RIP as its routing protocol but is considering moving to OSPF. Should it stay with RIP or move to OSPF? Why?

IV. **General Stores** General Stores is a large retail store chain operating about 1,300 stores across the United States and Canada. Each store is connected into the corporate data network. At the end of each day, each store transmits sales and payroll information to the corporate head office in Seattle. Inventory data are transmitted in real time as products are sold to one of a dozen regional distribution centers across North America. The network is also used for credit card validations as customers check out and pay for their purchases. The network supports email traffic, but its

use is restricted to department managers and above. The network is designed much like the Internet: One connection from each store goes into a regional network that typically has a series of network connections to other parts of the network. Network volumes have been growing, but at a fairly predictable rate, as the number of stores and overall sales volume increase. General Stores is considering implementing a digital telephone service that will allow it to transmit internal telephone calls to other General Stores offices or stores through the data network. Telephone services outside of General Stores will continue to be done normally. General Stores currently uses RIP as its routing protocol but is considering moving to OSPF. Should it stay with RIP or move to OSPF? Why?

CASE STUDY

NEXT-DAY AIR SERVICE

See the Web site at www.wiley.com/college/fitzgerald.

HANDS-ON ACTIVITY 5A

Using TCP/IP

In this chapter, we've discussed the basic components of TCP/IP such as IP addresses, subnet masks, DNS requests, and ARP requests. In this activity, we'll show you how to explore these items on your computer. Although this activity is designed for Windows computers, most of these commands will also work on Apple computers.

This activity will use the command prompt, so start by clicking START, then RUN, and then type CMD and press enter. You should see the command window, which in Windows is a small window with a black background. Like all other windows, you can change its shape by grabbing the corner and stretching it.

IPCONFIG: Reading your computer's settings

In a focus box earlier in the chapter, we showed you how to find your computer's TRCP/IP settings using Windows. You can also do it by using the IPCONFIG command. In the command window, type IPCONFIG/ALL and press enter.

You should see a screen like that shown in Figure 5-19. The middle of the screen will show the TCP/IP information about your computer. You can see the IP address (192.168.1.102 in Figure 5-19); the subnet mask (255.255.255.0); the default gateway, which is the IP address of the router leading out of your subnet

(192.168.1.1); the DHCP server (192.168.1.1); and the available DNS servers (e.g., 63.240.76.4). Your computer will have similar, but different, information. As discussed in Technical Focus 5.3, your computer might be using "private" IP addresses the same as my computer shown in Figure 5-19, so your addresses may be identical to mine. We'll explain how network address translation (NAT) is done in Chapter 11.

Deliverables

1. Use the ipconfig/all command on your computer. What is the IP address, subnet mask, IP address of default gateway, and MAC of your computer?

2. Why does every computer on the Internet need to have these four numbers?

PING: Finding other computers

The PING sends a small packet to any computer on the Internet to show you how long it takes the packet to travel from your computer to the target computer and back again. You can ping a computer using its IP address or Web URL. Not all computers respond to ping commands, so not every computer you ping will answer.

Start by pinging your default gateway: just type PING followed by the IP address of your gateway. Figure 5-20

```
C:\Documents and Settings\Administrator>ipconfig/all

Windows IP Configuration

        Host Name . . . . . . . . . . . . . : ALAN
        Primary Dns Suffix . . . . . . . . .:
        Node Type . . . . . . . . . . . . . : Unknown
        IP Routing Enabled . . . . . . . . .: No
        WINS Proxy Enabled . . . . . . . . .: No
        DNS Suffix Search List . . . . . . .: insightbb.com

Ethernet adapter Local Area Connection:

        Connection-specific DNS Suffix . . .: insightbb.com
        Description . . . . . . . . . . . . : Intel(R) PRO/1000 MT Network Connect
ion
        Physical Address . . . . . . . . . .: 00-0D-56-D8-8D-96
        Dhcp Enabled . . . . . . . . . . . .: Yes
        Autoconfiguration Enabled . . . . . : Yes
        IP Address . . . . . . . . . . . . .: 192.168.1.102
        Subnet Mask . . . . . . . . . . . . : 255.255.255.0
        Default Gateway . . . . . . . . . . : 192.168.1.1
        DHCP Server . . . . . . . . . . . . : 192.168.1.1
        DNS Servers . . . . . . . . . . . . : 63.240.76.4
                                              204.127.198.4
                                              63.240.76.135
        Lease Obtained . . . . . . . . . . .: Wednesday, February 20, 2008 8:09:37
 AM
        Lease Expires  . . . . . . . . . . .: Tuesday, February 26, 2008 8:09:37 A
M

C:\Documents and Settings\Administrator>
```

FIGURE 5-19 IPCONFIG command

shows that the PING command sends four packets to the target computer and then displays the maximum, minimum, and average transit times. In Figure 5-20, you can see that pinging my gateway is fast: less than 1 millisecond for the packet to travel from my computer to my router and back again.

Next, ping a well-known Web site in the United States to see the average times taken. Remember that not all Web sites will respond to the ping command. In Figure 5-20, you can see that it took an average of 52 milliseconds for a packet to go from my computer to Google and back again. Also note that www.google.com has an IP address of 216.239.37.99.

Now, ping a Web site outside the United States. In Figure 5-20, you can see that it took an average of 239 milliseconds for a packet to go from my computer to the City University of Hong Kong and back again. If you think about it, the Internet is amazingly fast.

Deliverables

1. Ping your own default gateway. How many packets were returned? How long did it take for your default gateway to respond?

2. Ping google.com. How many packets were returned? How long did it take for you default gateway to respond?

3. Ping National Australian University www.anu.edu.au. How many packets were returned? How long did it take for your default gateway to respond?

ARP: Displaying Physical Addresses

Remember that to send a message to other computers on the Internet, you must know the physical address (aka data link layer address) of the next computer to send the message to. Most computers on the Internet will be outside your subnet, so almost all messages your computer sends will be sent to your gateway (i.e., the router leaving your subnet). Remember that computers use ARP requests to find physical addresses and store them in their ARP tables. To find out what data link layer addresses your computer knows, you can use the ARP command.

At the command prompt, type ARP-A and press enter. This will display the contents of your ARP table. In Figure 5-21, you can see that the ARP table in my computer has only one entry, which means all the messages from my computer since I turned it on have only gone to this one computer—my router. You can also see the physical address of my router: 00-04-5a-0b-d1-40.

If you have another computer on your subnet, ping it and then take a look at your ARP table again. In Figure 5-21, you can see the ping of another computer on my subnet (192.168.1.152) and then see the ARP table with this new entry. When I pinged 192.168.1.152, my computer had to find its physical address, so it issued an ARP request, and 192.168.1.152 responded with an ARP response, which

```
C:\Documents and Settings\Administrator>ping 192.168.1.1

Pinging 192.168.1.1 with 32 bytes of data:

Reply from 192.168.1.1: bytes = 32 time < 1ms TTL = 64
Reply from 192.168.1.1: bytes = 32 time < 1ms TTL = 64
Reply from 192.168.1.1: bytes = 32 time < 1ms TTL = 64
Reply from 192.168.1.1: bytes = 32 time < 1ms TTL = 64

Ping statistics for 192.168.1.1:
  Packets: Sent = 4, Received = 4, Lost = 0 (0% loss),
Approximate round trip times in milli-seconds:
  Minimum = 0ms, Maximum = 0ms, Average = 0ms
```

```
C:\Documents and Settings\Administrator>ping www.google.com

Pinging www.1.google.com [216.239.37.99] with 32 bytes of data:

Reply from 216.239.37.99: bytes = 32 time = 53ms TTL = 235
Reply from 216.239.37.99: bytes = 32 time = 52ms TTL = 236
Reply from 216.239.37.99: bytes = 32 time = 52ms TTL = 236
Reply from 216.239.37.99: bytes = 32 time = 53ms TTL = 235

Ping statistics for 216.239.37.99:
  Packets: Sent = 4, Received = 4, Lost = 0 (0% loss),
Approximate round trip times in milli-seconds:
  Minimum = 52ms, Maximum = 53ms, Average = 52ms
```

```
C:\Documents and Settings\Administrator>ping www.cityu.edu.hk

Pinging amber.cityu.edu.hk [144.214.5.218] with 32 bytes of data:

Reply from 144.214.5.218: bytes = 32 time = 240ms TTL = 236
Reply from 144.214.5.218: bytes = 32 time = 239ms TTL = 236
Reply from 144.214.5.218: bytes = 32 time = 239ms TTL = 236
Reply from 144.214.5.218: bytes = 32 time = 240ms TTL = 236

Ping statistics for 144.214.5.218:
  Packets: Sent = 4, Received = 4, Lost = 0 (0% loss),
Approximate round trip times in milli-seconds:
  Minimum = 239ms, Maximum = 240ms, Average = 239ms
```

FIGURE 5-20 PING command

my computer added into the ARP table before sending the ping.

Deliverables

1. Type ARP-A at the command prompt. What are the entries in your ARP table?
2. Suppose that there are no entries in your ARP table. Is this a problem? Why or why not?

NSLOOKUP: Finding IP Addresses

Remember that to send a message to other computers on the Internet, you must know their IP addresses. Computers use DNS servers to find IP addresses. You can issue a DNS request by using the NSLOOKUP command.

Type NSLOOKUP and the URL of a computer on the Internet and press enter. In Figure 5-22, you'll see that www.cnn.com has several IP addresses and is also known as cnn.com

Deliverable

Find the IP address of google.com and of another Web site of your choice.

```
C:\Documents and Settings\Administrator>arp.-a.

Interface: 192.168.1.102 --- 0x10003
  Internet Address        Physical Address   Type
  192.168.1.1   00-04-5a-0b-d1-40            dynamic
```

```
C:\Documents and Settings\Administrator>ping 192.168.1.152

Pinging 192.168.1.152 with 32 bytes of data:

Reply from 192.168.1.152: bytes = 32 time < 1ms TTL = 64
Reply from 192.168.1.152: bytes = 32 time < 1ms TTL = 64
Reply from 192.168.1.152: bytes = 32 time < 1ms TTL = 64
Reply from 192.168.1.152: bytes = 32 time < 1ms TTL = 64

Ping statistics for 192.168.1.152:
    Packets: Sent = 4, Received = 4, Lost = 0 (0% loss),
Approximate round trip times in milli-seconds:
    Minimum = 0ms, Maximum = 0ms, Average = 0ms
```

```
C:\Documents and Settings\Administrator>arp -a

Interface: 192.168.1.102 --- 0x10003
  Internet Address        Physical Address   Type
  192.168.1.1             00-04-5a-0b-d1-40  dynamic
  192.168.1.152           00-08-e1-00-21-f6  dynamic
```

FIGURE 5-21 ARP command

```
C:\Documents and Settings\Administrator>nslookup www.cnn.com
Server: ns1.insightbb.com
Address: 63.240.76.135

Non-authoritative answer:
Name: cnn.com
Addresses: 64.236.16.116, 64.236.24.12, 64.236.24.20, 64.236.24.28
         64.236.29.120, 64.236.16.20, 64.236.16.52, 64.236.16.84
Aliases: www.cnn.com
```

FIGURE 5-22 NSLOOKUP command

```
C:\Documents and Settings\administrator>ipconfig /displaydns

Windows IP Configuration

        mp-rtp-2-w2dm2.cisco.com
        ----------------------------------------
        Record Name . . . . . : mp-rtp-2-w2dm2.cisco.com
        Record Type . . . . . : 1
        Time To Live  . . . . : 82349
        Data Length . . . . . : 4
        Section . . . . . . . : Answer
        A (Host) Record . . . : 64.102.242.44


        Record Name . . . . . : ns1.cisco.com
        Record Type . . . . . : 1
        Time To Live  . . . . : 82349
        Data Length . . . . . : 4
        Section . . . . . . . : Additional
        A (Host) Record . . . : 128.107.241.185


        Record Name . . . . . : ns2.cisco.com
        Record Type . . . . . : 1
        Time To Live  . . . . : 82349
        Data Length . . . . . : 4
        Section . . . . . . . : Additional
        A (Host) Record . . . : 64.102.255.44


        1.0.0.127.in-addr.arpa
        ----------------------------------------
        Record Name . . . . . : 1.0.0.127.in-addr.arpa.
        Record Type . . . . . : 12
        Time To Live  . . . . : 0
        Data Length . . . . . : 4
        Section . . . . . . . : Answer
        PTR Record  . . . . . : localhost


        www.austria.ipv6tf.org
        ----------------------------------------
        Record Name . . . . . : www.austria.ipv6tf.org
        Record Type . . . . . : 1
        Time To Live  . . . . : 85235
        Data Length . . . . . : 4
        Section . . . . . . . : Answer
        A (Host) Record . . . : 80.120.160.184


        Record Name . . . . . : ns1.v6.telekom.at
        Record Type . . . . . : 1
        Time To Live  . . . . : 85235
        Data Length . . . . . : 4
        Section . . . . . . . : Additional
        A (Host) Record . . . : 80.120.160.188


        Record Name . . . . . : ns1.v6.telekom.at
        Record Type . . . . . : 28
        Time To Live  . . . . : 85235
        Data Length . . . . . : 16
        Section . . . . . . . : Additional
        AAAA Record . . . . . : 2001:890:600:d1::100
```

FIGURE 5-23   DNS cache

DNS Cache

The IPCONFIG/DISPLAYDNS command can be used to show the contents of the DNS cache. You can experiment with this by displaying the cache, visiting a new Web site with your browser, and then displaying the cache again. Figure 5-23 shows part of the cache on my computer after visiting a number of sites. The DNS cache contains information about all the Web sites I've visited, either directly or indirectly (by having a Web page on one server pull a graphics file off of a different server).

For example, the second entry in this figure is ns1 .cisco.com, which has an IP address of 128.107.241.185 (a 4-byte long address). The record type is one, which means this is a "host"—that is, a computer on the Internet using IPv4. Because the DNS information might change, all entries have a maximum time to live set by the DNS that provides the information (usually 24 hours); the time to live value is the time in seconds that this entry will remain in the cache until it is removed.

The very last entry in this figure is for ns1.v6 .telekom.at. The record type of 28 means that this is a host that uses IPv6, which you can see from the 16-byte long address in the record (2001:890:600:d1: :100).

Deliverables

1. Display your DNS cache using the command ipconfig /displaydns.

2. How many entries are there in your cache?

3. Open your browser and visit www.ietf.org. Once the page loads, display your DNS cache again. Copy the DNS entry for this Web site.

TRACERT: Finding Routes through the Internet

The TRACERT command will show you the IP addresses of computers in the route from your computer to another computer on the Internet. Many networks have disabled TRACERT for security reasons, so it doesn't always work. Type TRACERT and the URL of a computer on the Internet and press enter. In Figure 5-24, you'll see the route from my computer, through the Insight network, through the AT&T network, through the Level 3 network, and then through the Google network until it reaches the server. TRACERT usually sends three packets, so beside each hop is the total time to reach that hop for each of the three packets. You'll see that it took just over 50 milliseconds for a packet to go from my computer to Google. You'll also see that the times aren't always "right," in that the first packet took 50 milliseconds to reach the bbr1 Washington Level 3 router (step 9) but only 40 milliseconds to reach the next hop to the car2 Washington Level 3 router (step 10). The time to each hop is measured separately, each with a different packet, so sometimes a packet is delayed longer on one hop or another.

Deliverables

1. Type tracert google.com in your comand window.

2. How many computers/hops did it take the packet to reach Google?

3. What was the shortest hop (in terms of time)? Why do you think this is the shortest hop?

```
C:\Documents and Settings\Administrator>tracert www.google.com

Tracing route to www.1.google.com [216.239.37.104]
over a maximum of 30 hops:
  1    1 ms    1 ms    1 ms  192.168.1.1
  2    7 ms   10 ms    8 ms  12-220-5-129.client.insightBB.com [12.220.5.129]
  3   11 ms   12 ms   11 ms  12-220-1-78.client.insightBB.com [12.220.1.78]
  4   17 ms   16 ms   16 ms  12-220-0-26.client.insightBB.com [12.220.0.26]
  5   19 ms   18 ms   18 ms  tbr1-p011 901.cgcil.ip.att.net [12.123.4.226]
  6   18 ms   16 ms   16 ms  ggr2-p310.cgcil.ip.att.net [12.123.6.65]
  7   19 ms   18 ms   18 ms  so-9-1.car4.Chicago1.Level3.net [4.68.127.165]
  8   19 ms   18 ms   19 ms  ae-2-52.bbr2.Chicago1.Level3.net [4.68.101.33]
  9   50 ms   39 ms   39 ms  ae-2-0.bbr1.Washington1.Level3.net [4.68.128.201]
 10   40 ms   40 ms   39 ms  ae-12-53.car2.Washington1.Level3.net [4.68.121.83]
 11   53 ms   78 ms   56 ms  unknown.Level3.net [166.90.148.174]
 12   54 ms   52 ms   51 ms  72.14.232.106
 13   55 ms   54 ms   53 ms  216.239.48.96
 14   55 ms   55 ms   54 ms  216.239.48.110
 15   52 ms   51 ms   52 ms  216.239.37.104
Trace complete.
```

FIGURE 5-24 TRACERT command

HANDS-ON ACTIVITY 5B

Exploring DNS Request and DNS Response

In this chapter, we talked about address resolution. This activity will help you see how your computer sends a DNS request for a Web site you never visited, before it can create a HTTP request packet to display the Web site on your browser. We will use Wireshark for this activity. Use of Wireshark was explained in Chapter 2.

1. Use ipconfig/all command to find the IP address of your computer and your DNS server.

2. So that we can explore the DNS request and response properly, the first step is to empty your DNS cache. Use ipconfig/flushdns command in the command prompt window to empty the DNS of your computer.

3. Open Wireshark and enter "ip.addr==your IP address" into the filter to only capture packets that either originate or are destined for your computer.

4. Start packet capture in Wireshark.

5. With your browser, visit www.ietf.org.

6. Stop packet capture after the Web page is loaded.

Deliverables

1. Locate the DNS query and response message for www.ietf.org. In Figure 5-25, they are packets 27 and 28. Are these packets sent over UDP or TCP?

2. What is the destination port for the DNS query message? What is the source port of the DNE response message?

3. To what IP address is the DNS query message sent? Compare this IP address to your local DNS server IP address. Are these two IP addresses the same?

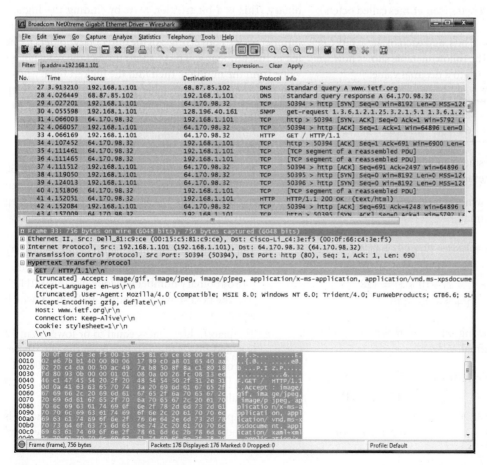

FIGURE 5-25 DNS capture

4. The www.ietf.org contains several images. Before retrieving each image, does your host issue a new DNS query? Why or why not?

5. Now locate the HTTP Get message. What is the source and destination IP address? Compare the source to your IP address. Are these the same?

6. Approximately how many HTTP GET request messages did your browser send? Why was there a need to send additional HTTP GET messages?

HANDS-ON ACTIVITY 5C

Converting Decimal Values into Binary, and Vice Versa.

Part A

Being able to convert decimal values to binary (and vice versa) is very important in networking because this is the basis for how subnetting is done. You may have done some of these exercises in high school and probably didn't know why it was important to be able to convert decimal values into binary, and vice versa. This hands-on activity will help you recall how this is done or will teach how to do it in case you never seen this before.

As you know, an IPv4 address consists of 32 bits that have been separated into 4 bytes (sometimes called octets), for example, 129.79.126.1. This is called the dotted decimal address. Each byte has 8 bits, and each of these bits can assume a value of 0 or 1. The following table shows how we convert each binary position to a decimal value:

Binary position	2^7	2^6	2^5	2^4	2^3	2^2	2^1	2^0
Decimal value	128	64	32	16	8	4	2	1

To practice the conversion from binary to decimal, let's do a couple problems together:

1. You have the following binary number: 10101010. Convert it into decimal.

$$10101010 = (1 * 128) + (0 * 64) + (1 * 32)$$
$$+ (0 * 16) + (1 * 8) + (0 * 4)$$
$$+ (1 * 2) + (0 * 1) = 128$$
$$+ 31 + 8 + 2 = 170$$

2. You have the following binary number: 01110111. Convert it into decimal.

$$01110111 = (0 \times 128) + (1 * 64) + (1 * 32)$$
$$+ (1 * 16) + (0 * 8) + (1 * 4)$$
$$+ (1 * 2) + (1 * 1)$$
$$= 64 + 32 + 16 + 4 + 2 + 1 = 119$$

It is important to notice what the range of possible decimal values for each byte is. The lower bound is given when each bit is 0 and the upper bound is when each bit is 1. So 00000000 will give us 0 and 11111111 will give us 255. This is the reason why IPv4 addresses cannot go above the value of 255.

Deliverable

Calculate the decimal values of the following binary numbers: 11011011, 01111111, 10000000, 11000000, 11001101.

Part B

Now let's practice the conversion of decimal value to binary. This is a bit trickier. Start by finding the highest binary position that is equal to or smaller than the decimal number we are converting. All the other placeholders to the left of this number will be 0. Then subtract the placeholder value from the number. Then find the highest binary position that is equal to or smaller than the remainder. Keep repeating these steps until the remainder is 0. Now, let's practice.

3. Convert 60 into a binary number.

   a. The placeholder that is equal to or lower than 60 is 32. Therefore the first two bits for 60 are 0 and the third one is 1 – 001_ _ _ _ _ . The next step is to subtract 32 from 60, which equals 60 − 32 = 28.

   b. The placeholder that is equal to or lower than 32 is 16, which is the fourth bite from the left. Therefore our binary number will look like this: 0011_ _ _ _. The next step is to subtract 16 from 28, which equals 28 − 16 = 12.

   c. The placeholder that is equal to or lower than 12 is 8, and this is the fifth bite from the left. Therefore our binary number will look like this: 00111_ _ _. The next step is to subtract 8 from 12, which equals 12 − 8 = 4.

   d. The placeholder that is equal to or lower than 4 is 4, and this is the sixth bite from the left. Therefore

our binary number will look like this: 001111_ _.
The next step is to subtract 4 from 4, which equals
$4 - 4 = 0$.

   e. Given that our remainder is 0, the additional bits
      are 0, and we find our answer: 60 in binary is
      00111100.

4. Convert 182 into a binary number.

$182 = 10110110$
(Because $182 - 128 = 54$, $54 - 32 = 22$, $22 - 16 = 6$,
and $6 - 4 = 2$)

Deliverable

Calculate the binary value for each of the following binary
numbers: 126, 128, 191, 192, 223.

HANDS-ON ACTIVITY 5D

Introduction to Subnetting

If you are not familiar with binary numbers, you may want
to do Hands-On Activity 5C before you do this activity.

A subnet mask is a 32-bit binary number that tells us to
which subnet a device belongs. A 1 indicates that that bit is
part of the subnet network address, and a 0 indicates that
that bit is part of the unique host address for the individual
computer. The subnet mask is a continuous stream of ones
followed by all zeros, so the subnet mask can assume only

certain values. For example, a subnet mask could never
have a value of 11111111.11111111.00000000.10000000.

The following table shows the subnet mask values in
both binary and decimal notation for classes A, B, and C.
For example, a subnet mask of 255.255.255.0 for a computer with an address of 192.168.1.101 tells us that the
computer is in subnet 192.168.1.0 and has a unique address
of 101 within that subnet.

Class	First Byte Range	Byte Allocation	Subnet Mask in Binary Notation	Subnet Mask in Decimal Notation
A	1–126	Network.Host.Host.Host	11111111.00000000.00000000.00000000	255.0.0.0
B	128–191	Network.Network.Host.Host	11111111.11111111.00000000.00000000	255.255.0.0
C	192–223	Network.Network.Network.Host	11111111.11111111.11111111.00000000	2555.255.255.0

Deliverable

Fill in the following table and find the admissible values for
a subnet mask.

Binary Representation of a Byte	Decimal Value
10000000	
11000000	
11100000	
11110000	
11111000	
11111100	
11111110	
11111111	

Suppose you were assigned the network 209.98.208.0,
which is a Class C address. The usual subnet mask for
a Class C address is 255.255.255.0, which provides one
subnet with 253 host computers (there are 255 possible

addresses, but the .255 address is reserved and cannot
be assigned to a computer because this is the broadcast
address for this subnet, and the .0 address is reserved for
the subnet itself). Suppose you need to create 10 subnets within this address space. This means that part of the
address usually used for host addresses must be used as
part of the subnet address. How many bits do you need to
use from the host space to create 10 subnets?

Solution: If we use 1 bit, we will be able to create 2 subnets (they will have the following binary representation: 11111111.11111111.11111111.00000000 and
111111111.11111111.11111111.10000000). If we use 2 bits,
we will be able to create 2^2 subnets, which is 4. Using
3 bits will give us 2^3 subnets, which is 8. Therefore we
need to use 4 bits ($2^4 = 16$), which will give us 16 subnets. This is more than we need, but if we use 3 bits, it
will not meet our needs. The subnet mask for this network will be 1111111.11111111.11111111.11110000, or
255.255.255.240.

This also means that we now only have 4 bits to use for the host address on each network. So this means the maximum number of host addresses on each subnet is $2^4 = 16$.

Deliverables

Now that you understand how to make decisions regarding subnet masks, work on the following problems:

1. Given a Class C network and a number of subnets required, complete the table to identify the number of bits to borrow from the host field to use for the subnet field and the maximum number of host addresses available per subnet.

Number of Subnets Required	Number of Bits to Borrow for the Subnet Field	Maximum Number of Hosts per Subnet	Subnet Mask in Binary and Decimal Representation
2			
5			
12			
24			
40			

2. Given a Class B network and a number of subnets required, complete the table to identify the number of bits to borrow from the host field for the subnet field and the maximum number of host addresses available per subnet.

Number of Subnets Required	Number of Bits to Borrow for the Subnet Field	Maximum Number of Hosts per Subnet	Subnet Mask in Binary and Decimal Representation
5			
8			
35			
200			
400			

3. Given a Class A network and a number of subnets required, complete the table to identify the number of bits to borrow from the host field for the subnet field and the maximum number of host addresses available per subnet.

Number of Subnets Required	Number of Bits to Borrow for the Subnet Field	Maximum Number of Hosts per Subnet	Subnet Mask in Binary and Decimal Representation
10			
20			
80			
400			
2000			

HANDS-ON ACTIVITY 5E

Subnetting Class C Addresses

To do this activity, you need to do Hands-On Activity 5D. First, we explain how to find the subnet address for each subnet, the range of host addresses, and the direct broadcast address. Then you will be asked to do a similar exercise by yourself.

Assume that you have been assigned the 192.168.1.0/24 network. You need to create 6 subnets.

a. How many bits do you need to borrow from the host field for the subnet field?
   We need to borrow 3 bits: 1 bit would give us 2 subnets, 2 would give us 4, and 3 would give us 8.

b. What is the maximum number of subnets that can be created with this number of bits?
   We can create $2^3 = 8$ subnets.

c. How many bits can be used to create the host space?
   Each byte has 8 bits—we are using 3 bits to define the subnets, and this leaves us with 5 bits for the host space.

d. What is the maximum number of host addresses available per subnet?
   $2^5 - 2 = 32 - 2 = 30$. We have 5 bits for the host space, and each bit can assume a value of 1 or 0 (2^5). However, two addresses on each subnet are reserved—the first one (all zeros) for the subnet address and last address (all ones) for the broadcast address.

e. What prefix would you use? What is the subnet mask, in binary and decimal format?
   Recall that the prefix indicates the number of bits used to identify the network. Given that this is a Class C address and we use 3 bytes plus 3 additional bits for subnets ($8 + 8 + 8 + 3 = 27$), our prefix will be /27. Recall that the subnet mask is a continuous stream of 1s—in our case, 27 of them. Therefore the subnet mask in binary is 11111111.11111111.11111111.11100000.
   We need to convert this binary number into a decimal to get the subnet mask. Hands-On Activity 5C might come in handy here. The subnet mask in decimal is 255.255.255.224.

f. What is the increment value?
   The increment value is the amount by which the subnet address increases from one subnet to the next and is given by the placeholder value of the last 1 in the subnet mask. Because the last byte in the subnet mask has three 1s, the third number 1 represents 32 (see Hands-On Activity 5C). So, the increment value is 32.

g. Complete the following table; define each of the subnets, the range of host addresses on the subnet, and the directed broadcast address on the subnet.

Subnet Number	Subnet Address (first address on the subnet)	Range of Host Addresses	Direct Broadcast Address (last address on the subnet)
0	192.168.1.0	192.168.1.1 - 192.168.1.30	192.168.1.31
1	192.168.1.32	192.168.1.33 - 192.168.1.62	192.168.1.63
2	192.168.1.64	192.168.1.65- 192.168.1.94	192.168.1.95
3	192.168.1.96	192.168.1.97 - 192.168.1.126	192.168.1.127
4	192.168.1.128	192.168.1.129 - 192.168.1.158	192.168.1.159
5	192.168.1.160	192.168.1.161 - 192.168.1.190	192.168.1.191
6	192.168.1.192	192.168.1.193 - 192.168.1.222	192.168.1.223
7	192.168.1.224	192.168.1.225 - 192.168.1.254	192.168.1.255

Explanation of this table:

In part b we indicated that there were eight subnets. The best way to fill out the table is to identify the subnet addresses for all subnets. The very first subnet's IP address is when all the bits in the last byte are 0, giving us the following decimal value: 192.168.1.0. Recall from part f that the incremental value is 32, which means that the second subnet's IP address will have the third placeholder equal to 1, giving us the following address: 192.168.1.32. To find the third subnet's IP address, we need to multiply the increment value (32) by 2, resulting in 192.168.1.64. You would continue until the eighth subnet, in which all the first 3 bits in the last byte equal 1, giving us 192.168.1.224.

The direct broadcast address's value is one less than the next subnet's IP address. Also, this address will have all the host bits in the last byte equal to 1. For simplicity, I will only convert the last byte of several broadcast addresses to binary to illustrate this:

Broadcast Address	Last Byte Converted to Binary (network bits | host bits)
192.168.1.31	0 0 0 | 1 1 1 1 1
192.168.1.63	0 0 1 | 1 1 1 1 1
192.168.1.95	0 1 0 | 1 1 1 1 1
192.168.1.127	0 1 1 | 1 1 1 1 1

The addresses between the subnet address and the broadcast address can be assigned to any hosts on the network.

Deliverables

Assume that you have been assigned 192.168.111.129/28.

1. How many bits are borrowed to create the subnet field? _____

2. What is the maximum number of subnets that can be created with this number of bits? _____

3. How many bits can be used to create the host space? _____

4. What is the maximum number of host addresses available per subnet? _____

5. What is the subnet mask, in binary and decimal format? _____

6. Complete the following table and calculate the subnet that this address is on, and define all the other subnets (the range of host addresses on the subnet and the directed broadcast address on the subnet).

Subnet Number	Subnet Address	Range of Host Addresses	Direct Broadcast Address
0			
1			
2			
3			
4			
5			
6			
7			
...			
Last subnet number			

7. Answer the following:

   a. What subnet is 192.168.111.129 on?

   b. A junior network administrator is trying to assign 192.168.111.127 as a static IP address for a computer on the network but is getting an error message. Why?

   c. Can 192.168.111.39 be assigned as an IP address?

HANDS-ON ACTIVITY 5F

IPv6 Addresses

The IPv4 address space provides approximately 4.3 billion addresses, but only 3.7 billion addresses are assignable because the IPv4 addressing system separates the addresses into classes and reserves some addresses for multicasting, testing, and other specific uses. The IPv4 address space has almost been exhausted, which is why it is vital to understand the IPv6 protocol.

The 32-bit IPv4 address is a series of four 8-bit fields separated by dots, such as 129.79.126.1. However, larger 128-bit IPv6 addresses need a different representation because of their size. IPv6 addresses use colons to separate entries in a series of 16-bit hexadecimal.

A sample IPv6 address is **2031:0000:130F:0000:0000:09 C0:876A:130B**. IPv6 does not require explicit address string notation. Because the IPv6 addresses are much longer than their IPv4 counterparts, several rules to shorten the addresses were developed:

- Leading zeros in a field are optional. For example, the field 09C0 equals 9C0, and the field 0000 equals 0. So 2031:0000:130F:0000:0000:09C0:876A :130B can be written as 2031:0:130F:0:0:9C0:876A: 130B.

- Successive fields of zeros can be represented as two colons "::". However, this shorthand method can only be used once in an address, for example, 2031:0:130F:0000:0000:9C0:876A:130B can be written as 2031:0:130F::9C0:876A:130B.

- An unspecified address is written as "::" because it contains only zeros.

Deliverable

Use the preceding guidelines to compress the following IPv6 addresses into the shortest forms possible.

Preferred Representation	Compressed Representation
A0B0:10F0:A110:1001:5000:0000:0000:0001	
0000:0000:0000:0000:0000:0000:0000:0001	
2001:0000:0000:1234:0000:0000:0000:45FF	
3ffe:0000:0010:0000:1010:2a2a:0000:1001	
3FFE:0B00:0C18:0001:0000:1234:AB34:0002	
FEC0:0000:0000:1000:1000:0000:0000:0009	
FF80:0000:0000:0000:0250:FFFF:FFFF:FFFF	

HANDS-ON ACTIVITY 5G

IPv4 Subnetting Game

It's game time! Cisco has created a great game for you to practice subnetting:

"Does Subnetting frighten you? Imagine being a system administrator in top secret Area 51! This game helps you master your subnetting skills to use on the job or to prepare for your Cisco CCENT or CCNA Certification."

Step 1

Before you can play the game you will have to create an account at https://learningnetwork.cisco.com/docs/DOC-1802

a. Click "Play Now" button under "Subnet Game" Image

b. Click "Register Now" button in the "New User" area

c. Fill out the required fields and click "Submit"

d. You will be sent an email to your email account to verify the registration

e. Use your newly created Cisco account to start playing Cisco's "Subnet Game"

Step 2

Familiarize yourself with the game by reading the Instructions

Step 3

To solve each puzzle of the Subnet Game, you need to complete two sections of the screen by

1. Setting the correct subnet mask

2. Setting the addresses

1. The subnet mask must fit the requirements given in the work order (on the right section of the screen). For example, if the work order states a need to have four subnets, the subnet mask must be set to 255.255.255.192 and then the "Set" button must be clicked.

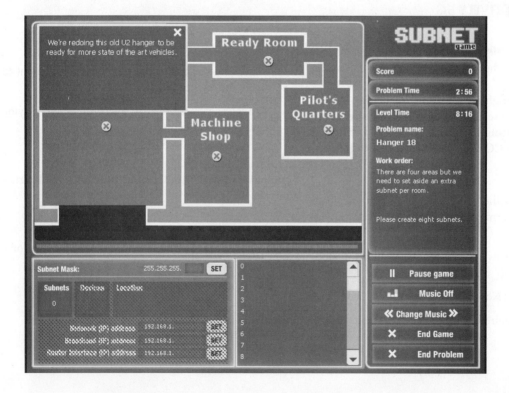

2. Enter the Network; Broadcast; and Router Interface Addresses and click the adjacent "Set" button for each. When all three have been entered, a green check mark is placed in that subnet.

If you have not entered the correct subnet mask, you may still see all green arrows, but you will be unable to proceed. Until you have entered the correct subnet mask, the problem is not complete.

Deliverables

1. Once you successfully complete a scenario, take a screenshot showing that you have successfully completed it and paste it into a Word document.

2. **Solve all five scenarios**, and when you are done, take a screenshot of the game screen showing the number of problems you have solved. Good luck, and have fun!

PART THREE **NETWORK TECHNOLOGIES**

CHAPTER 6

NETWORK DESIGN

The chapters in the first section of the book provided a fundamental understanding of how networks work using the five-layer model. This chapter starts the next section of the book, which focuses on how we design networks. We usually design networks in seven network architecture components: Local Area Networks (LANs), Building Backbone Networks, Campus Backbones that connect buildings, Wide Area Networks (WANs) that connect campuses, Internet access, e-commerce edge, and Data Centers. Network design is an interative process in which the designer examines users' needs, develops an initial set of technology designs, assesses their cost, and then revisits the needs analysis until the final network design emerges.

OBJECTIVES

- Understand the seven network architecture components
- Describe the overall process of designing and implementing a network
- Describe techniques for developing a logical network design
- Describe techniques for developing a physical network design
- Understand network design principles

OUTLINE

6.1 INTRODUCTION

All but the smallest organizations have networks, which means that most network design projects are the design of upgrades or extensions to existing networks, rather than the construction of entirely new networks. Even the network for an entirely new building is likely to be integrated with the organization's existing backbone network or Wide Area Network (WAN), so even new projects can be seen as extensions of existing networks. Nonetheless, network design is very challenging.

6.1.1 Network Architecture Components

Network designers usually think about networks as seven distinct network architecture components when they design networks. Figure 6-1 shows a typical network for a large

FIGURE 6-1

Network architecture
components

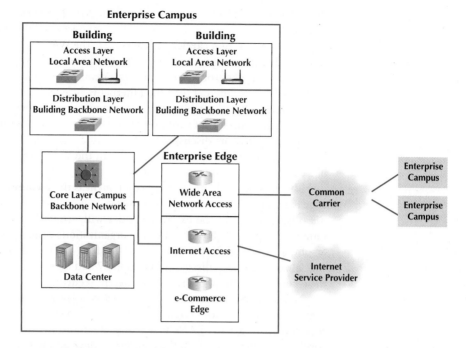

enterprise. This organization has three **enterprise campuses** in different cities that are connected by a WAN provided by a common carrier such as AT&T. Each campus has several buildings that are connected by a backbone network.

The first network architecture component is the **Local Area Network (LAN)**, which enables users to access the network. Some vendors call this component the **access layer** because it provides access to the network. Chapter 7 describes LANs, both wired and wireless, because when we build LANs today, we usually provide both wired and wireless access. The technologies we use in the LAN are probably familiar to you because you have used them, and perhaps you have even installed them in your home or apartment: They are network hubs, switches, and wireless access points.

The second network architecture component is the **building backbone network**, which some vendors call the **distribution layer**, because it distributes network traffic to and from the LANs. The building backbone typically uses the same basic technology that we use in the LAN (a network switch), but usually we buy faster switches because the building backbone carries more network traffic than a LAN. Chapter 8 describes building backbones.

The third network architecture component is the **campus backbone** (sometimes called the **core layer**), which connects all the buildings on one campus. The campus backbone is usually faster than the backbones we use inside buildings because it typically carries more traffic than they do. We use routers or layer 3 switches that do routing when we design the campus backbone. Chapter 8 also describes campus backbones.

The fourth network architecture component is the **data center**, which contains the organization's servers (e.g., database servers, email servers). The data center is essentially a LAN, but because so much traffic goes to and from the data center, it is typically designed and managed very differently than the LANs intended for user access. The data center is usually located centrally on the enterprise campus, with a very, very high speed connection into the campus backbone. There is usually one primary data center for the organization, typically found on its main headquarters campus. It is common for large organizations to have several data centers spread around the world. Many enterprise campuses have their own smaller data centers that store data just for that campus. We briefly discuss data center LAN design in Chapter 7.

The last three components of the network architecture make up the **enterprise edge**, the parts of the network that are at the edge of an enterprise campus and connect that campus to the rest of the world. One of these is the **Wide Area Network** (**WAN**), which is discussed in Chapter 9. A WAN is a private network that connects its different campus locations, usually leased from a **common carrier** such as AT&T. The WAN is for the private use of the organization and only carries its network traffic from one campus to another, unlike the Internet, which carries traffic from many different organizations. The circuits used in the WAN are traditionally very different than the Ethernet we use in the LAN, but this is changing.

Another network architecture component is the **Internet access** component, which enables the organization to connect to the Internet. The Internet and the technologies we use to connect to it are discussed in Chapter 10. Large organizations use the same technologies to connect to the Internet as they use in the WAN. Small companies and individuals like us typically use cable modem or DSL.

The final network architecture component is the **e-commerce edge**. The e-commerce edge is a special LAN with a group of severs that enables electronic data exchange between the organization and the external entities with which it does business (such as its customers or suppliers). For example, the organization's primary Web server is located in the e-commerce edge. Like the data center, the design of the LAN for the e-commerce edge is specialized; we briefly discuss it in Chapter 7 and again in Chapter 11 on security, because the e-commerce edge often requires different security.

Network design usually begins at the access layer, not the core layer. The needs of the users drive the network design (as well as the applications in the data center). This is the reason that we discuss LANs first (Chapter 7) and then move into the distribution and core layers (Chapter 8), with the enterprise edge coming last (WANs in Chapter 9 and the Internet in Chapter 10).

Most organizations put the last five components in the same building. The switches and routers that compose the campus backbone, the data center, and the enterprise edge are usually placed in one central building on campus so that data move very quickly between the enterprise edge, the campus backbone, and the data center.

6.1.2 The Traditional Network Design Process

The **traditional network design process** follows a very structured systems analysis and design process similar to that used to build application systems. First, the network analyst meets with users to identify user needs and the application systems planned for the network. Second, the analyst develops a precise estimate of the amount of data that each user will send and receive and uses this to estimate the total amount of traffic on each part of the network. Third, the circuits needed to support this traffic plus a modest increase in traffic are designed and cost estimates are obtained from vendors. Finally, 1 or 2 years later, the network is built and implemented.

This traditional process, although expensive and time consuming, works well for static or slowly evolving networks. Unfortunately, networking today is significantly different from what it was when the traditional process was developed. Three forces are making the traditional design process less appropriate for many of today's networks.

First, the underlying technology of the client and server computers, networking devices, and the circuits themselves is changing very rapidly. In the early 1990s, mainframes dominated networks, the typical client computer was an 8-MHz 386 with 1 megabyte (MB) of random access memory (RAM) and 40 MB of hard disk space, and a typical circuit was a 9,600-bps mainframe connection or a 1-Mbps LAN. Today, client computers and servers are significantly more powerful, and circuit speeds of 1 Gbps (one billion bits per second) are common. We now have more processing capability and network capacity than ever before; both are no longer scarce commodities that we need to manage carefully.

Second, the growth in network traffic is immense. The challenge is not in estimating today's user demand but in estimating its rate of growth. In the early 1990s, email and the Web were novelties primarily used by university professors and scientists. In the past, network demand essentially was driven by predictable business systems such as order processing. Today, much network demand is driven by less predictable user behavior, such as email and the Web. Many experts expect the rapid increase in network demand to continue, especially as video, voice, and multimedia applications become commonplace on networks. At a 10% growth rate, user demand on a given network will increase by one-third in 3 years. At 20%, it will increase by about 75% in 3 years. At 30%, it will double in less than 3 years. A minor mistake in estimating the growth rate can lead to major problems. With such rapid growth, it is no longer possible to accurately predict network needs for most networks. In the past, it was not uncommon for networks to be designed to last for 5–10 years. Today, most network designers use a 3- to 5-year planning horizon.

Finally, the balance of costs has changed dramatically over the years. In the early 1990s, the most expensive item in any network was the hardware (circuits, devices, and servers). Today, the most expensive part of the network is the staff members who design, operate, and maintain it. As the costs have shifted, the emphasis in network design is no longer on minimizing hardware cost (although it is important); the emphasis today is on designing networks to reduce the staff time needed to operate them.

The traditional process minimizes the equipment cost by tailoring the equipment to a careful assessment of needs but often results in a mishmash of different devices with different capabilities. Two resulting problems are that staff members need to learn to operate and maintain many different devices and that it often takes longer to perform network management activities because each device may use slightly different software.

Today, the cost of staff time is far more expensive than the cost of equipment. Thus, the traditional process can lead to a false economy—save money now in equipment costs but pay much more over the long term in staff costs.

MANAGEMENT	6-1 Average Life-Spans
FOCUS	

A recent survey of network managers found that most expect their network hardware to last 3–5 years—not because the equipment wears out, but because rapid changes in capabilities make otherwise good equipment obsolete.

Life expectancy for selected network equipment:

Rack mounted switch	4.5 years
Chassis switch	4.5 years
Backbone router	5 years
Branch office router	4 years

As Joel Snyder, a senior partner at OpusOne (a network consulting firm), puts it: "You might go buy a firewall for a 1.5 Mbps circuit at a remote office and then 2 weeks later have your cable provider offer you 50 Mbps."

Wi-Fi access point	3 years
Desktop PC	3.5 years
Laptop PC	2.5 years
Mainframe	8.5 years

Adapted from: "When to Upgrade," Network World, November 28, 2005, pp. 49–50.

6.1.3 The Building-Block Network Design Process

Some organizations still use the traditional process of network design, particularly for those applications for which hardware or network circuits are unusually expensive (e.g., WANs that cover long distances through many different countries). However, many other organizations now use a simpler approach to network design that we call the **building-block process**. The key concept in the building-block process is that networks that use a few standard components throughout the network are cheaper in the long run than networks that use a variety of different components on different parts of the network.

Rather than attempting to accurately predict user traffic on the network and build networks to meet those demands, the building-block process instead starts with a few standard components and uses them over and over again, even if they provide more capacity than is needed. The goal is simplicity of design. This strategy is sometimes called "narrow and deep" because a very narrow range of technologies and devices is used over and over again (very deeply throughout the organization). The results are a simpler design process and a more easily managed network built with a smaller range of components.

In this chapter, we focus on the building-block process to network design. The basic design process involves three steps that are performed repeatedly: needs analysis, technology design, and cost assessment (Figure 6-2). This process begins with **needs analysis**, during which the designer attempts to understand the fundamental current and future network needs of the various users, departments, and applications. This is likely to be an educated guess at best. Users' access needs and the needs of applications drive the network design process from the top into the center of the network. These needs are classified as typical or high volume. Specific technology needs are identified (e.g., the ability to dial in with current modem technologies).

The next step, **technology design**, examines the available technologies and assesses which options will meet users' needs. The designer makes some estimates about the network needs of each category of user and circuit in terms of current technology (e.g., 1 Gbps Ethernet) and matches needs to technologies. Because the basic network design is general, it can easily be changed as needs and technologies change. The difficulty, of course, lies in predicting user demand so one can define the technologies needed. Most organizations solve this by building more capacity than they expect to need and by designing networks that can easily grow and then closely monitoring growth so they expand the network ahead of the growth pattern.

In the third step, **cost assessment**, the relative costs of the technologies are considered. The process then cycles back to the needs analysis, which is refined using the technology and cost information to produce a new assessment of users' needs. This in turn triggers changes in the technology design and cost assessment, and so on. By cycling through these three processes, the final network design is established (Figure 6-3).

FIGURE 6-2

Network design

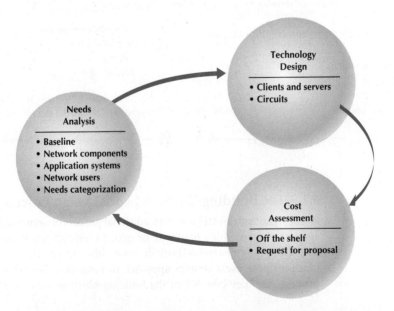

FIGURE 6-3

The cyclical nature of
network design

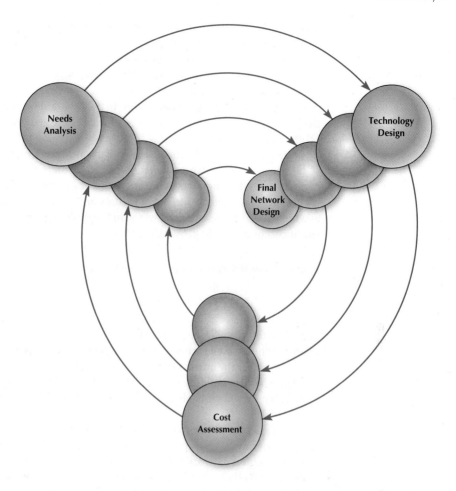

6.2 NEEDS ANALYSIS

The goal of needs analysis is to understand why the network is being built and what users
and applications it will support. In many cases, the network is being designed to improve
poor performance or enable new applications to be used. In other cases, the network is
upgraded to replace unreliable or aging equipment or to standardize equipment so that only
one type of equipment, one protocol (e.g., TCP/IP, Ethernet), or one vendor's equipment is
used everywhere in the network.

Often, the goals in network design are slightly different between LANs and backbones
(BNs) on the one hand and WANs on the other. In the LAN and BN environments, the organization owns and operates the equipment and the circuits. Once they are paid for, there are
no additional charges for usage. However, if major changes must be made, the organization
will need to spend additional funds. In this case, most network designers tend to err on the
side of building too big a network—that is, building more capacity than they expect to need.

In contrast, in most WANs, the organization leases circuits from a common carrier
and pays for them on a monthly or per-use basis. Understanding capacity becomes more
important in this situation because additional capacity comes at a noticeable cost. In this
case, most network designers tend to err on the side of building too small a network, because
they can lease additional capacity if they need it—but it is much more difficult to cancel a
long-term contract for capacity they are not using.

Much of the needs analysis may already have been done because most network design
projects today are network upgrades rather than the design of entirely new networks.
In this case, there is already a fairly good understanding of the existing traffic in the

network and, most important, of the rate of growth of network traffic. It is important to gain an understanding of the current operations (application systems and messages). This step provides a **baseline** against which future design requirements can be gauged. It should provide a clear picture of the present sequence of operations, processing times, work volumes, the current communication network (if one exists), existing costs, and user/management needs. Whether the network is a new network or a network upgrade, the primary objective of this stage is to define (1) the **geographic scope** of the network and (2) the users and applications that will use it.

The goal of the needs analysis step is to produce a **logical network design**, which is a statement of the network elements needed to meet the needs of the organization. The logical design does not specify technologies or products to be used (although any specific requirements are noted). Instead, it focuses on the fundamental functionality needed, such as a high-speed access network, which in the technology design stage will be translated into specific technologies (e.g., switched 100Base-T).

6.2.1 Network Architecture Component

The first step in needs analysis is to break the network into the seven network architecture components in Figure 6-1: LANs, building backbones, campus backbones, WANs, Internet access, e-commerce edge, and data centers. Not all layers are present in all networks. Small networks, for example, may not have a core backbone because there is only one building. Likewise, the Data Center is typically designed and managed separately.

Sometimes, the current network infrastructure imposes constraints. For example, if we are adding a new building to an existing office complex that used 1 Gbps Ethernet in the LANs, then we will probably choose to use the same in the new building. All such constraints are noted.

It is easiest to start with the highest level, so most designers begin by drawing a network diagram for any WANs with enterprise campuses that must be connected. A diagram that shows the logical network going between the locations is sufficient. Details such as the type of circuit and other considerations will be added later. Next, the individual enterprise campus diagrams are drawn, usually in a series of separate diagrams, but for a simple network, one diagram may be sufficient.

At this point, the designers gather general information and characteristics of the environment in which the network must operate. For example, they determine whether there are any legal requirements, such as local, state/provincial, federal, or international laws, regulations, or building codes, that might affect the network.

MANAGEMENT **6-2 A New Hospital Network**

FOCUS

Kingston Hospital is part of the National Health Service in the United Kingdom. The hospital is one of the largest in London, with more than 3,500 employees. As the health care industry moves into a digital environment, the network becomes critical. Mobile computing on tablets at the patient bedside enables doctors, nurses, and other staff to provide care without relying on paper notes, which can be easily lost or misunderstood because of poor handwriting.

The access layer is primarily wireless LAN, with 650 wireless access points spread throughout the hospital. The hospital provides more than 200 tablets to staff to review patient records, update observations, and order tests and medications. Pharmacists use laptops and workstations on wheels to manage and deliver prescriptions.

These access points and wired LANs are connected into building backbones that run at 1 Gbps. These in turn are connected into two large campus backbone switches that provide 10 Gbps.

Adapted from: "Laying Foundations for Digital Hospital Vision," Cisco Systems Inc., 2013.

6.2.2 Application Systems

Next, the designers must review the list of applications that will use the network and identify the location of each. This information should be added to the emerging network documentation. This process is called *baselining*. Next, those applications that are expected to use the network in the future are added.

In many cases, the applications will be relatively well defined. Specific internal applications (e.g., payroll) and external applications (e.g., Web servers) may already be part of the "old" network. However, it is important to review the organization's long-range and short-range plans concerning changes in company goals, strategic plans, development plans for new products or services, projections of sales, research and development projects, major capital expenditures, possible changes in product mix, new offices that must be served by the communications network, security issues, and future commitments to technology. For example, a major expansion in the number of offices or a major electronic commerce initiative will have a significant impact on network requirements.

It also is helpful to identify the hardware and software requirements of each application that will use the network and, if possible, the protocol each application uses (e.g., HTTP over TCP/IP, Windows file access). This knowledge helps now and will be particularly useful later when designers develop technological solutions.

6.2.3 Network Users

In the past, application systems accounted for the majority of network traffic. Today, much network traffic is produced by the discretionary use of the Internet. Applications such as email and the Web are generating significant traffic, so the network manager is no longer in total control of the network traffic generated on his or her networks. This is likely to continue in the future as network-hungry applications such as desktop videoconferencing become more common. Therefore, in addition to understanding the applications, you must also assess the number and type of users that will generate and receive network traffic and identify their location on the emerging network diagram. We usually assume that most users will want both wired and wireless access to the network, although there are exceptions. Hotels may only provide wireless access for guests, and some offices may only provide wired access.

6.2.4 Categorizing Network Needs

At this point, the network has been designed in terms of geographic scope, application systems, and users. The next step is to assess the relative amount of traffic generated in each part of the network. With the traditional design approach, this involves considerable detailed analysis. With the building-block approach, the goal is to provide some rough assessment of the relative magnitude of network needs. Each application system is assessed in general terms to determine the amount of network traffic it can be expected to generate today and in the future, compared with other applications. Likewise, each user is categorized as either a typical user or a high-traffic user. These assessments will be refined in the next stage of the design process.

This assessment can be problematic, but the goal is some relative understanding of the network needs. Some simple rules of thumb can help. For example, applications that require large amounts of multimedia data or those that load executables over the network are likely to be high-traffic applications. Applications that are time sensitive or need constant updates (e.g., financial information systems, order processing) are likely to be high-traffic applications.

Once the network requirements have been identified, they also should be organized into **mandatory requirements**, **desirable requirements**, and **wish-list requirements**. This information enables the development of a minimum level of mandatory requirements and a negotiable list of desirable requirements that are dependent on cost and availability. For example, desktop videoconferencing may be a wish-list item, but it will be omitted if it increases the cost of the network beyond what is desired.

At this point, the local facility network diagrams are prepared. For a really large network, there may be several levels. The choice is up to the designer, provided the diagrams and supporting text clearly explain the network's needs.

6.2.5 Deliverables

The key deliverable for the needs assessments stage is a set of logical network diagrams, showing the applications, circuits, clients, and servers in the proposed network, each categorized as either typical or high traffic. The logical diagram is the conceptual plan for the network and does not consider the specific physical elements (e.g., routers, switches, circuits) that will be used to implement the network.

Figure 6-4 shows the results of a needs assessment for a building that includes the access layer (LANs), the distribution layer (building backbone), and the core layer (campus backbone). This figure shows the distribution and access components in the building with the series of six access LANs connected by one building backbone, which is in turn connected to a campus core backbone. One of the six LANs is highlighted as a high-traffic LAN, whereas the others are typical. We normally would assume that the LANs need both wired and wireless access unless the requirements stated differently. Three mandatory applications are identified that will be used by all network users: email, Web, and file sharing. One wish-list requirement (desktop videoconferencing) is also identified for a portion of the network.

FIGURE 6-4

Sample needs assessment Logical network design for a single building. LAN = Local area network

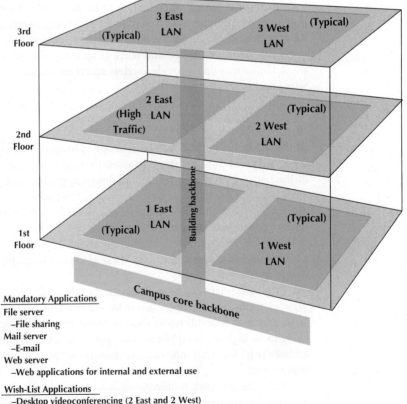

Mandatory Applications
File server
  –File sharing
Mail server
  –E-mail
Web server
  –Web applications for internal and external use

Wish-List Applications
  –Desktop videoconferencing (2 East and 2 West)

6.3 TECHNOLOGY DESIGN

Once the needs have been defined in the logical network design, the next step is to develop a **physical network design** (or set of possible designs). The physical network design starts with the client and server computers needed to support the users and applications. If the network is a new network, new computers will need to be purchased. If the network is an existing network, the servers may need to be upgraded to the newest technology. Once these are designed, then the circuits and devices connecting them are designed.

6.3.1 Designing Clients and Servers

The idea behind the building-block approach is to specify needs in terms of some standard units. Typical users are allocated the base-level client computers, as are servers supporting typical applications. Users and servers for applications needing more powerful computers are assigned some advanced computer. As the specifications for computers rapidly improve and costs drop (usually every 6 months), today's typical user may receive the type of computer originally intended for the advanced user when the network is actually implemented, and the advanced users may end up with a computer not available when the network was designed.

6.3.2 Designing Circuits

The same is true for network circuits and devices (e.g., hubs, routers, switches). There are two interrelated decisions in designing network circuits and devices: the fundamental technology and protocols (e.g., Ethernet) and the capacity of each circuit (e.g., 100 Mbps, 1000 Mbps). These are interrelated because each technology offers different circuit capacities.

Designing the circuit capacity means **capacity planning**, estimating the size and type of the standard and advanced network circuits for each type of network (LAN, backbone, WAN). As you will learn in Chapter 7 on LANs, wired and wireless circuits come in standard sizes. Most users with a desktop or laptop computer don't need to send files that are over a gigabyte in size at a time (i.e., 1000 Meg). And if they do, they understand there may be a slight delay. Therefore, circuits for wired LANs are typically 100 Mbps or 1 Gbps. Wireless circuits are a little different, so we'll avoid them until Chapter 7.

Designing circuit capacities for backbone networks is more challenging because backbones move traffic from many computers at one time and there are more choices in standard sizes. This requires some assessment of the current and future **circuit loading** (the amount of data transmitted on a circuit). This analysis can focus on either the *average* circuit traffic or the *peak* circuit traffic. For example, in an online banking network, traffic volume peaks usually are in the midmorning (bank opening) and just prior to closing. Airline and rental car reservations network designers look for peak volumes before and during holidays or other vacation periods, whereas telephone companies normally have their highest peak volumes on Mother's Day. Designing for peak circuit traffic is the ideal.

The designer usually starts with the total characters transmitted per day on each circuit or, if possible, the maximum number of characters transmitted per 2-second interval if peaks must be met. You can calculate message volumes by counting messages in a current network and applying some estimated growth rate. If an existing network is in place, network monitors/analyzers (see Chapter 12) may be able to provide an actual circuit character count of the volume transmitted per minute or per day.

A good rule of thumb is that 80% of this circuit loading information is easy to gather. The last 20% needed for very precise estimates is extremely difficult and expensive to find. However, precision usually is not a major concern because of the stairstep nature of communication circuits and the need to project future needs. For example, the difference between 100 Mbps and 1 Gbps is quite large, and assessing which level is needed for typical traffic does not require a lot of precision. Forecasts are inherently less precise than understanding current network traffic. The **turnpike effect** is an expression that means that traffic increases much faster than originally forecast. It comes from the traffic forecasting that was done for the construction of the early interstate highways. When a new, faster highway (or network) is built, people are more likely to use it than the old slow one because it is available, is very efficient, and provides new capabilities. The annual growth factor for network use may vary from 5% to 50% and, in some cases, may exceed 100% for high-growth organizations.

Although no organization wants to overbuild its network and pay for more capacity than it needs, in most cases, upgrading a network costs 50% to 80% more than building it right the first time. Few organizations complain about having too much network capacity, but being under capacity can cause significant problems. Given the rapid growth in network demand and the difficulty in accurately predicting it, most organizations intentionally overbuild (build more capacity into their network than they plan to use), and most end up using this supposedly unneeded capacity within 3 years.

In any network, there may be a **bottleneck**, a circuit that is filled almost to its capacity and thus is the critical point that determines whether users get good or bad response times. When users complain about a slow network, it is usually because there is a bottleneck circuit somewhere in the network. Of course, the bottleneck could also be a slow Web server that is simply receiving more traffic than it can handle, but usually the problem is a circuit.

Take another look at Figure 6-4. Suppose we specified 1 Gbps circuits as the standard for the LANs. If each LAN has 20 computers, then this is in theory a total capacity of 120 Gbps in the building (6 LANs × 20 computers each × 1 Gbps = 120 Gbps). Not all the computers will be sending or receiving at the same time, so this is artificially high, but it is a theoretical maximum.

If this is the case, what speed should we specify for the building backbone? We have a few standard speeds, as you will learn in Chapter 8: 1 Gbps, 10 Gbps, 40 Gbps, 100 Gbps. A 1 Gbps backbone is probably too slow and would end up being a bottleneck. Is 10 Gbps enough? It's hard to say without knowing the circuit loading. Without the circuit loading, most network designers would set the building backbone speed at one level above the standard LAN speed, which in this case would be 10 Gbps.

This problem continues at the next architecture component—the campus core backbone. If each building has a 10 Gbps backbone, what speed should the campus backbone that connects all the buildings be? Without a circuit loading, it's hard to say. Once again, most network designers would set the building backbone speed at one level above the building backbone speed, which in this case would be 40 Gbps. And this is where reality sets in. Today, the technology for 40 Gbps is very expensive—so expensive, in fact, that most organizations don't buy it unless they really need it. Chances are, the campus backbone would be designed at 10 Gbps, which means it might be the bottleneck—at least for traffic on campus.

Figure 6-5 shows the physical design for the network in Figure 6-4. Take a moment to look at it and compare Figures 6-4 and 6-5.

As we move beyond the campus to the enterprise edge, network design becomes a bit more difficult. As you will learn in Chapter 9, on WANs, and Chapter 10, on the Internet, the technologies we use for WANs and Internet access are quite different to what we use for LANs and backbones. Their speeds are much, much slower and much more expensive. A typical WAN circuit speed is between 1 Mbps and 50 Mbps. Yes, that was Mbps; in other words, more than *100 times slower* than the speed of our backbone networks. Thus the bottleneck in most enterprise networks is the WAN and the Internet, not the enterprise campus network.

This is also true for the network in your house or apartment. Most wireless LAN access points you buy today provide speeds of 100–400 Mbps, yet your Internet connection is usually less than 25 Mbps. This means the response times you experience when you're on the Internet will be the same whether you buy a really fast, state-of-the-art wireless access point

FIGURE 6-5

Physical network design
for a single building

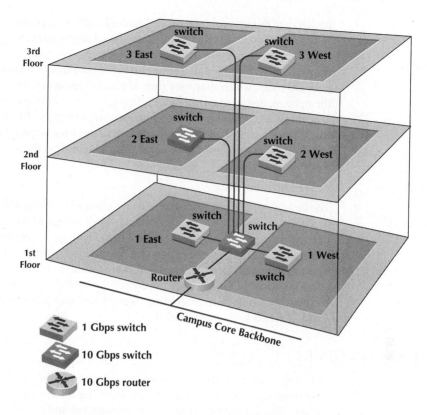

or an old one that provides only 50 Mbps, because the bottleneck is the Internet access, not the wireless LAN. Unless you're spending a lot of money on a really fast Internet connection, don't waste your money on a really fast wireless access point.

6.3.3 Network Design Tools

Network modeling and design tools can perform a number of functions to help in the technology design process. With most tools, the first step is to enter a diagram or model of the existing network or proposed network design. Some modeling tools require the user to create the network diagram from scratch. That is, the user must enter all of the network components by hand, placing each server, client computer, and circuit on the diagram and defining what each is.

Other tools can "discover" the existing network; that is, once installed on the network, they will explore the network to draw a network diagram. In this case, the user provides some starting point, and the modeling software explores the network and automatically draws the diagram itself. Once the diagram is complete, the user can then change it to reflect the new network design. Obviously, a tool that can perform network discovery by itself is most helpful when the network being designed is an upgrade to an existing network and when the network is very complex.

Once the diagram is complete, the next step is to add information about the expected network traffic and see if the network can support the level of traffic that is expected. **Simulation**, a mathematical technique in which the network comes to life and behaves as it would under real conditions, is used to model the behavior of the communication network. Applications and users generate and respond to messages while the simulator tracks the number of packets in the network and the delays encountered at each point in the network.

Simulation models may be tailored to the users' needs by entering parameter values specific to the network at hand (e.g., this computer will send an average of three 100-byte packets per minute and receive one hundred 1,500-byte packets per minute). Alternatively, the user may prefer to rely primarily on the set of average values provided by the network.

Once the simulation is complete, the user can examine the results to see the estimated response times throughout. It is important to note that these network design tools provide only estimates, which may vary from the actual results. At this point, the user can change the network design in an attempt to eliminate bottlenecks and rerun the simulation. Good modeling tools not only produce simulation results but also highlight potential trouble spots (e.g., servers, circuits, or devices that experienced long response times). The very best tools offer suggestions on how to overcome the problems that the simulation identified.

6.3.4 Deliverables

The key deliverable is a set of one or more physical network designs like that in Figure 6-5, which is the design for a single building. Most designers like to prepare several physical designs so they can trade-off technical benefits (e.g., performance) against cost. In most cases, the critical part is the design of the network circuits and devices. In the case of a new network designed from scratch, it is also important to define the client computers with care because these will form a large portion of the total cost of the network. Usually, however, the network will replace an existing network and only a few of the client computers in the existing network will be upgraded.

6.4 COST ASSESSMENT

The purpose of this step is to assess the costs of various physical network design alternatives produced in the previous step. The main items are the costs of software, hardware, and circuits. These three factors are all interconnected and must be considered along with the performance and reliability required. All factors are interrelated with regard to cost.

Estimating the cost of a network is quite complex because many factors are not immediately obvious. Some of the costs that must be considered are

- Circuit costs, including costs of circuits provided by common carriers or the cost of purchasing and installing your own cable
- Network devices such as switches and routers
- Hardware costs, including servers, printers, uninterruptible power supplies, and backup tape drives
- Software costs for network operating system, application software, and middleware
- Network management costs, including special hardware, software, and training needed to develop a network management system for ongoing redesign, monitoring, and diagnosis of problems
- Test and maintenance costs for special monitoring equipment and software, plus the cost of onsite spare parts
- Costs for WAN and Internet circuits leased from common carriers

6.4.1 Request for Proposal

Although some network components can be purchased off the shelf, most organizations develop a **request for proposal (RFP)** before making large network purchases. RFPs specify what equipment, software, and services are desired and ask vendors to provide their best prices. Some RFPs are very specific about what items are to be provided in what time frame. In other cases, items are defined as mandatory, important, or desirable, or several scenarios are provided and the vendor is asked to propose the best solution. In a few cases, RFPs specify generally what is required and the vendors are asked to propose their own network designs. Figure 6-6 provides a summary of the key parts of an RFP.

FIGURE 6-6
Request for proposal

Information in a Typical Request for Proposal

- **Background information**
  - **Organizational profile**
  - **Overview of current network**
  - **Overview of new network**
  - **Goals of new network**
- **Network requirements**
  - **Choice sets of possible network designs (hardware, software, circuits)**
  - **Mandatory, desirable, and wish-list items**
  - **Security and control requirements**
  - **Response-time requirements**
  - **Guidelines for proposing new network designs**
- **Service requirements**
  - **Implementation time plan**
  - **Training courses and materials**
  - **Support services (e.g., spare parts on site)**
  - **Reliability and performance guarantees**
- **Bidding process**
  - **Time schedule for the bidding process**
  - **Ground rules**
  - **Bid evaluation criteria**
  - **Availability of additional information**
- **Information required from vendor**
  - **Vendor corporate profile**
  - **Experience with similar networks**
  - **Hardware and software benchmarks**
  - **Reference list**

Once the vendors have submitted their proposals, the organization evaluates them against specified criteria and selects the winner(s). Depending on the scope and complexity of the network, it is sometimes necessary to redesign the network on the basis of the information in the vendors' proposals.

One of the key decisions in the RFP process is the scope of the RFP. Will you use one vendor or several vendors for all hardware, software, and services? Multivendor environments tend to provide better performance because it is unlikely that one vendor provides the best hardware, software, and services in all categories. Multivendor networks also tend to be less expensive because it is unlikely that one vendor will always have the cheapest hardware, software, and services in all product categories.

Multivendor environments can be more difficult to manage, however. If equipment is not working properly and it is provided by two different vendors, each can blame the other for the problem. In contrast, a single vendor is solely responsible for everything.

6.4.2 Selling the Proposal to Management

One of the main problems in network design is obtaining the support of senior management. To management, the network is simply a cost center, something on which the organization is spending a lot of money with little apparent change. The network keeps on running just as it did the year before.

The key to gaining the acceptance of senior management lies in speaking management's language. It is pointless to talk about upgrades from 100 Mbps to 1 Gbps on the backbone because this terminology is meaningless from a business perspective. A more compelling argument is to discuss the growth in network use. For example, a simple graph that shows network usage growing at 25% per year, compared with the network budget growing at 10% per year, presents a powerful illustration that the network costs are well managed, not out of control.

Likewise, a focus on network reliability is an easily understandable issue. For example, if the network supports a mission-critical system such as order processing or moving point-of-sale data from retail stores to corporate offices, it is clear from a business perspective that the network must be available and performing properly, or the organization will lose revenue.

6.4.3 Deliverables

There are three key deliverables for this step. The first is an RFP that goes to potential vendors. The second deliverable, after the vendor has been selected, is the revised physical network diagram (e.g., Figure 6-5) with the technology design complete. Exact products and costs are specified at this point (e.g., a 24-port 1000Base-T Cisco Ethernet switch). The third deliverable is the business case that provides support for the network design, expressed in business objectives.

6.5 IMPLICATIONS FOR MANAGEMENT

Network design was at one time focused on providing the most efficient networks custom-tailored to specific needs. Today, however, network design uses a building-block approach. Well-designed networks use a few common, standardized network technologies over and over again throughout the network, even though they might provide more capacity than needed. Under ideal circumstances, the organization will develop deep relationships with a very small set of vendors.

As the cost to operate and maintain networks gradually becomes more expensive than the cost to purchase network technologies in the first place, good network design commonly results in the purchase of more expensive equipment to save significantly more money in reduced network management costs over the life of the network. Although there is a temptation to go with the lowest bidder and buy inexpensive equipment, in many cases this can significantly increase the life cycle cost of a network. The use of sophisticated network design tools and network management tools has become a key part of almost all new networks installed today.

SUMMARY

Network Architecture Components Network designers usually think about networks as seven network architecture components. LANs (wired and wireless) provide users access to the network (access layer). Building backbones (distribution layer) connect the LANS inside one building. Campus backbones (core layer) connect the different buildings. The data center houses the organization's main servers. At the enterprise edge, we have WAN access that connects to other campuses operated by the organization, Internet access, and the e-commerce edge, which enables a business to support its customers and/or suppliers.

Traditional Network Design The traditional network design approach follows a very structured systems analysis and design process similar to that used to build application systems. It attempts to develop precise estimates of network traffic for each network user and network segment. Although this is expensive and time consuming, it works well for static or slowly evolving networks. Unfortunately, computer and networking technology is changing very rapidly, the growth in network traffic is immense, and hardware and circuit costs are relatively less expensive than they used to be. Therefore, use of the traditional network design approach is decreasing.

Building-Block Approach to Network Design The building-block approach attempts to build the network using a series of simple predefined building components, resulting in a simpler design process and a more easily managed network built with a smaller range of components. The basic process involves three steps that are performed repeatedly. Needs analysis involves developing a logical network design that includes the geographic scope of the network and a categorization of current and future network needs of the various network segments, users, and applications as either typical or high traffic. The next step, technology design, results in a set of one or more physical network designs. Network design and simulation tools can play an important role in selecting the technology that typical and high-volume users, applications, and network segments will use. The final step, cost assessment, gathers cost information for the network, usually through an RFP that specifies what equipment, software, and services are desired, and asks vendors to provide their best prices. One of the keys to gaining acceptance by senior management of the network design lies in speaking management's language (cost, network growth, and reliability), not the language of the technology (Ethernet, ATM, and DSL).

KEY TERMS

access layer, 167
baseline, 172
bottleneck, 176
building backbone
   network, 167
building-block process,
   169
campus backbone network,
   167
capacity planning, 175
circuit loading, 175

common carrier, 168
core layer, 167
cost assessment, 170
data center, 167
desirable requirements,
   173
distribution layer, 167
e-commerce edge, 168
enterprise campus, 167
enterprise edge, 167
geographic scope, 172

Internet access, 168
logical network design, 172
mandatory requirements,
   173
needs analysis, 170
network architecture
   component, 172
physical network design,
   175
request for proposal (RFP),
   178

simulation, 177
technology design, 170
traditional network design
   process, 168
turnpike effect, 176
Wide Area Network
   (WAN) access, 168
wish-list requirements, 173

QUESTIONS

1. What are the keys to designing a successful data communications network?
2. How does the traditional approach to network design differ from the building-block approach?
3. Describe the three major steps in current network design.
4. What is the most important principle in designing networks?
5. Why is it important to analyze needs in terms of both application systems and users?
6. Describe the key parts of the technology design step.
7. How can a network design tool help in network design?
8. On what should the design plan be based?
9. What is an RFP, and why do companies use them?

10. What are the key parts of an RFP?
11. What are some major problems that can cause network designs to fail?
12. What is a network baseline, and when is it established?
13. What issues are important to consider in explaining a network design to senior management?
14. What is the turnpike effect, and why is it important in network design?
15. What are the seven network architecture components?
16. What is the difference between a building backbone and a campus backbone, and what are the implications for the design of each?
17. What are typical speeds for the LAN, building backbone, and campus backbone? Why?

18. What is a bottleneck, and why do network managers care about them?

19. Is it important to have the fastest wireless LAN technology in your apartment? What about in the library of your school? Explain.

20. Why do you think some organizations were slow to adopt a building-block approach to network design?

21. For what types of networks are network design tools most important? Why?

EXERCISES

A. What factors might cause peak loads in a network? How can a network designer determine if they are important, and how are they taken into account when designing a data communications network?

B. Collect information about two network design tools and compare and contrast what they can and cannot do.

MINICASES

I. **Computer Dynamics** Computer Dynamics is a microcomputer software development company that has a 300-computer network. The company is located in three adjacent five-story buildings in an office park, with about 100 computers in each building. The LANs in each building are similar, but one building has the data center on the second floor. There are no other office locations. The current network is poorly designed for its current needs and must be completely replaced. Develop a logical design for this enterprise campus that considers the seven network architecture components. There are no other campuses, so you can omit WAN access. You will need to make some assumptions, so be sure to document your assumptions and explain why you have designed the network in this way.

II. **Drop and Forge** Drop and Forge is a manufacturing firm with a 60-computer network on its Toledo, Ohio, campus. The company has one very large manufacturing plant with an adjacent office building. The office building houses 50 computers, with an additional 10 computers in the plant. The current network is old and needs to be completely replaced. Develop a logical design for this enterprise campus that considers the seven network architecture components. There are no other campuses, so you can omit WAN access. You will need to make some assumptions, so be sure to document your assumptions and explain why you have designed the network in this way.

III. **AdviceNet** AdviceNet is a consulting firm with offices in Toronto, New York, Los Angeles, Dallas, and Atlanta. The firm currently uses the Internet to transmit data, but its needs are growing and it is concerned over the security of the Internet. The New York office is the primary headquarters with 200 computers spread across four floors and has the enterprise data center. Develop a logical design for the New York enterprise campus that considers the seven network architecture components. Describe the assumptions you have made.

IV. **Accurate Accounting** Accurate Accounting is a regional accounting firm that has 15 local offices throughout Georgia, Florida, and the Carolinas. The company is constructing a new office building for use as its main headquarters. The building will have two floors with a total of 40 offices, each with a desktop computer. Develop a logical design for the Atlanta headquarters enterprise campus that considers the seven network architecture components. You will need to make some assumptions, so be sure to document your assumptions and explain why you have designed the network in this way.

V. **Donald's Distributing** Donald's Distributing is a regional trucking firm that is constructing a new office building (its only office). The network has 80 desktop computers and 2 servers. Develop a logical design for the enterprise campus that considers the seven network architecture components. You will need to make some assumptions, so be sure to document your assumptions and explain why you have designed the network in this way.

CASE STUDY

NEXT-DAY AIR SERVICE

See the companion Web site at www.wiley.com/college/fitzgerald

HANDS-ON ACTIVITY 6A

Network Design Software

There are many different network design software tools. Some are simple drawing tools; others offer powerful network simulation modeling capabilities. One powerful tool that provides a free demo version that can be downloaded is SmartDraw.

The first step is to download and install the SmartDraw software. The software is available at www.smartdraw.com.

SmartDraw comes with a variety of network icons and templates that can be used to quickly build network diagrams. Figure 6-7 shows the main drawing screen in SmartDraw and a network diagram.

Deliverable

Select a network and draw it.

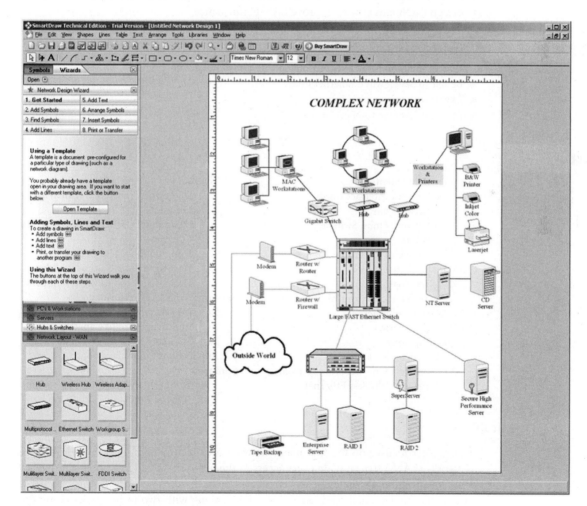

FIGURE 6-7 SmartDraw software

CHAPTER 7

WIRED AND WIRELESS LOCAL AREA NETWORKS

This chapter examines the three major network architecture components that use Local Area Networks (LANs): the LANs that provide network access to users, the data center, and the e-commerce edge. We focus on the LANs that provide network access to users as these are more common. This chapter draws together the concepts from the first section of the book on fundamental concepts to describe how wired and wireless LANs work. We first summarize the major components of LANs and then describe the two most commonly used LAN technologies: wired and wireless Ethernet. The chapter ends with a discussion of how to design LANs and how to improve LAN performance.

OBJECTIVES

- Understand the major components of LANs
- Understand the best practice recommendations for LAN design
- Be able to design wired Ethernet LANs
- Be able to design wireless Ethernet LANs
- Be able to improve LAN performance

OUTLINE

7.1 INTRODUCTION

This chapter focuses on the first major network architecture component: the Local Area Networks (LANs) that provide users access to the network. Most large organizations have numerous wired and wireless LANs connected by backbone networks. In this chapter, we discuss the fundamental components of a LAN, along with two technologies commonly used in LANs—traditional wired Ethernet (IEEE 802.3), which is commonly used to connect desktop computers, and wireless Ethernet (IEEE 802.11, commonly called Wi-Fi), which often is used to connect laptop computers and mobile devices. There used to be many different types of LAN technologies, but gradually the world has changed so that Ethernet dominates. The majority of LAN design is done for the LANs that enable users to access the network, whether wired or wireless, because there are more of these LANs than any other type. Therefore, this chapter focuses on the design of these access LANs. However, the data center and e-commerce edge also use LANs, so we include sections on the unique design needs of these two network architecture components.

A Day in the Life: LAN Administrator

Most days start the same way. The LAN administrator arrives early in the morning before most people who use the LAN. The first hour is spent checking for problems. All the network hardware and servers in the server room receive routine diagnostics. All the logs for the previous day are examined to find problems. If problems are found (e.g., a crashed hard disk), the next few hours are spent fixing them. Next, the daily backups are done. This usually takes only a few minutes, but sometimes a problem occurs and it takes an hour.

The next step is to see if there are any other activities that need to be performed to maintain the network. This involves checking email for security alerts (e.g., Windows updates and antivirus updates). If critical updates are needed, they are done immediately. There are usually emails from several users that need to be contacted, concerning either problems with the LAN or requests for new hardware or software to be installed. These new activities are prioritized into the work queue.

And then the real work begins. Work activities include tasks such as planning for the next roll out of software upgrades. This involves investigating the new software offerings, identifying what hardware platforms are required to run them, and determining which users should receive the upgrades. It also means planning for and installing new servers or network hardware such as firewalls.

Of course, some days can be more exciting than others. When a new virus hits, everyone is involved in cleaning up the compromised computers and installing security patches on the other computers. Sometimes virus attacks can be fun when you see that your security settings work and beat the virus.

Source: With thanks to Steve Bushert.

7.2 LAN COMPONENTS

There are several components in a traditional LAN (Figure 7-1). The first two are the client computer and the server. Clients and servers have been discussed in Chapter 2, so they

FIGURE 7-1

Local area network components

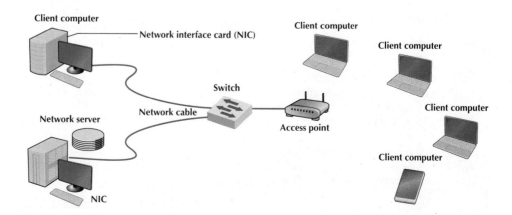

are not discussed further here. The other components are network interface cards (NICs), network circuits, hubs/switches/access points, and the network operating system.

7.2.1 Network Interface Cards

The **network interface card (NIC)** is used to connect the computer to the network cable in a wired network and is one part of the physical layer connection among the computers in the network. In a wireless network, the NIC is a radio transmitter that sends and receives messages on a specific radio frequency. All desktop computers have a wired NIC built in, while virtually all laptops have both a wired NIC and a wireless NIC. You can purchase a wireless NIC for a desktop computer (often as a USB device).

7.2.2 Network Circuits

Each computer must be physically connected by network circuits to the other computers in the network.

Wired LANs Most LANs are built with **unshielded twisted-pair (UTP) cable**, **shielded twisted-pair (STP) cable**, or **fiber-optic cable**. (Common cable standards are discussed on the next page. We should add that these cable standards specify the minimum quality cable required; it is possible, for example, to use category 5e UTP cable that is rated for 1000 Mbps in a LAN that runs at 100 Mbps.)

Many LANs use UTP cable. Its low cost makes it very useful. STP is only used in special areas that produce electrical interference, such as factories near heavy machinery or hospitals near MRI scanners.

Fiber-optic cable is even thinner than UTP wire and therefore takes far less space when cabled throughout a building. It also is much lighter, weighing less than 10 pounds per 1,000 feet. Because of its high capacity, fiber-optic cabling is perfect for BNs, although it is beginning to be used in LANs.

TECHNICAL FOCUS **7-1 Commonly Used Network Cable Standards**

Name	Type	Maximum Data Rate	Often Used By	Cost[1] ($/foot)
Category 1[2]	UTP	1 Mbps	Telephone	0.04
Category 3[3]	UTP	10 Mbps	10Base-T Ethernet	0.06
Category 5	UTP	100 Mbps	100Base-T Ethernet	0.07
Category 5	STP	100 Mbps	100Base-T Ethernet	0.18
Category 5e[4]	UTP	1 Gbps	1000Base-T Ethernet	0.10
Category 6	UTP	10 Gbps	10GBase-T	0.15
Category 7	STP	40 Gbps	40GBase-T	0.25
62.5/50	Fiber	1 Gbps	1000Base-F Ethernet	0.25

Notes

1. These costs are approximate costs for cable only (no connectors). They often change but will give you a sense of the relative differences in costs among the different options.
2. Category 1 is standard voice-grade twisted-pair wires but it can also be used to support low-speed analog data transmission.
3. Category 2 and category 4 cable are old standards no longer in use today.
4. Category 5e is an improved version of category 5 that has better insulation and a center plastic pipe inside the cable to keep the individual wires in place and reduce noise from cross-talk, so that it is better suited to 1000Base-T.

Wireless LANs Wireless LANs (WLANs) use radio transmissions to send data between the NIC and the access point (AP). Most countries (but not all) permit WLANs to operate in two frequency ranges: the 2.4 and 5 GHz range. These same frequency ranges can be used by cordless phones and baby monitors, which means that your WLAN and your cordless phone may interfere with each other. Under ideal conditions, the radio transmitters in the NICs and APs can transmit 100–150 meters (300–450 feet). In practice, the range is much shorter as walls absorb the radio waves. The other problem is that as the distance from the AP increases, the maximum speed drops, often very dramatically.

When we design a WLAN, it is important to ensure that the APs don't interfere with each other. If all APs transmitted on the same frequency, the transmissions of one AP would interfere with another AP. Therefore, each AP is set to transmit on a different **channel**, very much like the different channels on your TV. Each channel uses a different part of the 2.4 or 5 GHz frequency range so that there is no interference among the different channels. When a computer first starts using the WLAN, its NIC searches all available channels within the appropriate frequency range and then picks the channel that has the strongest signal.

7.2.3 Network Hubs, Switches, and Access Points

Network **hubs** and **switches** serve two purposes. First, they provide an easy way to connect network cables. A hub or a **switch** can be thought of as a junction box, permitting new computers to be connected to the network as easily as plugging a power cord into an electrical socket. Each connection point where a cable can be plugged in is called a **port**. Each port has a unique number. Switches can be designed for use in **small-office, home-office (SOHO)** environments (see Figure 7-2a) or for large enterprise environments (see Figure 7-2b).

Simple hubs and switches are commonly available in 4-, 8-, 16-, and 24-port sizes, meaning that they provide anywhere between 4 and 24 ports into which network cables can be plugged. When no cables are plugged in, the signal bypasses the unused port. When a cable is plugged into a port, the signal travels down the cable as though it were directly connected to the hub or switch. Some switches also enable different types of cables to be

(a) Small-Office, Home-Office (SOHO) switch with five 10/100/1000 Mbps ports

http://homestore.cisco.com/en-us/Switches/
linksys-EZXS55W_stcVVproductId53934575VVcatId543809VVviewprod.htm

(b) Data center chassis switch with 512 10 Gbps ports

Source: newsroom.cisco.com/dlls/2008/prod_012808b.html

FIGURE 7-2 Lan switches

Source: Courtesy Cisco Systems, Inc. Unauthorized use not permitted

connected and perform the necessary conversions (e.g., twisted-pair cable to coaxial cable and twisted-pair cable to fiber-optic cable).

MANAGEMENT **7-1 Cable Problems at the University of Georgia**

FOCUS

*L*ike many organizations, the Terry College of Business at the University of Georgia is headquartered in a building built before the computer age. When local area network cabling was first installed in the early 1980s, no one foresaw the rapid expansion that was to come. Cables and hubs were installed piecemeal to support the needs of the handful of early users.

The network eventually grew far beyond the number of users it was designed to support. The network cabling gradually became a complex, confusing, and inefficient mess. There was no logical pattern for the cables, and there was no network cable plan. Worse still, no one knew where all the cables and hubs were physically located. Before a new user was added, a network technician had to open up a ceiling and crawl around to find a

hub. Hopefully, the hub had an unused port to connect the new user, or else the technician would have to find another hub with an empty port.

To complicate matters even more, asbestos was discovered. Now network technicians could not open the ceiling and work on the cable unless asbestos precautions were taken. This meant calling in the university's asbestos team and sealing off nearby offices. Installing a new user to the network (or fixing a network cable problem) now took 2 days and cost $2,000.

The solution was obvious. The university spent $400,000 to install new category 5 twisted-pair cable in every office and to install a new high-speed fiber-optic backbone network between network segments.

Second, hubs and switches act as repeaters. Signals can travel only so far in a network cable before they attenuate and can no longer be recognized. (Attenuation was discussed in Chapter 4.) All LAN cables are rated for the maximum distance they can be used (typically 100 meters for **twisted-pair cable** and 400 meters to several kilometers for fiber-optic cable).

A wireless **access point** is a radio transceiver that plays the same role as a hub or switch in wired Ethernet LANs. It enables the computers near it to communicate with each other and it also connects them into wired LANs, typically using 100Base-T or 1000Base-T. All NICs in the WLAN transmit their frames to the AP, and then the AP retransmits the frames over the wireless network or over the wired network to their destination. Therefore, if a frame has to be transmitted from one wireless computer to another, it is transmitted twice, once from the sender to the AP and then from the AP to the destination. At first glance this may seem a bit strange because it doubles the number of transmissions in the WLAN. However, very few frames are ever sent from client computer to client computer in a WLAN. Most frames are exchanged between client computers and a server of some kind. Therefore, a server should never be placed on a WLAN because client computers cannot reach it directly but have to communicate with it via the AP. Even if they are intended to serve clients on a WLAN, they should always be placed on the wired portion of the LAN.

Figure 7-3a shows an AP for use in SOHO environments. This AP is wired into the regular Ethernet LAN and has a separate power supply that is plugged into a normal electrical outlet. Figure 7-3b shows an AP for use in large enterprises. It is also wired into the regular Ethernet LAN, but it uses **power over Ethernet (POE)** so it needs no external power; the power is provided from a POE switch over the unused wires in a category 5/5e cable. POE APs are more expensive, but can be located anywhere you can run Cat 5/5e cable, even if there are no power outlets nearby.

FIGURE 7-3

Wireless access points

Source: Courtesy of the author, Alan Dennis

(a) AP for SOHO use   (b) A power-over-Ethernet AP for enterprise use

Most WLANs are installed using APs that have **omnidirectional antennas**, which means that the antenna transmits in all directions simultaneously. Some antennas are built into the AP itself, while others stick up above it. One common omnidirectional antenna is the dipole antenna shown in Figure 7-3a; others are built into the AP box, as is Figure 7-3b.

The other type of antenna that can be used on APs is the **directional antenna**, which, as the name suggests, projects a signal only in one direction. Because the signal is concentrated in a narrower, focused area, the signal is stronger and therefore will carry farther than the signal from an AP using an omnidirectional antenna. Directional antennas are most often used on the inside of an exterior wall of a building, pointing to the inside of the building. This keeps the signal inside the building (to reduce security issues) and also has the benefit of increasing the range of the AP.

Many wireless routers are sold for use in SOHO environments. The wireless routers are both a wireless access point and a router, and many also contain a 1000Base-T switch. It is important not to use the term *wireless router* when you mean a *wireless access point*.

MANAGEMENT
FOCUS

7-2 Managing Network Cabling

You must consider a number of items when installing cables or when performing cable maintenance. You should:

- Perform a physical inventory of any existing cabling systems and document those findings in the network cable plan.

- Properly maintain the network cable plan. Always update cable documentation immediately on installing or removing a cable or hub. Insist that any cabling contractor provide "as-built" plans that document where the cabling was actually placed, in case of minor differences from the construction plan.

- Establish a long-term plan for the evolution of the current cabling system to whatever cabling system will be in place in the future.

- Obtain a copy of the local city fire codes and follow them. For example, cables used in airways without conduit need to be plenum-certified (i.e., covered with a fire-retardant jacket).

- Conceal all cables as much as possible to protect them from damage and for security reasons.

- Properly number and mark both ends of all cable installations as you install them. If a contractor installs cabling, always make a complete inspection to ensure that all cables are labeled.

7.2.4 Network Operating Systems

The **network operating system (NOS)** is the software that controls the network. Every NOS provides two sets of software: one that runs on the **network server(s)** and one that runs on the network client(s). The server version of the NOS provides the software that performs the functions associated with the data link, network, and application layers and usually the computer's own operating system. The client version of the NOS provides the software that performs the functions associated with the data link and the network layers and must interact with the application software and the computer's own operating system. Most NOSs provide different versions of their client software that run on different types of computers, so that Windows computers, for example, can function on the same network as Apple computers. In most cases (e.g., Windows and Linux), the client NOS software is included with the operating system itself.

NOS Server Software The NOS server software enables the file server, print server, or database server to operate. In addition to handling all the required network functions, it acts as the application software by executing the requests sent to it by the clients (e.g., copying a file from its hard disk and transferring it to the client, printing a file on the printer, executing a database request, and sending the result to the client). NOS server software replaces the normal operating system on the server. By replacing the existing operating system, it provides better performance and faster response time because a NOS is optimized for its limited range of operations. The most commonly used NOS are Windows Server and Linux.

NOS Client Software The NOS software running at the client computers provides the data link layer and network layer. Most operating systems today are designed with networking in mind. For example, Windows provides built-in software that will enable it to act as a client computer with a Windows Server.

One of the most important functions of a NOS is a *directory service*. Directory services provide information about resources on the network that are available to the users, such as shared printers, shared file servers, and application software. A common example of directory services is Microsoft's **Active Directory Service (ADS)**.

Active Directory Service works in much the same manner as TCP/IP's DNS service, and in fact ADS servers, called **domain controllers**, can also act as DNS servers. Network resources are typically organized into a hierarchical tree. Each branch on the tree contains a domain, a group of related resources. For example, at a university, one domain might be the resources available within the business school, and another domain might be the resources in the computer science school, while another might be in the medical school. Domains can contain other domains, and in fact the hierarchical tree of domains within one organization can be linked to trees in other organizations to create a *forest* of shared network resources.

Within each domain, there is a server (the domain controller) that is responsible for resolving address information (much like a DNS server resolves address information on the Internet). The domain controller is also responsible for managing authorization information (e.g., who is permitted to use each resource) and making sure that resources are available only to authorized users. Domain controllers in the same tree (or forest) can share information among themselves, so that a domain controller in one part of the tree (or forest) can be configured to permit access to resources to any user that has been approved by another domain controller in a different part of the tree (or forest).

If you login to a Microsoft server or domain controller that provides ADS, you can see all network resources that you are authorized to use. When a client computer wishes to view available resources or access them, it sends a message using an industry standard directory protocol called **lightweight directory access protocol (LDAP)** to the ADS domain controller. The ADS domain controller resolves the textual name in the LDAP request to a network address and—if the user is authorized to access the resource—provides contact information for the resource.

Network Profiles A **network profile** specifies what resources on each server are available on the network for use by other computers and which devices or people are allowed what access to the network. The network profile is normally configured when the network is established and remains in place until someone makes a change. In a LAN, the server hard disk may have various resources that can or cannot be accessed by a specific network user (e.g., data files and printers). Furthermore, a password may be required to grant network access to the resources.

If a device such as a hard disk on one of the network's computers is not included on the network profile, it cannot be used by another computer on the network. For example, if you have a hard disk (C) on your computer and your computer is connected to this LAN but the hard disk is not included on the network profile assignment list, then no other computer can access that hard disk.

In addition to profiling disks and printers, there must be a *user profile* for each person who uses the LAN, to add some security. Each device and each user is assigned various access codes, and only those users who log in with the correct code can use a specific device. Most LANs keep audit files to track who uses which resource. Security is discussed in Chapter 9.

7.3 WIRED ETHERNET

Almost all LANs installed today use some form of **Ethernet**. Ethernet was originally developed by DEC, Xerox, and Intel but has since become a standard formalized by the IEEE as **IEEE 802.3**.[1] The IEEE 802.3 version of Ethernet is slightly different from the original version but the differences are minor. Likewise, another version of Ethernet has also been developed that differs slightly from the 802.3 standard.

Ethernet is a layer 2 protocol, which means it operates at the data link layer. Every Ethernet LAN needs hardware at layer 1, the physical layer, that matches the requirements of the Ethernet software at layer 2.

7.3.1 Topology

Topology is the basic geometric layout of the network—the way in which the computers on the network are interconnected. It is important to distinguish between a logical topology and a physical topology. A **logical topology** is how the network works conceptually, much like a logical data flow diagram (DFD) or logical entity relation diagram (ERD) in systems analysis and design or database design. A **physical topology** is how the network is physically installed, much like a physical DFD or physical ERD.

Hub-Based Ethernet When we use hubs, Ethernet's logical topology is a **bus topology**. All computers are connected to one half-duplex circuit running the length of the network that is called the bus. The top part of Figure 7-4 shows Ethernet's logical topology. All **frames** from any computer flow onto the central cable (or bus) and through it to all computers on the LAN. Every computer on the bus receives *all* frames sent on the bus, even those intended for other computers. Before processing incoming frames, the Ethernet software on each computer checks the data link layer address and processes only those frames addressed to that computer.

---

[1] The formal specification for Ethernet is provided in the 802.3 standard on the IEEE standards Web site. The URL is www.ieee802.org/3

FIGURE 7-4

Ethernet topology using hubs

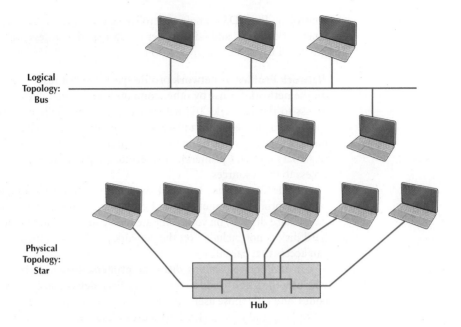

The bottom part of Figure 7-4 shows the physical topology of an Ethernet LAN when a hub is used. From the outside, an Ethernet LAN *appears* to be a star topology, because all cables connect to the central hub. Nonetheless, it is logically a bus.

With hubs, all computers share the same multipoint circuit and must take turns using it. This shared multipoint circuit is often called a **collision domain**, because if two computers ever did accidentally transmit at the same time, there would be a collision. When one computer transmits, all the other computers must wait, which is very inefficient. Because all frames are sent to all computers in the same collision domain, security is a problem because any frame can be read by any computer. Most companies don't use hub-based Ethernet today, but products are still available and are very cheap. Wireless Ethernet, which we discuss in a later section, works much the same as hub-based Ethernet.

Switch-Based Ethernet When we use switches, Ethernet's topology is a logical star and a physical star (Figure 7-5). From the outside, the switch looks almost identical to a hub, but inside, it is very different. A switch is an intelligent device with a small computer built in that is designed to manage a set of separate point-to-point circuits. That means that each circuit connected to a switch is *not* shared with any other devices; only the switch and the attached computer use it. The physical topology looks essentially the same as Ethernet's physical topology: a star. On the inside, the logical topology is a set of separate point-to-point circuits, also a star. Many switches support full duplex circuits, meaning that each circuit can simultaneously send and receive.

When a switch receives a frame from a computer, it looks at the address on the frame and retransmits the frame only on the circuit connected to that computer, not to all circuits as a hub would. Therefore, no computer needs to wait because another computer is transmitting; every computer can transmit at the same time, resulting in much faster performance. Today, no one buys a hub unless she or he can't afford a switch.

So how does a switch know which circuit is connected to what computer? The switch uses a **forwarding table** that is very similar to the routing tables discussed in Chapter 5. The table lists the Ethernet address of the computer connected to each port on the switch. When the switch receives a frame, it compares the destination address on the frame to the addresses in its forwarding table to find the port number on which it needs to transmit the

FIGURE 7-5

Ethernet topology using switches

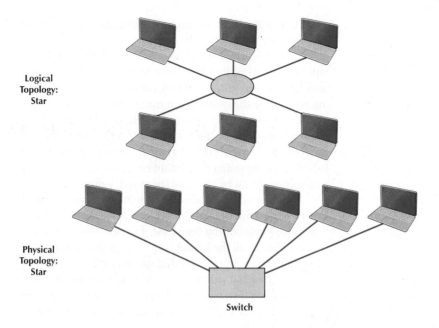

Logical
Topology:
Star

Physical
Topology:
Star

Switch

frame. Because the switch uses the Ethernet address to decide which port to use and because Ethernet is a data link layer or layer-2 protocol, this type of switch is called a **layer-2 switch**.

When switches are first turned on, their forwarding tables are empty; they do not know what Ethernet address is attached to what port. Switches *learn* addresses to build the forwarding table. When a switch receives a frame, it reads the frame's data link layer source address and compares this address to its forwarding table. If the address is not in the forwarding table, the switch adds it, along with the port on which the frame was received.

If a switch receives a frame with a destination address that is not in the forwarding table, the switch must still send the frame to the correct destination. In this case, it must retransmit the frame to all ports, except the one on which the frame was received. The attached computers, being Ethernet and assuming they are attached to a hub, will simply ignore all frames not addressed to them. The one computer for whom the frame is addressed will recognize its address and will process the frame, which includes sending an acknowledgement (ACK) or a negative acknowledgement (NAK) back to the sender. When the switch receives the ACK or NAK, it will add this computer's address and the port number on which the ACK or NAK was received to its forwarding table and then send the ACK or NAK on its way.

So, for the first few minutes until the forwarding table is complete, the switch acts like a hub. But as its forwarding table becomes more complete, it begins to act more and more like a switch. In a busy network, it takes only a few minutes for the switch to learn most addresses and match them to port numbers. To make a switch work faster, the most active connections are placed on the top of the forwarding table. If a computer is not communicating for more than 300 seconds, its entry is usually removed from the forwarding table.

There are three modes in which switches can operate. The first is **cut-through switching**. With cut-through switching, the switch begins to transmit the incoming packet on the proper outgoing circuit as soon as it has read the destination address in the frame. In other words, the switch begins transmitting before it has received the entire frame. The advantage of this is low **latency** (the time it takes a device from receiving a frame to transmitting it) and results in a very fast network. The disadvantage is that the switch begins transmitting before it has read and processed the frame check sequence at the end of the frame; the frame may contain an error, but the switch will not notice until after almost all of the frame has been transmitted. Cut-through switching can only be used when the incoming data circuit has the same data rate as the outgoing circuit.

With the second switching mode, called **store and forward switching**, the switch does not begin transmitting the outgoing frame until it has received the entire incoming frame and has checked to make sure it contains no errors. Only after the switch is sure there are no errors does the switch begin transmitting the frame on the outgoing circuit. If errors are found, the switch simply discards the frame. This mode prevents an invalid frame from consuming network capacity, but provides higher latency and thus results in a slower network (unless many frames contain errors). Store and forward switching can be used regardless of whether the incoming data circuit has the same data rate as the outgoing circuit because the entire frame must be stored in the switch before it is forwarded on its way.

The final mode, called **fragment-free switching**, lies between the extremes of cut-through switching and store and forward switching. With fragment-free switching, the first 64 bytes of the frame are read and stored. The switch examines the first 64 bytes (which contain all the header information for the frame), and if all the header data appear correct, the switch presumes that the rest of the frame is error free and begins transmitting. Fragment-free switching is a compromise between cut-through and store and forward switching because it has higher latency and better error control than cut-through switching, but lower latency and worse error control than store and forward switching. Most switches today use cut-through or fragment-free switching.

7.3.2 Media Access Control

When several computers share the same collision domain (i.e., multipoint circuit), it is important to control their access to the media. If two computers on the same circuit transmit at the same time, their transmissions will become garbled. These collisions must be prevented, or if they do occur, there must be a way to recover from them. This is called *media access control.*

Ethernet uses a contention-based media access control technique called **Carrier Sense Multiple Access with Collision Detection (CSMA/CD)**. CSMA/CD, like all contention-based techniques, is very simple in concept: wait until the circuit is free and then transmit. Computers wait until no other devices are transmitting, then transmit their frames. As an analogy, suppose you are talking with a small group of friends (four or five people). As the discussion progresses, each person tries to grab the floor when the previous speaker finishes. Usually, the other members of the group yield to the first person who jumps in right after the previous speaker.

Ethernet's CSMA/CD protocol can be termed "ordered chaos." As long as no other computer attempts to transmit at the same time, everything is fine. However, it is possible that two computers located some distance from one another can both listen to the circuit, find it empty, and begin simultaneously. This simultaneous transmission is called a **collision**. The two frames collide and destroy each other.

The solution to this is to listen while transmitting, better known as **collision detection (CD)**. If the NIC detects any signal other than its own, it presumes that a collision has occurred and sends a jamming signal. All computers stop transmitting and wait for the circuit to become free before trying to retransmit. The problem is that the computers that caused the collision could attempt to retransmit at the same time. To prevent this, each computer waits a random amount of time after the colliding frame disappears before attempting to retransmit. Chances are both computers will choose a different random amount of time and one will begin to transmit before the other, thus preventing a second collision. However, if another collision occurs, the computers wait a random amount of time before trying again. This does not eliminate collisions completely, but it reduces them to manageable proportions.

FIGURE 7-6

Types of Ethernet

Name	Maximum Data Rate
10Base-T	10 Mbps
100Base-T	100 Mbps
1000Base-T	1 Gbps
1000Base-F	1 Gbps
10 GbE	10 Gbps
40 GbE	40 Gbps

7.3.3 Types of Ethernet

Figure 7-6 summarizes the many different types of Ethernet in use today. The **10Base-T** standard revolutionized Ethernet and made it the most popular type of LAN in the world. Today, **100Base-T** and **1000Base-T** are the most common forms of Ethernet.

Other types of Ethernet include 1000Base-F (which runs at 1 Gbps and is sometimes called **1 GbE**), **10 GbE** (10 Gbps), **40 GbE** (40 Gbps), and **100 GbE** (100 Gbps). They can use Ethernet's traditional half-duplex approach, but most are configured to use full duplex. Each is also designed to run over fiber-optic cables, but some may also use traditional twisted-pair cables (e.g., Cat 5e). For example, two common versions of 1000Base-F are *1000Base-LX* and *1000Base-SX*, which both use fiber-optic cable, running up to 440 and 260 meters, respectively; *1000Base-T*, which runs on four pairs of category 5 twisted-pair cable, but only up to 100 meters;[2] and *1000Base-CX*, which runs up to 24 meters on one category 5 cable. Similar versions of 10 and 40 GbE that use different media are also available.

MANAGEMENT FOCUS   **7-3 Moving to Gigabit Ethernet**

Kotak Mahindra Group, one of India's leading financial services provider, offers comprehensive financial solutions such as commercial banking, stock brokering, mutual funds, life insurance, and investment banking. They employ 20,000 people at more than 1,300 branches in India and around the world.

Because of the high network traffic in their main data center location, Kotak installed gigabit Ethernet switches in their core network. The switches provide 512 ports of 10 GbE, with the ability to upgrade to 40 and 100 Gbps. The switches have an internal switching capacity of 15 Tbps (15 trillion bits per second), so there is room for growth.

Adapted from: "Kotak Group Builds State-of-the-Art Data Center on Cisco Nexus 7000 Switch," Cisco Customer Case Study, Cisco Systems, 2009.

Some organizations use **10/100/1000 Ethernet**, which is a hybrid that can run at any of these three speeds; 10/100/1000 NICs and switches detect the signal transmitted by the

---

[2]It would be reasonable to think that 1000Base-T would require 10 category 5 cables because 10×100 Mps = 1,000 Mbps. However, it is possible to push 100-Mbps cables to faster speeds over shorter distances. Therefore, the category 5 flavor of 1000Base-T uses only 4 pairs of category 5 (i.e., 8 wires) running at 125 Mbps, but over shorter distances than would be normal for 100Base-T. A special form of category 5 cable (called category 5e) has been developed to meet the special needs of 1000Base-T. This same approach is used to run 10 GbE over category 5.

computer or device on the other end of the cable and will use 10 Mbps, 100 Mbps, or 1 Gbps, depending on which the other device uses.

7.4 WIRELESS ETHERNET

Wireless Ethernet (commonly called **Wi-Fi**) is the commercial name for a set of standards developed by the **IEEE 802.11** standards group. A group of vendors selling 802.11 equipment trademarked the name Wi-Fi to refer to 802.11 because they believe that consumers are more likely to buy equipment with a catchier name than 802.11. Wi-Fi is intended to evoke memories of Hi-Fi, as the original stereo music systems in the 1960s were called.

The 802.11 family of technologies is much like the Ethernet family. They reuse many of the Ethernet 802.3 components and are designed to connect easily into Ethernet LANs. For these reasons, IEEE 802.11 is often called *wireless Ethernet*. Just as there are several different types of Ethernet (e.g., 10Base-T, 100Base-T, and 1000Base-T), there are several different types of 802.11.

7.4.1 Topology

The logical and physical topologies of Wi-Fi are the same as those of hub-based Ethernet: a physical star and a logical bus. There is a central AP to which all computers direct their transmissions (star), and the radio frequencies are shared (bus) so that all computers must take turns transmitting.

7.4.2 Media Access Control

Media access control in Wi-Fi is **Carrier Sense Multiple Access with Collision Avoidance (CSMA/CA)**, which is similar to the contention-based CSMA/CD approach used by Ethernet. With CSMA/CA, computers listen before they transmit, and if no one else is transmitting, they proceed with transmission. Detecting collisions is more difficult in radio transmission than in transmission over wired networks, so Wi-Fi attempts to avoid collisions to a greater extent than traditional Ethernet. CSMA/CA has two media access control approaches. However, before a computer can transmit in a WLAN, it must first establish an **association** with a specific AP, so that the AP will accept its transmissions.

Associating with an AP Searching for an available AP is called *scanning*, and a NIC can engage in either active or passive scanning. During *active scanning*, a NIC transmits a special frame called **probe frame** on all active channels on its frequency range. When an AP receives a probe frame, it responds with a probe response that contains all the necessary information for a NIC to associate with it. A NIC can receive several probe responses from different APs. It is up to the NIC to choose with which AP to associate. This usually depends on the speed rather than distance from an access point. Once a NIC associates with an access point, they start exchanging packets over the channel that is specified by the access point.

During *passive scanning*, the NIC listens on all channels for a special frame called a **beacon frame** that is sent out by an access point. The beacon frame contains all the necessary information for a NIC to associate with it. Once a NIC detects this beacon frame, it can decide to associate with it and start communication on the frequency channel set by the access point.

Distributed Coordination Function The first media access control method is the **distributed coordination function (DCF)** (also called **physical carrier sense method** because it relies on the ability of computers to physically listen before they transmit). With DCF, each frame in CSMA/CA is sent using stop-and-wait ARQ. After the sender transmits one frame, it immediately stops and waits for an ACK from the receiver before attempting to send another frame. When the receiver of a frame detects the end of the frame in a transmission, it waits a fraction of a second to make sure the sender has really stopped transmitting, and then immediately transmits an ACK (or a NAK). The original sender can then send another frame, stop and wait for an ACK, and so on. While the sender and receiver are exchanging frames and ACKs, other computers may also want to transmit. So when the sender ends its transmission, you might ask, why doesn't some other computer begin transmitting before the receiver can transmit an ACK? The answer is that the physical carrier sense method is designed so that the time the receiver waits after the frame transmission ends before sending an ACK is significantly less time than the time a computer must listen to determine that no one else is transmitting before initiating a new transmission. Thus, the time interval between a frame and the matching ACK is so short that no other computer has the opportunity to begin transmitting.

Point Coordination Function The second media access control technique is called the **point coordination function (PCF)** (also called the **virtual carrier sense** method). Not all manufacturers have implemented PCF in their APs. DCF works well in traditional Ethernet because every computer on the shared circuit receives every transmission on the shared circuit. However, in a wireless environment, this is not always true. A computer at the extreme edge of the range limit from the AP on one side may not receive transmissions from a computer on the extreme opposite edge of the AP's range limit. In Figure 7-1, all computers may be within the range of the AP, but may not be within the range of each other. In this case, if one computer transmits, the other computer on the opposite edge may not sense the other transmission and transmit at the same time causing a collision at the AP. This is called the *hidden node problem* because the computers at the opposite edges of the WLAN are hidden from each other.

When the hidden node problem exists, the AP is the only device guaranteed to be able to communicate with all computers on the WLAN. Therefore, the AP must manage the shared circuit using a controlled-access technique, not the contention-based approach of traditional Ethernet. With this approach, any computer wishing to transmit first sends a **request to send (RTS)** to the AP, which may or may not be heard by all computers. The RTS requests permission to transmit and to reserve the circuit for the sole use of the requesting computer for a specified time period. If no other computer is transmitting, the AP responds with a **clear to send (CTS)**, specifying the amount of time for which the circuit is reserved for the requesting computer. All computers hear the CTS and remain silent for the specified time period. The virtual carrier sense method is optional. It can always be used, never used, or used just for frames exceeding a certain size, as set by the WLAN manager.

Controlled-access methods provide poorer performance in low-traffic networks because computers must wait for permission before transmitting rather than just waiting for an unused time period. However, controlled-access techniques work better in high-traffic WLANs, because without controlled access, there are many collisions. Think of a large class discussion in which the instructor selects who will speak (controlled access) versus one in which any student can shout out a comment at any time.

7.4.3 Wireless Ethernet Frame Layout

An 801.11 data frame is illustrated in Figure 7-7. We notice two major differences when we compare the 802.11 frame to the 802.3 frame used in wired Ethernet (see Chapter 4). First, the wireless Ethernet frame has four address fields rather than two like the wired Ethernet. These four address fields are source address, transmitter address, receiver address, and destination address. The source and destination address have the same meaning as in wired Ethernet. However, because every NIC has to communicate via an access point (it cannot directly communication with another NIC), there is a need to add the address of the access point and also any other device that might be needed to transmit the frame. To do this, the transmitter and received address fields are used.

Frame Control (2 bytes)	Duration (2 bytes)	Address 1 (6 bytes)	Address 2 (6 bytes)	Address 3 (6 bytes)	Sequence Control (2 bytes)	Address 4 (6 bytes)	Data (0-2312 bytes)	FCS (6 bytes)

FIGURE 7-7   A wireless Ethernet frame

Second, there is new field called sequence control that indicates how a large frame is fragmented—split into smaller pieces. Recall that in wired networks this is done by the transport layer, not the data link layer. Moving the segmentation to the data link layer for wireless makes the transmission transparent to the higher layers. The price, however, is less efficiency because of the size of the frame and thus also a higher error rate.

7.4.4 Types of Wireless Ethernet

Wi-Fi is one of the fastest changing areas in networking. There are six versions of Wi-Fi; all but the last two or three versions are obsolete but may still be in use in some companies. All the different types are backward compatible, which means that laptops and APs that use new versions can communicate with laptops and APs that use older versions. However, this backward compatibility comes with a price. These old laptops become confused when other laptops operate at high speeds near them, so when an AP detects the presence of a laptop using an old version, it prohibits laptops that use the newer versions from operating at high speeds. Thus one old laptop will slow down all the other new laptops around it.

802.11a IEEE **802.11a** is an obsolete, legacy technology, and no new products are being developed. Under perfect conditions, it provides eight channels of 54 Mbps each with a maximum range of 50 meters or 150 feet. Speeds of 20 Mbps at 50 foot ranges are more common in the face of interference such as drywall or brick walls.

802.11b IEEE **802.11b** is another obsolete, legacy technology. Under perfect conditions, it provides three channels of 11 Mbps each with a maximum range of 150 meters or 450 feet, although in practice both the speed and range are lower.

802.11g IEEE **802.11g** is another obsolete, legacy technology. Under perfect conditions, it provides three channels of 54 Mbps each with a maximum range of 150 meters or 450 feet, although in practice both the speed and range are lower.

802.11n IEEE **802.11n** is another obsolete version, but many organizations continue to use it because it is cheap. Under perfect conditions, it provides three channels of 450 Mbps each with a maximum range of 100 meters or 300 feet, although in practice both the speed and range are lower. Older versions of 802.11n provide a maximum speed of 300 Mbps. You would probably think the three channels are numbered 1, 2, and 3, but they aren't. The three channels are numbered 1, 6, and 11, because the underlying technology provides 11 channels, with channels 1, 6, and 11 designed so they do not overlap and cause interference with each other. It is also possible to configure a **dual-band** AP so it combines all the channels into one "dual-band" channel that provides 600 Mbps.

802.11ac IEEE **802.11ac** is the latest version. This version runs in two different frequency spectrums simultaneously (2.4 and 5 GHz) to provide very high speed data rates. Some vendors have introduced products that conform to the standard but operate only in the 2.4 GHz spectrum. These products offer fewer channels and/or slower data rates, so we now need to read product labels very carefully before buying equipment. To make things more confusing, there are two different versions of the standard. One version provides eight channels each running at 433 Mbps with a maximum range of 100 meters (300 feet) under perfect conditions. The actual throughput after you consider the symbol structure (to prevent errors, it uses six symbols to send 5 bits, rather than sending multiple bits on each symbol; see Chapter 3) and the efficiency of the data link protocol (see Chapter 4) is about 300 Mbps. As you get farther from the AP, the speed drops, so users will only see the maximum speed within 20–30 meters of the AP, depending on the interference in the environment. At maximum range, data rates are likely to be about 90 Mbps per channel (60 Mbps throughput). The other version of the standard provides eight channels of 867 Mbps under perfect conditions (with an effective throughput of 610 Mbps). Work is progressing on a version that will combine the eight channels into one channel that provides a total of 6.9 Gbps (or a throughput of 4.9 Gbps).

802.11ad   IEEE **802.11ad** (sometimes called **WiGig**) is a specialized version of wireless Ethernet that has a maximum range of 10 meters (30 feet). WiGig cannot penetrate walls, so it can only be used in the same room as the AP. Current products have data rates of 7 Gbps (throughput of 5 Gbps) in each channel, and future versions are expected to reach 50 Gbps per channel (throughput of 35 Gbps). Some experts believe WiGig is best suited to SOHO environments with digital entertainment needs. Other experts expect it to be used in high-density office areas that have many cubicles in the same open space or in sports stadiums and university classrooms, which often have many mobile devices seeking network access.

7.4.5 Security

Security is important to all networks and types of technology, but it is especially important for wireless networks. With a WLAN, anyone walking or driving within the range of an AP (even outside the offices) can begin to use the network.

Finding WLANs is quite simple. You just walk or drive around different office buildings with your WLAN-equipped client computer and see if it picks up a signal. There are also many special-purpose software tools available on the Internet that will enable you to learn more about the WLANs you discover, with the intent of helping you to break into them. This type of wireless reconnaissance is often called **wardriving** (see www.wardriving.com). **Warchalking** refers to the practice of writing symbols in chalk on sidewalks and walls to indicate the presence of an unsecured WLAN (see www.warchalking.org).

WEP   One wireless security technique is **Wired Equivalent Privacy (WEP)**. With WEP, the AP requires the user to have a *key* to communicate with it. All data sent to and from the AP are encrypted so that they can only be understood by computers or devices that have the key (encryption is discussed in more detail in Chapter 11). If a computer does not have the correct WEP key, it cannot understand any messages transmitted by the access point, and the access point will not accept any data that are not encrypted with the correct key.

The WEP keys are produced dynamically, much like the way in which a DHCP server is used to dynamically produce IP addresses. When an AP first discovers a new client computer, it requires the user to log in before it will communicate with the client computer. The user ID and password supplied by the user are transmitted to a login server, and if the server determines that they are valid, the server generates a WEP key that will be used by the AP and client computer to communicate for this session. Once the client logs out or leaves the WLAN, the WEP key is discarded, and the client must log in again and receive a new WEP key.

WEP has a number of serious weaknesses, and most experts agree that a determined hacker can break into a WLAN that uses only WEP security. A good way to think about WEP is that it is like locking your doors when you leave: It won't keep out a professional criminal, but it will protect against a casual thief.

WPA **Wi-Fi Protected Access (WPA)** is a newer, more secure type of security. WPA works in ways similar to WEP: Every frame is encrypted using a key, and the key can be fixed in the AP or can be assigned dynamically as users login. The difference is that the WPA key is longer than the WEP key and thus is harder to break. More importantly, the key is changed for *every* frame that is transmitted to the client. Each time a frame is transmitted, the key is changed.

802.11i **802.11i** (also called WPA2) is the newest, most secure type of WLAN security. The user logs in to a login server to obtain the master key. Armed with this master key, the user's computer and the AP negotiate a new key that will be used for this session until the user leaves the WLAN. 802.11i uses the Advanced Encryption Standard (AES) discussed in Chapter 11 as its encryption method.

MAC Address Filtering With **MAC address filtering**, the AP permits the owner to provide a list of MAC addresses (i.e., layer-2 addresses). The AP only processes frames sent by computers whose MAC address is in the address list; if a computer with a MAC address not in the list sends a frame, the AP ignores it. Unfortunately, this provides no security against a determined hacker. There is software available that will change the MAC address on a wireless NIC, so a determined hacker could use a packet sniffer (e.g., Wireshark) to discover a valid MAC address and then use the software to change his MAC address to one the AP would accept. MAC address filtering is like WEP; it will protect against a casual thief, but not a professional.

MANAGEMENT

FOCUS

7-4 Mooching Wi-Fi

*I*f you connect into someone else's Wi-Fi network and start using his or her Internet connection, are you:

    a. Guilty of stealing from the owner because you haven't paid him or her
    b. Guilty of stealing from the ISP because you haven't paid them
    c. Committing an unethical but not illegal act
    d. Really frugal, and not unethical
    e. All of the above

According to the St. Petersburg, Florida, police department, the answer is a. They arrested a man named Benjamin Smith for "willfully, knowingly, and without authorization" accessing the network of a homeowner while sitting in a car parked on the street.

According to Verizon and most ISPs, which explicitly prohibit sharing, the answer is b. "It's obviously not good for Verizon to have its services given away for free, just as a cable company won't want someone funneling their cable connection next door," said a Verizon spokeswoman.

According to Miss Manners, the answer is c. It's not nice to use other people's stuff without asking their permission.

According to Jennifer Granick, executive director of the Center for Internet and Society at Stanford Law School, the answer is d. "Such use (i.e., sharing) might be allowed or even encouraged (by the owner)." Unless the owner states you can't enter a network, how do you know you're not invited?

As Lee Tien, a senior staff attorney at the Electronic Frontier Foundation, says, "Right now, we don't have a way of saying 'Even though my wireless signal is open, I'm saying you can't use it.'" Until we do, the answer is e. So, tread carefully. Don't leave your WLAN unsecured or you may be legally inviting others to use it as well as your Internet connection. Likewise, don't intentionally enter someone else's WLAN and use his or her Internet connection or you might end up like Benjamin Smith—spending the night in jail.

Adapted from: John Cox, "Mooching Wi-Fi," Network World, August 8, 2005, pp. 1, 49.

7.5 THE BEST PRACTICE LAN DESIGN

This section focuses on the design of wired and wireless LANs that provide network access to users. The data center and e-commerce edge also use LANs, so we include sections on the unique needs of these two network architecture components. The past few years have seen major changes in LAN technologies (e.g., gigabit Ethernet and high-speed wireless Ethernet). As technologies have changed and costs have dropped, so too has our understanding of the best practice design for LANs.

One of the key questions facing network designers is the relationship between Wi-Fi and wired Ethernet. The data rates for Wi-Fi have increased substantially with the introduction of each new version of 802.11, so they are similar to the data rates offered by 100Base-T wired Ethernet. The key difference is that 100Base-T wired Ethernet using switches provides 100 Mbps to each user, whereas Wi-Fi shares its available capacity among every user on the same AP, so as more users connect to the APs, the network gets slower and slower.

Wi-Fi is considerably cheaper than wired Ethernet because the largest cost of LANs is not the equipment, but in paying someone to install the cables. The cost to install a cable in an existing building is typically between $150 and $400 per cable, depending on whether the cable will have to be run through drywall, brick, ceilings, and so on. Installing cable in a new building during construction is cheaper, typically $50 to $100 per cable.

Most organizations today install wired Ethernet to provide access for desktop users and install Wi-Fi as **overlay networks**. They build the usual **switched Ethernet** networks as the primary LAN, but they also install Wi-Fi for laptops and mobile devices. Some organizations have begun experimenting with Wi-Fi by moving groups of users off the wired networks onto Wi-Fi as their primary network to see whether Wi-Fi is suitable as a primary network.

Today, we still believe the best practice is to use wired Ethernet for the primary LAN, with Wi-Fi as an overlay network. However, this may change. Stay tuned.

MANAGEMENT

FOCUS

7-5 Will Wi-Fi Replace Wired LANS?

As KPMG, one of the largest consulting firms in the world, began to build a new 2,800-person headquarters near Amsterdam, KPMG's IT group realized that their traditional wired network approach would have required 18,000 cable runs, 55 chassis switches, and 260 LAN switches. The up-front cost was expected to exceed $6 million, and the recurring operating costs would run into the millions annually as well.

KPMG began to wonder if there was a better way. Could they build an entirely wireless network that would meet their needs?

After careful analysis, KPMG decided they were not ready to go completely wireless. However, they decided to shift a substantial portion of their traditionally wired users to wireless. They cut their wired network by half and installed more than 500 802.11n access points throughout the new facility to provide complete coverage for data and voice. The new network design cut the initial cost by $2 million and reduced annual operating costs by $750,000 per year.

The new design also delivered substantial green benefits. Access Points use about 5% of the electricity that 48-port switches require for power and cooling. By eliminating half the switches, the new design eliminated more than 350 metric tons of carbon dioxide emissions each year.

Adapted from: "KPMG Netherlands Counts on Aruba for Network Rightsizing," Enterprise Case Study, Aruba Networks, 2009.

7.5.1 Designing User Access with Wired Ethernet

Many organizations today install switched 100Base-T or 1000Base-T over category 5e wiring for their wired LANs. It is relatively low cost and fast.

In the early days of LANs, it was common practice to install network cable wherever it was convenient. Little long-term planning was done. The exact placement of the cables was often not documented, making future expansion more difficult—you had to find the cable before you could add a new user.

With today's explosion in LAN use, it is critical to plan for the effective installation and use of LAN **cabling**. The cheapest point at which to install network cable is during the construction of the building; adding cable to an existing building can cost significantly more. Indeed, the costs to install cable (i.e., paying those doing the installation and additional construction) are usually substantially more than the cost of the hubs and switches, making it expensive to reinstall the cable if the cable plan does not meet the organization's needs.

Most buildings under construction today have a separate LAN **cable plan**, as they have plans for electrical cables. Each floor has a data wiring closet that contains one or more network hubs or switches. Cables are run from each room on the floor to this wiring closet.

7.5.2 Designing User Access with Wireless Ethernet

Selecting the best practice wireless technology is usually simple. You pick the newest one, cost permitting. Today, 802.11ac is the newest standard, but in time, there will be a new one.

Designing the physical WLAN is more challenging than designing a wired LAN because the potential for radio interference means that extra care must be taken in the placement of access points. With the design of LANs there is considerable freedom in the placement of switches, subject to the maximum limits to the length of network cables. In WLANs, however, the placement of the access points needs to consider both the placement of other access points and the sources of interference in the building.

The physical WLAN design begins with a **site survey**. The site survey determines the feasibility of the desired coverage, the potential sources of interference, the current locations of the wired network into which the WLAN will connect, and an estimate of the number of APs required to provide coverage. WLANs work very well when there is a clear line of sight between the AP and the wireless computer. The more walls there are between the AP and the computer, the weaker the wireless signal becomes. The type and thickness of the wall also has an impact; traditional drywall construction provides less interference than does concrete block construction.

An access point with an omnidirectional antenna broadcasts in all directions. Its coverage area is a circle with a certain radius. Wi-Fi has a long range, but real-world tests of Wi-Fi in typical office environments have shown that data rates slow down dramatically when the distance from a laptop to the AP exceeds 50 feet. Therefore, many wireless designers use a radius of 50 feet when planning traditional office environments, which ensures access high-quality coverage. It is also expensive, because many APs will need to be purchased. Costs may be reduced by using a longer radius (e.g., 100 feet), so that fewer APs are needed, but this may result in slower data rates.

One may design wireless LANs using this 50-foot radius circle, but because most buildings are square, it is usually easier to design using squares. Figure 7-8 shows that a 50-foot radius translates into a square that is approximately 70 feet on each edge. For this reason, most designers plan wireless LANs using 50- to 75-foot squares, depending on the construction of the building: smaller squares in areas where there are more walls that can cause more interference and larger squares in areas with fewer walls.

FIGURE 7-8

Design parameters for
Wi-Fi access point range

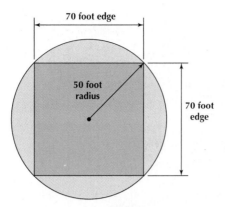

Figure 7-9 shows a sample building that has two parts. The lower left corner is a 150 feet × 150 feet square, while the rest of the building is a 150 feet × 450 feet rectangle. Let's assume that the large rectangle part is an open office environment, while the smaller part uses drywall. If we put two rows of APs in the large rectangle part, we could probably space them so that each AP covered a 75-foot square. This would take a total of 12 APs for this area (see Figure 7-9). This same spacing probably won't work for the small area with drywall, so we would probably design using 50-foot squares, meaning we need nine APs in this area (see Figure 7-9).

When designing a wireless LAN, it is important to ensure that the APs don't interfere with each other. If all APs transmitted on the same frequency, the transmissions of one AP would interfere with another AP where their signals overlapped—just like what happens on your car radio when two stations are in the same frequency. Therefore, each AP is set to transmit on a different **channel**, very much like the different channels on your TV. Figure 7-9 shows how we could set the APs to the three commonly used channels (1, 6, and 11) so that there is minimal overlap between APs using the same channel.

After the initial design is complete, a site survey is done using a temporary AP and a computer or device that can actually measure the strength of the wireless signal. The temporary AP is installed in the area as called for in the initial design, and the computer or device

FIGURE 7-9

A Wi-Fi design (the numbers indicate the channel numbers)

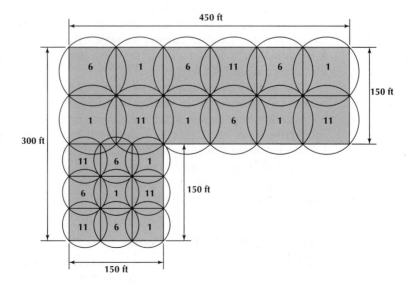

FIGURE 7-10

A Wi-Fi design in the
three dimensions (the
numbers indicate the
channel numbers)

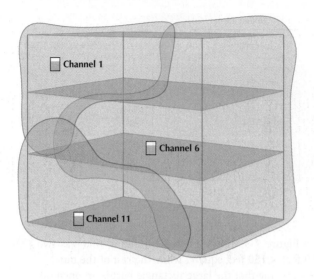

is carried throughout the building measuring the strength of the signal. Actually measuring the strength of the signal in the environment is far more accurate than relying on estimated ranges.

Design becomes more difficult in a multistory building because the signals from the APs travel up and down as well as in all horizontal directions. The design must include the usual horizontal mapping but also an added vertical mapping to ensure that APs on different floors do not interfere with one another (Figure 7-10). Because floors are usually thicker than walls, signals travel further horizontally than vertically, making design a bit more difficult. It becomes even more difficult if your set of floors in a large office tower is surrounded by APs of other companies. You have to design your network not to interfere with theirs.

Most wireless LAN APs offer the ability to provide two separate wireless networks. The primary network is secured by a password that is entered when you first connect to the network. This password is remembered by the device so that you never have to enter the password a second time. This password secures the access to the network, and all connections use some form of encryption, such as WPA2, so that no one can read your messages (even if someone accesses the same AP using the same password). This network is typically used by regular users of the network such as employees of an organization or the homeowner in a SOHO network.

The second network is a guest network that is secured by a separate password that is entered on a Web page when you first connect to the network. This network is not secure, meaning that other users with the right hacking software can read the messages you send and receive. However, because the network will not allow users on the network without the password, it means that access can be controlled so that only authorized users have access. This network is typically used by guests who need temporary access. The guest network is often configured so it provides slower speeds than the primary network, so if the AP gets busy, it prioritizes traffic for regular users over traffic for guest users.

7.5.3 Designing the Data Center

The data center is where the organization houses its primary servers. In most large organizations, the data center is huge because it contains the data center as well as the campus backbone switches and the enterprise edge. Figure 7-11 shows the data center building at

FIGURE 7-11

The data center at
Indiana University
Source: Courtesy of the author,
Alan Dennis

Indiana University. This building, which is built partially underground to withstand an F5 tornado, is 87,000 square feet, of which 33,000 square feet is used for servers. The servers can store about 50 petabytes of data (about 50 million gigabytes).

Designing the data center requires considerable expertise, because most data on a network flow from or to the data center. In all large-scale networks today, servers are placed together in server farms or clusters, which sometimes have hundreds of servers that perform the same task. Yahoo.com, for example, has more than a thousand Web servers that do nothing but respond to Web search requests. In this case, it is important to ensure that when a request arrives at the server farm, it is immediately forwarded to a server that is not busy—or that is the least busy.

A special device called a **load balancer** or **load balancing switch** acts as a router at the front of the server farm (Figure 7-12). All requests are directed to the load balancer at its IP address. When a request hits the load balancer, it forwards it to one specific server using its IP address. Sometimes a simple round-robin formula is used (requests go to each server one after the other in turn); in other cases, more complex formulas track how busy each server actually is. If a server crashes, the load balancer stops sending requests to it, and the network continues to operate without the failed server. Load balancing makes it simple to add servers (or remove servers) without affecting users. You simply add or remove the server(s) and change the software configuration in the load balancing switch; no one is aware of the change.

Server virtualization is somewhat the opposite of server farms and load balancing. Server virtualization is the process of creating several logically separate servers (e.g., a Web server, an email server, and a file server) on the same physical computer. The virtual servers run on the same physical computer but appear completely separate to the network (and if one crashes, it does not affect the others running on the same computer).

Over time, many firms have installed new servers to support new projects, only to find that the new server was not fully used; the server might only be running at 10% of its capacity and sitting idle for the rest of the time. One underutilized server is not a problem, but imagine if 20–30% of a company's servers are underutilized. The company has spent too much money to acquire the servers, and more importantly, it is continuing to spend money to monitor, manage, and update the underused servers. Even the space and power used by having many separate computers can noticeably increase operating costs. Server virtualization enables firms to save money by reducing the number of physical servers they buy and operate, while still providing all the benefits of having logically separate devices and operating systems.

FIGURE 7-12

Network with load
balancer

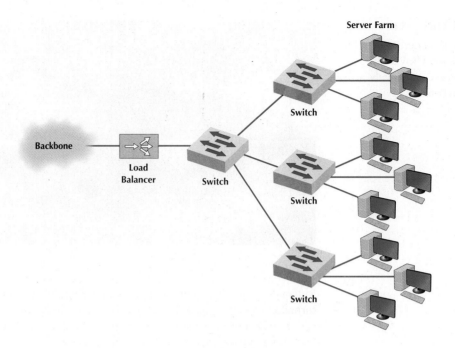

Some operating systems enable virtualization natively, which means that it is easy to configure and run separate virtual servers. In other cases, special-purpose virtualization software (e.g., VMware) is installed on the server and sits between the hardware and the operating systems; this software means that several different operating systems can be installed on the same physical computer.

A **storage area network (SAN)** is a LAN devoted solely to data storage. When the amount of data to be stored exceeds the practical limits of servers, the SAN plays a critical role. The SAN has a set of high-speed storage devices and servers that are networked together using a very high speed network. When data are needed, clients send the request to a server on the LAN, which obtains the information from the devices on the SAN and then returns it to the client.

The devices on the SAN may be a large set of database servers or a set of network-attached disk arrays. In other cases, the devices may be **network-attached storage (NAS)** devices. A NAS is not a general-purpose computer, such as a server that runs a server operating system (e.g., Windows and Linux); instead, it has a small processor and a large amount of disk storage and is designed solely to respond to requests for files and data. NAS can also be attached to LANs, where they function as fast file servers. Figure 7-13 shows the SAN for the Kelley School of Business at Indiana University. This SAN stores 125 terabytes of data.

7.5.4 Designing the e-Commerce Edge

The e-commerce edge contains the servers that are designed to serve data to customers and suppliers, such as the corporate Web server. The e-commerce edge is essentially a smaller, specialized version of the data center. It contains all the same equipment as the data center (e.g., load balancer, SAN, and UPS), but this equipment supports access by users external to the organization. It is often connected directly to the Internet access part of the network via a very high speed circuit as well as the campus backbone.

The e-commerce edge often has different security requirements than the servers in the data center intended for use by employees inside the organization because the e-commerce

FIGURE 7-13

The storage area network (SAN) at the Kelley School of Business at Indiana University
Source: Courtesy of the author, Alan Dennis

edge is primarily intended to serve those external to the organization. We discuss the special security needs of the e-commerce edge in Chapter 11.

7.5.5 Designing the SOHO Environment

Most of what we have discussed so far has focused on network design in large enterprises. What about LAN design for SOHO environments? SOHO environments can be small versions of enterprise designs, or can take a very different approach.

Figure 7-14a shows a SOHO LAN designed similar to a small enterprise design that provides both wired and wireless Ethernet (it's in Alan's house). Virtually all of the rooms in the house are wired with 1000Base-T Ethernet over Cat 5e cable, which terminates in a 24-port patch panel. You can see from the figure that only five of the rooms are actually wired from the patch panel into the 16-port switch; one of those wires connects the AP mounted in an upstairs hallway (not shown) that provides wireless access throughout the house and onto the back deck and gazebo. There is a separate router and cable modem. The AP, switch, and router are all Cisco or Linksys equipment and are the original 2001 equipment, and still work well. The cable modem is an off-brand provided by the ISP and has broken and been replaced every 3 years.

Figure 7-14b shows a more modern—and probably more common—SOHO LAN that provides only wireless access (it's in Alexandra's house). This has a cable modem that connects into a wireless router; the wireless router is a wireless AP, a router, and a switch for wired Ethernet all in one box. This network is simpler and cheaper because it contains fewer devices and is used only for wireless access. Alexandra doesn't have a desktop computer at home, but she could easily connect one if she wanted by adding a wireless NIC into a desktop; the 802.11n WLAN provides ample capacity for a small SOHO network.

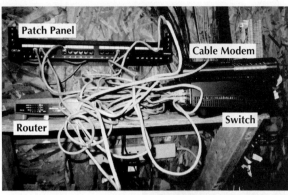

(a) Alan's home network (b) Alexandra's home network

FIGURE 7-14 SOHO LAN designs

Source: Photos courtesy of the authors, Alan Dennis and Alexandra Durcikova

7.6 IMPROVING LAN PERFORMANCE

When LANs had only a few users, performance was usually very good. Today, however, when most computers in an organization are on LANs, performance can be a problem. Performance is usually expressed in terms of throughput (the total amount of user data transmitted in a given time period) or in response time (how long it takes to get a response from the destination). In this section, we discuss how to improve throughput. We focus on dedicated-server networks because they are the most commonly used type of LANs, but many of these concepts also apply to peer-to-peer networks.

TECHNICAL FOCUS **7-2 Error Control in Wired Ethernet**

*E*thernet provides a strong error control method using stop and wait ARQ with a CRC-32 error detection field (see Chapter 4). However, the normal way of installing wired Ethernet doesn't use stop and wait ARQ.

In the early days of Ethernet, LAN environments were not very reliable, so error control was important. However, today's wired Ethernet LANs are very reliable; errors seldom occur. Stop and wait ARQ uses considerable network capacity because every time a frame is transmitted, the sender must stop and wait for the receiver to send an acknowledgment. By eliminating the need to stop and wait and the need to send acknowledgments, Ethernet can significantly improve network performance—almost doubling the number of messages that can be transmitted in

the same time period. Ethernet does still add the CRC and does still check it for errors, but any frame with an error is simply discarded.

If Ethernet doesn't provide error control, then higher layers in the network model must. In general, TCP is configured to provide error control by using continuous ARQ (see Chapter 5) to ensure that all frames that have been sent are actually received at the final destination. If a frame with an error is discarded by Ethernet, TCP will recognize that a frame has been lost and ask the sender to retransmit. This moves responsibility for error control to the edges of the network (i.e., the sender and receiver) rather than making every computer along the way responsible for ensuring reliable message delivery.

To improve performance, you must locate the **bottleneck**, the part of the network that is restricting the data flow. Generally speaking, the bottleneck will lie in one of two places.

The first is the network server. In this case, the client computers have no difficulty sending requests to the network server, but the server lacks sufficient capacity to process all the requests it receives in a timely manner. The second location is a network circuit, either the access LAN, the building backbone, the campus backbone, or the circuit into the data center. In this case, the server (or more likely, a server farm) can easily process all the client requests it receives, but a circuit lacks enough capacity to transmit all the requests to the server.

The first step in improving performance, therefore, is to identify whether the bottleneck lies in a circuit or the server. To do so, you simply watch the utilization of the server during periods of poor performance. If the server utilization is high (e.g., 80–100%), then the bottleneck is the server; it cannot process all the requests it receives in a timely manner. If the server utilization is low during periods of poor performance, then the problem lies with a network circuit; some circuits cannot transmit messages as quickly as necessary.

Most organizations focus on ways to improve the server and the circuits to remove bottlenecks. These actions address only the supply side of the equation—that is, increasing the capacity of the LAN as a whole. The other way to reduce performance problems is to attack the demand side: reduce the amount of network use by the clients, which we also discuss. Figure 7-15 provides a performance checklist.

7.6.1 Improving Server Performance

Improving server performance can be approached from two directions simultaneously: software and hardware.

Software The NOS is the primary software-based approach to improving network performance. Some NOSs are faster than others, so replacing the NOS with a faster one will improve performance.

Each NOS provides a number of software settings to fine-tune network performance. Depending on the number, size, and type of messages and requests in your LAN, different

FIGURE 7-15

Improving local area
network performance

```
                  Performance Checklist
Increase Server Performance
• Software
• Fine-tune the network operating system settings
• Hardware
• Add more servers and spread the network applications
  across the servers to balance the load
• Upgrade to a faster computer
• Increase the server's memory
• Increase the number and speed of the server's hard disk(s)

Increase Circuit Capacity
• Upgrade to a faster circuit
• Increase the number of circuits

Reduce Network Demand
• Move files from the server to the client computers
• Increase the use of disk caching on client computers
• Change user behavior
```

settings can have a significant effect on performance. The specific settings differ by NOS but often include things such as the amount of memory used for disk caches, the number of simultaneously open files, and the amount of buffer space.

Hardware One obvious solution if your network server is overloaded is to buy a second server (or more). Each server is then dedicated to supporting one set of application software (e.g., one handles email, another handles the financial database, and another stores customer records). The bottleneck can be broken by carefully identifying the demands each major application software package places on the server and allocating them to different servers.

Sometimes, however, most of the demand on the server is produced by one application that cannot be split across several servers. In this case, the server itself must be upgraded. The first place to start is with the server's CPU. Faster CPUs mean better performance. If you are still using an old computer as a LAN server, this may be the answer; you probably need to upgrade to the latest and greatest. Clock speed also matters: the faster, the better. Most computers today also come with CPU-cache (a very fast memory module directly connected to the CPU). Increasing the cache will increase CPU performance.

A second bottleneck is the amount of memory in the server. Increasing the amount of memory increases the probability that disk caching will work, thus increasing performance.

A third bottleneck is the number and speed of the hard disks in the server. The primary function of the LAN server is to process requests for information on its disks. Slow hard disks give slow network performance. The obvious solution is to buy the fastest disk drive possible. Even more important, however, is the number of hard disks. Each computer hard disk has only one read/write head, meaning that all requests must go through this one device. By using several smaller disks rather than one larger disk (e.g., five 200 gigabyte disks rather than one 1 terabyte disk), you now have more read/write heads, each of which can be used simultaneously, dramatically improving throughput. A special type of disk drive called **RAID (redundant array of inexpensive disks)** builds on this concept and is typically used in applications requiring very fast processing of large volumes of data, such as multimedia. Of course, RAID is more expensive than traditional disk drives, but costs have been shrinking. RAID can also provide fault tolerance, which is discussed in Chapter 11.

Several vendors sell special-purpose network servers that are optimized to provide extremely fast performance. Many of these provide RAID and use **symmetric multiprocessing (SMP)** that enables one server to use up to 16 CPUs. Such servers provide excellent performance but cost more (often $5,000 to $15,000).

7.6.2 Improving Circuit Capacity

Improving the capacity of a circuit means increasing the volume of simultaneous messages the circuit can transmit from network clients to the server(s). One obvious approach is simply to buy a bigger circuit. For example, if you are now using a 100Base-T LAN, upgrading to 1000Base-T LAN will improve capacity. Or if you have 802.11n, then upgrade to 802.11ac. You can also add more circuits so that there are two or even three separate high speed circuits between busy parts of the network, such as the core backbone and the data center. Most Ethernet circuits can be configured to use full duplex (see Chapter 4), which is often done for backbones and servers.

Another approach is to segment the network. If there is more traffic on a LAN than it can handle, you can divide the LAN into several smaller segments. Breaking a network into smaller parts is called **network segmentation**. In a wired LAN, this means adding one of more new switches and spreading the computers across these new switches. In a wireless LAN, this means adding more access points that operate on different channels. If wireless performance is significantly worse than expected, then it is important to check for sources of interference near the AP and the computers such as Bluetooth devices and cordless phones.

7.6.3 Reducing Network Demand

One way to reduce network demand is to move files to client computers. Heavily used software packages that continually access and load modules from the network can place unusually heavy demands on the network. Although user data and messages are often only a few kilobytes in size, today's software packages can be many megabytes in size. Placing even one or two such applications on client computers can greatly improve network performance (although this can create other problems, such as increasing the difficulty in upgrading to new versions of the software).

Most organizations now provide both wired and wireless networks, so another way to reduce demand is to shift it from wired networks to wireless networks, or vice versa, depending on which has the problem. For example, you can encourage wired users to go wireless or install wired Ethernet jacks in places where wireless users often sit.

Because the demand on most LANs is uneven, network performance can be improved by attempting to move user demands from peak times to off-peak times. For example, early morning and after lunch are often busy times when people check their email. Telling network users about the peak times and encouraging them to change their habits may help; however, in practice, it is often difficult to get users to change. Nonetheless, finding one application that places a large demand on the network and moving it can have a significant impact (e.g., printing several thousand customer records after midnight).

7.7 IMPLICATIONS FOR MANAGEMENT

As LANs have standardized on Ethernet, local area networking technology has become a commodity in most organizations. As with most commodities, the cost of LAN equipment (i.e., network interface cards, cabling, hubs, and switches) has dropped significantly. Some vendors are producing high-quality equipment, whereas some new entrants into the market are producing equipment that meets standards but creates opportunities for problems because it lacks the features of more established brands. It becomes difficult for LAN managers to explain to business managers why it's important to purchase higher-quality, more expensive equipment when low-cost "standardized" equipment is available.

Most SOHO users are moving quickly to wireless, which means that wired Ethernet is a legacy technology for small SOHO devices; there is little profit to be made in this market, and many manufacturers will abandon it. We have seen a rise in the sales of wireless cards for desktop computers, and desktop computers targeted for sale to the SOHO market will come standard with wireless cards in addition to the wired Ethernet cards we see today.

Decreasing costs for LAN equipment also means that network-enabled microprocessor-controlled devices that have not normally been thought of as computer technology are becoming less expensive. Therefore, we have seen devices such as copiers turned into network printers and scanners. This trend will increase as electrical appliances such as refrigerators and ovens become network devices. Don't laugh; networked vending machines are already in use.

SUMMARY

LAN Components The NIC enables the computer to be physically connected to the network and provides the physical layer connection among the computers. Wired LANs use UTP wires, STP wires, and/or fiber-optic cable. Network hubs and switches provide an easy way to connect network cables and act as repeaters. Wireless NICs provide radio connections to access points that link wireless computers into the wired network. The NOS is the software that performs the functions associated with the data link and the network layers and interacts with the application software and the computer's own operating system. Every NOS provides two sets of software: one that runs on the network server(s) and one that runs on the network client(s). A network profile specifies what resources on each server are available for network use by other computers and which devices or people are allowed what access to the network.

Ethernet (IEEE 802.3) Ethernet, the most commonly used LAN protocol in the world, uses a contention-based media access technique called CSMA/CD. There are many different types of Ethernet that use different network cabling (e.g., 10Base-T, 100Base-T, 1000Base-T, and 10 GbE). Switches are preferred to hubs because they are significantly faster.

Wireless Ethernet Wireless Ethernet (often called Wi-Fi) is the most common type of wireless LAN. It uses physical star/logical bus topology with both controlled and contention-based media access control. 802.11n, the newest version, provides 200 Mbps over three channels or faster speeds over fewer channels.

Best Practice LAN Design Most organizations install 100Base-T or 10/100/1000 Ethernet as their primary LAN and also provide wireless LANs as an overlay network. For SOHO networks, the best LAN choice may be wireless. Designing the data center and e-commerce edge often uses specialized equipment such as server farms, load balancers, virtual servers, SANs, and UPS.

Improving LAN Performance Every LAN has a bottleneck, a narrow point in the network that limits the number of messages that can be processed. Generally speaking, the bottleneck will lie in either the network server or a network circuit. Server performance can be improved with a faster NOS that provides better disk caching, by buying more servers and spreading applications among them or by upgrading the server's CPU, memory, NIC, and the speed and number of its hard disks. Circuit capacity can be improved by using faster technologies (100Base-T rather than 10Base-T), by adding more circuits, and by segmenting the network into several separate LANs by adding more switches or access points. Overall LAN performance also can be improved by reducing the demand for the LAN by moving files off the LAN, moving users from wired Ethernet to wireless or vice versa, and by shifting users' routines.

KEY TERMS

access point (AP), 188
Active Directory Service
   (ADS), 190
association, 196
beacon frame, 196
bottleneck, 208
bus topology, 191

cable plan, 202
cabling, 202
Carrier Sense Multiple
   Access with Collision
   Detection (CSMA/CD),
   194

Carrier Sense Multiple
   Access with Collision
   Avoidance (CSMA/CA),
   196
channel, 203
clear to send (CTS), 197
collision, 194

collision detection (CD),
   194
collision domain, 192
cut-through switching, 193
directional antenna, 189
distributed coordination
   function (DCF), 196

QUESTIONS

1. Define *local area network*.
2. Describe at least three types of servers.
3. Describe the basic components of a wired LAN.
4. Describe the basic components of a wireless LAN.
5. What types of cables are commonly used in wired LANs?
6. Compare and contrast category 5 UTP, category 5e UTP, and category 5 STP.
7. What is a cable plan and why would you want one?
8. What does a NOS do? What are the major software parts of a NOS?
9. How does wired Ethernet work?
10. How does a logical topology differ from a physical topology?
11. Briefly describe how CSMA/CD works.
12. Explain the terms 100Base-T, 100Base-F, 1000Base-T, 10 GbE, and 10/100/1000 Ethernet.
13. How do Ethernet switches know where to send the frames they receive? Describe how switches gather and use this knowledge.
14. Compare and contrast cut-through, store and forward, and fragment-free switching.
15. Compare and contrast the two types of antennas.
16. How does Wi-Fi perform media access control?
17. How does Wi-Fi differ from shared Ethernet in terms of topology, media access control, and error control, Ethernet frame?
18. Explain how CSMA/CA DCF works.
19. Explain how CSMA/CA PCF works.
20. Explain how association works in WLAN.
21. What are the best practice recommendations for wired LAN design?
22. What are the best practice recommendations for WLAN design?
23. What is a site survey, and why is it important?
24. How do you decide how many APs are needed and where they should be placed for best performance?
25. How does the design of the data center differ from the design of the LANs intended to provide user access to the network?
26. What are three special purpose devices you might find in a data center and what do they do?
27. What is a bottleneck and how can you locate one?
28. Describe three ways to improve network performance on the server.

29. Describe three ways to improve network performance on circuits.
30. Many of the wired and wireless LANs share the same or similar components (e.g., error control). Why?
31. As WLANs become more powerful, what are the implications for networks of the future? Will wired LANS still be common or will we eliminate wired offices?

EXERCISES

A. Survey the LANs used in your organization. Are they wireless or wired? Why?
B. Document one LAN (or LAN segment) in detail. What devices are attached, what cabling is used, and what is the topology? What does the cable plan look like?
C. You have been hired by a small company to install a simple LAN for its 18 Windows computers. Develop a simple LAN and determine the total cost; that is, select the cables, hubs/switches, and so on, and price them. Assume that the company has no network today and that the office is small enough that you don't need to worry about cable length.

MINICASES

I. **Designing a New Ethernet** One important issue in designing Ethernet lies in making sure that if a computer transmits a frame, any other computer that attempts to transmit at the same time will be able to hear the incoming frame before it stops transmitting, or else a collision might go unnoticed. For example, assume that we are on earth and send an Ethernet frame over a very long piece of category 5 wire to the moon. If a computer on the moon starts transmitting at the same time as we do on earth and finishes transmitting before our frame arrives at the moon, there will be a collision, but neither computer will detect it; the frame will be garbled, but no one will know why. So, in designing Ethernet, we must make sure that the length of cable in the LAN is shorter than the length of the shortest possible frame that can be sent. Otherwise, a collision could go undetected.

a. Let's assume that the smallest possible message is 64 bytes (including the 33-byte overhead). If we use 100Base-T, how long (in meters) is a 64-byte message? While electricity in the cable travels a bit slower than the speed of light, once you include delays in the electrical equipment in transmitting and receiving the signal, the effective speed is only about 40 million meters per second. (*Hint*: First calculate the number of seconds it would take to transmit the frame then calculate the number of meters the signal would travel in that time, and you have the total length of the frame.)

b. If we use 10 GbE, how long (in meters) is a 64-byte frame?

c. The answer in part b is the maximum distance any single cable could run from a switch to a computer in an Ethernet LAN. How would you overcome the problem implied by this?

II. **Pat's Petunias** You have been called in as a network consultant by your cousin Pat, who operates a successful mail-order flower business. She is moving to a new office and wants to install a network for her telephone operators, who take phone calls and enter orders into the system. The number of operators working varies depending on the time of day and day of the week. On slow shifts, there are usually only 10 operators, whereas at peak times, there are 50. She has bids from different companies to install (1) Wi-Fi or (2) a switched Ethernet 100Base-T network. She wants you to give her some sense of the relative performance of the alternatives so she can compare that with their different costs. What would you recommend?

III. **Eureka!** Eureka! is a telephone- and Internet-based concierge service that specializes in obtaining things that are hard to find (e.g., Super Bowl tickets, first-edition books from the 1500s, and Fabergé eggs). It currently employs staff members who work 24 hours per day (over three shifts), with usually 5–7 staff members working at any given time. Staff members answer the phone and respond to requests entered on the Eureka! Web site. Much of their work is spent on the phone and on computers searching on the Internet. They have just leased a new office and are about to wire it. They have bids from different companies to install (a) a 100Base-T network or (b) a Wi-Fi network. What would you recommend? Why?

IV. **Tom's Home Automation** Your cousin Tom runs a small construction company that builds custom houses. He has just started a new specialty service that he is offering to other builders on a subcontracting basis: home automation. He provides a complete service of installing cable in all the rooms in which the homeowner wants data access and installs the necessary networking devices to provide a LAN that will connect all the computers in the house to the Internet. Most homeowners choose to install a DSL or cable modem Internet connection that provides a 12–25 Mbps from the house to the Internet. Tom has come to you for advice about whether he should continue to offer wiring services (which often cost $50 per room) or whether wireless is a better direction. What type of LAN would you recommend?

V. **Sally's Shoes** Sally Smith runs a shoe store in the mall that is about 30 feet by 50 feet in size, including a small office and a storage area in the rear. The store has one inventory computer in the storage area and one computer in the office. She is replacing the two cash registers with computers that will act as cash registers but will also be able to communicate with the inventory computer. Sally wants to network the computers with a LAN. What sort of LAN design would you recommend? Draw a picture.

VI. **South West State University** South West State University installed a series of four Wi-Fi omnidirectional APs spread across the ceiling of the main floor of its library. The main floor has several large, open areas plus two dozen or so small offices spread around the outside walls. The WLAN worked well for one semester, but now more students are using the network, and performance has deteriorated significantly. What would you recommend that they do? Be sure to support your recommendations.

VII. **Household Wireless** Your sister is building a new two-story house (which measures 50 feet long by 30 feet wide) and wants to make sure that it is capable of networking her family's three computers together. She and her husband are both consultants and work out of their home in the evenings and a few days a month (each has a separate office with a computer, plus a laptop from the office that are occasionally used). The kids also have a computer in their playroom. They have several options for networking their home:

a. Wire the two offices and playroom with Ethernet Cat 5e cable and put in a 1000Base-T switch for $40

b. Install one Wi-Fi access point ($85) and put Wi-Fi cards in the three computers for $50 each (their laptops already have Wi-Fi)

c. Any combination of these options

What would you recommend? Justify your recommendation.

VIII. **Ubiquitous Offices** Ubiquitous Offices provides temporary office space in cities around the country. They have a standard office layout that is a single floor with outside dimensions of 150 feet wide by 150 feet long. The interior is drywall offices. They have 1000Base-T but want to add wireless access as well. How many access points would you buy, and where would you put them? Draw the office and show where the access points would go.

IX. **ABC Warehouse** ABC Warehouse is a single-floor facility with outside dimensions of 100 feet wide by 350 feet long. The interior is open, but there are large metal shelving units throughout the building to hold all the goods in the warehouse. How many access points would you buy, and where would you put them? Draw the warehouse and show where the access points would go.

X. **Metro Motel** Metro Motel is a four-story motel on the outskirts of town. The outside dimensions of the motel are 60 feet wide by 200 feet long, and each story is about 10 feet high. Each floor (except the ground floor) has 20 rooms (drywall construction). There is a central corridor with rooms on both sides. How many access points would you buy, and where would you put them? Draw the motel and show where the access points would go.

CASE STUDY

NEXT-DAY AIR SERVICE

See the companion Web site at www.wiley.com/college/fitzgerald

HANDS-ON ACTIVITY 7A

Windows Peer-to-Peer Networking

In this chapter, we've discussed two types of LANs: peer-to-peer LANs and dedicated server LANs. This activity will show you how to set up a peer-to-peer LAN for your house or apartment. We first describe file sharing and then discuss printer sharing.

Windows File Sharing

Windows file sharing enables you to select folders on your computer that you can permit other users on your LAN to read and write. There are three steps to creating a shared folder.

Step 1. Give your computer an Application Layer Name within a Workgroup

1. Go to Settings → Control Panel → System
2. Click on the Computer Name Tab
3. Click Change
4. Type in a New Computer Name and Workgroup Name. All computers must have the same workgroup name to share files. Each computer within a workgroup must have a unique name.

Step 2. Enable File Sharing

1. Go to Settings → Control Panel → Windows Firewall
2. Click on the Exceptions tab
3. Make sure the box in front of File and Printer Sharing is checked
4. Go to Settings → Control Panel → Network Connections
5. Right click on the LAN connection and click Properties
6. Ensure that the box in front of File and Printer Sharing for Microsoft Networks is checked.

Step 3. Create the Shared Folder

1. Open Windows Explorer
2. Create a new folder
3. Right click the folder name and choose Properties
4. Click on the Sharing tab
5. Avoid the Network Wizard and make sure the boxes in front of Share This Folder and Allow Network Users to change are checked

Once you have created a shared folder, other computers in your workgroup can access it. Move to another computer on your LAN and repeat steps 1 and 2 (and step 3 if you like). Now you can use the shared folder:

1. Double click on My Network Places
2. Double click on a shared folder
3. Create a file (e.g., using Word) and save it in your shared directory
4. Move the file(s) across computers in your workgroup

If you do this on your home network, anyone with access to your network can access the files in your shared folder. It is much safer to turn off file sharing unless you intentionally want to use it (see Step 2 and make sure the boxes are not checked if you want to prevent file sharing).

Windows Printer Sharing

In the same way you can share folders with other computers in your workgroup, you can share printers. To share a printer, do the following on the computer that has the printer connected to it:

1. Go to Settings → Control Panel → Printers and Faxes
2. Right click on a printer and select Properties
3. Click on the Sharing tab
4. Click on Share This Printer

Once you have done this, you can move to other computers on your LAN and install the network on them:

1. Go to Settings → Control Panel → Printers and Faxes
2. Click on Add a Printer
3. In the Welcome to Add a Printer Wizard, click Next
4. Click the Radio Button in front of A Network Printer and click Next
5. Click the Radio Button in front of Browse for a Printer and click Next
6. Select the Network Printer and click Next
7. You can make this printer your default printer or not, and click Next

Deliverables

1. Do a print screen of Windows Explorer to show the folders on another computer you can access.

2. Do a print screen to show you can print to the networked printer.

HANDS-ON ACTIVITY 7B

Tracing Ethernet

TracePlus Ethernet is a network monitoring tool that enables you to see how much network capacity you are using. If you're working from home with a broadband Internet connection, you'll be surprised how little of the Ethernet capacity you're actually using. Your LAN connection is probably 1000 Mbps (or 300 Mbps if you're using wireless), while the broadband connection into your home or apartment is only 20–30 Mbps. The bottleneck is the broadband connection, so you use only a small percentage of your LAN capacity.

1. Download and install TracePlus. A free trial version of TracePlus is available at TUCows

(www.tucows.com/preview/230332/TracePlus-Ethernet?q=Traceplus+). The URL might move, so if this link doesn't work, search on the Internet. Just be careful what you download and where you get it. We like TuCows and Cnet as safe download sites, but you can also check Norton SafeWeb for their ratings of sites (safeweb.norton.com).

2. Start TracePlus and monitor your network. Leave it open in one part of your screen as you surf the Internet, check email, or watch a video.

Figure 7-16 shows a sample TracePlus screen while I was surfing the Internet and checking email with Microsoft Outlook. The dashboard at the bottom of the screen shows

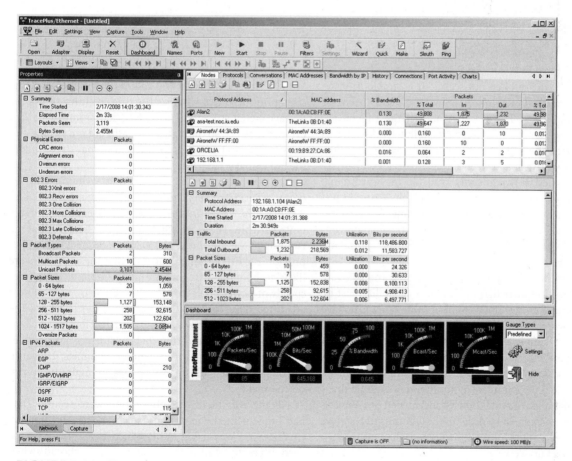

FIGURE 7-16 TracePlus

the real-time usage. You can see that when I took this screen shot, my computer was sending and receiving about 100 packets per second (or if you prefer, 100 frames per second), for a total of just under 1 Mbps of data. This is less than 1% of the total Ethernet bandwidth (i.e., network capacity), because I have switched to 100Base-T on my computer. The dashboard also shows that I'm sending and receiving almost no broadcast or multicast data.

Immediately above the dashboard is the summary for my computer (192.1681.104 (Alan 2)). In the 2 minutes and 30 seconds of monitoring, my computer received 1,875 inbound packets with a total of 2.236 megabytes of data for a utilization of 0.118%. The average bits per second was about 118 Kbps. During the same time, my computer sent slightly fewer outbound packets (1,232), but the average packet was about 10 times smaller because the total amount of data sent was only 218,569 bytes. Most packets were 128–511 bytes in length, but some were smaller and some were larger.

The Nodes tab in the upper right of the screen shows the nodes on my network that TracePlus can monitor.

These include my computer (Alan2), a second computer (Orcelia), my router (192.168.1.1), a wireless access point (Aironet) with two connections (into the LAN and out to the wireless LAN), and the Indiana University VPN server (because I had my VPN connected; Chapter 11 discusses VPNs). You can see that all of these devices have little utilization (under 1%), as well as the total number of packets these devices have sent and received. You can click through the other tabs in this area to see the packet distribution.

The panel on the left of the screen shows additional information about the types of packets, errors, and packet sizes.

Deliverables

1. How many packets can your computer send and receive?

2. What is the total data rate on your network?

3. What is your network utilization?

HANDS-ON ACTIVITY 7C

Wardriving and Warwalking

Wireless LANS are often not secure. It is simple to bring your laptop computer into a public area and listen for wireless networks. This is called wardriving (if you are in a car) or warwalking (if you're walking). As long as you do not attempt to use any networks without authorization, wardriving and warwalking are quite legal. There are many good software tools available for wardriving. My favorites are Net Surveyor (available from http://nutsaboutnets.com/netsurveyor-wifi-scanner/) or Wireless NetView (available from http://download.cnet.com/WirelessNetView/3000-2162_4-191039.html). Both are simple to use, yet powerful.

The first step is to download and install the software on a laptop computer that has wireless capability. Just be careful what you download as these sites sometimes have other software on the same page. Once you have installed the software, simply walk or drive to a public area and start it up. Figure 7-17 shows an example of the 13 networks I discovered in my home town of Bloomington, Indiana, when I parked my car in a neighborhood near the university that has a lot of rental houses and turned on Wireless Netview. I rearranged the order of the columns in Netview, so your screen might look a little different than mine when you first start up Netview.

NetView displays information about each wireless LAN it discovers. The first column shows the name of the WLAN (the ssid). The second column shows the last signal strength it detected, whereas the third column shows the average signal strength. I used NetView from my parked car on the street, so the signal strengths are not strong, and because I wasn't moving, the average signal strength and the last signal strength are the same.

You can examine the "PHY Types" column and see that most APs are 802.11n, although there are three older 802.11g APs. Values in the "Maximum Speed" column are quite variable. There are some newer 8011.n APs that are running at the top speed of 450 Mbps. Some 802.11n APs provide 144 Mbps, which suggests that these WLANs are likely to be older APs that are not capable of the higher speeds of newer 802.11n APs. You can also see that there are three 802.11g APs that provide only 54 Mbps. The "Channel" column shows a fairly even distribution of channels 1, 6, and 11, indicating that most users have configured them to use the three standard channels. However, the owner of the FatJesse WLAN has configured it to run on channel 2.

All the APs in this neighborhood were secure. They had implemented encryption. However, the very first AP (2WIRE935) was using WEP, which is a very old standard. It's better than nothing, but its owner should switch to WPA or WPA2.

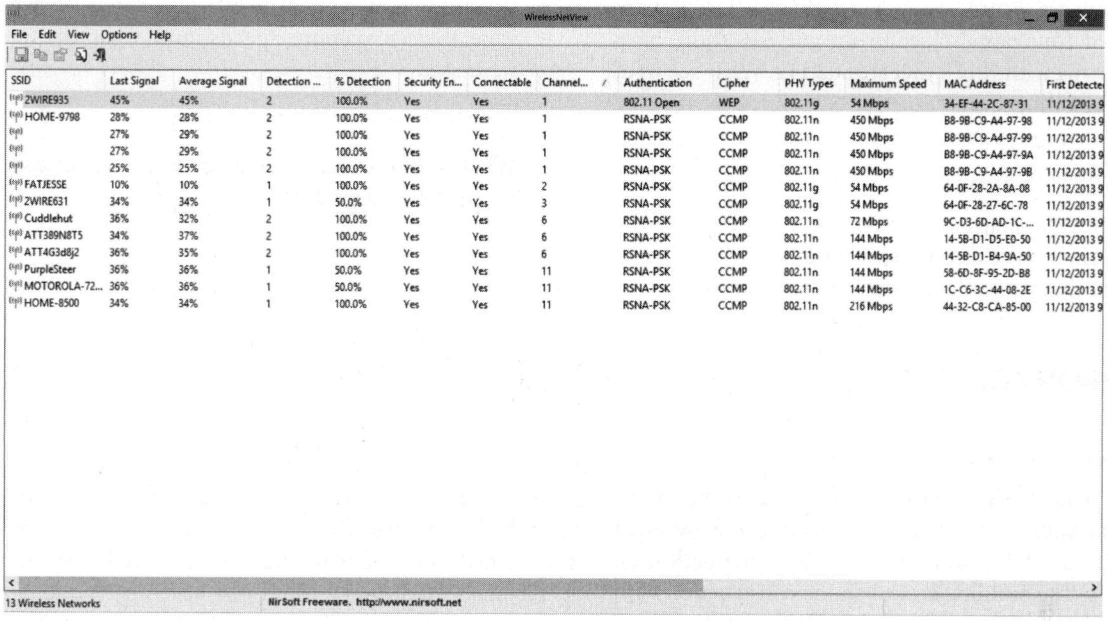

FIGURE 7-17   WLANs in a neighborhood in Bloomington, Indiana

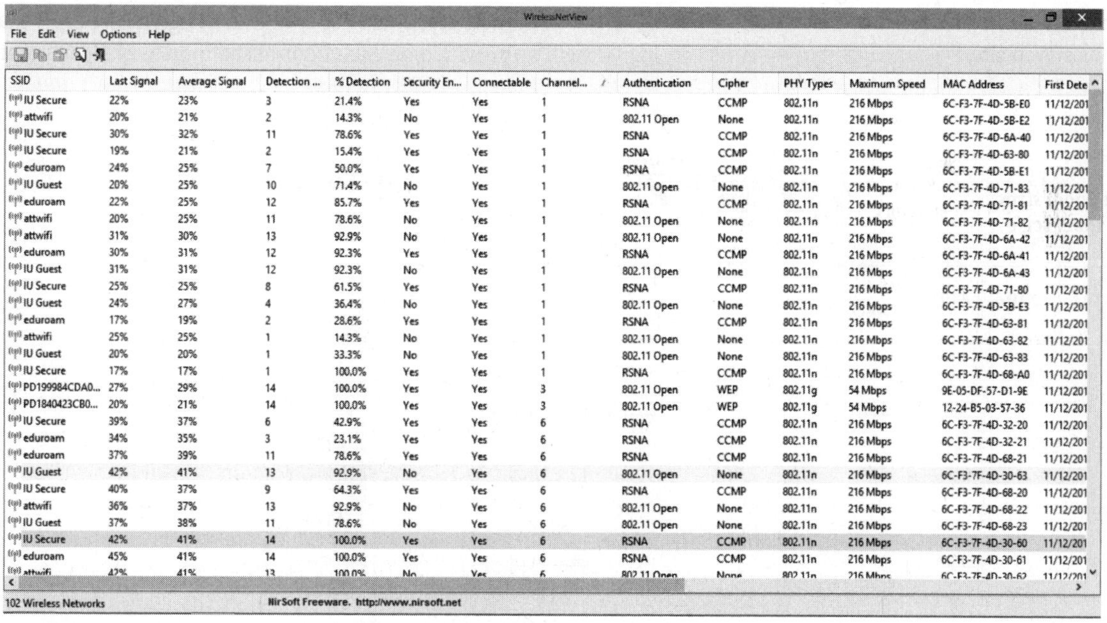

FIGURE 7-18   WLANs at Indiana University

Figure 7-18 shows a similar screen capture in the Kelley School of Business at Indiana University. If you look closely, you'll see that this only shows a small subset of the APs that were visible to NetView. There were more than 50 APs in total. In this case, you'll see a more standard configuration, with virtually all the APs being 802.11n running at 216 Mbps in channels 1, 6, and 12 (although you can't see the ones in channel 12). All the APs on the IU Secure or eduaroam are secured, whereas attwifi and IU Guest are not secured. You can also see two rogue APs (both have names starting with "PD") that are 802.11g, WEP-secured, running at 54 Mbps.

Deliverables

1. Capture a snapshot for the screen having all the information related to the various network connections that you collected during your warwalking.

2. What different versions of 802.11 did you see, what were their maximum speeds, and what channels were used?

3. How many networks were secure?

4. What is your overall assessment of the WLAN usage with respect to security?

HANDS-ON ACTIVITY 7D

Apollo Residence Access LAN Design

Apollo is a luxury residence hall that will serve honor students at your university. The residence will be eight floors, with a total of 162 two-bedroom, one-bathroom apartments. The building is steel-frame construction with concrete on the outside and drywall on the inside that measures 240 feet by 150 feet. The first floor has an open lobby with a seating area and separate office area, whereas the second floor has meeting rooms. Floors 3–8 each contain apartments and a large open lounge with a seating area (see Figure 7-19). Visio files for the residence are available on this book's Web site.

Your team was hired to design a network for this residence hall. To improve its quality of service, the university has decided to install wired network connections in each apartment so that every room can have an IP phone as well as network access. For security reasons, the university wants two separate networks: a LAN that will provide secure wired and wireless access to all registered students and a public wireless LAN that will provide Internet access to visitors.

This activity focuses only on the design of the LAN that will be provided on each floor of six floors with apartments

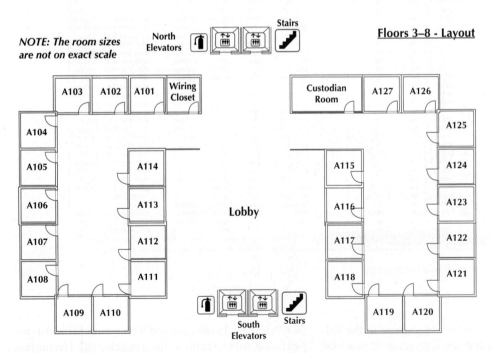

FIGURE 7-19 Plans for Floors 3–8 of Apollo Residence

Ethernet Hub and Switches	Price (each)
Ethernet 100Base-T 8 port Switch	30
Ethernet 100Base-T 16 port Switch	70
Ethernet 100Base-T 24 port Switch	80
Ethernet 100Base-T 48 port Switch	130
Ethernet 10/100/1000Base-T 8 port Switch	70
Ethernet 10/100/1000Base-T 16 port Switch	130
Ethernet 10/100/1000Base-T 24 port Switch	200
Ethernet 10/100/1000Base-T 48 port Switch	300
Upgrade any switch to include POE	75
Cable (Including Installation)	**Price (per drop)**
UTP Cat 5e (1000Base-T or slower)	50
UTP Cat 6 (1000Base-T or slower)	60
STP Cat 5e (1000Base-T or slower)	60
Wireless Access Points	**Price (each)**
802.11 wireless access point	60
802.11 wireless access point with POE	120

FIGURE 7-20   LAN equipment price list

(floors 3–8). Do not consider floors 1 and 2 at this point; we will add those in the Hands-On Activity at the end of the next chapter. We have not yet discussed how to design a building backbone or campus backbone, so just assume that the backbone will connect into a LAN switch using one 100Base-T or 1000Base-T.

Deliverables

1. Design the network for this residence hall and draw where the network equipment would be placed (use the floor plans provided).

2. Specify the products in your design and provide their cost and the total cost of the network. There are two options for specifying product. Option 1 is to use the generic LAN equipment list in Figure 7-20. Option 2 is to use CDW (www.cdw.com) to find LAN equipment. If you use CDW, you must use only Cisco devices (to ensure quality).

CHAPTER 8

BACKBONE NETWORKS

This chapter examines backbone networks (BNs) that are used in the distribution layer (within-building backbones) and the core layer (campus backbones). We discuss the three primary backbone architectures and the recommended best practice design guidelines on when to use them. The chapter ends with a discussion of how to improve BN performance and of the future of BNs.

8.1 INTRODUCTION

Chapter 6 outlined the seven major components in a network (see Figure 6.1). Chapter 7, on LANs, described how to design the LANs that provide user access to the network as well as the LANs in the data center and e-commerce edge. This chapter focuses on the next two major network architecture components: the backbone networks that connect the access LANs with a building (called the distribution layer) and the backbone networks that connect the different buildings on one enterprise campus (called the core layer).

Backbones used to be built with special technologies, but today most BNs use high-speed Ethernet. There are two basic components to a BN: the network cable and the hardware devices that connect other networks to the BN. The cable is essentially the same as that used in LANs, except that it is often fiber optic to provide higher data rates. Fiber optic is also used when the distances between the buildings on an enterprise campus are farther apart than the 100 meters that standard twisted-pair cable can reach. The hardware devices can be computers or special-purpose devices that just transfer messages from one network to another. These include switches, routers, and VLAN switches.

Switches operate at the data link layer. These are the same **layer-2 switches** discussed in Chapter 7 in that they use the data link layer address to forward packets between network segments. They learn addresses by reading the source and destination addresses.

Routers operate at the network layer. They connect two different TCP/IP subnets. Routers are the "TCP/IP gateways" that we first introduced in Chapter 5. Routers strip off the data link layer packet, process the network layer packet, and forward only those messages that need to go to other networks on the basis of their network layer address. Routers may be special-purpose devices or special network modules in other devices (e.g., wireless access points for home use often include a built-in router). In general, they perform more processing on each message than switches and therefore operate more slowly.

VLAN switches are a special combination of layer-2 switches and routers. They are complex devices intended for use in large networks that have special requirements. We discuss these in Section 8.4.

In the sections that follow, we describe the three basic BN architectures and discuss at which layer they are often used. We assume that you are comfortable with the material on TCP/IP in Chapter 5; if you are not, you may want to go back and review Section 5.6 of the chapter, entitled "TCP/IP Example," before you continue reading. We then explain the best practice design guidelines for the distribution layer and the core layer and discuss how to improve performance.

8.2 SWITCHED BACKBONES

Switched backbones are probably the most common type of BN used in the distribution layer (i.e., within a building); most new building BNs designed today use switched backbones.

Switched backbone networks use a star topology with one switch at its center. Figure 8-1 shows a switched backbone connecting a series of LANs. There is a switch serving each LAN (access layer) that is connected to the backbone switch at the bottom of the figure (distribution layer). Most organizations now use switched backbones in which all network devices for one part of the building are physically located in the same room, often in a **rack** of equipment. This has the advantage of placing all network equipment in one place for easy maintenance and upgrade, but it does require more cable. In most cases, the cost of the cable is only a small part of the overall cost to install the network, so the cost is greatly outweighed by the simplicity of maintenance and the flexibility it provides for future upgrades.

The room containing the rack of equipment is sometimes called the **main distribution facility (MDF)** or *central distribution facility* (CDF). Figure 8-2 shows a photo of an MDF room at Indiana University. Figure 8-3 shows the equipment diagram of this same room. The cables from all computers and devices in the area served by the MDF (often hundreds of cables) are run into the MDF room. Once in the room, they are connected into the various devices. The devices in the rack are connected among themselves using very short cables called **patch cables**.

With rack-mounted equipment, it becomes simple to move computers from one LAN to another. Usually, all the computers in the same general physical location are connected to the same switch and thus share the capacity of the switch. Although this often works well, it can cause problems if many of the computers on the switch are high-traffic computers. For example, if all the busy computers on the network are located in the upper left area of the figure, the switch in this area may become a bottleneck.

With an MDF, all cables run into the MDF. If one switch becomes overloaded, it is straightforward to unplug the cables from several high-demand computers from the overloaded switch and plug them into one or more less-busy switches. This effectively spreads the traffic around the network more efficiently and means that network capacity is no longer tied to the physical location of the computers; computers in the same physical area can be connected into different network segments.

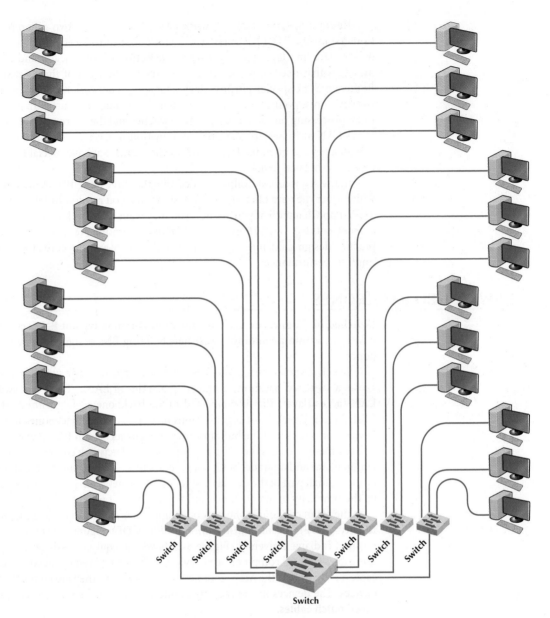

FIGURE 8-1 Rack-mounted switched backbone network architecture

Sometimes a **chassis switch** is used instead of a rack. A chassis switch enables users to plug **modules** directly into the switch. Each module is a certain type of network device. One module might be a 16-port 100Base-T switch, another might be a router, whereas another might be a 4-port 1000Base-F switch, and so on. The switch is designed to hold a certain number of modules and has a certain internal capacity, so that all the modules can be active at one time. For example, a switch with four 1000Base-T switches (with 24 ports each) and one 1000Base-F port would have to have an internal switching capacity of at least 97 Gbps ($[4 \times 24 \times 1 \text{ Gbps}] + [1 \times 1 \text{Gbps}]$).

The key advantage of chassis switches is their flexibility. It becomes simple to add new modules with additional ports as the LAN grows and to upgrade the switch to use new technologies. For example, if you want to add gigabit Ethernet, you simply lay the cable and insert the appropriate module into the chassis switch.

FIGURE 8-2

An MDF with rack-mounted equipment. A layer-2 chassis switch with five 100Base-T modules (center of photo) connects to four 24-port 100Base-T switches. The chassis switch is connected to the campus backbone using 1000Base-F over fiber-optic cable. The cables from each room are wired into the rear of the patch panel (shown at the top of the photo), with the ports on the front of the patch panel labeled to show which room is which. Patch cables connect the patch panel ports to the ports on the switches. *Source:* Photo courtesy of the author, Alan Dennis

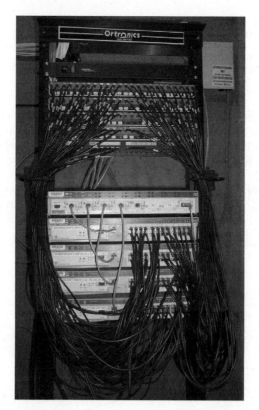

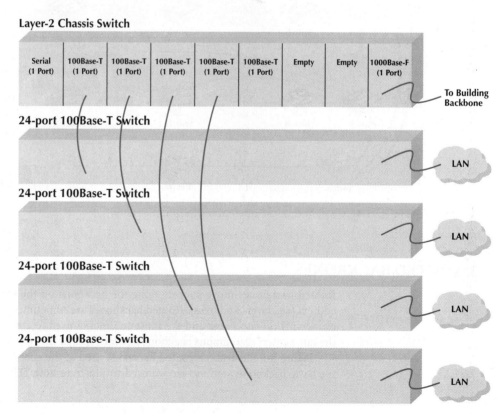

FIGURE 8-3   MDF network diagram

MANAGEMENT	8-1 Switched Backbones at Indiana University
FOCUS	

At Indiana University we commonly use switched back-bones in our buildings. Figure 8-4 shows a typical design. Each floor in the building has a set of switches and access points that serve the LANs on that floor. Each of these LANs and WLANs are connected into a switch for that floor, thus forming a switched backbone on each floor. Typically, we use switched 100Base-T within each floor.

The switch forming the switched backbone on each floor is then connected into another switch in the basement, which provides a switched backbone for the entire building. The building backbone is usually a higher speed network running over fiber-optic cable (e.g., 100Base-F or 1 GbE). This switch, in turn, is connected into a high-speed router that leads to the campus backbone (a routed back-bone design).

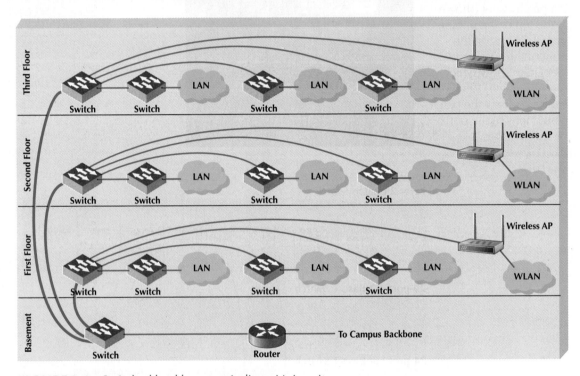

FIGURE 8-4 Switched backbones at Indiana University

8.3 ROUTED BACKBONES

Routed backbones move packets along the backbone on the basis of their network layer address (i.e., layer-3 address). Routed backbones are sometimes called *subnetted backbones* or *hierarchical backbones* and are most commonly used to connect different buildings on the same enterprise campus backbone network (i.e., at the core layer).

Figure 8-5 illustrates a routed backbone used at the core layer. A routed backbone is the basic backbone architecture we used to illustrate how TCP/IP worked in Chapter 5.

There are a series of LANs (access layer) connected to a switched backbone (distribution layer). Each backbone switch is connected to a router. Each router is connected to a core router (core layer). These routers break the network into separate subnets. The LANs in one building are a separate subnet from the LANs in a different building. Message traffic stays within each subnet unless it specifically needs to leave the subnet to travel elsewhere on the network, in which case the network layer address (e.g., TCP/IP) is used to move the packet. For example, in a switched backbone, a broadcast message (such as an ARP) would be sent to every single computer in the network. A routed backbone ensures that broadcast

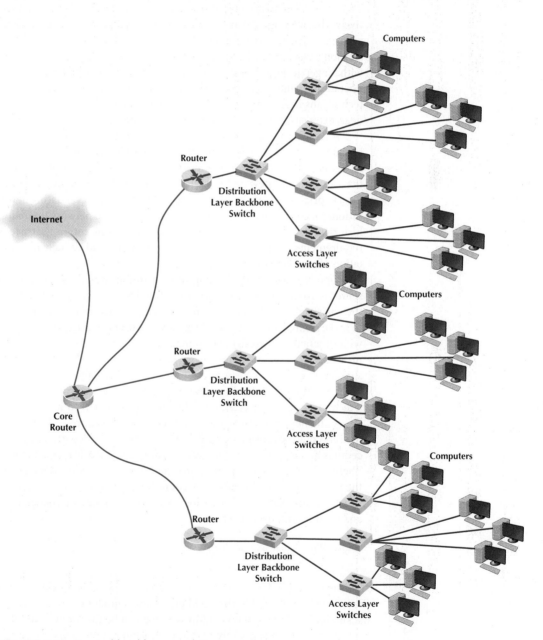

FIGURE 8-5　Routed backbone architecture

messages stay in the one network segment (i.e., subnet) where they belong and are not sent to all computers. This leads to a more efficient network.

Each set of LANs is usually a separate entity, relatively isolated from the rest of the network. There is no requirement that all LANs share the same technologies. Each set of LANs can contain its own server designed to support the users on that LAN, but users can still easily access servers on other LANs over the backbone, as needed.

A Day in the Life: Network Operations Manager

The job of the network operations manager is to ensure that the network operates effectively. The operations manager typically has several network administrators and network managers that report to him or her and is responsible for both day-to-day operations and long-term planning for the network. The challenge is to balance daily firefighting with longer-term planning; they're always looking for a better way to do things. Network operations managers also meet with users to ensure their needs are met. While network technicians deal primarily with networking technology, a network operations manager deals extensively with both technology and the users.

A typical day starts with administrative work that includes checks on all servers and backup processes to ensure that they are working properly and that there are no security issues. Then it's on to planning. One typical planning item includes planning for the acquisition of new desktop or laptop computers, including meeting with vendors to discuss pricing, testing new hardware and software, and validating new standard configurations for computers. Other planning is done around network upgrades, such as tracking historical data to monitor network usage, projecting future user needs, surveying user requirements, testing new hardware and software, and actually planning the implementation of new network resources.

One recent example of long-term planning was the migration from a Novell file server to Microsoft ADS file services. The first step was problem definition; what were the goals and the alternatives? The key driving force behind the decision to migrate was to make it simpler for the users (e.g., now the users do not need to have different accounts with different passwords) and to make it simpler for the network staff to provide technical support (e.g., now there is one less type of network software to support). The next step was to determine the migration strategy: a Big Bang (i.e., the entire network at once) or a phased implementation (several groups of users at a time). The migration required a technician to access each individual user's computer, so it was impossible to do a Big Bang. The next step was to design a migration procedure and schedule whereby groups of users could be moved at a time (e.g., department by department). A detailed set of procedures and a checklist for network technicians were developed and extensively tested. Then each department was migrated on a 1-week schedule. One key issue was revising the procedures and checklist to account for unexpected occurrences during the migration to ensure that no data were lost. Another key issue was managing user relationships and dealing with user resistance.

Source: With thanks to Mark Ross.

The primary advantage of the routed backbone is that it clearly segments each part of the network connected to the backbone. Each segment (usually a set of LANs or switched backbone) has its own subnet addresses that can be managed by a different network manager. Broadcast messages stay within each subnet and do not move to other parts of the network.

There are two primary disadvantages to routed backbones. First, the routers in the network impose time delays. Routing takes more time than switching, so routed networks can sometimes be slower. Second, routers are more expensive and require more management than switches.

Figure 8-5 shows one core router. Many organizations actually use two core routers to provide better security, as we discuss in Chapter 11.

8.4 VIRTUAL LANs

For many years, the design of LANs remained relatively constant. However, in recent years, the introduction of high-speed switches has begun to change the way we think about LANs. Switches offer the opportunity to design radically new types of LANs. Most large organizations today have implemented the **virtual LAN (VLAN)**, a new type of LAN-BN architecture made possible by intelligent, high-speed switches.

Virtual LANs are networks in which computers are assigned to LAN segments by software rather than by hardware. In the first section, we described how in rack-mounted collapsed BNs a computer could be moved from one hub to another by unplugging its cable and plugging it into a different hub. VLANs provide the same capability via software so that the network manager does not have to unplug and replug physical cables to move computers from one segment to another.

Often, VLANs are faster and provide greater opportunities to manage the flow of traffic on the LAN and BN than do the traditional LAN and routed BN architectures. However, VLANs are significantly more complex, so they usually are used only for large networks.

The simplest example is a **single-switch VLAN**, which means that the VLAN operates only inside one switch. The computers on the VLAN are connected into the one switch and assigned by software into different VLANs (Figure 8-6). The network manager uses special software to assign the dozens or even hundreds of computers attached to the switch to different VLAN segments. The VLAN segments function in the same way as physical LAN segments or subnets; the computers in the same VLAN act as though they are connected to the same physical switch or hub in a certain subnet. Because VLAN switches can create multiple subnets, they act like routers, except the subnets are *inside* the switch, not between switches. Therefore, broadcast messages sent by computers in one VLAN segment are sent only to the computers on the same VLAN.

Virtual LANs can be designed so that they act as though computers are connected via hubs (i.e., several computers share a given capacity and must take turns using it) or via switches (i.e., all computers in the VLAN can transmit simultaneously). Although switched circuits are preferred to the shared circuits of hubs, VLAN switches with the capacity to provide a complete set of switched circuits for hundreds of computers are more expensive than those that permit shared circuits.

We should also note that it is possible to have just one computer in a given VLAN. In this case, that computer has a dedicated connection and does not need to share the network capacity with any other computer. This is commonly done for servers.

Benefits of VLANs Historically, we have assigned computers to subnets based on geographic location; all computers in one part of a building have been placed in the same subnet. With VLANs, we can put computers in different geographic locations in the same subnet. For example, in Figure 8-6, a computer in the lower left could be put on the same subnet as one in the upper right—a separate subnet from all the other computers.

A more common implementation is a **multiswitch VLAN**, in which several switches are used to build the VLANs (Figure 8-7). VLANs are most commonly found in building backbone networks (i.e., access and distribution layers) but are starting to move into core

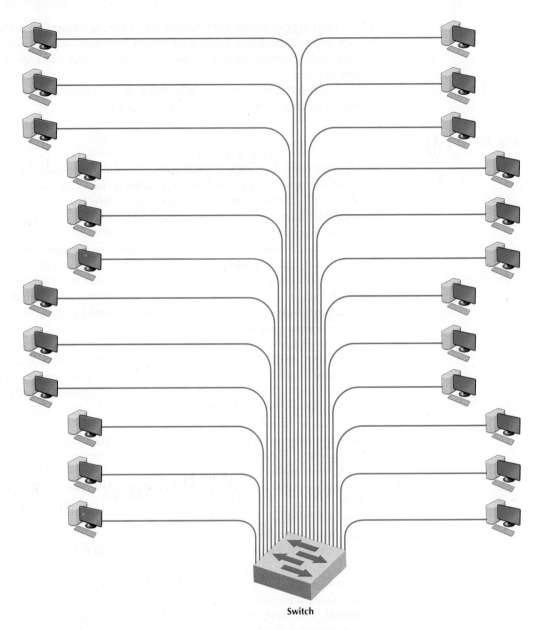

Switch

FIGURE 8-6 VLAN-based backbone network architecture

backbones between buildings. In this case, we can now create subnets that span buildings. For example, we could put one of the computers in the upper left of Figure 8-7 in the same subnet as the computers in the lower right, which could be in a completely different building. This enables us to create subnets based on *who* you are, rather than on *where* you are; we have an accounting subnet and a marketing subnet, not a Building A and a Building B subnet. We now manage security and network capacity by who you are, not by where your computer is. Because we have several subnets, we need to have a router—but more on that shortly.

Virtual LANs offer two other major advantages compared to the other network architectures. The first lies in their ability to manage the flow of traffic on the LAN and backbone very precisely. VLANs make it much simpler to manage the broadcast traffic, which has the potential to reduce performance and to allocate resources to different types of traffic more

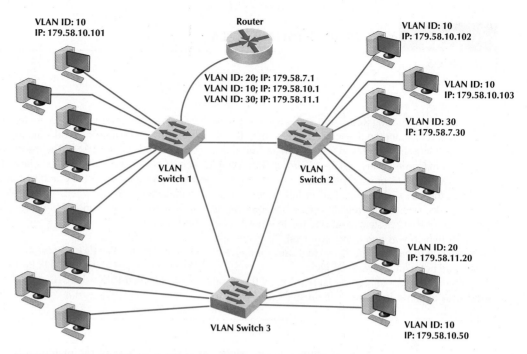

FIGURE 8-7 Multiswitch VLAN-based backbone network design

precisely. The bottom line is that VLANs often provide faster performance than the other backbone architectures.

The second advantage is the ability to prioritize traffic. The VLAN tag information included in the Ethernet packet defines the VLAN to which the packet belongs and also specifies a priority code based on the **IEEE 802.1q** standard (see Chapter 4). As you will recall from Chapter 5, the network and transport layers can use RSVP quality of service (QoS), which enables them to prioritize traffic using different classes of service. RSVP is most effective when combined with QoS capabilities at the data link layer. (Without QoS at the hardware layers, the devices that operate at the hardware layers [e.g., layer-2 switches] would ignore QoS information.) With the Ethernet packet's ability to carry VLAN information that includes priorities, we now have QoS capabilities in the data link layer. This means we can connect VOIP telephones directly into a VLAN switch and configure the switch to reserve sufficient network capacity so that they will always be able to send and receive voice messages.

The biggest drawbacks to VLANs are their cost and management complexity. VLAN switches also are much newer technologies that have only recently been standardized. Such "leading-edge" technologies sometimes introduce other problems that disappear only after the specific products have matured.

How VLANs Work VLANs work somewhat differently than the traditional Ethernet/IP approach described in the previous chapters. Each computer is assigned into a specific VLAN that has a **VLAN ID** number (which ranges from 1 to 1,005 or to 4,094, depending on whether the extended range standard is used). Each VLAN ID is matched to a traditional IP subnet, so each computer connected to a VLAN switch also receives a traditional IP address assigned by the VLAN switch (the switch acts as a DHCP server; see Chapter 5). Most VLAN switches can support only 255 separate VLANs simultaneously, which means each switch can support up to 255 separate IP subnets, which is far larger than most organizations want in any single device.

MANAGEMENT	8-2 VLANs IN SHANGRI-LA
FOCUS	

*S*hangri-La's Rasa Sayang Resort and Spa is a five-star luxury resort hotel located on the scenic Batu Feringgi Beach in Penang, Malaysia. The resort has two main buildings, the 189-room Garden Wing and the 115-room Rasa Wing, with an additional 11 private spa villas.

Over the years, the resort had installed three separate networks: one for the resort's operations, one for its POS (point-of-sales) system, and one for Internet access for guests (which was wired, not wireless). The networks were separate to ensure security, so that users of one network could not gain access to another.

As part of a multi-million-dollar renovation, the resort decided to upgrade its network to gigabit speeds and to offer wireless Internet access to its guests. Rather than build three separate networks again, it decided to build one network using VLANs. The resort installed 12 wireless access points and 24 VLAN switches, plus two larger core VLAN switches. The VLAN architecture provides seamless management of the wired and wireless components as one integrated network and ensures robust performance and security.

Adapted from: "Wireless Access amidst Lush Greenery of Penang Shangri-La's Resort," HP ProCurve Customer Case Study, Hewlett-Packard, 2010.

Computers are assigned into the VLAN (and the matching IP subnet) based on the physical port on the switch into which they are connected.[1] Don't confuse the physical port on the switch (which is the jack the cable plugs into) with the TCP port number from Chapter 5; they are different—it's another example of networking using the same word ("port") to mean two different things. The network manager uses software to assign the computers to specific VLANs using their physical port numbers, so it is simple to move a computer from one VLAN to another.

When a computer transmits an Ethernet frame, it uses the traditional Ethernet and IP addresses we discussed in previous chapters (e.g., Chapters 4 and 5) to move the frame through the network because it doesn't know that it is attached to a VLAN switch. Recall that as a message moves through the network, the IP address is used to specify the final destination and the Ethernet address is used to move the message from one computer to the next along the route to the final destination. Some devices, such as layer-2 switches, are transparent; the Ethernet frame passes through them unchanged. Other devices, such as routers, remove the Ethernet frame and create a new Ethernet frame to send the message to the next computer. VLANs are transparent—although they do change the frame at times.

Let's use Figure 8-7 to explain how VLAN switches work. We'll assume this network uses the first 3 bytes to specify the IP subnet. In this example, we have three VLAN switches with three IP subnets (179.58.10.x, 179.58.3.x, and 179.58.11.x) and three VLANs (10, 20, and 30). A router is used to enable communication among the different IP subnets.

Suppose a computer connected to switch 2 (IP 179.58.10.102) sends a message to a computer on the same IP subnet that is also connected to switch 2 (IP 179.58.10.103). The sending computer will recognize that the destination computer is in the same IP subnet, create an Ethernet frame with the destination computer's Ethernet address (using ARP if needed to find the Ethernet address), and transmit the frame to VLAN switch 2. When a VLAN switch receives a frame that is destined for another computer in the *same* subnet on the *same* VLAN switch, the switch acts as a traditional layer-2 switch: it forwards the frame unchanged to the correct computer. Remember from Chapter 7 that switches build a forwarding table that

---

[1]One type of VLAN switch used to enable computers to be assigned into VLANs is based on dynamic criteria such as Ethernet address, but this type of switch has essentially disappeared. The extra cost of dynamic VLAN switches outweighed the benefits they provided, and they lost in the marketplace.

lists the Ethernet address of every computer connected to the switch. When a frame arrives at the switch, the switch looks up the Ethernet address in the forwarding table, and if it finds the address, then it forwards the frame to the correct computer. We discuss what happens if the Ethernet address is not in the forwarding table in a moment.

Suppose that a computer wants to send a message to a computer in the same subnet, but that the destination computer is actually on a different VLAN switch. For example, in Figure 8-7, suppose this same computer (IP 179.58.10.102) sends a message to a computer on switch 3 (179.58.10.50). The sending computer will act exactly the same because to it, the situation is the same. It doesn't know where the destination computer is; it just knows that the destination is on its own subnet. The sending computer will create an Ethernet frame with the destination computer's Ethernet address (using ARP if needed to find the Ethernet address) and transmit the frame to VLAN switch 2. Switch 2 receives the frame, looks up the destination Ethernet address in its forwarding table, and recognizes that the frame needs to go to switch 3.

Virtual LAN switches use Ethernet 802.1q tagging to move frames from one switch to another. Chapter 4 showed that the layout of an Ethernet frame contains a **VLAN tag** field which VLAN switches use to move frames among switches. When a VLAN switch receives an Ethernet frame that needs to go to a computer on another VLAN switch, it changes the Ethernet frame by inserting the VLAN ID number and a priority code into the VLAN tag field. When a switch is configured, the network administrator defines which VLANs span which switches and also defines **VLAN trunks**—circuits that connect two VLAN switches and enable traffic to flow from one switch to another. As a switch builds its forwarding table, it receives information from other switches and inserts the Ethernet addresses of computers attached to them into its forwarding table along with the correct trunk to use to send frames to them.

In this case, switch 2 receives the frame and uses the forwarding table to identify that it needs to send the frame over the trunk to switch 3. It changes the frame by inserting the VLAN ID and priority code into the tag field and transmits the frame over the trunk to switch 3. Switch 3 receives the frame, looks the Ethernet address up in its forwarding table, and identifies the specific computer to which the frame needs to be sent. The switch removes the VLAN tag information and transmits the revised frame to the destination computer. In this way, neither the sending computer nor the destination computer is aware that the VLAN exists. The VLAN is transparent.

Suppose the same sending computer (179.58.10.102) wants to send a message to a computer on a *different* subnet in the same VLAN (e.g., 179.58.7.30 on the same switch or 179.58.11.20 on switch 3). The sending computer recognizes that the destination is on a different subnet and therefore creates an Ethernet frame with a destination Ethernet address of its router (179.58.10.1) and sends the frame to switch 2.

At this point, everything works the same as in the previous example. Switch 2 looks up the destination Ethernet address in its forwarding table and recognizes that the frame needs to go to switch 1 because the router's Ethernet address is listed in the forwarding table as being reachable through switch 1. Switch 2 sets the VLAN tag information and sends the frame over the trunk to switch 1. Switch 1 looks up the destination Ethernet address in its forwarding table and sees that the router is attached to it. Switch 2 removes the VLAN tag field and sends the frame to the router.

The router is a layer-3 device, so when it receives the message, it strips off the Ethernet frame and reads the IP packet. It looks in its routing table and sees that the destination IP address is within a subnet it controls (either 179.58.7.x or 179.58.11.x, depending on to which destination computer the packet was sent). The router creates a new Ethernet frame and sets the destination Ethernet address to the destination computer (using an ARP if needed) and sends the frame to switch 1.

Switch 1 reads the Ethernet address and looks it up in its forwarding table. It discovers the frame needs to go to switch 2 (for 179.58.7.30) or switch 3 (for 179.58.11.20), sets the

VLAN tag field, and forwards the frame over the trunk to the correct switch. This switch in turn removes the VLAN tag information and sends the frame to the correct computer.

Until now, we've been talking about unicast messages—messages from one computer to another—that are the majority of network traffic. However, what about broadcast messages, such as ARPs, that are sent to all computers in the same subnet? Each computer on a VLAN switch is assigned into a subnet with a matching VLAN ID. When a computer issues a broadcast message, the switch identifies the VLAN ID of the sending computer and then sends the frame to all other computers that have the same VLAN ID. These computers may be on the same switch or on different switches. For example, suppose computer 179.58.10.102 issues an ARP to find an Ethernet address (e.g., the router's address). Switch 2 would send the broadcast frame to all attached computers with the same VLAN ID (e.g., 179.58.10.103). Switch 2's trunking information also tells it that VLAN 10 spans switch 1 and switch 3, so it sends the frame to them. They, in turn, use their tables to send it to their attached computers that are in the same VLAN (which includes the router). Note that the router has multiple IP addresses and VLAN IDs because it is connected to several different VLANs and subnets (three, in our example here).

We have also assumed that the VLAN switch has a complete forwarding table—a table that lists all the Ethernet addresses of all the computers in the network. Just like a layer-2 switch, the VLAN switch learns Ethernet addresses as it sends and receives messages. Where the VLAN switch is first turned on, the forwarding table is empty, just like the forwarding table of a layer-2 switch; however, its VLAN ID and trunk tables are complete because these are defined by the network administrator. Suppose the switch has just been turned on and has an empty forwarding table. It receives an Ethernet frame, looks up the destination address in the forwarding table, and does not find where to send it. What happens?

If the VLAN switch were a layer-2 switch, it would send the frame to all ports. However, a VLAN switch can be a bit smarter than this. If you think about how IP works, you will see that an Ethernet frame is *always* sent to a computer in the same IP subnet as the sending computer. Any time a frame needs to move to a different subnet, it goes through a router which sits on both subnets. Think about it for a minute before you continue reading. Therefore, any time the VLAN switch can't find a destination Ethernet address in the forwarding table, it treats the frame as a broadcast frame and sends it to all the computers in the same subnet, which in VLAN terms means all the computers with the same VLAN ID.

This means that a VLAN architecture can improve performance by reducing traffic in the network compared with a switched backbone architecture. Because a switched backbone uses layer-2 switches, all the computers are in the same subnet, and all broadcast traffic goes to all computers. By using a VLAN we can limit where broadcast traffic flows by dividing the network into separate subnets, so that broadcast messages only go to computers in the same subnet.

8.5 THE BEST PRACTICE BACKBONE DESIGN

The past few years have seen radical changes in the backbone, both in terms of new technologies (e.g., gigabit Ethernet) and in architectures (e.g., VLANs). Fifteen years ago, the most common backbone architecture was the routed backbone, connected to a series of shared 10Base-T hubs in the LAN.

Today, the most effective architecture for the distribution layer in terms of cost and performance is a switched backbone (either rack-mounted or using a chassis switch) because it provides the best performance at the least cost. For the core layer, most organizations use a routed backbone. Many large organizations are now implementing VLANs, especially those

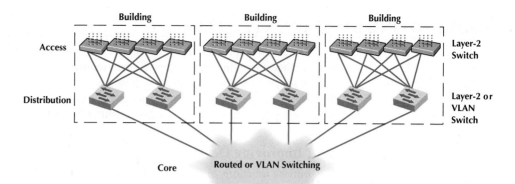

FIGURE 8-8 The best practice network design

that have departments spread over multiple buildings, but VLANs add considerable cost and complexity to the network.

Given the trade-offs in costs, there are several best practice recommendations. First, the best practice architecture is a switched backbone or VLAN for the distribution layer and a routed backbone for the core layer. Second, the best practice recommendation for backbone technology is gigabit Ethernet. Considering the LAN and backbone environments together, the ideal network design is likely to be a mix of layer-2 and VLAN Ethernet switches. Figure 8-8 shows one likely design. The access layer (i.e., the LANs) uses 1000Base-T layer-2 Ethernet switches running on Cat 5e or Cat 6 twisted-pair cables to provide flexibility for 100Base-T or 1000Base-T. The distribution layer uses layer-2 or VLAN switches that use 100Base-T or more commonly 1000Base-T/F (over fiber or Cat 6) to connect to the access layer. To provide good reliability, some organizations may provide redundant switches, so if one fails, the backbone continues to operate. The core layer uses routers or VLAN Ethernet switches running 10 GbE or 40 GbE over fiber.

TECHNICAL FOCUS | **8-1 Multiprotocol Label Switching**

Multiprotocol Label Switching (MPLS) is an approach to improving QoS and the movement of packets with different layer-2 protocols through TCP/IP networks.

With MPLS, routers called **Label Switched Routers (LSRs)** are used. The network manager defines a series of **Forwarding Equivalence Classes (FEC)** through the network of LSRs. Each FEC has a reserved data rate and a QoS.

When a packet arrives at the edge of the MPLS network, an edge LSR reads the destination address on the incoming packet. The edge LSR can be configured to use the IP address, the IP address and the source or destination port, or the address in any protocol understood by the LSR. The edge LSR accepts the incoming packet and attaches an MPLS *label* (a packet that contains the FEC address). The edge LSR then forwards the packet to the next LSR as defined in the FEC.

This LSR reads the MPLS label and removes it from the incoming packet, consults its MPLS address table to find the packet's next destination, attaches a new MPLS label with the new FEC address, and forwards the packet to the next LSR in the FEC.

This process continues until the packet reaches the edge LSR closest to its final destination. This edge LSR strips off the MPLS label and forwards the packet outside of the MPLS network in exactly the same format in which it entered the MPLS network.

The advantage of MPLS is that it can easily integrate layer-2 protocols and also provide QoS in an IP environment. It also enables traffic management by enabling the network manager to specify FEC based on both the IP address and the source or destination port.

8.6 IMPROVING BACKBONE PERFORMANCE

The method for improving the performance of BNs is similar to that for improving LAN performance. First, find the bottleneck, then remove it (or, more accurately, move the bottleneck somewhere else). You can improve the performance of the network by improving the performance of the devices in the network, by upgrading the circuits between them, and by changing the demand placed on the network (Figure 8-9).

8.6.1 Improving Device Performance

The primary functions of computers and devices in BNs are forwarding/routing messages and serving up content. If the devices and computers are the bottleneck, routing can be improved with faster devices or a faster routing protocol. Distance vector routing is faster than dynamic routing (see Chapter 5) but obviously can impair circuit performance in high-traffic situations. Link state routing is usually used in WANs because there are many possible routes through the network. BNs often have only a few routes through the network, so link state routing may not be too helpful because it will delay processing and increase the network traffic because of the status reports sent through the network. Distance vector routing will often simplify processing and improve performance.

Most backbone devices are store-and-forward devices. One simple way to improve performance is to ensure that they have sufficient memory. If they don't, the devices will lose packets, requiring them to be retransmitted.

8.6.2 Improving Circuit Capacity

If network circuits are the bottlenecks, there are several options. One is to increase circuit capacity (e.g., by going from 100Base-T Ethernet to gigabit Ethernet). Another option is to add additional circuits alongside heavily used ones so that there are several circuits between some devices.

In many cases, the bottleneck on the circuit is only in one place—the circuit to the server. A switched network that provides 100 Mbps to the client computers but a faster circuit to the server (e.g., 1000Base-T) can improve performance at very little cost.

8.6.3 Reducing Network Demand

One way to reduce network demand is to restrict applications that use a lot of network capacity, such as desktop videoconferencing, medical imaging, or multimedia. In practice, it is often difficult to restrict users. Nonetheless, finding one application that places a large demand on the network and moving it can have a significant impact.

FIGURE 8-9

Facility map of the Western Trucking headquarters

```
                    Performance Checklist
Increase Device Performance
• Change to a more appropriate routing protocol (either distance vector or link state)
• Increase the devices' memory

Increase Circuit Capacity
• Upgrade to a faster circuit
• Add circuits

Reduce Network Demand
• Change user behavior
• Reduce broadcast messages
```

Much network demand is caused by broadcast messages, such as those used to find data link layer addresses (see Chapter 5). Some application software packages and NOS modules written for use on LANs also use broadcast messages to send status information to all computers on the LAN. For example, broadcast messages inform users when printers are out of paper or when the server is running low on disk space. When used in a LAN, such messages place little extra demand on the network because every computer on the LAN gets every message.

This is not the case for routed backbones because messages do not normally flow to all computers, but broadcast messages can consume a fair amount of network capacity in switched backbones. In many cases, broadcast messages have little value outside their individual LAN. Therefore, some switches and routers can be set to filter broadcast messages so that they do not go to other networks. This reduces network traffic and improves performance.

8.7 IMPLICATIONS FOR MANAGEMENT

As the technologies used in LANs and WLANs become faster and better, the amount of traffic the backbone network needs to support is increasing at an even faster rate. Coupled with the significant changes in the best practice recommendations for the design of backbone networks, this means that many organizations have had to replace their backbones. We would like to think that these have been one-time expenditures, but, as traffic grows, demand placed on the backbone will continue to increase, meaning the amount spent on switches and routers for use in the backbone will increase. Designing backbone networks to be easily upgradable is now an important management goal.

As Ethernet moves more extensively into the backbone, the costs associated with buying and maintaining backbone devices and training networking staff will decrease, because now there will be one standard technology in use throughout the LAN, WLAN, and backbone. The new focus is on faster and faster versions of Ethernet. Although we will spend more on new equipment, performance will increase much more quickly, and the cost to operate the equipment will decrease.

SUMMARY

Switched Backbones These use the same layer-2 switches as LANs to connect the different LANs together. The switches are usually placed in a rack in the same room (called an IDF or MDF) to make them easy to maintain.

Routed Backbones These use routers to connect the different LANs or subnets. Routed backbones are slower than switched backbones, but they prevent broadcast traffic from moving between the different parts of the network.

VLAN Backbones These combine the best features of switched and routed backbones. They are very complex and expensive, so they are mostly used by large companies.

Best Practice Backbone Design The best practice backbone architecture for most organizations is a switched backbone (using a rack or a chassis switch) or VLAN in the distribution layer and a routed backbone in the core layer. The recommended technology is gigabit Ethernet.

Improving Backbone Performance Backbone performance can be improved by choosing the best network layer routing protocols. Upgrading to faster circuits and adding additional circuits on very busy backbones can also improve performance. Finally, one could move servers closer to the end users or reduce broadcast traffic to reduce backbone traffic.

KEY TERMS

chassis switch, 224	layer-2 switch, 222	multiswitch VLAN, 229	switched backbone, 223
forwarding equivalence	main distribution facility	patch cables, 223	virtual LAN (VLAN), 229
class FEC, 235	(MDF), 223	rack, 223	VLAN ID, 231
IEEE 802.1q, 231	module, 224	routed backbone, 226	VLAN switch, 223
label switched router (LSR),	multiprotocol label	router, 223	VLAN tag, 233
235	switching (MPLS), 235	single-switch VLAN, 229	VLAN trunk, 233

QUESTIONS

1. How does a layer-2 switch differ from a router?
2. How does a layer-2 switch differ from a VLAN?
3. How does a router differ from a VLAN?
4. Under what circumstances would you use a switched backbone?
5. Under what circumstances would you use a routed backbone?
6. Under what circumstances would you use a VLAN backbone?
7. Explain how routed backbones work.
8. In Figure 8.5, would the network still work if we removed the routers in each building and just had one core router? What would be the advantages and disadvantages of doing this?
9. Explain how switched backbones work.

10. What are the key advantages and disadvantages of routed and switched backbones?
11. Compare and contrast rack-based and chassis-based switched backbones.
12. What is a module and why are modules important?
13. Explain how single-switch VLANs work.
14. Explain how multiswitch VLANs work.
15. What is IEEE 802.1q?
16. What are the advantages and disadvantages of VLANs?
17. How can you improve the performance of a BN?
18. Why are broadcast messages important?
19. What are the preferred architectures used in each part of the backbone?
20. Some experts are predicting that Ethernet will move into the WAN. What do you think?

EXERCISES

A. Survey the BNs used in your organization. Is the campus core backbone different from the distribution backbones used in the buildings? Why?
B. Document one BN in detail. What devices are attached, what cabling is used, and what is the topology? What networks does the backbone connect?
C. You have been hired by a small company to install a backbone to connect four 100base-T Ethernet LANs (each using one 24-port hub) and to provide a connection to the Internet. Develop a simple backbone

and determine the total cost (i.e., select the backbone technology and price it, select the cabling and price it, select the devices and price them, and so on). Prices are available at www.datacommwarehouse.com, but use any source that is convenient. For simplicity, assume that category 5, category 5e, category 6, and fiber-optic cable have a fixed cost per circuit to buy and install, regardless of distance, of $50, $60, $120, and $300, respectively.

MINICASES

I. **Pat's Engineering Works** Pat's Engineering Works is a small company that specializes in complex engineering consulting projects. The projects typically involve one or two engineers who do data-intensive analyses

for companies. Because so much data are needed, the projects are stored on the company's high-capacity server but moved to the engineers' workstations for analysis. The company is moving into new offices and wants you to design its network. It has a staff of 8 engineers (which is expected to grow to 12 over the next 5 years), plus another 8 management and clerical employees who also need network connections but whose needs are less intense. Design the network. Be sure to include a diagram.

II. **Hospitality Hotel** Hospitality Hotel is a luxury hotel whose guests are mostly business travelers. To improve its quality of service, it has decided to install network connections in each of its 600 guest rooms and 12 conference meeting rooms. Last year, the hotel upgraded its own internal networks to switched 100Base-T, but it wants to keep the public network (i.e., the guest and meeting rooms) separate from its private network (i.e., its own computer systems). Your task is to design the public network and decide how to connect the two networks together. Be sure to include a diagram.

III. **Indiana University** Reread Management Focus 8-1. What other alternatives do you think Indiana University considered? Why do you think they did what they did?

IV. **Shangri-La** Reread Management Focus 8-2. What other alternatives do you think the Shangri-La Resort considered? Why do you think they did what they did?

V. **Chicago Consulting** You are the network manager for a consulting firm that needs to install a backbone to connect four 100Base-T Ethernet LANs (each using a 24-port switch). Develop a simple backbone and determine the total cost (i.e., select the device and price it). Prices are available at www.cdw.com, but you can use any source that is convenient.

VI. **Western Trucking** Western Trucking operates a large fleet of trucks that deliver shipments for commercial shippers such as food stores, retailers, and wholesalers. Their main headquarters building and secondary building are shown in Figure 8-10. They want to upgrade to a faster network. Design a new network for them, including the specific backbone and LAN technologies to be used. Assume that the main office building is 170 feet by 100 feet in size and that the secondary building is 100 feet by 50 feet. The two buildings are 100 feet apart.

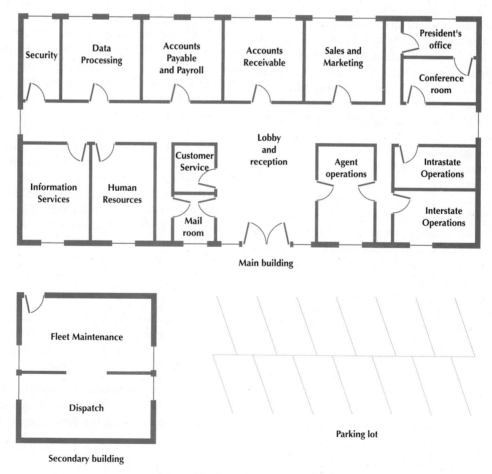

FIGURE 8-10 Facility map of the Western Trucking headquarters

NEXT-DAY AIR SERVICE

See the companion Web site at www.wiley.com/college/fitzgerald.

HANDS-ON ACTIVITY 8A

Network Mapping

Network mapping software enables you to generate a map of the computers on all the LANs connected to a backbone. There are many good network mapping packages. Two of my favorites are LANState and Network Topology Mapper (www. solarwinds. com/network-topology-mapper . aspx). LANState is simpler to use but works best for small networks. Network Topology Mapper is more complex but can map large networks. This activity will focus on LANState.

Mapping a Small Network

The first step is to download and install LANState. A demo version of the software is available free of charge from 10-Strike Software (www.10-strike.com/lanstate).

You begin by creating a new network map; choose File and then select the Map Creation Wizard. Then choose Scan IP address range and click Next. You will be asked to enter an address range. Choose some range, ideally the address range of a small network. I choose to use my home network range (192.168.1.1 through 192.168.2.254), which has two wireless routers (192.168.1.1. and 192.168.2.1). After you have added the address range to scan, click Next. Step 2 is to select how you will detect the devices on your network. The most common approach is to use an ICMP ping, which was discussed in Chapter 5. This approach sends an ICMP to each possible address in the range you specified. Not all computers are configured to respond to pings for security reasons, so this approach may not reveal all the computers and devices in your network. Make sure that the box in front of ICMP Ping is checked.

The second approach is to send an ARP request for every computer in the address range you specified (see Chapter 5). The advantage of this approach is that every device will respond to an ARP request. The disadvantage is that you can only use ARPs for devices and computers in your same subnet. Make sure that the box in front of ARP ping is checked.

To speed up your network, make sure the box in front of Search SNMP hosts is not checked. SNMP is a network management protocol that we will discuss in Chapter 12. If you're using a small network, it probably does not have SNMP. If you're using a large network that uses SNMP, you probably don't have the password required (unless you're the network manager).

Click Next, and after 10–20 seconds, you should see a list of devices and computers that were discovered.

Figure 8-11 shows the small network in Alan's house. I have a router (192.168.1.1) that connects a number of computers to the Internet. I also have a second wireless access router (192.168.2.1) and a printer (192.168.1.186). When I did this map, four computers and my networked TV were turned on and responded to LANState's pings (192.168.1.104, 192.168.1.129, 192.168.1.130, 192.168.131, and 192.168.1.188). You will also see that the broadcast address of 192.168.1.255 showed up, although there is no device on this address. Computers and devices that are not turned on do not respond to the pings and therefore are not mapped. Because I use dynamic addressing, the addresses of my computers will change every time I turn them on.

Click Next and the network map will be shown. See Figure 8.12. You can also left click on any device and choose System Information and General to learn more about that device. Figure 8-13 also shows the information about one computer (192.168.1.188). It shows the MAC address (i.e., the Ethernet address), the card manufacturer, and the DNS name (i.e., application layer address) for this computer.

Deliverables

1. Use the 10-Strike Software to draw a map of your home network or some other network. Describe two to five components on your map just like the example in the textbook shows.

2. Use the System Information and provide additional information (e.g., MAC address and card manufacturer) about at least two devices on your network.

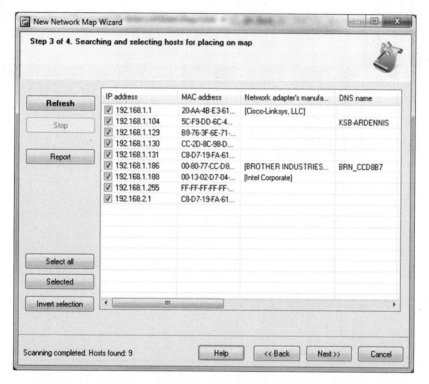

FIGURE 8-11   Computers and devices at Alan's house

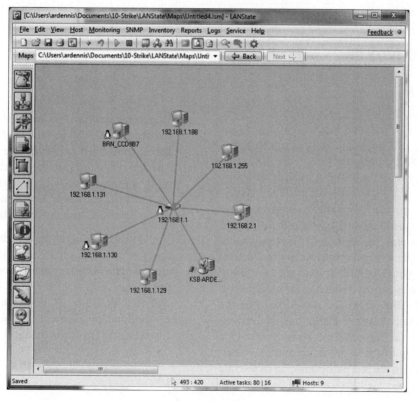

FIGURE 8-12   Network map for Alan's house

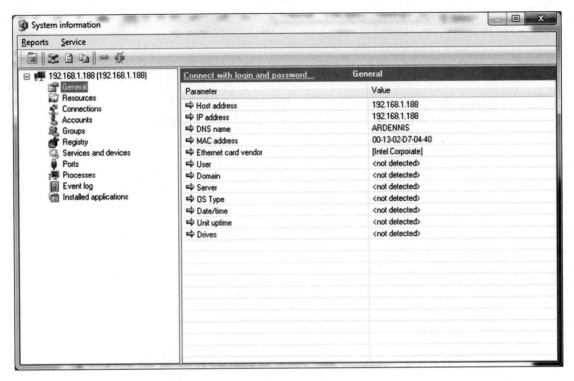

FIGURE 8-13   System information for 192.168.1.188

HANDS-ON ACTIVITY 8B

Apollo Residence Network Design

Apollo is a luxury residence hall that will serve honor students at your university. The residence will be eight floors, with a total of 162 two-bedroom, one-bathroom apartments on floors 3–8. Read Hands-On Activity 7D, which provides the description of the building and a figure showing floors 3–8.

The first floor has an open lobby with a seating area and separate office area (see Figure 8-14), whereas the second floor has meeting rooms (see Figure 8-15). Floors 1 and 2 are smaller than the upper floors (100 feet by 70 feet) because a parking garage is built around the outside of these floors. Visio files for the residence are available on this book's Web site. The offices and server room on the first floor is for the university's residence hall administration, which manages all the university's residences. One design goal is to keep this network as separate as possible from the network in the rest of the building to provide greater security.

Deliverables

1. Your team was hired to design the network for this residence hall. Design the LANs for each floor, the distribution layer backbone that will connect the different floors in the building, and the part of the network that will connect into the campus core backbone. Draw where the network equipment would be placed (use the floor plans provided).

2. Specify the products in your design and provide their cost and the total cost of the network. There are two options for specifying product. Option 1 is to use the generic LAN equipment list in Figure 8-16. Option 2 is to use CDW (www.cdw.com) to find LAN equipment. If you use CDW, you must use only Cisco devices (to ensure quality).

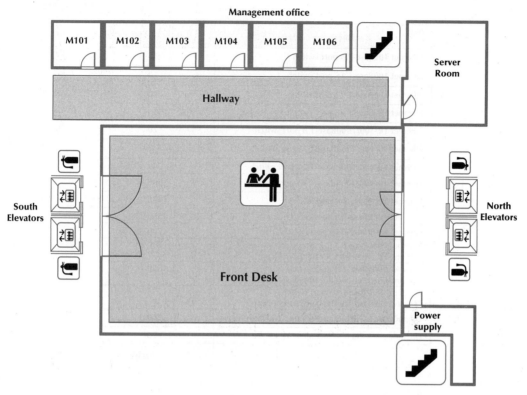

FIGURE 8-14 Apollo Residence first floor

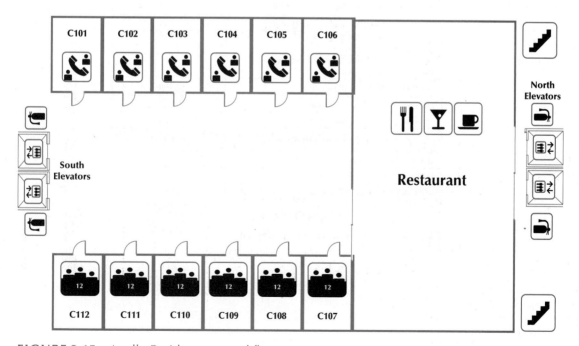

FIGURE 8-15 Apollo Residence second floor

Ethernet Switches	Price (each)
Ethernet 100Base-T 8 port switch	30
Ethernet 100Base-T 16 port switch	70
Ethernet 100Base-T 24 port switch	80
Ethernet 100Base-T 48 port switch	130
Ethernet 10/100/1000Base-T 8 port switch	70
Ethernet 10/100/1000Base-T 16 port switch	130
Ethernet 10/100/1000Base-T 24 port switch	200
Ethernet 10/100/1000Base-T 48 port switch	300
Ethernet 1000Base-F 4 port switch	400
Ethernet 1000Base-F 8 port switch	500
Ethernet 1000Base-F 16 port switch	700
Ethernet 1000Base-F 4 port switch Plus one Ethernet 10/100/1000Base-T port	450
Ethernet 1000Base-F 8 port switch Plus one Ethernet 10/100/1000Base-T port	550
Ethernet 1000Base-F 16 port switch Plus one Ethernet 10/100/1000Base-T port	750
Upgrade any switch to include one 1000Base-F port	200
Upgrade any switch to include POE	75
Wireless Access Point	**Price (each)**
802.11 wireless access point	60
802.11 wireless access point with POE	100
Routers	**Price (each)**
Ethernet 10/100/1000 Base-T 2 port router	100
Ethernet 10/100/1000 Base-T 4 port router	120
Ethernet 10/100/1000 Base-T 8 port router	150
Ethernet 10/100/1000 Base-T 4 port router Plus one 1000BaseF port	350
Ethernet 10/100/1000 Base-T 8 port router Plus one 1000BaseF port	400
Ethernet 1000BaseF 2 port router	500
Ethernet 1000BaseF 4 port router	800
Ethernet 1000BaseF 8 port router	1000
Cable (Including Installation)	**Price (each)**
UTP Cat 5e (1000Base-T or slower)	50
UTP Cat 6 (1000Base-T or slower)	60
STP Cat 5e (1000Base-T or slower)	60
Fiber 1GbE	100

FIGURE 8-16   Equipment price list

CHAPTER 9

WIDE AREA NETWORKS

The Wide Area Network (WAN) is a key part of the enterprise edge. Most organizations do not build their own WAN communication circuits, preferring instead to lease them from common carriers or to use the Internet. This chapter focuses on the WAN architectures and telecommunications services offered by common carriers for use in enterprise WANs, not the underlying technology that the carriers use to provide them. We discuss the three principal types of WAN services that are available: dedicated-circuit services, packet-switched services, and virtual private network (VPN) services. We conclude by discussing how to improve WAN performance and how to select services to build WANs.

OBJECTIVES

- Understand dedicated-circuit services and architectures
- Understand packet-switched services and architectures
- Understand Internet-based VPN services and architectures
- Understand the best practice recommendations for WAN design
- Be familiar with how to improve WAN performance

OUTLINE

9.1 INTRODUCTION

Wide area networks (WANs) typically run long distances, connecting different offices in different cities or countries. Some WANs run much shorter distances, connecting different buildings in the same city. Most organizations do not own the land across which WANs are built, so instead they rent or lease circuits from **common carriers**—private companies such as AT&T, Bell Canada, Sprint, and BellSouth that provide communication services to the public. As a customer, you do not lease physical cables per se; you simply lease circuits that provide certain transmission characteristics. The carrier decides whether it will use twisted-pair cable, coaxial cable, fiber optics, or other media for its circuits.

Common carriers are profit oriented, and their primary products are services for voice and data transmissions, both over traditional wired circuits as well as cellular services. A common carrier that provides local telephone services (e.g., BellSouth) is commonly called a **local exchange carrier (LEC)**, whereas one that provides long-distance services (e.g., AT&T) is commonly called an **interexchange carrier (IXC)**. As the LECs move into the long-distance market and IXCs move into the local telephone market, this distinction may disappear.

In this chapter, we examine the WAN architectures and technologies from the viewpoint of a network manager rather than that of a common carrier. We focus less on internal operations and how the specific technologies work and more on how these services are offered to network managers and how they can be used to build networks because network managers are less concerned with how the services work and more concerned with how they can use them effectively.

Likewise, we focus on WAN services in North America because the majority of our readers are in North America. Although there are many similarities in the way data communications networks and services have evolved in different countries, there also are many differences. Most countries have a federal government agency that regulates data and voice communications. In the United States, the agency is the **Federal Communications Commission (FCC)**; in Canada, it is the **Canadian Radio-Television and Telecommunications Commission (CRTC)**. Each state or province also has its own **public utilities commission (PUC)** to regulate communications within its borders.

We discuss two WAN services that use common carrier networks (dedicated-circuit services and packet-switched services) and one that uses the public Internet (virtual private network). The first two enable the customer to more precisely design and manage the WAN and offer more reliable services, so these services are most commonly chosen by large organizations that view the WAN as an important part of their business operations. The public Internet is usually much cheaper than these services, but less reliable, so it is usually only attractive to small organizations that are more price sensitive.

9.2 DEDICATED-CIRCUIT NETWORKS

With a dedicated-circuit network, the user leases circuits from the common carrier for his or her exclusive use 24 hours per day, 7 days per week. It is like having your own private network, but it is managed by the common carrier. Dedicated-circuit networks are sometimes called *private line services*. Dedicated circuit networks became popular in the early 1990s, so the fundamental technology is more than 20 years old. Dedicated services have evolved and improved over the years, but their basic design is old. Some experts believe that they will slowly disappear over the next 10 years, as packet-switched services become more popular.

9.2.1 Basic Architecture

With a dedicated-circuit network, you lease circuits from common carriers. All connections are point to point, from one building in one city to another building in the same or a different city. The carrier installs the circuit connections at the two end points of the circuit and makes the connection between them. The circuits run through the common carrier's cloud, but the network behaves as if you have your own physical circuits running from one point to another (Figure 9-1).

The user leases the desired circuit from the common carrier (specifying the physical end points of the circuit) and installs the equipment needed to connect computers and devices (e.g., routers or switches) to the circuit. This equipment may include multiplexers or a **channel service unit (CSU)** and/or a **data service unit (DSU)**; a CSU/DSU is the WAN equivalent of a NIC in a LAN. The device takes the outgoing packet (usually an Ethernet packet at the data link layer and an IP packet at the network layer) and translates it to use the data link layer and network protocols used in the WAN.

FIGURE 9-1

Dedicated-circuit services.
CSU = channel service unit; DSU = data service unit; and MUX = multiplexer

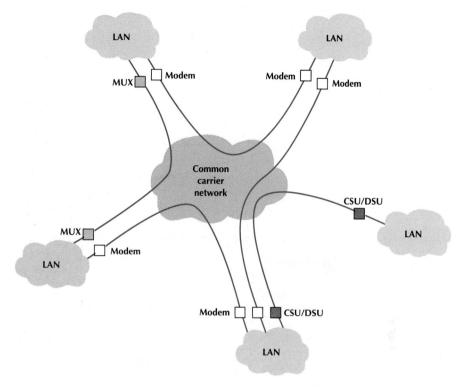

Dedicated circuits are billed at a flat fee per month, and the user has unlimited use of the circuit. Once you sign a contract, making changes can be expensive because it means rewiring the buildings and signing a new contract with the carrier. Therefore, dedicated circuits require careful planning, both in terms of locations and the amount of capacity you purchase.

There are three basic architectures used in dedicated-circuit networks: ring, star, and mesh. In practice, most networks use a combination of architectures.

Ring Architecture A **ring architecture** connects all computers in a closed loop with each computer linked to the next (Figure 9-2). The circuits are full-duplex or half-duplex circuits, meaning that messages flow in both directions around the ring. Computers in the ring may send data in one direction or the other, depending on which direction is the shortest to the destination.

One disadvantage of the ring topology is that messages can take a long time to travel from the sender to the receiver. Messages usually travel through several computers and circuits before they reach their destination, so traffic delays can build up very quickly if one circuit or computer becomes overloaded. A long delay in any one circuit or computer can have significant impacts on the entire network.

In general, the failure of any one circuit or computer in a ring network means that the network can continue to function. Messages are simply routed away from the failed circuit or computer in the opposite direction around the ring. However, if the network is operating close to its capacity, this will dramatically increase transmission times because the traffic on the remaining part of the network may come close to doubling (because all traffic originally routed in the direction of the failed link will now be routed in the opposite direction through the longest way around the ring).

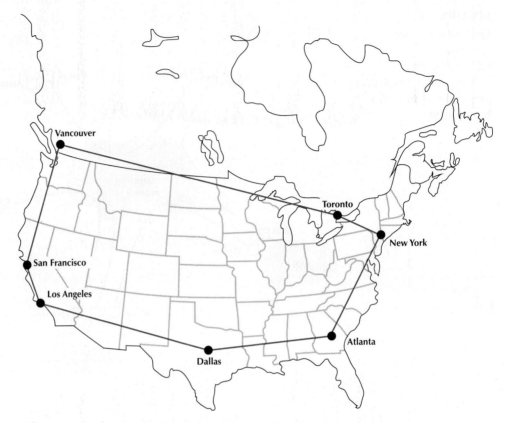

FIGURE 9-2   Ring-based design

Star Architecture   A **star architecture** connects all computers to one central computer that routes messages to the appropriate computer (Figure 9-3). The star topology is easy to manage because the central computer receives and routes all messages in the network. It can also be faster than the ring network because any message needs to travel through at most two circuits to reach its destination, whereas messages may have to travel through far more circuits in the ring network. However, the star topology is the most susceptible to traffic problems because the central computer must process all messages on the network. The central computer must have sufficient capacity to handle traffic peaks, or it may become overloaded and network performance will suffer.

In general, the failure of any one circuit or computer affects only the one computer on that circuit. However, if the central computer fails, the entire network fails because all traffic must flow through it. It is critical that the central computer be extremely reliable.

Mesh Architecture   In a **full-mesh architecture**, every computer is connected to every other computer (Figure 9-4a). Full-mesh networks are seldom used because of the extremely high cost. **Partial-mesh architecture** (usually called just **mesh architecture**), in which many, but not all, computers are connected, is far more common (Figure 9-4b). Most WANs use partial-mesh topologies.

The effects of the loss of computers or circuits in a mesh network depend entirely on the circuits available in the network. If there are many possible routes through the network, the loss of one or even several circuits or computers may have few effects beyond the specific computers involved. However, if there are only a few circuits in the network, the loss of even one circuit or computer may seriously impair the network.

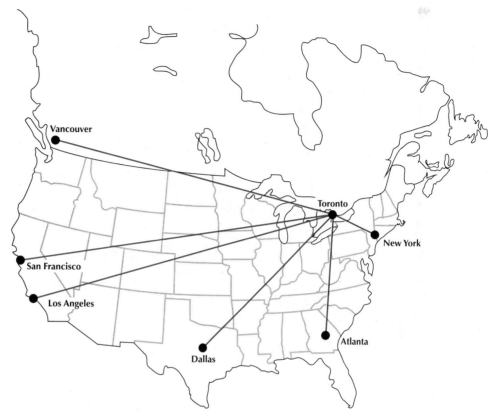

FIGURE 9-3   Star-based design

In general, mesh networks combine the performance benefits of both ring networks and star networks. Mesh networks usually provide relatively short routes through the network (compared with ring networks) and provide many possible routes through the network to prevent any one circuit or computer from becoming overloaded when there is a lot of traffic (compared with star networks, in which all traffic goes through one computer).

The drawback is that mesh networks use decentralized routing so that each computer in the network performs its own routing. This requires more processing by each computer in the network than in star or ring networks. Also, the transmission of network status information (e.g., how busy each computer is) "wastes" network capacity.

There are two types of **dedicated-circuit services** in common use today: T carrier services and synchronous optical network (SONET) services. Both T carrier and SONET have their own data link protocols, which are beyond the scope of this chapter.

9.2.2 T Carrier Services

T carrier circuits are the most commonly used form of dedicated-circuit services in North America today. As with all dedicated-circuit services, you lease a dedicated circuit from one building in one city to another building in the same or different city. Costs are a fixed amount per month, regardless of how much or how little traffic flows through the circuit. There are several types of T carrier circuits as shown in Figure 9-5, but only T1 and T3 are in common use today.

A **T1 circuit** (also called a *DS1 circuit*) provides a data rate of 1.544 Mbps. T1 circuits can be used to transmit data but often are used to transmit both data and voice. In this

FIGURE 9-4

Mesh design

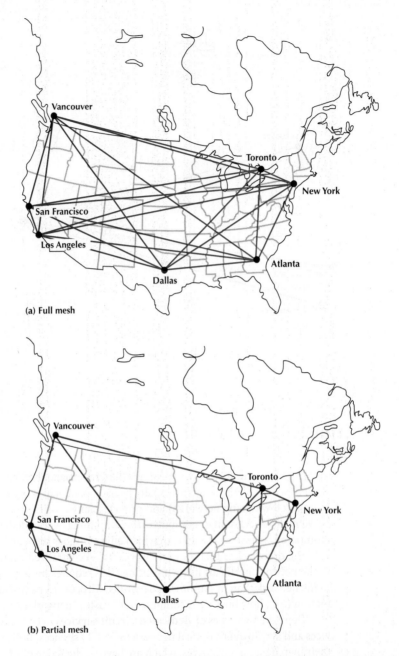

(a) Full mesh

(b) Partial mesh

case, inverse TDM provides 24 64-Kbps circuits.[1] Digitized voice using PCM requires a 64-Kbps circuit (see Chapter 3), so a T1 circuit enables 24 simultaneous voice channels. Most common carriers make extensive use of PCM internally and transmit most of their voice telephone calls in digital format using PCM, so you will see many digital services offering combinations of the standard PCM 64-Kbps circuit.

A **T3 circuit** allows transmission at a rate of 44.736 Mbps, although most articles refer to this rate as 45 megabits per second. This is equal to the capacity of 28 T1 circuits. T3

---

[1] If you multiply 24 circuits by 64 Kbps per circuit, you will get 1.536 Mbps, not 1.544 Mbps. This is because some of the 1.544-Mbps circuit capacity is used by the common carrier for control signals used to frame the data (i.e., mark the start and stop of packets).

FIGURE 9-5

T carrier services

T Carrier Designation	DS Designation	Speed
FT1	DS0	64 Kbps
T1	DS1	1.544 Mbps
T2	DS2	6.312 Mbps
T3	DS3	44.376 Mbps
T4	DS4	274.176 Mbps

FIGURE 9-6

SONET (synchronous optical network) and SDH (synchronous digital hierarchy) services. OC = optical carrier (level)

SONET Designation	SDH Designation	Speed
OC-1		51.84 Mbps
OC-3	STM-1	155.52 Mbps
OC-12	STM-4	622.08 Mbps
OC-24	STM-8	1.244 Gbps
OC-48	STM-16	2.488 Gbps
OC-192	STM-24	9.953 Gbps
OC-768	STM-256	39.813 Gbps
OC-3072	STM-1024	159.25 Gbps

circuits are becoming popular as the transmission medium for corporate MANs and WANs because of their higher data rates. Although T2 and T4 circuits are defined standards, they are not commercially available, and therefore we don't discuss them here.

Fractional T1, sometimes called **FT1**, offers portions of a 1.544-Mbps T1 circuit for a fraction of its full cost. Many (but not all) common carriers offer sets of 64 Kbps DS-0 channels as FT1 circuits. The most common FT1 services provide 128 Kbps, 256 Kbps, 384 Kbps, 512 Kbps, and 768 Kbps.

9.2.3 SONET Services

The **synchronous optical network (SONET)** is the American standard (ANSI) for high-speed dedicated-circuit services. The ITU-T recently standardized an almost identical service that easily interconnects with SONET under the name **synchronous digital hierarchy (SDH)**.

SONET transmission speeds begin at the OC-1 level (optical carrier level 1) of 51.84 Mbps. Each succeeding rate in the SONET fiber hierarchy is defined as a multiple of OC-1, with SONET data rates defined as high as 160 Gbps. Figure 9-6 presents the commonly used SONET and SDH services. Each level above OC-1 is created by an inverse multiplexer. Notice that the slowest SONET transmission rate (OC-1) of 51.84 Mbps is slightly faster than the T3 rate of 44.376 Mbps.

9.3 PACKET-SWITCHED NETWORKS

Packet-switched networks operate more like Ethernet and IP networks used in the LAN and BN than like dedicated circuit networks. With dedicated-circuit networks, a circuit is established between the two communicating routers that provides a guaranteed data transmission capability that is available for use by only those two devices. In contrast, packet-switched services enable multiple connections to exist simultaneously between computers over the same physical circuit, just like LANs and BNs.

FIGURE 9-7

Packet-switched services. LAN = local area network and PAD = packet assembly/disassembly device

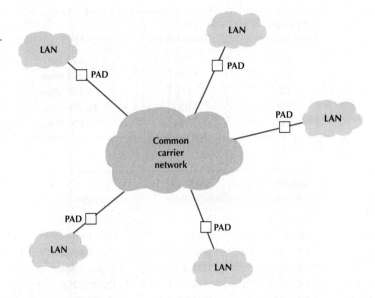

9.3.1 Basic Architecture

With packet-switched services, the user buys a connection into the common carrier cloud (Figure 9-7). The user pays a fixed fee for the connection into the network (depending on the type and capacity of the service) and is charged for the number of packets transmitted.

The user's connection into the network is a **packet assembly/disassembly device (PAD)**, which can be owned and operated by the customer or by the common carrier. The PAD converts the sender's data into the network layer and data link layer packets used by the packet network and sends them through the packet-switched network. At the other end, another PAD reassembles the packets back into the network layer and data link layer protocols expected by the destination (usually Ethernet and IP) and delivers them to the appropriate computer router.

MANAGEMENT 9-1 Cleveland Transit

FOCUS

*T*he Greater Cleveland Regional Transit Authority (GCRTA) has about 2,400 employees and provides bus, trolley, and rail service to about 1.3 million people in the Cleveland area. It has many office locations throughout the region, and more than half of its employees are on the move as they work.

A recent blackout highlighted how vulnerable GCRTA was to network outages. Communications were knocked out, including systems supporting the transit police.

GCRTA redesigned its WAN to use a SONET ring. SONET provides high-speed data services, and the ring topology ensures maximum reliability. Even if one part of the ring is knocked out, whether by power failures or someone accidentally cutting a line, the network will continue to operate.

Adapted from: "Staying on Track," Case Study, AT&T.

One of the key advantages of packet-switched services is that different locations can have different connection speeds into the common carrier cloud. The PAD compensates for differences in transmission speed between sender and receiver; for example, the circuit at the sender might be 50 Mbps, whereas the receiver only has a 1.5 Mbps circuit. In contrast, a dedicated circuit must have the same speed at both the sender and receiver.

Packet-switched networks enable packets from separate messages with different destinations to be *interleaved* for transmission, unlike dedicated circuits, which have one sender and one receiver.

The connections between the different locations in the packet network are called **permanent virtual circuits (PVCs)**, which means that they are defined for frequent and consistent use by the network. They do not change unless the network manager changes the network. Some common carriers also permit the use of **switched virtual circuits (SVCs)**, which change dynamically based on traffic, although this is not common. Changing PVCs is done using software, but common carriers usually charge each time a PVC is established or removed.

Some common carriers permit users to specify two different types of data rates that are negotiated per connection and for each PVC as it is established. The **committed information rate (CIR)** is the data rate the PVC guarantees to transmit. If the network accepts the connection, it guarantees to provide that level of service. Most connections also specify a **maximum allowable rate (MAR)**, which is the maximum rate that the network will attempt to provide, over and above the CIR. The circuit will attempt to transmit all packets up to the MAR, but all packets that exceed the CIR are marked as **discard eligible (DE)**. If the network becomes overloaded, DE packets are discarded. So although users can transmit more data than the CIR, they do so at a risk of lost packets and the need to retransmit them.

Packet-switched services are often provided by different common carriers than the one from which organizations get their usual telephone and data services. Therefore, organizations often lease a dedicated circuit (e.g., T1) from their offices to the packet-switched network **point of presence (POP)**. The POP is the location at which the packet-switched network (or any common carrier network, for that matter) connects into the local telephone exchange.

There are four types of packet-switched services: frame relay, MPLS, Ethernet services, and IP services. Some common carriers have hinted that they plan to discontinue all packet services except IP services, so over the next few years, many WAN technologies may disappear.

9.3.2 Frame Relay Services

Frame relay is one of the most commonly used WAN services in the United States. Like wired Ethernet LANs, it is an unreliable packet service because it does not perform error control. Frame relay checks for errors but simply discards packets with errors. It is up to the software at the source and destination to control for lost messages.

MANAGEMENT 9-2 **Frame Relay at Air China**

FOCUS

Air China is the largest airline in China, both in terms of traffic and assets. The airline has more than 200 aircraft that serve 81 domestic and 42 international destinations, with about 6,000 scheduled flights per week. The airline industry has become more competitive because of China's rapid economic growth, so the airline sought to improve its global WAN.

Air China needed a strong global network to link its headquarters in Beijing with its 40 offices in Asia, Europe, the Middle East, Africa, and North America. It partnered with AT&T to provide a frame relay in all countries. For local equipment, it chose Cisco routers and PADs to connect into the network.

Adapted from: "Managed Networking Solutions Offer Competitive Advantage for China's Largest Global Airline," Case Study, AT&T.

Frame relay does not yet provide QoS capabilities, but this is under development. Different common carriers offer frame relay networks with different transmission speeds. Most offer a range of CIR speeds that include 64 Kbps, 128 Kbps, 1.5 Mbps, and 45 Mbps. You will recognize these speeds as the same speeds of T carrier networks, because frame relay uses the T carrier networks for its physical transmission.

A Day in the Life: Networking and Telecommunications Vice President

A vice president is a person in an executive-level position whose focus is to set the strategic direction for the organization. A vice president has very little to do with the day-to-day operations; much like an admiral in a navy fleet, he or she defines the direction, but the individual captains running each ship actually make sure that everything that needs to happen gets done.

The vice president works with the chief information officer (CIO) and other executive leadership of the organization to identify the key organizational goals that have implications for the network. The vice president works with his or her staff to revise the strategic networking plan to ensure that the network is capable of supporting the organization's goals. The key elements of the strategic plan are the networking architectures, key technologies, and vendors. Once the strategy has been set, the vice president's job is to instruct the senior managers to execute the strategy and then let them do their jobs.

In most cases, the changes to the networking strategic plan are relatively minor, but sometimes there are dramatic changes that require a major shift in strategic direction. For example, in recent years, we've seen a major change in the fundamental capabilities of network tools and applications. Our architecture strategy during the 1990s was driven by the fact that network management tools were poor and maintenance costs per server were high; the fundamental architecture strategy was to minimize the number of servers. Today, network management tools are much better, maintenance costs per server are significantly lower, and network traffic has changed both in volume and in the number and complexity of services supported (e.g., Web, email, H.323, and IPv6); the strategy today is to provide a greater number of servers, each of which is dedicated to supporting one specific type of traffic.

Source: With thanks to Brian Voss.

9.3.3 Ethernet Services

Although we have seen rapid increases in capacities and sharp decreases in costs in LAN and BN technologies, changes in WAN services offered by common carriers saw only modest changes in the 1990s. That changed in 2000 with the introduction of several Internet start-ups (e.g., Yipes) offering **Ethernet services**.

Most organizations today use Ethernet and IP in the LAN and BN environments, yet the WAN packet network services (T carrier, SONET, and frame relay) discussed earlier use different layer-2 protocols. Any LAN or BN traffic, therefore, must be translated or encapsulated into a new protocol and destination addresses generated for the new protocol. This takes time, slowing network throughput. It also adds complexity, meaning that companies must add staff knowledgeable in the different WAN protocols, software, and hardware these technologies require. This is one reason many common carriers are starting to call these technologies "legacy technologies," signaling their demise.

Each of the preceding **packet services** uses the traditional public switched telephone network (PSTN) provided by the common carriers such as AT&T and BellSouth. In contrast, Ethernet services bypass the PSTN; companies offering Ethernet services have laid their own gigabit Ethernet fiber-optic networks in large cities. When an organization signs up for service, the packet network company installs new fiber-optic cables from their citywide backbone into the organization's office complex and connects it to an Ethernet switch. The organization simply plugs its network into its Ethernet switch and begins using the service. All traffic entering the packet network must be Ethernet, using IP.

Currently, Ethernet services offer CIR speeds of 1 Mbps to 40 Gbps, in 1-Mbps increments, at a lower cost than traditional packet-switched networks. Because this is an emerging technology, we should see many changes in the next few years.

MANAGEMENT

FOCUS

9-3 A Georgia Ethernet WAN

Marietta City Schools (MCS) is a school district northwest of Atlanta, Georgia, that has 8,000 students and 1,200 employees at 13 schools plus an administrative office. Its WAN was a traditional SONET network using OC-1 circuits in a star design connecting each school to the MCS administrative office.

The network was expensive and did not offer sufficient room for growth as MCS contemplated moving to more digital education. MCS implemented an Ethernet WAN and then gradually phased out the old SONET WAN.

MCS contracted with Zayo, a large common carrier that provides services to businesses and governments but not the consumer market (which is why you've probably never heard of them). Each school and the administrative office now has its own 1 Gbps Ethernet over fiber connection into the Zayo network and can easily send data to any of MCS's 14 sites. Because it is a packet-switched network, each location can have a different speed, and MCS is already considering upgrading the busier sites to 10 Gbps.

Adapted from: Education/E-Rate: Multi-Campus Network Upgrade; Ethernet Augmentation for Georgia School District, Zayo Group, LLC.

9.3.4 MPLS Services

Multiprotocol label switching (MPLS) is another relatively new WAN technology that is designed to work with a variety of commonly used layer-2 protocols. It is sometimes called a layer-2.5 technology because it inserts a 4-byte header that contains its own information between the layer-2 frame and the layer-3 IP packet.

With MPLS, the customer connects to the common carrier's network using any common layer-2 service (e.g., T carrier, SONET, frame relay, and Ethernet). The carrier's switch at the network entry point examines the incoming frame and converts the incoming layer-2 or layer-3 address into an MPLS address label. This label and some other control information (e.g., quality of service) form the MPLS header, which is inserted into the layer-2 frame for transmission inside the carrier's network. The carrier can use the same layer-2 protocol inside its network as the customer, or it can use something different; for example, the customer could connect to the MPLS network using frame relay, but the carrier could use SONET inside its network.

The address in MPLS label is used to move through the frame through the carrier network until it reaches the edge of the network at the customer's destination. The MPLS switch at this exit point removes the MPLS header and delivers the packet into the customer's network using whatever layer-2 protocol the customer has used to connect into the carrier's network at this point (e.g., frame and T1).

MPLS offers a wide variety of data speeds because it depends on the underlying physical circuits used. It is common to see MPLS services running at the lower speeds of T carrier circuits (e.g., 64 Kpbs, 1.5 Mbps and 45 Mbps) as well as the higher speeds of SONET (e.g., 51 Mbps, 155 Mbps, and 622 Mbps).

MANAGEMENT

FOCUS

9-4 MPLS at Cisco

For years, Cisco Systems Inc. had supported its Europe/Middle East/Africa (EMEA) offices with a series of star networks connected to stars (called a hub-and-spoke design). The WAN core was three offices (London, Amsterdam, and Brussels) connected to each other in a full mesh using OC-3 circuits. Each of these three offices was the center of a star network that connected to three other secondary star networks and 10 major sites (9 stars and 30 major sites in total). The nine secondary stars connected a total of 85 other offices.

The network was at capacity, and any time one of the three core offices (or one of the hubs of the secondary stars) needed to be taken down for maintenance, it shut down a major part of the network. Worse still, it looked like the London office would need to move to a new building, which meant significant rewiring of the network.

Cisco chose to implement a full mesh MPLS network to provide greater capacity and better flexibility. Each office is connected into the MPLS carrier's cloud with two separate MPLS circuits that are laid in physically separate routes to provide better reliability in case a circuit is accidentally cut. Each of the two circuits is sized for the needs of the specific office, ranging from 64 Kbps up to 45 Mbps. Since the three core offices no longer route traffic for the entire network, they don't need as much network capacity as they did with the hub and spoke design. The new network has significantly increased capacity, reliability, and flexibility, while keeping costs about the same.

Adapted from: "How Cisco IT in Europe Migrated to MPLS VPN WAN," Cisco IT Case Study, Cisco.

9.3.5 IP Services

Many experts predict that in 5 years, IP services will be the only type of packet-switched services available in the market. With IP services, the PAD at the sending site takes the outgoing message (which usually is an Ethernet frame containing an IP packet), strips off the Ethernet frame, and uses the IP address in the IP packet to route the packet though the carrier's packet-switched network to its final destination. The PAD at the destination has an Ethernet port, so a new Ethernet packet is added before the packet enters the customer's network at the destination. Because the carrier's packet-switched network uses IP addresses, this network looks and feels like the Internet, although it is a separate network for use only by customers of the carrier.

The data link layer protocol used inside the common carrier's network is whatever the carrier chooses to use, and the customer never really knows—or cares. Most IP services use MPLS as the data link layer protocol, but as long as the customer receives the contracted data speeds and packets are delivered in a reliable manner, the customer never needs to know what protocol(s) are used. Because MPLS is often used as the underlying network protocol, there is the same wide variety of data speeds as we see in MPLS services (e.g., 1.5 Mbps, 45 Mbps, 155 Mbps, and 622 Mbps).

9.4 VIRTUAL PRIVATE NETWORKS

A **virtual private network (VPN)** provides the equivalent of a private packet-switched network over the public Internet.[2] It involves establishing a series of PVCs that run over the Internet so that the network acts like a set of dedicated circuits even though the data flows over the Internet.

9.4.1 Basic Architecture

With a VPN, you first lease an Internet connection at whatever access rate and access technology you choose for each location you want to connect. For example, you might lease a T1 circuit from a common carrier that runs from your office to your **Internet Service Provider (ISP)**. Or you might use a DSL or cable modem, which are discussed in the next chapter. You pay the common carrier for the circuit and the ISP for Internet access. Then you connect a **VPN gateway** (a specially designed router) to each Internet access circuit to provide access from your networks to the VPN. The VPN gateways enable you to create PVCs through the Internet that are called *tunnels* (Figure 9-8).

The VPN gateway at the sender takes the outgoing packet and encapsulates it with a protocol that is used to move it through the tunnel to the VPN gateway on the other side. The VPN gateway at the receiver strips off the VPN packet and delivers the packet to the destination network. The VPN is transparent to the users; it appears as though a traditional packet-switched network PVC is in use. The VPN is also transparent to the ISP and the Internet as a whole; there is simply a stream of Internet packets moving across the Internet.

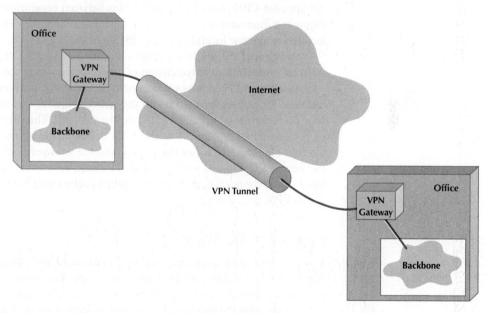

FIGURE 9-8 A virtual private network (VPN).
ISP = Internet service provider

[2]Some common carriers and third-party vendors are now providing VPN services that use their own networks rather than the Internet. These networks, sometimes called Private VPNs, offer an additional measure of security because in addition to flowing through the carrier's private network, they provide the same security benefits as VPNs on the public Internet. In the interest of simplicity, we will focus on Internet-based VPN services.

VPN software is commonly used on home computers or laptops to provide the same secure tunnels to people working from offsite.

VPNs operate either at layer 2 or layer 3. A **layer-2 VPN** uses the layer-2 packet (e.g., Ethernet) to select the VPN tunnel and encapsulates the entire packet, starting with the layer-2 packet. Layer-2 tunneling protocol (**L2TP**) is an example of a layer-2 VPN. A **layer-3 VPN** uses the layer-3 packet (e.g., IP) to select the VPN tunnel and encapsulates the entire packet, starting with the layer-3 packet; it discards the incoming layer-2 packet and generates an entirely new layer-2 packet at the destination. **IPSec** is an example of a layer-3 VPN.

The primary advantages of VPNs are low cost and flexibility. Because they use the Internet to carry messages, the major cost is Internet access, which is inexpensive compared with the cost of dedicated-circuit services and packet-switched services from a common carrier. Likewise, anywhere you can establish Internet service, you can quickly put in a VPN.

There are two important disadvantages. First, traffic on the Internet is unpredictable. Sometimes packets travel quickly, but at other times, they take a long while to reach their destination. Although some VPN vendors advertise QoS capabilities, these apply only in the VPN devices themselves; on the Internet, a packet is a packet. Second, because the data travel on the Internet, security is always a concern. Most VPN networks encrypt the packet at the source VPN device before it enters the Internet and decrypt the packet at the destination VPN device. (See Chapter 11 for more on encryption.)

9.4.2 VPN Types

Three types of VPNs are in common use: intranet VPN, extranet VPN, and access VPN. An **intranet VPN** provides virtual circuits between organization offices over the Internet. Figure 9-8 illustrates an intranet VPN. Each location has a VPN gateway that connects the location to another location through the Internet.

An **extranet VPN** is the same as an intranet VPN, except that the VPN connects several different organizations, often customers and suppliers, over the Internet.

An **access VPN** enables employees to access an organization's networks from a remote location. Employees have access to the network and all the resources on it in the same way as employees physically located on the network. The user uses VPN software on his or her computer to connect to the VPN device at the office. The VPN gateway accepts the user's log-in, establishes the tunnel, and the software begins forwarding packets over the Internet. Compared with a typical ISP-based remote connection, the access VPN is a more secure connection than simply sending packets over the Internet. Figure 9-9 shows an access VPN.

9.4.3 How VPNs Work

When packets move across the Internet, they are much like postcards in the paper mail. Anyone can read what they contain. VPNs provide security by encapsulating (i.e., surrounding) packets in a separate, secure packet that is encrypted. No one can read the encapsulated data without knowing the password that is used to decrypt the packet. Layer-2 and layer-3 VPNs work very similarly, except that layer-2 VPNs encapsulate the user's data starting with the layer-2 packet (the Ethernet frame) while layer-3 VPNs encapsulate the user's data starting with the layer-3 packet (the IP packet).

Figure 9-9 shows how a layer-3 access VPN using IPSec works. Suppose an employee is working at home with a LAN that uses a router to connect to the Internet via an Internet Service Provider (ISP) using DSL (we explain how DSL works in the next chapter). When the employee wants to use the VPN, he or she starts the VPN software on his or her computer

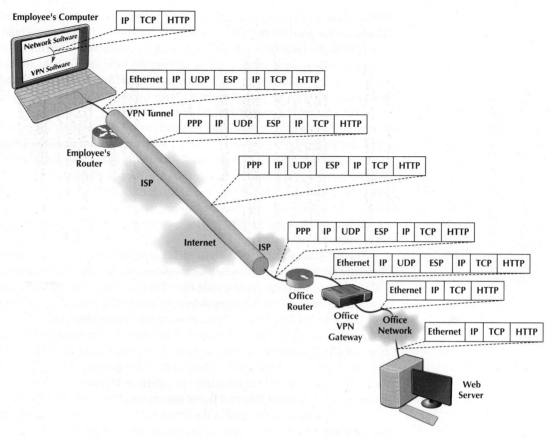

FIGURE 9-9 Using VPN software

and uses it to log in to the VPN gateway at the office. The VPN software creates a new "interface" on the employee's computer that acts exactly like a separate connection into the Internet. Interfaces are usually hardware connections, but the VPN is a software interface, although the employee's computer doesn't know this—it's just another interface. Computers can have multiple interfaces; a laptop computer often has two interfaces, one for wire Ethernet and one for wireless Wi-Fi.

The VPN gateway at the office is also a router and a DCHP server. The VPN gateway assigns an IP address to the VPN interface on the employee's computer that is an IP address in a subnet managed by the VPN gateway. For example, if the VPN gateway has an IP address of 156.56.198.1 and managed the 156.56.198.x subnet, it would assign an IP address in this subnet domain (e.g., 156.56.198.55).

The employee's computer now thinks it has two connections to the Internet: the traditional interface that has the computer's usual IP address and the VPN interface that has an IP address assigned by the VPN gateway. The VPN software on the employee's computer makes the VPN interface the default interface for all network traffic to and from the Internet, which ensures that all messages leaving the employee's computer flow through the VPN interface to the VPN gateway at the office.

Suppose the employee sends an HTTP request to a Web server at the office (or somewhere else on the Internet). The Web browser software will create an HTTP packet that is passed to the TCP software (which adds a TCP segment), and this in turn is passed to the IP software managing the VPN interface. The IP software creates the IP packet using the source IP address assigned by the VPN gateway. Normally, the IP software would then pass the IP packet to the Ethernet software that manages the Ethernet interface into the employee's LAN, but because the IP packet is being sent out the VPN interface, the IP packet is passed to the VPN software managing the VPN interface. Figure 9-9 shows the message as it leaves the network software and is passed to the VPN for transmission: an HTTP packet, surrounded by a TCP segment, surrounded by an IP packet.

The VPN software receives the IP packet, encrypts it, and encapsulates it (and its contents: the TCP segment and the HTTP packet) with an **Encapsulating Security Payload (ESP)** packet using IPSec encryption. The contents of the ESP packet (the IP packet, the TCP segment, and the HTTP packet) are encrypted so that no one except the VPN gateway at the office can read them. You can think of the IPSec packet as an application layer packet whose destination is the office VPN gateway. How do we send an application layer packet over the Internet? Well, we pass it to the TCP software, which is exactly what the VPN software does.

The VPN software passes the ESP packet (and its encrypted contents) to the employee's computer normal Internet interface for transmission. This interface has been sitting around waiting for transmissions, but because the VPN interface is defined as the primary interface to use, it has received no messages to transfer except those from the VPN software.

This interface treats the ESP packet as an application layer packet that needs to be sent to the VPN gateway at the office. It attaches a transport layer packet (a UDP datagram in this case, not a TCP segment). It then passes the ESP packet to the IP software, which creates an IP packet with an IP destination address of the VPN gateway at the office and a source IP of the employee's computer's normal Internet interface. It passes this IP packet to the Ethernet software, which adds an Ethernet frame and transmits it to the employee's router.

The employee's router receives the Ethernet frame, strips off the frame, and reads the IP packet. It sees that the packet needs to be sent to the VPN gateway at the office, which means sending the packet to the employee's ISP over the DSL circuit. Because DSL uses PPP as its layer-2 protocol, it adds a PPP frame and sends the packet over the DSL circuit to the ISP.

The router at the ISP strips off the PPP frame and reads the IP packet, which it uses to route the packet through the Internet. As the packet moves over the Internet, the layer-2 frame changes at each hop, depending on the circuit in use. For example, if the ISP uses a T3 circuit, then the ISP creates an appropriate layer-2 frame to move the packet over the T3 circuit (which usually is a PPP frame).

The packet travels from the Internet to the ISP that connects the office to the Internet and arrives at the office's router. This router will strip off the incoming layer-2 frame (suppose the office uses a T-3 connection with PPP as shown in the figure), read the IP packet, and create an Ethernet frame that will send the packet to the office VPN gateway. The VPN gateway will strip off the Ethernet frame, read the IP packet, strip it off, read the UDP datagram, strip it off, and hand the ESP packet to its VPN software. The VPN gateway's software will decrypt the ESP packet and deencapsulate the IP packet (and the TCP segment and HTTP packet it contains) from the ESP packet. The VPN gateway now has the IP packet (and the TCP segment and HTTP packet) that was originally created by the software on the employee's computer. The VPN gateway reads this IP packet and creates an Ethernet frame to send it on the next hop to its destination and transmits it into the office network, where it ultimately reaches the Web server. On this last leg of the journey after it leaves the VPN gateway, the packet is not encrypted and can be read like a normal packet on the Internet.

The return path from the Web server back to the employee's computer is very similar. The Web server will process the HTTP request packet and create an HTTP response packet that it sends back to the employee's computer. The source address on the IP packet that the Web server received was the IP address associated with the VPN interface on the employee's computer, so the Web server uses this address as the destination IP address. This packet is therefore routed back to the VPN gateway, because the subnet for this IP address is defined as being in the subnet that the VPN gateway manages. Once again, the return packet is not encrypted on this part of the journey.

When the packet arrives at the VPN gateway, it looks up the VPN IP address in its table and sees the usual IP address of the computer associated with that VPN address. The VPN gateway creates an ESP packet and encrypts the IP packet from the Web server (and the TCP segment and HTTP packet it contains). It then treats the ESP packet as an application layer packet that needs to be sent to the VPN software on the employee's computer; it passes it to its TCP software for a UDP datagram, then to its IP software for an IP packet, and then to its Ethernet software for an Ethernet frame and transmission back through the VPN tunnel.

When the packet eventually reaches the employee's computer, it comes in the normal Internet interface and eventually reaches the TCP software that strips off the UDP datagram. The TCP software sees that the ESP packet inside the UDP datagram is destined for the VPN software (remember that TCP port numbers are used to identify to which application layer software a packet should go). The VPN software removes the ESP packet and passes the IP packet it contains to the IP software, which in turn strips off the IP packet, and passes the TCP segment it contains to the TCP software, which strips off the TCP segments and passes the HTTP packet it contains to the Web browser.

9.5 THE BEST PRACTICE WAN DESIGN

Developing best practice recommendations for WAN design is more difficult than for LANs and backbones because the network designer is buying services from different companies rather than buying products. The relatively stable environment enjoyed by the WAN common carriers is facing sharp challenges by VPNs at the low end and Ethernet and MPLS services at the high end. As larger IT and equipment firms enter the VPN and Ethernet services markets, we should see some major changes in the industry and in the available services and costs.

We also need to point out that the technologies in this chapter are primarily used to connect different corporate locations. Technologies primarily used for Internet access (e.g., DSL and cable modem) are discussed in the next chapter.

We use the same two factors as we have previously for LANs and backbones (effective data rates and cost), plus add one additional factor: reliability.

Figure 9-10 summarizes the major services available today for the WAN, grouped by the type of service. A few patterns should emerge from the table. For small WANs with low

FIGURE 9-10

WAN services

Type of Service	Data Rates	Relative Cost	Reliability
Dedicated-Circuit Services			
T Carrier	64 Kbps to 45 Mbps	Moderate	High
SONET	50 Mbps to 10 Gbps	High	High
Packet-Switched Services			
Frame Relay	64 Kbps to 45 Mbps	Moderate	High
Ethernet	1 Mbps to 40 Gbps	Moderate	High
MPLS	64 Kbps to 10 Gbps	Moderate	High
IP	64 Kbps to 1 Gbps	Moderate	High
VPN Services			
VPN	64 Kbps to 50 Mbps	Low	Moderate

FIGURE 9-11

Best practice WAN
recommendations

Network Needs	Recommendation
Low to Moderate Traffic **(10 Mbps or less)**	**VPN if reliability is less important** **Frame relay otherwise**
High Traffic **(10–50 Mbps)**	**Ethernet, IP, or MPLS if available** **T3 if network volume is stable and predictable** **Frame relay otherwise**
Very High Traffic **(50 Mbps to 100 Gbps)**	**Ethernet, IP, or MPLS if available** **SONET if network volume is stable and predictable**

to moderate data transmission needs, VPN services are a good alternative, provided the lack of reliability is not a major issue. Otherwise, frame relay is a good choice. See Figure 9-11.

For networks with high data transmission needs (10–50 Mbps) there are several distinct choices. If cost is more important than reliability, then a VPN is a possible choice. If you need flexibility in the location of your network connections and you are not completely sure of the volume of traffic you will have between locations, frame relay, IP, or MPLS are good choices. If you have a mature network with predictable demands, then T3 is probably a good choice.

For very-high-traffic networks (50 Mbps to 100 Gbps), Ethernet or MPLS services are a dominant choice. And again, some organizations may prefer the more mature SONET services, depending on whether the greater flexibility of packet services provides value or a dedicated circuit makes more sense.

Unless their data needs are stable, network managers often start with more flexible packet-switched services and move to the usually cheaper dedicated-circuit services once their needs have become clear and an investment in dedicated services is safer. Some packet-switched services even permit organizations to establish circuits with a zero-CIR (and rely entirely on the availability of the MAR) so network managers can track their needs and lease only what they need.

Network managers often add a packet network service as an overlay network on top of a network built with dedicated circuits to handle peak data needs; data usually travel over the dedicated-circuit network, but when it becomes overloaded with traffic, the extra traffic is routed to the packet network.

9.6 IMPROVING WAN PERFORMANCE

Improving the performance of WANs is handled in the same way as improving LAN performance. You begin by checking the devices in the network, by upgrading the circuits between the locations, and by changing the demand placed on the network (Figure 9-12).

9.6.1 Improving Device Performance

In some cases, the key bottleneck in the network is not the circuits; it is the devices that provide access to the circuits (e.g., routers). One way to improve network performance is to upgrade the devices and computers that connect backbones to the WAN. Most devices are rated for their speed in converting input packets to output packets (called **latency**). Not all devices are created equal; some vendors produce devices with lower latencies than others.

Another strategy is examining the routing protocol, either static or dynamic. Dynamic routing will increase performance in networks that have many possible routes from one

FIGURE 9-12

Improving performance
of metropolitan and
local area networks

Performance Checklist

Increase Computer and Device Performance
• **Upgrade devices**
• **Change to a more appropriate routing protocol (either static or dynamic)**

Increase Circuit Capacity
• **Analyze message traffic and upgrade to faster circuits where needed**
• **Check error rates**

Reduce Network Demand
• **Change user behavior**
• **Analyze network needs of all new systems**
• **Move data closer to users**

---

computer to another and in which message traffic is "bursty"—that is, in which traffic occurs in spurts, with many messages at one time, and few at others. But dynamic routing imposes an overhead cost by increasing network traffic. In some cases, the traffic and status information sent between computers accounts for more than 50% of all WAN message traffic. This is clearly a problem because it drastically reduces the amount of network capacity available for users' messages. Dynamic routing should use no more than 10–20% of the network's total capacity.

9.6.2 Improving Circuit Capacity

The first step is to analyze the message traffic in the network to find which circuits are approaching capacity. These circuits then can be upgraded to provide more capacity. Less-used circuits can be downgraded to save costs. A more sophisticated analysis involves examining *why* circuits are heavily used. For example, in Figure 9-2, the circuit from San Francisco to Vancouver may be heavily used, but much traffic on this circuit may not originate in San Francisco or be destined for Vancouver. It may, for example, be going from Los Angeles to Toronto, suggesting that adding a circuit here would improve performance to a greater extent than upgrading the San Francisco-to-Vancouver circuit.

The capacity may be adequate for most traffic but not for meeting peak demand. One solution may be to add a packet-switched service that is used only when demand exceeds the capacity of the dedicated circuit network. The use of a service as a backup for heavy traffic provides the best of both worlds. The lower-cost dedicated circuit is used constantly, and the backup service is used only when necessary to avoid poor response times.

Sometimes a shortage of capacity may be caused by a faulty circuit. As circuits deteriorate, the number of errors increases. As the error rate increases, throughput falls because more messages have to be retransmitted. Before installing new circuits, monitor the existing ones to ensure that they are operating properly or ask the common carrier to do it.

9.6.3 Reducing Network Demand

There are many ways to reduce network demand. One step is to require a network impact statement for all new application software developed or purchased by the organization. This focuses attention on the network impacts at an early stage in application development. Another simple approach is to use data compression techniques for all data in the network.

Another more difficult approach is to shift network usage from peak or high-cost times to lower-demand or lower-cost times. For example, the transmission of detailed sales and inventory reports from a retail store to headquarters could be done after the store closes. This takes advantage of off-peak rate charges and avoids interfering with transmissions requiring higher priority such as customer credit card authorizations.

The network also can be redesigned to move data closer to the applications and people who use them. This also will reduce the amount of traffic in the network. Distributed database applications enable databases to be spread across several different computers. For example, instead of storing customer records in one central location, you could store them according to region.

9.7 IMPLICATIONS FOR MANAGEMENT

As the amount of digital computer data flowing through and WANs has increased and as those networks have become increasingly digital, the networking and telecommunications vice president role has significantly changed over the past 10 years. Traditionally this vice president has been responsible for computer communications; today in most companies, this individual is also responsible for telephone and voice services.

T carrier, SONET, and old technologies such as ATM have traditionally dominated the WAN market. However, with the growing use of VPNs and Ethernet and MPLS services, we are beginning to see a major change. In the early 1990s, the costs of WANs were quite high relative to other types of networks. As these networks have changed to increasingly digital technologies, and as competition has increased with the introduction of new companies and new technologies (e.g., VPNs and Ethernet services), costs have begun to drop. More firms are now moving to implement software applications that depend on low-cost WANs, and cloud architectures are becoming common.

The same factors that caused the LAN and BN to standardize on a few technologies (Ethernet and wireless Ethernet) are now acting to shape the future of the WAN. We believe that within 5 years, T carrier and frame relay will disappear and will be replaced by Ethernet, IP, and MPLS services.

These changes have also had significant impacts on the manufacturers of networking equipment designed for WANs. Market shares and stock prices have shifted dramatically over the last 5 years in favor of companies with deep experience in backbone technologies (e.g., Ethernet) and Internet technologies (e.g., IP) as those technologies spread into the WAN market.

SUMMARY

Dedicated-Circuit Networks A dedicated circuit is leased from the common carrier for exclusive use 24 hours per day, 7 days per week. You must carefully plan the circuits you need because changes can be expensive. The three common architectures are ring, star, and mesh. T carrier circuits have a set of digital services ranging from FT1 (64 Kbps) to T1 (1.5 Mbps) to T3 (45 Mbps). A SONET service uses fiber optics to provide services ranging from OC-1 (51 Mbps) to OC-192 (10 Gbps).

Packet-Switched Networks Packet switching is a technique in which messages are split into small segments. The user buys a connection into the common carrier cloud and pays a fixed fee for the connection into the network and for the number of packets transmitted. Frame relay is an older service that provides data rates of 64 Kbps to 45 Mbps.

Ethernet services use Ethernet and IP to transmit packets at speeds between 1 Mbps and 100 Gbps. Two newer services are MPLS and IP that provide speeds from 64 Kbps to as much as 40 Gbps.

VPN Networks A VPN provides a packet service network over the Internet. The sender and receiver have VPN devices that enable them to send data over the Internet in encrypted form through a VPN tunnel. Although VPNs are inexpensive, traffic delays on the Internet can be unpredictable.

The Best Practice WAN Design For small WANs with low to moderate data transmission needs, VPN or frame relay services are reasonable alternatives. For high-traffic networks (10–50 Mbps), Ethernet, IP, or MPLS services are a good choice, but some organizations may prefer the more mature—and therefore proven—T3 services. For very high-traffic networks (50 Mbps to 100 Gbps), Ethernet, IP, or MPLS services are a dominant choice, but again some organizations may prefer the more mature SONET services. Unless their data needs are stable, network managers often start with more flexible packet-switched services and move to the usually cheaper dedicated-circuit services once their needs have become clear and an investment in dedicated services is safer.

Improving WAN Performance One can improve network performance by improving the speed of the devices themselves and by using a better routing protocol. Analysis of network usage can show what circuits need to be increased or decreased in capacity, what new circuits need to be leased, and when additional switched circuits may be needed to meet peak demand. Reducing network demand may also improve performance. Including a network usage analysis for all new application software, using data compression, shifting usage to off-peak times, establishing priorities for some applications, or redesigning the network to move data closer to those who use it are all ways to reduce network demand.

KEY TERMS

access VPN, 258
Canadian Radio-Television and Telecommunications Commission (CRTC), 246
channel service unit/data service unit (CSU/DSU), 246
committed information rate (CIR), 253
common carrier, 245
dedicated-circuit services, 249
discard eligible (DE), 253
Ethernet services, 254
Encapsulating Security Payload (ESP), 260
extranet VPN, 258

Federal Communications Commission (FCC), 246
fractional T1 (FT1), 251
frame relay, 253
full-mesh architecture, 248
interexchange carrier (IXC), 246
Internet Service Provider (ISP), 257
intranet VPN, 258
IPSec, 258
L2TP, 258
latency, 262
layer-2 VPN, 258
layer-3 VPN, 258
local exchange carrier (LEC), 246

maximum allowable rate (MAR), 253
mesh architecture, 248
multiprotocol label switching (MPLS), 255
packet assembly/disassembly (PAD), 252
packet services, 255
Packet-switched services, 251
partial-mesh architecture, 248
permanent virtual circuits (PVC), 253
point of presence (POP), 253

public utilities commission (PUC), 246
ring architecture, 247
star architecture, 248
switched virtual circuit (SVC), 253
synchronous digital hierarchy (SDH), 251
synchronous optical network (SONET), 251
T carrier circuit, 249
T1, T2, T3, T4 circuits, 249
virtual private network (VPN), 257
VPN gateway, 257
VPN software, 258

QUESTIONS

1. What are common carriers, local exchange carriers, and interexchange carriers?
2. Who regulates common carriers and how is it done?
3. How does MPLS work?
4. Compare and contrast dedicated-circuit services and packet-switched services.
5. Is a WAN that uses dedicated circuits easier or harder to design than one that uses packet-switched circuits? Explain.
6. Compare and contrast ring architecture, star architecture, and mesh architecture.
7. What are the most commonly used T carrier services? What data rates do they provide?
8. Distinguish among T1, T2, T3, and T4 circuits.
9. Describe SONET. How does it differ from SDH?
10. How do packet-switching services differ from other WAN services?
11. Where does packetizing take place?
12. Compare and contrast frame relay, MPLS, and Ethernet services.
13. Which is likely to be the longer-term winner: IP, MPLS, or Ethernet services?
14. Explain the differences between CIR and MAR.
15. How do VPN services differ from common carrier services?
16. Explain how VPN services work.
17. Compare the three types of VPN.
18. How can you improve WAN performance?
19. Describe five important factors in selecting WAN services.
20. Are Ethernet services a major change in the future of networking or a technology blip?
21. Are there any WAN technologies that you would avoid if you were building a network today? Explain.
22. Suppose you joined a company that had a WAN composed of SONET, T carrier, and frame relay services, each selected to match a specific network need for a certain set of circuits. Would you say this was a well-designed network? Explain.
23. It is said that frame relay services and dedicated-circuit services are somewhat similar from the perspective of the network designer. Why?

EXERCISES

A. Find out the data rates and costs of T carrier services in your area.
B. Find out the data rates and costs of packet-switched and dedicated-circuit services in your area.
C. Investigate the WAN of a company in your area. Draw a network map.
D. Using Figure 9-9:
   a. Suppose the example used a layer-2 VPN protocol called L2TP. Draw the messages and the packets they would contain.
   b. Suppose the Web server was an email server. Draw the messages from the email server to the employee's computer. Show what packets would be in the message.
   c. Suppose the office connects to its ISP using metro Ethernet. What packets would be in the message from the office router to the ISP?
   d. Suppose the employee connects to the ISP using a layer-2 protocol called XYZ. What packets would be in the message from the employes's router to the ISP?

MINICASES

I. **Cookies Are Us** Cookies Are Us runs a series of 100 cookie stores across the midwestern United States and central Canada. At the end of each day, the stores send sales and inventory data to headquarters, which uses the data to ship new inventory and plan marketing campaigns. The company has decided to move to a new WAN. What type of a WAN architecture and WAN service would you recommend? Why?

II. **MegaCorp** MegaCorp is a large manufacturing firm that operates five factories in Dallas, four factories in Los Angeles, and five factories in Albany, New York. It operates a tightly connected order management system that coordinates orders, raw materials, and inventory across all 14 factories. What type of WAN architecture and WAN service would you recommend? Why?

III. **Sunrise Consultancy** Sunrise Consultancy is a medium-sized consulting firm that operates 17 offices around the world (Dallas, Chicago, New York, Atlanta, Miami, Seattle, Los Angeles, San Jose, Toronto, Montreal, London, Paris, Sao Paulo, Singapore, Hong Kong, Sydney, and Bombay). They have been using Internet connections to exchange email and files, but the volume of traffic has increased to the point that they now want to connect the offices via a WAN. Volume is low but expected to grow quickly once they implement a new knowledge management system. What type of a WAN topology and WAN service would you recommend? Why?

IV. **Cleveland Transit** Reread Management Focus 9-1. What other alternatives do you think Cleveland Transit considered? Why do you think they did what they did?

V. **Air China** Reread Management Focus 9-2. What other alternatives do you think Air China considered? Why do you think they did what they did?

VI. **Marietta City Schools** Reread Management Focus 9-3. What alternatives do you think Marietta City Schools considered? Why do you think they did what they did?

VII. **Cisco** Reread Management Focus 9-4. What other alternatives do you think that Cisco considered? Why do you think they did what they did?

CASE STUDY

NEXT-DAY AIR SERVICE

See the companion Web site at www.wiley.com/college/fitzgerald.

HANDS-ON ACTIVITY 9A

Examining Wide Area Neworks

There are millions of WANs in the world. Some are run by common carriers and are available to the public. Others are private networks run by organizations for their internal use only. Thousands of these networks have been documented on the Web.

Explore the Web to find networks offered by common carriers and compare the types of network circuits they have. Now do the same for public and private organizations to see what they have. Figure 9-13 shows the network map for Zayo, a large common carrier (see zayo.com). This

figure shows the circuits running at 100 Gbps that connect major cities in the United States. Zayo has a much larger network that includes portions that run slower than 100 Gbps, but the network has hundreds of sites and is too hard to show in one figure.

Deliverable

Print or copy two different WAN maps. Does the WAN use only one type of circuits, or are there a mix of technologies in use?

HANDS-ON ACTIVITY 9B

Examining VPNs with Wireshark

If you want to see VPNs in action and understand how they protect your data as they move over the Internet, you can sniff your packets with Wireshark. To do this lab, you'll have to have a VPN you can use. This will normally be available from your school.

In this exercise, you'll use Wireshark to sniff the packets with and without the VPN. Before you start, you'll need to download and install Wireshark, a packet sniffer software package, on your computer.

1. Start the VPN software on your computer.

2. Start a Web browser (e.g., Internet Explorer) and go to a Web site.

3. Start Wireshark and click on the Capture menu item. This will open up a new menu (see the very top of Figure 9-14). Click on Interfaces.

4. This will open a new window that will enable you to select which interface you want to capture packets from. Figure 9-14 shows you the three

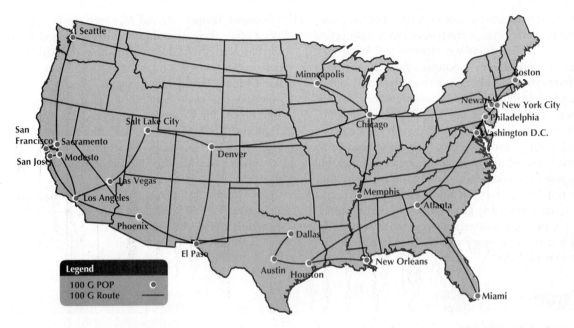

FIGURE 9-13 100 Gbps network for a U.S. Internet Service Provider

interfaces I have on my computer. The first interface is a dial-up modem that I never use. The second interface (labeled "Broadcom NetXtreme Gigabit Ethernet Driver") is my Ethernet local area network. It has the IP address of 192.168.1.104. The third interface (labeled "WN (PPP/SLIP) Interface") is the VPN tunnel; it has an IP address of 156.56.198.144 and only appears when you start the VPN software and log in to a VPN gateway. If you do a WhoIs on this IP address (see Chapter 5 for WhoIs), you will see that this IP address is owned by Indiana University. When I logged into my VPN software, it assigned this IP address to the tunnel so that all IP packets that leave my computer over this tunnel will appear to be from a computer on a subnet on the Indiana University campus that is connected to the VPN gateway. Your computer will have different interfaces and IP addresses because your network is different than mine, but the interfaces should be similar.

5. Start by capturing packets on your regular Ethernet interface. In my case, this is the second interface. Click on the Start button beside the Ethernet driver (which is 192.168.1.104 on my computer).

6. Go to your Web browser and use it to load a new Web page, which will cause some packets to move through your network.

7. A screen similar to that in Figure 9-15 will appear. After a few seconds, go back to Wireshark and click the Interface menu item and then click Stop.

8. The top window in Figure 9-15 shows the packets that are leaving the computer through the tunnel. Click on a packet to look at it. The middle window in this figure shows what's inside the packet. We see an Ethernet frame, an IP packet, a UDP datagram, and an Encapsulating Security Payload packet (which is the ESP packet). Notice that you cannot see anything inside the ESP packet because its contents are encrypted. All packets in this tunnel will *only* flow to and from my computer (192.168.1.104) and the VPN gateway (156.56.245.15).

9. Now we want to look at the packets that are sent by your computer *into* the VPN tunnel. No one else can see these packets. You can see them only because they are on your computer and you're looking at them as they move from your traditional network software to your VPN software.

10. Click on the Wireshark Capture menu item and click Interfaces.

11. Click on the Start button beside your VPN interface, which in my case in Figure 9-14 is the button in front of 156.56.198.144.

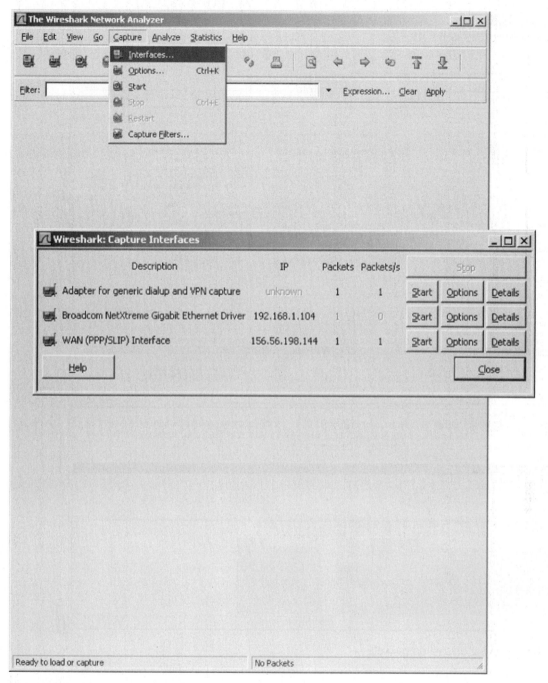

FIGURE 9-14 Starting Wireshark

12. Go to your Web browser and use it to load a new Web page, which will cause some packets to move through your network.

13. A screen similar to that in Figure 9-16 will appear. After a few seconds, go back to Wireshark and click the Interface menu item, and then click Stop.

14. The top window in Figure 9-16 shows the packets that are entering the VPN tunnel. Click on an HTTP packet to look at it (you may need to scroll to find one). The middle window in this figure shows what's inside the packet. We see an Ethernet frame, an IP packet, a TCP segment, and an HTTP request (for a page called/enterprise/on www.tatacommunications.com). We can see these because they have not yet entered the VPN software to be encrypted. These are the packets that would normally be sent over the Internet

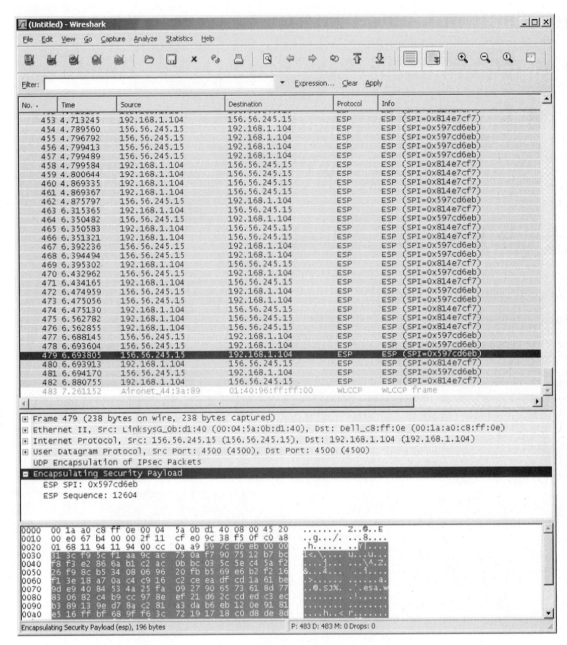

FIGURE 9-15 Viewing encrypted packets

if we have not started the VPN software. Like all normal Internet messages, they can be read by anyone with sniffer software such as Wireshark.

Deliverables

1. What layer-2, -3, and -4 protocols are used on your network to transmit an HTTP packet without a VPN?

2. What layer-2, -3, and -4 protocols are used on your network to transmit an HTTP packet when your VPN is active?

3. Look inside the VPN tunnel as was done in step 14. What layer-2, -3, and -4 protocols are used inside the encrypted packet?

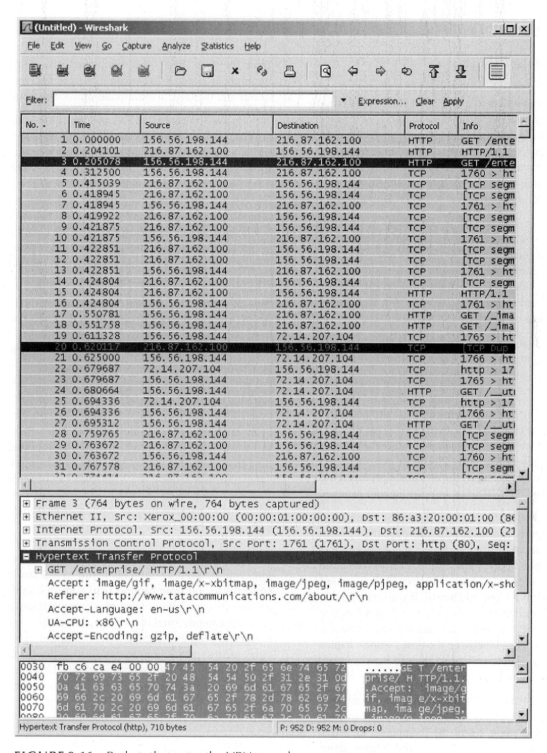

FIGURE 9-16 Packets that enter the VPN tunnel

HANDS-ON ACTIVITY 9C

Examining VPNs with Tracert

Tracert is a useful tool for seeing how VPNs affect routing. To do this lab, you'll have to have a VPN you can use. This will normally be available from your school.

Tracert is a simple command that comes preinstalled on all Windows and Mac computers. Tracert enables you to see the route that an IP packet takes as it moves over the Internet from one computer to another. Do this activity when you are not on campus.

1. Tracert is a command line command, so you first need to start the CMD window. Click Start, then Run, and then type CMD and press enter. This will open the command window, which is usually a small window with a black background. You can change the size and shape of this window, but it is not as flexible as a usual window.

2. We will first trace the route from your computers to two other computers without using the VPN. So make sure your VPN is *not* connected.

3. We'll start by tracing the route from your computer to a computer on the campus of the site you VPN into. In my case, I VPN into my university, which is Indiana University. I can choose to trace the route to any computer on campus. I'll choose our main Web server (www.iu.edu). At the command prompt, type tracert and the URL of a computer on your campus.

4. The top half of Figure 9-17 shows the route from my computer to www.iu.edu. There are 18 hops and it takes about 35 ms. The first hop does not report information because this feature is turned off in the router at my house for security reasons. You can see that my ISP is Comcast (hop 6). If you compare this to the tracert at the end of Chapter 5, you'll notice that my ISP changed (and thus the route into the Internet changed) between the time I wrote Chapter 5 and this chapter; Comcast bought Insight in my town of Bloomington, Indiana.

5. Now trace the route from your computer to another computer on the Internet. The bottom of Figure 9-17 shows the route from my computer to www.google.com. There are 17 hops, and it takes about 35 ms. You'll see that the routes to IU and Google are the same until step 6, and then they diverge.

6. Next we want to see what happens when you have a VPN connection. Start your VPN software and connect into the VPN gateway at your school.

7. Trace the route from your computer to the same computer as in step 3. At the command prompt, type tracert and the URL of a computer on your campus.

8. The top half of Figure 9-18 shows the route from my computer to www.iu.edu. There are two hops and it takes about 35 ms. The VPN is in operation and is transparent to my networking software, which thinks it is on the same subnet as the VPN gateway. Therefore, it thinks there is just one hop from my computer to the subnet's gateway, the VPN gateway. You'll see that the time is still about 35 ms, so the packet is still traveling the same 18 hops to get there; it's just that the tracert packet is encapsulated and doesn't see all the hops through the VPN tunnel.

9. Now do a tracert to the same computer as you did in step 5. The bottom of Figure 9-18 shows the route from my computer to www.google.com. There are nine hops and it takes about 43 ms. Of course, the first hop is really 17 hops and 35 ms; this is again hidden from view. As we explained in the text, when the VPN is connected, all packets go from your computer to the VPN gateway on your campus before being routed to the final destination. You can see from this figure that this adds additional hops and time to packets that are not going to your campus, compared to not using the VPN. You can also see that once the packets leave the VPN gateway, they are ordinary packets; they are no longer encrypted and protected from view.

The VPN provides security only to and from the VPN gateway on your campus, not beyond it. Therefore, you should use your VPN if you have security concerns to and from campus (e.g., someone sniffing your packets). But if most of your work is going to be off campus, then the VPN increases the time it takes to send and receive packets and only provides security protection over the last section from your computer to your school's campus. Using the VPN may not be worth the additional response time it imposes on you.

Deliverables

1. What are the routes from your computer to your campus Web server with and without the VPN?

2. What are the routes from your computer to www.google.com with and without the VPN?

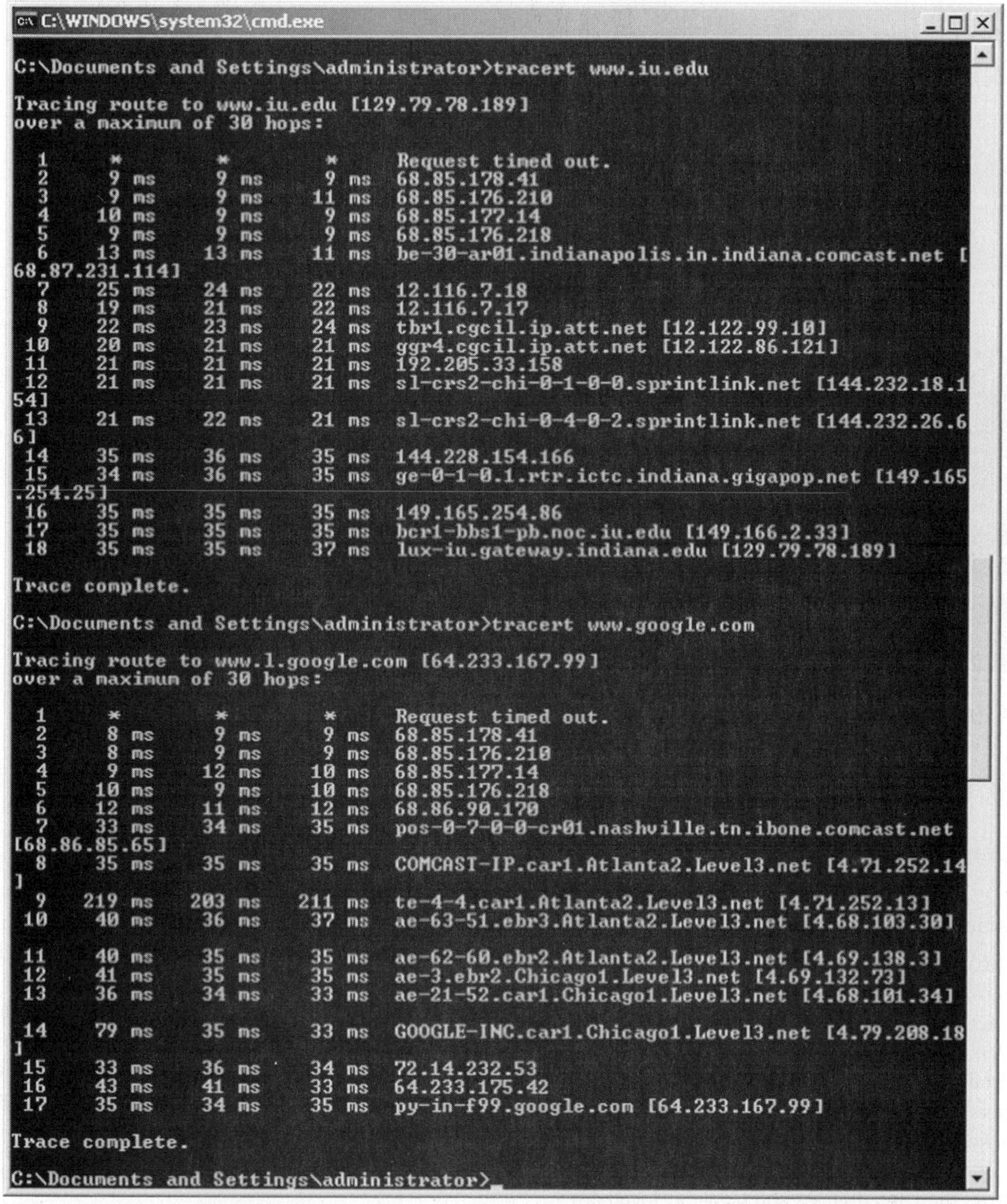

```
C:\WINDOWS\system32\cmd.exe                                              _ □ ×

C:\Documents and Settings\administrator>tracert www.iu.edu

Tracing route to www.iu.edu [129.79.78.189]
over a maximum of 30 hops:

  1     *          *          *        Request timed out.
  2     9 ms       9 ms       9 ms     68.85.178.41
  3     9 ms       9 ms      11 ms     68.85.176.210
  4    10 ms       9 ms       9 ms     68.85.177.14
  5     9 ms       9 ms       9 ms     68.85.176.218
  6    13 ms      13 ms      11 ms     be-30-ar01.indianapolis.in.indiana.comcast.net [
68.87.231.114]
  7    25 ms      24 ms      22 ms     12.116.7.18
  8    19 ms      21 ms      22 ms     12.116.7.17
  9    22 ms      23 ms      24 ms     tbr1.cgcil.ip.att.net [12.122.99.10]
 10    20 ms      21 ms      21 ms     ggr4.cgcil.ip.att.net [12.122.86.121]
 11    21 ms      21 ms      21 ms     192.205.33.158
 12    21 ms      21 ms      21 ms     sl-crs2-chi-0-1-0-0.sprintlink.net [144.232.18.1
54]
 13    21 ms      22 ms      21 ms     sl-crs2-chi-0-4-0-2.sprintlink.net [144.232.26.6
6]
 14    35 ms      36 ms      35 ms     144.228.154.166
 15    34 ms      36 ms      35 ms     ge-0-1-0.1.rtr.ictc.indiana.gigapop.net [149.165
.254.25]
 16    35 ms      35 ms      35 ms     149.165.254.86
 17    35 ms      35 ms      35 ms     bcr1-bbs1-pb.noc.iu.edu [149.166.2.33]
 18    35 ms      35 ms      37 ms     lux-iu.gateway.indiana.edu [129.79.78.189]

Trace complete.

C:\Documents and Settings\administrator>tracert www.google.com

Tracing route to www.l.google.com [64.233.167.99]
over a maximum of 30 hops:

  1     *          *          *        Request timed out.
  2     8 ms       9 ms       9 ms     68.85.178.41
  3     8 ms       9 ms       9 ms     68.85.176.210
  4     9 ms      12 ms      10 ms     68.85.177.14
  5    10 ms       9 ms      10 ms     68.85.176.218
  6    12 ms      11 ms      12 ms     68.86.90.170
  7    33 ms      34 ms      35 ms     pos-0-7-0-0-cr01.nashville.tn.ibone.comcast.net
[68.86.85.65]
  8    35 ms      35 ms      35 ms     COMCAST-IP.car1.Atlanta2.Level3.net [4.71.252.14
]
  9   219 ms     203 ms     211 ms     te-4-4.car1.Atlanta2.Level3.net [4.71.252.13]
 10    40 ms      36 ms      37 ms     ae-63-51.ebr3.Atlanta2.Level3.net [4.68.103.30]

 11    40 ms      35 ms      35 ms     ae-62-60.ebr2.Atlanta2.Level3.net [4.69.138.3]
 12    41 ms      35 ms      35 ms     ae-3.ebr2.Chicago1.Level3.net [4.69.132.73]
 13    36 ms      34 ms      33 ms     ae-21-52.car1.Chicago1.Level3.net [4.68.101.34]

 14    79 ms      35 ms      33 ms     GOOGLE-INC.car1.Chicago1.Level3.net [4.79.208.18
]
 15    33 ms      36 ms      34 ms     72.14.232.53
 16    43 ms      41 ms      33 ms     64.233.175.42
 17    35 ms      34 ms      35 ms     py-in-f99.google.com [64.233.167.99]

Trace complete.

C:\Documents and Settings\administrator>
```

FIGURE 9-17   Tracert without a VPN

FIGURE 9-18 Tracert with a VPN

HANDS-ON ACTIVITY 9D

Apollo Residence Network Design

Apollo is a luxury residence hall that will serve honor students at your university. We described the residence in Hands-On Activities at the end of Chapters 7 and 8.

The university has recognized that work is going virtual, with more and more organizations building virtual teams with members drawn from different parts of the organization who work together from different cities, instead of meeting face-to-face. It has joined together with five universities across the United States and Canada (located in Boston, Los Angeles, Atlanta, Dallas, and Toronto) to form a consortium of universities that will build virtual team experiences into their programs.

The universities have decided to start with their honors programs, and each has created a required course that involves its students working with students at the other universities to complete a major project. The students will use collaboration software such as email, chat, Google Docs, Skype, and WebEx to provide text, audio, and video communication. These tools can be used over the Internet, but to ensure that there are no technical problems, the universities have decided to build a separate private WAN that connects the six honors residences on each university campus (in the five cities listed, plus your university).

Deliverable

Your team was hired to design the WAN for this six-university residence network. Figure 9-19 provides a list of possible WAN services you can use. Specify what services you will use at each location and how the six locations will be connected. Provide the estimated monthly operating cost of the network.

WAN Service	Data Rate	Monthly Cost per Circuit
T1	1.5 Mbps	$500
T3	45 Mbps	$5000
SONET OC-1	52 Mbps	$5500
SONET OC-3	155 Mbps	$12,000
SONET OC-12	622 Mbps	$30,000
Frame Relay	1.5 Mbps	$250, plus $.01 per 10,000 packets and $10 per PVC routing table entry; MAR available at $50 per 1.5 Mbps
Frame Relay	45 Mbps	$3500, plus $.01 per 10,000 packets and $10 per PVC routing table entry; MAR available at $50 per 1.5 Mbps
Ethernet	1 Mbps	$1000, plus $.01 per 10,000 packets
Ethernet	5 Mbps	$1200, plus $.01 per 10,000 packets
Ethernet	10 Mbps	$1500, plus $.01 per 10,000 packets
Ethernet	20 Mbps	$2000, plus $.01 per 10,000 packets
Ethernet	50 Mbps	$2500, plus $.01 per 10,000 packets
Ethernet	100 Mbps	$3000, plus $.01 per 10,000 packets
Ethernet	200 Mbps	$3500, plus $.01 per 10,000 packets
Ethernet	500 Mbps	$4000, plus $.01 per 10,000 packets
Ethernet	1 Gbps	$5000, plus $.01 per 10,000 packets
MPLS	1.5 Mbps	$500, plus $.01 per 10,000 packets
MPLS	45 Mbps	$2500, plus $.01 per 10,000 packets
MPLS	52 Mbps	$3000, plus $.01 per 10,000 packets
MPLS	155 Mbps	$5000, plus $.01 per 10,000 packets
MPLS	622 Mbps	$10,000, plus $.01 per 10,000 packets
IP Services	1.5 Mbps	$500, plus $.01 per 10,000 packets
IP Services	45 Mbps	$2500, plus $.01 per 10,000 packets
IP Services	52 Mbps	$3000, plus $.01 per 10,000 packets
IP Services	155 Mbps	$5000, plus $.01 per 10,000 packets
IP Services	622 Mbps	$10,000, plus $.01 per 10,000 packets

FIGURE 9-19 Monthly costs for WAN services

CHAPTER 10

THE INTERNET

This chapter examines the Internet in more detail to explain how it works and why it is a network of networks. The chapter also examines Internet access technologies, such as DSL and cable modem, as well as the possible future of the Internet.

OBJECTIVES

- Understand the overall design of the Internet
- Be familiar with DSL, cable modem, fiber to the home, and WiMax
- Be familiar with possible future directions of the Internet

OUTLINE

10.1 INTRODUCTION

The Internet is the most used network in the world, but it is also one of the least understood. There is no one network that is *the* Internet. Instead, the Internet is a network of networks—a set of separate and distinct networks operated by various national and state government agencies, nonprofit organizations, and for-profit corporations. The Internet exists only to the extent that these thousands of separate networks agree to use Internet protocols and to exchange data packets among one another.

When you are on the Internet, your computer (iPad, smart phone, etc.) is connected to the network of an Internet Service Provider (ISP) that provides network services for you. Messages flow between your client device and the ISP's network. Suppose you request a Web page on CNN.com, a Web site that is outside of your ISP's network. Your HTTP request flows from your device through your ISP's network and through other networks that link your ISP's network to the network of the ISP that provides Internet services for CNN. Each of these networks is separate and charges its own customers for Internet access but permits traffic from other networks to flow through them. In many ways, the Internet is like the universe (see Figure 10-1). Each of us works in his or her own planet with its own rules (i.e., ISP) but each planet is interconnected with all the others.

The Internet is simultaneously a strict, rigidly controlled club in which deviance from the rules is not tolerated and a freewheeling, open marketplace of ideas. All networks that connect to the Internet must rigidly conform to an unyielding set of standards for the transport and network layers; without these standards, data communication would not be possible. At the same time, content and new application protocols are developed freely and without restriction, and quite literally anyone in the world is allowed to comment on proposed changes.

FIGURE 10-1

The Internet is a lot like
the universe—many
independent systems
linked together
Source: NASA

In this chapter, we first explain how the Internet really works and look inside the
Seattle Internet exchange point, at which more than 150 separate Internet networks meet
to exchange data. We then turn our attention to how you as an individual can access the
Internet and what the Internet may look like in the future.

10.2 HOW THE INTERNET WORKS

10.2.1 Basic Architecture

The Internet is hierarchical in structure. At the top are the very large national **Internet
Service Providers (ISPs)**, such as AT&T and Sprint, that are responsible for large Inter-
net networks. These **national ISPs**, called **tier 1 ISPs**, connect together and exchange data
at **Internet exchange points (IXPs)** (Figure 10-2). For example, AT&T, Sprint, Verizon,
Qwest, Level 3, and Global Crossing are all tier 1 ISPs that have a strong presence in North
America.

In the early 1990s, when the Internet was still primarily run by the U.S. National Science
Foundation (NSF), the NSF established four main IXPs in the United States to connect the
major tier 1 ISPs (the 1990s name for an IXP was network exchange point or NAP). When
the NSF stopped funding the Internet, the companies running these IXPs began charging the ISPs for connections, so today the IXPs in the United States are all not-for-profit
organizations or commercial enterprises run by various common carriers such as AT&T
and Sprint. As the Internet has grown, so too has the number of IXPs; today there are
several dozen IXPs in the United States with more than a hundred more spread around
the world.

IXPs were originally designed to connect only large tier 1 ISPs. These ISPs in turn
provide services for their customers and also to **regional ISPs** (sometimes called **tier 2
ISPs**) such as Comcast or BellSouth. These tier 2 ISPs rely on the tier 1 ISPs to transmit their
messages to ISPs in other countries. Tier 2 ISPs, in turn, provide services to their customers
and to local ISPs (sometimes called **tier 3 ISPs**) who sell Internet access to individuals. As

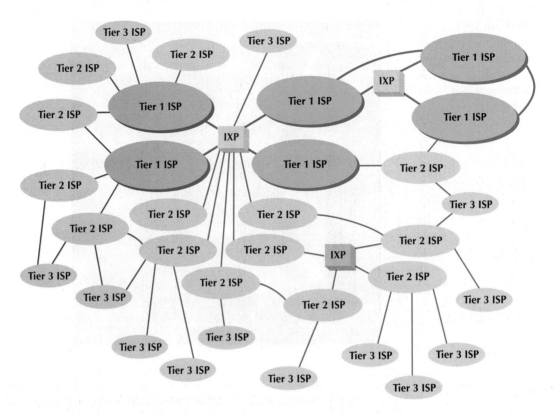

FIGURE 10-2   Basic Internet architecture.
ISP = Internet service provider and IXP = Internet exchange point

the number of ISPs grew, smaller IXPs emerged in most major cities to link the networks of these regional ISPs.

Because most IXPs and ISPs now are run by commercial firms, many of the early restrictions on who could connect to whom have been lifted. Most now openly solicit business from all tiers of ISPs and even large organizations. Regional and local ISPs often will have several connections into other ISPs to provide backup connections in case one Internet connection fails. In this way, they are not dependent on just one higher-level ISP.

In general, ISPs at the same level do not charge one another for transferring messages they exchange. That is, a national tier 1 ISP does not charge another national tier 1 ISP to transmit its messages. This is called **peering**. Figure 10-2 shows several examples of peering. It is peering that makes the Internet work and that has led to the belief that the Internet is free. This is true to some extent, but higher-level ISPs normally charge lower-level ISPs to transmit their data (e.g., a tier 1 will charge a tier 2 and a tier 2 will charge a tier 3). And of course, any ISP will charge individuals like us for access!

In October 2005, an argument between two national ISPs shut down 45 million Web sites for a week. The two ISPs had a peering agreement, but one complained that the other was sending it more traffic than it should, so it demanded payment and stopped accepting traffic, leaving large portions of the network isolated from the rest of the Internet. The dispute was resolved, and they began accepting traffic from each other and the rest of the Internet again.

In Figure 10-2, each of the ISPs is an **autonomous system**, as defined in Chapter 5. Each ISP is responsible for running its own interior routing protocols and for exchanging routing information via the Border Gateway Protocol (BGP) exterior routing protocol (see Chapter 5) at IXPs and at any other connection points between individual ISPs.

10.2.2 Connecting to an ISP

Each of the ISPs is responsible for running its own network that forms part of the Internet. ISPs make money by charging customers to connect to their part of the Internet. Local ISPs charge individuals for access, whereas national and regional ISPs (and sometimes local ISPs) charge larger organizations for access.

Each ISP has one or more **points of presence (POP)**. A POP is simply the place at which the ISP provides services to its customers. To connect into the Internet, a customer must establish a circuit from his or her location into the ISP POP. For individuals, this is often done using a DSL modem or cable modem, as we discuss in the next section. Companies can use these same technologies, or they can use the WAN technologies we discussed in the previous chapter. Once connected, the user can begin sending TCP/IP packets from his or her computer to the POP.

MANAGEMENT

FOCUS

10-1 Inside the Seattle Internet Exchange Point

The Seattle Internet Exchange (SIX) was established as a nonprofit organization in April 1997 by two small ISPs with offices in Seattle's Westin Building. The ISPs had discovered that to send data to each other's network in the same building, their data traveled to Texas and back. They decided to peer and installed a 10Base-T Ethernet hub connecting their two networks so that traffic flowed between them much more quickly.

In June 1997, a third small ISP joined and connected its network into the hub. Gradually word spread and other small ISPs began to connect. In May 1998, the first tier 1 ISP connected its network, and traffic grew enough so that the old 10 Mbps hub was replaced by a 10/100 Ethernet switch. As an aside, we'll note that the switch you have in your house or apartment today probably has more capacity than this switch. In February 1999, Microsoft connected its network, and traffic took off again. In September 2001, the 10/100 Ethernet switch was replaced by a 10/100/1000 Ethernet switch.

The current configuration is a set of 3 large GbE switches connected together with 80 Gbps Ethernet circuits. There are an additional 4 GbE switches located in the Westin Building connected to these three core switches with 1 Gbps Ethernet. SIX also has additional facilities located around the Seattle area that connect to the three core switches via 10–40 Gbps Ethernet, depending on location.

Today, SIX offers several types of Ethernet connections to its clients. The first 1 Gbps connection is free; all subsequent 1 Gbps connections cost a one-time fee of $1,000, whereas 10 Gbps connections cost a one-time fee of $5,000. Of course, you have to pay a common carrier to provide a network circuit into the Westin Building and then pay the Westin Building a small fee to run a fiber cable from the building's MDF to the SIX network facility. Traffic averages between 100 and 250 Gbps across the SIX network.

More than 150 ISPs (e.g., AT&T, World Communications, Bell Canada, and Saskatchewan Telecommunications) and corporations (e.g., Google, Facebook, and Yahoo) are members of SIX. About half of the members are open to peering with anyone who joins SIX. The rest, mostly tier 1 ISPs and well-known corporations, are selective or restrictive in their peering agreements, which means that they are already well-connected into the Internet and want to ensure that any new peering agreements make business sense.

Adapted from: www.seattleix.net

It is important to note that the customer must pay for both Internet access (paid to the ISP) and for the circuit connecting from the customer's location to the POP (usually paid to the local exchange carrier [e.g., BellSouth and AT&T], but sometimes the ISP also can provide circuits). For a T1 connection, for example, a company might pay the local exchange carrier $250 per month to provide the T1 circuit from its offices to the ISP POP and *also* pay the ISP $250 per month to provide the Internet access.

An ISP POP is connected to the other POPs in the ISP's network. Any messages destined for other customers of the same ISP would flow within the ISP's own network. In most cases, the majority of messages entering the POP are sent outside of the ISP's network and thus must flow through the ISP's network to the nearest IXP and, from there, into some other ISP's network.

This can be less efficient than one might expect. For example, suppose you are connected to the Internet via a local tier 3 ISP in Minneapolis and request a Web page from another organization in Minneapolis. A short distance, right? Maybe not. If the other organization uses a different local tier 3 ISP, which in turn uses a different regional tier 2 ISP for its connection into the Internet, the message may have to travel all the way to the nearest IXP, which could be in Chicago, Dallas, or New York, before it can move between the two separate parts of the Internet.

10.2.3 The Internet Today

Figure 10-3 shows the North American backbone of a major ISP as it existed while we were writing this book; it will have changed by the time you read this. As you can see, it has many Internet circuits across the United States and Canada. Many interconnect in Chicago, where many ISPs connect into the Chicago IXP. It also connects into major IXPs in Reston, Virginia; Miami; Los Angeles; San Jose; Palo Alto; Vancouver; Calgary; Toronto; and Montreal.

Today, the backbone circuits of the major U.S. national ISPs operate at SONET OC-192 (10 Gbps). A few are now experimenting with OC-768 (80 Gbps), and several are in the planning stages with OC-3072 (160 Gbps). This is good because the amount of Internet traffic has been growing rapidly.

As traffic increases, ISPs can add more and faster circuits relatively easily, but where these circuits come together at IXPs, bottlenecks are becoming more common. Network vendors such as Cisco and Juniper are making larger and larger switches capable of handling these high-capacity circuits, but it is a daunting task. When circuit capacities increase by

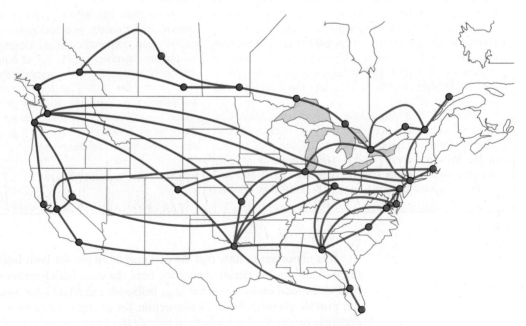

FIGURE 10-3 A typical Internet backbone of a major ISP

100%, switch manufacturers also must increase their capacities by 100%. It is simpler to go from a 622 Mbps circuit to a 10 Gbps circuit than to go from a 20 Gbps switch to a 200 Gbps switch.

10.3 INTERNET ACCESS TECHNOLOGIES

There are many ways in which individuals and organizations can connect to an ISP. Most individuals use DSL or cable modem. As we discussed in the preceding section, many organizations lease T1, T3, or Ethernet circuits into their ISPs. DSL and cable modem technologies are commonly called **broadband technologies** because they provide high-speed communications.[1]

It is important to understand that Internet access technologies are used only to connect from one location to an ISP. Unlike the WAN technologies in the previous chapter, Internet access technologies cannot be used for general-purpose networking from any point to any point. In this section, we discuss four principal Internet access technologies (DSL, cable modem, fiber to the home, and WiMax). Of course, many users connect to the Internet using Wi-Fi on their laptops from public access points in coffee shops, hotels, and airports. Since we discussed Wi-Fi in Chapter 7, we won't discuss it here.

10.3.1 Digital Subscriber Line (DSL)

Digital subscriber line (DSL) is a family of point-to-point technologies designed to provide high-speed data transmission over traditional telephone lines.[2] The reason for the limited capacity on traditional telephone circuits lies with the telephone and the switching equipment at the end offices. The actual cable in the **local loop** from a home or office to the telephone company end office is capable of providing much higher data transmission rates. So DSL usually requires just changing the telephone equipment, not rewiring the local loop, which is what has made it so attractive.

Architecture DSL uses the existing local loop cable but places different equipment on the customer premises (i.e., the home or office) and in the telephone company end office. The equipment that is installed at the customer location is called the **customer premises equipment (CPE)**. Figure 10-4 shows one common type of DSL installation. (There are other forms.) The CPE in this case includes a **line splitter** that is used to separate the traditional voice telephone transmission from the data transmissions. The line splitter directs the telephone signals into the normal telephone system so that if the DSL equipment fails, voice communications are unaffected.

The line splitter also directs the data transmissions into a **DSL modem**, which is sometimes called a *DSL router*. This is both a modem and an FDM multiplexer (see Chapter 3). The DSL modem produces Ethernet packets so it can be connected directly into a computer or to a router and can serve the needs of a small network. Most DSL companies targeting home users combine all of these devices (and a wireless access point) into one device so that consumers just have to install one box, rather than separate line splitters, modems, routers, switches, and access points.

Figure 10-4 also shows the architecture within the local carrier's end office (i.e., the telephone company office closest to the customer premises). The local loops from many customers enter and are connected to the **main distribution facility (MDF)**. The MDF

---

[1] *Broadband* is a technical term that means "analog transmission" (see Chapter 3). The new broadband technologies often use analog transmission, so they were called broadband. However, the term *broadband* has been corrupted in common usage so that to most people it usually means "high-speed."

[2] More information can be found from the DSL forum (www.adsl.com) and the ITU-T under standard G.992.

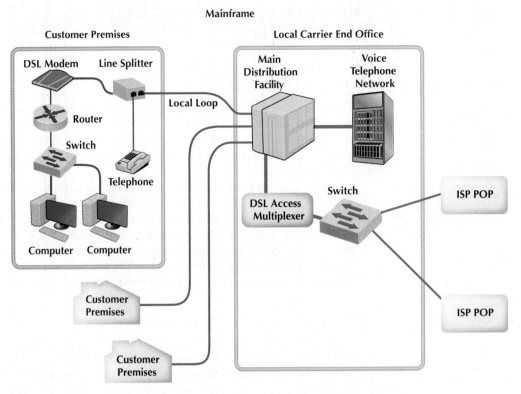

FIGURE 10-4   Digital subscriber line (DSL) architecture.
ISP = Internet service provider and POP = point of presence

works like the CPE line splitter; it splits the voice traffic from the data traffic and directs the voice traffic to the voice telephone network and the data traffic to the **DSL access multiplexer (DSLAM)**. The DSLAM demultiplexes the data streams and converts them into digital data, which are then distributed to the ISPs. Some ISPs are collocated, in that they have their POPs physically in the telephone company end offices. Other ISPs have their POPs located elsewhere.

Types of DSL   There are many different types of DSL. The most common type today is **asymmetric DSL (ADSL)**. ADSL uses frequency division multiplexing (see Chapter 3) to create three separate channels over the one local loop circuit. One channel is the traditional voice telephone circuit. A second channel is a relatively high-speed data channel downstream from the carrier's end office to the customer. The third channel is a slightly slower data channel upstream from the customer to the carrier's end office.[3] ADSL is called asymmetric because its two data channels have different speeds. Each of the two data channels is further multiplexed using time division multiplexing so they can be subdivided.

The size of the two digital channels depends on the distance from the CPE to the end office. The shorter the distance, the higher the speed, because with a shorter distance, the circuit suffers less attenuation and higher-frequency signals can be used, providing a greater bandwidth for modulation. Figure 10-5 lists the common types of DSL.

---

[3]Because the second data channel is intended primarily for upstream data communication, many authors imply that this is a simplex channel, but it is actually a set of half-duplex channels.

FIGURE 10-5

Some typical digital subscriber line data rates

Maximum Downstream Rate	Maximum Upstream Rate
3 Mbps	512 Kbps
6 Mbps	640 Kbps
12 Mbps	1.5 Mbps
18 Mbps	1.5 Mbps
24 Mbps	3 Mbps

10.3.2 Cable Modem

One alternative to DSL is the **cable modem**, a digital service offered by cable television companies. The **Data over Cable Service Interface Specification (DOCSIS)** standard is the dominant one. DOCSIS is not a formal standard but is the one used by most vendors of **hybrid fiber coax (HFC)** networks (i.e., cable networks that use both fiber-optic and coaxial cable). As with DSL, these technologies are changing rapidly.[4]

Architecture Cable modem architecture is very similar to DSL—with one very important difference. DSL is a point-to-point technology, whereas cable modems use *shared* multipoint circuits. With cable modems, each user must compete with other users for the available capacity. Furthermore, because the cable circuit is a multipoint circuit, all messages on the circuit go to all computers on the circuit. If your neighbors were hackers, they could use pocket sniffers such as Wireshark (see Chapter 4) to read all messages that travel over the cable, including yours.

Figure 10-6 shows the most common architecture for cable modems. The cable TV circuit enters the customer premises through a cable splitter that separates the data transmissions from the TV transmissions and sends the TV signals to the TV network and the data signals to the cable modem. The cable modem (both a modem and frequency division multiplexer) translates from the cable data into Ethernet packets, which then are directed into a computer to a router for distribution in a small network. As with DSL, cable modem companies usually combine all of these separate devices into one or two devices to make it easier for the home consumer to install.

The cable TV cable entering the customer premises is a standard coaxial cable. A typical segment of cable is shared by anywhere from 300 to 1,000 customers, depending on the cable company that installed the cable. These 300–1,000 customers share the available data capacity, but of course, not all customers who have cable TV will choose to install cable modems. This coax cable runs to a *fiber node*, which has an **optical-electrical (OE) converter** to convert between the coaxial cable on the customer side and fiber-optic cable on the cable TV company side. Each fiber node serves as many as half a dozen separate coaxial cable runs.

The fiber nodes are in turn connected to the cable company **distribution hub** (sometimes called a *headend*) through two separate circuits: an upstream circuit and a downstream circuit. The upstream circuit, containing data traffic from the customer, is connected into a **cable modem termination system (CMTS)**. The CMTS contains a series of cable modems/multiplexers and converts the data from cable modem protocols into protocols needed for Internet traffic, before passing them to a router connected to an ISP POP. Often, the cable company is a regional ISP, but sometimes it just provides Internet access to a third-party ISP.

---

[4]More information can be found at www.cablemodem.com.

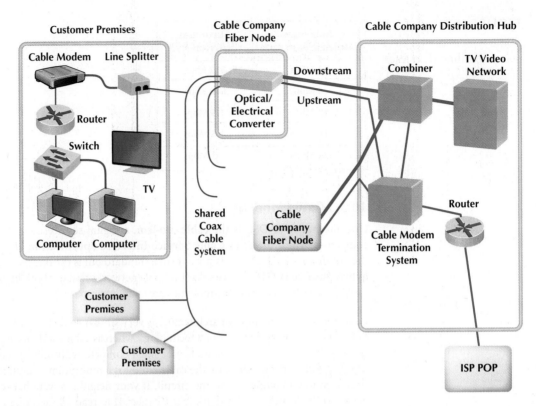

FIGURE 10-6 Cable modem architecture.
ISP = Internet service provider and POP = point of presence

The downstream circuit to the customer contains both ordinary video transmissions from the cable TV video network and data transmissions from the Internet. Downstream data traffic enters the distribution hub from the ISP POP and is routed through the CMTS, which produces the cable modem signals. This traffic is then sent to a *combiner*, which combines the Internet data traffic with the ordinary TV video traffic and sends it back to the fiber node for distribution.

Types of Cable Modems The DOCSIS standard provides many types of cable modems. The maximum speed is about 150 Mbps downstream and about 100 Mbps upstream, although most cable TV companies provide at most 50 Mbps downstream and 10 Mbps upstream. Cable modems can be configured to limit capacity, so the most common speeds offered by most cable providers range from 1 to 20 Mbps downstream and from 1 to 5 Mbps upstream. Of course, this capacity is shared, so an individual user will only see this when no other computers on his or her segment are active.

MANAGEMENT
FOCUS

10-2 Internet Speed Test

*T*he speed of your Internet connection depends on many things, such as your computer's settings, the connection from your computer to your ISP, and the connections your ISP has into the Internet. Many Internet sites enable you to test how fast your Internet connection actually is. Our favorite is speedtest.net

10.3.3 Fiber to the Home

Fiber to the home (FTTH) is exactly what it sounds like: running fiber-optic cable into the home. The traditional set of hundreds of copper telephone lines that run from the telephone company switch office is replaced by one fiber-optic cable that is run past each house or office in the neighborhood. Data are transmitted down the signal fiber cable using wavelength division multiplexing (WDM), providing hundreds or thousands of separate channels. As of 2014, FTTH was installed in about 10 million homes in the United States. The largest implementations were in test market cities in North Dakota, Virginia, and Pennsylvania.

Architecture FTTH architecture is very similar to DSL and cable modem. At each subscriber location, an **optical network unit (ONU)** (also called an *optical network terminal* [*ONT*]) acts like a DSL modem or cable modem and converts the signals in the optical network into an Ethernet format. The ONU acts as an Ethernet switch and can also include a router. FTTH is a dedicated point-to-point service like DSL, not a shared multipoint service like cable modem.

Providers of fiber to the home can use either active optical networking or passive optical networking to connect the ONU in the customer's home. Active networking means that the optical devices require electrical power and works in much the same way as traditional electronic switches and routers. Passive optical networking devices require no electrical current and thus are quicker and easier to install and maintain than traditional electrical-based devices, but because they are passive, the optical signal fades quickly, giving a maximum range of about 10 miles.

Types of FTTH There are many types of FTTH, and because FTTH is a new technology, these types are likely to evolve as FTTH enters the market and becomes more widely adopted. Common types provide 10–100 Mbps downstream and 1–10 Mbps upstream. The most commonly used type provides 15 Mbps downstream and 4 Mbps upstream. Newer versions have been announced targeted at business users that provide 1 Gbps down and 100 Mbps up.

10.3.4 WiMax

WiMax (short for Worldwide Interoperability for Microwave Access) is the commercial name for a set of standards developed by the IEEE 802.16 standards group. WiMax is a family of technologies that is much like the 802.11 Wi-Fi family. It reuses many of the Wi-Fi components and was designed to connect easily into Ethernet LANs. WiMax can be used as a fixed wireless technology to connect a house or an office into the Internet, but its future lies in its ability to connect mobile laptops and smart phones into the Internet.

WiMax is a relatively old technology. The problem is that computer manufacturers have been waiting for ISPs to build WiMax networks before they build WiMax into their computers. Meanwhile, ISPs have been waiting for computer manufacturers to provide WiMax-capable computers before they build WiMax networks. And so we have a catch-22.

This changed in 2011 when Intel developed a cheap WiMax chip set. Many computer manufacturers are including WiMax on their laptops, so ISPs have started building WiMax networks. Many large cities now have WiMax networks, and this will gradually spread to other parts of the country.

Most experts envision a future where both Wi-Fi and WiMax coexist. Laptops and smart phones will connect to Wi-Fi networks in home and office locations where Wi-Fi is available. If Wi-Fi is not available and the user has subscribed to WiMax services, then the laptop or smart phone will connect to the WiMax network.

Architecture Although WiMax can be used in fixed locations to provide Internet access to homes and offices, we will focus on mobile use as this is likely to be the most common use. Mobile WiMax works in much the same way as Wi-Fi. The laptop or smart phone has a WiMax network interface card (NIC) and uses it to establish a connection to a WiMax access point (AP). Many devices use the same AP, so WiMax is a shared multipoint service in which all computers must take turns transmitting. Media access control is controlled access, using a version of the 802.11 point coordination function (PCF).

WiMax uses the 2.3, 2.5, and 3.5 GHz frequency ranges in North America, although additional frequency ranges may be added. The maximum range is from 3 to 10 miles, depending on interference and obstacles between the device and the AP. Most WiMax providers in the United States are using effective ranges of 0.5–1.5 miles when they install WiMax APs.

Types of WiMax There are several types of WiMax available, with new versions under development. The most common type of **mobile wireless** provides speeds of 40 Mbps, shared among all users of the same AP. Some providers have versions that run at 70 Mbps. New versions under development promise speeds of 300 Mbps.

10.4 THE FUTURE OF THE INTERNET

10.4.1 Internet Governance

Because the Internet is a network of networks, no one organization operates the Internet. The closest thing the Internet has to an owner is the **Internet Society** (internetsociety.org). The Internet Society is an open-membership professional society with about 150 organizational members and 65,000 individual members in more than 100 countries, including corporations, government agencies, and foundations that have created the Internet and its technologies. Because membership is open, anyone, including students, is welcome to join and vote on key issues facing the Internet.

Its mission is to ensure "the open development, evolution and use of the Internet for the benefit of all people throughout the world." It works in three general areas: public policy, education, and standards. In terms of public policy, the Internet Society participates in the national and international debates on important issues such as censorship, copyright, privacy, and universal access. It delivers training and education programs targeted at improving the Internet infrastructure in developing nations. Its most important activity lies in the development and maintenance of Internet standards. It works through four interrelated standards bodies: the Internet Engineering Task Force, Internet Engineering Steering Group, Internet Architecture Board, and Internet Research Task Force.

The **Internet Engineering Task Force (IETF)** (www.ietf.org) is a large, open international community of network designers, operators, vendors, and researchers concerned with the evolution of the Internet architecture and the smooth operation of the Internet. The IETF works through a series of working groups, which are organized by topic (e.g., routing, transport, and security). The **request for comments (RFCs)** that form the basis for Internet standards are developed by the IETF and its working groups.

Closely related to the IETF is the **Internet Engineering Steering Group (IESG)**. The IESG is responsible for technical management of IETF activities and the Internet standards process. It administers the process according to the rules and procedures that have been ratified by the Internet Society trustees. The IESG is directly responsible for the actions associated with entry into and movement along the Internet "standards track," including final approval of specifications as Internet standards. Each IETF working group is chaired by a member of the IESG.

| TECHNICAL | 10-1 Registering an Internet Domain Name |
| FOCUS | |

Until the 1990s, there was only a moderate number of computers on the Internet. One organization was responsible for registering domain names (sets of application layer addresses) and assigning IP addresses for each top-level domain (e.g., .COM). Network Solutions, for example, was the sole organization responsible for domain name registrations for the .COM, .NET, and .ORG domains. In October 1998, the **Internet Corporation for Assigned Names and Numbers (ICANN)** was formed to assume responsibility for the IP address space and domain name system management.

In spring 1999, ICANN established the Shared Registration System (SRS) that enabled many organizations to perform domain name registration and address assignment using a shared database. More than 1,000 organizations are now accredited by ICANN as registrars and are permitted to use the SRS. Each registrar has the right to assign names and addresses in one or more top-level domains. For a list of registrars and the domains they serve, see www.internic.com

If you want to register a new domain name and obtain an IP address, you can contact any accredited registrar for that top-level domain. One of the oldest privately operated registrars is register.com. Each registrar follows the same basic process for registering a name and assigning an address, but each may charge a different amount for its services. To register a name, you must first check to see if it is available (i.e., that no one else has registered it). If the name has already been registered, you can find out who owns it and perhaps attempt to buy it from the owner.

If the domain name is available, you will need to provide the IP address of the DNS server that will be used to store all IP addresses in the domain. Most large organizations have their own DNS servers, but small companies and individuals often use the DNS of their ISP.

Whereas the IETF develops standards and the IESG provides the operational leadership for the IETF working groups, the **Internet Architecture Board (IAB)** provides strategic architectural oversight. The IAB attempts to develop conclusions on strategic issues (e.g., top-level domain names, use of international character sets) that can be passed on as guidance to the IESG or turned into published statements or simply passed directly to the relevant IETF working group. In general, the IAB does not produce polished technical proposals but rather tries to stimulate action by the IESG or the IETF that will lead to proposals that meet general consensus. The IAB appoints the IETF chairperson and all IESG members, from a list provided by the IETF nominating committee. The IAB also adjudicates appeals when someone complains that the IESG has failed.

The **Internet Research Task Force (IRTF)** operates much like the IETF: through small research groups focused on specific issues. Whereas IETF working groups focus on current issues, IRTF research groups work on long-term issues related to Internet protocols, applications, architecture, and technology. The IRTF chairperson is appointed by the IAB.

10.4.2 Building the Future

The Internet is changing. New applications and access technologies are being developed at lightning pace. But these innovations do not change the fundamental structure of the Internet. It has evolved more slowly because the core technologies (TCP/IP) are harder to change gradually; it is difficult to change one part of the Internet without changing the attached parts.

Many organizations in many different countries are working on dozens of different projects in an attempt to design new technologies for the next version of the Internet. The two primary American projects working on the future Internet got started at about the same

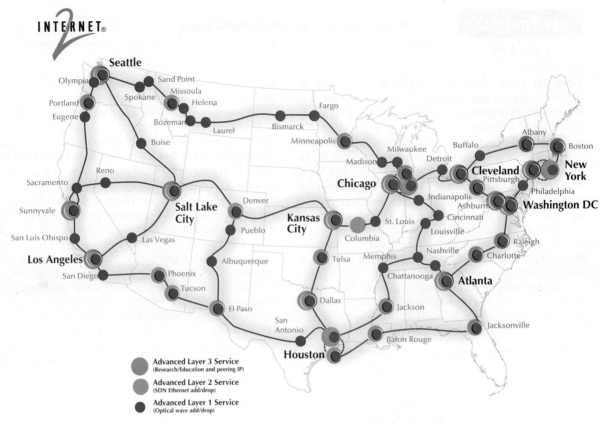

FIGURE 10-7 Internet2 network map. Reproduced by permission of Internet2®

time in 1996. The U.S. National Science Foundation provided $100 million to start the **Next Generation Internet (NGI)** program, and 34 universities got together to start what turned into **Internet2®**. Internet2® comprises about 400 universities, corporations, government agencies, and organizations from more than 100 countries with a primary focus to develop advanced networking as well as other innovative technologies for research and education.

Figure 10-7 shows the major high-speed circuits in the Internet2® network. All the circuits in Internet2® are at least OC-192 (10 Gbps). Many circuits are 100 Gbps, with 1 Tbps circuits being tested.

The access points are called **gigapops**, so named because they provide a point of presence at gigabit speeds. Gigapops also usually provide a wider range of services than traditional IXPs, which are primarily just data exchange points. All of the gigapops provide connections at layer 1, the physical layer. Many of the gigapops also provide layer 2 connections (usually Ethernet) and layer 3 connections (usually IPv6). Typical connection fees range from $6,000 per year for 1 Gbps to $165,000 per year for 100 Gbps.

Besides providing very high-speed Internet connections, these networks are intended to experiment with new protocols that 1 day may end up on the future Internet. For example, most circuits run IPv6 as the primary network layer protocol rather than IPv4. Most are also working on new ways to provide quality of service (QoS) and multicasting. Internet2® is also developing new applications for a high-speed Internet, such as tele-immersion and videoconferencing.

10.5 IMPLICATIONS FOR MANAGEMENT

Several years ago, there was great concern that the traffic on the Internet would exceed its capacity. The growth of traffic on the Internet was increasing significantly faster than the construction of new Internet circuits; several experts predicted the collapse of the Internet. It did not happen for the simple reason that companies could make money by building new circuits and charging for their use. Today, there are a large number of fiber-optic circuits that have been built but not yet turned on. Wavelength division multiplexing technologies mean that 10–20 times more data can now be transmitted through the same fiber-optic cable (see Chapter 3). Many countries, companies, and universities are now building the Next Generation Internet using even newer, experimental, very high-speed technologies. The Internet will not soon run out of capacity.

In recent years, there has been a blossoming of new "broadband" technologies for higher speed Internet access. Individuals and organizations can now access the Internet at relatively high speeds—much higher speeds than we would have even considered reasonable 5–10 years ago. This means that it is now simple to move large amounts of data into most homes and businesses in North America. As a result, software applications that use the Internet can provide a much richer multimedia experience than ever before.

In previous chapters, we described how there has been a significant reduction in a number of different technologies in use in LANs, backbones, and WANs over the past few years. We have entered that stage with regard to Internet access technologies. Today there are many choices, but over the next 2 years a few dominant standards will emerge, and the market will solidify around those standards. Organizations that invest in the technologies that ultimately become less popular will need to invest significant funds to replace those technologies with the dominant standards. The challenge, of course, is to figure out which technology standards will become dominant. Will it be cable modem and DSL or fiber to the home? Only time will tell.

SUMMARY

How the Internet Works The Internet is a set of separate networks, ranging from large national ISPs to midsize regional ISPs to small local ISPs, that connect with one another at IXPs. IXPs charge the ISPs to connect, but similar-sized ISPs usually do not charge each other to exchange data. Each ISP has a set of points of presence through which it charges its users (individuals, businesses, and smaller ISPs) to connect to the Internet. Users connect to a POP to get access to the Internet. This connection may be via DSL, cable modem, or a WAN circuit such as T1 or Ethernet.

DSL DSL enables users to connect to an ISP POP over a standard point-to-point telephone line. The customer installs a DSL modem that connects via Ethernet to his or her computer system. The modem communicates with a DSLAM at the telephone company office, which sends the data to the ISP POP. ADSL is the most common type of DSL and often provides 24 Mbps downstream and 3 Mbps upstream.

Cable Modem Cable modems use a shared multipoint circuit that runs through the cable TV cable. They also provide the customer with a modem that connects via Ethernet to his or her computer system. The modem communicates with a CMTS at the cable company office, which sends the data to the ISP POP. The DOCSIS standard is the dominant standard, but there are no standard data rates today. Typical downstream speeds range between 10 and 20 Mbps, and typical upstream speeds range between 1 and 5 Mbps.

Fiber to the Home FTTH is a new technology that is not widely implemented. It uses fiber-optic cables to provide high-speed data services (e.g., 100 Mbps) to homes and offices.

WiMax WiMax works similarly to Wi-Fi in that it enables mobile users to connect into the Internet at speeds of 40–70 Mbps.

The Future of the Internet The closest the Internet has to an owner is the Internet Society, which works on public policy, education, and Internet standards. Standards are developed through four related organizations governed by the Internet Society. The IETF develops the actual standards through a series of working groups. The IESG manages IETF activities. The IAB sets long-term strategic directions, and the IRTF works on future issues through working groups in much the same way as the IETF. Many different organizations are currently working on the next generation of the Internet, including Internet2.

KEY TERMS

asymmetric DSL (ADSL), 282
autonomous systems, 278
broadband technologies, 281
cable modem, 283
cable modem termination system (CMTS), 283
customer premises equipment (CPE), 281
Data over Cable Service Interface Specification (DOCSIS), 283
digital subscriber line (DSL), 281

distribution hub, 283
DSL access multiplexer (DSLAM), 282
DSL modem, 281
fiber to the home (FTTH), 285
gigapop, 288
Internet Architecture Board (IAB), 287
Internet Corporation for Assigned Names and Numbers (ICANN), 287
Internet Engineering Steering Group (IESG), 286

Internet Engineering Task Force (IETF), 286
Internet exchange point (IXP), 277
Internet Research Task Force (IRTF), 287
Internet Service Provider (ISP), 277
Internet Society, 286
Internet2®, 288
line splitter, 281
local loop, 281
main distribution facility (MDF), 281
mobile wireless, 286

national ISP, 277
optical-electrical (OE) converter, 283
optical network unit (ONU), 285
peering, 278
point of presence (POP), 279
regional ISP, 277
request for comment (RFC), 286
tier 1 ISP, 277
tier 2 ISP, 277
tier 3 ISP, 277
WiMax, 285

QUESTIONS

1. What is the basic structure of the Internet?
2. Explain how the Internet is a network of networks.
3. What is an IXP?
4. What is a POP?
5. Explain one reason why you might experience long response times in getting a Web page from a server in your own city.
6. What type of circuits are commonly used to build the Internet today? What type of circuits are commonly used to build Internet2®?
7. Compare and contrast cable modem and DSL.
8. Explain how DSL works.
9. How does a DSL modem differ from a DSLAM?
10. Explain how ADSL works.
11. Explain how a cable modem works.
12. What is an OE converter? A CMTS?

13. Which is better, cable modem or DSL? Explain.
14. Explain how FTTH works.
15. What are some future technologies that might change how we access the Internet?
16. Explain how WiMax works.
17. What are the principal organizations responsible for Internet governance, and what do they do?
18. How is the IETF related to the IRTF?
19. What is the principal American organization working on the future of the Internet?
20. What is Internet2®?
21. What is a gigapop?
22. Today, there is no clear winner in the competition for broadband Internet access. What technology or technologies do you think will dominate in 2 years' time? Why?

23. Would you be interested in subscribing to 100 Mbps FTTH for a monthly price of $100? Why or why not?

24. Many experts predicted that small, local ISPs would disappear as regional and national ISPs began offering local access. This hasn't happened. Why?

EXERCISES

A. Describe the current network structure of Internet2®.

B. Provide the service details (e.g., pricing and data rates) for at least one high-speed Internet access service provider in your area.

C. Some people are wiring their homes for 100Base-T. Suppose a friend who is building a house asks you what—if any—network to put inside the house and what Internet access technology to use. What would you recommend?

D. Provide service details (e.g., pricing and data rates) for WiMax in your area or a large city such as New York or Los Angeles.

E. Report the prices and available connections for one IXP, such as the Seattle IXP.

MINICASES

I. Cathy's Collectibles Your cousin Cathy runs a part-time business out of her apartment. She buys and sells collectibles such as antique prints, baseball cards, and cartoon cells and has recently discovered the Web with its many auction sites. She has begun buying and selling on the Web by bidding on collectibles at lesser-known sites and selling them at a profit at more well-known sites. She downloads and uploads lots of graphics (pictures of the items she's buying and selling). She asks you for advice. Figure 10-8 shows some of the available Internet services and their prices. Explain the differences in these services and make a recommendation.

II. Surfing Sam Sam likes to surf the Web for fun, to buy things, and to research for his classes. Figure 10-8 shows some of the available Internet services and their prices. Explain the differences in these services and make a recommendation.

III. Cookies Are Us Cookies Are Us runs a series of 100 cookie stores across the midwestern United States and central Canada. At the end of each day, the stores express-mail a diskette or two of sales and inventory data to headquarters, which uses the data to ship new inventory and plan marketing campaigns. They have decided to move data over a WAN or the Internet. What type of a WAN topology and service (see Chapter 9) or Internet connection would you recommend? Figure 10-8 shows some of the available Internet services and their prices, whereas Figure 9-19 in the previous chapter shows faster circuits that could be used to connect to an ISP for Internet services. You should increase the prices in Figure 9-19 by 50% to get the price that an ISP would charge to provide both the faster circuit and Internet services on it. Why?

IV. Organic Foods Organic Foods operates organic food stores in Toronto. The store operates like a traditional grocery store but offers only organically grown produce and meat, plus a wide array of health food products. Organic Foods sells memberships, and its 3,000 members receive a discount on all products they buy. There are also special member events and sales promotions each month. Organic Foods wants to open a new Internet site that will enable it to email its members monthly and provide up-to-date information and announcements about new products, sales promotions, and member events on its Web site. It has two options. First, it could develop the software on its own server in its office and connect the office (and the server) to the Internet via DSL, T1, or similar connection from its offices to an ISP. Alternately, it could pay the ISP to host the Web site on its servers and just connect the office to the ISP for Internet service. Figure 10-8 shows some of the available Internet services and their prices, whereas Figure 9-19 in the previous chapter shows faster circuits that could be used to connect to an ISP for Internet services. You should increase the prices in Figure 9-19 by 50% to get the price that an ISP would charge to provide both the faster circuit and Internet services on it. Web hosting would cost $500 to $1,000 per month, depending on the traffic. Which would you recommend, and what size of an Internet connection would you recommend if you choose to host it yourself? Justify your choice.

Service	Speed	Cost
DSL	3 Mbps down; 512 Kbps up	$30
	6 Mbps down; 640 Kbps up	$35
	12 Mbps down; 1.5 Mbps up	$40
	18 Mbps down; 1.5 Mbps up	$45
	24 Mbps down; 3 Mbps up	$55
	45 Mbps down; 6 Mbps up	$65
	50 Mbps down; 25 Mbps up	$200
	50 Mbps down; 50 Mbps up	$300
Cable Modem	5 Mbps down; 1 Mbps up	$40
	10 Mbps down; 1.5 Mbps up	$45
	16 Mbps down; 3 Mbps up	$70
	50 Mbps down; 10 Mbps up	$110
	75 Mbps down; 15 Mbps up	$150
	100 Mbps down; 20 Mbps up	$200
FTTH	15 Mbps down; 5 Mbps up	$50
	50 Mbps down; 25 Mbps up	$70
	75 Mbps down; 35 Mbps up	$100
WiMax	5 Mbps down; 5 Mbps up	$50 for up to 6 Gb of data per month; $80 for up to 12 Gb of data per month
	10 Mbps down; 10 Mbps up	$80 for up to 6 Gb of data per month; $120 for up to 12 Gb of data per month
	20 Mbps down; 20 Mbps up	$120 for up to 6 Gb of data per month; $150 for up to 12 Gb of data per month

FIGURE 10-8   Internet prices

CASE STUDY

NEXT-DAY AIR SERVICE

See the Web site at www.wiley.com/college/fitzgerald

HANDS-ON ACTIVITY 10A

Seeing the Internet

The Internet is a network of networks. One way to see this is by using the VisualRoute software. VisualRoute is a commercial package but provides a demonstration on its Web site. Go to visualroute.com and register to use their free service. Then enter a URL and watch as the route from your computer to the destination is traced and graphed. Figure 10-9 shows the route from my house in Indiana to the City University of Hong Kong.

FIGURE 10-9 Visual trace route

Another interesting site is the Internet Traffic Report (www.internettrafficreport.com). This site shows how busy the parts of the Internet are in real time. The main page enables you to see the current status of the major parts of the world, including a "traffic index" that rates performance on a 100-point scale. You can also see the average response time at key Internet NAPs, MAEs, and peering points (at least those that have agreed to be monitored), which is an average of 135 milliseconds. It also shows the global packet loss rates—the percentage of packets discarded due to transmission errors (an average of 3% today).

By clicking on a region of the world, you can see the same statistics for routers in that region. If you click on a specific router, you can see a graph of its performance over the past 24 hours. Figure 10-10 shows the statistics for one router operated by Sprint.

You can also get traffic reports for Internet2® at noc.net.internet2.edu/i2network/live-network-status.html. The "weathermap," as Internet2® calls it, shows traffic in both directions because the circuits are full duplex. You can also click on any circuit to see a graph of traffic over the last 24 hours.

Deliverables

1. Trace the route from your computer to CNN.com and to the University of Oxford www.ox.ac.uk

2. Use the Internet traffic report to find the average response time and packet loss in Asia, Australia, and North America. Pick a router in North America and report its typical response time for the past 24 hours.

3. How busy are the Internet2® links from Chicago to Atlanta right now? What was the peak traffic on these circuits over the last 24 hours?

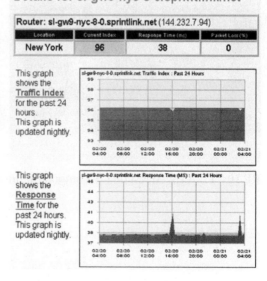

FIGURE 10-10 Internet traffic reports

HANDS-ON ACTIVITY 10B

Measuring Your Speed

The download and upload speeds you get on the Internet depend partly on the type of Internet access you have. The speeds also depend on how your ISP is connected to other ISPs, how busy the Internet is today, and how busy the Web site you're working with is. The last two factors (Internet traffic and Web traffic at the server) are beyond your control. However, you can chose what type of Internet connection you have and who your ISP is.

Many sites on the Internet can test the speed of your Internet connection. Our favorite speed site is speedtest.net. Speedtest.net has lots of advertising; ignore it (and any "windows scan" offer) and just do the speed test. You begin by selecting a server for the test. I selected a server in Nova Scotia and tested how fast the connection was between it and my computer in Indiana, which is connected to the Internet using Comcast's cable modem service. Figure 10-11 shows that my download speed was 28.86 Mbps and my upload speed was 5.63 Mbps. I ran the same test to a server closer to my computer in Indiana and got about the same speeds. The speeds to a server in Mexico were about 1.5 Mbps down and 1.0 up.

Deliverable

1. Test the upload and download speeds to a server close to your computer and to one far away from you.

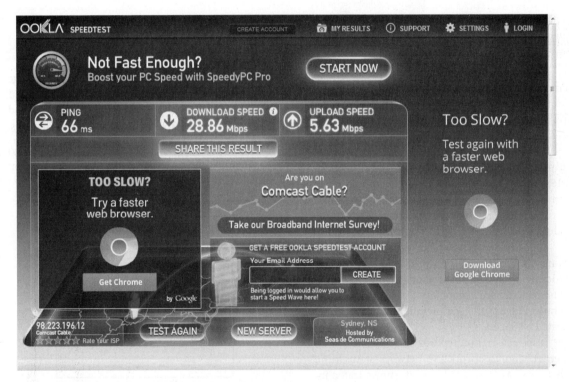

FIGURE 10-11   A speed test on my computer in Indiana

HANDS-ON ACTIVITY 10C

Apollo Residence Network Design

Apollo is a luxury residence hall that will serve honor students at your university. We described the residence in Hands-On Activities at the end of Chapters 7 and 8.

Your university has a good connection to the Internet through the high-speed Internet2® network, which you'll recall is a network that connects about 400 research and education organizations around the world over some very high-speed Internet circuits. While much of the Internet traffic from the university goes to and comes from the other universities and organizations that are part of Internet2®, a substantial portion of traffic goes to and comes from the commercial Internet. This is especially true for traffic generated by undergraduate students who make up the majority of the intended population of the Apollo Residence.

Therefore, the university has decided to build a second connection into the Internet for primary use by the students of the Apollo Residence. This Internet connection will also provide a backup connection for the university's main Internet connection, just in case Internet2® experiences problems.

Deliverables

Your team was hired to select the Internet circuit. Figure 10-8 provides a list of possible Internet services you can use. Figure 9-19 in the previous chapter shows faster circuits that could be used to connect to an ISP for Internet services. You should increase the prices in Figure 9-19 by 50% to get the price that an ISP would charge for providing both the faster circuit and Internet services on it. Specify what service(s) you will use. Provide the estimated monthly operating cost of the circuit(s).

PART FOUR NETWORK MANAGEMENT

CHAPTER 11

NETWORK SECURITY

This chapter describes why networks need security and how to provide it. The first step in any security plan is risk assessment, understanding the key assets that need protection, and assessing the risks to each. A variety of steps can be taken to prevent, detect, and correct security problems due to disruptions, destruction, disaster, and unauthorized access.

OBJECTIVES

- Be familiar with the major threats to network security
- Be familiar with how to conduct a risk assessment
- Understand how to ensure business continuity
- Understand how to prevent intrusion

OUTLINE

11.1 INTRODUCTION

Business and government have always been concerned with physical and information security. They have protected physical assets with locks, barriers, guards, and the military since organized societies began. They have also guarded their plans and information with coding systems for at least 3,500 years. What has changed in the last 50 years is the introduction of computers and the Internet.

The rise of the Internet has completely redefined the nature of information security. Now companies face global threats to their networks and, more importantly, to their data. Viruses and worms have long been a problem, but credit card theft and identity theft, two of the fastest-growing crimes, pose immense liability to firms who fail to protect their customers' data. Laws have been slow to catch up, despite the fact that breaking into a computer in the United States—even without causing damage—is now a federal crime punishable by a fine and/or imprisonment. Nonetheless, we have a new kind of transborder cyber crime against which laws may apply but that will be very difficult to enforce. The United States and Canada may extradite and allow prosecution of digital criminals operating within their borders, but investigating, enforcing, and prosecuting transnational cyber crime across different borders is much more challenging. And even when someone is caught, he or she faces a lighter sentence than a bank robber.

Computer security has become increasingly important over the last 10 years with the passage of the Sarbanes-Oxley Act (SOX) and the Health Insurance Portability and Accountability Act (HIPAA). However, despite these measures, the number of security incidents is growing. For example, Verizon's 2013 security report concluded that at least 174 million electronic records had been compromised in more than 855 separate security incidents. These incidents included not only viruses but also industrial espionage, fraud, extortion, and identity theft. The years when creating a virus was for fun are long gone. The goal of these attacks was money.

You probably heard on the news that the large companies Zappos and Target had been victims of cyberattacks and that millions of the credit card information of millions of their customers had been stolen. However, a company of any size can be the target of an attack. According to Symantec, more than 50% of all targeted companies had fewer than 2,500 employees because they often have weaker security.

Many organizations, private and public, focus on helping individuals, organizations, and governments to protect themselves from criminals operating on the Internet (cyber-criminals). These include CERT (Computer Emergency Response Team) at Carnegie Mellon University, APWG (Anti-Phishing Working Group), the Russian-based Kaspersky Lab, McAfee, and Symantec.

There are three main reasons why there has been an increase in computer security over the past few years. First, in the past, hacking into somebody's computer was considered to be a hobby, but today being a cybercriminal is a profession. There are professional organizations that one can hire to break into computer networks of specific targets to steal information. We are not talking about ethical hacking (when a company hires another company to test its security) but rather hackers who, for a fee, will steal information, intellectual property, or computer code. These attacks are called targeted attacks, in which cybercriminals not only try to exploit technical vulnerabilities but also try to "hack the human" via social engineering or phishing emails. These targeted attacks can be very sophisticated, and any organization can become a victim because every organization has data that can be of value to cybercriminals.

Second, hacktivism (the use of hacking techniques to bring attention to a larger political or social goal) has become more common. Hacktivism combines illegal hacking techniques with digital activism and usually targets large organizations and governments by sabotaging or defacing their public Web sites to bring attention to the hackers' social or political cause. For example, in 2010, the group called Anonymous took down Web sites owned by Visa and MasterCard to protest their denial of payments to the WikiLeaks. This type of threat is not as pervasive as that from cybercriminals, but it has increased in the past few years.

Third, the increase in mobile devices offers a very fertile environment for exploitation. More and more frequently, we access our bank accounts, buy items on Amazon, and access our business data through our mobile devices, so cybercriminals are now targeting these mobile devices. These types of attacks often are easier to develop because mobile security is typically weaker than computer security, so they offer a potentially high yield.

These trends will increase the value of personal data, and therefore the potential threat to our privacy and the privacy of businesses will increase. It is thus very important for businesses and also individuals to understand their assets, potential threats to these assets, and the way they can protect them. We explore these in the next section of this chapter.

11.1.1 Why Networks Need Security

In recent years, organizations have become increasingly dependent on data communication networks for their daily business communications, database information retrieval, distributed data processing, and the internetworking of LANs. The rise of the Internet with opportunities to connect computers and mobile devices anywhere in the world has significantly increased the potential vulnerability of the organization's assets. Emphasis on network security also has increased as a result of well-publicized security break-ins and as government regulatory agencies have issued security-related pronouncements.

The losses associated with the security failures can be huge. An average annual loss of about $350,000 sounds large enough, but this is just the tip of the iceberg. The potential loss of consumer confidence from a well-publicized security break-in can cost much more in lost business. More important than these, however, are the potential losses from the disruption of application systems that run on computer networks. As organizations have come to depend on computer systems, computer networks have become "mission-critical." Bank of America, one of the largest banks in the United States, estimates that it would cost the bank $50 million if its computer networks were unavailable for 24 hours. Other large organizations have produced similar estimates.

Protecting customer privacy and the risk of identity theft also drive the need for increased network security. In 1998, the European Union passed strong data privacy laws that fined companies for disclosing information about their customers. In the United States, organizations have begun complying with the data protection requirements of HIPAA and a California law providing fines up to $250,000 for each unauthorized disclosure of customer information (e.g., if someone were to steal 100 customer records, the fine could be $25 million).

As you might suspect, the value of the data stored on most organizations' networks and the value provided by the application systems in use far exceeds the cost of the networks themselves. For this reason, the primary goal of network security is to protect organizations' data and application software, not the networks themselves.

11.1.2 Types of Security Threats

For many people, security means preventing intrusion, such as preventing an attacker from breaking into your computer. Security is much more than that, however. There are three primary goals in providing security: confidentiality, integrity, and availability (also known as CIA). **Confidentiality** refers to the protection of organizational data from unauthorized disclosure of customer and proprietary data. **Integrity** is the assurance that data have not been altered or destroyed. **Availability** means providing continuous operation of the organization's hardware and software so that staff, customers, and suppliers can be assured of no interruptions in service.

There are many potential threats to confidentiality, integrity, and availability. Figure 11-1 shows some threats to a computer center, the data communication circuits, and the attached computers. In general, security threats can be classified into two broad categories: ensuring business continuity and preventing unauthorized access.

Ensuring **business continuity** refers primarily to ensuring availability, with some aspects of data integrity. There are three main threats to business continuity. *Disruptions* are the loss of or reduction in network service. Disruptions may be minor and temporary. For example, a network switch might fail or a circuit may be cut, causing part of the network to cease functioning until the failed component can be replaced. Some users may be affected, but others can continue to use the network. Some disruptions may also be caused by or result in the *destruction* of data. For example, a virus may destroy files, or the "crash" of a hard disk may cause files to be destroyed. Other disruptions may be catastrophic. Natural (or human-made) *disasters* may occur that destroy host computers or large sections of

FIGURE 11-1

Some threats to a
computer center, data
communication circuits,
and client computers

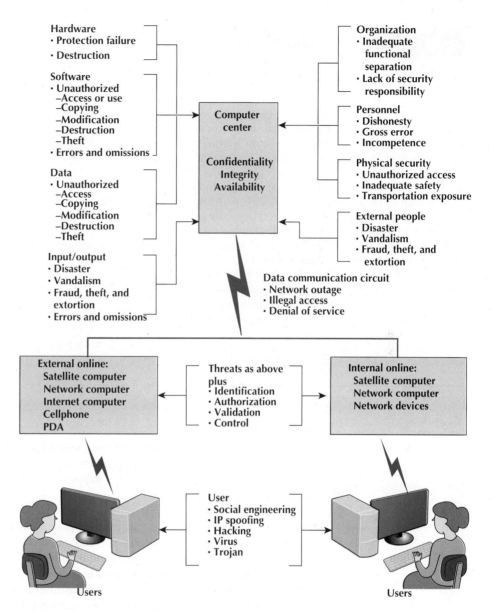

the network. For example, hurricanes, fires, floods, earthquakes, mudslides, tornadoes, or terrorist attacks can destroy large parts of the buildings and networks in their path.

Preventing unauthorized access, also referred to as *intrusion*, refers primarily to confidentiality, but also to integrity, as an intruder may change important data. Intrusion is often viewed as external attackers gaining access to organizational data files and resources from across the Internet. However, almost half of all intrusion incidents involve employees. Intrusion may have only minor effects. A curious intruder may simply explore the system, gaining knowledge that has little value. A more serious intruder may be a competitor bent on industrial espionage who could attempt to gain access to information on products under development, or the details and price of a bid on a large contract, or a thief trying to steal customer credit card numbers or information to carry out identity theft. Worse still, the intruder could change files to commit fraud or theft or could destroy information to injure the organization.

MANAGEMENT

FOCUS

11-1 Same Old Same Old

*N*o matter the industry, every company should consider itself to be a target of cybercrime – Target learned this the hard way in December 2013. Russian hacker(s) were able to install malware on the company's point-of-sale systems (cash registers) and steal the credit card information of more than 40 million individuals.

Hackers probably got access to Target's network using credentials of an HVAC vendor. Investigators said that the malware installed on the point-of-sale systems was neither sophisticated nor novel and was detected by two security systems that Target had installed on its network. Why didn't security specialists listen to the warnings from their security software? Target, just like any other company, gets bombarded by thousands of attacks each day, and the likelihood of one of them getting through increases each day – just a simple logic of probability. Although some attacks are sophisticated in nature, most of them are well known.

One can say, same old same old. Cyberattackers are playing the game of numbers – the more persistent they are in their attacks, the more likely they will get inside a network and gain access to critical information such as credit card numbers.

This only reminds us that cybersecurity is a global problem and that everybody who uses the Internet can be and probably is under attack. Therefore, learning about security and investing in it is necessary to survive and strive in the Internet era.

Adapted from: "Missed Alarms and 40 Million Stolen Credit Card Numbers: How Target Blew It," by Michael Riley, Ben Elgin, Dune Lawrence, and Carol Matlack, March 13, 2014, *Bloomberg Businessweek* (www.businessweek.com) and Krebs on Security (krebsonsecuirty.com)

11.1.3 Network Controls

Developing a secure network means developing **controls**. Controls are software, hardware, rules, or procedures that reduce or eliminate the threats to network security. Controls *prevent, detect*, and/or *correct* whatever might happen to the organization because of threats facing its computer-based systems.

Preventive controls mitigate or stop a person from acting or an event from occurring. For example, a password can prevent illegal entry into the system, or a set of second circuits can prevent the network from crashing. Preventive controls also act as a deterrent by discouraging or restraining someone from acting or proceeding because of fear or doubt. For example, a guard or a security lock on a door may deter an attempt to gain illegal entry.

Detective controls reveal or discover unwanted events. For example, software that looks for illegal network entry can detect these problems. They also document an event, a situation, or an intrusion, providing evidence for subsequent action against the individuals or organizations involved or enabling corrective action to be taken. For example, the same software that detects the problem must report it immediately so that someone or some automated process can take corrective action.

Corrective controls remedy an unwanted event or an intrusion. Either computer programs or humans verify and check data to correct errors or fix a security breach so it will not recur in the future. They also can recover from network errors or disasters. For example, software can recover and restart the communication circuits automatically when there is a data communication failure.

The remainder of this chapter discusses the various controls that can be used to prevent, detect, and correct threats. We also present a general risk assessment framework for identifying the threats and their associated controls. This framework provides a network manager with a good view of the current threats and any controls that are in place to mitigate the occurrence of threats.

Nonetheless, it is important to remember that it is not enough just to establish a series of controls; someone or some department must be accountable for the control and security of the network. This includes being responsible for developing controls, monitoring their operation, and determining when they need to be updated or replaced.

Controls must be reviewed periodically to be sure that they are still useful and must be verified and tested. Verifying ensures that the control is present, and testing determines whether the control is working as originally specified.

It is also important to recognize that there may be occasions in which a person must temporarily override a control, for instance, when the network or one of its software or hardware subsystems is not operating properly. Such overrides should be tightly controlled, and there should be a formal procedure to document this occurrence should it happen.

11.2 RISK ASSESSMENT

The first step in developing a secure network is to conduct a **risk assessment**. There are several commonly used **risk assessment frameworks** that provide strategies for analyzing and prioritizing the security risks to information systems and networks. A risk assessment should be simple so that both technical and nontechnical readers can understand it. After reading a risk assessment, anyone should be able to see which systems and network components are at high risk for attack or abuse and which are at low risk. Also, the reader should be able to see what controls have been implemented to protect him or her and what new controls need to be implemented.

Three risk assessment frameworks are commonly used:

1. Operationally Critical Threat, Asset, and Vulnerability Evaluation (OCTAVE) from the Computer Emergency Readiness Team
2. Control Objectives for Information and Related Technology (COBIT) from the Information Systems Audit and Control Association
3. Risk Management Guide for Information Technology Systems (NIST guide) from the National Institute of Standards and Technology

Each of these frameworks offers a slightly different process with a different focus. However, they share five common steps:

1. Develop risk measurement criteria
2. Inventory IT assets
3. Identify threats
4. Document existing controls
5. Identify improvements

11.2.1 Develop risk measurement criteria

Risk measurement criteria are the measures used to evaluate the way a security threat could affect the organization. For example, suppose that a hacker broke in and stole customer credit card information from a company server. One immediate impact to the organization is *financial*, because some customers are likely to stop shopping, at least in the short term. Depending where the company is located, there may also be some *legal* impact because some countries and/or states have laws concerning the unauthorized release of personal information. There also may be longer-term impacts to the company's *reputation*.

Each organization needs to develop its own set of potential business impacts, but the five most commonly considered impact areas are financial (revenues and expenses), productivity (business operations), reputation (customer perceptions), safety (health of customers and employees), and legal (potential for fines and litigation). However, some organizations add other impacts and not all organizations use all of these five because some may not apply. It is important to remember that these impacts are for information systems and networks,

Impact Area	Priority	Low Impact	Medium Impact	High Impact
Financial	High	Sales drop by less than 2%	Sales drop by 2%–10%	Sales drop by more than 10%
Productivity	Medium	Increase in annual operating expenses by less than 3%	Increase in annual operating expenses between 3% and 6%	Increase in annual operating expenses by more than 6%
Reputation	High	Decrease in number of customers by less than 2%	Decrease in number of customers by 2%–15%	Decrease in number of customers by more than 15%
Legal	Medium	Incurring fines or legal fees less than $10,000	Incurring fines or legal fees between $10,000 and $60,000	Incurring fines or legal fees exceeding $60,000

FIGURE 11-2   Sample risk measurement criteria for a Web-based bookstore

so although safety is important to most organizations, there may be little impact on safety from information system and network problems.

Once the impact areas have been identified, the next step is to prioritize them. Not all impact areas are equally important to all organizations. Some areas may be high priority, some medium, and some low. For example, for a hospital, safety may be the highest priority and financial the lowest. In contrast, for a restaurant, information systems and networks may pose a low (or nonexistent) safety risk (because they are not involved in food safety) but a high priority reputation risk (if, for example, credit card data were stolen). There may be a temptation to say every impact is high priority, but this is the same as saying that all impacts are medium, because you cannot distinguish between them when it comes time to take action.

The next step is to develop specific measures of what could happen in each impact area and what we would consider a high, medium, and low impact. For example, one financial impact could be a decrease in sales. What would we consider a low financial impact in terms of a decrease in sales: 1%? 2%? What would be a high impact on sales? These are business decisions, not technology decisions, so they should be made by the business leaders.

Figure 11-2 has sample risk measurement criteria for a Web-based bookstore. As you can see, only four of the impact areas apply for this company, because information systems and network security problems would not harm the safety of employees or customers. However, it would be a different case if this were a pharmaceutical company. A threat, such as malware, could cause changes in how a drug is prepared, potentially harming customers (patients) and also employees.

As Figure 11-2 suggests, our fictional Web-based book company believes that financial and reputation impacts have high priority, whereas productivity and legal impacts are medium. This figure also provides metrics for assessing the impact of each risk. For example, our fictitious company considers it a low financial impact if their sales were to drop by 2% because of security problems. The financial impact would be high if they were to lose more than 10% of sales.

11.2.2 Inventory IT assets

An **asset** is something of value and can be either hardware, software, data, or applications. Figure 11-3 defines six common categories of IT assets.

An important type of asset is the **mission-critical application,** which is an information system that is critical to the survival of the organization. It is an application that cannot be permitted to fail, and if it does fail, the network staff drops everything else to fix it. For example, for an Internet bank that has no brick-and-mortar branches, the Web site is a mission-critical application. If the Web site crashes, the bank cannot conduct business with its customers. Mission-critical applications are usually clearly identified so that their importance is not overlooked.

TECHNICAL	11-1 Basic Control Principles of a Secure Network
FOCUS	

- The less complex a control, the better.
- A control's cost should be equivalent to the identified risk. It often is not possible to ascertain the expected loss, so this is a subjective judgment in many cases.
- Preventing a security incident is always preferable to detecting and correcting it after it occurs.
- An adequate system of internal controls is one that provides "just enough" security to protect the network, taking into account both the risks and costs of the controls.
- Automated controls (computer-driven) always are more reliable than manual controls that depend on human interaction.
- Controls should apply to everyone, not just a few select individuals.
- When a control has an override mechanism, make sure that it is documented and that the override procedure has its own controls to avoid misuse.
- Institute the various security levels in an organization on the basis of "need to know." If you do not need to know, you do not need to access the network or the data.
- The control documentation should be confidential.
- Names, uses, and locations of network components should not be publicly available.
- Controls must be sufficient to ensure that the network can be audited, which usually means keeping historical transaction records.

- When designing controls, assume that you are operating in a hostile environment.
- Always convey an image of high security by providing education and training.
- Make sure the controls provide the proper separation of duties. This applies especially to those who design and install the controls and those who are responsible for everyday use and monitoring.
- It is desirable to implement entrapment controls in networks to identify attackers who gain illegal access.
- When a control fails, the network should default to a condition in which everyone is denied access. A period of failure is when the network is most vulnerable.
- Controls should still work even when only one part of a network fails. For example, if a backbone network fails, all local area networks connected to it should still be operational, with their own independent controls providing protection.
- Don't forget the LAN. Security and disaster recovery planning has traditionally focused on host mainframe computers and WANs. However, LANs now play an increasingly important role in most organizations but are often overlooked by central site network managers.
- Always assume your opponent is smarter than you.
- Always have insurance as the last resort should all controls fail.

FIGURE 11-3

Types of assets.
DNS = Domain Name
Service; DHCP =
Dynamic Host Control
Protocol; LAN = local
area network; WAN =
wide area network

Hardware	• Servers, such as mail servers, Web servers, DNS servers, DHCP servers, and LAN file servers • Client computers • Devices such as switches and routers
Circuits	• Locally operated circuits such as LANs and backbones • Contracted circuits such as WAN circuits • Internet access circuits
Network software	• Server operating systems and system settings • Application software such as mail server and Web server software
Client software	• Operating systems and system settings • Application software such as word processors
Organizational data	• Databases with organizational records
Mission-critical applications	• For example, for an Internet bank, its Web site is mission-critical

The next most important type of asset is the organization's data. For example, suppose someone were to destroy a mainframe computer worth $10 million. The computer could be replaced simply by buying a new one. It would be expensive, but the problem would be solved in a few weeks. Now suppose someone were to destroy all the student records at your university so that no one would know what courses anyone had taken or their grades. The cost would far exceed the cost of replacing a $10 million computer. The lawsuits alone would easily exceed $10 million, and the cost of staff to find and reenter paper records would be enormous and certainly would take more than a few weeks.

Once all assets are identified, they need to be rated for importance. To order them, you need answer questions such as, what would happen if this information asset's *confidentiality, integrity, or accessibility* were compromised? This will allow you to assess the importance of this asset as either low, medium, or high. You need also to document each asset, not just information assets, and briefly describe why each asset is critical to the organization. Finally, the owners of each asset are recorded. Figure 11-3 summarizes some typical assets found in most organizations.

11.2.3 Identify Threats

A **threat** is any potential occurrence that can do harm, interrupt the systems using the network, or cause a monetary loss to the organization.

Figure 11-5 summarizes the most common types of threats and their likelihood of occurring based on several surveys in recent years. This figure shows the percentage of organizations affected each year by each threat but not whether the threat caused damage; for example, 100% of companies reported experiencing one or more viruses each year, but in most cases, the antivirus software prevented any problems. The actual probability of a threat to your organization depends on your business. An Internet bank, for example, is more likely to be a target of theft of information than a restaurant with a simple Web site. Nonetheless, Figure 11-5 provides some general guidance.

The next step is to create **threat scenarios**. A threat scenario describes how an asset can be compromised by one specific threat. An asset can be compromised by more than one threat, so it is common to have more than one threat scenario for each asset. For example, the confidentiality, integrity, and/or availability of the client data database in Figure 11-4 can be compromised by information theft (confidentiality), sabotage (integrity), or a natural disaster such as a tornado (availability). When preparing a threat scenario, we name the asset, describe the threat, explain the consequence (violation of confidentiality, integrity or availability), and estimate the likelihood of this threat happening (high, medium, or low).

Figure 11-6 provides an example of a threat scenario for one asset (the customer database) of a Web-based bookstore. The top half of the threat scenario describes the risk associated with the asset from the threat, while the bottom half (shaded in color) describes the existing controls that have been implemented to protect the asset from this threat. This step focuses on the top half of the threat scenario, whereas the next step (11.2.4) describes the bottom half.

A threat scenario begins with the name of the asset and the threat being considered. The threat is described and the likelihood of its occurrence is assessed as high, medium, or low. Then the potential impact is identified, whether this be to confidentiality, integrity, or availability. Some threats could have multiple impacts.

Next the consequences of the threat are assessed, using the impact areas identified in step 1 and their priority (e.g., reputation, financial, productivity, safety, and legal). We identify the impact that each scenario could have on each priority area, high, medium, or low, using the risk measurement criteria defined in step 1. We calculate an impact score by multiplying the priority of each area by the impact the threat would have, using a 1 for a low value, a 2 for a medium value, and a 3 for a high value, and summing all the results to produce an **impact score**.

Asset	Importance	Most Important Security Requirement	Description	Owner(s)
Customer database	High	■ **Confidentiality** ■ Integrity ■ Availability	This database contains all customers' records, including address and credit card information.	VP of Marketing CIO
Web server	High	■ Confidentiality ■ Integrity ■ **Availability**	This is used by our customers to place orders. It is very important that it would be available 24/7.	CIO
Mail server	Medium	■ Confidentiality ■ **Integrity** ■ Availability	This is used by employees for internal communication. It is very important that no one intercepts this communication as sensitive information is shared via email.	CIO
Financial records	High	■ **Confidentiality** ■ Integrity ■ Availability	These records are used by the C-level executives and also by the VP of operations. It is imperative that nobody else but the C-team be able to access this mission information.	CFO
Employees' computers	Low	■ Confidentiality ■ Integrity ■ **Availability**	Each employee is assigned to a cubical that has a desktop computer in it. Employees provide customer service and support for our Web site using these computers.	Division directors

FIGURE 11-4   Sample inventory of assets for a Web-based bookstore

Finally, we can calculate the relative **risk score** by multiplying the impact score by the likelihood (using 1 for low likelihood, 2 for medium likelihood, and 3 for high likelihood).

Figure 11-6 shows that the risk score for information theft from the customer database is 50. The absolute number does not really tell us anything. Instead, we compare the risk scores among all the different threat scenarios to help us identify the most important risks we face.

Figure 11-7 shows the threat scenario for a tornado strike against our customer database. Take a moment and compare the two threat scenarios. You can see that the tornado risk score is 14, which shows that information theft is a greater risk than a tornado.

FIGURE 11-5
Likelihood of a threat

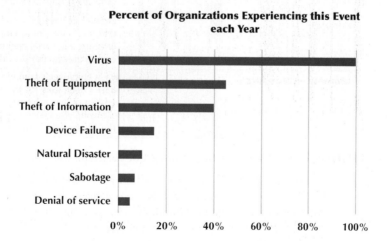

Percent of Organizations Experiencing this Event each Year

Asset	Customer database
Asset Importance	High
Threat	Theft of information
Description	An external hacker or a disgruntled current or former employee can gain unauthorized access to the client data and distribute it to a third party.
Likelihood	Medium (2)
Impact on	√ Confidentiality ____ Integrity ____ Availability

Impact Area	Priority	Impact	Score
Financial	High (3)	Medium (2)	6
Productivity	Medium (2)	High (3)	6
Reputation	High (3)	High (3)	9
Legal	Medium (2)	Medium (2)	4
		Impact Score	25

Risk Score (Likelihood × Impact Score)	50
Adequacy of Existing Controls	Medium
Risk Control Strategy	____ Accept √ Mitigate ____ Share ____ Defer
Risk Mitigation Controls	
Encryption	The database is encrypted.
Firewall	A firewall is installed on the router in front of the database to prevent unauthorized access.
Personnel Policy	All employees have their log-in credentials removed within 24 hours of their resignation or termination.
Training	Employees have to attend annual security training that focuses on information disclosure policy, phishing and social engineering techniques to ensure they do not provide their passwords to anyone.
Automatic screen lock	Each employee's computer will lock if the computer hasn't been used for five minutes so that if an employee leaves his or her desk without logging off, someone else cannot gain unauthorized access to the employee's computer.

FIGURE 11-6   Threat scenario for theft of customer information

In these examples, we have used only three values (high, medium, and low) to assess likelihood, priority, and impact. Some organizations use more complex scoring systems. And nothing says that likelihood, priority, and impact have to use the same scales. Some organizations use 5-point scales for priority, 7-point scales for impact, and 100-point scales for likelihood.

Asset	Client database
Asset Importance	High
Threat	Natural disaster (tornado)
Description	Our data center could be hit by an F4 or F5 tornado that would destroy the database
Likelihood	Low (1)
Impact on	_____ Confidentiality _____ Integrity √_____ Availability

Impact Area	Ranking	Impact	Score
Financial	High (3)	Low (1)	3
Productivity	Medium (2)	High (3)	6
Reputation	High (3)	Low (1)	3
Legal	Medium (2)	Low (1)	2
		Risk Score	**14**

Risk Score (Likelihood × Impact Score)	**14**
Adequacy of Existing Controls	**Medium**
Risk Control Strategy	___ Accept √_ Mitigate ___ Share ___Defer

Risk Mitigation Controls	**Description**
Backup of Database	Each night, the database will be copied to a second secure data center located 500 miles from the main data center.
Disaster Recovery Plan	A disaster recovery plan is in place and will be tested every two years to ensure that the database can be successfully restored to an alternate data center that can be operational within 48 hours.

FIGURE 11-7   Threat scenario for destruction of customer information by a tornado

11.2.4 Document Existing Controls

Once the specific assets, threat scenarios, and their risk scores have been identified, you can begin to work on the **risk control strategy**, which is the way an organization intends to address a risk. In general, an organization can **accept** the risk, **mitigate** it, **share** it, or **defer** it. If an organization decides to _accept_ a risk, it means the organization will be taking no action to address it and accept the stated consequences. In general, these risks have very low impact on the organization.

  Risk mitigation involves implementation of some type of a **control** to counter the threat or to minimize the impact. An organization can implement several types of controls, such as using antivirus software, implementing state-of-the-art firewalls, or providing security training for employees.

An organization can decide to *share* the risk. In this case, it purchases insurance against the risk. For example, you share a risk for getting into a car accident. It is quite unlikely that you will be in a car accident, but if it were to happen, you want to make sure that the insurance company can step in and pay for all the damages. Similarly, an organization may decide to purchase insurance against information theft or damage from a tornado. Sharing and mitigation can be done simultaneously.

Finally, the organization can *defer* the risk. This usually happens when there is a need to collect additional information about the threat and the risk. These risks are usually not imminent and, if they were to occur, would not significantly impact the organization.

For each threat scenario, the risk control strategy needs to be specified. If the organization decides to mitigate and/or share the risk, specific controls need to be listed. The next two sections in this chapter describe numerous controls that can be used to mitigate the security risks organizations face.

Once the existing controls have been documented, an overall assessment of their adequacy is done. This assessment produces a value that is relative to the risk, such as high adequacy (meaning the controls are expected to strongly control the risks in the threat scenario), medium adequacy (meaning some improvements are possible), or low adequacy (meaning improvements are needed to effectively mitigate or share the risk). Once again, some organizations use more complex scales such as a letter grade (A, A−, A+, B, etc.) or 100-point scales.

The bottom sections of the threat scenarios in Figures 11-6 and 11-7 show the strategy, controls, and their adequacy for both threat scenarios. For the theft of information, the Web-based bookstore has already implemented several risk mitigation strategies: encryption, a firewall, personnel policies, training, and automatic screen lock. For the tornado, the company implemented a database backup and a disaster recovery plan. Both have been assessed as medium adequacy.

At this point, you may or may not understand the controls described in these figures. However, after you read the rest of the chapter, you will understand what each control is and how it works to mitigate the risk from the threat.

11.2.5 Identify Improvements

The final step in risk assessment—and its ultimate goal—is to identify what improvements are needed. Most organizations face so many threats that they cannot afford to mitigate all of them to the highest level. They need to focus first on the highest risks; the threat scenarios with the highest risk scores are carefully examined to ensure that there is at least a medium level of control adequacy. In addition, the most important assets' security requirements (labeled as high in Figure 11-4) are adequately protected. Additional controls that could be implemented to improve the risk mitigation are considered, as are ways to share the risk. As mentioned earlier, Sections 11.3 and 11.4 describe many different controls that can be implemented to mitigate the risks associated with the loss of business continuity and unauthorized access.

The second focus is on threat scenarios whose mitigation controls have low adequacy. Ideally, these will all be low-risk threats, but they are examined to ensure the level of expenditure matches the level of risk.

11.3 ENSURING BUSINESS CONTINUITY

Business continuity means that the organization's data and applications will continue to operate even in the face of disruption, destruction, or disaster. A business continuity plan has two major parts: the development of controls that will prevent these events from having a major impact on the organization, and a disaster recovery plan that will enable the organization to recover if a disaster occurs. In this section, we discuss controls designed to prevent, detect, and correct these threats. We focus on the major threats to business continuity: viruses, theft, denial of service, attacks, device failure, and disasters. Business continuity planning is sometimes overlooked because intrusion is more often the subject of news reports.

11.3.1 Virus Protection

Special attention must be paid to preventing computer **viruses**. Some are harmless and just cause nuisance messages, but others are serious, such as by destroying data. In most cases, disruptions or the destruction of data are local and affect only a small number of computers. Such disruptions are usually fairly easy to deal with; the virus is removed and the network continues to operate. Some viruses cause widespread infection, although this has not occurred in recent years.

Most viruses attach themselves to other programs or to special parts on disks. As those files execute or are accessed, the virus spreads. *Macro viruses*, viruses that are contained in documents, emails, or spreadsheet files, can spread when an infected file is simply opened. Some viruses change their appearances as they spread, making detection more difficult.

A **worm** is special type of virus that spreads itself without human intervention. Many viruses attach themselves to a file and require a person to copy the file, but a worm copies itself from computer to computer. Worms spread when they install themselves on a computer and then send copies of themselves to other computers, sometimes by emails, sometimes via security holes in software. (Security holes are described later in this chapter.)

The best way to prevent the spread of viruses is to install **antivirus software** such as that by Symantec. Most organizations automatically install antivirus software on their

---

MANAGEMENT 11-2 **Attack of the Auditors**

FOCUS

Security has become a major issue over the past few years. With the passage of HIPAA and the Sarbanes-Oxley Act, more and more regulations are addressing security. It takes years for most organizations to become compliant, because the rules are vague and there are many ways to meet the requirements.

"If you've implemented commonsense security, you're probably already in compliance from an IT standpoint," says Kim Keanini, chief technology officer of nCricle, a security software firm. "Compliance from an auditing standpoint, however, is something else." Auditors require documentation. It is no longer sufficient to put key network controls in place; now you have to provide documented proof that a control is working, which usually requires event logs of transactions and thwarted attacks.

When it comes to security, Bill Randal, MIS director of Red Robin Restaurants, can't stress enough the importance of documentation. "It's what the auditors are really looking for," he says. "They're not IT folks, so they're looking for documented processes they can track. At the start of our [security] compliance project, we literally stopped all other projects for another three weeks while we documented every security and auditing process we had in place."

Software vendors are scrambling not only to ensure that their security software performs the functions it is designed to do but also to improve its ability to provide documentation for auditors.

Adapted from: Oliver Rist, "Attack of the Auditors," *InfoWorld*, March 21, 2005, pp. 34–40.

computers, but many people fail to install them on their home computers. Antivirus software is only as good as its last update, so it is critical that the software be updated regularly. Be sure to set your software to update automatically or do it manually on a regular basis.

Viruses are often spread by downloading files from the Internet, so do not copy or download files of unknown origin (e.g., music, videos, screen savers), or at least check every file you do download. Always check all files for viruses before using them (even those from friends!). Researchers estimate that 10 new viruses are developed every day, so it is important to frequently update the virus information files that are provided by the antivirus software.

11.3.2 Denial-of-Service Protection

With a **denial-of-service (DoS) attack**, an attacker attempts to disrupt the network by flooding it with messages so that the network cannot process messages from normal users. The simplest approach is to flood a Web server, mail server, and so on, with incoming messages. The server attempts to respond to these, but there are so many messages that it cannot.

One might expect that it would be possible to filter messages from one source IP so that if one user floods the network, the messages from this person can be filtered out before they reach the Web server being targeted. This could work, but most attackers use tools that enable them to put false source IP addresses on the incoming messages so that it is difficult to recognize a message as a real message or a DoS message.

A **distributed denial-of-service (DDoS) attack** is even more disruptive. With a DDoS attack, the attacker breaks into and takes control of many computers on the Internet (often several hundred to several thousand) and plants software on them called a **DDoS agent** (or sometimes a *zombie* or a *bot*). The attacker then uses software called a **DDoS handler** (sometimes called a *botnet*) to control the agents. The handler issues instructions to the computers under the attacker's control, which simultaneously begin sending messages to the target site. In this way, the target is deluged with messages from many different sources, making it harder to identify the DoS messages and greatly increasing the number of messages hitting the target (see Figure 11-8). Some DDos attacks have sent more than one million packets per second at the target.

There are several approaches to preventing DoS and DDoS attacks from affecting the network. The first is to configure the main router that connects your network to the Internet (or the firewall, which will be discussed later in this chapter) to verify that the source address of all incoming messages is in a valid address range for that connection (called **traffic filtering**). For example, if an incoming message has a source address from inside your network, then it is obviously a false address. This ensures that only messages with valid addresses are permitted into the network, although it requires more processing in the router and thus slows incoming traffic.

A second approach is to configure the main router (or firewall) to limit the number of incoming packets that could be DoS/DDoS attack packets that it allows to enter the network, regardless of their source (called **traffic limiting**). Technical Focus 11-2 describes some of the types of DoS/DDoS attacks and the packets used. Such packets have the same content as legitimate packets that should be permitted into the network. It is a flood of such packets that indicates a DoS/DDoS attack, so by discarding packets over a certain number that arrive each second, one can reduce the impact of the attack. The disadvantage is that during an attack, some valid packets from regular customers will be discarded, so they will be unable to reach your network. Thus the network will continue to operate, but some customer packets (e.g., Web requests, emails) will be lost.

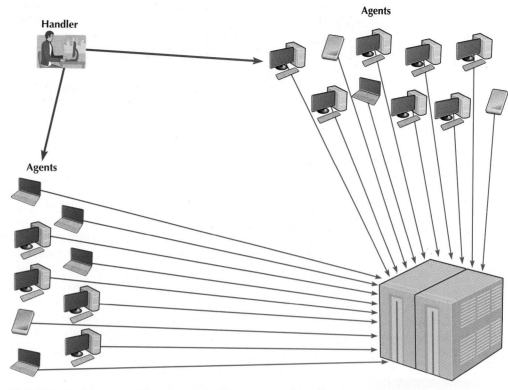

FIGURE 11-8 A distributed denial-of-service attack

A third and more sophisticated approach is to use a special-purpose security device, called a **traffic anomaly detector**, that is installed in front of the main router (or firewall) to perform **traffic analysis**. This device monitors normal traffic patterns and learns what normal traffic looks like. Most DoS/DDoS attacks target a specific server or device so when the anomaly detector recognizes a sudden burst of abnormally high traffic destined for

MANAGEMENT

FOCUS

11-3 DDoS Attacks for Hire?

*A*lthough the idea of DDoS is not new, they have increased by 1,000% since 2005, partially because you can now hire a hacker who will attack anyone you like for a fee. On hacker forums, hackers advertise their ability to take Web sites down. All you need to do is to reach them via a message on this forum and negotiate the fee.

DDoS attacks are also used as a test for hackers wanting to join these hacker groups. The leader of a hacker group will give a target Web site to an aspiring member, and the hacker has to prove that he or she can bring the Web site down. The target Web sites are selected based on the security measures they have to protect themselves against attacks, so this task can be simple or quite complex based on the test target selected.

DDoS attacks are here to stay because they are no longer a hobby but a source of income for cybercriminals. Attackers are now able to bombard a target at 300+ Gbps, which is six times the size of the largest attack in 2009.

Adapted from: "The New Normal: 200–400 Gbps DDoS Attacks," posted February 14, 2014, on Krebs on Security (krebsonsecurity.com).

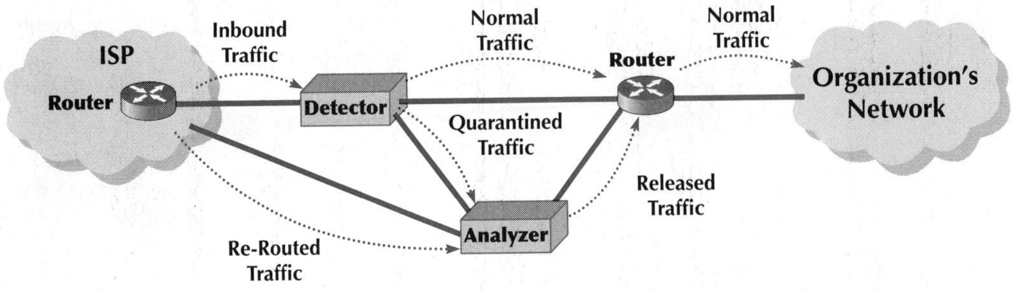

FIGURE 11-9 Traffic analysis reduces the impact of denial of service attacks

a specific server or device, it quarantines those incoming packets but allows normal traffic to flow through into the network. This results in minimal impact to the network as a whole. The anomaly detector reroutes the quarantined packets to a **traffic anomaly analyzer** (see Figure 11-9). The anomaly analyzer examines the quarantined traffic, attempts to recognize valid source addresses and "normal" traffic, and selects which of the quarantined packets to release into the network. The detector can also inform the router owned by the ISP that is sending the traffic into the organization's network to reroute the suspect traffic to the anomaly analyzer, thus avoiding the main circuit leading into the organization. This process is never perfect, but it is significantly better than the other approaches.

TECHNICAL FOCUS

11-2 Inside a DoS Attack

A DoS attack typically involves the misuse of standard TCP/IP protocols or connection processes so that the target for the DoS attack responds in a way designed to create maximum trouble. Five common types of attacks include the following:

- **ICMP Attacks** The network is flooded with ICMP echo requests (i.e., pings) that have a broadcast destination address and a faked source address of the intended target. Because it is a broadcast message, every computer on the network responds to the faked source address so that the target is overwhelmed by responses. Because there are often dozens of computers in the same broadcast domain, each message generates dozens of messages at the target.
- **UDP Attacks** This attack is similar to an ICMP attack, except that it uses UDP echo requests instead of ICMP echo requests.
- **TCP SYN Floods** The target is swamped with repeated SYN requests to establish a TCP connection, but when the target responds (usually to a faked source address), there is no response. The target continues to allocate TCP control blocks,

expects each of the requests to be completed, and gradually runs out of memory.

- **UNIX Process Table Attacks** This is similar to a TCP SYN flood, but instead of TCP SYN packets, the target is swamped by UNIX open connection requests that are never completed. The target allocates open connections and gradually runs out of memory.
- **Finger of Death Attacks** This is similar to the TCP SYN flood, but instead the target is swamped by finger requests that are never disconnected.
- **DNS Recursion Attacks** The attacker sends DNS requests to DNS servers (often within the target's network) but spoofs the from address so the requests appear to come from the target computer that is overwhelmed by DNS responses. DNS responses are larger packets than ICMP, UDP, or SYN responses, so the effects can be stronger.

Adapted from: "Web Site Security and Denial of Service Protection," www.nwfusion.com.

Another possibility under discussion by the Internet community as a whole is to require Internet Service Providers (ISPs) to verify that all incoming messages they receive from their customers have valid source IP addresses. This would prevent the use of faked IP addresses and enable users to easily filter out DoS messages from a given address. It would make it virtually impossible for a DoS attack to succeed and much harder for a DDoS attack to succeed. Because small- to medium-sized businesses often have poor security and become the unwilling accomplices in DDoS attacks, many ISPs are beginning to impose security restrictions on them, such as requiring firewalls to prevent unauthorized access (firewalls are discussed later in this chapter).

11.3.3 Theft Protection

One often overlooked security risk is theft. Computers and network equipment are commonplace items that have a good resale value. Several industry sources estimate that more than $1 billion is lost to computer theft each year, with many of the stolen items ending up on Internet auction sites (e.g., eBay).

Physical security is a key component of theft protection. Most organizations require anyone entering their offices to go through some level of physical security. For example, most offices have security guards and require all visitors to be authorized by an organization employee. Universities are one of the few organizations that permit anyone to enter their facilities without verification. Therefore, you'll see most computer equipment and network devices protected by locked doors or security cables so that someone cannot easily steal them.

One of the most common targets for theft is laptop computers. More laptop computers are stolen from employee's homes, cars, and hotel rooms than any other device. Airports are another common place for laptop thefts. It is hard to provide physical security for traveling employees, but most organizations provide regular reminders to their employees to take special care when traveling with laptops. Nonetheless, they are still the most commonly stolen device.

11.3.4 Device Failure Protection

Eventually, every computer network device, cable, or leased circuit will fail. It's just a matter of time. Some computers, devices, cables, and circuits are more reliable than others, but every network manager has to be prepared for a failure.

The best way to prevent a failure from impacting business continuity is to build **redundancy** into the network. For any network component that would have a major impact on business continuity, the network designer provides a second, redundant component. For example, if the Internet connection is important to the organization, the network designer ensures that there are at least two connections into the Internet—each provided by a different common carrier, so that if one common carrier's network goes down, the organization can still reach the Internet via the other common carrier's network. This means, of course, that the organization now requires two routers to connect to the Internet, because there is little use in having two Internet connections if they both run through the same router; if that one router goes down, having a second Internet connection provides no value.

This same design principle applies to the organization's internal networks. If the core backbone is important (and it usually is), then the organization must have two core backbones, each served by different devices. Each distribution backbone that connects to the core backbone (e.g., a building backbone that connects to a campus backbone) must also have two connections (and two routers) into the core backbone.

The next logical step is to ensure that each access layer LAN also has two connections into the distribution backbone. Redundancy can be expensive, so at some point, most organizations decide that not all parts of the network need to be protected. Most organizations build redundancy into their core backbone and their Internet connections but are very careful in choosing which distribution backbones (i.e., building backbones) and access layer LANs will have redundancy. Only those building backbones and access LANs that are truly important will have redundancy. This is why a risk assessment is important, because it is too expensive to protect the entire network. Most organizations only provide redundancy in mission-critical backbones and LANs (e.g., those that lead to servers).

Redundancy also applies to servers. Most organizations use a server farm, rather than a single server, so that if one server fails, the other servers in the server farm continue to operate and there is little impact. Some organizations use **fault-tolerant servers** that contain many redundant components so that if one of its components fails, it will continue to operate.

Redundant array of independent disks (RAID) is a storage technology that, as the name suggests, is made of many separate disk drives. When a file is written to a RAID device, it is written across several separate, redundant disks.

There are several types of RAID. RAID 0 uses multiple disk drives and therefore is faster than traditional storage, because the data can be written or read in parallel across several disks, rather than sequentially on the same disk. RAID 1 writes duplicate copies of all data on at least two different disks; this means that if one disk in the RAID array fails, there is no data loss because there is a second copy of the data stored on a different disk. This is sometimes called **disk mirroring**, because the data on one disk is copied (or mirrored) onto another. RAID 2 provides error checking to ensure no errors have occurred during the reading or writing process. RAID 3 provides a better and faster error checking process than RAID 2. RAID 4 provides slightly faster read access than RAID 3 because of the way it allocates the data to different disk drives. RAID 5 provides slightly faster read and write access because of the way it allocates the error checking data to different disk drives. RAID 6 can survive the failure of two drives with no data loss.

Power outages are one of the most common causes of network failures. An **uninterruptable power supply (UPS)** is a device that detects power failures and permits the devices attached to it to operate as long as its battery lasts. UPS for home use are inexpensive and often provide power for up to 15 minutes—long enough for you to save your work and shut down your computer. UPS for large organizations often have batteries that last for an hour and permit mission-critical servers, switches, and routers to operate until the organization's backup generator can be activated.

11.3.5 Disaster Protection

A disaster is an event that destroys a large part of the network and computing infrastructure in one part of the organization. Disasters are usually caused by natural forces (e.g., hurricanes, floods, earthquakes, fires), but some can be humanmade (e.g., arson, bombs, terrorism).

Avoiding Disaster Ideally, you want to avoid a disaster, which can be difficult. For example, how do you avoid an earthquake? There are, however, some commonsense steps you can take to avoid the full impact of a disaster from affecting your network. The most fundamental is again redundancy; store critical data in at least two very different places, so if a disaster hits one place, your data are still safe.

Other steps depend on the disaster to be avoided. For example, to avoid the impact of a flood, key network components and data should never be located near rivers or in the

MANAGEMENT	11-4 Recovering from Katrina
FOCUS	

*A*lthough natural disasters don't happen frequently, people remember them long after their time. The last natural disaster to have been categorized among the 10 worst disasters of the last 101 years is Katrina. This Category 5 hurricane caused terrifying damage but also allowed us to better prepare for future natural disasters.

As Hurricane Katrina swept over New Orleans, Ochsner Hospital lost two of its three backup power generators, knocking out air-conditioning in the 95-degree heat. Fans were brought out to cool patients, but temperatures inside critical computer and networking equipment reached 150 degrees. Kurt Induni, the hospital's network manager, shut down part of the network and the mainframe with its critical patient records system to ensure they survived the storm. The hospital returned to paper-based record keeping, but Induni managed to keep email alive, which became critical when the telephone system failed and a main fiber line was cut. E-mail through the hospital's T-3 line into Baton Rouge became the only reliable means of communication. After the storm, the mainframe was turned back on and the patient records were updated.

While Ochsner Hospital remained open, Kindred Hospital was forced to evacuate patients (under military protection from looters and snipers). The patients' files, all electronic, were simply transferred over the network to other hospitals with no worry about lost records, X-rays, CT scans, and such.

In contrast, the Louisiana court system learned a hard lesson. The court system is administered by each individual parish (i.e., county) and not every parish had a disaster recovery plan or even backups of key documents–many parishes still used old paper files that were destroyed by the storm. "We've got people in jails all over the state right now that have no paperwork and we have no way to offer them any kind of means for adjudication," said Freddie Manit, CIO for the Louisiana Ninth Judicial District Court. No paperwork means no prosecution, even for felons with long records, so many prisoners would simply be released. Sometimes losing data is not the worst thing that can happen.

Adapted from: http://www.popularmechanics.com/science/environment/natural-disasters/4219861; Phil Hochmuth, "Weathering Katrina," *NetworkWorld*, September 19, 2005, pp. 1, 20; and M. K. McGee, "Storm Shows Benefits, Failures of Technology," *Information week*, September 15, 2005, p. 34.

basement of a building. To avoid the impact of a tornado, key network components and data should be located underground. To reduce the impact of fire, a fire suppression system should be installed in all key data centers. To reduce the impact of terrorist activities, the location of key network components and data should be kept a secret and should be protected by security guards.

Disaster Recovery A critical element in correcting problems from a disaster is the **disaster recovery plan**, which should address various levels of response to a number of possible disasters and should provide for partial or complete recovery of all data, application software, network components, and physical facilities. A complete disaster recovery plan covering all these areas is beyond the scope of this text. Figure 11-10 provides a summary of many key issues. A good example of a disaster recovery plan is MIT's business continuity plan at web.mit.edu/security/www/pubplan.htm. Some firms prefer the term *business continuity plan.*

The most important elements of the disaster recovery plan are **backup** and **recovery controls** that enable the organization to recover its data and restart its application software should some portion of the network fail. The simplest approach is to make backup copies of all organizational data and software routinely and to store these backup copies off-site.

FIGURE 11-10

Elements of a disaster recovery plan

A good disaster recovery plan should include the following:

- The name of the decision-making manager who is in charge of the disaster recovery operation. A second manager should be indicated in case the first manager is unavailable.
- Staff assignments and responsibilities during the disaster.
- A preestablished list of priorities that states what is to be fixed first.
- Location of alternative facilities operated by the company or a professional disaster recovery firm and procedures for switching operations to those facilities using backups of data and software.
- Recovery procedures for the data communication facilities (backbone network, metropolitan area network, wide area network, and local area network), servers, and application systems. This includes information on the location of circuits and devices, whom to contact for information, and the support that can be expected from vendors, along with the name and telephone number of the person at each vendor to contact.
- Action to be taken in case of partial damage or threats such as bomb threats, fire, water or electrical damage, sabotage, civil disorders, and vendor failures.
- Manual processes to be used until the network is functional.
- Prodecures to ensure adequate updating and testing of the disaster recovery plan.
- Storage of the data, software, and the disaster recovery plan itself in a safe area where they cannot be destroyed by a catastrophe. This area must be accessible, however, to those who need to use the plan.

Most organizations make daily backups of all critical information, with less important information (e.g., email files) backed up weekly. Backups used to be done on tapes that were physically shipped to an off-site location, but more and more, companies are using their WAN connections to transfer data to remote locations (it's faster and cheaper than moving tapes). Backups should always be encrypted (encryption is discussed later in the chapter) to ensure that no unauthorized users can access them.

Continuous data protection (CDP) is another option that firms are using in addition to or instead of regular backups. With CDP, copies of all data and transactions on selected servers are written to CDP servers as the transaction occurs. CDP is more flexible than traditional backups that take snapshots of data at specific times or than disk mirroring, which duplicates the contents of a disk from second to second. CDP enables data to be stored miles from the originating server and time-stamps all transactions to enable organizations to restore data to any specific point in time. For example, suppose a virus brings down a server at 2:45 P.M. The network manager can restore the server to the state it was in at 2:30 p.m. and simply resume operations as though the virus had not hit.

Backups and CDP ensure that important data are safe, but they do not guarantee the data can be used. The disaster recovery plan should include a documented and tested approach to recovery. The recovery plan should have specific goals for different types of disasters. For example, if the main database server was destroyed, how long should it take the organization to have the software and data back in operation by using the backups? Conversely, if the main data center was completely destroyed, how long should it take? The answers to these questions have very different implications for costs. Having a spare network server or a server with extra capacity that can be used in the event of the loss of the primary server is one thing. Having a spare data center ready to operate within 12 hours (for example) is an entirely different proposition.

Many organizations have a disaster recovery plan, but only a few test their plans. A **disaster recovery drill** is much like a fire drill in that it tests the disaster recovery plan and provides staff the opportunity to practice little-used skills to see what works and what doesn't work before a disaster happens and the staff must use the plan for real. Without regular disaster recovery drills, the only time a plan is tested is when it must be used. For example, when an island-wide blackout shut down all power in Bermuda, the backup generator in the British Caymanian Insurance office automatically took over and kept the company operating. However, the key-card security system, which was not on the generator, shut down, locking out all employees and forcing them to spend the day at the beach. No one had thought about the security system and the plan had not been tested.

Organizations are usually much better at backing up important data than are individual users. When did you last back up the data on your computer? What would you do if your computer was stolen or destroyed? There is an inexpensive alternative to CDP for home users. **Online backup** services such as mozy.com enable you to back up the data on your computer to their server on the Internet. You download and install client software that enables you to select what folders to back up. After you back up the data for the first time, which takes a while, the software will run every few hours and automatically back up all changes to the server, so you never have to think about backups again. If you need to recover some or all of your data, you can go to their Web site and download it.

MANAGEMENT FOCUS   11-5 **Disaster Recovery Hits Home**

"*T*he building is on fire" were the first words she said as I answered the phone. It was just before noon and one of my students had called me from her office on the top floor of the business school at the University of Georgia. The roofing contractor had just started what would turn out to be the worst fire in the region in more than 20 years, although we didn't know it then. I had enough time to gather up the really important things from my office on the ground floor (memorabilia, awards, and pictures from 10 years in academia) when the fire alarm went off. I didn't bother with the computer; all the files were backed up off-site.

Ten hours, 100 firefighters, and 1.5 million gallons of water later, the fire was out. Then our work began. The fire had completely destroyed the top floor of the building, including my 20-computer networking lab. Water had severely damaged the rest of the building, including my office, which, I learned later, had been flooded by almost 2 feet of water at the height of the fire. My computer, and virtually all the computers in the building, were damaged by the water and unusable.

My personal files were unaffected by the loss of the computer in my office; I simply used the backups and continued working—after making new backups and giving them to a friend to store at his house. The Web server I managed had been backed up to another server on the opposite side of campus 2 days before (on its usual weekly backup cycle), so we had lost only 2 days' worth of changes. In less than 24 hours, our Web site was operational; I had our server's files mounted on the university library's Web server and redirected the university's DNS server to route traffic from our old server address to our new temporary home.

Unfortunately, the rest of our network did not fare as well. Our primary Web server had been backed up to tape the night before, and though the tapes were stored off-site, the tape drive was not; the tape drive was destroyed and no one else on campus had one that could read our tapes; it took 5 days to get a replacement and reestablish the Web site. Within 30 days we were operating from temporary offices with a new network, and 90% of the office computers and their data had been successfully recovered.

Living through a fire changes a person. I'm more careful now about backing up my files, and I move ever so much more quickly when a fire alarm sounds. But I still can't get used to the rust that is slowly growing on my "recovered" computer.

Source: Alan Dennis

Disaster Recovery Outsourcing Most large organizations have a two-level disaster recovery plan. When they build networks, they build enough capacity and have enough spare equipment to recover from a minor disaster such as loss of a major server or a portion of the network (if any such disaster can truly be called minor). This is the first level. Building a network that has sufficient capacity to quickly recover from a major disaster such as the loss of an entire data center is beyond the resources of most firms. Therefore, most large organizations rely on professional disaster recovery firms to provide this second-level support for major disasters.

Many large firms outsource their disaster recovery efforts by hiring **disaster recovery firms** that provide a wide range of services. At the simplest, disaster recovery firms provide secure storage for backups. Full services include a complete networked data center that clients can use when they experience a disaster. Once a company declares a disaster, the disaster recovery firm immediately begins recovery operations using the backups stored on site and can have the organization's entire data network back in operation on the disaster recovery firm's computer systems within hours. Full services are not cheap, but compared to the potential millions of dollars that can be lost per day from the inability to access critical data and application systems, these systems quickly pay for themselves in time of disaster.

11.4 INTRUSION PREVENTION

Intrusion is the second main type of security problem and the one that tends to receive the most attention. No one wants an intruder breaking into his or her network.

Four types of intruders may attempt to gain unauthorized access to computer networks. The first are casual intruders who have only a limited knowledge of computer security. They simply cruise along the Internet trying to access any computer they come across. Their unsophisticated techniques are the equivalent of trying doorknobs, and, until recently, only those networks that left their front doors unlocked were at risk. Unfortunately, a variety of hacking tools are now available on the Internet that enable even novices to launch sophisticated intrusion attempts. Novice attackers who use such tools are sometimes called *script kiddies*.

The second type of intruders are experts in security, but their motivation is the thrill of the hunt. They break into computer networks because they enjoy the challenge and enjoy showing off for friends or embarrassing the network owners. These intruders are called **hackers** and often have a strong philosophy against ownership of data and software. Most cause little damage and make little attempt to profit from their exploits, but those who do can cause major problems. Hackers who cause damage are often called **crackers**.

The third type of intruder is the most dangerous. They are professional hackers who break into corporate or government computers for specific purposes, such as espionage, fraud, or intentional destruction. The U.S. Department of Defense (DoD), which routinely monitors attacks against U.S. military targets, has until recently concluded that most attacks are individuals or small groups of hackers in the first two categories. While some of their attacks have been embarrassing (e.g., defacement of some military and intelligence Web sites), there have been no serious security risks. However, in the late 1990s, the DoD noticed a small but growing set of intentional attacks that they classify as exercises, exploratory attacks designed to test the effectiveness of certain software attack weapons. Therefore, they established an **information warfare** program and a new organization responsible for coordinating the defense of military networks under the U.S. Space Command.

The fourth type of intruder is also very dangerous. These are organization employees who have legitimate access to the network but who gain access to information they are not authorized to use. This information could be used for their own personnel gain, sold to competitors, or fraudulently changed to give the employee extra income. Many security break-ins are caused by this type of intruder.

The key principle in preventing intrusion is to be *proactive*. This means routinely testing your security systems before an intruder does. Many steps can be taken to prevent intrusion and unauthorized access to organizational data and networks, but no network is completely safe. The best rule for high security is to do what the military does: Do not keep extremely sensitive data online. Data that need special security are stored in computers isolated from other networks. In the following sections, we discuss the most important security controls for preventing intrusion and for recovering from intrusion when it occurs.

11.4.1 Security Policy

In the same way that a disaster recovery plan is critical to controlling risks due to disruption, destruction, and disaster, a **security policy** is critical to controlling risk due to intrusion. The security policy should clearly define the important assets to be safeguarded and the important controls needed to do that. It should have a section devoted to what employees should and should not do. Also, it should contain a clear plan for routinely training employees—particularly end-users with little computer expertise—on key security rules and a clear plan for routinely testing and improving the security controls in place (Figure 11-11). A good set of examples and templates is available at www.sans.org/resources/policies.

11.4.2 Perimeter Security and Firewalls

Ideally, you want to stop external intruders at the perimeter of your network so that they cannot reach the servers inside. There are three basic access points into most networks: the

FIGURE 11-11

Elements of a security policy

> **A good security policy should include the following:**
>
> - The name of the decision-making manager who is in charge of security
> - An incident reporting system and a rapid-response team to respond to security breaches in progress
> - A risk assessment with priorities as to which assets are most important
> - Effective controls placed at all major access points into the network to prevent or deter access by external agents
> - Effective controls placed within the network to ensure that internal users cannot exceed their authorized access
> - Use of minimum number of controls possible to reduce management time and to provide the least inconvenience to users
> - An acceptable use policy that explains to users what they can and cannot do, including guidelines for accessing others' accounts, password security, email rules, and so on
> - A procedure for monitoring changes to important network components (e.g., routers, DNS servers)
> - A plan to routinely train users regarding security policies and build awareness of security risks
> - A plan to routinely test and update all security controls that includes monitoring of popular press and vendor reports of security holes
> - An annual audit and review of the security practices

FIGURE 11-12

Using a firewall to protect networks

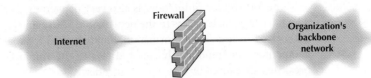

Internet, LANS, and WLANs. Recent surveys suggest that the most common access point for intrusion is the Internet connection (70% of organizations experienced an attack from the Internet), followed by LANs and WLANs (30%). External intruders are most likely to use the Internet connection, whereas internal intruders are most likely to use the LAN or WLAN. Because the Internet is the most common source of intrusions, the focus of perimeter security is usually on the Internet connection, although physical security is also important.

A **firewall** is commonly used to secure an organization's Internet connection. A firewall is a router or special-purpose device that examines packets flowing into and out of a network and restricts access to the organization's network. The network is designed so that a firewall is placed on every network connection between the organization and the Internet (Figure 11-12). No access is permitted except through the firewall. Some firewalls have the ability to detect and prevent denial-of-service attacks as well as unauthorized access attempts. Three commonly used types of firewalls are packet-level firewalls, application-level firewalls, and NAT firewalls.

Packet-Level Firewalls A **packet-level firewall** examines the source and destination address of every network packet that passes through it. It only allows packets into or out of the organization's networks that have acceptable source and destination addresses. In general, the addresses are examined only at the transport layer (TCP port ID) and network layer (IP address). Each packet is examined individually, so the firewall has no knowledge of what packets came before. It simply chooses to permit entry or exit based on the contents of the packet itself. This type of firewall is the simplest and least secure because it does not monitor the contents of the packets or why they are being transmitted and typically does not log the packets for later analysis.

The network manager writes a set of rules (called an **access control list [ACL]**) for the packet-level firewall so it knows what packets to permit into the network and what packets to deny entry. Remember that the IP packet contains the source IP address and the destination address and that the TCP segment has the destination port number that identifies the application-layer software to which the packet is going. Most application layer software on servers uses standard TCP port numbers. The Web (HTTP) uses port 80, whereas email (SMTP) uses port 25.

Suppose that the organization had a public Web server with an IP address of 128.192.44.44 and an email server with an address of 128.192.44.45 (see Figure 11-13). The network manager wants to make sure that no one outside of the organization can change the contents of the Web server (e.g., by using telnet or FTP). The ACL could be written to include a rule that permits the Web server to receive HTTP packets from the Internet (but other types of packets would be discarded). For example, the rule would say if the source address is anything, the destination IP address is 128.192.44.44, and the destination TCP port is 80, then permit the packet into the network; see the ACL on the firewall in Figure 11-13. Likewise, we could add a rule to the ACL that would permit SMTP packets to reach the email server: If the source address is anything, the destination is 128.192.44.45 and the destination TCP port is 25, then permit the packet through (see Figure 11-13). The last line in the ACL is usually a rule that says to deny entry to all other packets that have

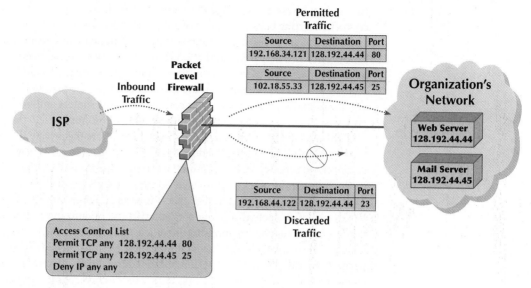

FIGURE 11-13 How packet-level firewalls work

not been specifically permitted (some firewalls come automatically configured to deny all packets other than those explicitly permitted, so this command would not be needed). With this ACL, if an external intruder attempted to use telnet (port 23) to reach the Web server, the firewall would deny entry to the packet and simply discard it.

Although source IP addresses can be used in the ACL, they often are not used. Most hackers have software that can change the source IP address on the packets they send (called **IP spoofing**), so using the source IP address in security rules is not usually worth the effort. Some network managers do routinely include a rule in the ACL that denies entry to all packets coming from the Internet that have a source IP address of a subnet inside the organization, because any such packets must have a spoofed address and therefore obviously are an intrusion attempt.

Application-Level Firewalls An **application-level firewall** is more expensive and more complicated to install and manage than a packet-level firewall, because it examines the contents of the application-level packet and searches for known attacks (see Security Holes later in this chapter). Application-layer firewalls have rules for each application they can process. For example, most application-level firewalls can check Web packets (HTTP), email packets (SMTP), and other common protocols. In some cases, special rules must be written by the organization to permit the use of application software it has developed.

Remember from Chapter 5 that TCP uses connection-oriented messaging in which a client first establishes a connection with a server before beginning to exchange data. Application-level firewalls can use *stateful inspection*, which means that they monitor and record the status of each connection and can use this information in making decisions about what packets to discard as security threats.

Many application-level firewalls prohibit external users from uploading executable files. In this way, intruders (or authorized users) cannot modify any software unless they have physical access to the firewall. Some refuse changes to their software unless it is done by the vendor. Others also actively monitor their own software and automatically disable outside connections if they detect any changes.

Network Address Translation Firewalls **Network address translation (NAT)** is the process of converting between one set of public IP addresses that are viewable from the Internet and a second set of private IP addresses that are hidden from people outside of the organization. NAT is transparent, in that no computer knows it is happening. Although NAT can be done for several reasons, the most common reasons are IPv4 address conservation and security. If external intruders on the Internet can't see the private IP addresses inside your organization, they can't attack your computers. Most routers and firewalls today have NAT built into them, even inexpensive routers designed for home use.

The **NAT firewall** uses an address table to translate the private IP addresses used inside the organization into proxy IP addresses used on the Internet. When a computer inside the organization accesses a computer on the Internet, the firewall changes the source IP address in the outgoing IP packet to its own address. It also sets the source port number in the TCP segment to a unique number that it uses as an index into its address table to find the IP address of the actual sending computer in the organization's internal network. When the external computer responds to the request, it addresses the message to the firewall's IP address. The firewall receives the incoming message, and after ensuring the packet should be permitted inside, changes the destination IP address to the private IP address of the internal computer and changes the TCP port number to the correct port number before transmitting it on the internal network.

This way systems outside the organization never see the actual internal IP addresses, and thus they think there is only one computer on the internal network. Most organizations also increase security by using private internal addresses. For example, if the organization has been assigned the Internet 128.192.55.X address domain, the NAT firewall would be assigned an address such as 128.192.55.1. Internal computers, however, would *not* be assigned addresses in the 128.192.55.X subnet. Instead, they would be assigned unauthorized Internet addresses such as 10.3.3.55 (addresses in the 10.X.X.X domain are not assigned to organizations but instead are reserved for use by private intranets). Because these internal addresses are never used on the Internet but are always converted by the firewall, this poses no problems for the users. Even if attackers discover the actual internal IP address, it would be impossible for them to reach the internal address from the Internet because the addresses could not be used to reach the organization's computers.

Firewall Architecture Many organizations use layers of NAT, packet-level, and application-level firewalls (Figure 11-14). Packet-level firewalls are used as an initial screen from the Internet into a network devoted solely to servers intended to provide public access (e.g., Web servers, public DNS servers). This network is sometimes called the *DMZ* (*demilitarized zone*) because it contains the organization's servers but does not provide complete security for them. This packet-level firewall will permit Web requests and similar access to the DMZ network servers but will deny FTP access to these servers from the Internet because no one except internal users should have the right to modify the servers. Each major portion of the organization's internal networks has its own NAT firewall to grant (or deny) access based on rules established by that part of the organization.

This figure also shows how a packet sent by a client computer inside one of the internal networks protected by a NAT firewall would flow through the network. The packet created by the client has the client's source address and the source port number of the process on the client that generated the packet (an HTTP packet going to a Web server, as you can tell from the destination port address of 80). When the packet reaches the firewall, the firewall changes the source address on the IP packet to its own address and changes the source port number to an index it will use to identify the client computer's address and port number. The destination address and port number are unchanged. The firewall then sends the packet

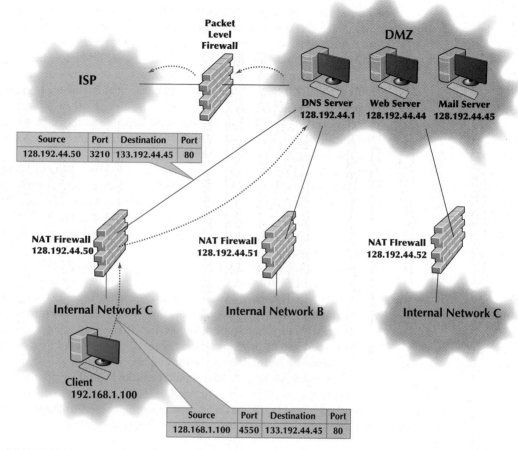

FIGURE 11-14 A typical network design using firewalls

on its way to the destination. When the destination Web server responds to this packet, it will respond using the firewall's address and port number. When the firewall receives the incoming packets, it will use the destination port number to identify what IP address and port number to use inside the internal network, change the inbound packet's destination and port number, and send it into the internal network so it reaches the client computer.

Physical Security One important element to prevent unauthorized users from accessing an internal LAN is *physical security*: preventing outsiders from gaining access into the organization's offices, server room, or network equipment facilities. Both main and remote physical facilities should be secured adequately and have the proper controls. Good security requires implementing the proper access controls so that only authorized personnel can enter closed areas where servers and network equipment are located or access the network. The network components themselves also have a level of physical security. Computers can have locks on their power switches or passwords that disable the screen and keyboard.

In the previous section we discussed the importance of locating backups and servers at separate (off-site) locations. Some companies have also argued that by having many servers in different locations, you can reduce your risk and improve business continuity. Does having many servers disperse risk, or does it increase the points of vulnerability? A clear disaster recovery plan with an off-site backup and server facility can disperse risk, like distributed server systems. Distributed servers offer many more physical vulnerabilities to an attacker: more machines to guard, upgrade, patch, and defend. Many times these dispersed machines are all part of the same logical domain, which means that breaking into one of them often can give the attacker access to the resources of the others. It is our feeling that a well-backed-up, centralized data center can be made inherently more secure than a proliferated base of servers.

Proper security education, background checks, and the implementation of error and fraud controls are also very important. In many cases, the simplest means to gain access is to become employed as a janitor and access the network at night. In some ways this is easier than the previous methods because the intruder only has to insert a listening device or computer into the organization's network to record messages. Three areas are vulnerable to this type of unauthorized access: wireless LANs, network cabling, and network devices.

Wireless LANs are the easiest target for **eavesdropping** because they often reach beyond the physical walls of the organization. Chapter 7 discussed the techniques of WLAN security, so we do not repeat them here.

Network cables are the next easiest target for eavesdropping because they often run long distances and usually are not regularly checked for tampering. The cables owned by the organization and installed within its facility are usually the first choice for eavesdropping. It is 100 times easier to tap a local cable than it is to tap an interexchange channel because it is extremely difficult to identify the specific circuits belonging to any one organization in a highly multiplexed switched interexchange circuit operated by a common carrier. Local cables should be secured behind walls and above ceilings, and telephone equipment and switching rooms (wiring closets) should be locked and their doors equipped with alarms. The primary goal is to control physical access by employees or vendors to the connector cables and modems. This includes restricting their access to the wiring closets in which all the communication wires and cables are connected.

TECHNICAL FOCUS **11-3 Data Security Requires Physical Security**

The general consensus is that if someone can physically get to your server for some period of time, then all of your information on the computer (except perhaps strongly encrypted data) is available to the attacker.

With a Windows server, the attacker simply boots the computer from the CD drive with a Knoppix version of Linux. (Knoppix is Linux on a CD.) If the computer won't boot from the CD, the attacker simply changes the BIOS to make it boot from the CD. Knoppix finds all the drivers for the specific computer and gives you a Linux desktop that can fully read all of the NTFS or FAT32 files.

But what about Windows password access? Nothing to it. Knoppix completely bypasses it. The attacker can then read, copy, or transmit any of the files on the Windows machine. Similar attacks are also possible on a Linux or Unix server, but they are slightly more difficult.

Certain types of cable can impair or increase security by making eavesdropping easier or more difficult. Obviously, any wireless network is at extreme risk for eavesdropping because anyone in the area of the transmission can easily install devices to monitor the radio or infrared signals. Conversely, fiber-optic cables are harder to tap, thus increasing security. Some companies offer armored cable that is virtually impossible to cut without special tools.

Other cables have built-in alarm systems. The U.S. Air Force, for example, uses pressurized cables that are filled with gas. If the cable is cut, the gas escapes, pressure drops, and an alarm is sounded.

Network devices such as switches and routers should be secured in a locked wiring closet. As discussed in Chapter 7, all messages within a given local area network are actually received by all computers on the WLAN, although they only process those messages addressed to them. It is rather simple to install a **sniffer program** that records all messages received for later (unauthorized) analysis. A computer with a sniffer program could then be plugged into an unattended switch to eavesdrop on all message traffic. A **secure switch** makes this type of eavesdropping more difficult by requiring a special authorization code to be entered before new computers can be added.

11.4.3 Server and Client Protection

Security Holes Even with physical security and firewalls, the servers and client computers on a network may not be safe because of **security holes**. A security hole is simply a bug that permits unauthorized access. Many commonly used operating systems have major security holes well known to potential intruders. Many security holes have been documented and "patches" are available from vendors to fix them, but network managers may be unaware of all the holes or simply forget to update their systems with new patches regularly.

A complete discussion of security holes is beyond the scope of this book. Many security holes are highly technical; for example, sending a message designed to overflow a memory buffer, thereby placing a short command into a very specific memory area that performs some function. Others are rather simple, but not obvious. For example, the attacker sends a message that lists the server's address as both the sender and the destination, so the server repeatedly sends messages to itself until it crashes.

MANAGEMENT | **11-6 Fake Antivirus?**

FOCUS

The world of computer viruses is constantly evolving and becoming more and more advanced. At the beginning of Internet, viruses were designed to do funny things (such as turn text on your screen upside down), but today they are designed to get your money and private information. Once a virus is installed on a computer, it will interact with a remote computer and transfer sensitive data to that computer. Antivirus software was developed to prevent viruses from being installed on computers. However, not all antivirus software is made equal.

There are many antivirus software companies that offer to scan your computer for free. Yes, for free! An old saying relates that if something sounds too good to be true, it probably is. Free antivirus software is not an

exception. Chester Wisniewky, at Sophos Labs, explains that once you have downloaded a free antivirus on to your computer, you have actually downloaded malware. Once you launch this software on your computer, it looks and behaves like a legitimate antivirus. Many of these free antivirus software packages are fully multilingual. The software has a very user-friendly GUI (graphical user interface) that looks and behaves like a legitimate antivirus. However, once you start scanning your computer, it will mark legitimate files on your computer as worms and Trojans and will give you a warning that your computer is infected. A regular user gets scared at this point and allows the software to remove the infected files. What is really happening is that malware is installed on your computer that will scan for any sensitive information and send this information to a host.

Rather than trying to get a free antivirus, spend money on a legitimate product such as Sophos, Symantec, or McAfee. Popular news magazines, such as *PC Magazine*, provide annual reviews of legitimate antivirus software and also the free antivirus. Your best protection against exploits of this kind is education.

Adapted from: "Which Antivirus Is the Best" (www.pc antivirusreviews.com); "Fake Antivirus: What Are They and How Do You Avoid Them?" by Cassie Bodnar, October 11, 2013 (blog.kaspersky.com)

Once a security hole is discovered, it is quickly circulated through the Internet. The race begins between hackers and security teams; hackers share their discovery with other hackers and security teams share the discovery with other security teams. CERT is the central clearinghouse for major Internet-related security holes, so the CERT team quickly responds to reports of new security problems and posts alerts and advisories on the Web and emails them to those who subscribe to its service. The developer of the software with the security hole usually works quickly to fix the security hole and produces a **patch** that corrects the hole. This patch is then shared with customers so they can download and apply it to their systems to prevent hackers from exploiting the hole to break in. Attacks that take advantage of a newly discovered security hole before a patch is developed are called **zero-day attacks**. One problem is that many network managers do not routinely respond to such security threats and immediately download and install the patch. Often it takes many months for patches to be distributed to most sites. Do you regularly install all the Windows or Mac updates on your computer?

Other security holes are not really holes but simply policies adopted by computer vendors that open the door for security problems, such as computer systems that come with a variety of preinstalled user accounts. These accounts and their initial passwords are well documented and known to all potential attackers. Network managers sometimes forget to change the passwords on these well-known accounts, thus enabling an attacker to slip in.

Operating Systems The American government requires certain levels of security in the operating systems and network operating systems it uses for certain applications. The minimum level of security is C2. Most major operating systems (e.g., Windows) provide at least C2. Most widely used systems are striving to meet the requirements of much higher security levels such as B2. Very few systems meet the highest levels of security (A1 and A2).

There has been a long running debate about whether the Windows operating system is less secure than other operating systems such as Linux. Every new attack on Windows systems ignites the debate; Windows detractors repeat "I told you so" while Windows defenders state that this happens mostly because Windows is the obvious system to attack since it is the most commonly used operating system and because of the hostility of the Windows detractors themselves.

There is a critical difference in what applications can do in Windows and in Linux. Linux (and its ancestor Unix) was first written as a multiuser operating system in which different users had different rights. Only some users were system administrators and had the rights to access and make changes to the critical parts of the operating system. All other users were barred from doing so.

11-4 Exploiting a Security Hole

*T*o exploit a security hole, the hacker has to know it's there. So how does a hacker find out? It's simple in the era of automated tools.

First, the hacker has to find the servers on a network. The hacker could start by using network scanning software to systematically probe every IP address on a network to find all the servers on the network. At this point, the hacker has narrowed the potential targets to a few servers.

Second, the hacker needs to learn what services are available on each server. To do this, he or she could use port scanning software to systematically probe every TCP/IP port on a given server. This would reveal which ports are in use and thus what services the server offers. For example, if the server has software that responds to port 80, it is a Web server, while if it responds to port 25, it is a mail server.

Third, the hacker would begin to seek out the exact software and version number of the server software providing each service. For example, suppose the hacker decides to target mail servers. There are a variety of tools that can probe the mail server software, and based on how the server software responds to certain messages, determine which manufacturer and version number of software is being used.

Finally, once the hacker knows which package and version number the server is using, the hacker uses tools designed to exploit the known security holes in the software. For example, some older mail server software packages do not require users to authenticate themselves (e.g., by a user id and password) before accepting SMTP packets for the mail server to forward. In this case, the hacker could create SMTP packets with fake source addresses and use the server to flood the Internet with spam (i.e., junk mail). In another case, a certain version of a well-known e-commerce package enabled users to pass operating system commands to the server simply by including a UNIX pipe symbol (|) and the command to the name of a file name to be uploaded; when the system opened the uploaded file, it also executed the command attached to it.

In contrast, Windows (and its ancestor DOS) was first written as an operating system for a single personal computer, an environment in which the user was in complete control of the computer and could do anything he or she liked. As a result, Windows applications regularly access and make changes to critical parts of the operating system. There are advantages to this. Windows applications can do many powerful things without the user needing to understand them. These applications can be very rich in features, and more important, they can appear to the user to be very friendly and easy to use. Everything appears to run "out-of-the-box" without modification. Windows has built these features into the core of their systems. Any major rewrite of Windows to prevent this would most likely cause significant incompatibilities with all applications designed to run under previous versions of Windows. To many, this would be a high price to pay for some unseen benefits called "security."

But there is a price for this friendliness. Hostile applications can easily take over the computer and literally do whatever they want without the user knowing. Simply put, there is a trade-off between ease of use and security. Increasing needs for security demand more checks and restrictions, which translates into less friendliness and fewer features. It may very well be that there is an inherent and permanent contradiction between the ease of use of a system and its security.

Trojan Horses One important tool in gaining unauthorized access is a **Trojan horse**. Trojans are remote access management consoles (sometimes called **rootkits**) that enable users to access a computer and manage it from afar. If you see free software that will enable you to control your computer from anywhere, be careful; the software may also permit an attacker to control your computer from anywhere! Trojans are more often concealed in other software that unsuspecting users download over the Internet (their name alludes to the original Trojan horse). Music and video files shared on Internet music sites are common carriers of Trojans. When the user downloads and plays a music file, it plays normally and the attached Trojan software silently installs a small program that enables the attacker to take complete control of the user's computer, so the user is unaware that anything bad has happened. The attacker then simply connects to the user's computer and has the same access and controls as the user. Many Trojans are completely undetectable by the very best antivirus software.

One of the first major Trojans was Back Orifice, which aggressively attacked Windows servers. Back Orifice gave the attacker the same functions as the administrator of the infected server, and then some: complete file and network control, device and registry access, with packet and application redirection. It was every administrator's worst nightmare, and every attacker's dream.

More recently, Trojans have morphed into tools such as MoSucker and Optix Pro. These attack consoles now have one-button clicks to disable firewalls, antivirus software, and any other defensive process that might be running on the victim's computer. The attacker can choose what port the Trojan runs on, what it is named, and when it runs. They can listen in to a computer's microphone or look through an attached camera—even if the device appears to be off. Figure 11-15 shows a menu from one Trojan that illustrates some of the "fun stuff" that an attacker can do, such as opening and closing the CD tray, beeping the speaker, or reversing the mouse buttons so that clicking on the left button actually sends a right click.

Not only have these tools become powerful, but they are also very easy to use—much easier to use than the necessary defensive countermeasures to protect oneself from them. And what does the near future hold for Trojans? We can easily envision Trojans that schedule themselves to run at, say 2:00 A.M., choosing a random port, emailing the attacker that the machine is now "open for business" at port # NNNNN. The attackers can then step in, do whatever they want to do, run a script to erase most of their tracks, and then sign out and shut off the Trojan. Once the job is done, the Trojan could even erase itself from storage. Scary? Yes. And the future does not look better.

FIGURE 11-15

One menu on the control console for the Optix Pro Trojan

Source: windowsecurity.com

Spyware, **adware**, and DDoS agents are three types of Trojans. DDoS agents were discussed in the previous section. As the name suggests, spyware monitors what happens on the target computer. Spyware can record keystrokes that appear to be userids and passwords so the intruder can gain access to the user's account (e.g., bank accounts). Adware monitors a user's actions and displays pop-up advertisements on the user's screen. For example, suppose you clicked on the Web site for an online retailer. Adware might pop-up a window for a competitor, or, worse still, redirect your browser to the competitor's Web site. Many antivirus software packages now routinely search for and remove spyware, adware, and other Trojans and special-purpose antispyware software is available (e.g., Spybot). Some firewall vendors are now adding anti-Trojan logic to their devices to block any transmissions from infected computers from entering or leaving their networks.

11.4.4 Encryption

One of the best ways to prevent intrusion is **encryption**, which is a means of disguising information by the use of mathematical rules known as *algorithms*. Actually, *cryptography* is the more general and proper term. *Encryption* is the process of disguising information, whereas **decryption** is the process of restoring it to readable form. When information is in readable form, it is called **plaintext**; when in encrypted form, it is called **ciphertext**. Encryption can be used to encrypt files stored on a computer or to encrypt data in transit between computers.

There are two fundamentally different types of encryption: symmetric and asymmetric. With **symmetric encryption**, the key used to encrypt a message is the *same* as the one used to decrypt it. With **asymmetric encryption**, the key used to decrypt a message is *different* from the key used to encrypt it.

MANAGEMENT 11-7 **Sony's Spyware**

FOCUS

Sony BMG Entertainment, the music giant, included a spyware rootkit on audio CDs sold in the fall of 2005, including CDs by such artists as Celine Dion, Frank Sinatra, and Ricky Martin. The rootkit was automatically installed on any PC that played the infected CD. The rootkit was designed to track the behavior of users who might be illegally copying and distributing the music on the CD, with the goal of preventing illegal copies from being widely distributed.

Sony made two big mistakes. First, it failed to inform customers who purchased its CDs about the rootkit, so users unknowingly installed it. The rootkit used standard spyware techniques to conceal its existence to prevent users from discovering it. Second, Sony used a widely available rootkit, which meant that any knowledgeable user on the Internet could use the rootkit to take control of the infected computer. Several viruses have been written that exploit the rootkit and are now circulating on the Internet. The irony is that rootkit infringes on copyrights held by several open source projects, which means Sony was engaged in the very act it was trying to prevent: piracy.

When the rootkit was discovered, Sony was slow to apologize, slow to stop selling rootkit-infected CDs, and slow to help customers remove the rootkit. Several lawsuits have been filed in the United States and abroad seeking damages. The Federal Trade Commission (FTC) found on January 30, 2007, that Sony BMG's CD copy protection had violated Federal Law. Sony BMG had to reimburse consumers up to $150 to repair damages that were caused by the illegal software that was installed on users' computers without their consent. This adventure proved to be very costly for Sony BMG.

Adapted from: J.A. Halderman and E.W. Felton, "Lessons from the Sony CD DRM Episode," working paper, Princeton University, 2006; and "Sony Anti-Customer Technology Roundup and Time-Line," *www.boingboing.net*, February 15, 2006. Wikipedia.com

MANAGEMENT	11-8 Trojans at Home
FOCUS	

*I*t started with a routine phone call to technical support—one of our users had a software package that kept crashing. The network technician was sent to fix the problem but couldn't, so thoughts turned to a virus or Trojan. After an investigation, the security team found a remote FTP Trojan installed on the computer that was storing several gigabytes of cartoons and making them available across the Internet. The reason for the crash was that the FTP server was an old version that was not compatible with the computer's operating system. The Trojan was removed and life went on.

Three months later the same problem occurred on a different computer. Because the previous Trojan had been logged, the network support staff quickly recognized it as a Trojan. The same hacker had returned, storing the same cartoons on a different computer. This triggered a complete investigation. All computers on our Business School network were scanned and we found 15 computers that contained the Trojan. We gathered forensic evidence to help identify the attacker (e.g., log files, registry entries) and filed an incident report with the university incident response team, advising them to scan all computers on the university network immediately.

The next day, we found more computers containing the same FTP Trojan and the same cartoons. The attacker had come back overnight and taken control of more computers. This immediately escalated the problem. We cleaned some of the machines but left some available for use by the hacker to encourage him not to attack other computers. The network security manager replicated the software and used it to investigate how the Trojan worked. We determined that the software used a brute force attack to break the administrative password file on the standard image that we used in our computer labs. We changed the password and installed a security patch to our lab computer's standard configuration. We then upgraded all the lab computers and only then cleaned the remaining machines controlled by the attacker.

The attacker had also taken over many other computers on campus for the same purpose. With the forensic evidence that we and the university security incident response team had gathered, the case is now in court.

Source: Alan Dennis

Single-Key Encryption Symmetric encryption (also called *single-key encryption*) has two parts: the **algorithm** and the **key**, which personalizes the algorithm by making the transformation of data unique. Two pieces of identical information encrypted with the same algorithm but with different keys produce completely different ciphertexts. With symmetric encryption, the communicating parties must share the one key. If the algorithm is adequate and the key is kept secret, acquisition of the ciphertext by unauthorized personnel is of no consequence to the communicating parties.

Good encryption systems do not depend on keeping the algorithm secret. Only the keys need to be kept secret. The key is a relatively small numeric value (in terms of the number of bits). The larger the key, the more secure the encryption because large "key space" protects the ciphertext against those who try to break it by **brute-force attacks**—which simply means trying every possible key.

There should be a large enough number of possible keys that an exhaustive brute-force attack would take inordinately long or would cost more than the value of the encrypted information.

Because the same key is used to encrypt and decrypt, symmetric encryption can cause problems with **key management**; keys must be shared among the senders and receivers very carefully. Before two computers in a network can communicate using encryption, both must have the same key. This means that both computers can then send and read any messages that use that key. Companies often do not want one company to be able to read messages they send to another company, so this means that there must be a separate key used for communication with each company. These keys must be recorded but kept secure so that they cannot be stolen. Because the algorithm is known publicly, the disclosure of the key means the total compromise of encrypted messages. Managing this system of keys can be challenging.

One commonly used symmetric encryption technique is the **Data Encryption Standard (DES)**, which was developed in the mid-1970s by the U.S. government in conjunction with IBM. DES is standardized by the National Institute of Standards and Technology (NIST). The most common form of DES uses a 56-bit key, which experts can break in less than a day (i.e., experts with the right tools can figure out what a message encrypted using DES says without knowing the key in less than 24 hours). DES is no longer recommended for data needing high security, although some companies continue to use it for less important data.

Triple DES (3DES) is a newer standard that is harder to break. As the name suggests, it involves using DES three times, usually with three different keys to produce the encrypted text, which produces a stronger level of security because it has a total of 168 bits as the key (i.e., 3 times 56 bits).

The NIST's new standard, called **Advanced Encryption Standard (AES)**, has replaced DES. AES has key sizes of 128, 192, and 256 bits. NIST estimates that, using the most advanced computers and techniques available today, it will require about 150 trillion years to crack AES by brute force. As computers and techniques improve, the time requirement will drop, but AES seems secure for the foreseeable future; the original DES lasted 20 years, so AES may have a similar life-span.

Another commonly used symmetric encryption algorithm is **RC4**, developed by Ron Rivest of RSA Data Security, Inc. RC4 can use a key up to 256 bits long but most commonly uses a 40-bit key. It is faster to use than DES but suffers from the same problems from brute-force attacks: Its 40-bit key can be broken by a determined attacker in a day or two.

Today, the U.S. government considers encryption to be a weapon and regulates its export in the same way it regulates the export of machine guns or bombs. Present rules prohibit the export of encryption techniques with keys longer than 64 bits without permission, although exports to Canada and the European Union are permitted, and American banks and Fortune 100 companies are now permitted to use more powerful encryption techniques in their foreign offices. This policy made sense when only American companies had the expertise to develop powerful encryption software. Today, however, many non-American companies are developing encryption software that is more powerful than American software that is limited only by these rules. Therefore, the American software industry is lobbying the government to change the rules so that they can successfully compete overseas.

Public Key Encryption The most popular form of asymmetric encryption (also called **public key encryption**) is **RSA**, which was invented at MIT in 1977 by Rivest, Shamir, and Adleman, who founded RSA Data Security in 1982. The patent expired in 2000, so many new companies entered the market and public key software dropped in price. The RSA technique forms the basis for today's **public key infrastructure (PKI)**.

Public key encryption is inherently different from symmetric single-key systems like DES. Because public key encryption is asymmetric, there are two keys. One key (called the **public key**) is used to encrypt the message and a second, very different **private key** is used to decrypt the message. Keys are often 512 bits, 1,024 bits, or 2,048 bits in length.

Public key systems are based on one-way functions. Even though you originally know both the contents of your message and the public encryption key, once it is encrypted by the one-way function, the message cannot be decrypted without the private key. One-way functions, which are relatively easy to calculate in one direction, are impossible to "uncalculate" in the reverse direction. Public key encryption is one of the most secure encryption techniques available, excluding special encryption techniques developed by national security agencies.

Public key encryption greatly reduces the key management problem. Each user has its public key that is used to encrypt messages sent to it. These public keys are widely publicized (e.g., listed in a telephone book-style directory)—that's why they're called "public" keys. In addition, each user has a private key that decrypts only the messages that were encrypted by its public key. This private key is kept secret (that's why it's called the "private" key). The net result is that if two parties wish to communicate with one another, there is no need to exchange keys beforehand. Each knows the other's public key from the listing in a public directory and can communicate encrypted information immediately. The key management problem is reduced to the on-site protection of the private key.

Figure 11-16 illustrates how this process works. All public keys are published in a directory. When Organization A wants to send an encrypted message to Organization B, it looks through the directory to find its public key. It then encrypts the message using B's public key. This encrypted message is then sent through the network to Organization B, which decrypts the message using its private key.

FIGURE 11-16

Secure transmission with public key encryption

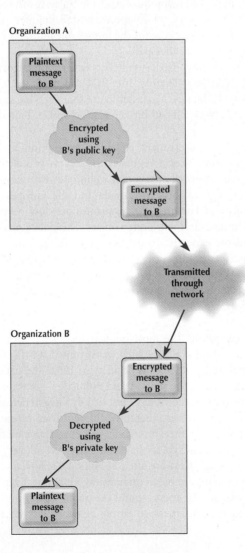

FIGURE 11-17
Authenticated and
secure transmission with
public key encryption

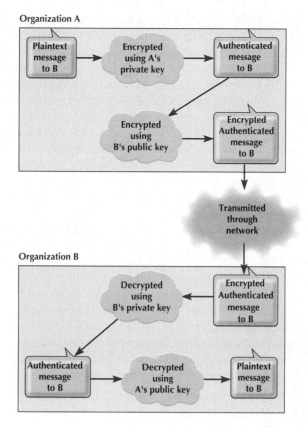

Authentication Public key encryption also permits the use of *digital signatures* through a process of **authentication**. When one user sends a message to another, it is difficult to legally prove who actually sent the message. Legal proof is important in many communications, such as bank transfers and buy/sell orders in currency and stock trading, which normally require legal signatures. Public key encryption algorithms are *invertable*, meaning that text encrypted with either key can be decrypted by the other. Normally, we encrypt with the public key and decrypt with the private key. However, it is possible to do the inverse: encrypt with the private key and decrypt with the public key. Because the private key is secret, only the real user could use it to encrypt a message. Thus, a digital signature or authentication sequence is used as a legal signature on many financial transactions. This signature is usually the name of the signing party plus other *key-contents* such as unique information from the message (e.g., date, time, or dollar amount). This signature and the other key-contents are encrypted by the sender using the private key. The receiver uses the sender's public key to decrypt the signature block and compares the result to the name and other key contents in the rest of the message to ensure a match.

Figure 11-17 illustrates how authentication can be combined with public encryption to provide a secure and authenticated transmission with a digital signature. The plaintext message is first encrypted using Organization A's private key and then encrypted using Organization's B public key. It is then transmitted to B. Organization B first decrypts the message using its private key. It sees that part of the message (the key-contents) is still in cyphertext, indicating it is an authenticated message. B then decrypts the key-contents part of the message using A's public key to produce the plaintext message. Since only A has the private key that matches A's public key, B can safely assume that A sent the message.

The only problem with this approach lies in ensuring that the person or organization who sent the document with the correct private key is actually the person or organization it claims to be. Anyone can post a public key on the Internet, so there is no way of knowing for sure who they actually are. For example, it would be possible for someone to create a Web site and claim to be "Organization A" when in fact the person is really someone else.

This is where the Internet's public key infrastructure (PKI) becomes important. The PKI is a set of hardware, software, organizations, and polices designed to make public key encryption work on the Internet. PKI begins with a **certificate authority (CA)**, which is a trusted organization that can vouch for the authenticity of the person or organization using authentication (e.g., VeriSign). A person wanting to use a CA registers with the CA and must provide some proof of identity. There are several levels of certification, ranging from a simple confirmation from a valid email address to a complete police-style background check with an in-person interview. The CA issues a digital *certificate* that is the requestor's public key encrypted using the CA's private key as proof of identity. This certificate is then attached to the user's email or Web transactions, in addition to the authentication information. The receiver then verifies the certificate by decrypting it with the CA's public key—and must also contact the CA to ensure that the user's certificate has not been revoked by the CA.

For higher security certifications, the CA requires that a unique "fingerprint" be issued by the CA for each message sent by the user. The user submits the message to the CA, who creates the unique fingerprint by combining the CA's private key with the message's authentication key contents. Because the user must obtain a unique fingerprint for each message, this ensures that the CA has not revoked the certificate between the time it was issued and the time the message was sent by the user.

Encryption Software Pretty Good Privacy (PGP) is a freeware public key encryption package developed by Philip Zimmermann that is often used to encrypt email. Users post their public key on Web pages, for example, and anyone wishing to send them an encrypted message simply cuts and pastes the key off the Web page into the PGP software, which encrypts and sends the message.

Secure Sockets Layer (SSL) is an encryption protocol widely used on the Web. It operates between the application-layer software and the transport layer (in what the OSI model calls the presentation layer). SSL encrypts outbound packets coming out of the application layer before they reach the transport layer and decrypts inbound packets coming out of the transport layer before they reach the application layer. With SSL, the client and the server start with a handshake for PKI authentication and for the server to provide its public key and preferred encryption technique to the client (usually RC4, DES, 3DES, or AES). The client then generates a key for this encryption technique, which is sent to the server encrypted with the server's public key. The rest of the communication then uses this encryption technique and key.

IP Security Protocol (IPSec) is another widely used encryption protocol. IPSec differs from SSL in that SSL is focused on Web applications, whereas IPSec can be used with a much wider variety of application layer protocols. IPSec sits between IP at the network layer and TCP/UDP at the transport layer. IPSec can use a wide variety of encryption techniques, so the first step is for the sender and receiver to establish the technique and key to be used. This is done using **Internet Key Exchange (IKE)**. Both parties generate a random key and send it to the other using an encrypted authenticated PKI process, and then put these two numbers together to produce the key. The encryption technique is also negotiated between the two, often being 3DES. Once the keys and technique have been established, IPSec can begin transmitting data.

IP Security Protocol can operate in either transport mode or tunnel mode for VPNs. In **IPSec transport mode**, IPSec encrypts just the IP payload, leaving the IP packet header unchanged so it can be easily routed through the Internet. In this case, IPSec adds an additional packet (either an Authentication Header [AH] or an Encapsulating Security Payload [ESP]) at the start of the IP packet that provides encryption information for the receiver.

In **IPSec tunnel mode**, IPSec encrypts the entire IP packet and must therefore add an entirely new IP packet that contains the encrypted packet as well as the IPSec AH or ESP packets. In tunnel mode, the newly added IP packet just identifies the IPSec encryption agent at the next destination, not the final destination; once the IPSec packet arrives at the encryption agent, the excrypted packet is VPN decrypted and sent on its way. In tunnel mode, attackers can only learn the endpoints of the VPN tunnel, not the ultimate source and destination of the packets.

11.4.5 User Authentication

Once the network perimeter and the network interior have been secured, the next step is to develop a way to ensure that only authorized users are permitted into the network and into specific resources in the interior of the network. This is called **user authentication**.

The basis of user authentication is the **user profile** for each user's **account** that is assigned by the network manager. Each user's profile specifies what data and network resources he or she can access and the type of access (read only, write, create, delete).

User profiles can limit the allowable log-in days, time of day, physical locations, and the allowable number of incorrect log-in attempts. Some will also automatically log a user out if that person has not performed any network activity for a certain length of time (e.g., the user has gone to lunch and has forgotten to log off the network). Regular security checks throughout the day when the user is logged in can determine whether a user is still permitted access to the network. For example, the network manager might have disabled the user's profile while the user is logged in, or the user's account may have run out of funds.

Creating accounts and profiles is simple. When a new staff member joins an organization, that person is assigned a user account and profile. One security problem is the removal of user accounts when someone leaves an organization. Often, network managers are not

---

TECHNICAL FOCUS | **11-5 Cracking a Password**

*T*o crack Windows passwords, you just need to get a copy of the security account manager (SAM) file in the WINNT directory, which contains all the Windows passwords in an encrypted format. If you have physical access to the computer, that's sufficient. If not, you might be able to hack in over the network. Then, you just need to use a Windows-based cracking tool such as LophtCrack. Depending on the difficulty of the password, the time needed to crack the password via brute force could take minutes or up to a day.

Or that's the way it used to be. Recently the *Cryptography and Security Lab* in Switzerland developed a new password-cracking tool that relies on very large amounts of RAM. It then does indexed searches of possible passwords that are already in memory. This tool can cut cracking times to less than 1/10 of the time of previous tools. Keep adding RAM and mHertz and you could reduce the crack times to 1/100 that of the older cracking tools. This means that if you can get your hands on the Windows-encrypted password file, then the game *is over*. It can literally crack complex passwords in Windows in seconds.

It's different for Linux, Unix, or Apple computers. These systems insert a 12-bit random "salt" to the password, which means that cracking their passwords will take 4,096 (2^{12}) times longer to do. That margin is probably sufficient for now, until the next generation of cracking tools comes along. Maybe.

So what can we say from all of this? That you are 4,096 times safer with Linux? Well, not necessarily. But what we may be able to say is that strong password protection, by itself, is an oxymoron. We must combine it with other methods of security to have reasonable confidence in the system.

informed of the departure and accounts remain in the system. For example, an examination of the user accounts at the University of Georgia found 30% belonged to staff members no longer employed by the university. If the staff member's departure was not friendly, there is a risk that he or she may attempt to access data and resources and use them for personal gain, or destroy them to get back at the organization. Many systems permit the network manager to assign expiration dates to user accounts to ensure that unused profiles are automatically deleted or deactivated, but these actions do not replace the need to notify network managers about an employee's departure as part of the standard human resources procedures.

MANAGEMENT

FOCUS

11-9 Selecting Passwords

The keys to users' accounts are passwords—we all know this. The stronger the password, the more secure is your account. But what does it mean to have a "strong" password? We all heard that we shouldn't pick keyboard patterns or names of family members or pets. But then different organizations have different rules for how to create strong passwords. Some might not give you any guidelines, whereas others are strict about how many uppercase letters you should use, numbers, and special characters you should use.

The National Institute of Standards and Technology (NIST) advises that the password strength boils down to the number of bits of entropy that a password has. So how can we calculate these bits of entropy? NIST has proposed the following rules to calculate the number of bits of entropy for a password:

1. The first byte counts as 4 bits.
2. The next 7 bytes count as 2 bits each.
3. The next 12 bytes count as 1.5 bits each.
4. Anything beyond that counts as 1 bit each.
5. Mixed case + nonalphanumeric = 2 to 6 more bits, depending on complexity.

For example, let's evaluate the following password's entropy: Pa$$w0rd (one you shouldn't use). Recall that each letter is represented as 1 byte.

- The first byte counts as 4 bits; therefore, "P" gives us 4 bits of entropy.
- The next 7 bytes count as 2 bits each; therefore, "a$$w0rd" gives us 7 × 2 bits = 14 additional bits of entropy.
- Mixed case + nonalphanumeric can give us up to 6 extra bits. Let's stay conservative and count 2 bits for these characters in our password, because the symbols are a close match for letters.

The total number of bits of entropy for our password is 20. How long will it take to crack this password using a brute force attack? Well, we have 2^{20} possibilities, and if a computer can guess 1,000 guesses per second it would take us approximately 17 minutes to break this password. We can agree that this is a very easy password to remember, but it is also very easy to break.

So how can we increase our password strength without making it almost impossible to remember it? More companies are moving to passphrases instead of passwords. A passphrase is simply four or more words that is not a common phrase such as a line from a song or movie. Let's look at the following password that uses four common words: horses love eating apples (without the spaces between the words). This password has 4 (for "h") + 14 (for "orseslov") + 18 (for "eeatingapple") + 1 (for "s") = 37 bits of entropy. It would take 4.35 years for a computer guessing 1,000 guesses per second to break this password. You can increase the strength of this password by adding spaces between the words or a few numbers at the end. This will then become a very easy password to remember but a very difficult one to crack.

General rules:

- Use passphrases, not passwords. Choose three or four easily remembered words.
- Longer is better. We recommend passphrases that are at least 15 characters long.
- Don't use the same passphrase everywhere. Instead, create a general passphrase you use but customize it for each site that requires a password by adding some numbers to it. For example, count the number of times the letter "a" appears in the URL of the website you are logging in to and add that to the end of your usual passphrase to create a unique passphrase just for that site.
- Always choose a unique passphrase for every high-risk site, such as your bank.

Gaining access to an account can be based on **something you know**, **something you have**, or **something you are**.

Passwords The most common approach is *something you know*, usually a **password**. Before users can log in, they need to enter a password. Unfortunately, passwords are often poorly chosen, enabling intruders to guess them and gain access. Some organizations are now requiring that users choose passwords that meet certain security requirements, such as a minimum length or including numbers and/or special characters (e.g., $, #, !). Some have moved to **passphrases** which, as the name suggests, are a series of words separated by spaces. Using complex passwords and passphrases has also been called one of the top five least effective security controls because it can frustrate users and lead them to record their passwords in places from which they can be stolen. Management Focus 11.9 offers some suggestions on how to create a strong password that is easy to remember.

Access Cards Requiring passwords provides, at best, midlevel security (much like locking your doors when you leave the house); it won't stop the professional intruder, but it will slow amateurs. Nonetheless, most organizations today use only passwords. About a third of organizations go beyond this and are requiring users to enter a password in conjunction with *something they have*, an **access card**. A **smart card** is a card about the size of a credit card that contains a small computer chip. This card can be read by a device, and to gain access to the network, the user must present both the card and the password. Intruders must have access to both before they can break in. The best example of this is the automated teller machine (ATM) network operated by your bank. Before you can gain access to your account, you must have both your ATM card and the access number.

Another approach is to use **one-time passwords**. The user connects into the network as usual, and after the user's password is accepted, the system generates a one-time password. The user must enter this password to gain access, otherwise the connection is terminated. The user can receive this one-time password in a number of ways (e.g., via a pager). Other systems provide the user with a unique number that must be entered into a separate hand-held device (called a **token**), which in turn displays the password for the user to enter. Other systems use **time-based tokens** in which the one-time password is changed every 60 seconds. The user has a small card (often attached to a key chain) that is synchronized with the server and displays the one-time password. With any of these systems, an attacker must know the user's account name and password and have access to the user's password device before he or she can log in.

Biometrics In high-security applications, a user may be required to present *something he or she is*, such as a finger, hand, or the retina of the eye for scanning by the system. These **biometric systems** scan the user to ensure that the user is the sole individual authorized to access the network account. About 15% of organizations now use biometrics. Although most biometric systems are developed for high-security users, several low-cost biometric systems are now on the market. The most popular biometric system is the fingerprint scanner. Several vendors sell devices for less than $100 that are the size of a mouse and that can scan a user's fingerprint. Some laptops now come with built-in fingerprint scanners that replace traditional Windows logins. Although some banks have begun using fingerprint devices for customer access to their accounts over the Internet, use of such devices has not become widespread, which we find a bit puzzling. The fingerprint is unobtrusive and means users no longer have to remember arcane passwords.

Central Authentication One long-standing problem has been that users are often assigned user profiles and passwords on several different computers. Each time a user wants to access a new server, he or she must supply his or her password. This is cumbersome for the users, and even worse for the network manager who must manage all the separate accounts for all the users.

More and more organizations are adopting **central authentication** (also called *network authentication, single sign-on, or directory services*), in which a log-in server is used to authenticate the user. Instead of logging into a file server or application server, the user logs into the **authentication server**. This server checks the user ID and password against its database and, if the user is an authorized user, issues a **certificate** (also called *credentials*). Whenever the user attempts to access a restricted service or resource that requires a user ID and password, the user is challenged, and his or her software presents the certificate to the authentication server (which is revalidated by the authentication server at the time). If the authentication server validates the certificate, then the service or resource lets the user in. In this way, the user no longer needs to enter his or her password to be authenticated to each new resource or service he or she uses. This also ensures that the user does not accidentally give out his or her password to an unauthorized service—it provides mutual authentication of both the user and the service or resource. The most commonly used authentication protocol is **Kerberos**, developed at MIT (see web.mit.edu /kerberos/www).

Although many systems use only one authentication server, it is possible to establish a series of authentication servers for different parts of the organization. Each server authenticates clients in its domain but can also pass authentication credentials to authentication servers in other domains.

11.4.6 Preventing Social Engineering

One of the most common ways for attackers to break into a system, even master hackers, is through **social engineering**, which refers to breaking security simply by asking. For example, attackers routinely phone unsuspecting users and, imitating someone such as a technician or senior manager, ask for a password. Unfortunately, too many users want to be helpful and simply provide the requested information. At first, it seems ridiculous to believe that someone would give his or her password to a complete stranger, but a skilled social engineer is like a good con artist: he—and most social engineers are men—can manipulate people.

Most security experts no longer test for social engineering attacks; they know from experience that social engineering will eventually succeed in any organization and therefore assume that attackers can gain access at will to normal user accounts. Training end users not to divulge passwords may not eliminate social engineering attacks, but it may reduce their effectiveness so that hackers give up and move on to easier targets. Acting out social engineering skits in front of users often works very well; when employees see how they can be manipulated into giving out private information, it becomes more memorable and they tend to become much more careful.

Phishing is a very common type of social engineering. The attacker simply sends an email to millions of users telling them that their bank account has been shut down due to an unauthorized access attempt and that they need to reactivate it by logging in. The email contains a link that directs the user to a fake Web site that appears to be the bank's Web site. After the user logs into the fake site, the attacker has the user's user ID and password and can break into his or her account at will. Clever variants on this include an email informing you that a new user has been added to your PayPal account, stating that the IRS has issued you a refund and you need to verify your social security number, or offering a mortgage at very low rate for which you need to provide your social security number and credit card number.

TECHNICAL	11-6 Inside Kerberos
FOCUS	

*K*erberos, the most commonly used central authentication protocol, uses symmetric encryption (usually DES). Kerberos is used by a variety of central authentication services, including Windows active directory services. When you log in to a Kerberos-based system, you provide your user ID and password to the Kerberos software on your computer. This software sends a request containing the user ID but *not* the password to the Kerberos authentication server (called the Key Distribution Center [KDC]).

The KDC checks its database for the user ID, and if it finds it, then it accepts the log-in and does two things. First, it generates a service ticket (ST) for the KDC that contains information about the KDC, a time stamp, and, most importantly, a unique session key (SK1), which will be used to encrypt all further communication between the client computer and the KDC until the user logs off. SK1 is generated separately for each user and is different every time the user logs in. Now, here's the clever part: The ST is encrypted using a key based on the password that matches the user ID. The client computer can only decrypt the ST if it knows the password that matches the user ID used to log in. If the user enters an incorrect password, the Kerberos software on the client can't decrypt the ST and asks the user to enter a new password. This way, the password is never sent over the network.

Second, the KDC creates a Ticket-Granting Ticket (TGT). The TGT includes information about the client computer and a time stamp that is encrypted using a secret key known only to the KDC and other validated servers. The KDC sends the TGT to the client computer encrypted with SK1, because all communications between the client and the server are encrypted with SK1 (so no one else can read the TGT). The client decrypts the transmission to receive the TGT, but because the client does not know the KDC's secret key, it cannot decrypt the contents of the TGT. From now until the user logs off, the user does not need to provide his or her password again; the Kerberos client software will use the TGT to gain access to all servers that require a password.

The first time a user attempts to use a server that requires a password, that server directs the user's Kerberos software to obtain a service ticket (ST) for it from the KDC. The user's Kerberos software sends the TGT to the KDC along with information about which server the user wants to access (remember that all communications between the client and the KDC are encrypted with SK1). The KDC checks to make sure that the user has not logged off, and if the TGT is validated, the KDC sends the client an ST for the desired server and a new session key (SK2) that the client will use to communicate with that server, both of which have been encrypted using SK1. The ST contains authentication information and SK2, both of which have been encrypted using the secret key known only to the KDC and the server.

The client presents a log-in request (which specifies the user ID, a time and date stamp, and other information) that has been encrypted with SK2 and the ST to the server. The server decrypts the ST using the KDC's secret key to find the authentication information and SK2. It uses the SK2 to decrypt the log-in request. If the log-in request is valid after decrypting with SK2, the server accepts the log-in and sends the client a packet that contains information about the server that has been encrypted with SK2. This process authenticates the client to the server and also authenticates the server to the client. Both now communicate using SK2. Notice that the server never learns the user's password.

11.4.7 Intrusion Prevention Systems

Intrusion prevention systems (IPS) are designed to detect an intrusion and take action to stop it. There are two general types of IPS, and many network managers choose to install both. The first type is a **network-based IPS**. With a network-based IPS, an **IPS sensor** is placed on key network circuits. An IPS sensor is simply a device running a special operating system that monitors all network packets on that circuit and reports intrusions to an **IPS management console**. The second type of IPS is the **host-based IPS**, which, as the name suggests, is a software package installed on a host or server. The host-based IPS monitors activity on the server and reports intrusions to the IPS management console.

There are two fundamental techniques that these types of IPSs can use to determine that an intrusion is in progress; most IPSs use both techniques. The first technique is **misuse detection**, which compares monitored activities with signatures of known attacks.

11-10 Social Engineering Wins Again

*D*anny had collected all the information he needed to steal the plans for the new product. He knew the project manager's name (Bob Billings), phone number, department name, office number, computer user ID, and employee number, as well as the project manager's boss's name. These had come from the company Web site and a series of innocuous phone calls to helpful receptionists. He had also tricked the project manager into giving him his password, but that hadn't worked because the company used one-time passwords using a time-based token system called Secure ID. So, after getting the phone number of the computer operations room from another helpful receptionist, all he needed was a snowstorm.

Late one Friday night, a huge storm hit and covered the roads with ice. The next morning, Danny called the computer operations room:

Danny:	"Hi, this is Bob Billings in the Communications Group. I left my Secure ID in my desk and I need it to do some work this weekend. There's no way I can get into the office this morning. Could you go down to my office and get it for me? And then read my code to me so I can log in?"
Operations:	"Sorry, I can't leave the Operations Center."
Danny:	"Do you have a Secure ID yourself?"
Operations:	"There's one here we keep for emergencies."

Danny:	"Listen. Can you do me a big favor? Could you let me borrow your Secure ID? Just until it's safe to drive in?"
Operations:	"Who are you again?"
Danny:	"Bob Billings. I work for Ed Trenton."
Operations:	"Yeah, I know him."
Danny:	"My office is on the second floor (2202B). Next to Roy Tucker. It'd be easier if you could just get my Secure ID out of my desk. I think it's in the upper left drawer." (Danny knew the guy wouldn't want to walk to a distant part of the building and search someone else's office.)
Operations:	"I'll have to talk to my boss."

After a pause, the operations technician came back on and asked Danny to call his manager on his cell phone. After talking with the manager and providing some basic information to "prove" he was Bob Billings, Danny kept asking about having the Operations technician go to "his" office.

Finally, the manager decided to let Danny use the Secure ID in the Operations Center. The manager called the technician and gave permission for him to tell "Bob" the one-time password displayed on their Secure ID any time he called that weekend. Danny was in.

Adapted from: Kevin Mitnick and William Simon, *The Art of Deception*, John Wiley and Sons, 2002.

Whenever an attack signature is recognized, the IPS issues an alert and discards the suspicious packets. The problem, of course, is keeping the database of attack signatures up to date as new attacks are invented.

The second fundamental technique is **anomaly detection**, which works well in stable networks by comparing monitored activities with the "normal" set of activities. When a major deviation is detected (e.g., a sudden flood of ICMP ping packets, an unusual number of failed log-ins to the network manager's account), the IPS issues an alert and discards the suspicious packets. The problem, of course, is false alarms when situations occur that produce valid network traffic that is different from normal (e.g., on a heavy trading day on Wall Street, e-trade receives a larger than normal volume of messages).

Intrusion prevention systems are often used in conjunction with other security tools such as firewalls (Figure 11-18). In fact, some firewalls are now including IPS functions. One problem is that the IPS and its sensors and management console are a prime target for attackers. Whatever IPS is used, it must be very secure against attack. Some organizations deploy redundant IPSs from different vendors (e.g., a network-based IPS from one vendor and a host-based IPS from another) to decrease the chance that the IPS can be hacked.

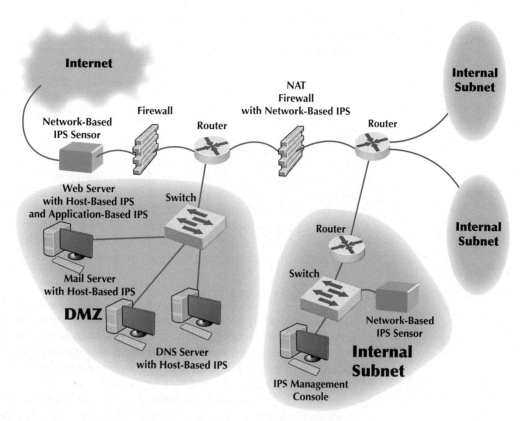

FIGURE 11-18 Intrusion prevention system (IPS)
DMZ = demilitarized zone; DNS = Domain Name Service; NAT = network address translation

Although IPS monitoring is important, it has little value unless there is a clear plan for responding to a security breach in progress. Every organization should have a clear response planned if a break-in is discovered. Many large organizations have emergency response "SWAT" teams ready to be called into action if a problem is discovered. The best example is CERT, which is the Internet's emergency response team. CERT has helped many organizations establish such teams.

Responding to an intrusion can be more complicated than it at first seems. For example, suppose the IPS detects a DoS attack from a certain IP address. The immediate reaction could be to discard all packets from that IP address; however, in the age of IP spoofing, the attacker could fake the address of your best customer and trick you into discarding packets from it.

11.4.8 Intrusion Recovery

Once an intrusion has been detected, the first step is to identify how the intruder gained unauthorized access and prevent others from breaking in the same way. Some organizations will simply choose to close the door on the attacker and fix the security problem. About 30% of organizations take a more aggressive response by logging the intruder's activities and working with police to catch the individuals involved. Once identified, the attacker will be charged with criminal activities and/or sued in civil court. Several states and provinces have introduced laws requiring organizations to report intrusions and theft of customer data, so the percentage of intrusions reported and prosecuted will increase.

A whole new area called **computer forensics** has recently opened up. Computer forensics is the use of computer analysis techniques to gather evidence for criminal and/or civil trials. The basic steps of computer forensics are similar to those of traditional forensics, but the techniques are different. First, identify potential evidence. Second, preserve evidence by making backup copies and use those copies for all analysis. Third, analyze the evidence. Finally, prepare a detailed legal report for use in prosecutions. Although companies are sometimes tempted to launch counterattacks (or counterhacks) against intruders, this is illegal.

Some organizations have taken their own steps to snare intruders by using **entrapment** techniques. The objective is to divert the attacker's attention from the real network to an attractive server that contains only fake information. This server is often called a **honey pot**. The honey pot server contains highly interesting, fake information available only through illegal intrusion to "bait" the intruder. The honey pot server has sophisticated tracking software to monitor access to this information that allows the organization and law enforcement officials to trace and legally document the intruder's actions. Possession of this information then becomes final legal proof of the intrusion.

11.5 BEST PRACTICE RECOMMENDATIONS

This chapter provides numerous suggestions on business continuity planning and intrusion prevention. Good security starts with a clear disaster recovery plan and a solid security policy. Probably the best security investment is user training: training individual users on data recovery and ways to defeat social engineering. But this doesn't mean that technologies aren't needed either.

Figure 11-19 shows the most commonly used security controls. Most organizations now routinely use antivirus software, firewalls, VPNs, encryption, and IPS.

Even so, rarely does a week pass without a new warning of a major vulnerability. Leave a server unattended for two weeks, and you may find that you have five critical patches to install.

People are now asking, "Will it end?" Is (in)security just a permanent part of the information systems landscape? In a way, yes. The growth of information systems, along with the new and dangerous ability to reach into them from around the world, has created new opportunities for criminals. Mix the possibilities of stealing valuable, marketable information with the low possibilities for getting caught and punished, and we would expect increasing numbers of attacks.

FIGURE 11-19

What security controls are used

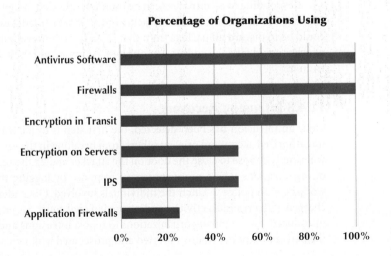

Perhaps the question should be: Does it have to be this bad? Unquestionably, we could be protecting ourselves better. We could better enforce security policies and restrict access. But all of this has a cost. Attackers are writing and distributing a new generation of attack tools right before us—tools that are very powerful, more difficult to detect, and very easy to use. Usually such tools are much easier to use than their defensive countermeasures.

The attackers have another advantage, too. Whereas the defenders have to protect *all* vulnerable points *all the time* to be safe, the attacker just has to break into *one place one time* to be successful.

So what may we expect in the future in "secure" organizational environments? We would expect to see strong **desktop management**, including the use of thin clients. Centralized desktop management, in which individual users are not permitted to change the settings on their computers, may become common, along with regular reimaging of computers to prevent Trojans and viruses and to install the most recent security patches. All external software downloads will likely be prohibited.

Continuous content filtering, in which all incoming packets (e.g., Web, email) are scanned, may become common, thus significantly slowing down the network. All server files and communications with client computers would be encrypted, further slowing down transmissions.

Finally, all written security policies would be rigorously enforced. Violations of security policies might even become a "capital offense" (i.e., meaning one violation and you are fired).

We may look forlornly back to the early days of the Internet when we could "do anything" as its Golden Days.

A Day in the Life: Network Security Manager

"Managing security is a combination of detective work and prognostication about the future."

A network security manager spends much of his or her time doing three major things. First, much time is spent looking outside the organization by reading and researching potential security holes and new attacks because the technology and attack opportunities change so fast. It is important to understand new attack threats, new scripting tools used to create viruses, remote access Trojans and other harmful software, and the general direction in which the hacking community is moving. Much important information is contained at Web sites such as those maintained by CERT (www.cert.org) and SANS (www.sans.org). This information is used to create new versions of standard computer images that are more robust in defeating attacks and to develop recommendations for the installation of application security patches. It also means that he or she must update the organization's written security policies and inform users of any changes.

Second, the network security manager looks inward toward the networks he or she is responsible for. He or she must check the vulnerability of those networks by thinking like a hacker to understand how the networks may be susceptible to attack, which often means scanning for open ports and unguarded parts of the networks and looking for computers that have not been updated with the latest security patches. It also means looking for symptoms of compromised machines such as new patterns of network activity or unknown services that have been recently opened on a computer.

Third, the network security manager must respond to security incidents. This usually means "firefighting"—quickly responding to any security breach, identifying the cause, collecting forensic evidence for use in court, and fixing the computer or software application that has been compromised.

Source: With thanks to Kenn Crook

11.6 IMPLICATIONS FOR MANAGEMENT

Network security was once an esoteric field of interest to only a few dedicated professionals. Today, it is the fastest-growing area in networking. The cost of network security will continue to increase as the tools available to network attackers become more sophisticated, as organizations rely more and more on networks for critical business operations, and as information warfare perpetrated by nations or terrorists becomes more common. As the cost of networking technology decreases, the cost of staff and networking technologies providing security will become an increasingly larger proportion of an organization's networking budget. As organizations and governments see this, there will be a call for tougher laws and better investigation and prosecution of network attackers.

Security tools available to organizations will continue to increase in sophistication, and the use of encryption will become widespread in most organizations. There will be an ongoing "arms race" between security officers in organizations and attackers. Software security will become an important factor in selecting operating systems, networking software, and application software. Those companies that provide more secure software will see a steady increase in market share, whereas those that don't will gradually lose ground.

SUMMARY

Types of Security Threats In general, network security threats can be classified into one of two categories: (1) business continuity and (2) intrusions. Business continuity can be interrupted by disruptions that are minor and temporary, but some may also result in the destruction of data. Natural (or man-made) disasters may occur that destroy host computers or large sections of the network. Intrusion refers to intruders (external attackers or organizational employees) gaining unauthorized access to files. The intruder may gain knowledge, change files to commit fraud or theft, or destroy information to injure the organization.

Risk Assessment Developing a secure network means developing controls that reduce or eliminate threats to the network. Controls prevent, detect, and correct whatever might happen to the organization when its computer-based systems are threatened. The first step in developing a secure network is to conduct a risk assessment. This is done by identifying the key assets and threats and comparing the nature of the threats to the controls designed to protect the assets. A company can pick one of several risk assessment frameworks that are considered to be industry standards.

Business Continuity The major threats to business continuity are viruses, theft, denial of service attacks, device failure, and disasters. Installing and regularly updating antivirus software is one of the most important and commonly used security controls. Protecting against denial of service attacks is challenging and often requires special hardware. Theft is one of the most often overlooked threats and can be prevented by good physical security, especially the physical security of laptop computers. Devices fail, so the best way to prevent network outages is to ensure that the network has redundant circuits and devices (e.g., switches and routers) on mission-critical network segments (e.g., the Internet connection and core backbone). Avoiding disasters can take a few commonsense steps, but no disaster can be completely avoided; most organizations focus on ensuring important data are backed up off-site and having a good, tested disaster recovery plan.

Intrusion Prevention Intruders can be organization employees or external hackers who steal data (e.g., customer credit card numbers) or destroy important records. A security policy defines the key stakeholders and their roles, including what users can and cannot do. Firewalls often stop intruders at the network perimeter by permitting only authorized packets into the network, by examining application layer packets for known attacks, and/or by hiding the organization's private IP addresses from the public Internet. Physical and dial-up security are also useful perimeter security controls. Patching security holes—known bugs in an operating system or application software package—is important to prevent intruders from using these to break in. Single key or public key encryption can protect data in transit or data stored on servers. User authentication ensures only authorized users can enter the network and can be based on something you know (passwords), something you have (access cards), or something you are (biometrics). Preventing social engineering, where hackers trick users into revealing their passwords, is very difficult. Intrusion prevention systems are tools that detect known attacks and unusual activity and enable network managers to stop an intrusion in progress. Intrusion recovery involves correcting any damaged data, reporting the intrusion to the authorities, and taking steps to prevent the other intruders from gaining access the same way.

KEY TERMS

access card, 337
access control list (ACL), 320
account, 335
Advanced Encryption Standard (AES), 331
adware, 329
algorithm, 330
anomaly detection, 340
antivirus software, 309
application-level firewall, 321
asymmetric encryption, 329
authentication, 333
authentication server, 338
availability, 298
backup controls, 315
biometric system, 337
brute-force attack, 330
business continuity, 298
central authentication, 338
certificate, 338
certificate authority (CA), 334
ciphertext, 329
computer forensics, 342
confidentiality, integrity, and availability (CIA), 298
continuous data protection (CDP), 316
controls, 300
corrective control, 300

cracker, 318
DDoS agent, 310
DDoS handler, 310
decryption, 329
denial-of-service (DoS) attack, 310
desktop management, 343
detective control, 300
disaster recovery drill, 316
disaster recovery firm, 318
disaster recovery plan, 315
disk mirroring, 314
distributed denial-of-service (DDoS) attack, 310
eavesdropping, 324
encryption, 329
entrapment, 342
fault-tolerant server financial impact, 314
firewall, 320
hacker, 318
honey pot, 342
host-based, 339
information warfare, 318
integrity, 298
Internet Key Exchange (IKE), 334
intrusion prevention systems (IPS), 339
IP Security Protocol (IPSec), 334
IP spoofing, 321

IPS management console, 339
IPS sensor, 339
IPSec transport mode, 334
IPSec tunnel mode, 335
Kerberos, 338
key, 330
key management, 330
misuse detection, 339
NAT firewall, 322
network address translation (NAT), 322
network-based IPS, 339
one-time password, 337
online backup, 317
packet-level firewall, 320
passphrase, 337
password, 337
patch, 326
phishing, 338
physical security, 313
plaintext, 329
Pretty Good Privacy (PGP), 334
preventive control, 300
private key, 331
public key, 331
public key encryption 331
public key infrastructure (PKI) 331
RC4, 331
recovery controls, 315
redundancy, 313

redundant array of independent disks (RAID), 314
risk assessment, 301
risk assessment frameworks, 301
risk mitigation controls, 307
risk score, 305
rootkit, 327
RSA, 331
Secure Sockets Layer (SSL), 334
secure switch, 325
security hole, 325
security policy, 319
smart card, 337
sniffer program, 325
social engineering, 338
something you are, 337
something you have, 337
something you know, 337
spyware, 329
symmetric encryption, 329
threat, 304
threat scenario, 304
time-based token, 337
token, 337
traffic analysis, 311
traffic anomaly analyzer, 312
traffic anomaly detector, 311
traffic filtering, 310

QUESTIONS

1. What factors have brought increased emphasis on network security?
2. Briefly outline the steps required to complete a risk assessment.
3. Name and describe the main impact areas. Who should be responsible for assessing what is meant by low/medium/high impact for each of the impact areas? Explain your answer.
4. What are some of the criteria that can be used to rank security risks?
5. What are the most common security threats? What are the most critical? Why?
6. Explain the purpose of threat scenarios. What are the steps in preparing threat scenarios?
7. What is the purpose of the risk score, and how is it calculated?
8. In which step of the risk assessment should existing controls be documented?
9. What are the four possible risk control strategies? How do we pick which one to use?
10. Why is it important to identify improvements that are needed to mitigate risks?
11. What is the purpose of a disaster recovery plan? What are five major elements of a typical disaster recovery plan?
12. What is a computer virus? What is a worm?
13. Explain how a denial-of-service attack works.
14. How does a denial-of-service attack differ from a distributed denial-of-service attack?
15. What is a disaster recovery firm? When and why would you establish a contract with them?
16. What is online backup?
17. People who attempt intrusion can be classified into four different categories. Describe them.
18. There are many components in a typical security policy. Describe three important components.
19. What are three major aspects of intrusion prevention (not counting the security policy)?
20. How do you secure the network perimeter?
21. What is physical security, and why is it important?
22. What is eavesdropping in a computer security sense?
23. What is a sniffer?
24. How do you secure dial-in access?
25. What is a firewall?
26. How do the different types of firewalls work?
27. What is IP spoofing?
28. What is a NAT firewall, and how does it work?
29. What is a security hole, and how do you fix it?
30. Explain how a Trojan horse works.
31. Compare and contrast symmetric and asymmetric encryption.
32. Describe how symmetric encryption and decryption work.
33. Describe how asymmetric encryption and decryption work.
34. What is key management?
35. How does DES differ from 3DES? From RC4? From AES?
36. Compare and contrast DES and public key encryption.
37. Explain how authentication works.
38. What is PKI, and why is it important?
39. What is a certificate authority?
40. How does PGP differ from SSL?
41. How does SSL differ from IPSec?
42. Compare and contrast IPSec tunnel mode and IPSec transfer mode.
43. What are the three major ways of authenticating users? What are the pros and cons of each approach?
44. What are the different types of one-time passwords and how do they work?
45. Explain how a biometric system can improve security. What are the problems with it?
46. Why is the management of user profiles an important aspect of a security policy?
47. How does network authentication work, and why is it useful?
48. What is social engineering? Why does it work so well?
49. What techniques can be used to reduce the chance that social engineering will be successful?
50. What is an intrusion prevention system?
51. Compare and contrast a network-based IPS and a host-based IPS.
52. How does IPS anomaly detection differ from misuse detection?
53. What is computer forensics?
54. What is a honey pot?
55. What is desktop management?

56. A few security consultants have said that broadband and wireless technologies are their best friends. Explain.
57. Most hackers start their careers breaking into computer systems as teenagers. What can we as a community of computer professionals do to reduce the temptation to become a hacker?
58. Some experts argue that CERT's posting of security holes on its Web site causes more security break-ins than it prevents and should be stopped. What are the pros and cons on both sides of this argument? Do you think CERT should continue to post security holes?
59. What is one of the major risks of downloading unauthorized copies of music files from the Internet (aside from the risk of jail, fines, and lawsuits)?
60. Although it is important to protect all servers, some servers are more important than others. What server(s) are the most important to protect, and why?

EXERCISES

A. Conduct a risk assessment of your organization's networks. Some information may be confidential, so report what you can.
B. Investigate and report on the activities of CERT (the Computer Emergency Response Team).
C. Investigate the capabilities and costs of a disaster recovery service.
D. Investigate the capabilities and costs of a firewall.
E. Investigate the capabilities and costs of an intrusion prevention system.
F. Investigate the capabilities and costs of an encryption package.
G. Investigate the capabilities and costs of an online backup service.

MINICASES

I. **Belmont State Bank** Belmont State Bank is a large bank with hundreds of branches that are connected to a central computer system. Some branches are connected over dedicated circuits and others use Multiprotocol Label Switching (MPLS). Each branch has a variety of client computers and ATMs connected to a server. The server stores the branch's daily transaction data and transmits it several times during the day to the central computer system. Tellers at each branch use a four-digit numeric password, and each teller's computer is transaction-coded to accept only its authorized transactions. Perform a risk assessment.

II. **Western Bank** Western Bank is a small, family-owned bank with six branches spread over the county. It has decided to move onto the Internet with a Web site that permits customers to access their accounts and pay bills. Design the key security hardware and software the bank should use.

III. **Classic Catalog Company, Part 1** Classic Catalog Company runs a small but rapidly growing catalog sales business. It outsourced its Web operations to a local ISP for several years, but as sales over the Web have become a larger portion of its business, it has decided to move its Web site onto its own internal computer systems. It has also decided to undertake a major upgrade of its own internal networks. The company has two buildings, an office complex, and a warehouse. The two-story office building has 60 computers. The first floor has 40 computers, 30 of which are devoted to telephone sales. The warehouse, located 400 feet across the company's parking lot from the office building, has about 100,000 square feet, all on one floor. The warehouse has 15 computers in the shipping department located at one end of the warehouse. The company is about to experiment with using wireless handheld computers to help employees more quickly locate and pick products for customer orders. Based on traffic projections for the coming year, the company plans to use a T1 connection from its office to its ISP. It has three servers: the main Web server, an email server, and an internal application server for its application systems (e.g., orders, payroll). Perform a risk assessment.

IV. **Classic Catalog Company, Part 2** Read MINICASES III above. Outline a brief business continuity plan, including controls to reduce the risks in advance as well as a disaster recovery plan.

V. **Classic Catalog Company, Part 3** Read MINICASES III above. Outline a brief security policy and the controls you would implement to control unauthorized access.

VI. **Classic Catalog Company, Part 4** Read MINI-CASES III above. What patching policy would you recommend for Classic Catalog?

VII. **Personal Password Storage and Protection** To help us not forget our many passwords, there are several companies that provide password managers. Find the top 5 password manager programs, compare their features and costs, and make a presentation of your findings to your classmates.

CASE STUDY

NEXT-DAY AIR SERVICE

See the Web site at www.wiley.com/college/fitzgerald

HANDS-ON ACTIVITY 11A

Securing Your Computer

This chapter has focused on security, including risk analysis, business continuity, and intrusion prevention. At first glance, you may think security applies to corporate networks, not your network. However, if you have a LAN at your house or apartment, or even if you just own a desktop or laptop computer, security should be one of your concerns. There are so many potential threats to your business continuity—which might be your education—and to intrusion into your computer(s) that you need to take action.

You should perform your own risk analysis, but this section provides a brief summary of some simple actions you should take that will greatly increase your security. Do this this week; don't procrastinate. Our focus is on Windows security, because most readers of this book use Windows computers, but the same advice (but different commands) applies to Apple computers.

Business Continuity

If you run your own business, then ensuring business continuity should be a major focus of your efforts. But even if you are "just" an employee or a student, business continuity is important. What would happen if your hard disk failed just before the due date for a major report?

1. The first and most important security action you can take is to configure Windows to perform automatic updates. This will ensure you have the latest patches and updates installed.

2. The second most important action is to buy and install antivirus software such as that from Symantec. Be sure to configure it for regular updates too. If you perform just these two actions, you will be relatively secure from viruses, but you should scan your system for viruses on a regular basis, such as the first of every month, when you pay your rent or mortgage.

3. Spyware is another threat. You should buy and install antispyware software that provides the same protection that antivirus software does for viruses. Spybot is a good package. Be sure to configure this software for regular updates and scan your system on a regular basis.

4. One of the largest sources of viruses, spyware and adware are free software and music/video files downloaded from the Internet. Simply put, don't download any file unless it is from a trusted vendor or distributor of software and files.

5. Develop a disaster recovery plan. You should plan today for what you would do if your computer were destroyed. What files would you need? If there are any important files that you wouldn't want to lose (e.g., reports you're working on, key data, or precious photos), you should develop a backup and recovery plan for them. The simplest is to copy the files to a shared directory on another computer on your LAN. But this won't enable you to recover the files if your apartment or house was destroyed by fire, for example. A better plan is to suscribe to a free online backup service such as mozy.com (think CDP on the cheap). If you don't use such a site, buy a large USB drive, copy your files to it, and store it off-site in your office or at a friend's house. A plan is only good if it is followed, so your data should be regularly backed up, such as doing so the first of every month.

Deliverables

1. Perform risk analysis for your home network.

2. Prepare a disaster recovery plan for your home network.

3. Research antivirus and antispyware software that you can purchase for your home network.

HANDS-ON ACTIVITY 11B

How to set up encryption on your computer

If you want to protect the data on your computer, you need to encrypt it. Encryption is widely used on the Internet these days—when you are making a purchase on Amazon or another retailer, your computer encrypts your credit card information before it gets transferred over the Internet.

Should you encrypt the data on your computer? The answer is *yes*. What if your computer gets stolen? You might say that your computer is password protected. Well, breaking into a password-protected computer is extremely easy. Should you then encrypt only your files, or should you encrypt the entire drive? If you only encrypt your files, if your computer gets stolen, the criminal will not be able to read your files but will still be able to install anything on your computer and see all the nonencrypted files. If you encrypt the entire drive, it would make it extremely difficult for anybody even to boot your computer without the password. However, if you ever forget your password or your drive gets corrupted, you probably wouldn't be able to retrieve your data files at all. Therefore, we suggest that you only encrypt your files rather than the entire drive.

In this activity, we introduce TrueCrypt, a free, open source software that can be used on Windows/Mac OS and Linux. Here is what you need to do to download True-Crypt:

1. Go to http://www.truecrypt.org/downloads and download the version of the software for your current operating system.

2. Once it is downloaded, install it. Accept the license terms and accept the default settings that the program offers you.

3. If this is the first time you are using True-Crypt, accept the suggestion to read the Beginner's Tutorial. You can find this tutorial here: http://www.truecrypt.org/docs/tutorial

Now you are ready to encrypt files on your computer. Here is a step-by-step guide:

1. Launch TrueCrypt. If you are using Windows, it will appear in your Start Menu.

2. Click on Create Volume.

3. The Wizard window will appear, and you should choose the first option—Create an encrypted file container.

4. Choose to create the volume within a file. TrueCrypt calls this a container. (Later you can experiment with other options that TrueCrypt allows you.)

5. Select to create the Standard TrueCrypt volume.

6. Now you need to specify where you wish the volume to be created. This will be a file that you can delete or move just like any other file. You may want to create it in My Documents and name it "Volume1." Hit the Save button to save your volume. Click on the Next button in the Wizard window.

   Caution: Do not select any existing file. Selecting an existing file will not encrypt the file but overwrite it, and all your data will be lost.

7. Now select the encryption method—we suggest you go with the default, AES.

8. In this step, you need to specify the size of the container. We suggest you make it 1 MB, although you can create a larger container if you are planning on encrypting a lot of files.

9. This is the most important step—you need to select a password. Once you type and confirm your selected password, you will be allowed to click the Next button.

10. To create a strong key, move your mouse around randomly for a short period of time. Then click Next.

11. Click Exit—you have successfully created a True-Crypt volume or file container. The Wizard will disappear now.

12. Select a drive letter (let's say J:) where you want the container to be mounted and click Select File.

13. In the file selector, select the volume you created in Step 6—Volume1—and click Open.

14. In the TrueCrypt window, select Mount. A dialog box requesting the password you created in step 9 will appear. Enter the password and click OK.

15. You have successfully mounted the container as virtual disk J:. This virtual disk is entirely encrypted and behaves like a real disk. You can save or copy files to this disk and they will be encrypted on the fly.

While encryption will not protect you against malware or somebody accessing your files if you leave your computer turned on in public spaces, it provides an additional layer of security. This Hands-On Activity is a beginner's guide to encryption. The next Hands-On Activity shows you how to secure your email using PGP. However, there other controls you can implement on your laptop, such as encrypting your Dropbox folder or creating a decoy operating system. Now it's up to you to learn more about the exciting world of encryption. Enjoy!

Deliverable

Encrypt a folder on your home computer. Show a screen shot of the encrypted folder.

HANDS-ON ACTIVITY 11C

Encryption Lab

The purpose of this lab is to practice encrypting and decrypting email messages using a standard called PGP (Pretty Good Privacy) that is implemented in an open source software Gnu Privacy Guard. You will need to download and install the Kleopatra software on your computer from this Web site: http://ftp.gpg4win.org/Beta/gpg4win-2.1.0-rc2.exe. For Mac OS X users, please visit this Web site: http://macgpg.sourceforge.net/.

1. Open Kleopatra. The first step in sending encrypted messages is to create your personal OpenPGP key pair—your personal private and public key.

2. Click on File and select New Certificate and then select Create a personal OpenPGP key pair and click Next.

3. Fill out your name as you want it to be displayed with your public key and the email address from which you will be sending and receiving emails. The comment window is optional and you can leave it empty. Click Next. Check and make sure that your name and email address are correctly entered. If this is the case, click the Create Key.

4. The system will now prompt you to enter a passphrase. This is your password to access your key, and it will also allow you to encrypt and decrypt messages. If the passphrase is not secure enough, the system will tell you. The quality indicator has to be green and show 100% for an acceptable passphrase. Once your passphrase is accepted, the system will prompt you to reenter the passphrase. Once this is done, Kleopatra will create your public and private key pair.

5. The next screen will indicate that a "fingerprint" of your newly created key pair is generated. This fingerprint is unique, and no one else has this fingerprint. You don't need to select any of the next steps suggested by the system.

6. The next step is to make your public key public so that other people can send encrypted messages to you. In the Kleopatra window, right click on your certificate and select Export Certificates from the menu. Select a folder on your computer where you want to save the public key and name it YourName public key.asc.

7. To see your public key, open this file in Notepad. You should see a block of fairly confusing text and numbers. My public key is shown in Figure 11-20. To share this public key, post your asc file on the class Web site. This key should be made public, so don't worry about sharing it. You can even post it on your own Web site so that other people can send you encrypted messages.

FIGURE 11-20 Example of a public key

8. Now, you should import the public key of the person with whom you want to exchange encrypted messages. Save the asc file with the public key on your computer. Then click the Import Certificates icon in Kleopatra. Select the asc file you want to import and click OK. Kleopatra will acknowledge the successful import of the public key.

9. The final step in importing the public key is to set the trust level to full trust. Left click on the certificate and from the menu select Change Owner Trust, and select "I believe checks are very accurate."

10. Now you are ready to exchange encrypted messages! Open Webmail, Outlook, or any other email client and compose a message. Copy the text of the message into clipboard by marking it and hitting CTRL + X. Right-click the Kleopatra icon on your status bar and select Clipboard and Encrypt (Figure 11-21). Click on Add Recipient and select the person to whom you want to send this message (Figure 11-22). I will send a message to Alan. Once the recipient is selected, just click Next. Kleopatra will return a screen that Encryption was successful.

11. The encrypted message is stored in your computer's clipboard. Open the email message window and paste (CTRL+V) the encrypted message to the body of the email. Now you are ready to send your first encrypted email!

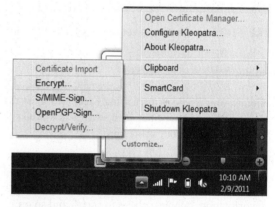

FIGURE 11-21 Encrypting a message using Kleopatra

12. To decrypt an encrypted message, just select the text in the email (you need to select the entire message from BEGIN PGP MESSAGE to END PGP MESSAGE). Copy the message to clipboard via CTRL+C. Right click the Kleopatra icon on your status bar, and then select Clipboard and Decrypt & Verify. This is very similar to how you encrypted the message. The decrypted message will be stored in the clipboard. To read it, just paste it to Word or any other text editor. You are done!

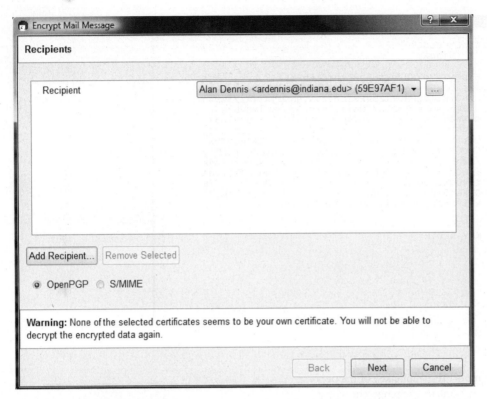

FIGURE 11-22 Selecting a recipient of an encrypted message

Deliverables

1. Create your PGP key pair using Kleopatra. Post the asc file of your public key on a server/class Web site as instructed by your professor.

2. Import the certificate (public key) of your professor to Kleopatra. Send your instructor an encrypted message that contains information about your favorite food, hobbies, places to travel, and so on.

3. Your professor will send you a response that will be encrypted. Decrypt the email and print its content so that you can submit a hard copy in class.

CHAPTER 12

NETWORK MANAGEMENT

Network managers perform two key tasks: (1) designing new networks and network upgrades and (2) managing the day-to-day operation of existing networks. The prior chapters have examined network design, so this chapter focuses on day-to-day network management, discussing the things that must be done to ensure that the network functions properly, although we do discuss some special-purpose equipment designed to improve network performance. Our focus is on the network management organization and the basic functions that a network manager must perform to operate a successful network.

OBJECTIVES

- Understand what is required to manage the day-to-day operation of networks
- Be familiar with the network management organization
- Understand configuration management
- Understand performance and fault management
- Be familiar with end user support
- Be familiar with cost management

12.1 INTRODUCTION

Network management is the process of operating, monitoring, and controlling the network to ensure it works as intended and provides value to its users. The primary objective of the data communications function is to move application-layer data from one location to another in a timely fashion and to provide the resources that allow this transfer to occur. This transfer of information may take place within a single department, between departments in an organization, or with entities outside the organization across private networks or the Internet.

Without a well-planned, well-designed network and without a well-organized network management staff, operating the network becomes extremely difficult. Unfortunately, many network managers spend most of their time **firefighting**—dealing with breakdowns and immediate problems. If managers do not spend enough time on planning and organizing the network and networking staff, which are needed to predict and prevent problems, they are destined to be reactive rather than proactive in solving problems.

MANAGEMENT FOCUS

12-1 What do Network Managers do?

If you were to become a network manager, some of your responsibilities and tasks would be to

- Manage the day-to-day operations of the network.
- Provide support to network users.
- Ensure the network is operating reliably.
- Evaluate and acquire network hardware, software, and services.
- Manage the network technical staff.
- Manage the network budget, with emphasis on controlling costs.
- Develop a strategic (long-term) networking and voice communications plan to meet the organization's policies and goals.

- Keep abreast of the latest technological developments in computers, data communications devices, network software, and the Internet.
- Keep abreast of the latest technological developments in telephone technologies and network services.
- Assist senior management in understanding the business implications of network decisions and the role of the network in business operations.

MANAGEMENT FOCUS

12-2 Five Key Management Tasks

Planning activities
- Forecasting
- Establishing objectives
- Scheduling
- Budgeting
- Allocating resources
- Developing policies

Organizing activities
- Developing organizational structure
- Delegating
- Establishing relationships
- Establishing procedures
- Integrating the smaller organization with the larger organization

Directing activities
- Initiating activities
- Decision making
- Communicating
- Motivating

Controlling activities
- Establishing performance standards
- Measuring performance
- Evaluating performance
- Correcting performance

Staffing activities
- Interviewing people
- Selecting people
- Developing people

One major organizational challenge is the integration of the voice communication function with the data communications function. Traditionally, voice communications were handled by a manager in the facilities department who supervised the telephone switchboard systems and also coordinated the installation and maintenance of the organization's voice telephone networks. By contrast, data communications traditionally were handled by the IT department because the staff installed their own communication circuits as the need arose, rather than coordinating with the voice communications staff.

This separation of voice and data worked well over the years, but today changing communication technologies are leading most organizations to combine the functions under the IT department. Voice communications are moving to VOIP, with VOIP phones replacing traditional analog phones.

We are moving from an era in which the computer system is the dominant IT function to one in which communications networks are the dominant IT function. In some organizations, the total cost of both voice and data communications will equal or exceed the total cost of the computer systems.

12.2 DESIGNING FOR NETWORK PERFORMANCE

At the end of the previous chapters we have discussed the best practice design for LANs, backbones, WANs, and WLANs and examined how different technologies and services offered different effective data rates at different costs. In the backbone and WAN chapters, we also examined different topologies and contrasted the advantages and disadvantages of each. So at this point, you should have a good understanding of the best choices for technologies and services and how to put them together into a good network design. In this section, we examine several higher-level concepts used to design the network for the best performance.

12.2.1 Managed Networks

The single most important element that contributes to the performance of a network is a **managed network** that uses **managed devices**. Managed devices are standard devices, such as switches and routers, that have small onboard computers to monitor the traffic that flows through the device as well as the status of the device and other devices connected to it. Managed devices perform their functions (e.g., routing, switching) and also record data on the traffic they process. These data can be sent to the network manager's computer when the device receives a special control message requesting the data, or the device can send an **alarm** message to the network manager's computer if it detects a critical situation such as a failing device or a huge increase in traffic.

In this way, network problems can be detected and reported by the devices themselves before problems become serious. In the case of the failing network card, a managed device could record the increased number of retransmissions required to successfully transmit messages and inform the network management software of the problem. A managed switch is often able to detect the faulty transmissions from a failing network card, disable the incoming circuit so that the card could not send any more messages, and issue an alarm to the network manager. In either case, finding and fixing problems is much simpler, requiring minutes, not hours.

Network Management Software A managed network requires both hardware and software: managed devices (e.g., switches, routers, APs) to monitor, collect, and transmit traffic reports and problem alerts; and network management software to store, organize, and analyze these reports and alerts. Managed devices are more expensive than unmanaged devices, because they have a CPU and software built into them. When we build a managed network, we normally buy all managed devices, rather than cutting costs by buying some managed devices and some unmanaged devices, although some organizations do install a mix of managed and unmanaged devices to cut costs. In this case, the managed devices are usually

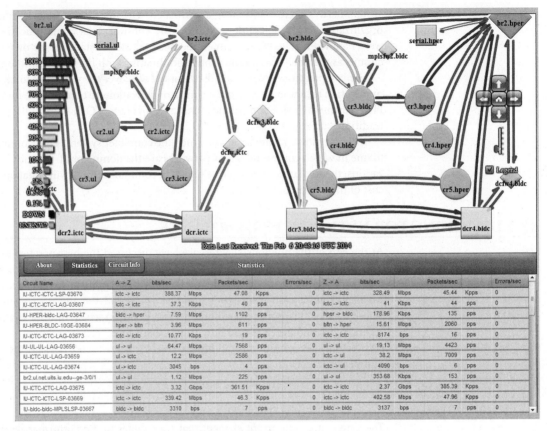

FIGURE 12-1 Device management software used on Indiana University's core backbone network.

placed on the backbone and unmanaged devices in the access layer. There are three fundamentally different types of network management software.

Device management software (sometimes called *point management software*) is designed to provide information about the specific devices on a network. It enables the network manager to monitor important devices such as servers, routers, and switches, and switches and to report configuration information, traffic volumes, and error conditions for each device. Figure 12-1 shows a sample display from a device management software package running at Indiana University. This figure shows the amount of traffic on the university's core backbone network. This chart is in color, which is hard to see in a black-and-white book. The chart shows that traffic is generally under control, with most circuits running at 10% or less of capacity. A few circuits are running at between 20% and 50% of capacity (e.g., the circuits between br2.ictc and br2.bldc). You can see that all circuits are full duplex because there are different traffic amounts in each direction.

System management software (sometimes called *enterprise management software* or a *network management framework*) provides the same configuration, traffic, and error information as device management systems but can analyze the device information to diagnose patterns, not just display individual device problems. This is important when a critical device fails (e.g., a router into a high-traffic building). With device management software, all of the devices that depend on the failed device will attempt to send warning messages to the network administrator. One failure often generates several dozen problem reports, called an **alarm storm**, making it difficult to pinpoint the true source of the problem quickly. The dozens of error messages are symptoms that mask the root cause. System management software tools correlate the individual error messages into a pattern to find the true cause, which is called **root cause analysis**, and then report the pattern to the network manager. Rather than first seeing pages and pages of error messages, the network manager instead is informed of the root cause of the problem.

Application management software also builds on the device management software, but instead of monitoring systems, it monitors applications. In many organizations, there are mission-critical applications that should get priority over other network traffic. For example, real-time order-entry systems used by telephone operators need priority over email. Application management systems track delays and problems with application layer packets and inform the network manager if problems occur.

Network Management Standards One important problem is ensuring that hardware devices from different vendors can understand and respond to the messages sent by the network management software of other vendors. By this point in the book, the solution should be obvious: standards. A number of formal and de facto standards have been developed for network management. These standards are application layer protocols that define the type of information collected by network devices and the format of control messages that the devices understand.

The most commonly used network management protocol is **Simple Network Management Protocol (SNMP)**. Each SNMP device (e.g., router, switch, server) has an **agent** that collects information about itself and the messages it processes and stores that information in a database called the **management information base (MIB)**. The network manager's management station that runs the **network management software** has access to the MIB. Using this software, the network manager can send control messages to individual devices or groups of devices asking them to report the information stored in their MIB.

Most SNMP devices have the ability for **remote monitoring (RMON)**. Most first-generation SNMP tools reported all network monitoring information to one central network management database. Each device would transmit updates to its MIB on the server every few minutes, greatly increasing network traffic. RMON SNMP software enables MIB information to be stored on the device itself or on distributed **RMON probes** that store MIB information closer to the devices that generate it. The data are not transmitted to the central server until the network manager requests, thus reducing network traffic (Figure 12-2).

Network information is recorded based on the data link layer protocols, network layer protocols, and application layer protocols so that network managers can get a very clear picture of the exact types of network traffic. Statistics are also collected based on network addresses so the network manager can see how much network traffic any particular computer is sending and receiving. A wide variety of alarms can be defined, such as instructing a device to send a warning message if certain items in the MIB exceed certain values (e.g., if circuit utilization exceeds 50%).

As the name suggests, SNMP is a simple protocol with a limited number of functions. One problem with SNMP is that many vendors have defined their own extensions to it. So the network devices sold by a vendor may be SNMP compliant, but the MIBs they produce contain additional information that can be used only by network management software produced by the same vendor. Therefore, although SNMP was designed to make it easier to manage devices from different vendors, in practice, this is not always the case.

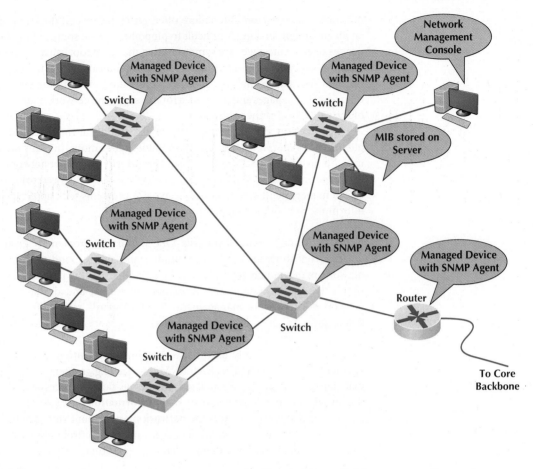

FIGURE 12-2 Network management with Simple Network Management Protocol (SNMP). MIB = management information base

---

12-3 Network Management at ZF Lenksysteme

ZF Lenksysteme manufactures steering systems for cars and trucks. It is headquartered in southern Germany but has offices and plants in France, England, the United States, Brazil, India, China, and Malaysia. Its network has about 300 servers and 600 devices (e.g., routers, switches).

ZF Lenksysteme had a network management system, but when a problem occurred with one device, nearby devices also issued their own alarms. The network management software did not recognize the interactions among the devices, and the resulting alarm storm meant that it took longer to diagnose the root cause of the problem.

The new HP network management system monitors and controls the global network from one central location with only three staff. All devices and servers are part of the system, and interdependencies are well defined, so alarm storms are a thing of the past. The new system has cut costs by 50% and also has extended network management into the production line. The robots on the production line now use TCP/IP networking, so they can be monitored like any other device.

Adapted from: ZF Lenksysteme, HP Case studies, hp.com

12.2.2 Managing Network Traffic

Most approaches to improving network performance attempt to maximize network speed. Another approach is to manage where and how we route traffic to improve network performance. This section examines two tools designed to better manage traffic with the ultimate goal of improving network performance.

Load Balancing As we mentioned in Chapter 7 on the design of the data center, servers are typically placed together in **server farms** or **clusters**, which sometimes have hundreds of servers that perform the same task. In this case, it is important to ensure that when a request arrives at the server farm, it is immediately forwarded to a server that is not busy—or is the least busy.

A special device called a **load balancer** or **virtual server** acts as a traffic manager at the front of the server farm (Figure 12-3). All requests are directed to the load balancer at its IP address. When a request hits the load balancer, it forwards it to one specific server using the server's IP address. Sometimes a simple round-robin formula is used (requests go to each server one after the other in turn); in other cases, more complex formulas track how busy each server actually is. If a server crashes, the load balancer stops sending requests to it, and the network continues to operate without the failed server. Load balancing makes it simple to add servers (or remove servers) without affecting users. You simply add or remove the server(s) and change the software configuration in the load balancer no one is aware of the change.

Policy-Based Management With **policy-based management** (sometimes called **application shaping** or **traffic shaping**), the network manager uses special software to set priority policies for network traffic that take effect when the network becomes busy. For example, the network manager might say that order processing and videoconferencing get the highest priority (order processing because it is the lifeblood of the company and videoconferencing because poor response time will have the greatest impact on it).

The policy management is usually implemented as a combination of hardware and software. A special traffic-shaping device is installed at a key point (usually between a building backbone and the campus backbone). The software to manage this device also configures

FIGURE 12-3
Network with load balancer

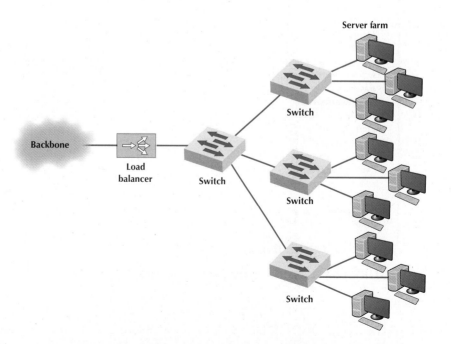

the network devices behind it using the quality of service (QoS) capabilities in TCP/IP and/or VLANs to give certain applications the highest priority when the devices become busy. Policy-based management requires managed devices that support QoS.

12.2.3 Reducing Network Traffic

A more radical approach to improving performance is to reduce the amount of traffic on the network. This may seem quite difficult at first glance—after all, how can we reduce the number of Web pages people request? We can't reduce all types of network traffic, but if we limit high-capacity users and move the most commonly used data closer to the users who need it, we can reduce traffic enough to have an impact on network performance. This section discusses three different tools that can be used.

Capacity Management **Capacity management** devices, sometimes called **bandwidth limiter** or **bandwidth shapers**, monitor traffic and can slow down traffic from users who consume a lot of network capacity. Capacity management is related to policy-based management but is simpler in that it only looks at the source of the traffic (i.e., the source IP address) rather than the nature of the traffic (e.g., videoconferencing, email, Web pages). These devices are installed at key points in the network, such as between a backbone and the core network. Figure 12-4 shows the control panel for one device made by NetEqualizer.

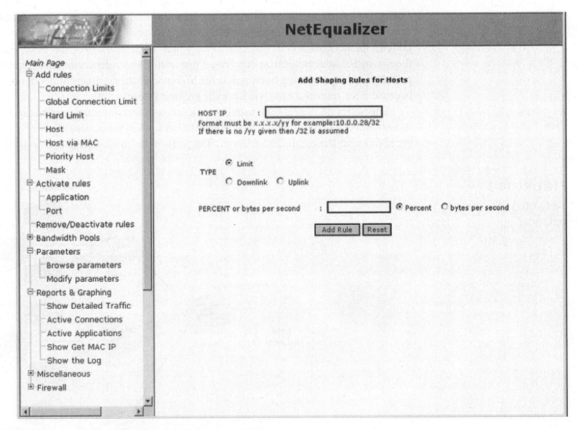

FIGURE 12-4 Capacity management software

FIGURE 12-5

Network with content engine

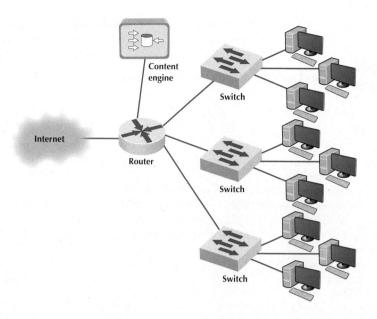

Content Caching The basic idea behind **content caching** is to store other people's Web data closer to your users. With content caching, you install a **content engine** (also called a **cache engine**) close to your Internet connection and install special content management software on the router (Figure 12-5). The router directs all outgoing Web requests and the files that come back in response to those requests to the cache engine. The content engine stores the request and the static files that are returned in response (e.g., graphics files, banners). The content engine also examines each outgoing Web request to see if it is requesting static content that the content engine has already stored. If the request is for content already in the content engine, it intercepts the request and responds directly itself with the stored file but makes it appear as though the request came from the URL specified by the user. The user receives a response almost instantaneously and is unaware that the content engine responded. The content engine is *transparent*.

Although not all Web content will be in the content engine's memory, content from many of the most commonly accessed sites on the Internet will be (e.g., yahoo.com, google.com, amazon.com). The contents of the content engine reflect the most common requests for each individual organization that uses it and changes over time as the pattern of pages and files changes. Each page or file also has a limited life in the cache before a new copy is retrieved from the original source so that pages that occasionally change will be accurate.

By reducing outgoing traffic (and incoming traffic in response to requests), the content engine enables the organization to purchase a smaller WAN circuit into the Internet. So not only does content caching improve performance, but it can also reduce network costs if the organization produces a large volume of network requests.

Content Delivery Content delivery, pioneered by **Akamai**,[1] is a special type of Internet service that works in the opposite direction. Rather than storing other people's Web files closer to their own internal users, a **content delivery provider** stores Web files for its clients closer to their potential users. Akamai, for example, operates almost 10,000 Web servers located near the busiest Internet IXPs and other key places around the Internet.

---

[1] Akamai (pronounced *AH-kuh-my*) is Hawaiian for "intelligent," "clever," and "cool." See www.akamai.com.

These servers contain the most commonly requested Web information for some of the busiest sites on the Internet (e.g., yahoo.com, monster.com, ticketmaster.com).

MANAGEMENT FOCUS

12-4 Load Balancing at Bryam Healthcare

Bryam Healthcare is a medical supply company serving more than 300,000 customers from 17 operating centers. When its sales representatives began complaining about the slow response times for email, Web, and other key applications, Anthony Acquanita, Byram's network manager, realized that the network architecture had reached its limits.

The old architecture was a set of four servers each running specific applications (e.g., one email server, one Web server). At different points in the week, a different server would become overloaded and provide slow response times for a specific application—the email server first thing Monday morning as people checked their email after the weekend, for example.

The solution was to install a load balancing switch in front of the servers and install all the major applications

on all the servers. This way, when the demand for one application peaks, there are four servers available rather than one. Because the demand for different applications peaks at different times, the result has been dramatically improved performance, without the need to buy new servers. The side benefit is that it is now simple to remove one server from operations at nonpeak times for maintenance or software upgrades without the users noticing (whereas in the past, server maintenance meant disabling an application [e.g., email] for a few hours while the server was worked on).

Adapted from: "Load Balancing Boosts Network," *Communications News*, November 2005, pp. 40–42.

When someone accesses a Web page of one of Akamai's customers, special software on the client's Web server determines if there is an Akamai server containing any static parts of the requested information (e.g., graphics, advertisements, banners) closer to the user. If so, the customer's Web server redirects portions of the request to the Akamai server nearest the user. The user interacts with the customer's Web site for dynamic content or HTML pages with the Akamai server providing static content. In Figure 12-6, for example, when a user in Singapore requests a Web page from yahoo.com, the main yahoo.com server farm responds with the dynamic HTML page. This page contains several static graphic files. Rather than provide an address on the yahoo.com site, the Web page is dynamically changed by the Akamai software on the yahoo.com site to pull the static content from the Akamai server in Singapore. If you watch the bottom action bar closely on your Web browser while some of your favorite sites are loading, you'll see references to Akamai's servers. On any given day, 15%–20% of all Web traffic worldwide comes from an Akamai server.

Akamai servers benefit both the users and the organizations that are Akamai's clients, as well as many ISPs and all Internet users not directly involved with the Web request. Because more Web content is now processed by the Akamai server and not the client organization's more distant Web server, the user benefits from a much faster response time; in Figure 12-6, for example, more requests never have to leave Singapore. The client organization benefits because it serves its users with less traffic reaching its Web server; Yahoo!, for example, need not spend as much on its server farm or the Internet connection into its server farm. In our example, the ISPs providing the circuits across the Pacific benefit because now less traffic flows through their network—traffic that is not paid for because of Internet peering agreements. Likewise, all other Internet users in Singapore (as well as users in the United States accessing Web sites in Singapore) benefit because there is now less traffic across the Pacific and response times are faster.

FIGURE 12-6
Network with content
delivery

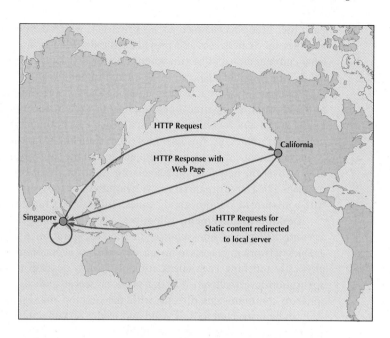

12-5 Content Delivery at Best Buy

*B*est Buy operates more than 1,150 retail electronic stores across the United States and Canada and has an extensive online Web store offering more than 600,000 products. Its Web store hosts more than 4,000 million visits a year, more than all of its 1,150 physical stores combined.

Best Buy wanted to improve its Web store to better customer experience and reduce operating costs. Akamai's extensive content delivery presence in North America enabled Best Buy to improve the speed of its Web transactions by 80%, resulting in substantial increases in sales. The shift to content delivery has also reduced the traffic to its own servers by more than 50%, reducing its operating costs.

Adapted from: Akamai Helps Best Buy, Akamai case studies, akamai.com

12.3 CONFIGURATION MANAGEMENT

We now turn our attention to the four basic management tasks that comprise network management. The first is configuration management. **Configuration management** means managing the network's hardware and software configuration, documenting it, and ensuring it is updated as the configuration changes.

12.3.1 Configuring the Network and Client Computers

One of the most common configuration activities is adding and deleting user accounts. When new users are added to the network, they are usually categorized as being a member of some group of users (e.g., faculty, students, accounting department, personnel department).

Each user group has its own access privileges, which define what file servers, directories, and files they can access and provide a standard log-in script. The log-in script specifies what commands are to be run when the user first logs in (e.g., setting default directories, connecting to public disks, running menu programs).

Another common activity is updating the software on the client computers attached to the network. Every time a new application system is developed or updated (or, for that matter, when a new version is released), each client computer in the organization must be updated. Traditionally, this has meant that someone from the networking staff has had to go to each client computer and manually install the software, either from CDs or by downloading over the network. For a small organization, this is time consuming but not a major problem. For a large organization with hundreds or thousands of client computers (possibly with a mixture of Windows and Apples), this can be a nightmare.

Desktop management, sometimes called *electronic software delivery* or *automated software delivery*, is one solution to the configuration problem. Desktop management enables network managers to install software on client computers over the network without physically touching each client computer. Most desktop management packages provide application-layer software for the network server and all client computers. The server software communicates directly with the desktop management software on the clients and can be instructed to download and install certain application packages on each client at some predefined time (e.g., at midnight on a Saturday). Microsoft and many antivirus software vendors use this approach to deliver updates and patches to their software.

Desktop management greatly reduces the cost of configuration management over the long term because it eliminates the need to update each and every client computer manually. It also automatically produces and maintains accurate documentation of all software installed on each client computer and enables network managers to produce a variety of useful reports. However, desktop management increases costs in the short term because it costs money (typically $25 to $50 per client computer) and requires network staff to install it manually on each client computer. Desktop Management Interface (DMI) is the emerging standard for desktop management.

12.3.2 Documenting the Configuration

Configuration documentation includes information about network hardware, network software, user and application profiles, and **network documentation**. The most basic information about network hardware is a set of network configuration diagrams that document the number, type, and placement of network circuits (whether organization owned or leased from a common carrier), network servers, network devices (e.g., hubs, routers), and client computers. For most organizations, this is a large set of diagrams: one for each LAN, BN, and WAN. Figure 12-7 shows a diagram of network devices in one office location.

These diagrams must be supplemented by documentation on each individual network component (e.g., circuit, hub, server). Documentation should include the type of device, serial number, vendor, date of purchase, warranty information, repair history, telephone number for repairs, and any additional information or comments the network manager wishes to add. For example, it would be useful to include contact names and telephone numbers for the individual network managers responsible for each separate LAN within the network and common carrier telephone contact information. (Whenever possible, establish a national account with the common carrier rather than dealing with individual common carriers in separate states and areas.)

A similar approach can be used for network software. This includes the network operating system and any special-purpose network software. For example, it is important to record

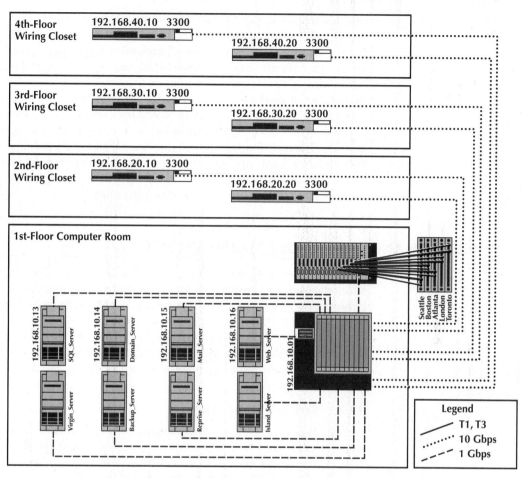

FIGURE 12-7   Network configuration diagram

which network operating system with which version or release date is installed on each network server. The same is true of application software. Sharing software on networks can greatly reduce costs, although it is important to ensure that the organization is not violating any software license rules.

Software documentation can also help in negotiating site licenses for software. Many users buy software on a copy-by-copy basis, paying the retail price for each copy. It may be cheaper to negotiate the payment of one large fee for an unlimited-use license for widely used software packages instead of paying on a per-copy basis.

The third type of documentation is the user and application profiles, which should be automatically provided by the network operating system or additional vendor or third-party software agreements. These should enable the network manager to easily identify the files and directories to which each user has access and each user's access rights (e.g., read-only, edit, delete). Equally important is the ability to access this information in the "opposite" direction, that is, to be able to select a file or directory and obtain a list of all authorized users and their access rights.

In addition, other documentation must be routinely developed and updated pertaining to the network. This includes network hardware and software manuals, application software manuals, standards manuals, operations manuals for network staff, vendor contracts and agreements, and licenses for software. The documentation should include details about performance and fault management (e.g., preventive maintenance guidelines and schedules, disaster recovery plan, and diagnostic techniques), end user support (e.g., applications software manuals, vendor support telephone numbers), and cost management (e.g., annual budgets, repair costs for each device). The documentation should also include any legal requirements to comply with local or federal laws, control, or regulatory bodies.

Maintaining documentation is usually a major issue for most organizations. Have you written programs? How well did you document them? Many technicians hate documentation because it is not "fun" and doesn't provide immediate value the same way that solving problems does. Therefore, it is often overlooked, so when someone leaves the organization, the knowledge of the network leaves with him or her.

12.4 PERFORMANCE AND FAULT MANAGEMENT

Performance management means ensuring the network is operating as efficiently as possible, whereas **fault management** means preventing, detecting, and correcting faults in the network circuits, hardware, and software (e.g., a broken device or improperly installed software). Fault management and performance management are closely related because any faults in the network reduce performance. Both require **network monitoring**, which means keeping track of the operation of network circuits and devices to ensure they are functioning properly and to determine how heavily they are used.

12.4.1 Network Monitoring

Most large organizations and many smaller ones use **network management software** to **monitor** and control their networks. One function provided by these systems is to collect operational statistics from the network devices. For small networks, network monitoring is often done by one person, aided by a few simple tools.

In large networks, network monitoring becomes more important. Large networks that support organizations operating 24 hours a day are often mission critical, which means a network problem can have serious business consequences. For example, consider the impact of a network failure for a common carrier such as AT&T or for the air traffic control system. These networks often have a dedicated **network operations center (NOC)** that is responsible for monitoring and fixing problems. Such centers are staffed by a set of skilled network technicians that use sophisticated network management software. When a problem occurs, the software immediately detects the problems and sends an alarm to the NOC. Staff members in the NOC diagnose the problem and can sometimes fix it from the NOC (e.g., restarting a failed device). Other times, when a device or circuit fails, they must change routing tables to route traffic away from the device and dispatch a technician to fix it.

A Day in the Life: Network Policy Manager

All large organizations have formal policies for the use of their networks (e.g., wireless LAN access, password, server space). Most large organizations have a special policy group devoted to the creation of network policies, many of which are devoted to network security. The job of the policy officer is to steer the policy through the policy-making process and ensure that all policies are in the best interests of the organization as a whole. Although policies are focused inside the organization, policies are influenced by events both inside and outside the organization. The policy manager spends a significant amount of time working with outside organizations such as the U.S. Department of Homeland Security, CIO and security officer groups, and industry security consortiums. The goal is to make sure all policies (especially security policies) are up to date and provide a good balance between costs and benefits.

A typical policy begins with networking staff writing a summary containing the key points of the proposed policy. The policy manager takes the summary and uses it to develop a policy that fits the structure required for organizational policies (e.g., date, rationale, scope, responsible individuals, and procedures). This policy manager works with the originating staff to produce an initial draft of the proposed policy. Once everyone in the originating department and the policy office are satisfied with the policy, it is provided to an advisory committee of network users and network managers for discussion. Their suggestions are then incorporated into the policy, or an explanation is provided as to why the suggestions will not be incorporated in the policy.

After several iterations, a policy becomes a draft policy and is posted for comment from all users within the organization. Comments are solicited from interested individuals, and the policy may be revised. Once the draft is finalized, the policy is then presented to senior management for approval. Once approved, the policy is formally published, and the organization charged with implementing the policy begins to use it to guide its operations.

Source: With thanks to Mark Bruhn

MANAGEMENT	12-6 **Network Management Salaries**
FOCUS	

Network management is not easy, but it doesn't pay too badly. Here are some typical jobs and their respective annual salaries:

Network Vice President	$150,000
Network Manager	90,000
Telecom Manager	77,000
LAN Administrator	70,000
WAN Administrator	75,000
Network Designer	80,000
Network Technician	60,000
Technical Support Staff	50,000
Trainer	50,000

Figure 12-8 shows part of the NOC at Indiana University (this is only about one-third of it). The NOC is staffed 24 hours a day, 7 days a week to monitor the university's networks. The NOC also has responsibility for managing portions of several very high-speed networks, including Internet2 (see Management Focus Box 12-7).

FIGURE 12-8   Part of the Network Operations Center at Indiana University. Photo courtesy of the author, Alan Dennis

Some types of management software operate passively, collecting the information and reporting it back to the central NOC. Others are active, in that they routinely send test messages to the servers or application being monitored (e.g., an HTTP Web page request) and record the response times. The network management software discussed in Section 12.2.2 is commonly used for network monitoring.

Performance tracking is important because it enables the network manager to be proactive and respond to performance problems before users begin to complain. Poor network reporting leads to an organization that is overburdened with current problems and lacks time to address future needs. Management requires adequate reports if it is to address future needs.

12.4.2 Failure Control Function

Failure control requires developing a central control philosophy for problem reporting, whether the problems are first identified by the NOC or by users calling in to the NOC or a help desk. Whether problem reporting is done by the NOC or the **help desk**, the organization should maintain a central telephone number for network users to call when any problem occurs in the network. As a central troubleshooting function, only this group or its designee should have the authority to call hardware or software vendors or common carriers.

Many years ago, before the importance (and cost) of network management was widely recognized, most networks ignored the importance of fault management. Network devices were "dumb" in that they did only what they were designed to do (e.g., routing packets) but did not provide any network management information.

For example, suppose a network interface card fails and begins to transmit garbage messages randomly. Network performance immediately begins to deteriorate because these random messages destroy the messages transmitted by other computers, which need to be retransmitted. Users notice a delay in response time and complain to the network support group, which begins to search for the cause. Even if the network support group suspects a failing network card (which is unlikely, unless such an event has occurred before), locating the faulty card is very difficult and time consuming.

Most network managers today are installing *managed devices* that perform their functions (e.g., routing, switching) and also record data on the messages they process (see Section 12.2.1). Finding and fixing the fault is much simpler, requiring minutes, not hours.

MANAGEMENT
FOCUS

12-7 Internet2 Weather Map

Internet2 is a high-performance backbone that connects about 400 Internet2 institutions in more than 100 countries. The current network is primarily a 10 Gbps fiber-optic network.

The network is monitored 24 hours a day, 7 days a week from the network operations center (NOC) located on the campus of Indiana University. The NOC oversees problem, configuration, and change management; network security; performance and policy monitoring; reporting; quality assurance; scheduling; and documentation. The center provides a structured environment that effectively coordinates operational activities with all participants and vendors related to the function of the network.

The NOC uses multiple network management software running across several platforms. One of the tools used by the NOC that is available to the general public is the Internet2 Weather Map (noc.net.internet2.edu). Each of the major circuits connecting the major Internet2 gigapops is shown on the map. Each link has two parts, showing the utilization of the circuits to and from each pair.

Adapted from: Internet2 Network NOC (noc.net.internet2 .edu)

Numerous software packages are available for recording fault information (Remedy is one of the more popular ones). The reports they produce are known as **trouble tickets**. The software packages assist the help desk personnel so they can type the trouble report immediately into a computerized failure analysis program. They also automatically produce various statistical reports to track how many failures have occurred for each piece of hardware, circuit, or software package. Automated trouble tickets are better than paper because they allow management personnel to gather problem and vendor statistics. There are four main reasons for trouble tickets: problem tracking, problem statistics, problem-solving methodology, and management reports.

Problem tracking allows the network manager to determine who is responsible for correcting any outstanding problems. This is important because some problems often are forgotten in the rush of a very hectic day. In addition, anyone might request information on the status of a problem. The network manager can determine whether the problem-solving mechanism is meeting predetermined schedules. Finally, the manager can be assured that all problems are being addressed. Problem tracking also can assist in problem resolution.

Are problems being resolved in a timely manner? Are overdue problems being flagged? Are all resources and information available for problem solving?

Problem statistics are important because they are a control device for the network managers as well as for vendors. With this information, a manager can see how well the network is meeting the needs of end users. These statistics also can be used to determine whether vendors are meeting their contractual maintenance commitments. Finally, they help to determine whether problem-solving objectives are being met.

Problem prioritizing helps ensure that critical problems get priority over less important ones. For example, a network support staff member should not work on a problem on one client computer if an entire circuit with dozens of computers is waiting for help. Moreover, a manager must know whether problem-resolution objectives are being met. For example, how long is it taking to resolve critical problems?

Management reports are required to determine network availability, product and vendor reliability (mean time between failures), and vendor responsiveness. Without them, a manager has nothing more than a "best guess" estimate for the effectiveness of either the network's technicians or the vendor's technicians. Regardless of whether this information is typed immediately into an automated trouble ticket package or recorded manually in a bound notebook-style trouble log, the objectives are the same.

The purposes of the trouble log are to record problems that must be corrected and to keep track of statistics associated with these problems. For example, the log might reveal that there were 37 calls for software problems (3 for one package, 4 for another package, and 30 for a third software package), 26 calls for cable modem problems evenly distributed among 2 vendors, 49 calls for client computers, and 2 calls to the common carrier that provides the network circuits. These data are valuable when the design and analysis group begins redesigning the network to meet future requirements.

TECHNICAL FOCUS

12-1 Technical Reports

*T*echnical reports that are helpful to network managers are those that provide summary information, as well as details that enable the managers to improve the network. Technical details include

- Circuit use
- Usage rate of critical hardware such as host computers, front-end processors, and servers
- File activity rates for database systems
- Usage by various categories of client computers

- Response time analysis per circuit or per computer
- Voice versus data usage per circuit
- Queue-length descriptions, whether in the host computer, in the front-end processor, or at remote sites
- Distribution of traffic by time of day, location, and type of application software
- Failure rates for circuits, hardware, and software
- Details of any network faults

12.4.3 Performance and Failure Statistics

Many different types of failure and recovery statistics can be collected. The most obvious performance statistics are those discussed earlier: how many packets are being moved on what circuits and what the response time is. Failure statistics also tell an important story.

One important failure statistic is **availability**, the percentage of time the network is available to users. It is calculated as the number of hours per month the network is available divided by the total number of hours per month (i.e., 24 hours per day $\times$ 30 days per month = 720 hours). The **downtime** includes times when the network is unavailable because of faults and routine maintenance and network upgrades. Most network managers strive for 99% to 99.5% availability, with downtime scheduled after normal working hours.

The **mean time between failures (MTBF)** is the number of hours or days of continuous operation before a component fails. Obviously, devices with higher MTBF are more reliable.

When faults occur, and devices or circuits go down, the **mean time to repair (MTTR)** is the average number of minutes or hours until the failed device or circuit is operational again. The MTTR is composed of these separate elements:

$$MTTRepair = MTTDiagnose + MTTRespond + MTTFix$$

The **mean time to diagnose (MTTD)** is the average number of minutes until the root cause of the failure is correctly diagnosed. This is an indicator of the efficiency of problem management personnel in the NOC or help desk who receive the problem report.

The **mean time to respond (MTTR)** is the average number of minutes or hours until service personnel arrive at the problem location to begin work on the problem. This is a valuable statistic because it indicates how quickly vendors and internal groups respond to emergencies. Compilation of these figures over time can lead to a change of vendors or internal management policies or, at the minimum, can exert pressure on vendors who do not respond to problems promptly.

TECHNICAL FOCUS

12-2 Elements of a Trouble Report

When a problem is reported, the trouble log staff members should record the following:

- Time and date of the report
- Name and telephone number of the person who reported the problem
- The time and date of the problem (and the time and date of the call)
- Location of the problem
- The nature of the problem
- When the problem was identified
- Why and how the problem happened

Finally, after the vendor or internal support group arrives on the premises, the last statistic is the **mean time to fix (MTTF)**. This figure tells how quickly the staff is able to correct the problem after they arrive. A very long time to fix in comparison with the time of other vendors may indicate faulty equipment design, inadequately trained customer service technicians, or even the fact that inexperienced personnel are repeatedly sent to fix problems.

For example, suppose your Internet connection at home stops working. You call your ISP, and they fix it over the phone in 15 minutes. In this case, the MTTRepair is 15 minutes, and it is hard to separate the different parts (MTTD, MTTR, and MTTF). Suppose you call your ISP and spend 60 minutes on the phone with them, and they can't fix it over the phone; instead, the technician arrives the next day (18 hours later) and spends 1 hour fixing the problem. In this case, MTTR = 1 hour + 18 hours + 1 hour = 20 hours.

The MTBF can be influenced by the original selection of vendor-supplied equipment. The MTTD relates directly to the ability of network personnel to isolate and diagnose failures and can often be improved by training. The MTTR (respond) can be influenced by showing vendors or internal groups how good or bad their response times have been in the past. The MTTF can be affected by the technical expertise of internal or vendor staff and the availability of spare parts on site.

| TECHNICAL | **12-3 Management Reports** |
| FOCUS | |

*M*anagement-oriented reports that are helpful to network managers and their supervisors provide summary information for overall evaluation and for network planning and design. Details include:

- Graphs of daily/weekly/monthly usage, number of errors, or whatever is appropriate to the network
- Network availability (**uptime**) for yesterday, the last 5 days, the last month, or any other specific period
- Percentage of hours per week the network is unavailable because of network maintenance and repair

- Fault diagnosis
- Whether most response times are less than or equal to 2 seconds for online real-time traffic
- Whether management reports are timely and contain the most up-to-date statistics
- Peak volume statistics as well as average volume statistics per circuit
- Comparison of activity between today and a similar previous period

Another set of statistics that should be gathered are those collected daily by the network operations group, which uses network management software. These statistics record the normal operation of the network, such as the number of errors (retransmissions) per communication circuit. Statistics also should be collected on the daily volume of transmissions (characters per hour) for each communication circuit, each computer, or whatever is appropriate for the network. It is important to closely monitor usage rates, the percentage of the theoretical capacity that is being used. These data can identify computers/devices or communication circuits that have higher-than-average error or usage rates, and they may be used for predicting future growth patterns and failures. A device or circuit that is approaching maximum usage obviously needs to be upgraded.

Such predictions can be accomplished by establishing simple **quality control charts** similar to those used in manufacturing. Programs use an upper control limit and a lower control limit with regard to the number of blocks in error per day or per week. Notice how Figure 12-9 identifies when the common carrier moved a circuit from one microwave channel to another (circuit B), how a deteriorating circuit can be located and fixed before it goes through the upper control limit (circuit A) and causes problems for the users, or how a temporary high rate of errors (circuit C) can be encountered when installing new hardware and software.

FIGURE 12-9

Quality control chart for circuits

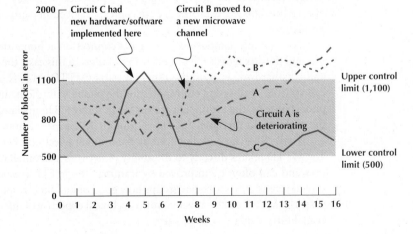

12.4.4 Improving Performance

The chapters on LANs, BNs, and WANs discussed several specific actions that could be taken to improve network performance for each of those types of networks. There are also several general activities to improve performance that cut across the different types of networks.

TECHNICAL
FOCUS

12-4 Inside a Service-Level Agreement

*T*here are many elements to a solid service-level agreement (SLA) with a common carrier. Some of the important ones include

- Network availability, measured over a month as the percentage of time the network is available (e.g., [total hours—hours unavailable]/total hours) should be at least 99.5%.
- Average round-trip permanent virtual circuit (PVC) delay, measured over a month as the number of seconds it takes a message to travel over the PVC from sender to receiver, should be less than 110 milliseconds, although some carriers will offer discounted services for SLA guarantees of 300 milliseconds or less.
- PVC throughput, measured over a month as the number of outbound packets sent over a PVC divided by the inbound packets received at the

destination (not counting packets over the committed information rate, which are discard eligible), should be above 99%—ideally, 99.99%.
- Mean time to respond, measured as a monthly average of the time from inception of trouble ticket until repair personnel are on site, should be 4 hours or less.
- Mean time to fix, measured as a monthly average of the time from the arrival of repair personnel on site until the problem is repaired, should be 4 hours or less.

Adapted from: "Carrier Service-Level Agreements," International Engineering Consortium Tutorial, www.iec.org, February

---

Most organizations establish **service-level agreements (SLAs)** with their common carriers and Internet service providers. An SLA specifies the exact type of performance and fault conditions that the organization will accept. For example, the SLA might state that network availability must be 99% or higher and that the MTBF for T1 circuits must be 120 days or more. In many cases, SLA includes maximum allowable response times. The SLA also states what compensation the service provider must provide if it fails to meet the SLA. Some organizations are also starting to use an SLA internally to define relationships between the networking group and its organizational "customers."

12.5 END USER SUPPORT

Providing **end user support** means solving whatever problems users encounter while using the network. There are three main functions within end user support: resolving network faults, resolving user problems, and training. We have already discussed how to resolve network faults, and now we focus on resolution of user problems and end user training.

12.5.1 Resolving Problems

Problems with user equipment (as distinct from network equipment) usually stem from three major sources. The first is a failed hardware device. These are usually the easiest to fix. A network technician simply fixes the device or installs a new part.

The second type of problem is a lack of user knowledge. These problems can usually be solved by discussing the situation with the user and taking that person through the process step by step. This is the next easiest type of problem to solve and can often be done by email or over the telephone, although not all users are easy to work with. Problematic users are sometimes called ID ten-T errors, written ID10T.

MANAGEMENT FOCUS

12-8 Network Manager Job Requirements

Being a network manager is not easy. We reviewed dozens of job postings for the key responsibilities, skills, and education desired by employers. The responsibilities listed below were commonly mentioned.

Responsibilities

- Determine network needs and architect solutions to address business requirements.
- Procure and manage vendor relations with providers of equipment and services.
- Deploy new network components and related network systems and services, including the creation of test plans and procedures, documentation of the operation, maintenance and administration of any new systems or services, and training.
- Develop, document, and enforce standards, procedures, and processes for the operation and maintenance of the network and related systems.
- Manage the efficiency of operations of the current network infrastructure, including analyzing network performance and making configuration adjustments as necessary.
- Administer the network servers and the network-printing environment.
- Ensure network security, including the development of applicable security, server, and desktop standards, and monitoring processes to ensure that mission critical processes are operational.
- Manage direct reports and contractors. This includes task assignments, performance monitoring, and regular feedback. Hire, train, evaluate, and terminate staff and contractors

under the direction of company policies and processes.
- Assist business in the definition of new product/service offerings and the capabilities and features of the systems to deliver those products and services to customers.

Skills required

- Strong technology skills in a variety of technologies
- LAN/WAN networking experience working with routers and switches
- Experience with Internet access solutions, including firewalls and VPN
- Network architecture design and implementation experience
- Information security experience
- Personnel management experience
- Project management experience
- Experience working in a team environment
- Ability to work well in an unstructured environment
- Excellent problem-solving and analytical skills
- Effective written and oral communication skills

Education

- Bachelor's degree in an information technology field
- Security Certification
- Microsoft MCSE Certification preferred
- Cisco CCNA Certification preferred

The third type of problem is one with the software, software settings, or an incompatibility between the software and network software and hardware. In this case, there may be a bug in the software, or the software may not function properly on a certain combination of hardware and software. Solving these problems may be difficult because they require expertise with the specific software package in use and sometimes require software upgrades from the vendor.

Resolving either type of software problem begins with a request for assistance from the help desk. Requests for assistance are usually handled in the same manner as network faults. A trouble log is maintained to document all incoming requests and the manner in which they are resolved. The staff member receiving the request attempts to resolve the problem in the best manner possible. Staff members should be provided with a set of standard procedures or scripts for soliciting information from the user about problems. In large organizations, this process may be supported by special software.

There are often several levels to the problem-resolution process. The first level is the most basic. All staff members working at the help desk should be able to resolve most of these. Most organizations strive to resolve between 75% and 85% of requests at this first level in less than an hour. If the request cannot be resolved, it is escalated to the second level of problem resolution. Escalation is a normal part of the process and not something that is "bad." Staff members who handle second-level support have specialized skills in certain problem areas or with certain types of software and hardware. In most cases, problems are resolved at this level. Some large organizations also have a third level of resolution in which specialists spend many hours developing and testing various solutions to the problem, often in conjunction with staff members from the vendors of network software and hardware.

12.5.2 Providing End User Training

End user training is an ongoing responsibility of the network manager. Training is a key part in the implementation of new networks or network components. It is also important to have an ongoing training program because employees may change job functions and new employees require training to use the organization's networks.

Training usually is conducted through in-class, one-on-one instruction and online self-paced courses. In-class training should focus on the 20% of the network functions that the user will use 80% of the time instead of attempting to cover all network functions. By getting in-depth instruction on the fundamentals, users become confident about what they need to do. The training should also explain how to locate additional information from online support, documentation, or the help desk.

12.6 COST MANAGEMENT

One of the most challenging areas of network management over the past few years has been **cost management**. Data traffic has been growing much more rapidly than has the network management budget, which has forced network managers to provide greater network capacity at an ever lower cost per megabyte (Figure 12-10). In this section, we examine the major sources of costs and discuss several ways to reduce them.

12.6.1 Sources of Costs

The cost of operating a network in a large organization can be very expensive. Figure 12-11 shows a recent cost analysis to operate the network for 1 year at Indiana University, a large Big Ten research university serving 40,000 students and 4,000 faculty and staff. This analysis includes the costs of operating the network infrastructure and standard applications such as email and the Web but does not include the costs of other applications such as course management software, registration, student services, accounting, and so on. Indiana University has a federal IT governance structure, which means that the different colleges and schools on campus also have budgets to hire staff and buy equipment for their faculty and staff. The budget in this figure omits these amounts, so the real costs are probably 50% higher than those shown. Nonetheless, this presents a snapshot of the costs of running a large network.

FIGURE 12-10

Network traffic versus
network management
budgets

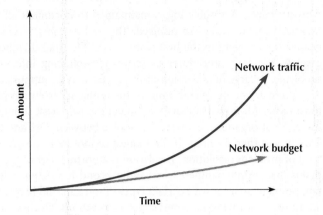

The largest area of costs in network operations is the $7.4 million spent on WAN circuits. Indiana University operates many high-speed networks (including Internet2), so these costs are higher than might be expected. This figure also shows the large costs of email, Web services, data storage, and security. The cost of end user support is the next largest cost item. This includes training as well as answering users' questions and fixing their problems. The remaining costs are purchasing new and replacement hardware and software. But, once again, remember that this does not include the hardware and software purchased by individual colleges and schools for their faculty and staff, which does not come from the central IT budget.

The **total cost of ownership (TCO)** is a measure of how much it costs per year to keep one computer operating. TCO includes the actual direct cost of repair parts, software upgrades, and support staff members to maintain the network, install software, administer the network (e.g., create user IDs, back up user data), provide training and technical support, and upgrade hardware and software. It also includes the indirect cost of time "wasted" by the user when problems occur, when the network is down, or when the user is attempting to learn new software.

Several studies over the past few years by Gartner Group, Inc., a leading industry research firm, suggest that the TCO of a computer is astoundingly high. Most studies suggest that the TCO for typical Windows computers on a network is about $7,000 *per computer per year*. In other words, it costs almost five times as much *each year* to operate a computer than it does to purchase it in the first place. Other studies by firms such as IBM and *Information Week*, an industry magazine, have produced TCO estimates of between $5,000 and $10,000 per year, suggesting that the Gartner Group's estimates are reasonable.

Although TCO has been accepted by many organizations, other firms argue against the practice of including indirect in the calculation. For example, using a technique that includes indirect, the TCO of a coffee machine is more than $50,000 per year—not counting the cost of the coffee or supplies. The assumption that getting coffee "wastes" 12 minutes per day multiplied by 5 days per week yields 1 hour per week, or about 50 hours per year, of wasted time. If you assume the coffeepot serves 20 employees who have an average cost of $50 per hour (not an unusually high number), you have a loss of $50,000 per year.

Some organizations, therefore, prefer to focus on costing methods that examine only the direct costs of operating the computers, omitting softer indirect costs such as "wasted" time. Such measures, often called **network cost of ownership (NCO)** or **real TCO**, have

Network Operations		$14,871,000
Account Administration	275,000	
Authentication Services	257,000	
Directory Services Infrastructure (incl DHCP, DNS)	746,000	
E-mail and Messaging	1,434,000	
Mainframe and Cluster Operations	633,000	
Mass Data Storage	1,424,000	
Policy Management	75,000	
Printing	201,000	
Security Administration	1,270,000	
WAN Operations	7,410,000	
Web Services	1,146,000	
End User Support		$6,544,000
Departmental Technology Support	553,000	
Instructional Technology Support	856,000	
Student Residence Halls Support	279,000	
Student Technology Centers Support	1,288,000	
Support Center (Help Desk)	2,741,000	
Training and Education	827,000	
Client Hardware		$3,901,000
Classroom Technology Equipment and Supplies	844,000	
Student Residence Halls Equipment and Supplies	601,000	
Student Technology Centers Equipment and Supplies	2,456,000	
Application Software		$3,729,000
Software Site Licenses	2,540,000	
Student Residence Halls Software	146,000	
Student Technology Centers Software	1,043,000	
Total		$29,045,000

FIGURE 12-11   Annual networking costs at Indiana University

found that NCO ranges between $1,500 and $3,500 *per computer per year*. The typical network management group for a 100-user network would therefore have an annual budget of about $150,000 to $350,000. The most expensive item is personnel (network managers and technicians), which typically accounts for 50% to 70% of total costs. The second most expensive cost item is WAN circuits, followed by hardware upgrades and replacement parts.

Calculating TCO for univerisites can be difficult. Do we calculate TCO for the number of computers or the number of users? Figure 12-11 shows an annual cost of $29 million. If we use the number of users, the TCO is about $659 ($29 million divided by 44,000 users). If we use the number of computers, TCO is $4,800 ($29 million divided by about 6,000 computers owned by the university).

There is one very important message from this pattern of costs. Because the largest cost item is personnel time, the primary focus of cost management lies in designing networks and developing policies to reduce personnel time, not to reduce hardware cost. Over the long term, it makes more sense to buy more expensive equipment if it can reduce the cost of network management.

Figure 12-12 shows the average breakdown of personnel costs by function. The largest time cost (where staff members spend most of their time) is systems management, which

FIGURE 12-12
Network management
personnel costs

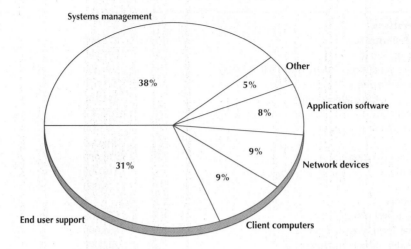

includes configuration, fault, and performance management tasks that focus on the network as a whole. The second largest item is end user support.

Network managers usually find it difficult to manage their budgets because networks grow so rapidly. They often find themselves having to defend ever-increasing requests for more equipment and staff. To counter these escalating costs, many large organizations have adopted **charge-back policies** for users of WANs and mainframe-based networks. (A charge-back policy attempts to allocate the costs associated with the network to specific users.) These users must "pay" for their network usage by transferring part of their budget allocations to the network group. Such policies are seldom used in LANs, making one more potential cultural difference between network management styles.

12.6.2 Reducing Costs

Given the huge amounts in TCO or even the substantial amounts spent in NCO, there is considerable pressure on network managers to reduce costs. Figure 12-13 summarizes five steps to reduce network costs.

The first and most important step is to develop standards for client computers, servers, and network devices (i.e., switches, routers). These standards define one configuration (or a small set of configurations) that are permitted for all computers and devices. Standardizing hardware and software makes it easier to diagnose and fix problems. Also, there are fewer software packages for the network support staff members to learn. The downside, of course, is that rigid adherence to standards reduces innovation.

FIGURE 12-13
Reducing network costs

Five Steps to Reduce Network Costs

- Develop standard hardware and software configurations for client computers and servers.
- Automate as much of the network management function as possible by deploying a solid set of network management tools.
- Reduce the costs of installing new hardware and software by working with vendors.
- Centralize help desks.
- Move to thin-client or cloud-based architectures.

MANAGEMENT	**12-9 Total Cost of Ownership in Minnesota**
FOCUS	

*T*otal cost of ownership (TCO) has come to the classroom. As part of a national TCO initiative, several school districts, including one in Minnesota, recently conducted a real TCO analysis. The school district was a system of eight schools (one high school, one middle school, and six elementary schools) serving 4,100 students in kindergarten through grade 12. All schools are connected via a frame relay WAN to the district head office.

Costs were assessed in two major groups: direct costs and indirect costs. The direct costs included the costs of hardware (replacement client computers, servers, networks, and printers and supplies), software, internal network staff, and external consultants. The indirect costs included staff training and development. "Wasted time" was not included in the TCO analysis.

The district examined its most recent annual budget and allocated its spending into these categories. The district calculated that it spent about $1.2 million per year

to support its 1,200 client computers, providing a TCO of about $1,004 per client computer per year. Figure 12-14 provides a summary of the costs by category.

A TCO of $1,004 is below average, indicating a well-managed network. The district had implemented several network management best practices, such as using a standardized set of software, using new standardized hardware, and providing professional development to teachers to reduce support costs. One other major contributing factor was the extremely low salaries paid to the IT technical staff (less than $25,000 per year) because of the district's rural location. Had the district been located in a more urban area, IT staff costs would have doubled, bringing TCO closer to the lower end of the national average.

Adapted from: "Minnesota District Case Study," Taking TCO to the Classroom, k12tco.gartner.com

FIGURE 12-14

Total cost of ownership (per client computer per year) for a Minnesota school district

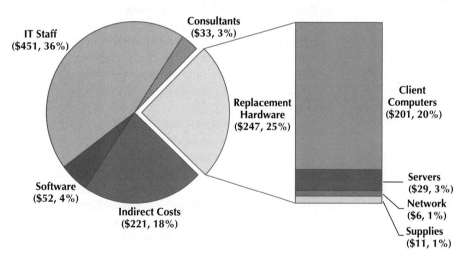

The second most important step is to automate as much of the network management process as possible. Desktop management can significantly reduce the cost to upgrade when new software is released. It also enables faster installation of new computers and faster recovery when software needs to be reinstalled and helps enforce the standards policies. The use of network management software to identify and diagnose problems can significantly reduce time spent in performance and fault management. Likewise, help desk software can cut the cost of the end support function.

A third step is to do everything possible to reduce the time spent installing new hardware and software. The cost of a network technician's spending half a day to install and configure new computers is often $300 to $500. Desktop management is an important step to reducing costs, but careful purchasing can also go a long way. The installation of standard hardware and software (e.g., Microsoft Office) by the hardware vendor can significantly reduce costs. Likewise, careful monitoring of hardware failures can quickly identify vendors of less reliable equipment who should be avoided in the next purchasing cycle.

Traditionally, help desks have been decentralized into user departments. The result is a proliferation of help desks and support staff members, many of whom tend to be generalists rather than specialists in one area. Many organizations have found that centralizing help desks enables them to reduce the number of generalists and provide more specialists in key technology areas. This results in faster resolution of difficult problems. Centralization also makes it easier to identify common problems occurring in different parts of the organization and take actions to reduce them.

Finally, many network experts argue that moving to thin-client or cloud-based architectures, just Web browsers on the client (see Chapter 2), can significantly reduce costs. Although this can reduce the cost to buy software, the real saving lies in the support costs. Because they are restricted to a narrow set of functions and generally do not need software installations, thin-client architectures become much easier to manage. TCO and NCO drop by 20% to 40%. Most organizations anticipate using thin-client and cloud-based architectures selectively, in areas where applications are well defined and can easily be restricted.

12.7 IMPLICATIONS FOR MANAGEMENT

Network management is one of the more challenging functions because it requires a good understanding of networking technologies, an ability to work with end users and management, and an understanding of the key elements driving networking costs. Normally no one notices it until something goes wrong.

As demand for network capacity increases, the costs associated with network management have typically increased in most organizations. Justifying these increased costs to senior management can be challenging because senior management often do not see greatly increasing amounts of network traffic—all they see are increasing costs. The ability to explain the business value of networks in terms understandable to senior management is an important skill.

As networks become larger and more complex, network management will increase in complexity. New technologies for managing networks will be developed, as vendors attempt to increase the intelligence of networks and their ability to "self-heal." These new technologies will provide significantly more reliable networks but will also be more expensive and will require new skills on the part of network designers, network managers, and network technicians. Keeping a trained network staff will become increasingly difficult because once staff acquire experience with the new management tools, they will be lured away by other firms offering higher salaries—which, we suppose, is not a bad thing if you're one of the network staff.

SUMMARY

Designing for Performance Network management software is critical to the design of reliable, high-performance networks. This software provides statistics about device utilizations and issues alerts when problems occur. SNMP is a common standard for network management software and the managed devices that support it. Load balancing, and policy-based management are tools used to better manage the flow of traffic. Capacity management, content caching, and content delivery are sometimes used to reduce network traffic.

Configuration Management
Configuration management means managing the network's hardware and software configuration, documenting it, and ensuring the documentation is updated as the configuration changes. The most common configuration management activity is adding and deleting user accounts. The most basic documentation about network hardware is a set of network configuration diagrams, supplemented by documentation on each individual network component. A similar approach can be used for network software. Desktop management plays a key role in simplifying configuration management by automating and documenting the network configurations. User and application profiles should be automatically provided by the network and desktop management software. There is a variety of other documentation that must be routinely developed and updated, including users' manuals and organizational policies.

Performance and Fault Management
Performance management means ensuring the network is operating as efficiently as possible. Fault management means preventing, detecting, and correcting any faults in the network circuits, hardware, and software. The two are closely related because any faults in the network reduce performance and because both require network monitoring. Today, most networks use a combination of managed devices to monitor the network and issue alarms and a help desk to respond to user problems. Problem tracking allows the network manager to determine problem ownership or who is responsible for correcting any outstanding problems. Problem statistics are important because they are a control device for the network operators as well as for vendors.

Providing End User Support
Providing end user support means solving whatever network problems users encounter. Support consists of resolving network faults, resolving software problems, and training. Software problems often stem from lack of user knowledge, fundamental problems with the software, or an incompatibility between the software and the network's software and hardware. There are often several levels to problem resolution. End user training is an ongoing responsibility of the network manager. Training usually has two parts: in-class instruction and the documentation and training manuals that the user keeps for reference.

Cost Management
As the demand for network services grows, so does its cost. The TCO for typical networked computers is about $7,000 per year per computer, far more than the initial purchase price. The network management cost (omitting "wasted" time) is between $1,500 and $3,500 per year per computer. The largest single cost item is staff salaries. The best way to control rapidly increasing network costs is to reduce the amount of time taken to perform management functions, often by automating as many routine ones as possible.

KEY TERMS

QUESTIONS

1. What skill does a network manager need?
2. What is firefighting?
3. Why is combining voice and data a major organizational challenge?
4. Describe what configuration management encompasses.
5. People tend to think of software when documentation is mentioned. What is documentation in a network situation?
6. What is desktop management, and why is it important?
7. What is performance and fault management?
8. What does a help desk do?
9. What do trouble tickets report?
10. Several important statistics related to network uptime and downtime are discussed in this chapter. What are they, and why are they important?
11. What is an SLA?
12. How is network availability calculated?
13. What is problem escalation?
14. What are the primary functions of end user support?
15. What is TCO?
16. Why is the TCO so high?
17. How can network costs be reduced?
18. What do network management software systems do and why are they important?
19. What is SNMP and RMON?
20. Compare and contrast device management software, system management software, and application management software.
21. How does a load balancer work?
22. What is server virtualization?
23. What is policy-based management?
24. What is capacity management?
25. How does content caching differ from content delivery?
26. How does network cost of ownership (aka real TCO) differ from total cost of ownership? Which is the most useful measure of network costs from the point of view of the network manager? Why?
27. Many organizations do not have a formal trouble reporting system. Why do you think this is the case?

EXERCISES

A. What factors might cause peak loads in a network? How can a network manager determine if they are important, and how are they taken into account when designing a data communications network?
B. Today's network managers face a number of demanding problems. Investigate and discuss three major issues.
C. Research the networking budget in your organization and discuss the major cost areas. Discuss several ways of reducing costs over the long term.
D. Explore the traffic on the networks managed by the Indiana University NOC as noc.net.internet2.edu. Compare the volume of traffic in two networks and how close to capacity the networks are.
E. Investigate the latest versions of SNMP and RMON and describe the functions that have been added in the latest version of the standard.
F. Investigate and report on the purpose, relative advantages, and relative disadvantages of two network management software tools.

MINICASES

I. City School District, Part 1 City School District is a large, urban school district that operates 27 schools serving 22,000 students from kindergarten through grade 12. All schools are networked into a regional WAN that connects the schools to the district central office and each other. The district has a total of 5,300 client computers. The table below shows the annual costs. Calculate the real TCO (without wasted time).

Budget Item	Annual Cost
IT staff salaries	$7,038,400
Consultants	1,340,900
Software	657,200
Staff training	545,900
Client computers	2,236,600
Servers	355,100
Network	63,600
Supplies and parts	2,114,700

II. City School District, Part 2 Read and complete Minicase I. Examine the TCO by category. Do you think that this TCO indicates a well-run network? What suggestions would you have?

III. Central Textiles Central Textiles is a clothing manufacturer that operates 16 plants throughout the southern United States and in Latin America. The Information Systems Department, which reports to the vice president of finance, operates the central mainframe and LAN at the headquarters building in Spartanburg, South Carolina, and the WAN that connects all the plants. The LANs in each plant are managed by a separate IT group at each plant that reports to the plant manager (the plant managers report to the vice president of manufacturing). The telephone communications system and long-distance agreements are managed by a telecommunications department in the headquarters that reports to the vice president of finance. The CEO of Central Textiles has come to you asking about whether this is the best arrangement, or whether it would make more sense to integrate the three functions under one new department. Outline the pros and cons of both alternatives.

IV. Indiana University Reread Management Focus 12-5. Take another look at Figure 12-1. If this is a typical traffic pattern, how would you suggest that they improve performance?

CASE STUDY

NEXT-DAY AIR SERVICE

See the Web site at www.wiley.com/college/fitzgerald

HANDS-ON ACTIVITY 12A

Monitoring Solarwinds Network

One of the key tasks of network management is monitoring the network to make sure everything is running well. There are many effective network monitoring tools available, and several have demonstrations you can view on the Web. One of my favorites is solarwinds.net. They have a live demonstration of their network management software available at npm.solarwinds.net. Log in with the provided guest access.

Figure 12-15 shows the top portion of the demo page. It shows a map of the network with circuits and locations color coded. On the left side of the screen is a list of all nodes showing their status (green for good, yellow for some problems, and red for major problems), although the colors are hard to see in the figure. The bottom left part of the figure shows the busiest servers. The bottom right of this figure shows the nodes with problems, so that a network manager can quickly see problems and act to fix them. For example, the Sales switch is down.

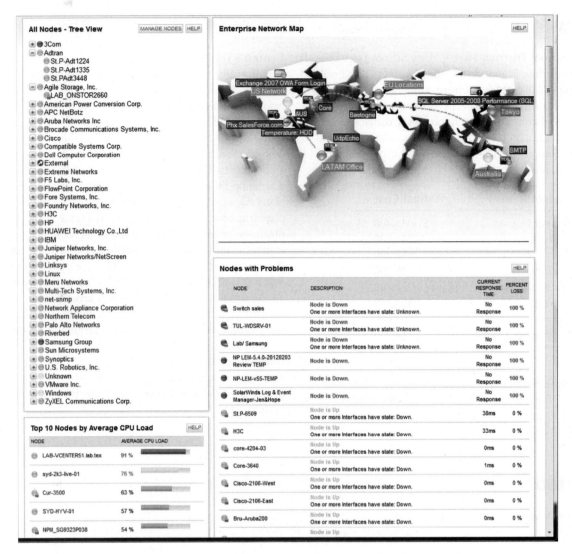

FIGURE 12-15 Solarwinds network management software, used with permission

Figure 12-16 shows the next part of the page after I scrolled down. We now see two pie charts on the right side that show application health, (which indicates that the software is an application management package as well as a network management package) and hardware health. You can click on any of the application or hardware categories to see which applications/hardware are in which status category. The table below these two pie charts shows the processes using the most memory, while pie chart on the right shows the busiest circuits (top five conversations). You'll note that the software is also a configuration management package, because below this pie chart there is a list of the last configuration changes.

Figure 12-17 shows the next part of the page. This includes the disk space that is closet to capacity and a summary of recent events. This software also integrates the help desk software, so it displays help desk requests that have not yet been completed, in order of priority. At the bottom of the screen is a weather radar map, because weather often causes network issues.

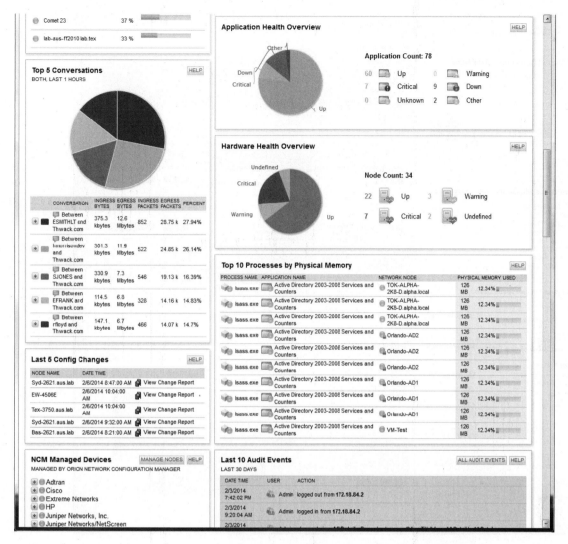

FIGURE 12-16 Solarwinds network management software, used with permission

This page is a summary page. Every element on the page can be clicked to go to the detail page to get more information about any item on the page.

Deliverables

1. What problem alerts are currently displayed for the Solarwinds network?

2. What are the top three nodes by CPU load? What are the top three conversations?

3. How many applications are in critical condition? Name one.

4. What is one help desk ticket that has not been completed?

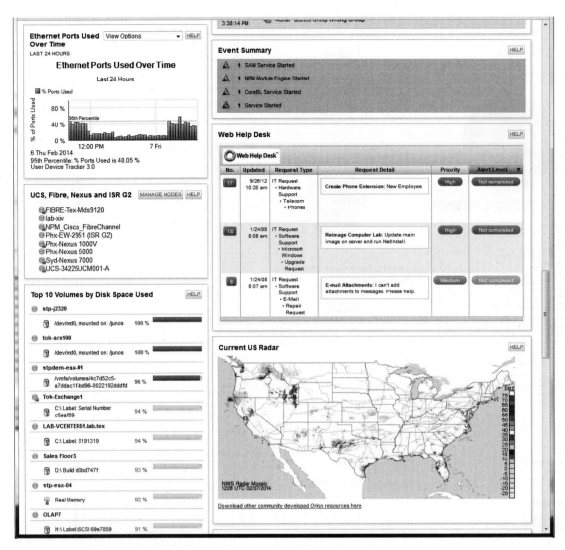

FIGURE 12-17 Solarwinds network management software, used with permission

HANDS-ON ACTIVITY 12B

Monitoring AT&T's WAN

AT&T permits you to monitor their Global IP network. Go to ipnetwork.bgtmo.ip.att.net and click on Look at your world wide network.

You'll see a screen that displays all the circuits at each of the major PoPs in their global IP network. You can select a city and see the round-trip delay (from the city to the other city and back again). It also displays the percentage of packets that have been lost in transit (due either to errors or overloading of circuits).

The tabs across the top of the screen (e.g., Network Delay, Network Loss, Averages) show summary data across the entire network.

Deliverables

1. What is the current latency and packet loss between Dallas and Austin?

2. What is the current latency and packet loss between Phoenix and New York?

HANDS-ON ACTIVITY 12C

Apollo Residence Network Design

Apollo is a luxury residence hall that will serve honor students at your university. We described the residence in Hands-On Activities at the end of Chapters 7, 8, 9, 10, and 11. In this activity, we want you to revisit the LAN design (Chapter 7), backbone design (Chapter 8), WAN design (Chapter 8), Internet design (Chapter 10), and security design (Chapter 11) and then add the design for good network management (this chapter).

Deliverables

Your team was hired to design the network for the Apollo residence. Design the entire network, including LANs, backbones, WAN, Internet, security, and network management. You will need to refer to the Hands-On Activities in Chapters 7–11 as well as this one. Figure 12-18 provides a list of possible hardware and software you can add, in addition to the equipment lists in these activities in prior chapters.

Device or Software	Price (each)
Add SNMP to any device	$200
SNMP device management software	$2,000
SNMP system management software	$4,000
SNMP application management software	$4,000
Load balancer (up to 10 servers) Includes management software	$1,500
Load balancer (up to 50 servers) Includes management software	$2,500
Load balancer (up to 100 servers) Includes management software	$4,000
Bandwidth shaper (runs at 1 Gbps) Includes management software	$1,000
Bandwidth shaper (runs at 10 Gbps) Includes management software	$3,000
Traffic shaper (runs at 1 Gbps) Includes management software	$10,000
Traffic shaper (runs at 10 Gbps) Includes management software	$30,000
Cache engine (runs at 1 Gbps) Includes management software	$1,000
Cache engine (runs at 10 Gbps) Includes management software	$3,000
Desktop management software	$1,000 plus $25 per desktop

FIGURE 12-18   Equipment list

INDEX